30697

D1801346

REF
296.03
J95
JUNIOR JUDAICA
OVER NIGHT
30697
V. 6

DATE DUE

| | | | |
|---|---|---|---|
| | | | |
| | | | |
| | | | |
| | | | |
| | | | |
| | | | |
| | | | |
| | | | |
| | | | |
| | | | |
| | | | |

# JUNIOR JUDAICA

## ENCYCLOPAEDIA JUDAICA FOR YOUTH

# JUNIOR JUDAICA

## ENCYCLOPAEDIA JUDAICA FOR YOUTH

editor in chief
Rabbi Dr. Raphael Posner

Revised Edition 1994

## 6
## Sp-Z
## Index
## Jewish Calendar 1920-2020

ENCYCLOPAEDIA JUDAICA

Copyright © 1994 by
KETER PUBLISHING HOUSE LTD.

All rights reserved including the right to reproduce
this book or portions thereof in any form.

Third, updated edition

Catalogue No. 258140

Printed and bound by Keterpress Enterprises, Jerusalem
Printed in Israel

REF
296.03
J95
V. 6

## TRANSLITERATION TABLE

There are many Hebrew words in *Junior Judaica;* some are printed in Hebrew letters but all are given in transliteration, that is, spelled out in English. The following table shows the system we have used in all cases except in a very few where there is an accepted English spelling.

**Consonants:**

| | |
|---|---|
| א | not transliterated |
| בּ | b |
| ב | v |
| ג | g |
| ד | d |
| ה | h |
| ו | v; when it is not a vowel |
| ז | z |
| ח | ḥ; pronounced like the "ch" in Loch Lomond |
| ט | t |
| י | y; when it is not a vowel |
| כּ | k |
| כ | kh; pronounced like the hard German "ch" as in *Ach!* |
| ך | kh; this is the final from of כ, i.e., the way it is written at the end of a word. |
| ל | l |
| מ | m |
| ם | m; final form of מ |
| נ | n |
| ן | n; final form of נ |
| ס | s |
| ע | not transliterated |
| פּ | p |
| פ | f |
| ף | f; final form of פ |
| צ | ẓ; pronounced "ts" as in tsetse fly |
| ץ | ẓ; final form of צ |
| ק | k |
| ר | r |
| שׁ | sh |
| שׂ | s |
| תּ | t |
| ת | t |

**Vowels:**

| | |
|---|---|
| *ַ *ָ *ֲ | a; as in calm |
| *ֶ *ֱ | e; as in bed |
| *ִ *ִי | i; as in tin |
| *ֵי *ֵ | ei; like the "a" in take |
| *ֹ *וֹ | o; as in or |
| *ֻ *וּ | u; as in zoo |

א and ע as pronounced by most Hebrew speakers have no sound but take the sound of the vowel. Occasionally, when they appear inside a word we use an apostrophe (') to indicate that the two vowels should be pronounced separately.

30697
[redacted]

**TEMPLE.** The main structure of the Second Temple as it is believed to have looked after the renovations undertaken by King Herod the Great. This is only a small corner of a massive scale-model reconstruction of the main buildings of the city of Jerusalem in the first century c.e. which is on display at the Holyland Hotel in the Bayit ve-Gan suburb of Jerusalem.

**SPACE EXPLORATION.** For ancient man, space travel was a miraculous phenomenon, reserved for gods and winged creatures. It seemed inconceivable that earth-bound humans would ever reach the heavens, and so scholars never dreamed of dealing with the subject.

But today the impossible has become reality. Man has walked on the moon and a new era has begun. Because it is such a fresh field, space exploration raises grave new questions for Judaism, for which there are no historical precedents. For example, according to Jewish moral traditions, can space exploration be justified as a venture which will ultimately benefit mankind, or is it a waste of money and effort which would be better spent in solving the problems existing right here on earth? Is man committing the sin of arrogance by moving beyond the bounds of God-given earth, much as his forefathers did in building the Tower of *Babel, or is he simply exploring the rest of God's universe? And if intelligent life is found on other planets, are they equal to man in the eyes of God?

On the lighter side are some of the practical implications of space travel. For example, a day is only about 90 minutes long for an astronaut: the time it takes to circle the globe and see both the sunrise and sunset. How can a man fulfill all the daily *mitzvot* in just 90 minutes? Would the space traveler have to recite the three daily services every 90 minutes? How would the orthodox Jew really handle these "time and space" problems, and would the same rules that apply on earth have to be followed in space and on other planets?

Until now there are no clear answers to these questions although various Jewish scholars have attempted to study the issue and give their opinions. Perhaps as exploration becomes more commonplace Judaism will gradually solve these problems and adapt to yet another stage in the progress of mankind.

**SPAIN** was once a thriving center of Jewish thought and achievement, yet today there are only a few thousand Jews left there, in a handful of communities struggling to maintain their Jewish identity. The medieval Jewish community of Spain nurtured great scholars and developed its own unique traditional flavor. But by the 15th century, all of this had been quashed by the Spanish authorities and Spanish Jews scattered to all corners of the globe.

According to legend, there were Jews living in

1

2

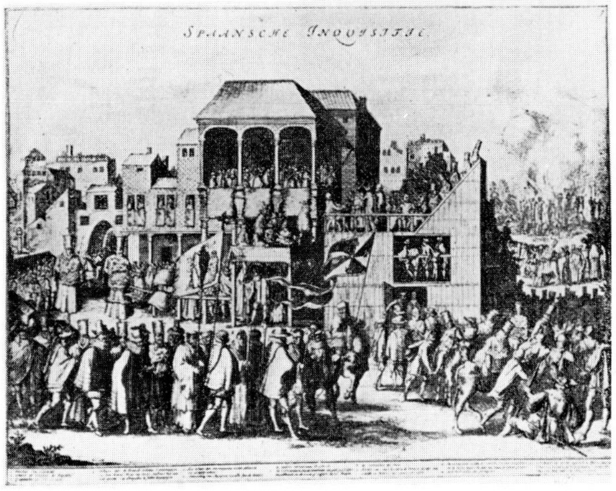

1. The synagogue built in the 1350s in Toledo, Spain, by the financier and community leader Samuel ben Meir ha-Levi Abulafia. The building was converted into a church in the 16th century (Church of El Transito) and it is still standing today.
2. A Dutch engraving from the 17th century of an *auto da fe* arranged by the Spanish Inquisition.

Spain in biblical times, but no proof exists in support of such stories. Most probably the first group of Jews settled there during the time of the Roman Empire.

When the Spaniards converted to Christianity, attempts were made to isolate members of different faiths and so, in 305 c.e., the Church Council at Elvira issued rules forbidding Christians to live in the houses of Jews or to eat in their company.

The Visigoths who took over Spain after the fall of the Romans, at first treated the Jews favorably. But in 589 they gave up their tolerant Arian Christian faith and adopted Catholicism as the official state religion. This national conversion became the root of all future problems for the Jews of Spain. The Catholics tried to convert the Jews by force. From 613, Jews were ordered to be baptized or leave the kingdom and this order was often revised in various forms, during subsequent centuries.

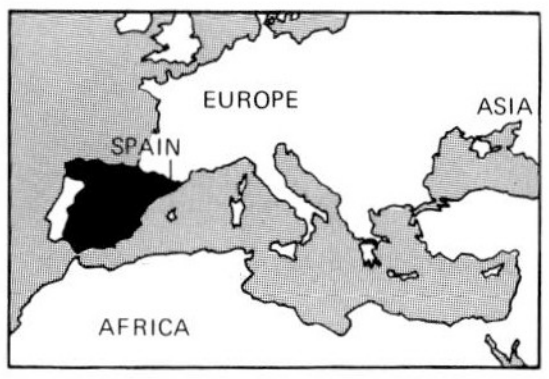

1

2

1. Stone embedded in the wall of a house in Barcelona, Spain, bearing a Hebrew inscription indicating that it marked a *hekdesh* (a gift donated in charity) by Rabbi Samuel of Cerdagne, who is believed to have lived in the 14th century. The inscription reads : "*Hekdesh* of Rabbi Samuel of Cerdagne, may his soul rest in peace."
2. Isaac Elchanan Spektor, one of the foremost Talmud scholars, educators and community leaders in Lithuania in the latter half of the 19th century.

By the time the Muslim *Arabs overran the Visigothic kingdom in 711, there were no communities of openly professing Jews left in Spain. But there remained many secret Jews who welcomed the Muslims as their saviors. Under Muslim protection the Jews prospered. Jewish scholarship and culture flourished and Jews attained high positions in many professions. One such leading figure, *Ḥisdai Ibn Shaprut, served as court physician in the 10th century and also assumed diplomatic duties. A yeshivah was established in Cordoba and during the Middle Ages, Spain saw such great Jewish scholars as Samuel Ha-Nagid, Isaac Alfasi, Rabbi Abraham *Ibn Ezra, and Abraham *Ibn Daud. Influential Jewish communities sprang up in Madrid, Granada, *Toledo and Seville. These communities absorbed the Arabic language and lifestyle while adapting it to Jewish needs. Hebrew poetry and philosophy flourished, largely based on Arabic literary forms.

During the 11th century, the Christians began to reconquer northern Spain while, in the south, more fanatic Muslim groups began persecuting the Jews. Caught between the two warring groups – Christians and Muslims – the Jews suffered at the hands of both and many wandered back and forth between the two territories seeking refuge. They were more successful in Christian Spain, but by the 13th century *blood libels started there and the Jews began to suffer under official anti-Semitic edicts. Outstanding Jewish figures such as Samuel *Abulafia in the 14th century and Isaac Abrabanel in the 15th managed to keep the spark of Jewish scholarship and culture burning, but the situation was rapidly deteriorating. The number of Conversos, *Marranos and New Christians (Jews forced by the Christians to convert; see *Conversion, Forced) increased and in 1478 the terrifying *Inquisition was introduced by which thousands of Jews were tortured and killed in the name of Christianity. Finally, in 1492, the Jews were expelled by *Ferdinand and Isabella and not a single professing Jew was left in the country. Yet Spanish Jewry had by no means disappeared, for almost everywhere refugees reconstituted their communities, clinging to their former language and culture. These Jews became known as *Sephardim (of Spanish origin) and their descendants formed Sephardic communities all over the world.

The edict of expulsion was formally repealed only in 1968. In time an official Jewish community was organized and in the late 1980s diplomatic relations with Israel were established.

During Hitler's rise to power, about 3,000 Jewish refugees fled to Spain, though they left again during the civil war there (1936–39). About 12,000 Jews lived in Spain in the early 1990s.

In 1992 events were held to acknowledge 500 years since the edict of expulsion. King Juan Carlos attended the convocation in Madrid's synagogue.

**SPEKTOR, ISAAC ELCHANAN** (1817-1896), Lithuanian rabbi and community leader. Born in the province of Grodno, Russia, Spektor spent most of his adult life as rabbi of Kovno (Kaunas), Lithuania. He worked tirelessly to better the lot of the Jews in their relations with the government and to alleviate the plight of the poor and the distressed. He organized aid for stricken communities, sought government permission for the provision of kosher food for Jewish soldiers and maintained a soup kitchen in Kovno until his death. He was instrumental in arousing the Jews of the West (in England and the U.S. in particular) to protest publicly to the Russian government concerning its harsh treatment of Jews, and the publicity aroused led to the establishment of welfare funds to aid the needy. He was an early and strong supporter of the Ḥovevei Zion (early Zionist) movement, and he publicly proclaimed the religious obligation of settling in Ereẓ Israel. A halakhic ruling of his concerning the prohibitions of the *shemitah* year enabled the Orthodox settler-farmers of Ereẓ Israel to maintain both their economic viability and full observance of Jewish law; although this ruling was disputed by many rabbis at the time, it has since been almost universally accepted as the authoritative position concerning *shemitah* practices in Israel (see *Sabbatical Year and Jubilee).

Among his written works are commentaries on the *Shulḥan Arukh* and a very large number of responsa. His broadmindedness and his peace-loving disposition won for him universal admiration. Many Torah institutions in the U.S. and Israel have been named in his honor, most notably the Isaac Elchanan Theological Seminary of *Yeshiva University, New York.

**SPINOZA, BARUCH** (1632-1677), Dutch philosopher and one of the leaders in the field of metaphysics.

Spinoza grew up during a period of intellectual and religious turmoil in Holland, when scholars and intellectuals began to openly question traditional beliefs. As an outstanding student, Spinoza became involved in those controversies. In 1656 he began to attract attention by questioning, among other matters, whether Moses really wrote the Bible and whether Adam was the first man. For the traditionalist Jewish community, these were radical, unthinkable ideas and on July 27 of that year he was excommunicated by the rabbinical council. "Having long known of the evil opinions and acts of Baruch de Spinoza . . . the council decided with the advice of the rabbis that the said Spinoza should be excommunicated and cut off from the Nation of Israel," read the declaration. All members of the Jewish community were forbidden to have any contact with him and there were even reports of attempts on his life.

Spinoza continued his university studies and his attacks on traditional religion. As a rationalist he rejected anything in religion that could not be logically explained. Thus he did not believe in prophecy or divine revelation. He felt that the Bible was written by men and must be interpreted only as a historical account. But he did not deny the existence of God, as he considered God to be the only rational explanation for the existence of the world and the laws of nature. He was a staunch supporter of intellectual and religious freedom.

In 1674 Spinoza completed his major work, called *Ethics,* but could not find a publisher because of its controversial nature. It was printed only after his death. He also wrote a *Political Treatise,* a Hebrew grammar book, and a historical critique of the Bible, in which he tries to identify the authors of the various sections and interpret miracles in a rational way.

Having been rejected by the Jewish community, he wrote most of his works for Christian friends, and even changed his name from Baruch to the Latin version, Benedict. His fame spread during his lifetime and he was consulted by scholars and statesmen alike. He died in the Hague.

**SPORTS.** In modern times, Jews have been actively involved in all forms of professional and social sports, as participants, organizers and financiers. In earlier times, however, Jewish participation in sports was not common. Sports as practiced by the Greeks and Romans were usually conducted in the nude and involved cruelties that made them repugnant to the Jews of the time. However, there is evidence that a sports association of young Jews existed in Asia Minor about 250 b.c.e. A Palestinian scholar of the Talmud, *Simeon ben Lakish was said to have been a gladiator in his youth, and during the last decades of the first century b.c.e. and the first few centuries of the common era, sports stadiums were erected in several cities in Ereẓ Israel. These, however, were not built to promote Jewish athletics, but as a means of Hellenizing Ereẓ Israel.

In the Middle Ages sporting activities were conducted in many places. In the 13th century it was the custom to hold tournaments and jousts as part of marriage celebrations; one medieval author describes "young men who go out on horseback to greet the bridegroom, and indulge in combats with one another, and tear one another's garments or cause injury to the horses." The most popular sports during medieval times were ballgames, which some rabbis even permitted to be played on the Sabbath. Exact details are not known about the nature of the games played but one was very similar to handball, although the ball was not struck by the hand but was caught in a long, narrow, scoop-like basket attached to the wrist and was thrown against a wall.

In the 19th century the number of Jews participating in sports increased, and many Jews in Europe and the United States did well in a variety of

Baruch Spinoza

1

2

1. One of the newest sports enjoyed by Israelis today – skiing on the slopes of Mount Herman, a snow-covered peak in the mountains bordering on Syria and Lebanon, which was captured in the Six-Day War of June 1967.
2. Students at the Wingate College of Physical Education race in training along the school's well-tended oval track.

1

2

4

3

5

1. Confined to a wheelchair, a contestant in an archery competition takes careful aim, during the 17th International Paraplegic Olympics held at Ramat Gan Sports Stadium, November 1968.
2. Ḥanan Keren, member of the Israel basketball team, takes a flying leap in front of the U. S. basket, during a match at the 1973 Maccabiah Games.
3. An Israel-Austria soccer game at Ramat Gan Stadium, December 1969.
4. Some of the more than 8,000 swimmers who participated in the 16th annual crossing of Lake Kinneret in September 1969.
5. Four simultaneous table-tennis matches, at the Seventh Maccabiah Games, July 1965.

sports. In 1896, seven Jewish athletes won 13 medals between them at the first modern Olympic Games in Athens. With the growth of the Zionist movement at the end of the century, Jewish interest in sports and physical fitness increased greatly. The Maccabi movement of sports clubs was then developed. By 1914, over 100 Maccabi clubs existed in Europe. The largest of these clubs – Ha-Koaḥ of Vienna, Bar Kochba of Berlin, and Ha-Gibor of Prague – became famous for their oustanding teams; however, it was Hungary that produced the most successful Jewish athletes in Europe.

Many Jewish children who went to the United States and Great Britain early in the 20th century learned the national games of these countries and became proficient in sports which required little space and equipment, such as boxing, handball, table tennis, basketball, gymnastics and wrestling. Professional sports, particularly boxing and basketball, attracted many Jews, who took advantage of the athletic scholarships offered by many universities to gain a college education.

Following World War II, the sports picture changed. Jews began to participate less in competition sports and diverted their attention to social sports such as tennis, golf, polo, yachting and squash. Most Jewish youth in college now play sports for recreation and not in order to receive scholarships.

In Israel, the first Jewish sports clubs, the Rishon le-Zion Club in Jaffa and the Ben Giora Club in Jerusalem, were established in 1906. In 1908 the first national sports competition – the Reḥovot Festival – was organized and held annually until the outbreak of World War I. Sports outside of school were organized by voluntary organizations. The first Maccabi club was established in Jerusalem in 1911 and soon had 300 members. By 1914 Maccabi had about 1,000 members in 15 clubs. The Maccabiah Games, an international competition of Jewish athletes, was organized in 1932.

At the second Maccabiah Games, in 1935, there were athletes from 27 countries. The Games were held again in 1951, 1953, and thereafter every four years, attracting many of the best Jewish athletes from the world over.

In 1980 over 40,000 athletes participated in organized competitive athletics in Israel. In international sports, Israel has participated in the Olympics since 1952 (except for 1980 which she boycotted); she was represented at the Asian Games from 1954 until debarred from further participation in 1974, due to Arab pressure. In 1992 Israel won its first Olympic medals and was admitted to the European Soccer Conference.

In non-competitive sports, Israel each year sponsors a "March to Jerusalem" and a swim across the Sea of Galilee. The march to Jerusalem draws thousands of of people of all ages and from many countries to join the soldiers in training who march. There is also the cross-country running corresponding to biblical events; on Hanukkah, for instance, relays of runners from Maccabi carry torches from Modi'in, birthplace of the *Hasmoneans, to the presidential residence in Jerusalem.

### INDIVIDUAL SPORTS

**Association Football (Soccer).** In soccer, the world's most popular sport, several Jews have distinguished themselves since 1900. Early in the 20th century the Danish brothers, Niels and Harald Bohr became famous soccer players; Harald won a silver medal in the first Olympic soccer competition in 1908. Other Jewish Olympic gold medallists in soccer have included Sandor Geller of Hungary (1952), Boris Razinsky of the Soviet Union (1956) and Arpad Orban of Hungary (1964). In 1967, Mark Lazarus became the first Jewish player to take part in a Wembley Cup (England) final. In the 1950s and 1960s Beta Guttman of Hungary was considered one of the world's greatest soccer coaches. Mikhail Romm was one of the organizers of soccer in the Soviet Union, and Mikhail Loshinsky played in the national team before World War II. Jack Swart and Jaap van Praag were members of the Netherlands soccer club, Ajax of Amsterdam, which won the European Cup and World Club championship in 1972.

**Baseball.** Baseball has been part of the American cultural scene since its origin in the 1840s. It is commonly played from elementary school through university and is considered the national pastime. Each week hundreds of thousands of fans troop to the ballpark to cheer on their favorite teams to victory and to suffer with them in their defeats. Many of the ballplayers are Jewish, and many Jews are managers, umpires and coaches.

In 1882 Louis Kramer (1849-1922) helped organize the American Association and was its president in 1891. Jacob C. (Jake) Morse (1860-1937) was a noted sportswriter, and manager of the Boston team in the Union League in 1884. Barney Dreyfuss, the owner of the Pittsburgh Pirates, founded the World Series in 1903. Other Jewish baseball executives include Harry (Judge) Goldman (1857-1941), an organiser of the American League, and Moses and Sydney Frank, officials of the Baltimore team in 1901-02.

The first Jewish professional baseball player was Lipman (Lip) Pike. In 1866 he played third base for the Philadelphia Athletics for $20 per week. Later he played for the Brooklyn Atlantics when they had a winning streak of more than 130 games, and he set the first homerun record when he hit six in one game. Jews who played on championship teams prior to 1900 include William M. (Billy) Nash (1865-1929), a major league player for 15 years; James T. (Chief) Roseman, an outfielder for New York in the American Association and manager of St. Louis; and Daniel E. Stearns (1861-1944), first baseman for Cincinnati.

Jewish ballplayers who achieved notable success after 1900 include Henry (Hank) Greenberg (1911- ), twice voted most valuable player and three times homerun champion; Sanford (Sandy) *Koufax; Al Rosen (1924- ), third baseman for the Cleveland Indians and American League home run champion in 1950 and 1953 and American League Most Valuable Player in 1953; Barney Pelty (1880-1939), pitcher for the St. Louis Browns, 1903-1912; Charles Solomon (Buddy) Myer (1904–74), American league infielder for Washington and Boston for 17 years, who won the league batting title in 1935; Larry Sherry (1935- ), pitching hero for the Los Angeles Dodgers in the 1959 World Series, and a major leaguer for 11 seasons; Arthur (Art) Shamsky (1941- ), a major league outfielder since 1965 who equaled a league record by hitting four home runs in four consecutive turns at bat and in 1969 batted .300 when the New York Mets won their first World Series; Kenneth (Ken) Holtzman, who pitched a no-hitter in 1969 for

Albert Leonard "Flip" Rosen, third baseman for the Cleveland Indians in the early 1950s, and winner of the American League Most Valuable Player Award in 1953.

1

2

1. U.S. champion walker, Henry Helmut Laskan (1916– ), who won a record 42 national championships.
2. Swinging the bat for the Boston Braves is Sidney Gordon (1918 – ), who was characterized as a "solid ballplayer."

Chicago and was a member of the World Champion Oakland Athletics in 1972 and 1973; and Alexander (Al) Schacht, baseball pitcher from 1919-1921 and "Clown Prince of Baseball."

**Basketball.** Basketball fans have cheered numerous Jewish players since Paul (Twister) Steinberg (1880- ) began his career at Little Falls, N.Y. in 1900. Today basketball is an extremely popular recreational sport and many Jews are involved in college and professional basketball as players, coaches and owners.

Early Jewish basketball personalities include Frank Basloe (1887-1966), professional player and coach who toured American from 1903-23 with his squad; Harry Baum (1882-1959), professor of engineering at City College of New York, was an outstanding coach. Henry Hart Elias (1882-1941), the first Jewish college player, played for Columbia and served as its first coach, and the first Jewish player to win collegiate honors was Samuel Melitzer (1880- ), in 1907, also for Columbia.

The leading school for Jewish basketball players was, however, the City College of New York. From 1908-1950, City College teams were among the best in the country and were nearly all Jewish. Nat Holman developed most of these teams; among his All-American players was William (Red) Holtzman (1920- ), who later coached the New York Knickerbockers to two world championships.

Many coaches and owners of basketball teams have been Jewish. These include Adolph Schayes; Harry Litwack, coach at Temple University, who has won more than 350 games; Arnold (Red) Auerbach; Abe Saperstein and Barney Sedran. Several members of the Basketball Hall of Fame are Leonard D. Sachs, David Tobey, Barney Sedran, Nat Holman, Red Auerbach, Abe Saperstein, Max Friedman and Edward Gottlieb.

**Boxing.** Though it is somewhat unusual to think of Jews as professional boxers, in earlier times Jews were at the top of the fight game. The most basic of sports, boxing was a natural pastime for many of the Jews growing up in urban New York city at the beginning of the 20th century; the availability of numerous boxing clubs and the popularity of the sport made boxing the perfect outlet for the aggressive youth of the ghetto. Jews held many world championships and also became successful managers and trainers.

The best boxers of the early era were Daniel *Mendoza; Samuel (Dutch Sam) Elias (1776-1816), who is credited with inventing the uppercut; Barney Aaron (1800-1850), Englishman known as the "Star of the East"; and Harry and Johnny Lazarus, brothers who emigrated to the U.S. in the 1850s and helped foster interest in boxing by giving lessons and exhibitions.

The first Jewish boxer to win a world championship under Marquis of Queensberry rules was Harry ("The Human Hairpin") Harris (1880-1959), bantamweight; and the Boxing Hall of Fame includes Daniel Mendoza, Benny Leonard, Abe Attell, Barney Ross, Joe Choynski, Lew Tendler, Ted "Kid" Lewis, Battling Levinsky, Barney "Young" Aaron, and Max Baer.

**Football.** In the third football game ever played, Moses Henry Epstein represented Columbia against Rutgers in 1870. In the next year Emil G. Hirsch, a future rabbi, appeared in the first game played at Pennsylvania University. Since that time football has become a major spectator sport, and the Sunday televised football game a national tradition. To the present day Jews have distinguished themselves in both the college and professional ranks.

Lucius Littauer, future "Glove King of America" and congressman for New York state, played for Harvard in 1875 and returned there in 1881 to become college football's first coach. Phil King was the first Jewish All-American. He and Benny Friedman (Michigan), Fred Sington (Alabama), Aaron Rosenberg (Southern California), Marshall Goldberg (Pittsburgh), and Sidney Luckman (Columbia), are members of the College Football Hall of Fame.

Although professional football began officially in 1895, the Syracuse, New York Athletic Association, with several Jews on its team, played the game for money before that date. Jews have been particularly involved in front office management of professional football clubs. Sidney Gillman (1911- ), coach of the Los Angeles Rams and San Diego Chargers, and Art Modell (1925- ), owner of the Cleveland Browns, are notable examples.

**Handball.** Though Jews have performed well in many sports, they have been among the masters of handball. Accounting for 35% of the membership of the United States Handball Association, Jewish champions have included Victor Hershkowitz (1919- ), handball's greatest all-round player, and Jimmy Jacobs (1931- ), the best player of the 1960s.

Handball held its first national championship in 1919, and the following year Max Gold won the title. Other players who gained national singles titles were

George Nelson, Ken Schneider, Paul Haber, Simon (Stuffy) Singer, Martin Decatur, Ken Davidoff, Fred Lewis, Steve Sandler, Michael Schmookler, Irving Jacobs, Harry Goldstein, Jack Londin, David Margolis, Joseph Garber, Arthur Wolfe, Seymour and Morton Alexander, and Sheila Maroshick. Members of the Helms Handball Hall of Fame include players Hershkowitz and Schneider and commissioners Hyman Goldstein and Judge Joseph Shane.

Other sports in which Jews have been leading participants include automobile racing, billiards, bowling, cricket, gymnastics, horse racing, rugby, tennis and track and field. In swimming the American Mark Spitz (1950- ) won four gold medals at the 1968 Olympiad and seven at the 1972 Games, establishing numerous world records in the process.

**STALIN** (Dzhugashvili), **JOSEF VISSARIONOVICH** (1879-1953). Throughout his career as Bolshevik revolutionary, ruler of the Soviet Union (see *Russia) and leader of world *Communism, Josef Stalin had to deal with the "Jewish question." His theory, in agreement with Lenin and the previous party line, was that the Jews were not a real and separate nation, and that eventually they would be assimilated and disappear.

Stalin, however, was not content to let events take what he thought was their natural course and attempted to speed up the process by imposing forced assimilation on the Jews. The Yiddish school system, publications, theaters and other institutions were liquidated, so that at the end of the 1930s only a few traces of Jewish culture remained.

After the German attack on the Soviet Union in 1941, in order to gain the support of western Jews for the Soviet war effort, Stalin established the Jewish Anti-Fascist Committee which was allowed to speak of Jewish nationality, solidarity and brotherhood. After the war, however, twenty six members of this committee were in 1952 charged with Jewish "nationalism" and maintaining contact with Western espionage, and were secretly executed.

An exceptional episode in Stalin's attitude toward Jewish nationhood was his energetic support in 1947-48 for the establishment of a Jewish state in Palestine. This policy, seemingly in contradiction to his anti-Zionist philosophy, was clearly a political move directed against Britain's position in the Middle East, and was reversed during the anti-Semitic and anti-Zionist stand of his last years.

From the end of 1948 until his death, Stalin displayed an extremely hostile attitude toward everything Jewish. There ensued mass arrests and executions of leading Jewish writers, artists, intellectuals and professionals in various fields. In the famous "Doctors' Plot" staged under Stalin's supervision in 1952, a number of Jewish doctors were accused of having conspired to kill government officials by incorrect medical treatment. Jews were ousted from their positions and rumors of an impending mass deportation of Jews to distant regions began to circulate. Stalin's death on March 5, 1953, however, prevented the execution of that final plan.

**STAMPS.** Stamp collectors (philatelists) often devote themselves to collecting stamps on a particular subject. Such a subject is "Judaica," the depiction of Jewish themes or famous "Jewish personalities" on stamps issued by various countries. Among the subjects in the Judaica collection are Nobel prize winners such as Niels Bohr and Albert Einstein; philosophers such as Maimonides; musicians such as Anton Rubinstein and Gustav Mahler; artists like Modigliani and Chagall; actors, writers, politicians and other outstanding figures.

In addition, there are stamps commemorating important events, places and themes in Jewish history. There is, for example, an Indian stamp depicting a synagogue there, a Polish stamp commemorating the Warsaw ghetto uprising, and a Brazilian stamp issued in honor of Israel President Zalman Shazar's visit to that country in 1966. There are also several stamps with Hebrew lettering on them (issued by the United Nations, Russia, Denmark and Jordan) and various treatments of biblical subjects. A field of special interest to collectors of Judaica is the period of the Holocaust, including anti-Semitic issues and ghetto stamps.

Of course, the greatest source of Judaica stamps is Israel. The first post offices in the Holy Land were established by the European powers in the mid-19th century. France began issuing special stamps for the Middle East in 1885. Austrian postage stamps for the area were issued in 1867, and the Italians were the first to issue stamps specially overprinted with the name of the city "Gerusalemme."

The British occupation forces issued the first stamp in Palestine on February 10, 1918 and it bears the initials E.E.F. ("Egyptian Expeditionary Forces"). In 1920, it was decided to issue stamps bearing inscriptions in the then official languages of

1. Stamp issued by the Hungarian Post Office in honor of Ludwik Lazar Zamenhof, the founder of the international language Esperanto.
2. The 19th-century Jewish poet Heinrich Heine, on a stamp issued by the East German "Deutsche Demokratische Republik."
3. Stamp issued by Ghana honoring both Albert Einstein and UNESCO (United Nations Educational, Scientific and Cultural Organization). In the center is a stylized drawing of an atom and beneath it Einstein's famous equation showing the relationship between matter and energy.

1

2

3

1

2

3

1. The Communist revolutionary Rosa Luxemberg, portrayed on a stamp issued by the U.S.S.R. Post Office.
2. A West German stamp issued in commemoration of the 20th-century German Jewish scholar and religious thinker, Leo Baeck.
3. U.S. violinist Isaac Stern, in a relaxed moment with his violin.

the country: English, Hebrew and Arabic. In 1927 the only pictorial set to be issued by the British government appeared and remained in use until the State of Israel was established in 1948.

During the War of Independence, communications were extremely difficult and from time to time the supply of postage stamps ran out. In order to overcome this shortage, and to continue a regular postal service, many local agencies issued their own stamps. Noteworthy among these and eagerly sought by philatelists are the Jewish National Fund labels overprinted with the word *Do'ar* ("post") and the local issues of Safed, Rishon le-Zion, and Petaḥ Tikvah.

On May 9, 1948, while Jerusalem was under siege, the first set of local stamps was issued. These were J.N.F. stamps showing the map of Ereẓ Israel with the frontiers of the Jewish state and the "International" city of Jerusalem as proposed by the United Nations.

On May 16, 1948, the *Do'ar Ivri* ("Hebrew Post") stamps bearing pictures of ancient Jewish coins went on sale throughout Israel. Since the name of the new state was not known until the day before issue (May 15, 1948), by which time the stamps had already been printed, the designation *Do'ar Ivri* was used instead. This set is today a highly-prized collector's item.

Since 1948 Israel has produced over 500 stamps, which have received international recognition for their attractive and colorful designs. The definitive series of ancient coins, the twelve tribes, the signs of the zodiac, and the emblems of towns and cities of Israel; annual Jewish New Year and Independence Day commemoratives; and the many other fascinating subjects have introduced Israel to philatelists throughout the world.

Many philatelic clubs, both in Israel and abroad, are devoted to the study of the postal history of Ereẓ Israel. There are also societies devoted to the study of Judaica stamps. One of these publishes the *Judaica Historical Philatelic Journal* in the United States.

**STEINER, HANNAH** (1894-1944), one of the founders of WIZO (Women's International Zionist Organization) in Czechoslovakia and its first president. Under her leadership, the Czechoslovakia WIZO trained young women to be pioneers, conducted Hebrew courses, and cared for impoverished Jews. When thousands of Jewish refugees fled from Germany to Czechoslovakia in 1933, Hannah helped organize a relief committee for them.

On March 16, 1939, the day after the Nazi occupation of Prague, Hannah Steiner was arrested but was released a few weeks later. She made arrangements for her son and daughter to go to Palestine, while she and her husband chose to remain in Czechoslovakia to help their fellow-Jews. Hannah and her husband were sent to the ghetto of Theresienstadt, where she was in charge of relief services for women. In 1944 she was deported to a concentration camp where she met her death.

**STERN, ISAAC** (1920-    ) is a celebrated U.S. violinist. At the outbreak of the war of October, 1973, the Israel government received an unusual telegram: "Have fiddle, will travel." The sender was Isaac Stern, who was informing the government of Israel that he was willing to come and perform before troops and civilians, as he had done during the Six-Day War.

Stern was born in the Ukraine, but was taken at an early age to San Francisco, where his mother worked as a pianist and teacher. He began studying the violin at the age of eight, and at 11 he was soloist with the San Francisco Orchestra. Besides his worldwide success as a violinist, he became known in New York for the active part he took in saving Carnegie Hall from destruction. He became president of the American-Israel Cultural Foundation, and appears frequently with the Israel Philharmonic Orchestra.

**STOCKADE AND WATCHTOWER.** When Arab-Jewish tensions mounted in Palestine, especially between the years 1936 and 1947, it became more and more difficult for Jews to establish agricultural settlements far from the guarded cities. Though large tracts of land had been bought up by the Jewish National Fund, the process of building kibbutzim on these lands involved weeks or even months of working in open, unprotected areas, with the Jewish pioneers exposed to Arab attack.

The Jewish settlers therefore evolved a plan for building "instant" kibbutzim, known as Stockade and Watchtower settlements. These were set up in surprise operations which left the Arabs no time or forewarning to plan an attack. Convoys carrying hundreds of Jewish helpers, prefabricated huts and fortifications set out at daybreak, protected by Jewish settlement police. By nightfall they had completed the erection of the entire settlement.

The "stockade" or outer wall, consisted of a double layer of planks with a filling of earth and stones. The "watchtower" stood at the center of the settlement, equipped with a searchlight and electric generator to permit the countryside to be scanned for signs of hostility. The 118 settlements established in this way include Tirat Ẓevi, Nir David and Sedeh Naḥum in the Beth Shean Valley; Massadah and Sha'ar ha-Golan in the Jordan Valley; and Ḥanitah in Upper Galilee.

**STREISAND, BARBRA** (1942– ), a U.S. actress, singer, director. Born in Brooklyn, N.Y., Barbra worked as a switchboard operator and theater usher until she won a singing contest at a Greenwich Village bar. After appearing several times on television, she made her first Broadway success in 1962 in the musical *I Can Get It For You Wholesale.* Two years later she played the leading role in the Broadway show *Funny Girl,* and became a great star. She won an Academy Award in 1968 for her role in the film version of *Funny Girl,* and she starred in *Yentl.* Her television show, *My Name Is Barbra,* received five Emmy awards in 1965. She was also a recording star.

1

2

**STRUCK, HERMANN** (1876-1944), German Jewish artist. Born into an Orthodox family, Struck studied at the Berlin Academy. He joined the Zionist movement at an early age, and in 1903 visited Palestine. On his way back to Germany he stopped in Vienna to visit Herzl and etch his portrait. In 1923 he moved to Palestine and settled in Haifa.

Struck's favorite technique was copper etching, although he did lithographs as well. His early work was usually signed with his Hebrew name, Ḥayyim Aharon ben David. A master of his craft, Struck taught graphic techniques to well-known artists such as Marc Chagall and Max Liebermann. He excelled as a portrait artist, but also did landscapes and scenes from Jewish life. Struck remained an Orthodox Jew all his life and attended several Zionist congresses as one of the leaders of the Mizrachi Party.

**STUDY.** Judaism considers study of the Torah (known in Hebrew as *talmud Torah*) as a most important religious duty; indeed the Mishnah gives a list of the most important *mitzvot* and says that *talmud Torah* is equal to all of them. The centrality of study is already clear from the Bible. In Moses' farewell speech to the Jews before he died, he said: "And these words [the Torah] which I command you

3

4

5

1. Members of Kibbutz Sha'ar ha-Golan put the finishing touches to a scale model of how their kibbutz looked as a "stockade and a watchtower" settlement on the very first day of its existence, May 3, 1938.
2. The usually vivacious U.S. actress Barbra Streisand, caught in a pensive mood.
3. "At the Synagogue," a painting completed by Lazar Krestin in 1918, showing the complementary function of the synagogue as a study hall for young and old alike.
4 and 5. Two paintings by the German-born Israel artist, Hermann Struck: "Self-Portrait" and "A Jewish Porter."

this day, shall be upon your heart; you should teach them to your children and you should talk about them at home, on journeys, when you lie down and when you get up" (Deuteronomy 6:6-8). This passage is so important that it is part of the *Shema which is recited twice a day, and it means that study of the Torah should be a person's main occupation.

Of course, people have to work in order to earn a living, but study is still the highest aspiration. According to the Talmud (a name which itself actually means study), a person must work hard at study and should be prepared to sacrifice a lot of his comforts for it. He should concentrate on it and ask again and again if he does not understand what his teacher is saying. Just as the student must be persistent, the teacher must be patient. Study is not, however, only for children or students. Everybody must devote himself to it.

Studying Torah has two purposes. Firstly it equips a person to be able to perform the other *mitzvot* correctly, which he cannot do if he does not know how. And secondly, it is a supreme *mitzvah* itself. This means that even if a person knows how to observe the commandments – and even if, theoretically, he knows "everything" – he is still required to study. This point is so important that some rabbis were of the opinion that one should not stop studying even in order to pray.

Because study is a *mitzvah,* there are special laws about it. Three benedictions should be recited before study; these are included in the beginning of the *Shaḥarit* service every morning. Everybody should set aside a fixed time every day for study and each community should establish a house of study *(bet ha-midrash)* which is holier even than the synagogue. If a person, for some good reason, cannot study, he should at least help others to by supporting them.

"Talmudists" by Lionel S. Reiss.

The rabbis worked out a program of study. At the age of five a child should start studying Bible, at ten years of age Mishnah, at 13 the commandments and at 15, the Talmud. A grown man should divide his study time equally between Bible, Mishnah and Talmud. In the course of time, the curriculum for children became adapted to different conditions and to the varying capacities of the students.

The *mitzvah* of study does not only include religious studies. In order to understand the Bible, Mishnah and Talmud, a knowledge of other disciplines is needed, particularly mathematics and the natural sciences. Thus, a person should study them as well. Some rabbis achieved eminence in these fields.

The tradition of study and learning has always occupied an important place in Jewish communal life. Wherever the Jews have wandered or been driven, one of the first things they always did was to set up schools. This accounts for their success in coming to terms with their new environment and for the outstanding number of great Jewish intellectuals who have made major contributions to world civilizations.

For more information about the methods of study, see *Education; *Yeshivah.

**SUFFERING.** One of the most serious challenges to religion is the problem of suffering. If God is all-powerful and good, as Judaism claims He is, how is it possible that He allows His creatures to suffer? This is not a new problem. The Bible is aware that suffering and pain are characteristic of human existence and many of the books of the Bible are concerned about the theological issues involved. The Book of Habakkuk, when it deals with one of the aspects of the problem, says that "the righteous man must live by his faith." This seems to mean that it is beyond the ability of human intelligence to understand the question and that man must have faith that God is doing the right thing.

The rabbis of the Talmud and the medieval Jewish philosophers were also troubled about the problem of suffering. Some thinkers suggested that the innocent suffer in this world so that their share in the world to come will be greater, but other philosophers rejected this idea. Another solution suggested was that suffering comes on a man in order to warn him to mend his ways and that "when a man sees that he is suffering, let him examine his deeds." The rabbis of the Talmud believed that it is a great religious virtue to bear one's suffering "with love," i.e., patiently and without becoming rebellious.

Whatever the solution to the theological problem of suffering, Judaism absolutely forbids inflicting suffering on other people and even on animals. Also, no man may ignore the suffering of others but must do everything in his power to help remedy the situation. This applies to physical suffering, to poverty and to psychological suffering. Furthermore, no man has the right to enjoy himself if the rest of the community is suffering. For other aspects of this subject see *Animals; *Good and Evil; *Reward and Punishment.

**SUKENIK, ELIEZER LIPA** (1889-1953), Israel archaeologist who played a central role in the acquisition and analysis of the Dead Sea Scrolls. Born in Poland, Sukenik settled in Ereẓ Israel when he was in his mid-20s and there enjoyed a long distinguished career as a teacher and field archaeologist. He directed excavations of the synagogues at *Bet Alfa and Hammat-Gader and he participated in the clearing of the Third (Herodian) Wall of Jerusalem. In 1938 he was appointed professor of archaeology at the Hebrew University and director of the University Museum of Jewish Antiquities. In 1947, when several ancients scrolls found in the region of the Dead Sea were offered for sale by Arab dealers, he was the first scholar to realize their significance and he succeeded in purchasing three of the most important ones. The remaining five years of his life he devoted to the study of these Dead Sea scrolls. His son, also a distinguished archaeologist, continued his studies of the Scrolls; for his biography, see Yigael *Yadin.

**SUKKOT** (Hebrew for "huts" or "tabernacles"), a seven-day festival beginning on the 15th day of the month of Tishrei, which falls in September or October. (In the Diaspora an extra eighth day is celebrated.) One of its main observances is living temporarily in huts, called *sukkot,* resembling those in which the Children of Israel dwelt during their forty years in the wilderness after the Exodus from Egypt.

This autumn festival was the last of the three "pilgrim" festivals connected with the farming year. From all corners of the Land of Israel throngs of pilgrims used to make their way up to Jerusalem carrying the gaily decorated baskets of fruit and grain which they brought to the Temple as a thanksgiving offering. At the gates of the city the townsfolk greeted them with music. The pilgrims then ascended the broad marble staircase that led from the City of David to the summit of the Temple Mount, where they would present their offerings to the Priests.

This holiday was also the occasion for the consecration of the Temple built by Solomon and every seventh year on Sukkot, the Torah was read by the king before the assembled people. In his vision of the end of days, the prophet *Zechariah foretells that all the nations of the world will assemble for the festival of Sukkot in Jerusalem to worship God.

1. Archaeologist Eliezer Lipa Sukenik, pictured with the type of earthenware jar in which the Dead Sea Scrolls were found.
2. The second week of the Yom Kippur War in October 1973 was also the week of the Sukkot festival. Even at the battlefront, Israel soldiers were able to observe the *mitzvah* of sitting in a *sukkah* – as in this highly unusual one perched on top of a half-track serving as a communications post in the Golan Heights.

1

2

2

3

1. A silver *etrog* container produced in Turkey in the 19th century. The top half of the oval lifts off for the *etrog* to be placed inside. The silver cut-out lettering consists of the verse from Leviticus, "And you shall take for yourselves . . .fruit of goodly trees," which has been interpreted by the rabbis as the *mitzvah* of taking the *etrog* as one of the "four species."
2. A young girl puts the finishing touches to a richly-decorated *sukkah,* located in Bene Berak, Israel. In addition to the generous selection of natural fruits hanging from the *sekhakh*-ceiling, the *sukkah* has been equipped with a floor rug and numerous paintings and plaques for the walls — all of which aid in making the *sukkah* a miniature, albeit temporary, home.
3. Bukharan Jews parading through the streets of Tel Aviv with Torah scrolls, on the eve of Simḥat Torah, 1969.

1

**The Sukkah.** The *sukkah* is a structure with at least three walls, made of any material. It must be at least ten handbreadths in height, and in area at least seven handbreadths square. The roof covering, or *sekhakh,* is usually leafy branches, and these must be arranged so that there is more covered than open space.

In present-day Israel, as in other countries, Jews construct *sukkot* in their gardens, on the sidewalks, and on the roofs and balconies of their houses, just as they did at the time of the return from the Babylonian exile, as described in the Book of Nehemiah: "So the people went forth . . . and made themselves booths, every one upon the roof of his house, and in their courts, and in the courts of the house of God . . . and there was very great gladness."

Though the *sukkah* is only a temporary dwelling for the week of the festival, it is used as if it were one's permanent home. Thus it is customary to beautify the *sukkah* with all sorts of decorations, such as hanging fruit from the ceiling, and adorning the walls with paper cut-outs and pictures of festival motifs and biblical scenes. And for the meals eaten there,the family's best china and silverware are used. Caucasian Jews build the walls of their *sukkot* with fir branches, while the Mountain Jews of Daghestan decorate their *sukkot* walls with tapestries and carpets. The Kurdish Jews sit on rugs in the *sukkah* as they do at home and in the synagogue, and in Aden, Jews were accustomed to decorate their *sukkot* with ornate glass lamps.

On the first night of the festival, a person is obliged to eat his festive meal in the *sukkah.* During the remainder of the festival, any full meal should be eaten in the *sukkah,* and the blessing "who commanded us to dwell in the *sukkah*" is recited, usually after the blessing over bread. However, if rain is likely to spoil one's food (the *sekhakh* must not be rainproof), one may continue the meal indoors. Living in the *sukkah* instead of in the security of one's home is thus a reminder that we are dependent on God's favors. Where the climate allows it, some people sleep in the *sukkah.* Synagogues usually build a *sukkah* for the benefit of members who have none of their own. The world over, the festive meals in the *sukkah* are accompanied by the happy singing of the family and its guests. Hospitality to the needy, which is always encouraged, is especially praiseworthy during this festival. Indeed, the Midrash states that the Children of Israel were divinely protected by "clouds of glory" during their 40-year wanderings in the wilderness, because the Patriarch Abraham had given shelter to three strangers in need. In fact, it is the opinion of Rabbi *Akiva in the Talmud that the *sukkot* mentioned in the Torah were not actual booths, but these protective clouds.

**Ushpizin.** When a family performs the *mitzvah* of the *sukkah* joyfully, they are said to be visited in the *sukkah* by seven "guests of the festival" (the *ushpizin*) who are present in spirit. Each day it is customary to invite and welcome one of these seven guests — Abraham, Isaac, Jacob, Moses, Aaron and David — by an appropriate recitation.

**The Arba'ah Minim.** Another distinctive observance of the festival of Sukkot is making a blessing over four kinds of plants, called the *arba'ah minim,* "the four species." The first is the citron *(etrog),* the second is the *lulav* (an unopened palm branch); the third is myrtle twigs *(hadasim);* and the fourth consist of sprigs of willow, called *aravot.* Because of the importance of this *mitzvah,* Jews generally spend time some days before the festival choosing their set of four species with loving care. In Israel, special market places are set up, where fathers and their children can be seen gathered around little stalls, patiently selecting an *etrog* that has a handsome shape, a clear skin, and an even yellow color. The fulfillment of the *mitzvah* of *arba'ah minim* as it appears in the Bible requires every male Jew to take the *arba'ah minim* in the hand on the first day of Sukkot. The *lulav* is held in the right hand, with the spine facing the holder. Strips of palm near its base bind three sprigs of myrtle to its right and two twigs of willow to its left. The *etrog* is held in the left hand. The *lulav*, the largest of the species, gives its name to the four, so that the benediction which is recited every morning of the festival is: "Blessed art Thou . . . King of the Universe, Who has sanctified us with His commandments and commanded us to take the *lulav*." Within the Temple, the *arba'ah minim* had to be taken each day of the festival. After its destruction, Johanan ben Zakkai ordained that wherever Jews celebrate Sukkot, the *arba'ah minim* should also be taken in the hand for seven days in commemoration of the Temple. During the morning prayers, while the thanksgiving Psalms of *Hallel* are chanted, the four species are waved – toward the east, south, west, and north, upward and downward – to remind oneself of God's rule over all of nature. Needless to say, a green sea of dozens of rhythmically waved *lulavim* in the synagogue makes an unforgettable sight.

Many symbolic interpretations of the four species have been offered over the generations. The Midrash, for example, compares them to four different kinds of Jews, each with a distinct "taste" and "fragrance." Some excel in the study of Torah as well as in their good deeds, some excel at one, some perhaps at neither. Others symbolically inferred from the fact that the *mitzvah* can be carried out only when the four species are held together that Jews must regard themselves and each other as parts of one body. Still other sages taught that the *lulav* represents the spine, the *etrog* the heart, the myrtle the eye, and the willow the mouth. The *mitzvah* of the four species is thus a reminder that all of one's organs should submit to the service of God.

Interestingly, archaeologists have recently shown that even during the rigors of war against the Romans in the second century c.e., Bar Kokhba took special care to see that his warriors were supplied with the four species. In more recent times, too, soldiers on duty in Israel, prisoners of war, and families living in remote hamlets or behind the Iron Curtain, have continued this tradition of defying hardship in order to observe the commandments of the Torah joyfully.

**The Water-Drawing Celebration.** In the days of the Temple, each day during the last six *ḥol ha-mo'ed* days of the festival (though not on the Sabbath), the priests used to fill a golden flagon with water drawn from the beautiful spring of *Siloam in the valley to the south of the Temple Mount, and carry it up the hill for a ceremony at the altar. This ceremony was called *Simḥat Bet ha-Sho'evah* (the joy of the water-drawing). According to the Mishnah, whoever failed to witness this ceremony in his lifetime "never witnessed real joy." Golden candlesticks, 50 cubits high, were lit with wicks made out of worn-out garments of the priests, and the light emitted was so bright that "there was not a courtyard in Jerusalem that did not reflect the light of the *Bet ha-Sho'evah.*" Men of piety and good deeds used to dance before the candlesticks with burning torches in their hands, singing songs and praises. And countless Levites played on harps, lyres, cymbals, trumpets and other musical instruments, on the 15 steps leading from the Court of the Israelites to the Court of the Women.

King Alexander *Yannai, who also acted as High Priest, once chose to ignore the traditional way of conducting this ceremonial. The vast throng of worshipers immediately reacted by pelting him with thousands of *etrogim*.

In Israel today, the celebration of *Simḥat Bet ha-Sho'evah* has been revived, especially in the *yeshivot* of Jerusalem. Anyone who wants to feel the joy of the *yom-tov* (festival) simply follows the sound of music until he traces it to one of several brightly-lit courtyards or old synagogues, where bearded instrumentalists set the lively rhythm, and visitors join in the singing and folk-dancing.

Part of the huge crowd of worshipers at the Western Wall in Jerusalem during the Sukkot holiday, with virtually every man equipped with his own set of the "four species."

A sketch of Sultan Suleiman I, "The Magnificent," at the age of 30, drawn by the German artist Alfred Duerer from a contemporary description.

**Hoshana Rabbah** is the seventh day of Sukkot. It takes its name from the word *hoshana* ("O save!") which frequently appears in the prayers of the day. Prayers for a good harvest in the year to come are recited during a procession with the four species around the *bimah*, at which a Torah scroll is held. Seven circuits are made, after which five *aravot* bound together are beaten on the ground. Since on this day the decrees of the Day of Atonement are finalized, it is customary to spend the night of Hoshana Rabbah in prayer and study. particularly the Book of Deuteronomy.
**Shemini Aẓeret**. "On the eighth day ye shall have a solemn assembly *(aẓeret):* ye shall do no manner of servile work." (Numbers 29:35). The rabbis have understood this verse as a commandment to celebrate the eighth day of Sukkot as a separate festival. On this day, the memorial service for the departed *(Yizkor)* and a special prayer for rain *(Tefillat Geshem)* are recited as part of the prayer service in the synagogue.
**Simḥat Torah**. The last day of the festival is Simḥat Torah ("rejoicing with the Torah"), which in Israel is celebrated on the same day as Shemini Aẓeret, and in the Diaspora on the day following. On this day, the cycle of reading the Torah which, throughout the year, is read each week portion by portion, is completed. The person called to the final reading is known as the *ḥatan Torah* ("bridegroom of the Torah"). The scroll is immediately rolled back to the beginning to show that the study of Torah never ends, and the *ḥatan Bereshit* ("bridegroom of Genesis") is called to the reading of the first portion of Genesis. It has also become customary to read and re-read the last portion in order to honor all congregants – including even boys under bar mitzvah age – by calling them to the Torah reading.

In the evening and morning, all the scrolls are taken from the ark and carried in procession around the synagogue, while happy songs of praise are sung by the congregation. These seven circuits are known as *hakkafot.* Congregants dance with the scrolls, and children wave gaily decorated flags. The "bridegrooms" then invite their fellow-congregants to a celebration in honor of the day.

**SULEIMAN I**, Ottoman sultan from 1520 to 1566. The epithet "The Magnificent" was given to him by the Europeans as a tribute to the prosperity enjoyed by the empire, thanks to his rule. The Jews called him "King Solomon," not only because it is the Hebrew version of "Suleiman" but also to emphasize his wisdom and legislative achievements.

There were a number of Jews who held important posts during Suleiman's reign, some acting as diplomatic agents of the Ottoman empire in European capitals. Moses Amon, the court physician, was one of his Jewish advisers and accompanied him on his travels and campaigns.

Don Joseph Nasi also played an important role in the Ottoman government, especially in foreign affairs. Deeply impressed by Nasi's abilities, the sultan made him one of his confidants and awarded him the title of Franji Bey. As ruler of Palestine, the sultan gave Nasi the ruined city of *Tiberias to rebuild and settle as a Jewish city. The project, however, was not successful. But Suleiman did leave a lasting mark on Ereẓ Israel: the walls around the Old City of Jerusalem were built at his command and are still standing today (see *Jerusalem).

Despite the fact that during Suleiman's rule the Jews of the Ottoman empire made great cultural and economic progress, the sultan also began imposing financial pressure on them, and it was only through the personal efforts of court Jews that this pressure was kept to a minimum.

**SUN** (Hebrew: *Shemesh*). As provider of life-giving warmth and light for the earth since time immemorial, this great fiery celestial body has been regarded with interest and awe by all mankind. In the biblical account of the creation, God made the sun, together with the moon and the stars, on the fourth day: "And God made the two great lights, the greater light to rule the day and the lesser light to rule the night."

Ancient peoples worshiped the "greater light" as a god, and the cult of the sun was very popular in Palestine among Israel's neighbors. This is evident in the names of ancient cities such as Bet Shemesh, En-Shemesh, and Ir-Shemesh. Though such sun-worshiping was forbidden in the Bible and punishable by death, there is evidence that it was introduced by various Israelite leaders. King *Manasseh of Judea, for example, placed altars in honor of the heavenly bodies in the Temple itself.

Many biblical references are made to the sun in miraculous and symbolic terms. In *Joseph's dream, the sun and moon personified his parents. In *Joshua, the sun is said to have stood still, thus lengthening the day and giving the Israelites time to defeat their enemy in battle while it was still light.

There are also various *aggadot* (legends) in rabbinic literature concerning the sun. One such *aggadah* tells that the sun and moon were originally created the same size. They were bitterly jealous of each other, however, and so God had to choose between them, making one smaller than the other. Since the moon is said to have unlawfully intruded on the sun's domain (that is, it can sometimes be seen during the day when only the sun should be shining), it was punished by being assigned the inferior position.

The times of the daily prayer services are fixed according to the rising and the setting of the sun. There is also a special prayer service in which a blessing is said over the sun, but this occurs only once every 28 years, when the sun supposedly returns to the exact position it occupied at the time of creation. The dates for the ceremony in the second half of the 20th century are April 8, 1953 and March 18, 1981.

**SUZMAN, HELEN** (1917- ), South African politician and member of parliament who strongly opposed her country's discriminatory apartheid policies. Born in Transvaal, South Africa, Helen Suzman was a university lecturer in economics before entering the political arena. She was first elected to Parliament in 1953 as a member of the United Party, the official opposition, but she broke away in 1959, because of disagreements on race policies. Then, together with 12 other party members, she formed the Progressive Party, and until 1974 was the party's only representative in Parliament, representing the constituency of Lower Houghton, Johannesburg.

A formidable debater, she has been a determined opponent of discrimination based on race or color, and a champion of the rights of the black South Africans. She retired from parliament in 1989.

**SWEDEN**, kingdom in northern Europe, part of the Scandinavian peninsula. It is unlikely that there were Jews in Sweden in pagan times, or in the Catholic Middle Ages. After Sweden turned Lutheran in the 16th century, several regulations were issued against the presence of Jews in the country, indicating that some had settled there illegally during certain periods. The regulations of 1685 referred to the Jews as "revilers of Christ and his communion."

The position changed, however, under the rule of the enlightened monarch Gustav III (1771-1792). He allowed Jews to settle there (the first being Aaron Isaac, in 1774). In 1779 Parliament granted Jews the right to settle in Stockholm, Goteborg and Norrkoping, under certain conditions and with a measure of religious freedom.

In 1838 the laws regarding Jews were liberalized even further. Swedish Jews, hitherto regarded as a colony of foreigners enjoying certain rights, were now incorporated into the Swedish state. From then on they were to be called "adherents of the Mosaic faith." Jewish autonomy was abolished and Jews became subject to Swedish law, like any other citizens. But because of anti-Jewish pressure, they were still restricted to residing only in Stockholm, Goteborg and Norrkoping as before, with the addition of Karlskrona. Despite these concessions to anti-Jewish feelings, no reform in the history of Swedish Jewry can compare in significance with the decree of June 1838, which marked the beginning of complete political emancipation and basic acceptance as citizens and members of the community. The emancipation of Swedish Jews was completed during the next few decades when they were entitled to reside in any part of the country, to acquire real estate, to intermarry, and to participate in municipal elections. The last barrier fell in 1870 when Jews were entitled to hold political office. And in 1951, the religious requirement for ministerial office was finally repealed.

As they became more emancipated, Swedish Jews also became more assimilated. But their numbers continued to grow, especially as immigrants arrived from Eastern Europe. In 1838 there were only about 900 Jews in Sweden, but by 1930 there were over 7,000.

During World War II Sweden at first had a strict immigration policy by which only a few Jews fleeing Nazi Europe could enter the country. But public opinion soon changed in favor of the refugees and a concerted effort was made to save thousands. Sweden received some 16,000 refugees from Denmark and Norway, supported the Danish resistance movement

2

1

1. Memorial to the victims of the Nazi Holocaust, located in the Jewish cemetery in Haga, Sweden.
2. Helen Suzman, South African parliamentarian and champion of civil rights.

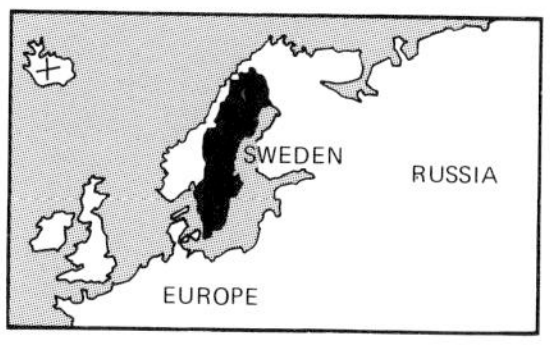

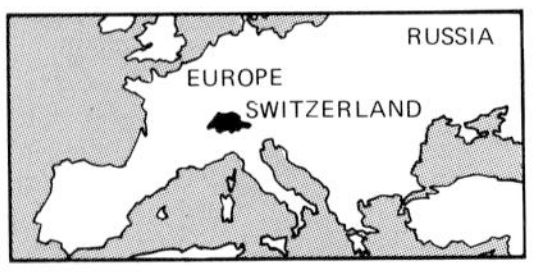


and, under the guidance of the World Jewish Congress, became a center for the dispatch of food parcels to concentration camps. Thanks to the efforts of Swedish officials, especially Count Folke Bernadotte who negotiated with Himmler, several thousand concentration camp victims were released and sent to Sweden. Altogether, more than 200,000 refugees reached Sweden during and after the war.

Today the approximately 15,000 Jews of Sweden are very much involved in Jewish religious and cultural activities. Jews are especially prominent in Swedish theater, arts and literature. In 1974 three Israeli citizens were arrested in Sweden for allegedly assassinating a suspected Arab agent. They were tried and sentenced by a Swedish court. Yet Swedish public opinion and official policy remain favorable towards Israel and Zionism.

**SWITZERLAND,** central European republic. Jewish settlement there dates back at least to the 13th century when Jews arrived from Germany and France. These early communities were relatively small and the principal occupation of the residents was limited to moneylending.

Disaster struck the Swiss Jews in 1348 when, plagued by the *Black Death, the Swiss blamed the Jews for starting the epidemic and tortured many into confessing their "guilt." Wave after wave of anti-Jewish persecutions ensued until the Jews in almost every Swiss community had either been burnt at the stake or expelled. A few years later some Jews made attempts to reestablish themselves in Switzerland, but very few succeeded and until the French Revolution in the 18th century, the only Jewish communities in Switzerland were those in Argau, Lengnau, and Oberendingen.

1. One of the many pro-Israel stickers that were widely seen throughout Switzerland during the oil embargo imposed by the Arab oil-producing nations in the winter of 1973, following the Yom Kippur War. "Better without car than without character" reads the text surrounding the *magen David.*
2. Double-domed synagogue of Basle, Switzerland, built in 1868.

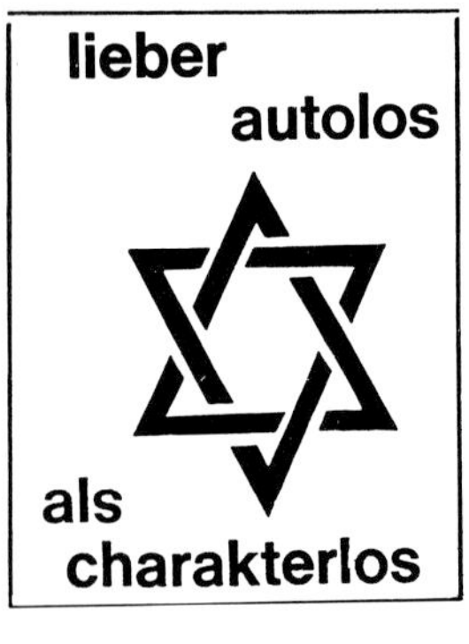

1

2

As French revolutionary ideals of equality began spreading to Switzerland, debates arose regarding the rights of Jews. Most Swiss opposed granting total emancipation and local governments maintained anti-Semitic restrictions. But by 1866 the federal constitution was finally revised, granting Jews the right to live anywhere in the country and gradually the individual localities began granting equal rights. However, the religious liberty of the Swiss Jews remains incomplete even today. A federal prohibition of *sheḥitah* – ritual slaughter of animals in keeping with the laws of *kashrut* – was passed in 1893 and never repealed, so that Swiss Jews still cannot prepare their own kosher meat and must import it from other countries.

During the Holocaust, Switzerland which maintains an official position of political neutrality and non-participation in all wars, could have provided the perfect refuge for European Jews. Unfortunately, the Swiss government failed to cooperate. An agreement between Switzerland and Germany resulted in the Germans stamping Jewish passports with a "J" so that the Swiss could weed out Jewish refugees and forbid their entry. In 1942 the Swiss passed a regulation refusing political asylum to persons who become "refugees only on racial grounds, e.g., Jews." By the end of the war, only 25,000 Jews had been allowed to take refuge there.

The Jewish population of Switzerland was put at 19,000 in the early 1990s. A federation of Jewish communities, known as the S.I.G. (Schweizerischer Israelitischer Gemeindebund) was formed in 1904, which now has about 5,000 members. The S.I.G. works towards solving the various problems of the Swiss Jewish community. Swiss Jews maintain active contact with Israel and the first Zionist Congress was held on Swiss soil. The Swiss government, while refusing to play any political role in the Middle East as part of its neutral policy, does maintain cordial diplomatic relations with Israel.

**SYMBOLISM** is the creation of a visible sign for something that is invisible. The invisible may be an idea which the artist or maker of the symbol tries to transmit to the viewer. Making beautiful, pleasing objects to have around you is not necessarily symbolism but merely decoration.

When discussing symbolism in the context of Judaism, the question of idolatry must arise. God is invisible and making any symbol to represent Him constitutes idolatry, and is expressly and completely forbidden in the Bible. Even if everybody is aware that the object is "only a symbol" and not the "real thing," it is still forbidden to make any image of anything whatsoever to represent God. This prohibition, which is one of the main principles of Judaism, led to a general rejection of symbols particularly if they had the human form, but even in the Bible there are many symbolic creations. Perhaps the most outstanding of these is the *Tabernacle which symbolized the "place where God dwelt," although God is everywhere, and certainly does not dwell in any specific place. The furnishings in the Tabernacle – and later in the *Temples – had symbolic significance and the rituals which were performed there were also symbolic. Judaism never understood the sacrifices in the same way the pagans did. The latter believed that the animals they offered were food for their gods. In the Bible it is quite clear that the Temple sacrifices were symbolic, and intended to educate the person who offered them.

Archaeologists have discovered synagogues from ancient times and other relics as well which bear pagan symbols. Among these is the famous figure of Helios, the sun god of the Greeks. Just how these came to be used by Jews is a mystery. It has been suggested by some scholars that by the time the Jews used them they had lost their original pagan significance or that the artists were unaware of that significance and used them as decorations and not as symbols.

In the Middle Ages, many Jewish symbols were used. These include the *shofar,* the *lulav* and the *etrog* that are used on the *Sukkot festival, depictions of the Ark of the Covenant, the **Menorah* and the tablets of the Ten Commandments. Very common today as a Jewish symbol is the *Magen David.

It seems that people need symbols in order to be able to focus their thoughts on an idea or a concept. As such the symbol performs a very important function. But, as Judaism sees it, great care must always be taken so that the symbol should not be confused with reality.

**SYNAGOGUE.** Throughout the ages, the synagogue has played a major role in the survival of the Jewish nation. It is perhaps the most important institution in Jewish religious and social life. However, there is no exact information about the origins of the synagogue. Some scholars claim that it dates back to the very beginnings of Judaism. Others point to the fact that in the days of the Temple, all sacrifices were

1

accompanied by prayer and so a place of prayer similar to a synagogue must have existed. The most reasonable explanation, however, is that the synagogue originated during the Babylonian exile (586 b.c.e.) when, deprived of the Temple in Jerusalem and feeling deserted in a strange land, the Jews would gather to read the Scriptures and pray for salvation. Upon return to Ereẓ Israel, they brought this tradition back with them, and records from the Second Temple period show that there were then numerous synagogues in existence, including one on the Temple Mount itself.

In the first century c.e., the synagogue emerged as a firmly-established institution. It is mentioned in all literary sources of that period, from various parts of the world. When the Second Temple was destroyed in 70 c.e., many of the rituals formerly conducted there were transferred to the synagogue, and organized *prayer became the substitute for sacrifice. The sages referred to the synagogue as *mikdash me'at* ("little sanctuary"), viewing it as a miniature Temple where Jewish congregations all over the world could gather and, to some extent, fill the void left by the destruction of the Temple in Jerusalem.

The remains of numerous synagogues dating back to the first few centuries of the Common Era have been uncovered, attesting to the widespread acceptance of the institution at that time. One of the largest such finds is the synagogue in Capernaum in the Galilee, probably built in the fourth century c.e. It was constructed entirely of stone around a courtyard, with a women's gallery on three sides. The *Dura Europos synagogue on the Euphrates river is one of the most famous discoveries of this period. Its decorative frescoes were found almost as clear as when first painted 1,700 years before. And the ruins of the synagogue in Ostia, Italy, constructed at the

2
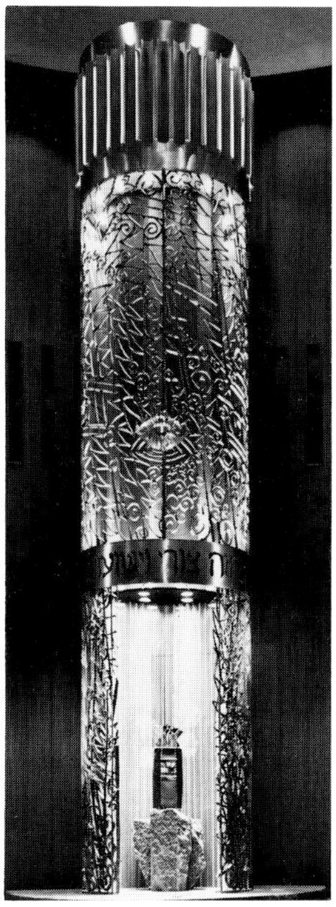

1. Commonly known as the "Kippah" this unusual structure was built in the mid-1960s to serve as the synagogue of the Hebrew University campus on Givat Ram, Jerusalem. Its formal name is the Israel Goldstein Synagogue.
2. The Ark of Temple Israel, New York City, made of lace-like aluminum, and with a base for the Torah scroll consisting of a slab of rough-hewn stone. Engraved at the center are the Hebrew words, "The Lord is my Rock and Redeemer."

The main sanctuary of the new (1973) complex of buildings of the Rockdale Reform Temple in Cincinnati, Ohio.

end of the first century and altered and enlarged during the next 300 years show that it was apparently a lavish edifice decorated in marble and mosaic.

During the Middle Ages, the social aspect of the synagogue became increasingly important. There was practically no activity in the daily life of the Jew which was not reflected in the life of the synagogue. Any person having a complaint could interrupt the service and petition for redress. Mourners were officially comforted in the synagogue – a custom which prevails to the present day – and the appearance of bridegrooms on the Sabbaths preceding and following their weddings were occasions for congregational rejoicing.

Democracy ruled the early synagogue well before it was applied to other contemporary institutions. The services were conducted by members of the congregation and officials were elected or appointed by the congregants. The ancient counterpart of the modern synagogue president was the *parnas;* the one who made administrative decisions and distributed honors was the *rosh knesset;* and the official charged with collecting and administering charity was the *gabbai.* The official positions of cantor and presiding rabbi originated only in the Middle Ages. At various periods there were also professional preachers, Torah readers and a **shammash* (or sexton) who took care of various maintenance duties.

In the 18th century, the rise of *Ḥasidism had a definite effect on the synagogue. The Ḥasidim disapproved of the formality of the synagogue service and so introduced a much more informal atmosphere. They abolished ornate furnishings, salaried officials, and overly structured services.

With the *Reform movement a century later, the synagogue took a turn in the opposite direction. The Reform synagogues were elaborate, impressive buildings. Many became known as "temples" and included an organ and choir loft.

These innovations caused much controversy within Judaism, and were regarded by Orthodoxy as sacrilegious imitations of Christian places of worship. In actual fact, there are very few laws concerning the appearance of the synagogue. *Halakhah* stipulates only that the room must have windows and that the ark which holds the Torah scrolls must be on the wall facing Jerusalem with the synagogue entrance directly opposite. The law recommends that the site of the synagogue be the highest spot in the city, but this has not always been feasible. Nevertheless, many traditions have arisen regarding the layout of the synagogue. The ark holding the Torah scrolls is usually covered with a decorative curtain called a *parokhet.* In front of the ark there is usually a light that is kept burning continuously *(ner tamid)* which serves as a symbolic reminder of the Temple **Menorah.* The honored members of the community sit along the eastern wall beside the ark. In Orthodox circles, the cantor's desk is usually in front of the ark, and the Torah is read from an elevated platform called a *bimah* in the center of the synagogue. The women are separated from the men by a *meḥiẓah* (partition) or else they are seated in a balcony above the main prayer area.

The Reform synagogues changed much of this traditional pattern. They moved the *bimah* to the front of the synagogue and allowed women and men to be seated together. These practices were also taken up by some Conservative congregations. The Sephardi synagogues also differ in some details from Ashkenazi ones. For example, Sephardim have no cantor's desk and the entire service is conducted from the *bimah.*

In modern times, a change has taken place, not only in the appearance of the synagogue but also in its functions. Mordecai *Kaplan of the United States formulated the concept of the "synagogue center" where the Jew would spend most of his leisure time. Its primary purpose would be not just prayer and study but cultural and social activities as well. Many Jewish centers today have, in addition to the synagogue, libraries, club rooms, classrooms, gymnasia and other facilities.

Despite external differences, synagogues the world over are treated with the same dignity and respect. The rabbis have ascribed to the synagogue a holiness patterned after that of the Temple. Frivolity, gossiping, eating, drinking, sleeping and transacting business (other than charity and the redemption of captives) are all forbidden in the synagogue. One may run when going to a synagogue, but on leaving, one must walk in order to indicate reluctance to part with the sanctity of the house of prayer.

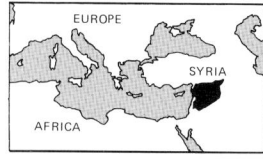

**SYRIA,** country in southwest Asia, bordering on northeast Israel. The ancient history of Syria is closely linked with that of Ereẓ Israel and in certain periods the two districts were even considered as one entity. In former times, Syria included the country known today as Lebanon.

The Syrians are thought to be descendants of the Arameans, a group of western-Semitic tribes which spread over the Fertile Crescent about 2000 b.c.e. Like the Israelite tribes, these people were soon subjected to the rivalries and domination of the great eastern powers such as Egypt, Assyria and Babylonia. During the Hellenistic period in the second century b.c.e., Syria served as the administrative center of the empire with Antioch as the capital. It was against this administration that the Maccabees revolted (164 b.c.e.) as commemorated by the festival of *Ḥanukkah.

The area was then captured by the Romans under Pompey (64 b.c.e.) and both Ereẓ Israel and Syria were placed by the Romans under the jurisdiction of a Syrian governor. The political situation, however, continued to be unstable and Syria was subsequently recaptured by the Persians, followed by the Byzantines and, in 636 c.e., by the Muslim Arabs.

Because of its proximity to Ereẓ Israel, Syria always had a large Jewish community and many of the rabbinic laws which applied to life in Ereẓ Israel were extended to include Syria. During the Arab period, the leading Jewish communities existed in Damascus, Aleppo and Pyre. They maintained regular contact with religious leaders in Palestine and produced many eminent scholars. But frequent changes in the leadership of the kingdom, invasions by the Mongols, Mamluks, and other foreign armies often resulted in oppressive decrees against non-Muslims and the Jewish community alternated between prosperity and misfortune.

In the 15th century, following the expulsions from Spain, Spanish Jews arrived in Syria and gradually brought about a decisive change in the nature of the Jewish community there. Eventually their leadership prevailed over Syrian Jewry, bringing with it the customs and lifestyle of *Sephardim.

In 1516 Syria was conquered by the Ottoman Turks, whose rule lasted for 400 years. After World War I, Syria was a French protectorate and in 1943 the country became an independent republic.

As the tension mounted between Jews and Arabs in Palestine in the 20th century, the situation of the Jews in Syria worsened. In 1947, violence broke out against the 10,000 Jews of Aleppo. All the synagogues were destroyed and about 6,000 Jews fled. By 1957 only about 5,300 Jews were left in all of Syria and at the present time there are less than 3,000. Many anti-Jewish laws have been passed by the Syrian government since the establishment of the State of Israel, including a prohibition on the sale of Jewish property, and the freezing of Jewish bank accounts. Many had their possessions confiscated by the authorities, and Palestinian refugees were housed in the dwellings vacated in the Jewish quarters of Damascus and Aleppo. Many Jews were put on trial because one of their relatives succeeded in escaping from Syria, others were obliged to report at police stations daily, and many were imprisoned without trial. In March 1964 a decree was enacted which prohibited Jews from traveling more than three miles beyond the limits of their home towns.

After the trial of the Israel intelligence agent Eli *Cohen, and at the time of his public hanging in Damascus in 1965, Jews were repeatedly assaulted. They suffered even more during the *Six-Day War and afterwards when many were arrested and others assaulted by the Muslim population.

Syrian hostility toward Israel has always been more extreme than that of any other Arab state. From 1948 to 1967, Syrian forces on the Golan Heights continuously bombarded Israeli settlements in the valley and attacked fishing boats on Lake Kinneret. After the Six-Day War, Israel occupied these strategic areas and succeeded in repelling a renewed Syrian attack during the *Yom Kippur War in 1973. Syria was the first Arab state to support the Palestinian terrorist activities, and encouraged the terrorist organizations to kill Jewish civilians, including women and children. In 1992 travel — but not emigration — restrictions on Syrian Jews were eased.

In peace talks with Israel, Syria demanded the return of the Golan Heights.

**SZENES, HANNAH** (1921-1944), poetess and Jewish freedom fighter who was tortured and executed by the Hungarian police after she parachuted into Nazi-occupied Europe to help organize Jewish resistance.

Born in Budapest of a cultured but assimilated family, Hannah became an ardent Zionist under the impact of the oppressive anti-Semitic atmosphere of Hungary, and in September 1939 she went to Palestine to study at the Nahalal agricultural school. At a young age she had revealed great literary talent and in Palestine she began to write Hebrew poems of great sensitivity and poignancy. Among the best-known are "Toward Caesarea" and "Blessed is the Match" *(Ashrei ha-Gafrur).* At the end of 1942, deeply concerned with the fate of European Jewry and that of her mother who was still living in Budapest, she joined the group of parachutists organized by the Haganah to help rescue Allied

1. A native Syrian spinning thread in a most primitive and basic manner.
2. Hannah Szenes, Jewish freedom fighter and heroine of World War II.

1

2

Henrietta Szold

"Ḥasidim Dancing," an illustration (originally in color) by Arthur Szyk.

prisoners of war and to organize Jewish resistance. In March 1944 she was parachuted over Yugoslavia, where she stayed for a while among Tito's partisans. On June 7, at the peak of the deportation of Hungarian Jewry to concentration camps, she crossed the border into Hungary and was almost immediately arrested by the Hungarian police. Though cruelly tortured, she did not reveal any information and on November 7, 1944 she was executed by a firing squad in a Budapest prison courtyard.

In Israel and among Jews everywhere, her name became a symbol of devotion and self-sacrifice and in 1950 her remains were taken to Ereẓ Israel and interred on Mount Herzl. A diary Hannah had kept from the age of 13 until her death was published in English in 1971.

**SZOLD, HENRIETTA** (1860-1945), U.S. educator, translator, Zionist activist and leader who founded Hadassah, the American Women's Zionist Organization. Henrietta was born in Baltimore, Maryland; her father, who was rabbi of the prestigious Oheb Shalom congregation, saw to it that she received a broad general and Jewish education (something quite rare for women in those days). After graduating from high school, she taught for the next 15 years at a private girls' academy, and at the same time she conducted classes at the congregational Hebrew school and gave adult education lectures on the Bible and Jewish history.

Following the Russian anti-Jewish pogroms of 1881, Baltimore received a large influx of Russian-Jewish immigrants, and Henrietta was instrumental in organizing the first night school geared to the needs of the new immigrants. Her interest in Jewish scholarship led to her appointment as secretary to the editorial board of the Jewish Publication Society, and she held this position for many years. She collaborated in the compilation of the *Jewish Encyclopaedia* and in the course of her lifetime she translated a dozen books (mainly from German), including the multi-volume *Legends of the Jews* by Louis Ginzberg.

She early became a Zionist, seeing in Zionism a balm for the wounds inflicted by history upon the Jewish people and "an ideal that can be embraced by all, no matter what their attitude may be to other Jewish questions." After moving to New York City in 1902, she became active in a women's study circle which held discussions on Zionism. A trip to Ereẓ Israel in 1909 impressed upon her the need to help alleviate the physical misery and disease suffered by many of the inhabitants, and she issued invitations for an organizational meeting of women interested in the "promotion of Jewish institutional enterprises in Palestine." In 1914 the first convention of the young organization, called Hadassah, was held and Henrietta was elected president.

By 1916 Hadassah had undertaken to organize an "American Zionist Medical Unit" to serve the needs of the residents of Palestine, and Henrietta accompanied the unit to Palestine and spent most of her remaining years there. In the 1930s she played a central role in the founding of Youth Aliyah, the organization which helped save tens of thousands of Jewish children from the Nazis and bring them to Ereẓ Israel. After her death in 1945, a fund she had established to provide a center for research publication and coordination of national youth activities was named Mosad Szold in her honor.

**SZYK, ARTHUR** (1894-1951). The solemn, lined, and suffering faces in the paintings by Arthur Szyk are not beautiful, but they are more stirring and more genuine than the fanciful creatures portrayed by many other artists. Bright and luminous like stained-glass windows and framed with intricate scrolls and figurework, his paintings are very distinctive and greatly admired.

Szyk was born to Jewish parents in Lodz, Poland, and studied in Cracow. During World War I, he served in the Russian army and was taken prisoner, but after the Revolution, he fought under General Sikorski against the Bolsheviks. Later, he moved to Paris and illustrated several books, including the biblical Book of Esther. In 1934, he was sent to the United States by the Polish government, where he exhibited his paintings at the prestigious Library of Congress in Washington, D.C., and several museums. He created a number of miniatures on the American Revolution which were presented to President Franklin D. Roosevelt by the government of Poland. After the outbreak of the Second World War, he took refuge in England and drew caricatures for British newspapers and magazines. When he settled in the United States a year later, he sketched cartoons satirizing Nazi leaders, and they were published as a collection called *The New Order.*

Many of Szyk's works were devoted to Jewish subjects; he illustrated the Passover *Haggadah,* The Book of Job, The Ten Commandments, and the Declaration of Independence of the State of Israel.

**TABERNACLE,** the portable sanctuary constructed by the Children of Israel and used by them for worship and communion with God during the period between the Exodus from Egypt and (perhaps) the building of the First Temple by Solomon (c.1220-970 b.c.e.).

**Hebrew Names for the Tabernacle.** The Bible uses a variety of Hebrew terms when speaking of the place where God and Israel communed:

a) *Mishkan* – "Dwelling " (God's dwelling place among the people of Israel ).

b) *Mishkan ha-Edut* – "The dwelling place of the Testimony" (the place where the two tablets containing the Ten Commandments were kept).

c) *Ohel Mo'ed* – "Tent of Meeting" (where God reveals Himself to Israel). It should be noted that the words *Mishkan* and *Ohel* are synonyms. In the Bible they are both used to denote the Tabernacle.

d) *Mikdash* – "Sanctuary" or the "Holy Place"; and especially *Kodesh ha-Kodashim,* the most holy place within the Tabernacle.

Some traditional commentators and many critical scholars believe that these terms may refer to more than one place; for the purposes of this article we are assuming that the biblical text is constantly referring to the one and only Tabernacle.

**The Role of the Tabernacle.** The Bible speaks of God, Who cannot be seen; God Who demands that His people act justly. But this God may be too abstract for some people to worship, and seem to be too far away to obey. On the other hand, to make an "image" of God to worship is idolatry. For these reasons, it seems, the ancient Israelites were commanded to build a sanctuary so that God may dwell amongst them (Exodus 25:8). The Tabernacle became the place to which sacrifices were brought in times of joy and in times of sadness. It became the place to which Moses retired when he wanted to communicate with God. When the Children of Israel camped in the desert, the Tabernacle was erected at the very center of the camp; when they moved, the Tabernacle was taken apart, and was moved with them. Physically and spiritually it was the central object for the Children of Israel and it was through the Tabernacle that they felt their connection with God.

**The Architecture of the Tabernacle.** According to the Bible, the chief architect of the Tabernacle, Bezalel, was assisted by Oholiab and other skilled artisans. Together they built the sanctuary and also made the special garments to be worn by the priests. The building materials were voluntarily contributed by the people of Israel. They consisted of gold, silver, bronze, acacia wood, linen, precious stones, and the hair and skins of animals.

The Tabernacle was designed so that it could be taken apart, moved, and reassembled with relative ease. Its most important component was the Sanctuary (*Mikdash*) which was divided into two separate rooms: the Holy of Holies which was 15 feet long, 15 feet wide and 15 feet high, and the Holy Place which was 30 feet long, 15 feet wide and 15 feet high. Only the High Priest was allowed to enter the Holy of Holies and even he could enter only on the Day of Atonement.

The sanctuary was surrounded by a rectangular courtyard which measured 150 feet from east to west and 75 feet from north to south. The walls of the courtyard consisted of curtains made of violet, scarlet and purple materials. They were supported by pillars made of acacia wood and covered with gold.

**Furniture.** The Torah describes the furniture of the Tabernacle before it details the structure itself. This is probably because the "furnishings" were considered more important than the Tabernacle which housed them.

The most important object in the Tabernacle was the Ark of the Covenant. It was a chest, made of acacia wood and measured three and three-quarter feet by two and a quarter feet. The wood was covered, on both sides, with pure gold. Within the Ark were placed the Tablets of the Decalogue (The Ten Commandments); in front of it was a pot of manna and Aaron's staff.

A slab of gold measuring three and three-quarter feet by two and a half feet, called the "mercy seat" *(kapporet)* rested on the Ark. From each end of the *kapporet,* and made out of the same piece of gold, there were two figures called cherubim. The cherubim had faces which were turned toward the *kapporet.* They also had wings which were arched so that they covered the *kapporet.* The whole structure was thought of as representing the "Throne of God" and it was kept in the Holy of Holies.

In the Holy Place (adjacent to the Holy of Holies), there was a table, made of gold on which were placed loaves of bread and jugs, bowls and ladles which were ordinarily used as part of the sacrificial service. Many modern scholars believe that these furnishings were similar to those found in pagan sanctuaries, which were considered as the "home" of the pagan gods. There is, however, one great difference. The God of

Drawing by the Austrian Ephraim Moses Lilien (1874–1925) of "The Tabernacle" in the desert, with the Israelites gathered before the entrance and with heavenly clouds above.

1

2

1. Moses displaying the Tablets of the Law (inscribed with the Ten Commandments) is the subject of this commemorative stamp, issued by the Post Office of Nicaragua. In this stamp, based on a painting by Rembrandt, the Tablets are represented in the less familiar form as two separate slabs of stone, while in the photograph below, the more common single-stone representation (with the Ten Commandments inscribed in two parallel columns) can be found.

2. The late former president of France, Charles De Gaulle, standing before the monument for French Jewish soldiers who fell in World War I. The central feature of the monument consists of huge, carved Tablets of the Law inscribed with the initial words of the Ten Commandments.

Israel is never thought of as consuming the bread; rather, the priests are explicitly instructed (Leviticus 24:9) that they are to eat the bread.

Other furnishings found in the Tabernacle included the *Menorah* (the golden candelabrum), an altar for sacrifices, and a bronze bowl resting on a bronze base.

**The Movements of the Tabernacle.** The Tabernacle was completed on the first day of the first month in the second year after the Exodus from Egypt. Moses himself supervised the final stages and he directed the dedication of the Tabernacle and the consecration of the priests. The Tabernacle stood in the center of the Israelite camp and a cloud rested over it. When the cloud lifted, it was considered a divine signal to move the camp. A silver trumpet was sounded, the Levites dismantled the Tabernacle and transported it to its next resting place.

After the Israelites left the wilderness and entered Ereẓ Israel, the Tabernacle was probably set up in Shiloh. After Shiloh was destroyed in 1050 b.c.e., the Ark of the Covenant was captured by the Philistines. David recaptured the Ark and built a new Tabernacle which, apparently, remained in use until Solomon built the Temple in Jerusalem. See also *Temple.

**TABLETS OF THE LAW,** the stones on which the *Ten Commandments were inscribed. In the description of the *Revelation on Mount Sinai related in the Book of Exodus, Moses is commanded to ascend the mountain to receive from God "the tablets of stone and the Torah and the commandments which I have written." The Ten Commandments were inscribed on the stones "on both their sides . . .and the writing was the writing of God." These first tablets of stone were smashed by Moses at the foot of the mountain when, after 40 days, he descended and saw the Jews worshiping the *golden calf. Subsequently he was commanded to hew two new tablets of stone and with them ascend the mountain a second time. On these tablets God wrote the same words which had been inscribed on the first tablets. The Tablets were housed in the Ark of the Covenant and were later brought into the Temple when it was built by Solomon. After the destruction of the Temple, the tablets and the ark were hidden and no trace of them was ever found.

The Tablets of the Law was a favorite subject of discussion among the authors of *aggadot.* They speculated that the Tablets were among the things created on the eve of the Sabbath of *Creation, and that in the spaces between the Ten Commandments all the 613 commandments of the Torah were also written.

As a Jewish art symbol, the two tablets have become very popular, and in the synagogue, a model of the two tablets is very frequently placed over the ark, inscribed with the first ten letters of the alphabet or with the first words of each of the Ten Commandments.

**TAILORING.** Almost every Jewish community, even in talmudic times, had its own tailor. Only a Jewish tailor could be trusted to obey the religious restrictions on clothing, such as *sha'atnez*, prohibiting the weaving together of wool and linen (see *Mixed Species). And only a Jewish tailor would be kept informed of the church-and government-imposed dress regulations for Jews which often required them to wear specific styles or colors.

Tailoring on a small and medium scale became an important element in Jewish communities in Islamic lands. In Yemen, for example, entire Jewish villages subsisted on weaving and tailoring until 1948. In Europe, Jewish tailors had to compete with Christian guilds and very often linked their trade to the sale and refurbishing of old clothes.

In the Russian *Pale of Settlement, tailoring both at home and as an itinerant craft became the mainstay of a growing section of the impoverished population of the **shtetl*. This way of life is expressed in Yiddish literature of the time and accompanied the immigrants to France, England and the United States.

In 19th-century England, Jews formed a major element in the clothing trade. Two Jewish firms in particular – Hyman and E. Moses & Son – developed the idea of producing cheaper quality new clothes for the working classes in the same styles as for the wealthy. These wholesalers needed hundreds of factories to supply the goods, so Jewish immigrants in Manchester and London were crowded into badly-ventilated "sweat shops" and worked long hours for low wages.

The same trend developed in the United States, where a few Jews became rich in the ready-made clothing industry while thousands of others suffered the unbearable working conditions of the garment trade. It was only with the formation of unions such as the International Ladies' Garment Workers' Union (1900) and the Amalgamated Clothing Workers' Union (1914) – under strong Jewish leadership – that conditions improved. In recent times, the ethnic character of these unions has become more diverse and the important role of the Jews in this field has decreased.

**TAITAZAK, JOSEPH,** 16th-century talmudist, Bible scholar and kabbalist. Few details are known of his early life beyond the fact that he was born in Spain and that he settled with his family in Salonika, Greece, some time after 1492, following the expulsion of Spanish Jewry. In Salonika he quickly rose to eminence as an outstanding scholar and halakhic authority, and in contemporary responsa he is referred to in such glowing terms as "holy one of Israel and crown of the Diaspora." Besides writing numerous responsa, he also composed commentaries on several books of the Bible, some of which have been published, while others are still in manuscript.

It was, however, as a kabbalist and teacher that Taitazak made his greatest mark. His lifestyle of ascetic piety and his kabbalist teachings seem to have had a formative impact upon almost all the mystical personalities who later formed the nucleus of the kabbalistic community of *Safed. Joseph *Caro, Solomon *Alkabeẓ and Moses Alsheikh, for example, all considered themselves to be among his devoted disciples. Taitazak was also believed to have a *maggid*, i.e., a divine voice which communicated with him about religious matters. He also established close personal contact with Solomon *Molcho when he was in Salonika and seems to have had an influence on him as well. One of Molcho's most famous epistles was specifically addressed to Joseph Taitazak. He died prior to 1545.

**TALLIT AND ẒIẒIT.** According to the Bible, God commanded the Jews to wear fringes on the corners of their garments as a reminder of the Lord's commandments: "And it shall be unto you for a fringe that ye may look upon it and remember all the commandments of the Lord" (Numbers 15:39). This fringe is called a *ẓiẓit.* In as much as most modern clothes are made without actual corners, the *ẓiẓit* is attached to a special four-cornered garment called a *tallit* worn by Jewish men in fulfillment of the commandment.

Originally the word *tallit* meant "gown" or "cloak" and referred to a rectangular fringed mantle resembling a blanket, worn by men in ancient times. But after the exile of the Jews from Ereẓ Israel in 70 c.e., it became inadvisable to wear these cloaks at all times in gentile company and so the *tallit* began to be used merely as a religious garment for prayer; hence its later meaning of "prayer shawl."

The *tallit* is usually white and made either of wool, cotton, or silk. The biblical commandment states that the fringe of each corner should contain one blue thread dyed in a special blue called *tekhelet.* This dye was extracted from a snail found only in certain areas. Because this dye became almost unobtainable in ancient times, however, rabbinic authorities in the second century c.e. waived the requirement for *tekhelet* in the *ẓiẓit.* Many modern *tallitot* are therefore decorated with blue stripes in remembrance of the missing blue thread.

Each of the four *ẓiẓit* on the *tallit* consists of one long and three short white threads which are passed through the holes in the four corners of the garment and folded so as to make eight threads. It is then knotted five times, each knot having a certain symbolic value. The *ẓiẓit* thus consists of five knots and eight threads – a total of 13. This number, together with the Hebrew numerical value of *ẓiẓit* (600), amounts to 613, the number of the biblical commandments of which the fringe itself is a reminder. Frequently the collar of the *tallit* has a special piece of cloth sewn in silver threads called *atarah* ("crown"). This is often embroidered with the words of the benediction recited when putting on the *tallit.*

A Georgian (U.S.S.R.) Jew, wrapped in a long, striped *tallit,* leading the congregation in prayer. Only one of the four corner *ẓiẓiyyot* is visible in this photograph.

The *tallit* is worn by males during the morning prayers (except on the Ninth of Av when, as a sign of mourning, it is not worn until the afternoon) as well as during all *Day of Atonement services. It is customary to press the fringes to the eyes and to kiss them three times during the recital of the last section of the **Shema* which deals with the commandment of the *ẓiẓit*.

The custom of wearing the *tallit* differs in many communities. In the Ashkenazi ritual, small children under bar mitzvah age wear *tallitot,* whereas in the Polish-Sephardi ritual only married men use them. In some cases the cantor and the rabbi wear *tallitot* at all services, and some bridegrooms wear them during the wedding ceremony. It is also customary to bury male Jews in their *tallitot* from which the fringes have been removed.

Although the ordinary *tallit* is worn only in the synagogue, strictly observant Jews wear the *tallit katan* (small *tallit*) under their upper garments the whole day.

**TALMUD.** The Hebrew term "Talmud" is derived from a word meaning "learning" or "study." The word is most commonly used to denote the book which includes both the Mishnah and the Gemara, and which constitutes a written record of the *Oral Law and the discussions of the *Sages concerning its interpretation. These discussions took place both in Ereẓ Israel (200-350 c.e.) and in Babylonia (200-500 c.e.); thus, there are two distinct versions of the Talmud, a Babylonian and a Palestinian.

The title page of a tractate of the Jerusalem Talmud, printed in Krotoszyn (Poland) in 1866 and patterned after the first printed edition of the Jerusalem Talmud, which was published in Venice in 1522.

**THE MISHNAH**

The term "Mishnah" is derived from the Hebrew root *shanah*, which means either "to repeat" or "to study and to teach." It is sometimes used to denote individual teachings which were once repeated and studied orally. In a more specific sense the term Mishnah refers to the collection of these oral teachings made by Rabbi *Judah ha-Nasi around the year 200 c.e. The Mishnah is written in pure Hebrew but not in the same style as the Bible; indeed, a special Hebrew style is known as Mishnaic Hebrew.

**Pre-history of Mishnah.** One of the leaders of the Jewish people upon the return to Ereẓ Israel (middle of fifth century b.c.e.) after the Babylonian exile was a priest and scribe named *Ezra. Under his leadership, the Bible, and particularly the five "Books of Moses" (Torah), was made the binding law of the land. Ezra's purpose, according to the modern scholar Morris Adler, was "to make of the Book the primary guide to action and belief; its words and teachings . . . the inspiration to good life and noble character." The biblical text records the fact that "Ezra had set his heart to seek (Hebrew: *lidrosh*) the Torah of the Lord . . . and to teach in Israel statutes and ordinances" (Ezra 7:10).

Naturally the new community faced many problems not directly anticipated by the Torah. The teachers, however, believed that God's Torah was given for all generations and that if they continued to seek (*lidrosh*) the correct interpretation, they would find the proper solution to all problems. Thus there developed a process of study known as **midrash,* whereby scholars diligently studied the Torah text in an effort to determine its meaning for their time. The *midrash* process continued for centuries,thereby creating a vast body of tradition which was conveyed orally from generation to generation.

It seems that various groups began to specialize in different aspects of this oral tradition. Priests, for example, collected many laws pertaining to sacrifice and other activities conducted in the Temple. Judges collected laws having to do with commerce, and students of revered scholars collected the interpretations of biblical passages taught by their teachers. Quite probably these laws and teachings were never written down. Specialists known as *tanna'im* ("repeaters") committed specific areas to memory. They then "repeated" the memorized material before the teacher who explained its meaning to his students.

**Rabbi Akiva.** Inevitably,different schools of interpretation developed, each with its own understanding of the law. (See *Law, Jewish; and also *Hillel and *Akiva.) After the destruction of the Temple by the Romans in 70 c.e., several leading scholars, fearing that the various traditions might be forgotten now that the central sanctuary had been destroyed, began collecting and arranging the vast oral law. We know from the Talmud that Rabbi Akiva (50-135 c.e.) was a pioneer in this area: "To whom can Akiva be compared? To a worker who took his basket and went forth. He found wheat and put it in, he found barley . . . and spelt and beans and lentils which he put in . . . he then separated the wheat by itself, the barley by itself . . . In a like manner Rabbi Akiva arranged the entire Torah." It seems that Akiva's contemporaries, Rabbi Joshua and Rabbi Eliezer, also collected and arranged segments of the oral law. These collections came to be called after their names, e.g., "Mishnah of Rabbi Eliezer."

Akiva's work was continued by his students, especially Rabbi *Meir. They added their own interpretations to the collection of Rabbi Akiva and even included opinions which Rabbi Akiva had rejected.

**Rabbi Judah ha-Nasi.** Finally, around the year 200, Judah ha-Nasi prepared a version of the previous teachings which became known as the Mishnah and was almost universally accepted. He arranged the individual laws *(halakhot)* into six *(shishah)* main "orders" (*sedarim*). [The acronym "*shas*," from the initial letters of *shishah sedarim*, thus refers to the entire Mishnah and the Gemara which accompanies it.] Each "order" was then subdivided into smaller, topical units, called *massekhtot* ("tractates"; singular: *massekhet*), and these added up to a total of 63 in number. Each *massekhet* was in turn divided into *perakim* ("chapters"; singular: *perek*). The tractates within each order and the chapters within each tractate were generally arranged according to length – the longer ones preceding the shorter ones.

**Rabbi Judah's Method.** Rabbi Judah did not include in his Mishnah all the *halakhot* (laws) in existence at the time. Those not included came to be known as *beraitot;* some of them were collected in a volume known as the *Tosefta* ("additional laws"). He made extensive use of the various statements of the law already in existence, often preserving their original order and exact wording. However, he also occasionally reworked older material, changing both its wording and its meaning and combining into one law the opinions of various authorities. Many laws are stated in the name of a more ancient authority; many are stated anonymously. Later students assumed that Rabbi Judah's method of expressing his agreement with an older opinion was to state that opinion anonymously.

Rabbi Judah deliberately chose to include opinions contrary to his own. His reasons, apparently, were both a desire to achieve acceptance for his Mishnah from diverse "schools" within the Jewish community and a recognition of the fact that future students ought to have before them a broad range of opinions. His Mishnah, therefore, became not only a code stating what the law should be, it also became a source book for the development of the Law to his time.

### THE GEMARA

Just as the rabbis of the Mishnah sought to interpret and to apply the Torah, so the rabbis of the Gemara sought to interpret and to apply the Mishnah. Those rabbis and scholars who were active up to and including the time of the Mishnah are known as *tanna'im*; those active during the period of the Gemara only, are known as *amora'im*. The *amora'im* had no authority to dispute the teachings of the *tanna'im*; they could only interpret the material received from earlier generations. Sometimes, however, the power to interpret really meant the power to re-interpret. When, for example, an *amora* comments on a law formulated in the Mishnah, *hakha be-mai askinan* ("this only refers to the following specific case . . ."), he has, in effect, taken a general law and limited it to a particular case. In this way, the law of the Mishnah has been "changed" and a new ( and sometimes contrary) law has come into general effect.

The *amora'im* not only "interpreted" the Mishnah, they also extended its principles into new areas, engaged in theological discussions on topics not covered by the Mishnah and reworked specific laws scattered throughout the teachings of the *tanna'im* so that they formed general legal principles which might be applied to future cases.

### THE BABYLONIAN TALMUD

The Babylonian Talmud (Talmud Bavli) contains the edited discussions on the Mishnah which took place in the academies of Babylonia from about 220-500 c.e.

The Jewish community in Babylonia ( the area of present-day Iraq) dated back to at least 597 b.c.e. In 219 c.e. a student of Rabbi Judah ha-Nasi returned from Ereẓ Israel to his native Babylonia and was soon appointed "head of the Jewish community in exile" *(resh galuta).* This student is known in talmudic literature as Rav (the teacher) and founded a great academy for study of his teacher's Mishnah in the city of Sura. Rav's colleague, Samuel, headed another school in Nehardea.

For almost 300 years these academies and others (Pumbedita, Mahoza, Mata Meḥasya) were centers of Jewish learning. Around the year 400 c.e., however, the policy of the Babylonian government changed and the status of the Jewish community was in danger. Leading teachers, like Rav Ashi (head of Sura 375-427) and Ravina (head of Sura 474-499) began to edit the records of the discussions held at the various academies. They had to sift, analyze, authenticate and arrange all the material which had developed in the many schools over the 300 year period. They also chose to reject some material and so there developed an "external Gemara" somewhat similar to the *beraitot* of the time of Rabbi Judah ha-Nasi. Most of this material is probably lost to

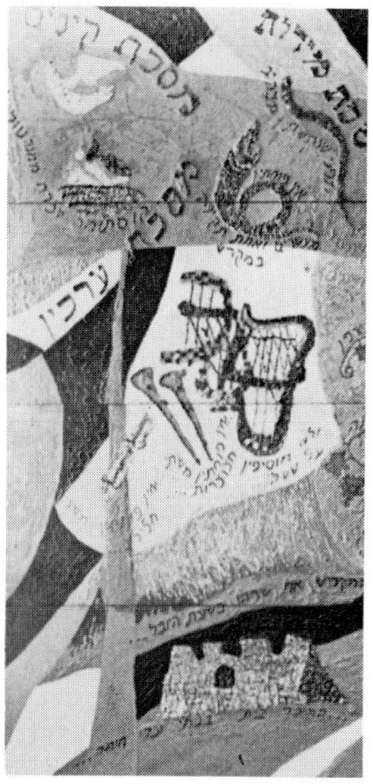

1

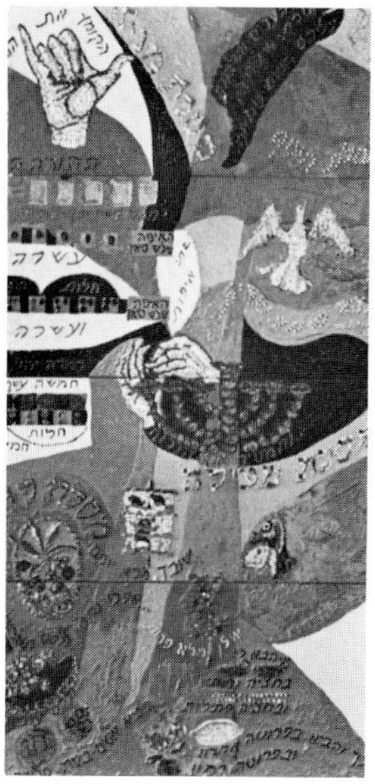

2

1 and 2. Two panels from one of six immense multi-color wall murals illustrating the Six Orders of the Mishnah, which were produced by the Israel artist Hannah Lerner and which adorn the dining hall of Boys' Town (an Orthodox technical high school) in Jerusalem. Shown are motifs drawn from the order *Kodashim* ("Holy Things"), including musical instruments played by the Levites in the Temple, birds used for sacrifices, and a hand of a *kohen* (priest).

30697
[redacted]

history. Even after the death of Ravina, additions were still made to the Talmud. Scholars, known as *savora'im* (scholars qualified to render decisions), completed the editing of the Talmud, clarified unsettled issues of Jewish law, and added explanations of existing materials.

The result of all these efforts is a series of volumes encompassing almost 6,000 folio pages and containing some two and a half million words. Only about one-third of the Babylonian Talmud is devoted to discussions of legal matters (*halakhah* – see *Law, Jewish); the remaining two-thirds is **aggadah* and is a storehouse of information of such topics as history, theology, medical practice, "superstitions" of both Jews and non-Jews, customs, beliefs, and theological disputes. The language of the Babylonian Talmud is the language Jews spoke then in Babylonia, Aramaic. Since the Babylonian Talmud is an edited record of oral discussions, it has a rather vague style. Just as in conversation mention of a topic only slightly related to the main subject may carry the discussion far afield, so in the Babylonian Talmud a tractate mainly concerned with the Temple sacrifices *(Menaḥot)* contains in it the laws of Torah scrolls, *ẓiẓit*, **tefillin*, and **mezuzah*.

### THE JERUSALEM (PALESTINIAN) TALMUD

The Jerusalem Talmud contains the edited discussions of *amora'im* who lived in Ereẓ Israel until around 350 C.E. During this period, major academies flourished in Tiberias, Caesarea, Sepphoris and Lydda. Constant unrest and rebellion against Roman rule led to the destruction of these centers and the emigration of large numbers of Jews from Palestine. It was during this difficult period that the *amora'im* decided to edit and write down their oral discussions, thus formulating the Jerusalem (Palestinian) Talmud.

**The Jerusalem Talmud's Relationship to the Babylonian Talmud.** Scholars have pointed out that the Jerusalem Talmud sometimes has a version of the Mishnah which differs from the one found in the Babylonian Talmud. The rabbis in Ereẓ Israel also display a greater readiness to change the text of the Mishnah rather than to interpret and reinterpret a received text. These differing approaches to the Mishnah sometimes result in legal decisions which are markedly different. Later tradition has, generally, preferred to follow the Babylonian decisions (see below).

The Jerusalem Talmud conveys discussions on the Mishnah which are absent from the Babylonian Talmud. This is especially true in the case of tractates dealing with agricultural practices in Ereẓ Israel. On the other hand, on most of the last two "orders" of the Mishnah, there exists almost no Gemara in the Jerusalem Talmud.

There are also marked differences in dialect between the two versions of the Talmud. In both, the predominant language is Aramaic, but the Babylonian Talmud contains mostly an eastern dialect and contains a considerable amount of Hebrew, whereas the Jerusalem Talmud employs western Aramaic mixed with a large number of Greek loan words.

The Jerusalem Talmud is generally less detailed, contains much less *aggadah* (about 40% of its total) and displays little interest in angels and demons. It is, however, not as well edited and therefore contains more contradictions and suffers from a lack of continuity. This is probably because the Jerusalem Talmud was edited in stages, by different schools and at different times.

Until the rise of Islam (seventh century C.E.) both Talmuds were of equal authority. When, however, the Jewish community in Ereẓ Israel shrunk, and when the center of the Islamic world moved to

Opening page of the tractate *Kiddushin* (dealing with the laws of marriage) from the edition of the Babylonian Talmud printed by Daniel Bomberg in Venice in 1520–23. This was the first complete printed edition of the Talmud, and Bomberg's arrangement of the page – text of the Talmud in the middle, set in square letters, and the commentaries of Rashi in the inner margin (in this case, on the right) and the *Tosafot* in the outer margin (here, left), both in "Rashi script" – served as the prototype for all subsequent printings of the Babylonian Talmud.

1

2

1 and 2. **Study.** Two paintings by Isidor Kaufmann, illustrating two typical "Study" scenes : a Ḥasidic *shtibl,* with both young and old engaged in prayer and study; and a solitary yeshivah student totally absorbed in his study of classical Jewish texts.

1. **Study.** "The Ḥeder," by Moritz Daniel Oppenheim, 19th century. Young pupils who have just started to study patiently wait their turn to recite the Hebrew alphabet.
2. **Study.** An oil painting by Leopold Pilichowski, early 20th century, showing a Ḥasidic sage endeavoring to convince a colleague of his interpretation of one of the points of Jewish law. The painting, entitled "Study," illustrates a basic feature of yeshivah study : learning in pairs or in small groups.

1

2

Baghdad, the Jerusalem Talmud became much less influential. Rabbi Isaac Alfasi (1013-1103) influenced later generations in favor of the Babylonian Talmud by reasoning that since it was revised later, its editors were aware of the arguments of the Jerusalem Talmud and had rejected them.

**COMMENTARIES OF THE MISHNAH AND TALMUD**

The best known commentaries on the Mishnah are those of Moses Maimonides (1157 in Arabic, 1297 Hebrew translation), Obadiah Bertinoro (1549), and a modern commentary by H. Albeck (1957, Jerusalem). By far the most popular commentary on the Babylonian Talmud was written by *Rashi (1040-1105). Many scholars in France and Germany in the 12th and 13th centuries wrote commentaries on Rashi's commentary, and these, known as *Tosafot*, are printed in most editions of the Talmud.

Hundreds of commentaries on the Talmud have been written through the ages; a new one is now being published by Adin Steinsalz in Ereẓ Israel. There are far fewer commentaries on the Jerusalem Talmud. Among the most important are those written by Moses Margolies (died 1786) in Lithuania, and Elijah Gaon (died 1797) of Vilna. More modern and of a scientific nature are those of Louis Ginzberg (1873-1953) and Saul Lieberman (1898- ).

**ENGLISH TRANSLATIONS**

The Mishnah has been translated into English by Herbert Danby (1933) and P. Blackman (1956). Soncino Press has published an English translation of the entire Talmud (1935-52), including the Mishnah, with Rabbi I. Epstein as editor. El Am (Israel) is publishing a "Talmud with English translation and commentary." There is, as yet, no English translation of the Jerusalem Talmud.

**PRINTED EDITIONS**

The Mishnah was first printed in Spain (1485) and Venice (1492). The Babylonian Talmud was printed by Gershom Soncino (1519) and a Christian, Daniel Bomberg (Venice, 1523). The format used by Bomberg has been followed by almost all publishers ever since. The edition which became almost standard and has been reproduced many times is that of the Widow and Brothers Romm of Vilna which was published from 1880 until 1886.

**TAM, JACOB BEN MEIR** (Rabbenu), leading 12th century French scholar and commentator on the Babylonian Talmud.

Rabbenu Tam (which means "our teacher, the righteous one") inherited his talent for careful explanation and sound reasoning from his grandfather, the great *Rashi. Jacob was recognized as an outstanding scholar by his contemporaries, and students flocked from all parts of Europe to his *bet midrash* in Northern France. These students, some of whom were older than he, spread his teachings to all corners of the globe, yet he himself never left France, where he lived comfortably on the profits of his vineyard and moneylending business.

Rabbenu Tam had a tremendous influence on the intellectual thought of his day. The *Tosafot*, commentaries to the Talmud written largely in the form of questions and answers, were heavily based on his teachings. He was also the author of works on ethics and Hebrew grammar, as well as the first collections of rhymed poetry written by a French scholar.

Rabbenu Tam was a very outspoken and high-handed leader who often became embroiled in controversy. He would not hesitate to change customs that did not appeal to him, or to introduce many important regulations dictated by the needs of the age. He was aggressive and attempted to impose his views on others. Yet despite his differences with other men of learning, his belief in the Torah as a model for peace and harmony in the Jewish community led to his being regarded by the majority as the greatest talmudic scholar of his generation.

**TAMMUZ, FAST OF,** communal fast occurring on the 17th of Tammuz (generally falling within the first weeks of July), which commemorates the breaching of the walls of Jerusalem by Titus in 70 c.e.; it thus marks the start of the last three tragic weeks which culminated in the destruction of the Temple on Tish'ah be-Av of that year. According to the Mishnah in the tractate *Ta'anit,* several other calamities also occurred on the 17th of Tammuz: the Tablets of the Law were broken by Moses when he descended the first time from Mount Sinai; the daily sacrifice ceased to be offered in the First Temple; and a Roman heathen by the name of Apostomos on that day burned the Torah in the sanctuary and set up an idol there. In the Jerusalem Talmud, it is also maintained that the 17th of Tammuz marks the date of the breaching of the walls of Jerusalem by *Nebuchadnezzar in 586 b.c.e., three weeks prior to the final destruction of the First Temple.

The Fast of Tammuz is thus closely linked with the fast of *Tish'ah be-Av. Exactly three weeks

Demnach von dem Allerdurchleichtigisten Großmächtigi-
Verzaichnuß
Welcher gestalten bey dem Fürstlichen HochStifft Eystett / der Newe Zoll auffgericht /

Upper portion of a list of customs tariffs, posted in Eichstaett, Germany, in 1656, which contains special rates for Jews. These rates were generally double the normal ones set for non-Jews, and there was even a special tax listed for the transportation of a dead Jew!

intervene between them, and these 21 days are known as *bein ha-meẓarim* ("between the straits") or as the "three weeks of mourning." During these three weeks, haircutting and the participation in joyous feasts are not allowed, as part of a modified regime of mourning. The liturgy for the Fast of Tammuz is similar to that of the other fast days: *seliḥot* are recited, the Torah is read and a special insertion is made in the *Amidah* prayer. For more information, see *Fasting and Fast Days.

The Fast of Tammuz is also traditionally associated with the fast mentioned by the prophet *Zechariah as the "Fast of the Fourth Month." According to the prophet, this fast in messianic times will be transformed into "joy and gladness and cheerful feasts for the house of Judah."

**TATTOO.** In biblical times, tattooing was used to mark slaves with the owner's brand. Jewish slaves were so marked by their owners and in ancient Egypt the slaves owned by Jews were also tattooed. Occasionally a man tattooed himself with a sign of his god, indicating that he was symbolically a slave to the deity.

The tattoo was made by cutting into the skin and filling the incision with ink or a dye. This method is clearly noted and condemned in the Mishnah: "If a man wrote pricked-in writing (tattoo), he deserves punishment . . . but only if he writes it and pricks it in with ink or eye-paint or anything that leaves a lasting mark." Earlier, the Bible categorically forbade this practice: "You shall not make gashes in your flesh for the dead or incise any marks on yourselves." While this was generally the rule, there seem to have been cases where Jews did incise God's name on their arms. Isaiah may be referring to this custom when he says: "One shall say, 'I am the Lord's'; and another shall inscribe his name, 'belonging to the Lord'."

**TAXATION**, the collecting of money or goods for the maintenance of political and social institutions and services, has been an integral part of organized communal life from earliest times, although in different ages and places in history, various forms of taxation have been imposed. From biblical times onward, the Jews have been subject to many types of taxes. The kings in the Bible imposed taxes on the people to maintain their own residences and households, to equip and maintain armies, and to provide for the needs of the Temple. Among the taxes collected were set portions of the annual yield of the fields, vineyards, flocks and olive groves. In addition, individuals would sometimes be "drafted" to perform required personal services for the king. The Book of Kings tells of King Solomon's division of the kingdom into 12 administrative units, each under the charge of an officer, each of which was responsible for providing the king and his household with food for one month of the year. In certain instances, for example after special acts of bravery, individuals would be rewarded with the lessening or elimination of their tax burden.

In the Bible itself, the concept of taxation actually has a very broad connotation. Thus the tithe given to the priest or to the poor, the obligation to leave a "corner of the field" for the poor, and the requirements of the *Sabbatical year and Jubilee, can also be seen as imposed duties, or as a form of taxation on the people. For more details on this, see *Tithes.

During the talmudic period in Babylonia, taxes were imposed by the local Jewish communities as well as by the central government, and this was also the normal situation in almost all the countries of the Diaspora. In Babylonia, on the local level, the taxpayers were required to assist in the building of a town wall and other defense features, and they had also to contribute to the synagogue and provide the poor with food and clothing.

A person was required to pay the assessed taxes only after he had owned land in the town for 12 months. The amount he had to pay depended upon his financial position and the benefit he would derive. Thus "a rich man nearer the wall shall pay more than one farther away, but a rich man further away will pay more than a poor man nearer the wall."

As part of the autonomy enjoyed by most of the Jewish communities in medieval Europe, taxes were generally imposed on the communities as a whole by the central and local rulers, and a committee of the community itself would determine the apportionment of the tax burden. (See *Self-Government, Jewish.) The assessment of the taxes to be paid by each member of the community was generally based on his net worth, and this was determined either on the basis of a voluntary declaration or by an evaluation made by a special committee of assessors who would base their decision on submitted documentary evidence. In general, those of limited financial means as well as scholars (those for whom "the Torah was their occupation") would be exempted from paying most taxes. The taxes which were collected, besides the standard poll tax and the other imposts which went to the coffers of the local and regional rulers, served a wide spectrum of municipal needs – such as maintaining the community's judicial and civic institutions, financing the town guard, providing health, education and religious services and funds for charity to the poor.

The urge to evade payment of taxes has always been strong, and as a result rabbinic leaders throughout the generations frequently stressed the need to be forthright in the payment of taxes. Tax evasion was seen as a form of robbery subject to severe punishment, for it was "robbery of the public" – it increased the burden on the remaining members of the community by obliging them to pay more than their due share for the satisfaction of the community's needs.

In the modern State of Israel, there is a taxation system similar to that found in most countries of the western world. However, because of the disproportionate defense burden, Israelis pay the highest tax rate in the world, approximating close to 50 percent of the average person's salary.

**TCHERNICHOWSKY, SAUL** (1875-1943), Hebrew poet who had a profound influence on the advancement of modern Hebrew poetry. Hebrew as a living, spoken language, was only beginning to develop in the 19th century, and most of Tchernichowsky's contemporaries relied on archaic biblical vocabulary and form as models for their literary work. But Tchernichowsky used modern poetic forms to describe familiar subjects, often emulating the style of the Romantic poets.

Born in the village of Mikhailovka, Russia, Tchernichowsky attended a Hebrew school and later a Russian school. Thus he received a background both in Jewish and Zionist thought and in secular subjects. He was especially interested in languages and later he began translating classical works (i.e., by Shakespeare, Homer, Longfellow and others) into Hebrew. He published his first two Hebrew poems in 1892, and his first book of verse, *Ḥezyonot u-Manginot* (Visions and Melodies) in 1898. These early works are mostly sensuous descriptions of nature, love, and beauty.

Tchernichowsky later studied medicine in Heidelberg and Lausanne, but on his return to Russia, found it difficult to obtain a permanent position as a doctor because he was Jewish. After World War I, he moved to Germany and in 1931 was commissioned to edit a medical textbook in Palestine, where he lived until his death.

The poetry of Tchernichowsky's later years reflects the trying times in which he lived. In some he reverted to describing the idyllic life of his childhood and in other poems he spoke bitterly of the Jewish struggle for survival. His works added a new dimension to contemporary Hebrew poetry.

Saul Tchernichowsky, pioneering modern Hebrew poet.

**TECHNION,** Israel Institute of Technology, is the only engineering university in Israel. Located in Haifa, it offers undergraduate and graduate level courses leading to degrees in architecture and town planning, the nuclear sciences, and all types of engineering – aeronautical, agricultural, chemical, civil and electrical. In 1991 there were 11,000 students, over 10 percent of whom were women. In its post-graduate research program, the Technion specializes in work on water desalination (rendering salt water fit for human use and for industry or agriculture), on medical electronics, construction techniques, aerodynamics and hydraulics.

The idea of establishing an institute of technology in Ereẓ Israel was first proposed in the early years of the century by the Hilfsverein der deutchen Juden ("Relief Organization of German Jews"). The organization canvassed donations from the heirs of Kalonymus Wissotzky, the tea merchant, and from Jacob *Schiff of New York, and the money collected was sufficient to erect a building and purchase all basic equipment. In 1912, the cornerstone was laid on the slopes of Mount Carmel in Haifa and the first classes were held in December, 1924.

In its planning stages, the school was known by the German name Technikum, and it was generally assumed that the language of instruction would be German, but as the date for the opening approached, a dispute arose among the members of the governing board (among whom were several prominent Zionist personalities) over this issue. A minority insisted that Hebrew be the language of instruction, but the majority voted for German. This aroused a storm of protest throughout the country, and the Hebrew Teachers' Association issued a ban against the acceptance by its members of teaching posts in the school. This language conflict delayed the opening of the school, and before the conflict was settled, World War I erupted, and the unoccupied building was turned into a military hospital. Following the war, the Zionist Organization acquired the property from the Hilfsverein and when the school finally opened in 1924, there was no longer any question that the language of instruction was to be Hebrew.

In 1953 the Technion acquired a 300-acre plot of land on the heights of Mount Carmel and began to build an extensive campus, which has come to be popularly called "Technion City."

**TEFILLIN,** two small black leather boxes containing tiny parchment scrolls inscribed with certain scriptural passages, and bound by black leather straps on the left arm and on the head. The *tefillin* are worn for all morning prayer services (except Sabbath and scripturally ordained festivals; in most rites they are not worn in the morning prayers of the Ninth of Av, but in the afternoon service) in observance of the biblical requirement that the Jew bind "these words" – that is, the words of the Torah – "for a sign upon thy hand and a frontlet between thine eyes." This commandment appears in four almost identical passages in the Torah, none of which mentions the actual term *tefillin.* There is, in fact, no biblical reference to the ceremony of donning *tefillin* and the manner in which it is to be carried out was designated by the rabbinic scholars of antiquity.

War orphans who have reached bar mitzvah age are directed by a young Ḥasid in the intricacies of properly putting on a pair of *tefillin.* They are at a communal bar mitzvah celebration held at Kefar Ḥabad, Israel, June 13, 1973.

Both the *tefillah* of the hand and of the head contain four biblical paragraphs. In the *tefillah* of the hand they are written on one piece of parchment which is inserted in the single hollowed cube. The *tefillah* of the head, however, is divided into four compartments and the four paragraphs, each written on a separate slip of parchment, are inserted in them. Two great scholars, *Rashi and Rabbenu *Tam disagreed as to the order in which these paragraphs should appear. Rashi's order is most universally accepted.

Rules as to the appearance and use of the *tefillin* are very strict. Both *tefillin* boxes and straps must be of leather, painted black. The parchment must be made from the skins of ritually clean animals, and the scriptural passages written on them by a duly qualified scribe in script like that of the Sefer Torah. The way in which the straps are cut and knotted is also specific and laden with symbolism.

The *tefillin* are put on immediately after the **tallit*. The *tefillah* of the hand is put on first, placed on the upper part of the weaker arm (i.e., a left-handed person places it on his right hand). The strap is wound seven times around the arm between the elbow and the wrist and the blessing for *tefillin* recited. The Ashkenazim wind the strap anti-clockwise and the Sephardim and Ḥasidim clockwise. The end of the strap is wrapped around the hand and the middle finger.

When the *tefillah* of the head is put on, care is taken that its front edge comes only as far forward as the hairline. It is held in place by a black strap that encircles the head, the knot resting on the nape of the neck. The two loose ends are left to hang down in front.

The duty of putting on *tefillin* begins when a boy reaches his religious maturity, that is at the age of 13 years and a day, though he usually begins to practice a few weeks earlier.

*Tefillin* are mentioned once in the New Testament under the peculiarly inappropriate name of "phylacteries," the Greek word for "amulet." However, this name has been universally adopted as the English equivalent of *tefillin.*

**TEL AVIV-JAFFA**. "From sand dunes to the biggest city in Israel in less than four decades" aptly describes the unparalleled development of Tel Aviv-Jaffa. Tel Aviv itself, the "first all-Jewish city in modern times," was founded in 1909; built on the sand dunes that stretched northward from the Arab city of Jaffa, it has developed since then into a kind of "megalopolis" (complex of cities) extending from Herzlia in the north to Reḥovot in the south, and merging in the east with such towns as Givatayim, Ramat Gan, *Bene Berak and *Petah Tikvah. In 1990 Tel Aviv-Jaffa contained close to 350,000 inhabitants and ever since the establishment of the State of Israel, has served as the business, entertainment, press and publication center of the country.

Like most large cities, Tel Aviv-Jaffa is a city of contrasts. In its southern districts, it embodies some of Israel's worst slums, while in the north and east there are attractive new suburbs such as Ramat Aviv, the location of Tel Aviv's rapidly-expanding university. These residential sections have a somewhat "Americanized" character. Tel Aviv's commercial and bohemian center is Dizengoff Street, one of the few localities in Israel with a pronounced "big city" rhythm of life. At the heart of the city rises Migdal Shalom, the highest skyscraper in the Middle East, and along the coast a whole chain of hotels has been built, most with their own beaches which serve as recreation and entertainment spots for tourists and residents alike.

Tel Aviv's beginnings actually date back to the early 19th century, when a Jewish community was reestablished in the all-Arab city of Jaffa. Throughout the Middle Ages, Jaffa's port had served as the "gateway to Zion" for Jewish pilgrims coming to Ereẓ Israel, but no Jewish residents had been allowed to settle there. In 1820, however, a Jewish traveler from Constantinople named Yeshaya Adjima, bought a house there (it was called Dar al-Yahud, the house of the Jew, by the local Arabs) and laid the foundations for a revived Jewish community. Merchants and artisans from North Africa followed him as settlers in Jaffa, and in the latter part of the century European Jews began to arrive as well. The First Aliyah swelled Jaffa's Jewish population and in 1887 the building of Jaffa's first Jewish quarter, Neveh Ẓedek, was initiated. This set the pattern for later Jewish settlements structured in tightly-knit, fraternal quarters within the midst of the Arab population.

The Second Aliyah further enlarged Jaffa's Jewish population, increasing it to 8,000 out of a total population of 17,000 in 1906. In 1909 it was decided to create a new suburb outside of Jaffa's boundaries which would constitute the "first all-Jewish city." The result was the city of Tel Aviv, whose foundations were then laid.

Tel Aviv grew steadily until World War I when the Jews were expelled from both Jaffa and Tel Aviv by the Turks. When the British took over, the Jews returned and Tel Aviv continued to expand. On May 12, 1934, Tel Aviv was officially given municipal status. In the same year, the Philharmonic Orchestra was founded, the Tel Aviv Museum was opened in the home of the city's long-time mayor, Meir Dizengoff, and the cornerstone was laid for the Habimah Theater building. After World War II, the city played a prominent role and suffered much in the struggle with the British authorities, for the *Haganah and the *Irgun had their headquarters there, and during the War of Independence, Tel Aviv was incessantly shelled from Jaffa's Arab quarters. On May 14, 1948, the State of Israel was proclaimed in Tel Aviv's museum building.

On April 24, 1949, Tel Aviv and Jaffa were united and the city's official name became Tel Aviv-Jaffa; one of the world's youngest cities had thus incorporated one of the oldest.

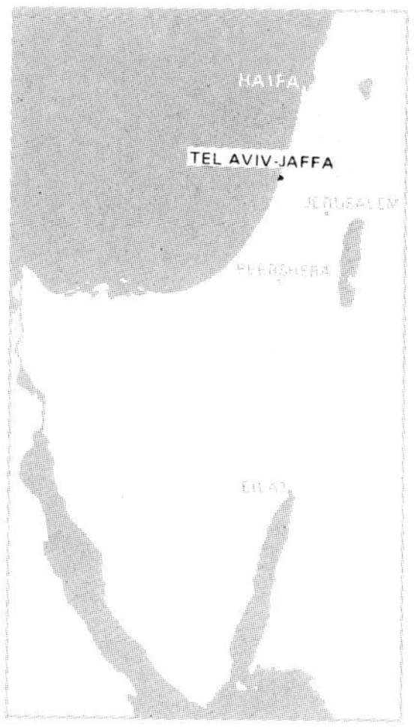


1

2

1. Dizengoff Circle, the center of Tel Aviv.
2. An aerial view of the city of Tel Aviv, showing the hotels along the coastline and the recently built marina.

1

2

1. One of the letter-tablets discovered at Tell El-Amarna, dating from the 18th Egyptian Dynasty. Inscribed in cuneiform characters, the tablet bears two letters addressed to the Egyptian pharaoh, written by the ruler of Tyre, stating that the pharaoh's commands have been carried out and that the whole region is in fear of his army.
2. A section of the Lithuanian town of Telsiai, original home of the Telz Yeshivah.
3. Tell el-Milḥ, located in the Negev near the town of Arad. This is a typical tell, with the artificial nature of the hill readily apparent from this photograph.

**TELL**, the Hebrew and Arabic word for the very common geographical feature of the Near East, the hill or mound artificially created over the course of centuries by the repeated building of cities on top of the uncleared ruins of earlier destroyed cities. In present-day Israel, *Bet Shean, *Megiddo and Hazor are among the most famous of the ancient tells so far discovered, and all have been the object of extensive archaeological investigation. The excavations at Bet Shean have revealed, for example, that there were no less than 18 separate levels of occupation of the site stretching over a period from the fourth millennium b.c.e. until the seventh century c.e. Throughout the Near East, tells have been among the most fruitful sites yielding important artifacts and documents. The tells at Nuzi and at el-Amarna, for example, have yielded large numbers of clay and stone tablets bearing inscriptions and texts which have been invaluable in clarifying many aspects of biblical history.

**TELL EL-AMARNA LETTERS**, a collection of cuneiform tablets discovered in the course of a series of archaeological excavations, begun in 1887, at an ancient city mound located 190 miles southeast of Cairo. This was the site of Akhetaten, the Egyptian capital city of the mid-14th century b.c.e., and the tablets uncovered represent a part of the diplomatic correspondence of the Pharaohs that was preserved in the royal archives.

The tablets proved invaluable both for linguistic and historical purposes. Almost all were written in Akkadian, the common language of the ancient Near East, but because they represent correspondence received from all corners of the region, they contain a large number of dialectical variations, and these greatly aided scholars in establishing the basic grammars of Akkadian as used in the various regions. As historical documents, the tablets provide a rare picture of the intricacies of the international political relations of the time, for most of the correspondents were either the kings of the major powers of the day or lesser rulers subject to them. On the surface, the letters give the impression that the period was one of relative peace and political stability, but closer scrutiny reveals that there was in fact a good deal of intrigue and shifty maneuvering on the part of many of the rulers, who attempted to strengthen their hand and consolidate their position. The situation in Palestine at the time, as disclosed by the letters, was quite chaotic. Petty kings were constantly at war with one another; the local Egyptian administration was corrupt and ineffective in maintaining order, and was concerned only with the payment of tribute to Pharaoh's coffers.

**TELZ**, Yiddish name for the city located in the northwest Lithuanian Soviet Socialist Republic and called in Russian Telshi (Telsiai).

The city is important in Jewish history primarily because of the yeshivah which was founded there in 1875 and which continued to exist uninterruptedly until the German invasion of *Lithuania in 1941. Throughout its 66 years of existence in Telz, the yeshivah was led by a series of outstanding talmudic scholars, beginning with its founder Rabbi Eliezer Gordon and including Joseph Leib Bloch, Simeon Shkop and Ḥayyim Rabinowitz. The Telz yeshivah pioneered the introduction of new teaching techniques into yeshivah education: the division of pupils into classes according to their knowledge and ability; the administration of periodic tests; and the stipulation of compulsory attendance. The Telz yeshivah became a stronghold of the *Musar movement, and after the closing of the *Volozhin yeshivah in 1892, it was one of the largest and most important yeshivot in Russia, numbering some 350 students.

In 1941, the Jewish community of Telz was wiped out by the invading German armies, but in the very same year the yeshivah was reestablished in Cleveland, Ohio. Under the leadership of Elijah Meyer

3

Bloch and Mordecai Gifter, the yeshivah flourished, and in the 1960s established for itself a large campus in a suburb of the city. Today there are over 400 students, and a parallel girls' school is conducted as well as a teachers' seminary, called Yavneh. A new suburb of Jerusalem is also named after Telz.

**TEMPLE**, the building in Jerusalem set aside for the worship of God and considered by the Bible as the only legitimate site to which sacrifice may be brought. Historians generally speak of two Temples: the first was built by King Solomon c. 960 b.c.e., and destroyed by the Babylonians in 586 b.c.e.; the second was built under the supervision of Ezra in 515 b.c.e. and destroyed by the Romans in 70 c.e.

### THE FIRST TEMPLE

**History**. The Bible relates that King David wanted to build a "House of the Lord" to replace the Tabernacle which had been in use since the Exodus from Egypt. He was, however, persuaded by the prophet Nathan to leave the project to his son, Solomon. Solomon built the Temple in Jerusalem, the "city of David," on the site where, according to tradition, the binding of Isaac took place (see *Akedah). This site was known as Mount Moriah, or the threshing floor of Araunah, the Jebusite.

The building was begun in the fourth year of Solomon's reign and was completed in the 11th year (c.955 b.c.e.). The Bible reports that 30,000 Israelites and 150,000 Canaanites were employed in the construction. Hiram, king of Tyre, was among the foreign potentates who contributed to its building. Materials for the Temple came from the treasury amassed by David (silver), the mines of King Solomon (copper), and the forests of Lebanon (cedar wood). From the moment of its dedication, the Temple in Jerusalem served as the central sanctuary for the Children of Israel. The Bible speaks of the existence of other "high places" at which sacrificial worship did take place. Although scholars differ as to whether these places had a legal status, they all agree that from the time of Josiah (622 b.c.e.) at least, there was no other legal sanctuary in Israel or Judea.

**Structure.** *Holy of Holies.* The Temple was built primarily to house the Ark of the Covenant, which was kept in its most important building, the Holy of Holies (*Devir;* see also *Tabernacle). The shape of this building was cubical (33 by 33 by 33 feet). It seems that its floor was somewhat higher and its ceiling lower than the adjacent building.

*Main Room.* The room to the east of the Holy of Holies was the *Heikhal* (the main room or holy place). It was twice as long (approximately 66 feet) and half again as high (approximately 50 feet) as the Holy of Holies. The rooms were separated, according to some scholars, by a thin wall of cedar.

A panoramic view of the Temple Mount and the Western Wall as the area looked on the fourth anniversary of the reunification of Jerusalem, May 23, 1971. On the Mount where the Temple once stood are located two giant mosques, the Dome of the Rock (left) and the al-Aqsa Mosque (far right).

*The Porch.* To the east of the *Heikhal* was a porch (*'Ulam*) which was approximately sixteen and a half feet by thirty-three feet. The porch served as an entrance to the holier sections and divided the holy precinct from the profane.

*The Adjacent Building.* A three-story building, known as *Yaẓi'a*, surrounded the Temple on every side except the east. The inner walls of the *Yaẓi'a* ran parallel to those of the Temple. Its three levels were each eight feet high, divided into approximately 30 chambers, and the building was used for storing the Temple vessels, utensils and treasures.

**Furniture.** *The Ark and Cherubim.* The Ark of the Covenant stood inside the Holy of Holies and contained the tablets of the Ten Commandments which were given to Moses on Mount Sinai. Hovering over the Ark were two cherubim, each 16 feet high, made of olive wood. Archaeologists believe that each of the cherubim was formed with a lion-like body, a man-shaped head, and two wings. The cherubim were believed to be servants of God whose main task was to guard the Ark.

*The Altars.* A relatively small altar (three feet by three feet by four and a half feet), made of cedar wood and overlaid with gold, stood before the entrance to the Holy of Holies. The main altar, used for burnt sacrifices, was made of bronze and stood in the court of the Temple which was in front of the porch. Two small incense altars were also found within the Temple. A full description of the Temple's furnishings is found in the Bible, in I Kings, Chapter 7.

**Religious Significance.** The Temple was even more than the place where the Ark of the Covenant was kept. It was also the only place where Israelites were permitted to offer sacrifices. (For a complete discussion of sacrificial worship in the Temple see *Sacrifices, *Priests, *Levites and *Music.) It was a place of assembly to which pilgrims would ascend on the holy days of Passover, Shavuot and Sukkot. Prayers were recited in the Temple and, when the worshiper was far away, he directed his prayers toward the Temple in the belief that through this action his words would reach God. Even today most synagogues are built facing towards Jerusalem, the site of the Temple.

The people of Israel also came to the Temple in times of distress when the priests would weep "between the porch (*'ulam*) and the altar." On fast days, large numbers would gather "in the court of the Lord's House"; often the prophets of Israel would use these occasions to speak to their people.

When the prophets of Israel spoke of the "end of days" when peace would be restored to the earth, they also spoke of many peoples coming "to the Mount of the Lord, to the House of the God of Jacob" to be taught the ways of God. The exiled of Israel will return to pay homage to God on the holy mountain in Jerusalem, and God's "house will be called a house of prayer for all peoples."

Not everything about the Temple was perfect. More than one prophet spoke of corruption amongst the priests and hypocrisy on the part of the people who thought that sacrificial worship was more important than moral behavior.

### THE SECOND TEMPLE

The first Temple was destroyed by the Babylonian armies under King Nebuchadnezzar during the first ten days of the month of Av (see *Tish'ah be-Av) in 586 b.c.e. Most of the inhabitants of Jerusalem and Judea were exiled to Babylonia. In 538 b.c.e., the Persian king Cyrus, who had conquered the Babylonians, issued a decree permitting the Jews to return to Jerusalem and to rebuild the Temple. Shortly thereafter the restoration was begun. Because of the many difficulties that had to be overcome, the project was not completed until March of 515 b.c.e. Ezra, Nehemiah, Zerubbabel, and the prophets Haggai and Zechariah all played major roles in the struggle to rebuild the Temple.

The Bible contains no description of the Second Temple or of its exact layout. Scholars, however, are of the opinion that it was much more modest in size than Solomon's Temple. In the fourth century, however, the Second Temple grew in size and significance due to the efforts of the Hasmonean kings, who attempted to enhance their own prestige by strengthening and enlarging the Temple. And in the first century b.c.e., under the rule of Herod, the Temple was completely renovated and it became one of the most impressive structures ever known.

### HEROD'S TEMPLE

**The Structure.** In the 18th year of his reign, Herod began to rebuild the Temple. One thousand priests were trained to be stonemasons and builders so that they could work in areas prohibited to laymen. In order to comply with Jewish law, stones were quarried without the use of iron tools and all preparations were made for the new structure before the old was demolished. Giant supporting walls were built and valleys were filled in so that the area of the Temple Mount could be doubled. The most famous of these, the Western Wall, still stands.

The Temple itself was raised 66 feet, widened by 50 feet, and rebuilt of huge pieces of white stone. The largest stone thus far found is 24 feet long and weighs over 100 tons. Huge walls, containing large and beautifully decorated gates, were built around the Temple area. Access to it was via a magnificent arch or a broad staircase which led into the Temple Mount area.

**The Courts.** Several courts were built near the Temple itself. The Court of the Women (220 feet by 220 feet) was situated on the eastern side. It was surrounded by a balcony so that the women could watch the Temple proceedings.

From the Court of the Women a staircase led to the Court of the Israelites, the area in which pilgrims gathered when they came to celebrate the Pilgrim Festivals. Gentiles also brought sacrifices to this court.

The archaeological excavations at the southern end of the Temple Mount, showing some of the remains dating back to the Second Temple period.

West of the Israelite Court was the Court of the Priests. Only priests and laymen bringing sacrifices were permitted to enter this Court. Before entering, non-priests immersed themselves in water and removed their shoes. A large altar, used for sacrificial offerings, was found there. Two vents were let into the southwest side so that the blood of sacrifices could drain through them into the Kidron valley.

**Temple Finances.** The expenses of the Temple were met in various ways. Gentile kings who had subjugated Judea often made large contributions to the Temple. Wealthy Jews also made generous contributions; widows and orphans, as well as the wealthy, used the Temple as a sort of bank. The most important source of income, however, was the half-shekel tax paid by every Jewish male from the age of 20 all over the world.

**Religious Significance.** The Second Temple evolved into much more than the only legitimate site for the sacrificial worship of God. It was also a place of prayer, study, and public assembly. The official copy of the *Bible was kept in the Temple and the authenticity of all other texts was checked by comparison to this version. The *Sanhedrin, the nation's highest court, met in the Chamber of Hewn Stone which was inside the Temple precincts. Only in the Temple, and only on the Day of Atonement was the full name of God pronounced. After Herod's restoration, the Temple also became a source of great national pride as well as a military structure of great significance. When in 70 c.e. it was destroyed by the Romans, the entire people of Israel observed a period of mourning which has continued,for many,until today.

**IN MEMORY OF THE TEMPLE**

The rabbis of that generation enacted new laws whose purpose was to fulfill the biblical verse, "If I forget thee, O Jerusalem . . ." (Psalm 137). They decreed that a corner of every house, a part of every meal, even some of every woman's jewelry, be set aside – in memory of the Temple. Special prayers were formulated to express the yearning of the people to return to Zion and to worship once again in the Temple of God. Instrumental music was banned from the synagogue service, a glass was broken at every wedding, and the words "Next year in Jerusalem" were recited on Passover and at the end of the Day of Atonement – all in memory of the Temple. Most historians believe that these prayers, customs, and hopes helped to unite the Jewish people and kept alive the hope of returning to Zion, a hope which was fulfilled in our days.

**TEN COMMANDMENTS.** According to the Bible, 49 days after the Israelites left Egypt, God revealed Himself to them at Mt. Sinai. The revelation consisted of God talking to the Jews and making a covenant with them. That "speech" of God is known as the Ten Commandments or the Decalogue and, in Hebrew, *Aseret ha-Dibrot,* the noun *dibrot* coming from the root "to speak." The Ten Commandments were written on two tablets of stone called the *luḥot ha-berit,* the "tablets of the covenant." Moses broke the first set when he saw the Israelites worshiping the *Golden Calf and later a second set was made. The tablets were kept in the Ark of the Covenant as a perpetual reminder to the Jews of their commitment to God. Nowadays a symbol of this is the two tablets that often adorn the top of the Torah ark in the synagogue.

The Ten Commandments appear twice in the Torah: once in Exodus 20:2-14 when the revelation took place and again in Deuteronomy 5:6-18 in Moses' farewell address to the nation when the aged leader repeated them. There are slight differences in wording between the two versions (with regard to the Sabbath Day commandment, see *Sabbath) but basically the Commandments are the same. Among the Bible commentators there is some difference of opinion as to how the Ten Commandments are to be divided but generally the following is the accepted scheme:

1. Belief in God
2. Against any form of idolatry
3. Against taking God's name in vain
4. Remembering and observing the Sabbath
5. Honoring parents
6. Against murder
7. Against adultery
8. Against stealing (interpreted by the rabbis as kidnapping)
9. Against false witness
10. Against coveting another man's possessions.

Although the Ten Commandments were spoken by God, the rabbis were at pains to point out that the rest of the Torah is just as authoritative as that section and that the whole Torah is the "word of God." This is one of the reasons why the Ten Commandments are not part of the normal prayer service – so that people should not say "only these verses were said by God." Nevertheless, when the Ten Commandments are read as part of the Torah reading in the synagogue, it is customary for the congregation to stand.

1. An Armenian Bible manuscript of the 13th century, illustrating Moses receiving the Ten Commandments from the "hand" of God at Mount Sinai.
2. One of two identical silver finials for a Torah scroll, decorated with a stylized representation of the Tablets of the Law containing the initial words of the Ten Commandments.

1

2

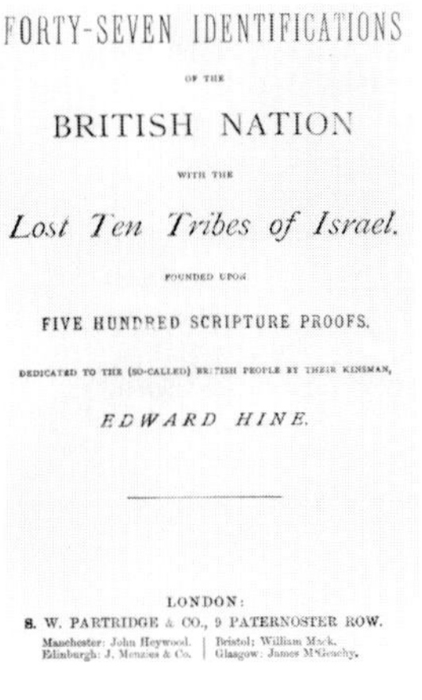
FORTY-SEVEN IDENTIFICATIONS

OF THE

BRITISH NATION

WITH THE

*Lost Ten Tribes of Israel.*

FOUNDED UPON

FIVE HUNDRED SCRIPTURE PROOFS.

DEDICATED TO THE (SO-CALLED) BRITISH PEOPLE BY THEIR KINSMAN,

*EDWARD HINE.*

LONDON:

S. W. PARTRIDGE & CO., 9 PATERNOSTER ROW.

Manchester: John Heywood. | Bristol: William Mack.
Edinburgh: J. Menzies & Co. | Glasgow: James M'Geachy.

Title page of a book printed in 1871, claiming to offer 47 "proofs" that the British were the authentic descendants of the Ten Lost Tribes of Israel.

**TEN LOST TRIBES,** the ten tribes which once inhabited the northern kingdom of Israel, were exiled in 722 b.c.e. and subsequently disappeared.

The Jewish nation originally consisted of twelve tribes: ten inhabited the north and were called the Kingdom of Israel, and two (Judah and Benjamin), in the south, were called the Kingdom of Judah. After the Kingdom of Israel was conquered by the Assyrians in 722 b.c.e., its inhabitants were exiled to "Halah and Habor by the river Gozan, and in the cities of the Medes" (II Kings 17:6 and 18:11). They were never seen again, and only the tribes of Judah and Benjamin, which were exiled to Babylon in 586 b.c.e., eventually succeeded in returning to their homeland.

Although the ten tribes disappeared, the prophets Isaiah, Jeremiah and Ezekiel promised that the time would come when they would be reunited with the remainder of the Jewish nation. This promise kept alive the hope that the ten tribes still existed and would be found.

Many legends were created to explain how the tribes disappeared, where they went and where they are now. Their inability to rejoin their brethren was attributed to the fact that they were exiled beyond the legendary river *Sambatyon, whose mysterious powers kept them from crossing.

Numerous attempts have been made by travelers and explorers to discover the ten tribes, or to identify them with different people. Almost every nation, including the Japanese, Persians, the *Falashas of Ethiopia, Red Indians, and the British, have been suggested as descendants of the lost tribes.

**TEN MARTYRS** (Hebrew: *asarah harugei malkhut),* collective name applied to ten sages of the Mishnah who lived in the mid-second century c.e. and who were tortured and put to death by the Romans after they continued to defy the prohibition against the teaching and practice of Judaism imposed by the emperors *Hadrian and Trajan. Many legendary accounts of their martyrdom have come down through the ages, and a common feature of all of them is the depiction in gruesome detail of the distinctively cruel fashion in which each of the sages met his death. Rabbi *Akiva, for example, had his flesh torn from him bit by bit; while Rabbi *Ḥananiah ben Teradyon was slowly burned to death wrapped in a Torah scroll. All the versions, however, also glorify the way each of the sages died – with head held high, disdainful of the Roman authorities, and accepting death as a judgment from heaven. The legendary accounts of the martyrdom of the ten present their deaths as having resulted from a collective sentence imposed upon them as a group by the emperor Hadrian, but this appears to be a "telescoping" of the actual historical facts, for not all of the ten were exact contemporaries and all of them could not have met their death at the same time.

The legend of the Ten Martyrs became a much-favored theme among the early *paytanim* and religious poets, and two poetic versions have actually been included in the standard liturgy – the poem *Elleh Ezkerah* ("These I will remember") is recited on the *Day of Atonement and *Arzei ha-Levanon Adirei ha-Torah* is included among the *kinot* recited by Ashkenazim on *Tish'ah be-Av.

In the Middle Ages, the legend of the Ten Martyrs came to be regarded as a type of national epic, providing moral and spiritual sustenance to those Jews who suffered endless religious persecution and oppression because of their adherence to their faith. Especially from the time of the First Crusade onward, the Ten Martyrs served as an exalted model for contemporaneous martyrs, who also came to be called *harugei malkhut.* Together with *Hannah and her seven sons, the Ten Martyrs thus became archetypes of Jewish martyrology.

**TERRITORIALISM** is the general name given to several minor movements which arose during the first decades of the 20th century which possessed the common aim of establishing Jewish settlements in various sparsely-populated areas of the world. It was envisaged that, in these territories, the Jewish population would eventually be predominant and, as a result, the Jews living there would enjoy the benefits of an autonomous Jewish life, free from the anti-Semitism and the disabilities which confronted them as a minority group in the Christian countries of Europe. In their vision of territorial autonomy as a solution to the "Jewish problem," the Territorialists were in full agreement with the Zionists; they differed from the Zionists, however, in not regarding Ereẓ Israel as the only possible place of settlement, and indeed, some Territorialists explicitly rejected Ereẓ Israel in favor of other locations.

The first of the Territorial movements was, in fact, an offshoot of the Zionist movement. It came into existence in response to the decision of the Seventh Zionist Congress (Basle, 1905), not to proceed with the *Uganda Scheme, the British-sponsored project of settling Jews in British East Africa. Led by Israel *Zangwill, 28 delegates who refused to accept the rejection of the scheme withdrew from the congress, and after meeting separately, decided to establish an "Independent Jewish Territorial Organization" (I.T.O.) which would be dedicated to "procuring a territory upon an autonomous basis for those Jews who cannot remain in the lands in which they at present live." The I.T.O. secured the collaboration of a great number of influential Jews, and entered into negotiations with many governments with a view to acquiring suitable territory. They sought to procure land in Angola, Cyrenaica, Mesopotamia, Australia, Mexico and elsewhere, but all the attempts ended in failure. Years later, Israel Zangwill confessed that "there was not a land on earth that we did not think about." In 1917, after the *Balfour Declaration, the I.T.O. ceased to function actively, and it was formally disbanded in 1925.

A second Territorialist organization was the Berlin-based "Allgemeine Juedische Kolonisations-Organisation" (A.I.K.O.). Established in 1908, the A.I.K.O. rejected the attempts made by the I.T.O. to settle Jews in far-flung parts of the globe, and concentrated its efforts on securing permission for a compact Jewish settlement either in Palestine, Syria, or the Sinai Peninsula. It rejected the political and national aspects of Zionism, and did not call for the attainment of political autonomy in the projected settled regions. The A.I.K.O. also had little success and was disbanded in 1920.

In 1935, the "Freeland League for Jewish Territorial Colonization" was formed, with the aim of "obtaining large-scale room in some sparsely populated area for the Jewish masses to live and develop according to their own views and culture and religion." The league negotiated for settlements in Angola, Ecuador, Australia (Kimberley), and Surinam, but all its efforts ended in failure. The league, however, has continued to exist until today, with a membership drawn largely from non-Zionists and those who emphasize Yiddish culture. Based in New York, the league publishes a Yiddish bi-monthly entitled *Freyland.* (See also *Zionism.)

**THEATER.** The substantial impact of the Jews on the world of theater – as performers, producers and playwrights – is a relatively recent phenomenon. For centuries,Jewish participation in this field was very limited, both as a result of traditional Judaism's disdain for the theater, and anti-Semitic restrictions on Jewish performers.

**In Ancient Times.** Neither biblical nor talmudic literature contains anything which can be described as "theater" or "drama." And even in the post-biblical period, when theaters and circuses became popular in the Hellenistic-Roman world, the Jews remained on the outskirts of the entertainment field. There is only one Jewish playwright known from that era, Ezekiel of Alexandria, who lived in the first century b.c.e. and wrote tragedies in Greek based on biblical themes. Despite rabbinic warnings against any contact with the theater, Jews were apparently avid theater-goers, though they did not participate in the production of plays.

The first Jewish performers appeared on the stage in Rome in the first century c.e. A Jewish actor, Aliturus, is known to have been among Emperor Nero's favorites and he is certainly not the only Jewish actor to find high favor in the royal court.

**The Middle Ages.** As Jews became increasingly unpopular in the Roman empire and later in various parts of the world, Jewish actors tended to either conceal their origins or form entirely Jewish theatrical companies performing for all-Jewish audiences. During the Middle Ages, these performances usually took place on special occasions such as festivals and weddings. The light-hearted *Purim play, for example, became especially popular both in and out of the ghettos.

1

2

1. Two of the most successful U.S. composers of theater musicals and stage shows, Oscar Hammerstein II (1895-1960) and Jerome Kern (1885-1945), pictured in the orchestra pit of the Alvin Theater, New York, during a rehearsal of *Music in the Air,* 1932.
2. Israel performers Hanna Meron and Shraga Friedman in the Hebrew version of *Hello Dolly,* Tel Aviv, 1969.

1

2

1. Hannah Maria Norsa, the first notable Jewish actress in England (died 1785).
2. The 18th-century English actress Harriet Abrams, pictured in her role as Sylvia in David Garrick's romantic drama *Cymon.*

In the 16th century, Mantua, Italy, gained fame as the center of the new Italian drama and Jews were among its foremost backers. The Jewish theater company of the Mantua ghetto acquired a high reputation and Jewish performers presented productions at state banquets. The success of the Mantuan community's theater group was due in large part to one man, Leone Portaleone Sommi, an impressario, well-known all over Europe, who stood at the threshold of modern times and modern theater.

**The Jewish Villain.** The Jews' participation in 17th and 18th century theatrical productions was at best insignificant. But as a stage character, the Jew, portrayed as a villain by non-Jewish actors, became a popular figure in the European theater.

This bleak period is typified by the theater in England where the Shakespearean age had made drama the most important art form in the country. Marlowe's *The Jew of Malta* (1591) and Shakespeare's *The Merchant of Venice* (1596), in both of which a Jew is the villain, set a pattern which was to endure.

But by the 19th century the tide began to turn. Jews comprised a considerable portion of theater audiences and they began protesting the anti-Semitic slurs. Disturbances broke out at various performances, often drowning out the play or stopping it completely. A revival of *The Jew of Malta* in 1818 led to a Jewish boycott of London theaters for the rest of the season.

Jews were also beginning to win distinction as actors, singers and writers. London's Hanna Norsa, France's Sarah *Bernhardt, Germany's Jacob Herzfeld, all became well-known performers. And Jewish playwrights began producing works which shed a much more favorable light on their co-religionists. British writer Israel *Zangwill's *The Melting Pot* and German writer G. E. Lessing's play *Nathan the Wise* (written in 1779 but popularized only much later) boldly attacked Christian prejudice, as did others during subsequent years.

Germany also fostered many talented directors and stage managers who developed the new trends of naturalistic (Otto Brahm), modernistic (Max Reinhardt) and expressionistic (Leopold Jessner) theater.

**The Yiddish Theater.** By the end of the 19th century, the main, flourishing centers of Jewish theater were New York and London, both cities with growing Jewish populations. Much of this development can be traced to the Yiddish theater, spreading rapidly in London's Whitechapel and New York's Second Avenue, which served as training grounds for Jewish actors.

The Yiddish theater developed in the 19th century in Russia as an offshoot of the ghetto Purim plays. Abraham *Goldfaden, regarded as the "father" of modern Yiddish theater, began as a Purim player and appeared in the first Yiddish play to be performed on stage, *Serkele,* in 1862.

Goldfaden set up his own theater, wrote plays and songs and hired traveling Yiddish troupes to perform. The best-known of these troupes were the Broder Singers, assembled in the 1860s.

A Russian edict of 1883 prohibiting Yiddish plays had the effect of sending Yiddish theater abroad first to London and then New York. The American Jewish public took to the Yiddish theater avidly, and scores of playhouses opened on Second Avenue, and in Philadelphia, Boston, Chicago, Detroit, and Cleveland. Their appeal for the most part was strictly sentimental, light-hearted comedies and tear-jerking melodramas about the old country. Some producers launched a reform movement, producing more serious plays and translations of great classics, thus starting a so-called "golden epoch" in Yiddish theater. Great Yiddish writers such as I.L.*Peretz, Sholem Asch, D. Pinski, M. Gordon and Sholem *Aleichem provided the inspiration for numerous productions.

But by World War I the Yiddish theater began to decline. The Jewish population of New York's Lower East Side started moving away and the new generation was growing up with English as its native tongue and not Yiddish. Jewish actors such as Rudolph Schildkraut, Bertha Kalish, Sophie Tucker and Molly Picon moved west to Broadway or even further west to Hollywood.

**Broadway.** The early and middle years of the 20th century saw the rise of Jews to unequaled prominence in New York theaters. Early outstanding figures on Broadway were playwrights Clifford Odets, Elmer Rice, and S. N. Behrman; showman Billy Rose; producers Sam and Ted Harris. In 1925, Samson Raphaelson wrote *The Jazz Singer* about a Jewish boy who had to choose between being a cantor and a musical comedy actor. Al *Jolson made the lead role famous, thus combining Jewish playwriting, musical talent, acting and theme, all in one package.

The musical comedy absorbed a high percentage of Jewish theatrical people, many of whom started out in burlesque and vaudeville — the music hall or variety theater which abounded in Jewish comedians and performers. Among the new stars were the *Marx Brothers, the Ritz Brothers, Zero Mostel, Danny *Kaye and Sid Caesar.

Jews were, in fact, among the originators of the musical comedy. Florenz Ziegfeld with his *Ziegfeld Follies* (1907-1931) introduced many singers, actors and composers like Irving Berlin and Jerome Kern. Elaborate revues were introduced by the Shubert brothers, theatrical entrepreneurs, who by 1956 owned 17 theaters on Broadway and about half the nation's legitimate theaters. The 1920s and following decades saw musical geniuses such as Richard Rogers, George and Ira *Gershwin, Lorenz Hart, George S. Kaufman, Morrie Ryskind, Oscar Hammerstein, and Frank Loesser. They created such big hits as *Porgy and Bess, Pal Joey, South Pacific, Carousel, Guys and Dolls, The Pajama Game, Damn Yankees, The Sound of Music,* and many more. Frederick Loewe composed the music for Alan J. Lerner's *My Fair Lady* and Leonard Bernstein introduced new musical trends in *West Side Story*.

The Jews have maintained their position of prominence in modern theater the world over and as the importance of film and television have increased, they have achieved renown in these areas as well (see also *Motion Pictures and *Hebrew Theater).

Below is an alphabetical listing of some outstanding Jewish performers, producers, directors, stage managers and playwrights not already mentioned:

**Allen, Woody** (originally Allen Stewart Konigsberg; 1936- ), U.S. comedian. Allen began his career writing jokes for television comedians and then appeared personally in comedy sequences based on the theme of failure. He is the author of the play *Don't Drink the Water* which opened on Broadway and has written and starred in numerous films including *Bananas, Take the Money and Run, Play It Again Sam,* and *Sleeper*.

**Benny, Jack** (formerly Benny Kubelsky; 1894-1975), U.S. vaudeville, film and radio entertainer. He won virtually every award in the entertainment industry, and his most memorable characterizations were of an unyielding skinflint, an atrocious fiddler, and a demanding boss.

**Berg, Gertrude** (1900-1966), U.S. actress, scriptwriter, and creator of the popular radio and TV family, "The Goldbergs." In later years she appeared in Broadway plays, including *A Majority of One*. "The Goldbergs" was transformed into a Broadway play, *Molly*, in 1973.

**Bernardi, Herschel** (1924–86), U.S. actor. Bernardi performed in *The World of Shalom Aleichem* (1954) and played Tevye in the Broadway production of *Fiddler on the Roof*.

**Berle, Milton** (formerly Berlinger; 1908- ), U.S. comedian, known as "Mr. Television." Berle played in nightclubs, films, and Broadway shows, including the *Ziegfeld Follies* of 1943. From 1948 to 1956 he did a weekly variety show on television in modern slapstick style. In the 1960s he also appeared in serious parts.

**Bikel, Theodore Meir** (1924- ), actor and folk singer. Born in Vienna, Bikel went to Palestine and joined kibbutz Massadah in 1941. In 1943 he worked at Habimah, Tel Aviv and in 1944 with Cameri. He was a founder of the Arts Chapter of the American Jewish Congress (1961). He has played in various Broadway shows and films, including *The Sound of Music, My Fair Lady,* and *The Russians are Coming*.

**Borge, Victor** (originally Borge Rosenbaum; 1909- ), Danish-U.S. satirical comedian. First a concert pianist, Borge made his debut as a comedian at 23. Much of his humor was anti-Nazi and he had to flee when the Germans occupied Denmark in 1940. In the U.S. he was featured on numerous variety shows. He was active in the civil rights movement and in the organization which gave scholarships in gratitude for Denmark's rescue of Jews during World War II.

**Bouwmeester, Louis Frederick Johannes** (1842-1925), Dutch actor, best known for his portrayal of Shakespearean characters.

**Brice (Borach), Fanny** (1891-1951), U.S. actress and singer. Born in New York, Fanny made her first appearance at the age of 14, and achieved her first success in the 1910 *Ziegfeld Follies*. She had a gift for mime and satire, and was noted for songs with a Brooklyn accent. The Broadway musical *Funny Girl* (1963) was based on her life story.

**Bruce, Lenny** (Leonard Alfred Schneider; 1926-1966), U.S. comedian. His obscene commentary on current affairs aroused widespread indignation and in 1964 he was arrested and convicted on obscenity charges. This brought almost 100 artists and professors to his defense. He was regarded by some as a satirist ahead of his time.

**Burstein**, family of actors appearing first in Yiddish productions in Eastern Europe, then on Broadway, finally settling in Israel in 1954. The son, Mike, starred in the Broadway show *Barnum* (1981).

**Dzigan, Shimon** (1905-1980), Yiddish satirical actor. Dzigan began his career in Poland where he became popular in comic dialogues with Israel Schumacher. During and after World War II, they gave

1

2

1. U.S. Yiddish-English actress, Molly Picon (1898–1992) in one of her early starring roles in *The Circus Girl,* produced in New York by her husband Jacob Kalich.
2. Keni Lipzin (1856–1918) in the title role of Jacob Gordin's Yiddish play *Mirele Efros.*

1

2

1. Israel actor Yehoshua Bertonoff, in a Habimah production of Aharon Megged's play *Genesis*.
2. U.S. actor Menashe Skulnik (1892–1970) in a Yiddish version of Franz Werfel's play, *Jacobowsky and the Colonel*.

performances in Russia, Western Europe and North and South America before settling in Israel in 1952.

**Epstein, Brian** (1934-1967), British impressario who revolutionized the world of "pop" music as manager of the Beatles.

**Grey, Joel** (1932- ), U.S. musical comedy actor. He gained international acclaim for his role as Master of Ceremonies in *Cabaret* and as George M. Cohan in *George M.*

**Hackett, Buddy** (Leonard Hacker; 1924- ), U.S. comedian. Born in Brooklyn, his wit and story-telling ability won him success on television in the 1960s and several movie roles. Hackett devoted much time to a foundation combating Tay-Sachs disease, which occurs mostly among Jewish children of Middle European background.

**Hurok, Solomon** (1890-1974), U.S. impressario responsible for assisting many great performers to achieve international fame. He took part in the discussions between Washington and Moscow that led to an agreement on cultural exchanges.

**Kaminska, Ida** (1899-1980), Polish actress, born into a family of Yiddish actors in Poland. She founded the Jewish State Theater in Poland and also achieved fame as a film actress. Her role in the film *The Shop on Main Street* (1967) was widely acclaimed.

**Kessler, David** (1860-1920), Yiddish actor and one of the leading actor-managers of the New York Yiddish theater during its heyday early in the century.

**Levenson, Samuel** (1914-1980), U.S. humorist. Born in Russia, Levenson was a high school teacher in Brooklyn before he gained a reputation as a humorist reciting stories about his childhood on New York's Lower East Side.

**Meskin, Aharon** (1898-1974), Israel actor and a founding member of Habimah. He was awarded the Israel Prize in 1960 and was the first chairman of the Israel section of the International Theater Institute.

**Miller, Arthur** (1915- ), U.S. playwright. He won the Pulitzer Prize for drama for *Death of a Salesman* (1949) and again for *A View from the Bridge* (1957).

**Pinter, Harold** (1930- ), English playwright known for symbolic, rather sinister plays such as *The Room, The Caretaker,* and *The Homecoming.*

**Rose, Billy** (William Samuel Rosenberg; 1899-1966), U.S. showman who pioneered nightclub-style entertainment and produced many Broadway shows.

**Sahl, Mort** (Morton Sahl Lyon; 1927- ), U.S. comedian and satirist. He excels in monologue, directing his satire mostly at political figures.

**Shore, Dinah** (Francis Rose Shore; 1917- ), U.S. singer. Born in Winchester, Tennessee, she sang on radio and on a regular television series.

**Shubert**, family of U.S. theater proprietors and producers who introduced more than 500 plays to American audiences.

**Simon, Neil** (1927- ), U.S. playwright who has written scores of successful Broadway comedies, including *Come Blow Your Horn, Barefoot in the Park, The Odd Couple, Sweet Charity, Plaza Suite, The Prisoner of Second Avenue, The Sunshine Boys,* and *The Good Doctor*. He also collaborated on several films including *The Heartbreak Kid*.

**Strasberg, Lee** (1901–82), U.S. theatrical director and teacher. He won the Pulitzer Prize for directing *Men in White* (1933). As director of the Actors' Studio from 1948, he developed the famous "Method" approach to acting.

**Thomashefsky, Boris** (1868-1939), U.S. actor and stage director. He was a pioneer of the Yiddish theater in America and one of its most active figures for nearly 50 years.

**Vaughan, Frankie** (Frank Ableson; 1928- ), English entertainer who became one of Britain's most popular and successful entertainers.

**THEFT AND ROBBERY.** Jewish law classifies the criminal act of theft or of robbery into seven broad categories: 1) fraud, that is, "stealing another person's mind"; 2) stealing by way of falsifying weights and measures; 3) stealing objects that are useless or have no value; 4) misappropriating documents, land or property consecrated to the Temple; 5) stealing personal items of worth; 6) stealing animals (sheep or oxen) and then slaughtering or selling them; 7) stealing a person, that is, kidnapping. Each of these categories carries a different penalty, ranging from death in the case of kidnapping to the payment of a double fine in the case of the theft of a personal item of worth and of a fourfold or fivefold fine in the case of the theft and subsequent slaughtering or selling of an animal. The distinction in Jewish law between theft and robbery is a formal one – theft being defined as an act of stealing done clandestinely, while robbery is an act of stealing done openly and with force.

Prohibitions against theft are scattered throughout the Torah, and the rabbis of the Talmud generally tended to see each as referring to a specific category of theft rather than as a prohibition against theft in general. Thus, the "Thou shalt not steal" of the Ten Commandments, because it appears in the context of prohibitions that carry the death penalty, was interpreted to be a reference to kidnapping, since that is the only type of theft punishable by death.

A thief who has been caught must, of course, return the objects he has stolen to their rightful owners. If he no longer has them in his possession, he must pay the value of the objects as they were assessed at the time of the robbery. The money to cover the value of the objects as well as for all the fines imposed, was drawn from the thief's possessions and property. If, after selling all he owns, the thief manages to accumulate sufficient funds to cover the cost value of the objects, he is allowed to pay the fines in instalments. However, if his net worth does not cover the value of the stolen objects, the court has the right to sell him into slavery and use the proceeds to repay the victim. Women, however, were never sold into slavery.

**THUNDER AND LIGHTNING.** The ancients were fine observers of nature since they were not isolated from it by modern comforts. They correctly associated thunder and lightning with clouds and rain, and saw their awesome magnificence as a demonstration of the power of God. It was said in the Talmud that thunder was created so that men should fear God, and the prophets said that shafts of lightning were His arrows hurled in anger. *Barak* (lightning) is mentioned more frequently than *ra'am* (thunder). Both, along with shooting stars, earthquakes and tempests, require the recitation of the blessing: "Whose strength and might fill the world."

**TIBBON, IBN,** a family of translators and authors who for four generations translated some of the greatest works in Jewish literature from Arabic to Hebrew, and thus made them accessible to all of world Jewry.

Judah ben Saul Ibn Tibbon (c.1120-c.1190) was the pioneer member of this family of gifted translators. Born in Granada, Spain, where the spoken and literary language of the Jews had, for several hundred years, been Arabic, he emigrated in the middle of the 12th century to Provence, in southern France. There he discovered that, on account of the language barrier, even the scholars and the highly-educated among the Jews of the region had no knowledge of the rich Jewish philosophic literature which had been composed in Spain and elsewhere in the Arab world. He also discovered, however, that there was a great thirst for this knowledge, and he spent much time conducting small study groups in which he would orally translate selections from the Judeo-Arabic literature. Soon, however, he was commissioned by a wealthy patron to commit his translations to writing. Thus began his formal career as a translator, and in a remarkably short time he succeeded in translating such classics as Baḥya ibn Paquda's *Ḥovot Ha-Levavot,* Judah Halevi's *Kuzari,* Saadiah Gaon's *Emunot ve-De'ot* and Jonah Ibn Janah's *Sefer ha-Rikma* and *Sefer ha-Shorashim.* Later generations would refer to him as the "Father of Translators" for this pioneering work which required unusual linguistic expertise and intellectual sharpness, for not only was the subject matter conceptually difficult, but the linguistic problems he had to surmount were also enormous. The Hebrew language of his day lacked the precise technical vocabulary employed by the Judeo-Arabic authors in their writings, and Ibn Tibbon was forced to coin a very large number of new Hebrew terms. In doing so, he enriched the Hebrew language immensely and his impact is still apparent in the modern Hebrew of today.

Judah's son, Samuel (c. 1160-1230), followed in his footsteps, and continued the family project of translating all the major Judeo-Arabic classics into Hebrew. He is most famous for his monumental translation of Maimonides' great philosophical work, the *Guide for the Perplexed.* Samuel's son, Moses, was also a translator, but he focused most of his attention upon general philosophic and scientific texts, including the Arabic editions of Greek authors such as Euclid.

Samuel's grandson, Jacob ben Machir (c.1236-1307) was the last in this line of translators; he translated numerous books on philosophy, mathematics and astronomy into Hebrew.

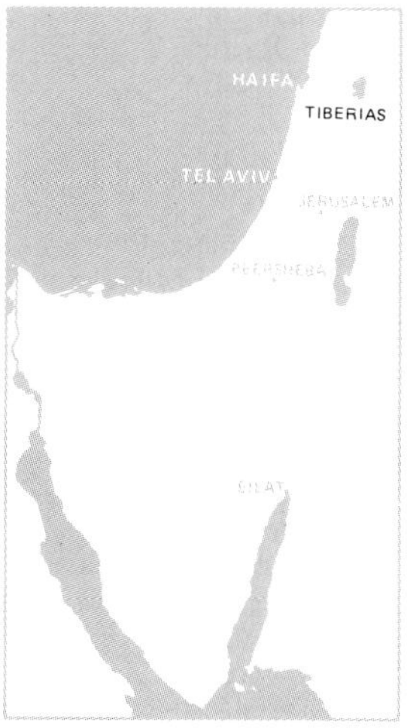


**TIBERIAS** (Hebrew: *Teveryah*), a city situated approximately at the mid-point of the western shore of Lake *Kinneret (the Sea of Galilee),is the largest urban settlement in the Jordan Valley and serves as the administrative, cultural and trade center of the surrounding region. Built on a steep slope rising up from the lake, the city is spread over a relatively large area, with the highest point some 1,500 feet above the level of the lake, with consequent differences in temperature, rainfall and vegetation, even within the city limits.

The city was founded in the first century c.e. by

Herod Antipas, son of *Herod, king of Judea, on the remains of the biblical city of Rakkath (Joshua 19:5), and was named after the then-reigning Roman emperor, Tiberius. For about 150 years the city remained a Roman enclave, with its city administration organized on a Greek model and its population consisting mainly of laborers and artisans. During the second century, however, it was chosen by the *Nasi (as the leader of the Jews was called) and the *Sanhedrin (supreme court) as their place of residence, and for hundreds of years thereafter the city played a central role in the development of Jewish culture and tradition. It remained the seat of the Nasi until the Arab conquest in the seventh century, and during this period the so-called "Palestinian Talmud" was actually composed there. In the seventh and eighth centuries, Tiberias was the home of the Masoretes, grammarians who established a definitive vocalization of the biblical text, as well as of the earliest group of post-biblical poets, the *paytanim.* The city suffered greatly during the Crusades, but it remained sufficiently intact to attract such a distinguished visitor as Moses *Maimonides, who journeyed to Tiberias from Egypt during the last years of his life, and whose alleged tomb can be seen there to this day. In the 16th century the city was given as a gift to Don Joseph Nasi by the Turkish sultan, and he attempted to re-establish a Jewish center there (see *Nasi, Gracia). Economic forces, however, favored the development of the more northernly city of *Safed, and it was not until the middle of the 19th century that Tiberias began to thrive again as a Jewish settlement.

For a long time, the Jewish and Arab populations of Tiberias maintained relatively cordial and tolerant relations, but during the War of Independence in 1948, all the Arab inhabitants fled, leaving the city totally Jewish. Since then, Tiberias has become a major center of absorption of new immigrants to Israel, and today has a population of about 34,000 the majority of whom originate from the countries of North Africa and Eastern Europe. The ancient part of the city is on the lake shore and on the hills above it there are new, modern housing projects. Tourism and recreation – particularly in the winter when the climate is warm and sunny – constitute Tiberias' principal economic foundation, with Lake Kinneret, the nearby hot springs, Roman and Crusader ruins, and tombs of saintly figures serving as the main attractions.

One of the many new resort hotels being built along the heights of Tiberias overlooking Lake Kinneret.

**TIME** is one of the basic dimensions of human existence. Everything we do takes place in the context of time; no human activity is outside it. We measure time by movement; in "clock time" an hour is the time it takes the minute hand to make a complete revolution around the face. Larger units of time are fixed according to the movements of the earth and the moon. For more on this,see *Calendar. But all these are merely methods of measuring time. Even if it is not measured, time is still there.

Ancient philosophers were divided over the issue of time and Jewish medieval philosophers followed that difference of opinion. Maimonides accepted the view of Aristotle that time is neither an independent substance nor is it identical with motion. Time is therefore not "real." Hasdai Crescas, another important Jewish philosopher, disagreed with that definition and described time as having an independent existence which movement is only used to measure.

Besides the questions of logic and philosophy these two views involve, an important theological problem is dependent on them. This is the question of God and time. Does God exist outside of time? Obviously this is an important issue as far as God's pre-knowledge of events is concerned. The general Jewish view is that time does not exist as far as God is concerned and indeed Maimonides is hard pressed to find an adequate formulation.

Of course, one of the great difficulties in discussing time is that the discussers, human beings, are so much within time that they cannot even imagine its absence.

**TISH'AH BE-AV** (the ninth day of the Hebrew month of Av, usually falling within the first week of August) is the traditional day of mourning for the

**Torah Ornaments.** An ornate mantle of Italian tissue made for the Scroll of Law in the Hambro Synagogue in London. Represented in miniature on the mantle are : Altar, Candelabrum, and a Scroll in a partially-opened Ark. The mantle is surmounted by a pair of silver finials with bells which were made by Abraham d'Oliveira, the earliest Anglo-Jewish silversmith known by name.

1

6

2

3

5

4

1. **Western Wall.** Stamp issued August 16, 1967, by the Israel Post Office, commemorating the victory of the Israel Defense Forces in the Six-Day War, and showing a portion of the Western Wall.
2. **Tel Aviv-Jaffa.** The port of Jaffa, depicted on one of a three-stamp series issued by the Israel Post Office, March 22, 1967.
3 and 4. **Sports.** A javelin thrower highlights the stamp issued by the Israel Post Office on April 18, 1961, to mark the Seventh International Congress of Hapoel (Israel Workers' Sports Organization); and a track and field runner is featured on the stamp issued October 1, 1950, to mark the Third Maccabiah Games.
5. **Yad Mordekhai.** One of three stamps issued by the Israel Post Office on April 29, 1952, Israel's fourth Independence Day, commemorating the strategically important role played by Kibbutz Yad Mordekhai in defending the southern border of Israel from Egyptian invasion.
6. **Weizmann.** Stamp issued December 9, 1952, in memory of Israel's first president, Chaim Weizmann.

destruction of the Temples in Jerusalem. It is the culmination of the three weeks of mourning that start on the 17th of Tammuz. On Tish'ah be-Av in the year 586 b.c.e., the Babylonian king *Nebuchadnezzar stormed the great *Temple built by Solomon, turned its marbled columns and gilded rooms into a useless pile of rubble and exiled Jerusalem's inhabitants.

After long years of suffering and effort, the Jews managed to rebuild the Temple, which stood for more than 600 years as a symbol of spiritual and national unity. But on the ninth of Av, in the year 70 c.e., the walls of the Temple were once again broken through – this time by the Romans – and the Temple and all its structures were completely razed. Only a small section of the exterior *Western Wall was preserved from destruction, and it has survived until today as a poignant memory of the glories of the past. In the sources there are slight discrepancies regarding the actual date; one opinion in the Talmud has it that the Second Temple was actually destroyed on the tenth of Av. But it is the ninth that was fixed for both Temples.

This tragic day has therefore been set aside as a time of sadness for all Jews, who are required to fast the whole day and observe most of the mourning rites which apply in the case of a death in the family, such as not wearing shoes or sandals made of leather. At the evening service in the synagogue, all decorations are removed from the ark, the lights are dimmed, a few candles are lit, and the whole congregation sits on low benches or on the floor listening in hushed silence to the mournful notes of *Eikhah,* the Book of Lamentations written by the prophet Jeremiah, an eye-witness to the destruction of the first Temple. The morning service for Tish'ah be-Av is unique in being the only non-festival day on which neither **tallit* nor **tefillin* are worn, for both are considered an adornment not suitable for the mourning period. (They are, however, worn for the afternoon service.)

Following a special reading from the Torah, the congregants once again seat themselves on the floor and chant, individually or in groups, special dirges and laments known as *kinot.* These bemoan, in addition to the destroyed Temples, all the tragedies that have happened to the Jews in history, for Tish'ah be-Av has come to be regarded as a symbol of all the historical tragedies of the Jewish people, among them the expulsion from Spain (according to tradition the expulsion was completed on the Ninth of Av), the Crusades and the Holocaust.

Religious poets throughout the ages attempted to give poetic expression to their grief over these various tragedies and it is their creations which have been collected in the book of *kinot* which are recited on Tish'ah be-Av. Among the most powerful laments which have been included in the various collections of *kinot* (like the *siddur* there are different collections for Sephardim and Ashkenazim) are those which retell the story of the *Ten Martyrs and those which detail the devastation wreaked upon the Jewish communities of France and Germany by the Crusaders. More recent additions to the book of *kinot* are poetic memorials to the six million who perished in the Holocaust in Europe. And in almost all collections of *kinot* there are also usually included several of the most poignant of the *Zionide* songs of the medieval Spanish poet *Judah Halevi.

In present day Israel,Tish'ah be-Av is observed by many tens of thousands at the Western Wall, where *kinot* are recited while seated on the ground facing the last remnant of the Second Temple.

**TITHES** (Hebrew: *terumot,* "heave offerings," and *ma'aserot,* "tithes"). During Temple times Israelites would set aside a portion of their agricultural products as tithes which were given to the priests, Levites, and alternately to the poor or were to be taken to Jerusalem and eaten there. The Bible only prescribes tithes for grain, wine and oil, but the rabbis extended this obligation to cover all agricultural and horticultural produce.

Before the produce was considered fit for consumption a small amount was first set aside for the priest: this was called *terumah gedolah* ("major heave offering"). The Bible itself does not stipulate a fixed amount but the rabbis said, "A generous person will give a fortieth, an average man a fiftieth, and a mean person a sixtieth." From what remained, a tenth was set aside for the levite: this was known as *ma'aser rishon* ("first tithe"); from this,the Levite himself would separate a tenth for the priest, called *terumat ma'aser* ("heave offering from the tithe"). During the third and sixth years of the seven-year sabbatical cycle,a special tithe was given to the poor, consisting of one-tenth of what remained, and called *ma'aser ani* ("tithe for the poor"). In the other years of the cycle, the poor man's tithe was not separated, but instead a second tithe *(ma'aser sheni)* was taken and either set aside to be eaten later in Jerusalem or redeemed for a sum of money which would be used to buy food in Jerusalem, to be consumed there.

The tithes served the purpose of supporting the

1 to 3. Three copperplate engravings used to illustrate the title pages of three tractates of a Hebrew-Latin edition of the Mishnah (printed in Amsterdam, 1700–1704), each of which deals with a different aspect of tithing. Figure 1 illustrates tractate *Demai,* and shows Jews tithing sacks of produce concerning which there are strong doubts whether the proper tithes have already been drawn from them (such doubtful produce is called *demai*); figure 2 illustrates tractate *Ma'aserot* and shows the selecting of lambs to be brought as part of the animal tithe; figure 3 illustrates tractate *Ma'aser Sheni,* and shows people eating the "second tithe" in Jerusalem.

1

2

3

priest and Levite who did not have any ancestral holdings of land and were occupied with the Temple service and other ritual duties, of supporting the poor, and of strengthening the position of Jerusalem in the consciousness of all the people of Israel. Basing themselves on the close similarity in sound between the words *te'aser* (give tithes) and *tit'asher* (become rich), Rabbi Johanan said: "Give tithes so that you will become rich," and Rabbi Akiva added that, "tithes are a fence which guards one's riches." After the exile from Ereẓ Israel, pious people became accustomed to give one-tenth of their earnings to charity, although this "tithe" is of comparatively modern origin.

It is still customary among Orthodox Jews to set aside tithes from all produce of the Land of Israel, and the produce marketed by Tnuva, the large agricultural collective, is tithed at source before it is sold. The *terumah* part is either destroyed or used as fodder for animals owned by priests; because they are ritually unclean, the *kohanim* themselves cannot eat it. The other tithes are distributed to the poor and needy.

Included in the commandments of tithing was the obligation to set aside a tithe of dough for baking, called *ḥallah,* to be given to the priest. Nowadays it is customary to set aside an olive's bulk from the dough and burn it.

**TITUS, FLAVIUS VESPASIANUS,** Roman leader who destroyed the Second Temple of Jerusalem in 70 c.e., razed the city and cruelly enslaved and massacred its inhabitants.

Titus and his father Vespasian were first sent to Judea in 66 c.e. by the Emperor Nero to suppress the Jewish revolt there. Titus captured Jotapata (where he spared the life of *Josephus who had been in command) and other cities in the Galilee. When his father became emperor in 69 c.e., Titus took charge of the entire campaign in Judea and began advancing on Jerusalem.

The Roman headquarters were established on Mount Scopus shortly before Passover, 70 c.e. Most of the trees around the outer walls were uprooted and embankments erected to enable the Roman soldiers to scale the barrier. But their efforts were constantly thwarted by the Jews who succeeded in undermining and destroying the embankments. After several futile attacks, Titus decided to resort to starving out his victims. He had the Temple area totally sealed off so that its inhabitants could not receive supplies.

1

2

1. A worker sorts tobacco leaves in the tobacco storage room of Kibbutz Yeḥi'am in the Upper Galilee.
2. The Arch of Titus in Rome, erected by the Roman emperor Titus in 81 c.e. in commemoration of his capture of Jerusalem in 70 c.e. It is decorated with relief work (not visible in this photograph) showing the spoils taken from the Jerusalem Temple.

Anyone caught trying to escape was tortured.

At various stages during the battle for Jerusalem, Josephus was sent by Titus to appeal to the Jews to surrender. The Jews scornfully rejected his pleas but in the end some members of the high priestly families were persuaded to surrender.

On the Ninth of Av, the Romans succeeded in scaling the wall around the Temple courtyard and set fire to the holy site. The Temple's destruction marked the end of organized Jewish resistance and Titus, after capturing the upper city as well, ordered the destruction of the whole city and its walls. Only the *Western Wall from the days of *Herod is left today as a reminder of past glory.

Titus was hailed as emperor by his soldiers and led a victory march back to Rome, carrying the sacred vessels from the Temple. An arch decorated with scenes from the procession was erected in Rome and is still standing today. During the Middle Ages, no Jew was allowed to (or would) pass under the Arch, paying instead a fee to be allowed to go through a neighboring house.

**TOBACCO** was introduced to the European continent by Christopher *Columbus, who learned of it from the Indians he met in the New World. Columbus relayed his find to his patrons in Spain, and from there it was spread throughout Europe by the *Marranos (secret Jews) then fleeing Spain after the expulsion in 1492.

Jews took up smoking in the 17th century and

snuff-taking – that is, the inhaling of tobacco dust through the nose – from the 18th century. Once they became mass consumers of the product, it was not long before they were involved in importing and trading in tobacco. In Amsterdam, for example, the first important tobacco importing and processing center in the 17th century, a Jew named Isak Italiaander was the largest importer and ten out of 30 leading tobacco importers were Jews. Jews also controled the tobacco monopolies in several German and Austrian provinces.

In Eastern Europe, snuff processing was widespread and tobacco was a staple ware of the Jewish peddler. When in the mid-19th century cigars and cigarettes entered the mass market, Leopold Kronenberg, the Jewish industrialist and financier, was one of the main entrepreneurs of Poland, owning 12 factories in 1867 and producing 25 percent of all snuff.

On the American continent Jews traded in tobacco as early as 1658. In the 19th century, poor Jewish immigrants from Eastern Europe entered the cigar and cigarette industry and, after the garment industry, it had the largest concentration of Jewish workers in the United States. The first professional cigarmakers were generally Jews of Dutch or German origin and Jewish tobacco workers spearheaded the labor movement of the 1870s and 1880s.

Similarly in England, cigarmaking was a widespread occupation in London's Jewish East End and Jews were very successful tobacconists on both a retail and wholesale level.

The role of Jews in the world tobacco industry has since declined, however, as large monopolies swallowed up the smaller firms.

**TOLEDO**, city in central Spain which served as a center of Jewish learning and culture during the Middle Ages. Jewish settlement in Toledo probably began when the town became the capital of the Visigoths (who then ruled Spain) in the sixth century. When the Visigoths converted to Catholicism in 589, the Church councils held in Toledo directed many decrees against the Jews and thus began the anti-Semitic tradition which was to continue in Spain for centuries.

The city was captured by Muslim Arabs in about 711 and for a time, under the Arab rulers, Jews enjoyed a degree of freedom and prosperity. By the 11th century Toledo had developed into a hub of Jewish scholarship where at least 4,000 Jews had gathered from various other cities in Spain to share in its wealth and culture. Even when the city was recaptured by the Christians in 1085, the situation remained good. The Jews of Toledo were known for their prowess in the fields of mathematics, astronomy and science, as well as in religious subjects. During this period some of the most distinguished Jewish personalities of their time lived in Toledo, including the families of *Ibn Ezra, *Judah Halevi and *Abulafia.

The Jews of this period lived mostly in the Jewish quarters situated in the western part of the city. The quarter spread as far as the gate known today as Cambron, formerly called "Gate of the Jews." The principal artery of the Jewish quarter, at present known as Calle del Angel, was formerly named Calle de la Juderia. At the height of their prosperity, the Jews probably formed one-third of the city's population. There were at least 10 synagogues in the city, and two of these have been converted into churches which are still standing. They are among the few Jewish buildings to have been preserved in Spain. One was founded in 1203 and is now the Church of Santa Maria la Blanca, and the other was built by Samuel Halevi in 1357, and is now called the Church of El Transito. These two synagogues are distinguished for the beauty of their Moorish architecture.

By the 14th century, the fortunes of the Jewish community in Toledo began to change. The plague of the Black Death took a heavy toll in 1348, and it was followed by anti-Semitic laws and persecutions. In 1391 almost all the synagogues were burned and many Jews murdered. The community remained impoverished until the expulsion from Spain in 1492. It never again regained its position of prominence in the Jewish world.

Toledo is also the name of an American town in the state of Ohio, which has about 6,300 Jews out of a total population of some 333,000.

**TOPOL, CHAIM** (1935- ), Israel actor who won international fame as Tevye the milkman in the musical *Fiddler on the Roof.* Born in Tel Aviv, Topol began his acting career in one of the entertainment units of the Israel army. After his release from service, he appeared at the Haifa Municipal Theater in Hebrew versions of classical and modern plays. In Tel Aviv he took part in the Hebrew production of *Fiddler on the Roof.* His fine performance led to an invitation to play the leading role in the English

1

2

1. Part of the inner courtyard of the Toledo mansion built in the 14th century by the Spanish financier and community leader, Samuel ben Meir ha-Levi Abulafia. It is now the El Greco Museum.
2. The Israel film star Chaim Topol playing in the Israel film *The Rooster,* 1971.

production of the play at the London West End Theater, and in the American film version. He has also appeared in several other films, including the Israel comedy, *Sallaḥ Shabbati.*

**TORAH.**

**Definition.** This article will deal with the Torah as the Five Books (Genesis, Exodus, Leviticus, Numbers and Deuteronomy) which, according to tradition, were revealed to Moses by God on Mount Sinai (see *Bible). The article will also discuss the reading of the Torah in the synagogue, the Torah as a sacred text which should be written in a prescribed way, and the ornaments associated with it.

**Other Definitions.** It is important to note that the term Torah has a wide variety of meanings in addition to the one presented here:

1) "Teaching" or "Instruction." The word Torah is derived from the Hebrew root which means "to teach."

2) "Law." The Bible often uses the term: "The Torah of . . ." followed by a series of laws. Some people, therefore, translate Torah as meaning law. This translation, however, is much too narrow. Torah contains law, but it also includes history, literature, folklore and ethical teachings.

3) "Written Torah" and "Oral Torah." According to tradition, when God revealed the Torah to Moses, He also revealed to him the proper way of interpreting it. These interpretations were conveyed orally from generation to generation. In this way there developed an Oral Torah (see *Oral Law), which supplemented the written Torah (i.e., the Five Books of Moses). Later generations expanded the concept of Torah to include acts of piety and kindness as well as the study of sacred texts. Torah came to encompass all of Jewish religion and life.

4) "System" or "Theory." In modern Hebrew the term Torah is used to indicate a scientific or philosophical system, i.e., "The Torah of Education," or "The Torah of Spinoza."

**The Torah's Message.** The Torah speaks of God as the sole creator of the Universe. Originally all creatures lived in peace, but after Adam had sinned, friction entered the world bringing violence in its wake. God destroyed the world, saving only one righteous man, Noah, and his family. Ten generations later God spoke to Abram (later called *Abraham) and told him to go to a new land (Ereẓ Israel) and to found there a people who would be a "source of blessing to all the families of the earth." Abraham's great-grandchildren left Ereẓ Israel and settled in Egypt where they subsequently became slaves to Pharaoh. God sent Moses to free the people, to lead them to Mount Sinai and, eventually, to bring them back to the land their forefathers had left.

At Mount Sinai God revealed Himself to the Israelite people. According to tradition, the Torah is the word of that revelation. The Torah addresses itself to the people of Israel, urging them to become a "kingdom of priests and a holy nation." It speaks to the individual, commanding him to love God with all his heart, all his soul and his might; to love his neighbor as himself; to pursue justice; and to "be holy as I the Lord your God am holy."

The Torah also tells of the problems faced by the Israelites after they left Egypt. It contains poems written by Moses as the Israelites crossed the Red Sea, and his talk to the Jews when he was about to die. The Torah's narrative ends with the death of Moses just before the Israelites return to the Promised Land. (A more detailed analysis of the contents of the Torah is found in the article *Bible.)

### THE READING OF THE TORAH

According to an ancient tradition, Moses commanded that the Israelites should read the Torah on the Sabbath, on festivals, and on the first day of each month; Ezra decreed that it should also be read on Monday and Thursday mornings as well as Sabbath afternoons. Scholars differ as to whether this tradition should be taken as a historical statement or not; however, even those who are skeptical about its literal truth believe that the tradition of reading the Torah in public is a very ancient one.

**The Cycle – One Year or Three Years.** The Babylonian Talmud relates that the Jews of "the West" (i.e., Ereẓ Israel) took three years to complete their

A Jaffa scribe carefully reviews a Torah scroll for mistakes and corrects those that do not permanently invalidate the scroll for use in the public reading of the Torah in the synagogue.

public reading of the Torah. They apparently divided the Torah into more than 150 different sections (*sedarim,* singular : *sidrah;* or *parashot,* singular : *parashah*). On the first Sabbath of their cycle they read the first few chapters of Genesis, on the next Sabbath a few more, and so on until, by the end of three years, they had read the entire Torah.

In Babylonia, the custom was different. There the Torah was divided into 54 different sections (naturally the Babylonian sections were about three times as long as the Palestinian sections) so that the entire cycle was completed in one year. Today, nearly all communities follow the Babylonian custom; however, some congregations, especially within the Conservative and Reform movements, are experimenting with a three-year cycle.

**The Preliminary Service.** Try to imagine the reading of the Torah in a traditional synagogue on a Sabbath morning. Assume that a *minyan* (ten adult Jews) is present. The Torah is in the *Aron Kodesh* (the Holy Ark). As the *ḥazzan* begins to chant special prayers, one or two members of the congregation move toward the ark. They have been honored with *petiḥat ha-aron* (the opening of the ark). At the proper moment one of them will open the ark; the other will take a Torah scroll from the ark and place it on the right shoulder of the *ḥazzan.* The entire congregation will have risen as a sign of respect. The *ḥazzan* chants the opening verse of the **Shema* and the congregation repeats his words. After some additional prayers the *ḥazzan* will walk with the Torah into the congregation. Congregants, as a token of their love for the Torah, will touch it and then touch their lips.

**The Ba'al Koreh.** When he has completed the procession, the *ḥazzan* will place the Torah on a special table from which it will be read. In ancient times seven different individuals each read one portion of the weekly *sidrah.* Nowadays in most congregations one person, called the *ba'al koreh* (the master reader) reads the entire *sidrah.* His task is rather difficult. The Torah text is without vowels, without punctuation and without musical notations. The *ba'al koreh* must memorize these aspects of the text so that his chanting is flawless. Generally two men stand with the *ba'al koreh,* one on each side of him. Their prime duty is to insure that he reads without error. If a mistake is made, these men must correct it and the *ba'al koreh* must re-read the word properly.

**Aliyah – Ascent to the Torah.** Before the *ba'al koreh* begins to read, a congregant will ascend to the Torah. This congregant has been honored with an *aliyah.* Generally, the first *aliyah* is given to a descendant of the priests (a *kohen*). If no *kohen* is present, the *aliyah* is given to a Levite; if neither is present, an Israelite is honored with the first *aliyah.* He is summoned to the Torah by his Hebrew name.

The *ba'al koreh* opens the Torah and indicates the words he is about to read. The person honored with the *aliyah* takes the corner of his *tallit* into his right hand, touches the words to be read and then brings the *tallit* to his lips. He then rolls the Torah closed and recites a benediction expressing thankfulness to God for giving the Torah to Israel. The *ba'al koreh* opens the Torah and reads approximately one-seventh of the weekly *sidrah* (one *aliyah*) after which the person honored with the *aliyah* recites a second benediction.

Now, a second person is called to the Torah. He is generally a Levite (if none is present, the *kohen* honored with the first *aliyah* is also given the second *aliyah*). The Levite follows the same procedure as the *kohen.* In all, at least seven persons ascend to the Torah, the last five being Israelites.

An *aliyah* is generally given to a person celebrating a joyous occasion (marriage, birth of a child, escape from potential danger), or to a learned member of the congregation. It has become customary, however, not to call a father and son or two brothers consecutively to the Torah.

In all Orthodox and in some Conservative congregations, only adult males are honored with *aliyot.* Reform congregations and a growing number of Conservative congregations also allow women to have *aliyot.*

**Maftir.** After the entire weekly *sidrah* has been read, a half *Kaddish* is chanted. Then an additional person is called for the *maftir* (completion) *aliyah.* The *ba'al koreh* usually re-reads the last few verses of the weekly *sidrah;* he seldom reads fresh material for the *maftir aliyah.* The exceptions are on holidays and some special Sabbaths when the *maftir* section deals with the theme of the day and is read from an additional Torah. In many synagogues the *maftir aliyah* is given to a young man (or woman) celebrating his bar mitzvah (or her bat mitzvah).

**Ha-Magbe'ah and Ha-Golel.** After the *maftir aliyah* has been read, two more people are called to the Torah. One of them (*ha-magbe'ah,* the lifter) lifts the Torah and shows it to the congregation. He should open the Torah so that at least three columns of

North African Torah ornaments dating from the 19th century: a richly embroidered Torah mantle and two silver finials with bells.

1. A Torah scroll and case from Persia, 1799.
2. A gold and silver Torah breastplate from late 18th-century Germany. It bears an engraved plaque indicating that it was to be used for the festival of Shavuot.

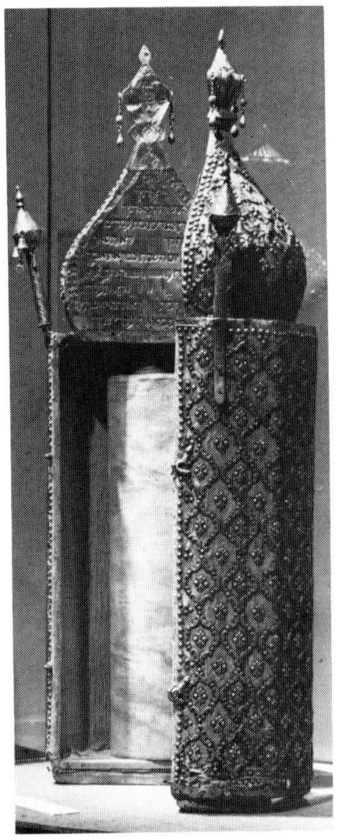
1

2

writing may be seen. The congregation responds by rising and chanting the Hebrew words which mean: "This is the Torah which Moses placed before the Children of Israel (spoken) by the mouth of God, (written) by the hand of Moses. *Ha-magbe'ah* then sits holding the Torah in both hands. The second person, *ha-golel* (the roller) then rolls the Torah closed. He must be careful to place the right hand (beginning) section above the left hand section and then ties the sections firmly together with a special ribbon (see Ornaments, below), places the mantle and other ornaments on the Torah and returns to his seat.

**Haftarah.** The person called for the *maftir aliyah* now recites a benediction thanking God for having chosen worthy prophets and then chants a selection from one of the prophetic books. The selection is known as the *Haftarah,* a term which probably means the closing section. The *Haftarah* section contains at least 21 verses and its theme is usually related to the theme of the Torah reading for that day. It is chanted with a melody different from the Torah melody. On holidays and on Special Sabbaths, the theme of the *Haftarah* is related to the special nature of the day. At the conclusion of the *Haftarah* several benedictions are chanted. This concludes the reading of the Torah. Shortly thereafter the Torah is returned to the ark.

**Weekdays and Holidays.** The Torah is also read on Sabbath afternoons and on Monday and Thursday mornings. On these occasions only the first section *(aliyah)* of the following week's *sidrah* is read. That reading is sub-divided into three *aliyot,* one for a *kohen,* one for a Levite, and one for an Israelite. No *Haftarah* is recited. On the New Moon as well as on the intermediate days of festivals *(ḥol ha-mo'ed)* there are four *aliyot.* On festivals two different Torah scrolls are used. The reading from the first scroll is divided into five *aliyot* (six on the Day of Atonement); it is followed by the chanting of a half *Kaddish.* The reading from the second scroll (the *maftir aliyah*) is always taken from the Book of Numbers, chapter 28 (which describes the additional Temple sacrifice for the individual festivals) and is always followed by the chanting of a *Haftarah.*

**The Torah as a Sacred Text.** The text of the Torah which is read in the synagogue must be transcribed according to very strict rules. It must be written on parchment produced from specified sections of the hide of a kosher animal. Special ink – black, durable, but not indelible – must be used. The text may be written only with a specially made quill, only by hand, and only by a qualified person known as a scribe. (For more details about the writing, see *Scribe.) It must be checked periodically to ensure that all its letters remain clear and distinct.

Because the Torah is the most sacred of all Jewish books, it must be treated with great respect. Every person should stand in its presence, should not touch the parchment on which it is written with his bare hands, and should try to have a Torah of his own in his possession. It is forbidden to sell a Torah scroll unless one uses the proceeds to marry, to continue his studies, or to redeem a person held captive. It is also forbidden to move a Torah scroll from place to place unless it will be read on at least three occasions in the new location. Should a Torah scroll accidentally fall, all those present are obliged to fast. When a scroll is damaged beyond repair, it is placed in an earthenware urn and buried in a special section of the cemetery.

**Torah Ornaments.** Because the Torah scroll is the most sacred object in Jewish tradition, Jews have always sought to ensure that it be preserved in the most aesthetically pleasing fashion possible. Over the generations, among both Ashkenazim and Sephardim, a distinctive set of protective and decorative "garments" have been designed for the Torah scrolls, and these can be seen today in any synagogue in the world when the scrolls are removed from the Ark for the public reading of the Torah.

Among *Ashkenazim, the scroll (which is made of individual pieces of parchment sewn together to form one continuous roll) is supported on two wooden staves known as the *aẓei ḥayyim,* "trees of life." Each end of the parchment scroll is attached to one of the staves and the scroll is rolled inward upon each of them. At the beginning of the yearly cycle of Torah readings, virtually all of the scroll is rolled up on the left stave, so that when the staves are pulled apart slightly, the first columns from the beginning of Genesis become visible. As the reading progresses, the portions read are rolled on to the right stave, and by Simḥat Torah (when the last section of Deuteronomy is read), virtually the complete text of the Torah has been transferred to it. The scroll is then rewound on the left stave and the reading of Genesis begins anew.

Mounted both on the top and bottom of each of the two staves are ornamental wooden projections, some decoratively carved, which serve as handles to facilitate the winding and carrying of the scroll. When the scroll is not in use, the two staves and the parchment wound around them are tightly bound

1
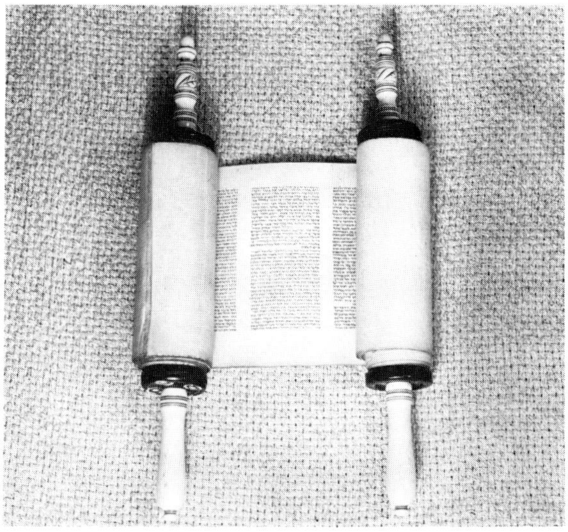

together by a wrapper which usually consists of a simple, long and wide white ribbon, but colorful, fancy velvet bands fastened with ornamented clasps are also used. In some Eastern European communities the wrapper was made of strips cut from a baby's swaddling cloth. The strips would be joined together to form a long runner which was then embroidered with the child's name and appropriate blessings for his welfare. When the child was old enough to be taken to the synagogue, the wrapper would be brought with him, and at his bar mitzvah the Torah from which he read would be clothed with his wrapper.

After being bound with the wrapper, the Torah scroll is then enclosed in a mantle – a circular sheath of fine velvet or silk material which is open at the bottom and closed at the top except for two holes through which the top handles of the *aẓei ḥayyim* protrude. The mantle is usually richly decorated with elaborate embroidered designs of columns, lions rampant, crowns and appropriate verses from the Torah.

When resting in the Ark and while being carried around the synagogue in procession both before and after the Torah reading, the scrolls are generally adorned with several other ornaments which are usually made of fine silver, and at times even of gold. Suspended on a chain from the top of the *aẓei ḥayyim* can be found 1) a breastplate or shield, engraved with various traditional symbols and sometimes including the name of the festival or special occasion for which the Torah has been taken from the Ark; and 2) a pointer, known as a *yad* which is used by the reader to locate his place in the unpunctuated manuscript of the Torah, since it is forbidden to touch the parchment with the bare hand during the reading of the Torah. The *yad* is frequently a miniature carved hand, with a pointing finger, and it is sometimes even encrusted with semi-precious stones, bracelets and rings. And mounted on top of the upper handles of the staves can be either a large crown, decorated with small bells and sparkling jewels, or a pair of finials, known as *rimmonim,* each of which is placed on one of the staves.

Among *Sephardim and in the Jewish communities of the East, the preservation and decoration of the Torah scrolls is in rather a different form. The scroll is also wound upon two wooden staves, but these are enclosed within a wooden box, formed by two arch-shaped sections joined at the center by a hinge. The case is flat at the bottom to enable it to stand securely on a table, and when the Torah is read, the box is opened like a book to reveal a column of text which is read without removing the scroll. The scroll is rolled to the appropriate place by manipulating the staves whose ends protrude through the top of the case. These staves are usually capped with permanent carved, wooden *rimmonim* and the box itself is covered in leather or metal engraved with traditional symbols. Inside,colorful and decorative kerchiefs called *mitpaḥot* are used to protect that part of the parchment exposed when the case is opened.

**TORONTO,** the capital of Canada's province of Ontario, is the city with the largest Jewish population in the country. Its 125,000 Jews make up a flourishing community with numerous synagogues, educational institutions and social service organizations.

Jewish communal life in Toronto began in 1856, when the first congregation, the Holy Blossom Synagogue, was founded by Jewish immigrants from Germany, England and Eastern Europe. With the influx of immigrants from Eastern Europe during the 1880s, many more synagogues were established, the most famous being the *Goel Tzedec* congregation and the *Beth Midrash Hagadol Chevra T'hillim.* At this time, several important religious educational institutions were founded as well, which have grown and expanded over the years so that at present, Toronto has many Jewish day and congregational schools.

2

1. A Torah scroll from 18th-century Poland, rolled upon two *aẓei ḥayyim* and opened to reveal the text from the end of the Book of Exodus (Chapter 35).
2. A silver *yad,* Torah pointer, made in Germany in the late 18th century.

1. Drawing of the 15th-century Dominican, Tomas de Torquemada, who in his capacity as the Grand Inquisitor of Spain was responsible for the torture and death of a great number of New Christians and Marranos.
2. Judah Touro, early American merchant and philanthropist.
3. Part of a crowd of over 10,000 Toronto Jews who demonstrated in front of the Inn on the Park Hotel in October 1971, on the occasion of the visit to Canada of Premier Alexei Kosygin of the U.S.S.R. They protested the harassment of Soviet Jews and demanded of the Soviet government, "Let My People Go!"

3

At the turn of the century, there was extensive Christian missionary activity, especially in the Jewish areas of Toronto. To combat the influence of the missionaries, the Jewish community organized its own social service institutions including hospitals, old age homes, family and child services, free loan societies and rehabilitation centers.

The influence of the Jewish community has also been notable in arts and theater, journalism and politics. Jews hold important editorial positions on the staff of the *Toronto Star,* and have served as aldermen and city board members. Toronto has also had two Jewish mayors: Nathan Phillips and Philip G. Given.

1

2

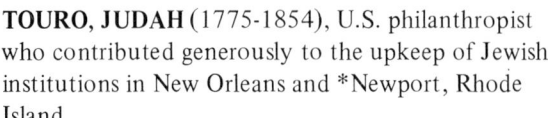

**TORQUEMADA, TOMAS DE** (1420-1498), first head of the Spanish *Inquisition and, as such, responsible for the mass torture, murder and exile of Spanish Jews.

Torquemada entered the Dominican Order of monks at the age of 14 and soon became known for his radical views. He rapidly rose in power and in about 1469 became confessor for Queen Isabella and King Ferdinand, thus acquiring powerful influence and protection from the royal couple. Together with Cardinal Mendoza, he drafted a petition to the Pope, requesting authorization for the establishment of a unified national Spanish Inquisition. Permission was received in 1478 and Torquemada appointed as its chief organizer.

By that time he was already known for his extreme anti-Semitic views and in his new position he began the complete eradication of Jews from Spain. He set up the supreme council of the Inquisition, appointed local tribunals in small towns and villages, and drew up instructions for the "trial" and torture of victims. By the time of his death, Torquemada had become a symbol of religious and ideological fanaticism.

**TOURO, JUDAH** (1775-1854), U.S. philanthropist who contributed generously to the upkeep of Jewish institutions in New Orleans and *Newport, Rhode Island.

Born in Newport, Touro grew up during the troubled times of the Revolutionary War. His father sided with the British and so the family was forced to leave their home and move to the British West Indies. Judah later returned to the United States, living first in Boston and then New Orleans, where he became a successful merchant and began accumulating his fortune.

He was severely wounded during the Battle of New Orleans in 1815, and became extremely withdrawn, refusing to join the New Orleans Jewish community. His friends eventually succeeded in arousing his sense of Jewish identity, and he provided the funds for the building of a new synagogue for the community. When he died, he bequeathed large sums of money for Jewish philanthropic causes.

A synagogue in Newport, a hospital in New Orleans and a Jewish college in New York City were all named in his honor.

**TRANSPLANTS.** Recent advances in medical knowledge and technology have made it possible to transplant organs (such as corneas of eyes, kidneys and even hearts) from a deceased or living person into another individual stricken with disease. Such operations have given rise to many pressing problems of a moral, theological and legal nature, concerning which rabbinic authorities as well as other spiritual leaders, have been called upon to offer guidance and direction.

From the point of view of Jewish law, three main difficulties presented themselves to those halakhic authorities who tackled the issue. Two relate to the transplantation of organs from deceased individuals. The first of these was determining a legal definition of death, for prior to death one is absolutely prohibited from moving or even touching a hopelessly ill patient or doing anything that might hasten his death. The second problem was finding a way of overcoming the explicit prohibition of the *halakhah* against deriving any benefit from the dead, of desecrating the body or of delaying the burial of the dead, all of which would apparently be the case in removing an organ for transplantation. As a solution, most halakhic authorities have accepted as a definition of death the state in which a person has stopped breathing altogether and his heart has stopped beating. And the resolution of the second problem was formulated in a classic *responsum* written by former Israel Chief Rabbi I. Unterman in 1953 in which he ruled that all the prohibitions are put aside because of *pikkuaḥ nefesh,* the possibility that through the use of the transplanted organ a life may be saved.

Transplantations from one living person to another present a third difficulty, and this arises from the general commandment to "take heed of thyself," which rabbinic authorities have interpreted to mean that a person cannot endanger his life willingly and knowingly. Here the basic halakhic position has been propounded by Britain's Chief Rabbi I. Jakobovits who has ruled that one may endanger one's life to donate a "spare" organ if the probability of saving the recipient's life is substantially greater than the risk to the donor's life or health. See also *Autopsies and Dissections.

**TRAVELERS AND EXPLORERS.** From the nomadic days of Abraham right down to the jet-age of today, the Jews have been travelers – moving from place to place in search of adventure, or riches, or just a place where they could live in peace. Our forefathers followed their herds from one green pasture to another, covering most of the Middle East in their wanderings. Later, when the Israelites had finally settled down in Ereẓ Israel, they built fleets of ships which enabled them to travel to the distant lands of Africa and Asia, bringing back riches and tales of adventure.

A drawing of a Zulu (African tribe) warrior and his daughter, drawn on the scene by the artist W. Bagg who accompanied the 19th-century South African trader, traveler and explorer, Nathaniel Isaacs, on his travels throughout Africa, and whose drawings illustrate Isaacs' book *Travels and Adventures in East Africa* (1836).

After the exile from the Land of Israel, Jews were forced to seek refuge in far-off places. Forbidden to own land or engage in regular occupations in these new lands, the Jews became traveling merchants and peddlers. In the ninth century, Jewish traders known as *Radaniya* traded between Western Europe and China, by land and sea. Later, Jewish traders made their way to Africa, sending geographical information about southern Morocco and the western Sahara back to Europe. Jewish travelers brought back elephants from Turkey, silk from China, and precious gems from India.

The most famous Jewish medieval traveler was *Benjamin of Tudela, who journeyed in the second half of the 12th century. He wrote a book on his travels which vividly describes the many Jewish communities he visited. His contemporary, the German traveler *Pethaḥiah of Regensburg, also journeyed through the Middle East and his account forms a valuable historical source.

During the age of discovery, when Europeans began making their way to the Americas and other points on the globe, Jews joined the explorers in various capacities. Jews are known to have been members of the crews of Vasco Da Gama, Columbus, and Cortez. Pedro Teixeira (1570-1650), a *Marrano from Lisbon, may have been the first Jew to travel around the world and is believed to have been the first white man to make a continuous journey up the River Amazon. Jews also participated in the Arctic explorations of the 18th and 19th centuries.

Of course, much Jewish travel concentrated on journeys to and from Ereẓ Israel. Actual descriptions of these travels exist only from the middle of the 12th century. The first known literary evidence of a journey towards Israel by a Jew was by *Judah Halevi. He left Spain in 1140, but never actually reached Ereẓ Israel. Benjamin of Tudela arrived in Ereẓ Israel about 1170 and described the people, places and conditions he found there. Other travelers who left diaries of their trips to the Holy Land included Judah al-Ḥarizi in 1218, Estori ha-Parḥi in 1322, groups of Italian Jews in the 15th century, *Karaite pilgrims in the 17th century, and ḥasidic immigrants in the 18th.

Travel literature and the history of travels in the 19th century accompany the first manifestations of Zionism. Moses *Montefiore and his wife Judith made seven trips to Ereẓ Israel. Others came from all parts of the world, many traveling thousands of miles on foot over mountains and rivers, in snow, rain and heat, to reach the Promised Land.

**TREBITSCH-LINCOLN, IGNATIUS TIMOTHY** (1879-1943), international adventurer. Born a Jew in Paks, Hungary, Trebitsch-Lincoln was baptized as a Lutheran in Hamburg in 1900. He then became a Presbyterian missionary in Canada. There he married a German girl, and the son born of the marriage professed Judaism throughout his life. In the next phase of his career, Trebitsch-Lincoln was an Anglican curate in England. Before long he turned Quaker, and was elected a Liberal Member of Parliament (1910). In World War I he served as a military censor. Suspected of spying for the Germans, he fled to the United States, but was deported to England, convicted of treason, and jailed for three years.

In 1920 Trebitsch-Lincoln participated in an abortive coup against the German republic, formed after World War I. He escaped death by fleeing first to the Balkans and then, in 1921, to China where he spent most of his remaining years. In 1925 he was given permission to return to England for a farewell visit to his son, a soldier, who had been sentenced to death for murder; but when his ship docked at Marseilles he learned that the execution had already taken place. He sought solace in Buddhism, and in 1931 was ordained a monk, adopting the name Chao Kung. Early in 1932 he became a collaborator of the Japanese military intelligence in Shanghai, as well as of the extreme Japanese Black Dragon Society. He worked for the Japanese in China until his death in a Shanghai hospital.

1. A pine tree growing in the outskirts of Jerusalem.
2. A palm tree located near Quseima in the Sinai desert.
3. *Tamarix mannifera,* the "manna" tree, located near the St. Catherine Monastery in the Sinai peninsula.

1

2

**TREES AND PLANTS.** The Bible mentions about 100 names of trees and plants, the bulk of them in Ereẓ Israel, and the Mishnah,Talmud and Midrashim add hundreds more to the list. It would seem that the Land of Israel was always covered with beautiful flowering shrubs and trees. The almond tree, for example, first to bloom in Israel's spring, is mentioned in the time of Jacob. The balsam tree, too, was one of the most profitable of Israel's trees, which grew in Jericho in ancient times. It was, in fact, often sold for its weight in gold. During the Roman-Jewish War of 60-70 c.e., the Jewish defenders cut down the balsam trees lest they fall into the hands of the enemy. Also abundant in those days were the olive tree, the sycamore, and the oak.

Scholars have tried to match up the names in the Bible with the plants and trees existing in Israel today. Though there are a multitude of trees and shrubs, making the labeling job more difficult, there are actually only three flowers mentioned in the Bible. These are the *shoshanah* (identified as the lily), *shoshanat ha-amakim* (lily of the valley), and *ḥavaẓẓelet ha-Sharon* (the rose of Sharon, considered by some to be the wild tulip).

Because trees and shrubs were so commonplace, the sages often used them to distinguish between various areas in Israel: "an indication of mountainous country is the presence of tall oaks; an indication of valleys is palm trees; an indication of streams is reeds; an indication of lowlands is sycamore trees."

Trees played a very special role in the lives of the ancient Jews. It was considered to be a sin to cut down a fruit tree which could have ultimately benefited the land and the people. A Jewish custom developed of planting a tree at the birth of a child (a cedar for a boy and a pine for a girl) and then cutting the trees down when the children married, to be used in the construction of the bridal canopy. The custom was meant to stress the everlasting bond between the nation and the land of Israel, but fell into disuse when the Jews were separated from their homeland.

Despite the honor accorded to trees and plants, the ancients were against having trees and large gardens in the town, especially in Jerusalem. It was felt that trees darkened the town and adversely affected the climate, while gardens required unsanitary fertilizers and attracted insects. Under the crowded living conditions of those days, it was important to let in as much sunlight as possible and keep out disease-spreading insects.

There are several laws regarding the growing and use of trees and plants. It is forbidden to graft two different kinds of plants or trees together (see *Mixed Species). It is also forbidden to eat the fruit of trees during the first three years after their planting.

Various festivals incorporate trees and plants in their traditions. *Tu be-Shevat is, of course, the most

3

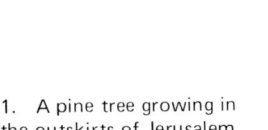

closely related as it celebrates the New Year of the Trees. On *Shavuot it is customary to decorate the synagogue with fragrant grass, flowers and branches of trees which have symbolic meaning. And on *Sukkot, the booths are covered with tree branches and decorated with fruits and greenery. (See also *Fruits and Vegetables.)

**TRENT, SIMON OF,** a Christian child born in 1475 in the city of Trent in northern Italy, whose brutal and unsolved murder gave rise to one of the worst *blood libels in Jewish history.

Simon's body was discovered near the house of the head of the Jewish community, and the whole community – men, women and children – were arrested. After 17 of them had been tortured for 15 consecutive days, they were so broken that they confessed to the crimes of which they had been accused in order to escape further torture. One of those tortured died in prison, six were burnt at the stake, and two (who had converted to Christianity) were strangled.

A papal commissary was then sent to Trent to investigate the circumstances of the incident, but was forced to leave when the results of his inquiries led him to contradict the findings of the local "trial." Proceedings were reopened in Trent in face of violent opposition from the commissary, and at the end of the year five more Jews were executed (two of them were converted to Christianity before their deaths). A papal court of inquiry in 1476 justified the libel, and in 1478, as a result of its proceedings, the Pope published a bull endorsing the "legality" of the trial. In the meantime four Jewish women of Trent had accepted the Christian faith and the property of the murdered Jews had been confiscated. Jews were thenceforth excluded from entering Trent.

Simon was eventually declared a saint. The libel had widespread repercussions and served for intense anti-Semitic propaganda both inside and outside Italy. According to legend, the rabbis of Italy imposed a ban on Jewish settlement in Trent after 1475; this was formally raised when Simon was de-beatified (the title "saint" was withdrawn from him) in 1965.

**TRIBES, TWELVE.** Until the Assyrian conquests in the eighth century b.c.e., the Israelites were grouped into 12 tribes held together by common religion and ancestry. These tribes were descended from the 12 sons of Jacob: a) The sons of his first wife Leah: Reuben, Simeon, Levi, Judah, Issachar and Zebulun; b) The sons of Leah's handmaiden Zilpah: Gad and Asher; c) The sons of Jacob's second wife Rachel: Joseph and Benjamin; and d) The sons of Rachel's handmaiden Bilhah: Dan and Naphtali.

The number 12 was a sacred number in ancient times, as evidenced by the fact that several other peoples living in those days were grouped into 12 clans. Therefore, although the tribe of Levi was appointed as priests and dispersed among the others to perform sacred duties, the tribe of Joseph was divided in two and named for his two sons – Manasseh and Ephraim – thus maintaining the balance of 12.

After the conquest of the Land of Canaan under Joshua, each of the 12 tribes received a portion of land. Reuben, Gad and half the tribe of Manasseh received territory east of the Jordan River, Naphtali and Asher in northern Galilee, Issachar and Zebulun in the Jezreel Valley, Ephraim and the other half of Manasseh in the mountains of Samaria, Benjamin and Judah in the Judean hills, Dan along the seacoast near Jaffa, and Simeon in the Negev.

Dan was later expelled from its territory by the Amorites and had to move north to the sources of the Jordan River. Other tribes also lost portions of their territories through battles and disputes.

Each of the 12 tribes enjoyed a good deal of autonomy, though there were no doubt certain administrative institutions common to all. The elders of the tribes were responsible for making the laws for the people and for dealing with foreign powers. It was the tribal elders, speaking for the entire nation, who eventually requested the prophet Samuel to appoint a king to rule over them all.

The Bible relates that at first the tribe of Reuben, descendants of Jacob's eldest son, was the dominant of the tribal league. This authority however, soon passed to Ephraim and then to Judah. When the monarchy was finally established, the tribal divisions and hierarchy began to disappear as the people united into one nation.

After the death of King Solomon, the tribes split along territorial and political lines, with Judah and Benjamin in the southern kingdom, called Judah, loyal to the Davidic dynasty and the rest of the tribes in the northern kingdom, called Israel, ruled by a succession of dynasties. Finally, in the eighth century b.c.e., the ten northern tribes, exiled by the Assyrians, vanished (see *Ten Lost Tribes) and with them went the traditional tribal structure of Israel.

1

2

3

1 to 3. Three of a twelve-stamp set issued by the Israel Post Office in the mid-1950s, each of which bears the emblem of one of the Twelve Tribes. Shown are the emblems of Simeon, Issachar and Naphtali.

Jews, however, remain conscious of their tribal origins and references are often made to these vanished clans. The only tribal distinction maintained in Judaism nowadays is that of *kohanim* (priests) and Levites who are from the tribe of Levi and all other Jews, who are known as *Yisre'elim* (Israelites).

**TROTSKY, LEV DAVIDOVICH** (1879-1940), Russian revolutionary, Soviet and Communist leader. Trotsky, whose real name was Bronstein, was the son of a Jewish farmer in the Ukraine. He studied mathematics at Odessa University, but gave up his studies to devote himself to the anti-czarist revolutionary activities and joined the illegal Social Democratic Party in 1896 (see *Russia). Arrested by the czarist authorities in 1898 and sent to Siberia, he escaped to England in October, 1902, arriving on a forged passport issued in the name of Trotsky.

It was in England that he met *Lenin and became increasingly involved in the Social Democratic cause. He went back to Russia at the outbreak of the 1905 revolution, was again arrested and sent to Siberia, and again escaped to England. But in 1917 he managed to return to Russia and this time became one of the main organizers and leaders of the October Revolution, an armed revolt which brought the Soviets to power.

In 1918 Trotsky became people's commissar for military affairs, organizing the Red Army and directing military operations on the various civil war fronts from his famous armored train. After Lenin's death in 1924, however, Trotsky's position in the communist hierarchy was weakened as a result of a campaign by *Stalin to discredit him. Within two years, Stalin succeeded in ousting Trotsky from the political life of both the Soviet Union and the Communist International and in January 1928 Trotsky was convicted of counter-revolutionary activities and sent to Alma-Ata in Turkestan. Even there he fearlessly continued to lead left-wing opposition to the Communist Party and a year later was expelled to Turkey with his wife and son. He then went to Norway and later settled in Mexico where, on August 21, 1940, he was assassinated in Mexico City by a "friend" who is generally assumed to have acted on Stalin's orders.

Trotsky had been convinced that there was no future for the Jews as a separate people, and favored their assimilation. But he was shocked at the anti-Semitic campaign conducted against him in the late 1920s in the Soviet Union. He was a remarkably gifted writer and orator who, unlike Stalin, wanted socialism on a world-wide, rather than just a national, scale. Because of his opposition to the official communist regime, however, Trotsky's name and the term Trotskyism in the Soviet Union have become officially synonomous with treason. Trotsky's role in the revolution has been erased from all official records in the Soviet Union, but he has continued to be supported and admired in many countries.

The Communist revolutionary, Lev Trotsky (center, foreground) marching through Red Square in Moscow during the early years after the Revolution when he was still "in favor" among the Communist leadership.

**TRUMAN, HARRY S.** (1884-1972) became 32nd president of the United States in April, 1945, just prior to the final capitulation of the German army and the end of World War II. Among the many difficult problems facing Truman as he took office were finding means of alleviating the plight of the hundreds of thousands of Jewish refugees left homeless and stateless on account of the war, and finding a solution to the troubled political state of Palestine. Truman recommended sending 100,000 Jewish refugees to Palestine and allowing many to enter the United States. In 1947 the United Nations Special Committee on Palestine supported his recommendation to allow Jewish displaced persons to enter Palestine, and the United States Congress passed special legislation in 1948 permitting 200,000 refugees, including Jews, to enter the United States.

In spite of his sympathetic attitude toward the Jews, Truman did not at first support the establishment of a Jewish state in Palestine and maintained that the United Nations should solve the Middle East problem; however, when the State of Israel was proclaimed on May 14, 1948, Truman personally made certain that the United States immediately recognized the new state.

There was much speculation concerning Truman's motives in reversing United States policy towards Palestine. Some suspected that Truman acted purely for political reasons, hoping to capture the American Jewish vote in the presidential elections of November 1948. Others believed that Truman was influenced by his long-time friend and former business partner, Eddie Jacobson, a Jew. Truman denied that his recognition was based on domestic political reasons. He explained in his memoirs that "the fate of the Jewish victims of Hitlerism was a matter of deep personal concern to me . . . ."

On the whole, Truman's liberal, "Fair Deal" administration, which lasted from 1948 to 1952, remained popular with Jewish voters even when the majority of the general public was against it as a result of the Korean war.

**TRUMPELDOR, JOSEPH** (1880-1920), soldier and early pioneer-settler in Ereẓ Israel whose life efforts to organize the military defense of the Jewish settlements in Ereẓ Israel and whose heroic death in a battle at Tel Ḥai in the north of the country became an inspirational symbol to pioneering youth from all parts of the Diaspora.

Born in a small town in the northern Caucasus, Trumpeldor was strongly influenced in his youth by the model of collective communal life which he witnessed at a nearby farming commune established by followers of the Russian writer Leo Tolstoy. In Trumpeldor's mind, the idea of collective living became merged with the Zionist ideal of settling Ereẓ Israel, and he dreamed of establishing agricultural communes in Ereẓ Israel which, if necessary, would be defended by armed force. He was however, drafted into the Russian army and lost an arm while fighting in the Russo-Japanese war. In 1912 he went to Ereẓ Israel and worked for a while at *kevuẓẓat* Deganyah, and participated in the defense of the Jewish settlements in the lower Galilee. When World War I broke out, he was deported to Egypt after he refused to join the Turkish army. In Alexandria, he called for the formation of a legion of volunteers drawn from the Ereẓ Israel deportees to be at the disposal of the British and help liberate the country from the Turks. The British allowed the formation of a Jewish brigade (the "Zion Mule Corps") of which Trumpeldor became the deputy commander and which participated in the Gallipoli campaign of 1915. Between 1915 and 1919 Trumpeldor traveled widely, spending much time in England and Russia, promoting the organization of Jewish regiments to fight the Turks and Jewish self-defense units to protect the settlements in Ereẓ Israel. In Russia, in particular, he was very active in the organization of the He-Ḥalutz movement whose aim was the training of young Jews for settling in Ereẓ Israel.

In 1919 he returned to Ereẓ Israel and in January 1920 was called to the northern Galilee to help organize the defense of the settlements there which had come under increasingly fierce Arab attack. On March 1 he was mortally wounded while participating in the defense of the settlements at Tel Ḥai; his dying words were:*Ein davar, tov lamut be'ad arẓenu* ("Never mind; it is good to die for our country").

Trumpeldor was buried near Tel Ḥai, and in 1934 a memorial was erected at his gravesite. Shortly after his death, a new settlement at the foot of Mount Gilboa was named Tel Yosef in his honor, and songs, poems and stories were written about him as a hero of the Jewish resettlement of Ereẓ Israel. His lifestory served as an inspirational model to both the pioneering socialist youth movements and the right-wing youth groups. One of the largest and most successful of the latter was named in his honor: Betar, an abbreviation of Berit Trumpeldor.

**TRUTH.** Being truthful is one of the most important virtues that a person can possess. In the Bible God is described as the "God of Truth" and truth is one of the 13 divine attributes. The rabbis taught that "truth has feet," i.e., is well founded and will endure. A sign of this was found in the very word itself. The Hebrew word for truth is *emet*; the first letter of the word is the first letter of the alphabet, the second is

1

2

3

1. A black and white photograph of Arthur Szyk's color illustration of the battle at Tel Ḥai, with a likeness of Joseph Trumpeldor (top) shown directing the defense of the settlement. At the bottom is a quotation attributed in the Mishnah to Hillel, "If I am not for myself, who is for me?" which epitomizes Trumpeldor's concept of Jewish self-defense.
2. U.S. President Harry Truman with the Torah scroll he received in 1948 from the first president of the State of Israel, Chaim Weizmann.
3. Joseph Trumpeldor, hero of the early 20th-century resettlement of Ereẓ Israel.

the middle letter of the alphabet and the last is the last letter of the alphabet. Thus, the three "feet" of truth are spread out and form a solid base. The Hebrew word for falsehood, however, is *sheker*, which is formed from the three letters of the alphabet before the last letter. The letters are not in their alphabetical order and represent feet which are too close together and not properly fixed. Falsehood has no foundation and will not last.

Being truthful does not only mean not telling lies. It also involves doing business honestly, abstaining from all deceit and hypocrisy, quoting correctly and in the name of the original author, and keeping promises. One rabbi in the Talmud said that a scholar may evade telling the truth in three instances: If he is asked whether he is a great scholar, he may – out of modesty – answer negatively even if he is one; if he is asked personal, intimate questions; and if he is asked whether his host was hospitable he may answer "no" even if it is untrue so that other people should not impose themselves on that person.

1. Woodcut from a *Minhagim Book* ("Book of Customs") printed in Amsterdam in 1707, which illustrates the section on the laws of Tu bi-Shevat. The table is decorated with various fruits and is surrounded by three trees in bloom.
2. The late actress and singer, Sophie Tucker. Her Yiddish and English songs and acts were widely acclaimed, particularly among the Jewish immigrant generation in America.

1

2

**TU BE-AV**, or the 15th day of the month of Av, was the date of a minor festival, observed only in the days of the Second Temple, which marked the beginning of the grape harvest in Ereẓ Israel. According to the Mishnah, each year on that date the daughters of Israel would dress in white clothes, which they would borrow from one another so that all would be dressed equally and no one would be embarrassed because of inferior clothes. They would go out to the vineyards to sing and dance. Single, eligible young men would follow them to the fields and each man would select the girl he wanted to be his wife. The festival celebration also included lighting torches and bonfires, and the bringing of a "wood offering" of kindling wood for the Temple altar.

In the Talmud, several additional reasons for the festivity of Tu be-Av are given. It was believed to be the day on which the Israelites in the desert ceased to die for the sins incurred following the return of the spies sent to spy out the land of Canaan; and it was also the day on which the Romans finally permitted the burial of the soldiers who had fallen in defense of *Bar Kokhba's last stronghold, the city of Betar.

In the Middle Ages, Tu be-Av assumed new, spiritual meaning. In some groups it was regarded as a day of forgiveness, similar to the Day of Atonement. For them, it marked the beginning of the days of judgment (which culminated in the Day of Atonement) and the time when one should make a reckoning of all one's misdeeds of the year. Also, from that day onward, many pietists would set aside extra evening hours of study in addition to the normal daytime schedule for the whole year round.

**TU BI-SHEVAT**, the fifteenth of the Hebrew month of Shevat (usually falling in January) which traditionally marks the festive "New Year of Trees." It is a joyous holiday celebrated by the donating of trees to Israel, the eating of fresh fruits, and the singing of psalms and songs.

This date was chosen because it marks the beginning of a new cycle of blossoming and fruit-bearing for the trees in Israel. All *mitzvot* relating to the annual growing and harvesting of fruits are also applied as of the 15th of Shevat (see *Tithes).

In Ashkenazi communities in Europe it was customary to eat 15 different kinds of fruit on Tu bi-Shevat, special preference being given to the varieties grown in Ereẓ Israel. The eating of fruits was accompanied by the recital of Psalms.

The Sephardi Jews gave the New Year of Trees a greater significance. The day was called "The Feast of Fruits" and special poems called "complas" were sung. A special service, believed to have been compiled by the 17th-century kabbalist Nathan of Gaza for this holiday, was modeled on the Passover *seder* and included the drinking of four cups of wine. This service was expanded and published in the 18th century under the name *Peri Eẓ Hadar* ("Citrus Fruits").

In Israel, the New Year of Trees has come to symbolize the modern transformation of the Land of Israel from desert sand to green fields and forests.

**TUCKER, SOPHIE** (1884-1966), vaudeville actress and singer, best-known for her songs *My Yiddishe Momma* and *Some of These Days.* Born in Russia as Sophie Kalish, she was taken to America by her parents while still a baby. As a child she worked in her parents' restaurant in Hartford, Connecticut. At 22, Sophie went to New York to appear in vaudeville acts, and became a star attraction at the Palace Theater. Her acts, presented in English or Yiddish, were filled with laughter and tears, and aroused the audience's sentimental feelings. They acclaimed her as "the last of the Red Hot Mamas."

Sophie became very wealthy but she shared her wealth with the needy by establishing the Sophie Tucker Foundation which distributed millions of dollars to charities. She also provided the funds for two youth centers in Israel which bear her name.

**TUNISIA**, a country in North Africa between *Libya and *Algeria, had, until recent times, an active and creative Jewish community whose history stretched back almost without interruption for more than 2,000 years. Communal legends and incidental references in the Talmud indicate that Jews were in that part of Africa as far back as the time of King Solomon, but indisputable archaeological and textual evidence prove the existence of Jewish communities there from the time of the Roman conquest (first century b.c.e.). During this early period, the Jews of Tunisia enjoyed great prosperity and economic stability, with the majority of them either large landowners or magnates in the maritime trade. Evidence attesting to the economic and social importance of the Jews within Tunisian life, especially during the first centuries of the common era, can be found in the numerous anti-Jewish polemical tracts composed by many of the early Church fathers (Tertullian, St. Cyprian, St. Augustine) which contain comments specifically directed at the Jews of Tunisia. However, with the conversion of the Roman Empire to Christianity and the subsequent submission of many parts of North Africa to Byzantine rule, the quality of Jewish life in Tunisia was greatly impaired. Fortunately the community remained stable enough to survive the tribulations of Christian rule, and it emerged with greatly renewed strength after the Arab conquest of North Africa in the seventh century.

A 19th-century Tunisian woman in native costume and high pointed hat.

Under Muslim rule, the Jews of Tunisia – like all Jews living in the territories of the Arab conquest – were granted the status of *dhimmis* ("protected persons," see *Islam) which allowed them, in exchange for the payment of a poll-tax, almost complete communal and religious freedom. Thanks to this benevolent rule, Tunisian Jewry experienced a period of great intellectual creativity which lasted for close to 400 years. For more on this see *Kairouan. During this period as well, the Jews of Tunisia played a central role in Mediterranean commerce, establishing far-flung business interests stretching from India in the east to Spain and northern Europe in the west.

The invasion, in the 1140s, of the Almohades, a fanatical and intolerant Muslim tribe of central north Africa, nearly destroyed Tunisian Jewry with one blow. Whole communities were wiped out and mass conversions to Islam were common throughout the country. Small groups, however, managed to survive and the next 300 years witnessed the slow but steady process of Tunisian Jewry regaining its strength and reconstructing its destroyed communities. Demographically, Tunisian Jewry received a big boost in the 15th century from large numbers of Spanish Jews who fled Spain as a result of the riots of 1391 and who continued to pour into North Africa all through the 15th century until the final, forced *expulsion of Spanish Jewry in 1492. These Spanish immigrants, however, did not become absorbed into the native population and sharp friction arose between the native Jews, the "Touans," and those of Spanish (later also Italian) extraction, the "Grana." In 1710, the Grana actually set up their own distinct communal structures (cemetery, slaughterhouse, school) and not until 1899 was communal unity once again achieved. In the 17th and 18th centuries, Tunisia once again became an important center of Jewish learning, producing scholars of note and authors of important halakhic and homiletical treatises. World War II, the establishment of the State of Israel, and Tunisia's winning its independence from France marked the beginning of the end for Tunisian Jewry. Although more moderate in its attitude to Israel than other Arab states, Tunisia began, in 1957, to dismantle many of the Jewish communal structures and undertook a campaign of harassment and humiliation against its Jewish inhabitants. Large numbers of Tunisia's Jews have already emigrated to Israel, and it is only a matter of time before the community disappears entirely. See also *Djerba.

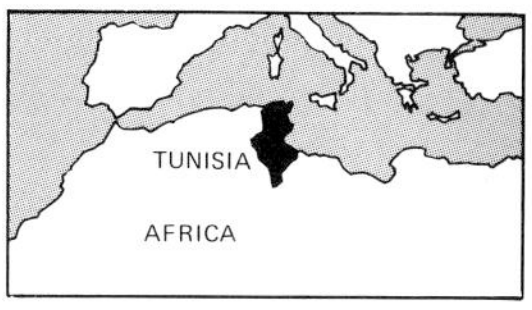

A drawing from 17th-century Turkey of "Dona Ebrea in Case" — a Jewish woman in her house. She is wearing the typical costume of the period, including a tall hat with a veil.

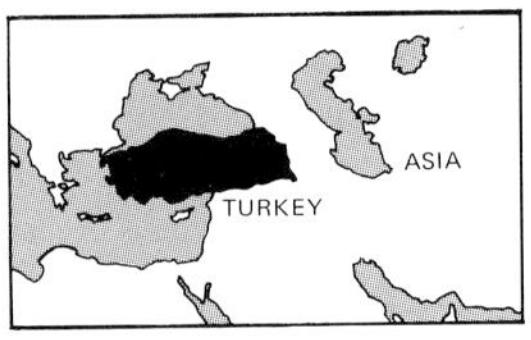


**TURKEY**, a republic bridging Asia Minor and Southeast Europe. Until the 14th century, the country now known as Turkey was a relatively insignificant area inhabited by small tribes. But in the 1300s these tribes, under the leadership of powerful sultans, began spreading their authority throughout Asia Minor and the Middle East, maintaining control of this enormous area for almost 700 years. For the story of this vast empire and the generations of Jews who lived within its realm, see *Ottoman Empire.

The 20th century, however, witnessed the end of Ottoman rule. The empire crumbled during the First World War, and instead the modern republic of Turkey emerged. The Treaty of Lausanne (1923), in which the new Turkish republic was recognized, guaranteed minority rights and as a result, the Jews were able to secure positions of prominence in almost every field of national life.

With the rise of Nazi power, however, anti-Semitism grew in Turkey. During the War, in order to meet special needs, the government imposed taxes on all citizens, but minorities were forced to pay much more than "ethnic Turks" and the Jews in particular were victimized. They were condemned as "alien blood," "Turks in name only," who were disloyal and ungrateful to the state. Jewish businesses were ruined, ordinary Jews were forced into bankruptcy or debt, and arrests and deportations were frequent.

With the German decline, this policy was relaxed and compensations promised. After the war, conditions improved and gradually life for the Jews returned to normal. But anti-Jewish propaganda and activities by extremist groups occasionally erupted. The Turkish government, in spite of Arab and Muslim pressure (most Turks are members of the Muslim faith) recognized Israel in 1949 and established diplomatic relations.

Considerable emigration to Israel took place after 1948, radically reducing the Jewish population of Turkey. Today there are about 19,000 Jews in the country, mainly in the city of Istanbul. Many of them are *Sephardim whose common language is a Spanish-Hebrew dialect known as Ladino.

**TYRE**, port city in *Lebanon. In ancient times it was an important port in the Phoenician empire (see *Phoenicians) and by the tenth century b.c.e. had become a dominant kingdom in its own right. Tyre was famous for its temple and craftsmen, and Hiram, king of Tyre, supplied *Solomon with wood for the building of the Temple. Later Hiram built a huge breakwater in front of the harbor, then situated on an impregnable island, which made Tyre one of the most important ports in the Mediterranean. In 332 b.c.e., after a siege of seven months, Alexander the Great captured Tyre by building a land bridge which linked the island to the mainland for the rest of its history.

In the Middle Ages Tyre was a rich and well-fortified city with a large Jewish community on a high economic and cultural level. The Jews of Tyre derived their income mainly from the manufacture of glass and the export of glass products. They also traded in spices and flax. In the 11th century it was the center of religious scholars who engaged in literary activities and maintained close contacts with the Ereẓ Israel academy. In 1071, when Jerusalem was conquered by the Seljuks, the academy was temporarily moved to Tyre. By the 13th century, however, the community seems to have declined and after the Mamluk conquest in 1291, the Tyre Jewish community ceased to exist. (See also *Ships and Sailing.)

# U

**UCEDA, SAMUEL BEN ISAAC** (1540- ?), talmudist, kabbalist and preacher. Uceda was born in Safed at a time when the town was becoming the major center of the *Kabbalah, and in his youth he was a pupil both of Isaac *Luria and Ḥayyim Vital, Luria's foremost disciple. At the age of 40, he established a yeshivah in Safed where both Talmud and Kabbalah were taught. The yeshivah was partially supported by the family of Gracia *Nasi of Constantinople. Uceda was a bibliophile and he owned a large library containing many manuscripts.

Uceda himself composed several volumes of commentaries – on the Five Scrolls and on the tractate *Avot.* These had wide circulation even in his lifetime. His sermons, however, were never printed and are still in manuscript.

**UGANDA SCHEME** is the name given to the proposal made by the British Government in 1903 to Theodor *Herzl, president of the Zionist Organization, to establish an autonomous Jewish colony in British East Africa (now Kenya). In advancing this proposal, the British were strongly motivated by colonialistic considerations – the desire to develop, for their own benefit, the unsettled areas of East Africa that had come under their control. Herzl, however, was attracted to the proposal for a combination of humanitarian and tactical reasons. He realized that the immediate establishment of an autonomous Jewish colony could serve as a temporary haven for the masses of East European Jews whose critically insecure position had only recently been demonstrated by the bloody pogroms of Kishinev. At the same time, the existence of such a political entity could serve to solidify the political ties of the Zionist Organization with the British government, and thus strengthen its position in the ensuing negotiations for a Jewish settlement in Palestine.

When Herzl presented the scheme to the Sixth Zionist Congress, which convened in August 1903, it met with violent opposition. To a large number of delegates, it seemed that the acceptance of the Uganda Scheme was tantamount to an abandonment of Zion, and they vigorously fought for its rejection. At one point, the opponents of the scheme actually walked out of the Congress, and Herzl was able to regain their support only after lengthy discussions in which he convinced them that even if the Uganda Scheme were implemented, he would continue to fight for the real goal of a Jewish settlement in Ereẓ Israel.

After the Congress, however, Herzl's opponents met at a separate conference in Kharkov, and again demanded that he abandon the scheme. Herzl flatly rejected their demand, but this time the unity of the Zionist Organization was saved by the sudden decision of the British Government to withdraw its offer to settle Jews in East Africa. The struggles over the proposal aggravated Herzl's already weakened physical condition, and he died before the next (the Seventh) Zionist Congress convened. At that Congress, the delegates established as the policy of the Organization that it should concern itself with settlement only in Ereẓ Israel.

**UGARIT**, ancient city in Syria, at which many important archaeological finds have been made, dating back to the very beginnings of civilization.

The first archaeological digs at this site took place in 1928, after a Syrian farmer accidentally uncovered an ancient tomb, and they were continued into the 1970s. During this time scholars have uncovered, among other things, an acropolis, two temples, a royal palace, and a high priest's house containing a rich collection of literary texts.

Most of these literary texts are from the Late Bronze Age (about 1500 to 1100 b.c.e.), the period when the Israelite tribes were conquering the neighboring Land of Canaan. The ancient inscriptions provide a unique source for the study of the social structure in the area during that historic time. Records were found in two languages: Akkadian, which was the standard language of the area, and Ugaritic, a West Semitic dialect. The texts were carved on clay tablets in one of the earliest alphabetic scripts yet found.

A stele of the "Baal of the Lightning," discovered in the excavations at Ra's Shamra, the ancient city of Ugarit. The god is shown standing on stylized mountains, brandishing a club in his right hand and a lance in the form of a lightning bolt in his left hand.

**ULLSTEIN**, family of German publishers whose newspaper and magazine empire was formerly one of the largest in the world. The company was founded by Leopold Ullstein (1826–1899) of Bavaria, who left his father's paper business at the age of 22 and went to Berlin, becoming a progressive member of the Berlin city council. In 1877 he bought a failing German newspaper and turned it into a successful evening paper with the name *Deutsche Union.* The paper reflected Ullstein's political views and was later merged with two other journals purchased by the company. The new paper's circulation reached the unprecedented figure of 40,000 and made the Ullstein company one of the biggest publishers in Germany.

1

1. Leopold Ullstein (1826–1899), founder of one of the world's largest magazine and newspaper empires, which was destroyed in the Nazi era.
2. Part of the mosaic floor uncovered during excavations of the palace built by the Umayyad caliph Hisham in Jericho, about 729 c.e.

All of Ullstein's five sons entered the family firm. In 1898, the three oldest sons founded the *Berliner Morgenpost* and raised its circulation to 600,000, the largest of any German daily. They managed the *Berliner Zeitung am Mittag* and made it the first German newspaper to be sold by street vendors instead of by subscription. They also published a series of other newspapers, had their own picture and news services, radio equipment, music division, dress pattern division, movie studios, and even a zoo to serve one of their children's newspapers. The other major ventures of the Ullstein company were its book and magazine empires.

The advent of Hitler, however, spelled the end of the Ullstein enterprise. The family was forced to sell the colossal empire to a Nazi-backed company for one-fifth of its value. After the war, the American authorities in West Berlin rebuilt the Ullstein plant and appointed Rudolf Ullstein as chairman, and by 1957 the *Berliner Zeitung* and *Morgenpost*, owned by the Ullstein group, once again had the largest circulation in West Berlin. In 1960, however, the controling interest in the group was sold and the Ullstein family interest in the concern came to an end.

**ULPAN.** Speaking a variety of languages and having widely differing backgrounds, the new immigrants to Israel often find it difficult to communicate and adjust. The ulpan, a center for intensive study of Hebrew and Jewish culture, has therefore become an essential Israeli service for immigrant absorption. Within a few months, newcomers of all ages learn the basics of everyday Hebrew and get a taste of Jewish history, traditions, folklore and literature.

The term "ulpan" comes from an Aramaic word meaning custom, or instruction. The term was coined in 1949 when the first center for intensive adult Hebrew study was opened at the Ezion immigrants' camp in Jerusalem.

Today there are close to 100 ulpanim all over the country. In many cases, the new immigrants live at the ulpan center, studying together 30 hours a week for four to five months. Here the Russian scientist, the Iranian farmer, and the American businessman all work side by side, struggling over their first Hebrew newspaper and learning to cope with their new environment. Many kibbutzim have resident ulpanim at which younger people study for half a day and help out in the kibbutz for the other half, thus covering the fees of the course, room and board. There are also part-time ulpanim which enable workers to study for a few hours a day in the mornings or evenings, while continuing to function in their jobs.

The success of the ulpan is due in part to the methods used. Only Hebrew is spoken from the moment the course begins, so the student is forced to use the language and develop a vocabulary. The curriculum deals in practicalities – everything from shopping lists to professional terminology – and gradually progresses from simple words to complex phrases.

More recently the term ulpan has also been used to refer to certain educational activities in the Diaspora, and in modern Hebrew it can also mean a broadcasting or artist's studio.

**UMAYYADS,** Arab dynasty (660-750), which established an empire extending from central Asia and the Indian border to the Atlantic Ocean. The capital of the Umayyad caliphate was Damascus, and Syria and Ereẓ Israel were the main centers.

Mu'awiya, the first Umayyad caliph (661-680), transformed the previously religious Muslim community into a secular Arab state. He and his successors confiscated land from the Jews of Ereẓ Israel and distributed it among the new Arab settlers. But, for the most part, they maintained religious freedom within their empire and many Jews attained high positions in the government. The only exception was the Caliph Omar II who was a religious fanatic and applied restrictions to minorities.

During the rule of the Umayyads, Ereẓ Israel was the scene of construction and development projects.

2

Umayyads built the Dome of the Rock on the Temple Mount and began the city of *Ramleh (see History section of *Israel article).

Towards the end, the Umayyad regime was plagued by natural catastrophes and internal strife. Between 746 and 749 there were a number of earthquakes in Ereẓ Israel, which caused heavy damage and much loss of life. This, coupled with civil strife and wars with the Byzantine invaders brought about the collapse of the Umayyad dynasty in Israel and paved the way for the rise of the *Abbasids.

The Umayyad dynasty also ruled in *Spain from 756, enduring for almost 200 years, and bringing cultural and material wellbeing for the Jews. For more on this see *Spain.

**UNITED NATIONS**. This world-wide organization, established in 1945 to maintain international peace and security in place of the defunct League of Nations, has become the controversial center of world diplomacy.

It was formed in the wake of World War II by a war-weary world in the hope that future problems between nations could be settled at the conference table rather than on the battlefield. But that dream of true international brotherhood has never been realized and the United Nations, although praised by some as the only forum for international debate, has been derided by others as completely inept. Its influence on world peace in general, and on Jewish survival in particular, remains questionable.

**The State of Israel.** It was a UN decision which gave Israel its legal status as an independent Jewish state. But, on the other hand, the UN has proved unable to furnish protection for that State.

When the UN was formed, Israel (then Palestine) was still a British *Mandate territory. On April 2, 1947, the British transmitted the Palestine issue to the UN requesting that they find a solution to the Jewish-Arab conflict. A special session of the UN General Assembly, the first of its kind, was summoned and the decision was taken to establish the UN Special Committee on Palestine (UNSCOP) consisting of representatives of 11 nations. UNSCOP members, after visiting Palestine, recommended that the area be partitioned into an Arab and a Jewish state, both to be granted independence (see *Partition of Palestine). On November 29, 1947, the plan was adopted in the General Assembly by a vote of 33 in favor, 13 against, with 10 abstentions. Thus the independent State of Israel was officially recognized, to take effect on May 15, 1948.

The partition resolution was hardly on record, however, before the Arab leadership decided to oppose it by force, and Israel's *War of Independence began. The Palestine Commission, which had been appointed by the UN to supervise the implementation of the partition, was now replaced by a UN mediator, Count Folke Bernadotte of Sweden who was to try to negotiate an end to the fighting.

The UN calls for a cease-fire were ignored by the Arab states and the international body proved incapable of enforcing any decisions. Armistice agreements were finally signed in the spring of 1949, under UN auspices, but it was almost entirely due to the Arab defeat on the battlefield rather than to the endless UN debates. The Israel War of Independence was the first armed conflict involving the UN, and the handling and outcome raised grave doubts as to the viability of the organization.

Many of the UN meetings in subsequent years were dominated by the Middle East question. The Arabs harped on the issue of "repatriating" the refugees who fled Israel during the war, but they themselves did little to improve the condition of these refugees and left them in disease-ridden, overcrowded camps. The plight of the refugees was used by the Arabs as a propaganda weapon against Israel. The Palestine Conciliation Committee (PCC) and later the UN Relief and Works Agency for Palestine Refugees (UNRWA) were formed to deal with this problem but proved ineffective mainly because of Arab resistance. Israel often complained of Arab belligerence but the UN decisions in this regard were ignored by the Arabs. In the 1950s the Arabs began submitting complaints about Israeli actions and the UN decisions became increasingly anti-Israel. During the following Arab-Israel wars (see *Sinai Campaign, *Six-Day War, and *Yom Kippur War), the UN called for the immediate withdrawal of Israel's troops, deplored Israel's "aggression" and completely

The United Nations presence in the Middle East has been strong since the signing of the armistice agreements between Israel and her Arab neighbors following the War of Independence in 1948. Shown in this photograph are United Nations "observers" in the region of the Syrian-Israel border, June 1957. They were charged with the task of supervising the military truce arranged after the Sinai Campaign of 1956, and it was their hasty withdrawal in June 1967 which helped to precipitate the Six-Day War.

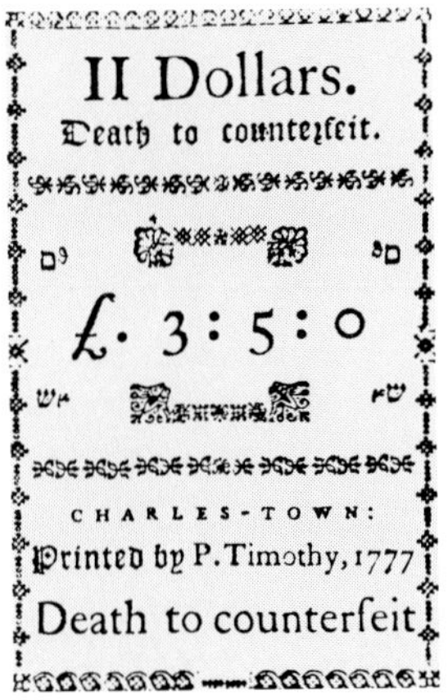

1

2

1. A $2 bill with Hebrew characters (the letters *shin* and *mem*) used as legal tender in Charleston, South Carolina, in 1777.
2. A notice board posted at the Polonies Talmud Torah, located at Congregation Shearith Israel in New York. The school opened on May 2, 1803, and by the turn of the century it was the oldest surviving Jewish religious school in America.

ignored or played down Arab terrorist and military action. Following the Sinai Campaign in 1956, the UN Emergency Force (UNEF) was established to "secure and supervise the cessation of hostilities." But in May 1967 Egypt demanded the withdrawal of UNEF troops and UN Secretary General U Thant immediately issued the necessary order without consulting Israel, thus precipitating the Six-Day War.

Following this conflict, on November 22, 1967, the Security Council adopted the famous Resolution 242, which affirmed that the establishment of a "just and lasting peace in the Middle East" was dependent both on withdrawal of Israel's forces and termination of hostilities, as well as respect for the right of every state in the area "to live in peace within secure and recognized boundaries." This decision served as a milestone in the Middle East conflict and its interpretation in exact terms is still being debated.

**The Anti-Israel Bloc.** Israel applied for membership in the UN in November 1948 but the application was not officially endorsed until May 1949. From the very beginning, Arab and Soviet intransigence blocked all Israel's efforts. She failed to gain election to any councils and most of her resolutions were immediately out-voted by the Arab-Communist bloc. At first the USSR had supported Israel and had even voted in favor of the partition plan, but in their endeavor to gain a foothold in the oil-rich Arab states, the Soviets began using their influence and power of veto in the UN to block pro-Israel moves.

The anti-Israel bias in the UN became especially vehement after the *Yom Kippur War. The so-called "Third World" nations (Asians and Africans) united behind the Arab terrorist movements and in Nov. 1974 Yasser Arafat, P.L.O. head, was given an official welcome at a UN session, a ceremony which is usually reserved only for heads of state. His flagrant advocation of violence and murder was received with cheers and ovations. At the same time, in an unprecedented action, Israel was barred from speaking in its own behalf in the Middle East debate and was also voted out of UNESCO (UN Educational, Scientific and Cultural Organization) on the fabricated and unfounded charge that UNESCO funds were being used by Israel to desecrate holy sites through archaeological excavation, particularly in Jerusalem.

These moves caused an angry reaction all over the world by Jews and non-Jews alike. Several countries (including the United States) and organizations withdrew their support of UNESCO.

The anti-Israel bloc also prevented the passage of resolutions on behalf of oppressed Jews in Syria and the U.S.S.R., although general resolutions regarding human rights and religious tolerance were supported.

In 1975 the UN passed a resolution equating Zionism with racism, which it repealed only in 1991 as the move toward peace in the Middle East progressed, and Israel's position at the UN improved.

**UNITED STATES OF AMERICA.** Jews started migrating to North America as early as the 17th century, lured by the opportunities and the freedom offered by the "New World." Typically the first Jews to settle in what later became the United States were *Sephardim, and although some were farmers, artisans or tailors, most were small shopkeepers who sold hardware, dry goods and liquor. They established small *kehillot* (communities) in the coastal cities and in the towns along the coastal plain, and after a while they generally had a *ḥazzan* (cantor), a *shoḥet* (ritual meat slaughterer) and a *shammash* to serve their religious needs. The earliest synagogues established in North America were in Newport (Rhode Island), New York, Philadelphia, Charlestown (South Carolina) and Savannah (Georgia). There were few anti-Jewish incidents to mar Jewish life in the early period of the North American colonies. Jews were accepted in the English North American settlements; their labor, money and talents were both needed and appreciated, and with the passage of time, there remained little to distinguish the American Jew from his gentile neighbor.

During the American Revolution (1775), many Jews served in the militia and some served as soldiers and officers. The most notable Jewish rebel was the Polish immigrant, Ḥayyim Salomon, an ardent patriot who served as an under-cover agent for the American forces while working for the British. With the adoption of the United States Constitution in 1788, Jews in common with all other citizens, gained full legal equality. Discrimination based on race or religion was formally outlawed, although in practice certain forms of social and legal discrimination persisted for a long time on a local and state level.

**The 19th century.** Between 1820 and 1880 United States Jewry increased from a small group to a major world Jewish community. This vast increase was largely due to immigration, especially from Germanic countries which were passing through an economic depression, and because of the repression of civil rights there following the revolutions of 1848-49. During these years Jewish settlement spread across the North American continent. Old coastal communities like Charleston, South Carolina, declined in importance while the Jewish population of such cities as Albany, Chicago, and Cleveland increased. A striking growth occurred in northern California during and after the Gold Rush of 1849-52. At that time San Francisco gained a large Jewish community. New York City's position as the home of the largest number of American Jews was well established by 1860. (See *New York.) In New England,on the other hand,there were very few Jews.

In terms of livelihood, the mid-19th century can be considered as the day of the German Jewish peddler. The progress of many of these immigrants followed a classic pattern. They began as simple peddlers serving the needs of their local communities on foot; then they acquired wagons and traveled great distances to service a wide and scattered clientele. At a later stage they would settle down and become managers or owners of stores strategically located at important crossroads. Finally the most successful among them would become large-scale merchants, setting up chains of stores and mail-order houses such as Sears and Roebuck, founded by Julius Rosenwald.

However during this period Jewish participation in the professions also increased greatly. Jews turned to banking, to industry and to the stock exchange. They entered the professions of law, medicine, engineering and journalism. By the mid-19th century it was Ashkenazi, not Sephardi, culture which dominated the American Jewish scene.

An important expression of the impact of German Jewry on American Jewish life was *Reform Judaism. Reform took root during the 1840s with the establishment of the Emanu-El Reformverein in New York City, and it reached the peak of its influence in the 1870s and 1880s when its organizational strength was solidified by the founding of the Union of American Hebrew Congregations, *Hebrew Union College and the Central Conference of American Rabbis. Isaac Mayer *Wise was one of the earliest organizers and among the most forceful spokesmen for American Reform Judaism. He faced strong opposition from Orthodox leaders like Isaac Leeser who was connected with the Spanish and Portuguese Synagogue in Philadelphia.

During the Civil War of 1861-65, Jews generally sided with the region in which they lived. More than 10,000 Jews served in the armies of the North and South, and after the conclusion of the fighting and the emancipation of the slaves, Jews played a prominent role in the commercial and economic development of the South. Several southern Jews, such as Raphael J. Moses in South Carolina, also reached important political positions. And in the larger coastal cities of the North, the German-Jewish merchant class expanded rapidly and made an important contribution to the post-Civil War industrial expansion.

**Until World War I.** Between 1880 and 1929 there was mass migration of Jews from Europe to the United States. This time the immigrants were mostly Eastern European in origin. The pogroms in Russia in 1881 gave strong impetus to this wave of immigration. Another reason was the tremendous natural growth of European Jewry which made it almost impossible for the economically restricted Jews to provide adequately for themselves and their families. From their earlier primary occupation as merchants, Jews now pursued more varied careers. More and more entered law, politics, banking, and medicine. An important group functioned as collectors and patrons of the arts, and as philanthropists. In the 1880s most Jews left the smaller towns of California, the South, and Middle West and concentrated in the great cities of the Northeast.

In almost every city in which they settled, the Jewish immigrants clustered in distinct neighborhoods. The streets where they lived became almost completely Jewish in population, and the

American Jews (foreground) and American Arabs holding counter demonstrations in front of the White House in Washington, June 8, 1967, the third day of the Six-Day War. The Jewish demonstrators had come to the White House to call for full U.S. support of Israel, and when it was announced that Egypt had accepted a cease-fire, the demonstration turned into a victory celebration.

stores, the festive air on the Sabbath and holidays, and the Yiddish heard in the streets reflected the Jewish character of the inhabitants. The largest of such neighborhoods was the Lower East Side of New York City.

By 1900 peddling had ceased to be a secure means of making an adequate living, and many of the newer East European immigrants joined the clothing industry as tailors, cutters and machinists. This was particularly true in New York, where unfortunately the men, women and children were taken unfair advantage of while they worked in the "sweat shops" of the clothing industry. As a result, a Jewish trade union movement was formed to organize the workers and fight for better working conditions. In 1911 a tragic fire at the Triangle Shirtwaist Factory, in which 146 workers, all women and young girls, were killed, resulted in a violent outcry and in the staging of a three-month strike by the International Ladies' Garment Workers' Union. The Union was then recognized as the official bargaining agent for the clothing workers, and under a settlement worked out by Louis D. Brandeis, vast improvements in working conditions were made.

The Jewish labor movement also helped to develop a vigorous and creative secular Yiddish culture in America. It flourished from the 1910s until the early 1930s, and helped sponsor several Yiddish daily newspapers, Yiddish theaters as well as Yiddish radio stations.

Very few of the Jewish immigrants, especially those who arrived before 1900, were particularly pious or learned. Confronted with the overpowering force of the secular, urban, industrial life into which they were cast as soon as they reached America, only a small percentage remained faithful to the orthodox religious values and practices which they had followed in Europe. After a while, for many, Rosh Ha-Shanah, Yom Kippur, bar mitzvahs and the recital of *Kaddish* remained their sole links with Judaism.

Until well into the 20th century, Jewish communal organization in the United States seldom went above the local synagogue level. A major exception was *B'nai Brith which was founded in 1843 and which developed outside the framework of the synagogue and on a national scale as a social and charitable organization. There were also *landsmannschaft* societies that united and served the particular needs of immigrants from the same European hometown, but neither these nor the synagogues offered American Jewry any type of organizational unity. This position

Advertisements which appeared in the directory of the city of Providence, Rhode Island, in 1857, showing the prominence of Jews at that time in the clothing industry.

was somewhat improved in 1917, with the founding of the Federation for the Support of Jewish Philanthropic Societies which began to coordinate Jewish fundraising activities in the country. Somewhat earlier (in 1906) the American Jewish Committee was established by a small group of prominent and wealthy Jews of German origin (among them Jacob H. *Schiff and Louis Marshall) with the aim of "preventing the infraction of the civil and religious rights of the Jews"; and the Committee soon became an influential spokesman for United States Jewry. During World War I the American Joint Distribution Committee was formed to provide relief and assistance to Jews made homeless by the war. During World War I as well, Zionism began to exert a strong influence in American Jewish life. Noted leaders among the early American Zionists were Henrietta *Szold, Stephen S. Wise and Louis D. *Brandeis.

Jewish educational opportunities in the United States prior to World War I were particularly meager. The Jewish immigrant parents were almost universally staunch believers in the American public school system as the ideal means of Americanizing their children as quickly and as thoroughly as possible; those parents who gave their children some sort of Jewish education generally sent them for a few hours each week to Hebrew school classes which were usually run by the local congregation and which met after public school hours. On a higher level, the *Jewish Theological Seminary was established in 1902 under the leadership of Solomon *Schechter to instruct rabbinical students in a more modern approach to Judaism so as to better serve the spiritual needs of American Jewry. (See *Conservative Judaism.)

**Between the Wars.** After World War I a great wave of anti-foreignism swept through America, and the extremely liberal immigration policy which had allowed over two and a half million Jews to enter the country from 1880, came to an end. In 1921 quotas were first imposed against immigrants from other than North or West European countries, and in 1924 the "Johnson Act" all but closed the doors of the United States to Jewish immigration. At the same time there was a noted increase in anti-Semitic feeling within the country, which manifested itself in the adoption of restrictive quotas in various professions, in the universities and elsewhere. The auto magnate, Henry Ford, used his great wealth to spread his violently anti-Semitic views through the dissemination of his own publication the *Dearborn Independent;* and during this period as well, the Ku Klux Klan, which had originally been a small, southern, anti-Negro vigilante group, acquired large numbers of new supporters in the country and turned their attention to the Jews as "obstacles to a real America."

However the '20s was also a period of great economic prosperity in the United States, and Jews took the opportunity to move out of their original immigrant quarters into more attractive urban districts, and out of immigrant trades into commercial and professional occupations. It was during this period as well that Jews began to figure prominently in American cultural life, both in literature and in the new *motion picture industry.

The depression, which began in the fall of 1929 and continued in effect until the beginning of World War II, dramatically affected all Americans, including the Jews. Thousands of small Jewish businesses were ruined and many established concerns fared no better. Even the Jewish philanthropies were drastically affected; they could no longer boast that "Jews take care of their own" for the numbers of those in need were far too great for them to supply all their requirements. Discrimination against Jews in employment also increased, and as a consequence many Jews then turned to government work and the civil service, where the laws against discrimination were more strictly observed.

1

With the rise of Nazism in Germany in the 1930s, many German Jews tried to emigrate to the U.S.; however, because of the continued restrictive immigration policy of the United States government, many were refused visas and large numbers of German Jews remained trapped in Germany, unable to flee before the devastation of the *Holocaust. One of the most famous German Jews who did manage to reach the U.S. was the great physicist and mathematician Albert *Einstein.

Until the depression, American Jews generally had been staunch supporters of the Republican Party. In the '30s, the Democratic Party became known as the party of reform, and under the leadership of Franklin D. *Roosevelt and with his "New Deal" program, it drew large numbers of Jews away from the Republicans and attracted enthusiastic Jewish support. Jews also began to figure prominently in American political life. In the '30s there was a Jewish cabinet member (Hans Morgenthau Jr.), three Jewish Supreme Court Justices, four Jewish governors, and many hundreds of Jewish politicians on the state and local level.

**World War II.** Until the Japanese attack on Pearl Harbor on December 7, 1941, a fierce debate raged in the United States over America's isolationism and non-involvement in the war against Nazism. U.S. Jews were prominent among those who early and forcefully called for American military support of England and France, and this provided fuel for the anti-Semites (among whom was numbered Charles A. Lindbergh, the aviation pioneer), who attempted to incite anti-Jewish feeling in the country by charging that the Jews were drawing America into a useless war. The U.S. decision to declare war on Japan and Germany following the Pearl Harbor attack ended the debate and proved a strong blow to anti-Semitism, which was now identified by most people with the Nazi enemy. During the war, approximately 550,000 Jews served in all branches of the U.S. armed forces and more than 36,000 were decorated for gallantry.

Nevertheless, America's Jews were still very fearful of appearing to want "special treatment," or of encouraging propaganda that it was a Jewish war, and

1. Tablet erected in 1903 at the site of the first Jewish cemetery in New York which was consecrated in 1656 near what is now the "Bowery" in Manhattan. What remains of the cemetery has been designated by the American Scenic and Historic Preservation Society as one of the historical landmarks of New York City.
2. Title page of one of the first issues (1824) of the earliest Jewish periodical to be published in English in the United States, *The Jew.* The magazine proclaimed its role to be one of providing "a defense of Judaism against all adversaries, and particularly against the insidious attacks of *Israel's Advocate*" (a Christian missionary publication).

2
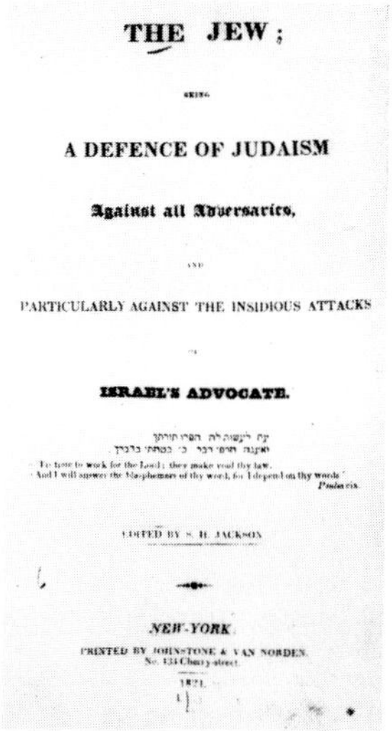

thus, even when information about the Nazi "final solution" for European Jewry became widely known, they refrained from demanding direct United States intervention to save Jews. The common view was that early victory was the sole means of rescuing Europe's Jews. However, in 1944, through the efforts of Secretary of the Treasury Henry Morgenthau Jr., who was deeply disturbed by the State Department's resistance to all rescue efforts, President Roosevelt established the War Refugees Board which attempted with some success to work through neutral countries and third parties to prevent further Nazi murders of Jews. Within the Jewish community, a *Va'ad Hazzalah* (Rescue Committee) was organized under Orthodox leadership to promote rescue work.

It was during World War II that Zionism finally won over United States Jewry. Under the vigorous leadership of Rabbi Abba Hillel *Silver, the American Zionist Emergency Council adopted aggressive tactics aimed at converting United States public opinion to the Zionist program, and it was at the Biltmore Hotel in New York in 1942 where an "extraordinary Zionist Conference" finally adopted as the official policy of the Zionist Organization the demand that a sovereign Jewish State be set up in the territory of the British Mandate in Palestine.

Drawing of the clothing store of Louis Lewisson, a pioneer Jewish merchant in Providence, Rhode Island. The store, located in Providence's main street, was first occupied in 1846.

**1945 to the Present.** In the years immediately following the war, United States Jewish communal life was dominated by concern for the care of the Jewish refugees in Europe and by the Jewish struggle in Palestine. Vast public meetings were frequently convened to publicize the plight of the Jewish war refugees and of the *yishuv* in Palestine. Funds raised for these and other overseas needs reached levels previously unattained and the Zionist Organization of America and Hadassah multiplied their membership manyfold, to include several hundreds of thousands of active supporters.

In common with American citizens generally, Jews enjoyed an era of prolonged prosperity during the post-World War II years. Homecoming servicemen found wellpaid jobs or attended colleges en masse under the liberal terms of the "GI Bill of Rights," and anti-Semitism all but disappeared from the public view.

Demographically the number of U.S. Jews increased only slightly after World War II. The birth rate was low and there was not a great deal of immigration which was still controled under a quota system. U.S. Jewry continued as a metropolitan group with about 40% living in the New York City area, and in all the cities there was large-scale movement to the suburbs.

After 1945 a new occupational pattern became evident in U.S. Jewry. Employment in the professions rose substantially and in addition to the continuing prominence of Jews as physicians (such as Jonas Salk who was instrumental in the development of the polio vaccine), lawyers, accountants and teachers, they also took leading parts as scientific professionals in such new industries as electronics.

Economic prosperity and the closing of the gap between natives and immigrants resulted in increased Jewish communal harmony. Communal interests now were focused mostly on local matters. Nearly every city conducted a combined campaign for overseas and domestic needs and had some form of central Jewish community organization.

At the national level, the National Community Relations Advisory Council of the B'nai Brith coordinated the various local defense organizations. The American Zionist Council similarly coordinated the various Zionist bodies, and the Synagogue Council achieved partial unity among synagogues.

By the end of the 1940s, the Jews were mostly American-born, largely college-educated and heavily concentrated in the merchant and professional classes. They began to excel in fields once closed to them. The novelists Saul Bellow, Bernard Malamud, Norman Mailer, and Herman *Wouk attained prominence as the authors of bestsellers. Playwrights like Arthur Miller, poets such as Allen Ginsberg, critics like Lionel Trilling and Leslie Fiedler and musicians such as Leonard Bernstein attained true distinction. Jewish professors could now be found in almost all colleges and universities, but especially in the "Ivy League" schools and public institutions.

U.S. Jewish religious life broadened after 1945, and Judaism became all but officially recognized as the "third U.S. religion." The philosophical writings of Martin *Buber and Abraham J. *Heschel received wide attention. Many interfaith institutes and assemblies were held. Many synagogues were built and were used not only for worship and study but also for elaborate social functions and even sports and social recreation centers. Orthodoxy changed its status as the Judaism of immigrants; it became intellectually active with the publication of many religious and philosophical books and journals. Rabbi Joseph Isaac *Schneersohn and his successor Menaḥem Mendel Schneersohn brought the *Ḥabad Lubavitch movement even greater popularity, spreading its doctrines the world over, and Rabbi Joseph Dov *Soloveitchik rose to prominence as a dynamic leader of a new vibrant Orthodoxy. The rabbinical seminaries and colleges of the three trends in American Judaism, Yeshiva University (Orthodox), Jewish Theological Seminary (Conservative) and Hebrew Union College (Reform) all increased tremendously in size and stature, and produced a large number of graduates trained to serve their various communities.

After 1950 Hebrew literary creativity almost disappeared from the United States. Yiddish also declined, although authors like Chaim Grade and Isaac Bashevis Singer continued to publish and became well-known through English translations of their works. On the other hand, Jewish cultural activity in English flourished.

Jewish education boomed and enrolment in Jewish schools increased. In the 1960s, 80% of U.S. Jewish children were estimated to have received some form of Jewish education during their school years. The number of Orthodox day schools also increased considerably.

Towards the end of the 1960s, in a generally stable situation, several new issues arose which created unusual interest and anxiety among America's Jews. One was the renewed efforts of the Catholic Church towards "ecumenism" and "dialogue" with Jews, which arose out of the Second Vatican Ecumenical Council convened by Pope John XXIII. The movement within the Church to "exonerate" the Jews from "deicide" (that is, the death of Jesus) and to formally recognize the theological legitimacy of Judaism stirred a reciprocal enthusiasm among many segments of America's Jewish population. Rabbi Abraham J. Heschel was among the most prominent American Jewish leaders who endorsed the renewed contact with the Church.

A second issue, and one which caused considerable anxiety among American Jews, was the rise of vocal and active anti-Semitism on the part of America's Black population. American Jews had early been staunch supporters of the movement to win for the Blacks full legal and social equality (see *Negro-Jewish relations). During the "civil rights summers" of the mid-1960s, young Jews made up as much as 50% of all the White student youth who went South to assist Negroes, according to some reports. But in the last years of the decade the waves of riots which swept through the northern Black districts shook the delicate balance of urban peace, and many small Jewish businesses located in these districts were violently destroyed. Militant Blacks denounced Whites in general and refused their assistance in terms that were sometimes markedly anti-Semitic. One response to the increased tension between Jews and Blacks living in the same neighborhoods was the establishment in Brooklyn, New York, of the Jewish Defense League, which later gained adherents in many parts of the country.

A third happening which stirred American Jewry greatly at the end of the '60s was the Six-Day War of June 1967. The crisis preceding the outbreak of fighting brought American Jewish concern for Israel to an unparalleled peak. Some youthful volunteers were able to leave for Israel before June 5, but the main contribution of American Jewry to Israel's war effort was money. As a consequence of the war, *aliyah* to Israel from the United States increased greatly as did tourism.

Anti-Semitic discrimination in the Soviet Union was also an important focus of Jewish communal concern at the end of the 1960s. The National Conference on Soviet Jewry, as well as the Academic

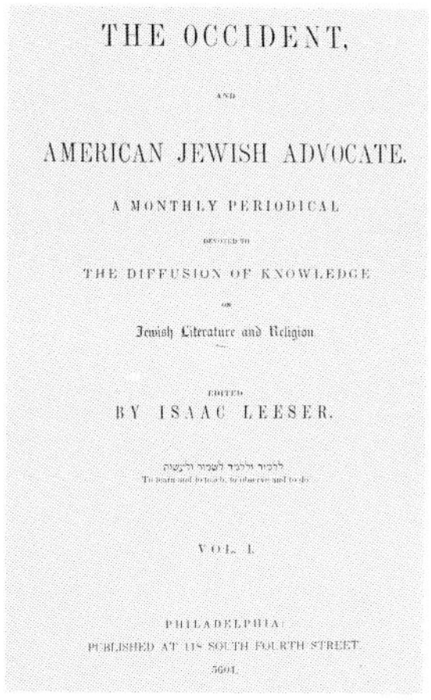
THE OCCIDENT,
AND
AMERICAN JEWISH ADVOCATE.
A MONTHLY PERIODICAL
DEVOTED TO
THE DIFFUSION OF KNOWLEDGE
ON
Jewish Literature and Religion
EDITED
BY ISAAC LEESER.
To learn and to teach, to observe and to do.
VOL. I.
PHILADELPHIA:
PUBLISHED AT 118 SOUTH FOURTH STREET.
5601.

1

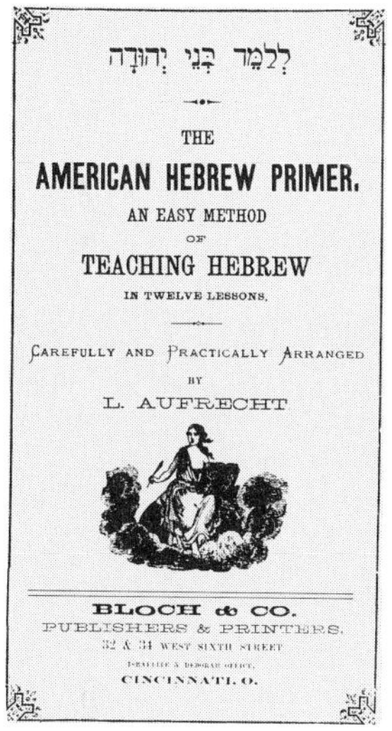
לְלַמֵּד בְּנֵי יְהוּדָה
THE
AMERICAN HEBREW PRIMER.
AN EASY METHOD
OF
TEACHING HEBREW
IN TWELVE LESSONS.
CAREFULLY AND PRACTICALLY ARRANGED
BY
L. AUFRECHT
BLOCH & CO.
PUBLISHERS & PRINTERS.
CINCINNATI, O.

2

1. Title page of Volume I of *The Occident and American Jewish Advocate,* edited by the Philadelphia rabbi and educator Isaac Leeser. First published in 1843, this monthly, "devoted to the diffusion of knowledge on Jewish literature and religion," was the first successful Jewish periodical in English in the United States. It was published uninterruptedly for 25 years and served as an important forum for popular Jewish education.
2. One of the first primers for teaching Hebrew to American children, printed in Cincinnati in 1868.

Council on Soviet Jewry and the Student Struggle for Soviet Jewry were established to organize demonstrations and publicize the plight of Soviet Jewry.

**U.S. and Israel.** U.S. policy in the Middle East has not always been consistent. This is because it depends on many factors: the rivalry with the USSR, the political persuasion of U.S. Jews and a widespread sympathy for Israel among the general American public.

On May 14, 1948, Israel was proclaimed a state and 11 minutes later, President Harry *Truman granted U.S. recognition of the new state. Since then, the U.S. and its subsequent presidents,Eisenhower, *Kennedy, *Johnson, *Nixon, Ford and *Reagan have supported Israel in varying degrees. The United States proved herself a true ally by supplying Israel with most of the military material she needed in the tense period following the Six-Day War of 1967 and the Yom Kippur War of 1973. Besides supplying most of Israel's arms, the U.S. grants loans, imports polished diamonds among other goods, and exports a great deal to Israel.

**Demography.** In 1990, the estimate for the United States Jewish population was 5,798,000. (This represented about 2.3% of the total U.S. population.) Forty-eight percent of the Jewish population lived in the Northeast states, 12% in the Midwest part of the country, 20% in the South and 20% in the West. The states with the largest Jewish populations were: New York (1,644,000), California (923,000), Florida (543,000), New Jersey (426,000), Pennsylvania (330,000), Massachusetts (275,000), and Illinois (257,000).

Close to two-thirds of the U.S. Jewish population are believed to be affiliated with one of the three trends in Judaism. The Conservative Movement in the U.S. claims at present to have 350,000 member families, comprising 1,500,000 souls; Reform claims 250,000 families, representing 1,000,000 souls; and Orthodoxy claims 300,000 families, comprising 1,500,000 souls. However, membership in an Orthodox synagogue cannot be regarded as identical with strict observance of Orthodox Judaism, and the number of strictly observant Jews in the United States is not now regarded to be higher than 300,000.

Major collections of Judaica and Hebraica have been amassed by many American university libraries in the 20th century, including those of Harvard and Yale. Shown here is one of the bookplates used by the Yale University Library for part of its Hebrew collection – in commemoration of the 19th-century Hungarian-U.S. scholar, Alexander Kohut, who is pictured on the bookplate with the *Arukh,* an 11th-century lexicon of talmudic terms which he masterfully edited, expanded and revised in an eight-volume work (1878–1892).

**UNIVERSITIES.** Jewish emphasis on education, including its advanced forms, is rooted in the early history of the Jewish people. Perhaps the very first institutions of higher learning were the Jewish academies of ancient Judea and Babylonia, established in the second century. They have been described as universities in which learned scholars pursued the most advanced studies of the Bible and Jewish law.

**Middle Ages.** During the Middle Ages, the Christian society began developing their own universities for the study of religious and secular subjects and for the first time Jews found themselves excluded from the general world of learning. Except for a few rare cases, the anti-Semitic attitude of these Christian universities kept the Jews away.

The limited number who did manage to enter Christian universities were all engaged in the study of medicine. On one rare occasion a 15th-century Hebrew grammarian was invited to teach Hebrew at the University of Paris but he refused.

It is not surprising that their exclusion from general universities should lead the Jews to formulate plans for establishing their own institutions. In 1466 King John of Sicily gave formal permission for the Jews to organize their own university, specializing in law and medicine, but the plan was never realized as the Jews were expelled from Sicily some years later. And in 1604 David Provençal of Mantua devised a plan for a Jewish university, but he too failed in the attempt to establish it.

Despite the discrimination,some Jews managed to obtain doctoral degrees from several Italian universities (the only country that would admit them to institutions of higher learning). The University of Padua in particular conferred 228 doctorates on Jews from 1517 to 1721.

Even when admitted to a university, the Jewish students were faced with special problems. They had to resort to devious means to avoid attending classes and examinations on the Sabbath, and they had to pay higher graduation fees than Christian students. Even if they acquired the degree, they were rarely able to practice their professions as Jewish doctors were forbidden to attend to Christian patients.

**Liberalization.** Slowly but surely, however, the barriers began to fall. In 1678 two Jews succeeded in gaining admission to the University of Frankfort which eventually developed a sizeable Jewish student body. And in 18th-century America, Jews studied at Harvard, Yale, the University of Pennsylvania, Columbia, and Brown (where they were excused from attendance on Saturdays). Rabbi Gershom Mendes *Seixas became regent of the University of the State of New York when it was founded in 1784 and served as a trustee of Columbia University, while

Joel Hart founded the College of Physicians and Surgeons in New York.

The 19th century saw the dawn of a period of tolerance in Europe and decrees were passed abolishing restrictive admission policies in many universities. The one country that still discriminated against Jews in this sphere was Russia and large numbers of young Russian Jews consequently enrolled at German universities where they made their mark as outstanding scholars.

**The 20th century**. In the last century, Jewish participation as both students and faculty members in universities has steadily increased, and their contributions to the growth of knowledge has gained international attention. Unfortunately, even in the 20th century many institutions insisted on quota systems to limit Jewish enrollment, especially in Eastern Europe and Nazi Germany. But the Jews were determined to maintain their place in university life. The opening of the Hebrew University in Jerusalem in 1925 and of Yeshiva College (now *Yeshiva University), in New York City, in 1928, indicated that Jews were now prepared to establish their own institutions if necessary and to take a leading role in the world of higher education. Jews' College in London became a recognized part of the University of London and provided a degree program in both religious and secular subjects. And in the United States, Gratz College was founded in 1897 for the training of Jewish teachers. The *Hebrew Union College and the *Jewish Theological Seminary, although rabbinical seminaries, also combine secular and religious studies and provide graduates with a nationally recognized degree. Brandeis University became the first nonsectarian liberal arts university to be founded and sponsored by Jews.

But even the supposedly equal-opportunity policy of the United States did not completely eliminate discriminatory practices in American universities. The use of quotas was rarely openly admitted but it was often a fact of life. In 1922, Harvard President Lowell defended the existence of a 10 percent quota for Jews as did the president of Dartmouth in 1945. Restrictive practices began to yield to public criticism after World War II so that Jewish enrollment at private institutions rose substantially, even reaching 20 percent of the student body at Ivy League schools. There are an estimated 400,000 Jewish students, and there are some 30,000 Jewish faculty members. In the 1990s Jews held the post of president at Harvard, Yale, Princeton, and other universities. A large proportion is concentrated in New York City which has the largest number and proportion of Jewish college students in the world. University admission policies instituted from the 1970s on to assist students from other minority groups in obtaining higher education did affect Jewish admissions in varying degrees.

Hundreds of American universities have full or partial Jewish Studies programs covering a wide range of sub-specialties, from Hebrew language through Latin American Jewish history. Though the Bible had long been taught even as part of Christian curricula, actual Jewish subjects were only incorporated towards the end of the 19th century. (For information on the universities in Israel, see the education section of the article *Israel. For more on the Jewish attitude towards learning, see *Education.)

**URIM AND THUMMIM**, a mysterious device employed by the high priest on behalf of the king or the high court, by means of which oracles or messages about the outcome of future events, would be obtained. The Bible provides no information about the appearance of the *Urim* and *Thummim*, about the material of which they were made, or how they were used. From the several oblique references to them found in the Bible (Numbers 27:21 and I Samuel 28:6), it appears that the *Urim* and *Thummim* were either a part of, or an appendage to, the breastplate worn by the high priest. On the breastplate were

Engraving from Jacques Basnage's *République des Hébreux* (Amsterdam, 1713) showing the high priest at the altar, wearing the *hoshen* (breastplate) upon which, or underneath which, the *Urim* and *Thummim* are believed to have been located.

The Zionist leader Abraham Menaḥem Ussishkin, photographed at Mount Scopus, Jerusalem in 1923.

embedded 12 precious stones, one for each of the tribes of Israel, and the Talmud speculates that the oracular message was miraculously spelled out by the protruding of letters out of the tribal names inscribed on the stones.

The first mention of the *Urim* and *Thummim* appears in the passage in Numbers which describes Moses' transfer of his authority to Joshua prior to his death. Joshua is told by God, through Moses, that in his capacity as leader of the Israelites, "he shall stand before Eleazar the priest, who shall inquire for him by the judgment of the *Urim* before the Lord." Much later, in the Book of *Samuel, King Saul unsuccessfully sought information from the *Urim* and *Thummim* about the outcome of an impending battle with the Philistines, and his failure to receive any response led him to seek advice from the witch of En-Dor who conjured up for him the spirit of the dead prophet Samuel.

It is not known exactly when the *Urim* and *Thummim* ceased to function, but the latest period for which there is evidence of their use is that of King David. Subsequently,oracles and predictions about future events were conveyed exclusively by the prophets.

The exact meaning of the words "*Urim*" and "*Thummim*" have puzzled scholars over the generations. Both in the Greek and Latin translations of the Bible they were rendered as "revelation and truth" or "teaching and truth" and this understanding gave rise to the incorporation of the Hebrew words *Urim ve-Thummim* on the official seal of Yale University in New Haven, Connecticut.

**URUGUAY** is a South American republic where Jews began to reside after the *Inquisition ceased there in 1813. However, only after the Constitution of 1918, which established the principle of the separation of church and state and defined the legal status of aliens, could an active Jewish community develop. In 1917-18 there were 1,700 Jews in the country, mostly Sephardim. As of 1990 about 24,000 Jews lived in Uruguay, almost all of them in the capital, Montevideo.

While the Jewish community tended to develop in a nationalist-secular direction, it showed great concern for the survival of its Jewish tradition. The Zionist movement began its activities in 1911 and by the 1960s the vast majority of the leadership of the community was Zionist.

Social contact between first-generation Uruguayan Jews and the non-Jewish community takes place mainly on the occupational level and tends to be superficial. But the second generation has achieved a greater degree of integration and assimilation, and intermarriage is fairly common. Anti-Semitic campaigns were unleashed at periods coinciding with economic crises, social instability, and authoritarian rule, and in reaction the Jewish community organized itself in self-defense.

Friendly relations between Uruguay and Israel began in 1947 with the enthusiastic support of Uruguay's UN representative for the plan to partition Palestine and establish a Jewish state. Since then relations have been marked by exchange visits of dignitaries and cultural, economic and scientific cooperation.

**USSISHKIN, ABRAHAM MENAḤEM MENDEL** (1863-1941), Zionist leader and president of the Jewish National Fund (JNF). Born in Russia, Ussishkin became an enthusiastic reader of the works of contemporary Hebrew writers in his teens, and from then on the revival of the Hebrew language was one of the main goals of his life work. Like many other early *Ḥibbat Zion members, he was shocked by the Russian pogroms of 1881, which emphasized to him the necessity for Jewish emigration. Ussishkin then began working actively for several Zionist groups. After graduating as a technical engineer from the Technological Institute in Moscow, he became active in Hebrew educational work as well as in Zionist propaganda and fund-raising in Russia.

Ussishkin was a "practical" Zionist who viewed agricultural settlement in Ereẓ Israel as the first and most important step toward attaining a Jewish state. He was thus active in recruiting youth for pioneer work and for agricultural settlement of the land. He was a delegate to the First Zionist Congress held in Basle in 1893, and was appointed Hebrew secretary of the Congress. At the Seventh Zionist Congress (1905), he was among the leaders of those who forced the abandonment of the *Uganda Scheme, and he then proposed a program of Zionism which was later adopted by the Zionist movement.

Under his influence the Zionist movement actively supported the establishment of agricultural settlements, educational and cultural institutions, and a Hebrew university. In 1919 Ussishkin himself settled in Ereẓ Israel, and in 1923 he was chosen to head the Jewish National Fund, a position he held for nearly twenty years.

**VA'AD LE'UMMI** (Hebrew for "National Committee"), the National Council of Jews of Palestine, which functioned from October 10, 1920 until the establishment of the provisional government of the State of Israel in May 1948. Though elected in 1920 and recognized immediately as a representative body in a letter from the high commissioner, Sir Herbert Samuel, the Va'ad Le'ummi achieved formal legal status only on January 1, 1928 when Keneset Yisrael, the organizational framework of the Jewish community of Palestine was legally established under the Religious Communities Organization Ordinance, 1926.

The Va'ad Le'ummi represented the Jewish community in its relations with the Mandatory government and the Arab leaders, and dealt with internal affairs (such as the school system). It cooperated closely with the *Jewish Agency executive, as well as the chief rabbinate and the local community councils. It served as the main organ of the Jews of Palestine before the League of Nations Permanent Mandates Commission and the numerous inquiry commissions into the "Palestine Problem" up to the United Nations Special Committee on Palestine, which in 1947 proposed the partition of Palestine into a Jewish and an Arab state.

**VATICAN**, residence of the Pope who is head of the Roman Catholic Church. The Vatican palace is situated in Vatican City, a unique independent state, only about 15 square miles (a few city blocks) located in the heart of Rome. This tiny state includes the famous St. Peter's Basilica, the Sistine Chapel, several museums and administrative offices. It has its own telephone system, postage stamps, coinage, and even a regular army of about 100 Swiss Guards. The importance of this state, however, is not in its minute size, but rather its enormous influence as the headquarters of the largest branch of the Christian religion. It is here that many of the decisions concerning Jewish-Christian relations and the attitude of millions of Catholics towards Jews and Israel originate.

The Church had, for several centuries, maintained control over a large area in Italy but in 1870 all this territory was seized and annexed to the new kingdom of Italy. It was not until 1929 that the Italian government granted the Holy See (the supreme governing body of the Catholic Church) independent control over Vatican City.

Jews who resided in the Church-owned territories had often been subject to restrictions and had been prevented from using the Vatican facilities. Although the Vatican had one of the most important archives of old manuscripts, including many talmudic sources, Jewish scholars were often barred from entering there.

As a member of the international community, the Vatican has had a somewhat varied attitude towards the State of Israel. It showed no enthusiasm for the Zionist cause and in 1947 the Vatican supported the idea of Jerusalem being an international zone. That plan, however, never materialized as the Jordanians seized a major portion of the city including most of the Christian holy sites. Israel, on the other hand, guaranteed the protection of holy places within her borders and free access for all pilgrims, and this move was well-received by the Vatican. Several representatives of the Jewish state have met with the Pope, and in 1964, Pope Paul VI visited Israel, the first Vatican state leader to do so. Though no formal diplomatic ties exist between the Vatican and Israel, mutual contacts are maintained. (See *Christianity; *Popes.)

**VEGETARIANISM.** Although Judaism is firmly opposed to cruelty to animals, it does allow man to use animals for his needs – to work for him and provide him with wool and milk, for instance – and it even permits him to kill them for food, though it insists that the pain caused to the animals in the process be reduced to a minimum. For more on this, see *Animals.

The Talmud points out that according to the biblical account, the consumption of meat was forbidden from Adam until Noah and was specifically permitted first to Noah. When Noah and his sons emerged from the Ark, they were allowed to use animals for food. This is perhaps because by saving the animals from the Flood, Noah became their master in the fullest sense of the word.

Apart from this, however, there is no suggestion of vegetarianism in the Bible. On the other hand, meat is

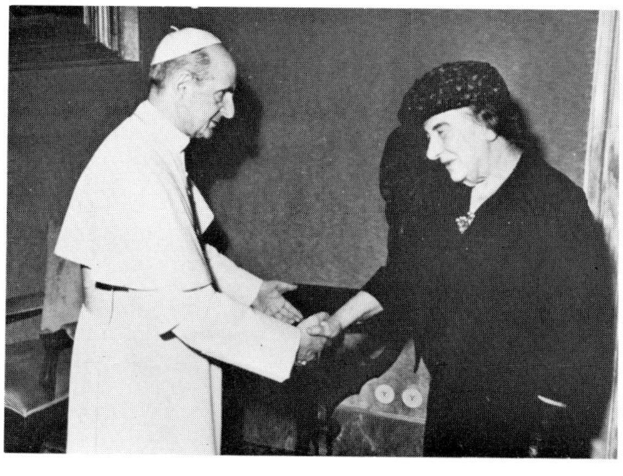

Pope Paul VI, greeting the former prime minister of Israel, Golda Meir, during a brief visit she made to the Vatican in January 1973.

never included in the staple diet of the Children of Israel, which is confined to agricultural products and, in fact, meat was regarded in the Bible as a luxury for which the Children of Israel would yearn, as they did in their lusting for the "fleshpots of Egypt." In the Talmud it is said that meat and wine are the means by which man "rejoices" and on this basis it has long been customary for Jews to eat meat and drink wine on the Sabbath and festivals.

There is, of course, no obligation for Jews to eat meat and there are even some Jewish vegetarian societies. However, in Temple times, every Jew had to partake of the Paschal lamb. It can be argued that for a Jew to adopt vegetarianism because he objects to killing animals for food is to introduce a moral and theological idea which is not included in Jewish teaching, and in fact suggests that Judaism is wrong not to advocate vegetarianism. For this reason many traditional Jews oppose the practice, regarding the Jewish way of life with its permission to eat meat as superior. However, some great rabbis advocated vegetarianism and pointed out that the permission to eat meat in the Bible is stated in a negative manner, as though the Bible is saying: "If you must, eat meat; but the ideal is not to." Of course, eating meat is severely limited by the dietary laws and the law of *sheḥitah;* for details see *Dietary Laws; *Sheḥitah.

**VEIL.** The veiled woman has traditionally been a symbol of chastity and modesty. It has been the custom since biblical times for the Jewish bride to cover her face before her groom, modestly hiding her beauty, just as Rebecca veiled herself on meeting *Isaac. In the 15th century, this custom was incorporated in the marriage ceremony (see *Marriage). The *bedeken,* as it is called, takes place in the presence of the groom, just before the couple is led under the canopy. Either the rabbi or the groom himself lowers the veil over the bride's face, lifting it again only after the ceremony is concluded. In 15th century Rhineland, bridal veils were part of the groom's presents to his bride. And in certain ḥasidic circles, brides have their faces completely wrapped and covered.

It also became customary in ancient societies for the married woman to keep her face covered before strangers. This custom still exists in oriental communities and among Bedouin tribes, whose black-veiled women have an air of mystery and intrigue.

Veils or face coverings are mentioned in the Bible with regard to persons other than brides. Thus Moses, after descending from Mount Sinai, wore some kind of mask to hide his radiant face. And the leper was instructed to cover his upper lip by pulling his head-covering over his face.

Engraving by Bernard Picart (18th century) of a German Jewish wedding ceremony. As is the custom even today among Ashkenazim, the bride is wearing a full veil which, just before the actual wedding, is lowered over her face by the groom in the ceremony called *bedeken.*

**VENGEANCE,** the inflicting of punishment upon a person for an offense or injury done to another, is explicitly prohibited in the Bible: "You shall not take vengeance . . . against your kinfolk. Love your neighbor as yourself." Even bearing a grudge against someone is forbidden, for it is merely a delayed form of vengeance which eventually emerges as an open act of revenge.

However, the Bible and the rabbis did recognize certain justified forms of vengeance, although all of these are outside the realm of personal relationships. A court of law, for example, performs necessary and justified vengeance when it imposes penalties and punishments on criminals and wrongdoers. Similarly, going to war against the enemies of Israel, after provocation and in legally justified circumstances, was also regarded as justified.

The prohibition against personal vengeance was put aside only in one case: to preserve the honor and dignity of the Torah as embodied in the person of a *talmid ḥakham,* a recognized pious Torah scholar. If a *talmid ḥakham* suffers public offense, he is not only allowed, but required, to take revenge. However, this dispensation was very severely limited: it was restricted to cases where the scholar suffered personal, not monetary, injury and the scholar was forbidden to take overt action; he may merely withhold interference if another comes to take up his cause. Furthermore, if the offender seeks forgiveness, the dispensation is terminated.

According to the Talmud, the ideal is to be among those "who are insulted but do not retaliate with insult, who hear themselves reproached without replying." Concerning such people, the rabbis declared that "he who forbears to retaliate will find forbearance from God for all his failings."

**VENICE**, city in north Italy, formerly an independent republic. It was here that the name "*ghetto" was first used to designate an enclosed section of the city, outside of which Jews were forbidden to reside. That occurred in 1516, when the rulers of Venice limited Jewish rights of residence to a particularly unhealthy area of the city near the foundry (*"geto"* in Italian). According to many historians, when Europeans rulers elsewhere subsequently introduced similar forms of segregation, they adopted the original Venetian term for the specific areas.

Within Venice itself, however, this was not the first hardship to which the Jews had been subjected. As early as 945 c.e. the Venetian senate forbade the captains of ships coming from or sailing to the Orient to accept Jews as passengers. By the 12th century Jewish merchants and moneylenders from Germany and the Middle East had been permitted to settle in the city. But they were subject to the hardships of severe taxation, as in 1290, were forced to wear a distinctive badge (1394) or hat (1496) and were often at the mercy of general outbreaks of violence. Thus in 1480 a *blood libel led to three Jews being burned at the stake.

These difficulties were largely surmounted during the 16th and 17th centuries, when the Jews became an increasingly important economic and commercial element in Venice. At a time when the city's traders were faced with a loss of markets, the overseas connections of the western and Levantine Jews became a decisive factor as far as the authorities were concerned. The latter therefore raised few objections to either the increase in the Jewish population, which rose to 4,800 in 1655 or to the influx of *Marrano refugees, whom they even protected from the worst excesses of the *Inquisition.

Under these favorable circumstances, the Jewish community experienced a remarkably rich social and cultural revival. Numerous welfare organizations were established, among the most outstanding of which was one primarily aimed at redeeming Jews taken captive by the Knights of St. John and held at Malta before being sold into slavery. Meanwhile, Venice itself became the home of several famous scholars, rabbis, physicians, writers and philosophers. It also attained renown as an important center of Hebrew *printing, and was the location of Daniel *Bomberg's famous press as well as several others. Moreover, during the 16th century many magnificent synagogues and yeshivot were erected; their rich and elegant interior decorations became one of the attractions of Venice, even for Christian visitors. Those which have since been reconstructed and restored are today still testimony to the prosperity and talent of the Venetian Jewish community during the period of its grandeur.

That golden age, however, was short-lived. By the 18th century the community was impoverished, subjected to severe trading and commercial restrictions, and its numbers were depleted by emigration. There was some improvement when the ghetto walls were torn down by Napoleon in 1797, and between 1848-49 the government was headed by a citizen of Jewish origin, Daniele Manin. However, although full emancipation was granted to the Jews in 1866, when the city was annexed to the independent kingdom of Italy, the community's fortunes did not revive. During World War II the Nazis deported 205 Jews from Venice to extermination camps, and in 1945 the community numbered only 1,050. The Jewish population has since declined further. The old ghetto is still a tourist attraction, but only one of the five surviving synagogues there remains open for regular worship.

The central square of the Venice ghetto as it looks today. It is believed that this was the first Jewish quarter to be known as a "ghetto," the name having been taken from the Italian word for a "foundry" located nearby. The section was enclosed by walls in 1516 and declared to be the only section of Venice open to Jewish settlement.

**VIENNA.** According to legend, Jews were among the first settlers sent by the Romans to colonize what later became the city of Vienna, capital of Austria. Documentary evidence, however, places Jews in Vienna only at the end of the 12th century. In 1194, Duke Leopold V of Austria appointed a Jew named Solomon as head of the royal mint. Two years later

Solomon and 15 other Jews residing in the city were brutally murdered by Crusader bands that swept through the city, and the synagogue was destroyed. However, a community was soon reestablished in the city and in 1238 a charter of privileges was granted by the emperor giving the Jews extensive autonomy and the right to lend money at relatively high rates of interest. A Church Council which convened in Vienna in 1267 attempted to revive ancient Church laws restricting Jewish rights, but these were not put into effect since the local rulers were heavily dependent upon the money that Jewish taxes poured into their coffers.

During the 14th century the community of Vienna was recognized as the leading community of German Jewry. There were then about a thousand Jews living in Vienna and the rabbinic leaders of the time, who were collectively known as the "Sages of Vienna," enjoyed great prestige throughout northwestern Europe. The most famous among them was Isaac ben Moses, known as the *Or Zaru'a,* after the massive halakhic compendium he edited containing extensive quotations from all the early halakhic authorities of northern Europe.

In the early 15th century, however, the Jewish community of Vienna was nearly wiped out as a result of cruel persecutions and the resultant forced conversion and martyrdom of many of its members. The community revived somewhat in the 16th and the early part of the 17th centuries – only to be faced with another expulsion in 1670. Close to 4,000 Jews were then forced to leave Vienna and seek new places of refuge in other parts of Europe.

The financial loss which Vienna suffered as a result of the expulsion of its Jews soon became unbearable, and by 1693 Jews were once again admitted to the city. However, this time, the number of Jews allowed to establish permanent residence was severely restricted and only the very wealthy were accepted as "tolerated subjects," in exchange for the payment of a very high tax. No provisions were made for an organized community and prayer services were only allowed in private homes.

Despite these restrictions, by the mid-18th century, Vienna had become an important Jewish center, numbering among its inhabitants many *court Jews (such as the Oppenheimer and Wertheimer families) and many wealthy Jews who were well-known philanthropists. In 1781 Austria's Emperor Joseph II issued the famous "Toleranz-Patent" which served as a forerunner to the emancipation decrees of the 19th century. In 1793 a printing press was set up in Vienna and the city soon became the leading center of Jewish publishing in central Europe. At the beginning of the 19th century Vienna was an important center of *Haskalah activity and by the end of the century it had become the center of Zionist activities, serving as the headquarters of the Zionist executive. The Zionist movement's organ, *Die Welt,* was also published there.

However, from the last decades of the 19th century onward, Vienna was also the home of virulent anti-Semitism and there were political parties, such as those led by Karl Lueger and Georg von Schoenerer, which based their whole political platform on anti-Semitic issues. The *Anschluss* (annexation) of Austria by Germany in 1938 marked the beginning of the liquidation of Austrian Jewry, and by the end of World War II only some 4,000 Viennese Jews had managed to survive, either in hiding or in the concentration and labor camps.

Following the War, the city's Jewish population again increased, largely because the city served as the main transit stop and first refuge for the hundreds of thousands of Eastern European Jewish refugees. In the 1970s Vienna was a transit point for Soviet Jews on their way to Israel. Vienna had 6,000 registered Jews in the early 1990s and some 10,000 Jewish immigrants from the former Soviet Union. It is also the home of the Documentation Center, established and directed by Simon Wiesenthal, for documenting the horrors of the Holocaust and tracing Nazi criminals still alive and at large.

Schoenau Castle, on the outskirts of Vienna, which served for several years as the temporary housing quarters of many thousands of Russian Jews who were permitted to leave the Soviet Union and were on their way to the State of Israel.

**VILNA,** capital of the Soviet Republic of Lithuania. Having served as a center of Jewish scholarship for over 300 years, it became known to East European Jews as the "Jerusalem of Lithuania."

Despite a ban on Jewish settlement there, issued in 1527, Jewish merchants resided in Vilna from the

**Sukkot.** Two decorated pages from the *Pesaro Siddur,* produced in Pesaro, Italy, 1880. The right-hand page contains the concluding hymns of the Yom Kippur service and the left-hand page the central portion of the *Amidah* prayer for the Sukkot festival. In a circular window at the bottom is a representative *sukkah.*

**Zechariah.** A full-page miniature depicting the *Menorah* described in a vision of the prophet Zechariah (Chapter 4). Two olive trees flank the *Menorah,* and two attached spouts pour oil into a bowl from which it is distributed to the *Menorah* by seven pipes. The *Menorah* symbolizes the restored Jewish state and the two olive trees represent the two future leaders, King and High Priest.

16th century onward and were permitted to engage in business, build a synagogue, and live in relative freedom. Although subjected to intermittent riots and anti-Semitic laws, the Jewish community survived and grew so that, by the 17th century, it claimed to be the leading Jewish community in Lithuania.

Scores of rabbinic scholars lived in Vilna during the 17th and 18th centuries, the most renowned being Rabbi Elijah ben Solomon Zalman, the *Gaon of Vilna. These scholars had a profound influence on Judaism in the sphere of both *Halakhah* (Jewish law) and Kabbalah (Jewish mysticism).

At the end of the 18th century, under the influence of the Gaon, Vilna became a center for the *Mitnaggedim* in their struggle against *Ḥasidism. In 1772 the community issued a ban *(*ḥerem)* against the Ḥasidim and the two groups engaged in a bitter political and religious struggle which lasted for the next 20 years.

Vilna also became an important center for the Enlightenment (*Haskalah) movement, which led to the modernization and secularization of many institutions there. The Russian authorities, eager to speed up "Russianization" encouraged this process, setting up modern Russian schools in Vilna.

Owing to the Russian government's prohibition on Jewish settlement in the villages in the late 19th century, many Jews in rural areas had to move to Vilna. The resulting congested conditions led to large-scale emigration to the United States, South Africa and, in some cases, to Ereẓ Israel.

Vilna became an active meeting ground for Jewish socialists in the 1890s, and a center of the Zionist movement in the 20th century. Several Zionist organizations (Ḥovevei Zion, Mizrachi, and others) held their inaugural conventions in Vilna. The city also saw the rise of a flourishing Hebrew and Yiddish literary society. In the 1920s, the *YIVO research institute for Yiddish language and culture was founded in Vilna, as were several Hebrew schools and numerous Yiddish and Hebrew periodicals.

This period, however, was not all tranquil for the Jews. From 1900 onward, there were *blood libels, massacres, and strong anti-Semitic agitation throughout the area. The age-old struggle between Poland, Russia and Lithuania for possession of Vilna often resulted in the massacre of Jews as scapegoats. In 1940 Lithuania was annexed to the USSR and the Soviet authorities closed down all Hebrew and Zionist organizations.

During World War II, the Jews of Vilna were herded into a ghetto. The community leaders organized a fighting force, headed by Yiẓḥak *Wittenberg, to defend the populace against the Nazis. But they were systematically murdered and by 1944 it is estimated that about 100,000 Vilna Jews were killed.

After the city was liberated by the Soviet army in 1944, several thousand survivors returned and tried to rebuild the Jewish community there. The Soviet authorities, however, arrested scores for "illegal" Zionist activities. In the early 1990s there were fewer than 9,000 Jews in Vilna. Relieved of Soviet repression, Jewish community life developed.

**VISIONS** are imaginary, supernatural, or prophetic sights seen in sleep or while in ecstasy. The Bible contains descriptions of many visions, especially of God and His angel (or angels). The prophets also had visions of simple or imaginary objects or persons which they interpreted in a symbolic way.

During the Second Temple period and later, visionary experiences were recorded. For example *Josephus records that John Hyrcanus, the second-century Hasmonean ruler of Judea, had a vision of God announcing to him which of his sons would be his heir. Rabbinic literature often mentions the appearance of the prophet *Elijah, who did not die but ascended to the heavens in a fiery chariot.

Medieval Jewish literature contains many descriptions of different kinds of visions. Some mystics described the glory of the heavenly world which they saw in visions, even including the songs of praise sung by the angels. Visions were most commonly seen in dreams and could also be deliberately invoked. Both scholars and simple folk told and retold numerous stories of visions said to have been seen. Countless medieval folktales recount how Elijah appeared to human beings in order to assist or punish them. It was also believed that

1

2

יונג ווילנע
1936

3

1. The narrow *Zydowska* ("Jews' Street") of Vilna, 1917.
2. The table of contents of the 1936 issue of *Yung Vilne,* the organ of a group of young Yiddish poets living in Vilna in the 1930s. Among the contributors were Chaim Grade, Abraham Sutzkever and Leizer Wolf.
3. Unusual tombstone of A. Weider, an early victim of a pogrom, located in the Vilna Jewish cemetery.

1

2

1. Sir Julius Vogel, prime minister of New Zealand in the 1870s, who is credited with spurring the economic development of New Zealand in the late 19th century.
2. Woodcut from the *Cologne Bible* (1478–80) illustrating Daniel's "Vision of the Ram and the He-Goat" (Daniel, Chapter 8). Daniel is shown kneeling before the angel Gabriel who interprets the vision for him.
3. Ḥayyim Meir Hager (center), leader of the Vizhnitz Ḥasidim, surrounded by family members and disciples.

demons and spirits of the dead appeared in visions to the living. Sometimes the dead appeared to pay a debt or to complain of a fault in the way or place in which they were buried. Demons could be invoked to perform a certain task by pouring oil on a bright surface, and were obliged to answer any request put to them. This practice was used even for catching a thief or finding a lost article. Early kabbalists recorded visions in which they were granted revelations of hidden truths from the heavenly spheres, and visions constituted an important element in the Shabbatean movement, many of whose adherents described messianic visions that were revealed to them. Many great legal authorities such as Joseph *Caro,the author of the *Shulḥan Arukh*, claimed to have had heavenly teachers who appeared to them in dreams and solved difficult halakhic problems. In fact a whole type of literature developed called *she'elot ḥalom*, "questions asked in dreams." As late as the 18th century the *Ba'al Shem Tov, founder of *Ḥasidism, described how his soul ascended to heaven and the visions he saw there.

**VIZHNITZ**, a ḥasidic dynasty founded in the mid-19th century in the Ukrainian town of Vizhnitz by Menaḥem Mendel ben Ḥayyim Hager (1830-1884). Menaḥem Mendel's father had been a ḥasidic *ẓaddik* and he himself became known at an early age as a

3

miracle worker and distributor of amulets. He served both as communal leader of the town and as head of the rabbinical court. A year after he died, a collection of his writings, *Ẓemaḥ Ẓaddik,* was published.

Menaḥem Mendel was succeeded by his son Baruch,and the latter's seven sons and three sons-in-law also became in turn heads of various branches of the dynasty. Today most of the descendants and adherents of Vizhnitz Ḥasidism can be found in Bene Berak, Israel.

**VOGEL, SIR JULIUS** (1835-1927), Jewish prime minister of New Zealand. Born in London, Vogel was attracted to Australia by the gold rush of the mid-1850s, and he settled in Melbourne. He failed, however, to make his fortune in the mines and in 1862 he moved to New Zealand. There he became a journalist and edited the colony's first daily newspaper, the *Otago Daily Times.* In the following few years he was elected first to the provincial council and then to the House of Representatives, and he gained a reputation as a master of financial affairs. Appointed colonial treasurer in 1869, he acquired even greater prestige and fame by successfully negotiating a significant loan deal with the British government, which facilitated the building of urgently-needed roads and railways. In 1873 he became prime minister, but his firm policy of centralizing the colony's political and administrative affairs and of curtailing local autonomy caused much opposition and lost him his widespread popular support. In 1875 he was forced to resign and he spent most of the rest of his life as agent-general of New Zealand in London. He was knighted by Queen Victoria in 1875.

**VOLOZHIN**, city in Belorussia, occupied at various times by both Russia and Poland, which acquired importance in Jewish life when the famous Eẓ Ḥayyim Yeshivah was founded there by Ḥayyim *Volozhiner in the 19th century.

The yeshivah served as the cornerstone of Eastern European Jewry. It became so highly esteemed that the military governor of neighboring Lithuania issued a document of protection to Rabbi Ḥayyim in 1813, instructing all military units to "safeguard the chief rabbi of Volozhin, Ḥayyim ben Isaac, his schools and educational institutions . . . ."

After Rabbi Ḥayyim's death in 1821, his son Isaac served as head of the yeshivah and as such was considered among the leaders of Russian Jewry.

Around this time (1824) the Russian authorities decided to close the yeshivah, but despite the official ban, the yeshivah continued to function and expand. Subsequent heads included Rabbi Eliezer Isaac Fried, Rabbi Naphtali Ẓevi Judah Berlin, and Rabbi Joseph Baer Soloveichik.

In the latter half of the 19th century, other influences began infiltrating the yeshivah: the *Musar movement, *Haskalah, and *Zionism all had their effects.

At various times the yeshivah was again closed down by the authorities but it always managed to reopen and resume activities. However, the final group of students were liquidated during the Holocaust, together with the entire Jewish population of the city which numbered approximately 3,000 of the city's 5,600 inhabitants. With this total devastation, the Jewish community of Volozhin, which had existed since the 16th century, ceased its profound influence on world Jewish scholarship.

**VOLOZHINER, ḤAYYIM BEN ISAAC** (1749-1821), Lithuanian rabbi and educator. In 1802 he founded the renowned yeshivah of *Volozhin (later to be named Eẓ Ḥayyim in his honor) which became the prototype and inspiration for the great talmudic academies of eastern Europe in the 19th and 20th centuries, and similar schools in Israel, the United States, and elsewhere. His yeshivah, which the poet Ḥ. N. *Bialik was later to call "the place where the soul of the nation was molded," raised religious scholarship in Lithuania to the unique status it was to enjoy there until the Holocaust.

Rabbi Ḥayyim ben Isaac set high standards for admission to his yeshivah, insisting on extreme diligence and hard work. He instituted the system of study in small groups (*ḥavruta*) rather than individual study, and insisted on "straight thinking" *(iyyun yashar)* rather than the complicated philosophical methods common in his day.

Rabbi Ḥayyim considered the study of Torah as the most important aspect of Jewish scholarship, seeing it as the direct form of communion with God. In opposition to the ḥasidic thinkers of his day, he felt that Torah should be studied for the sake of understanding rather than for any mystical benefits.

A leading disciple of the *Gaon of Vilna, Rabbi Ḥayyim followed in his teacher's footsteps in opposing the ḥasidic movement. But though he strongly criticized *Ḥasidism, he did not join in signing the ban against them, preferring a more moderate approach. He is said to have had a humble and pleasant personality which aided his recognition as the spiritual leader of a major portion of Russian Jewry.

Rabbi Ḥayyim's major work was the *Nefesh ha-Ḥayyim* published by his son Isaac three years after his death.

1

2

1. Selman A. Waksman, U.S. Nobel Prize-winning microbiologist who discovered streptomycin, the first important antibiotic.
2. Lilian Wald, U.S. social activist who worked tirelessly on behalf of the disadvantaged and the poor.

**WADI**, the bed of a stream in arid regions such as the Middle East and North Africa. During most of the year the wadi resembles a dry valley, but when the rains come, the wadi fills with storm water and can suddenly turn into a savagely rushing river.

Because the wadis were often the only source of water and irrigation in desert areas, primitive tribes settled around them and the archaeological remains of such early civilizations have been found near wadis all over Israel. Wadi al-Nattuf, for example, just north of Jerusalem, is the site of a prehistoric culture dating back 10,000 years. And Wadi Qumran near the Dead Sea was the source of the Dead Sea Scrolls. Wadi Qilt (or Kelt), between Jerusalem and Jericho, contains a Roman aqueduct which collected the rain water and conveyed it to Jerusalem. Today Wadi Qilt is a nature reserve attracting visitors to view the picturesque beauty of the lush green oasis at the bottom of the wadi, surrounded by barren desert mountains.

The rainfall causes deeper and deeper erosion in the mountains each year, leaving rugged cliffs and deep canyons. Such sites dot the countryside in Israel and neighboring countries which share the same seasonal climate.

**WAKSMAN, SELMAN ABRAHAM** (1888-1973), United States microbiologist and Nobel Prize winner. Born in the Ukraine, Waksman was barred, as a Jew, from attending a regular government high school; so he completed high school through correspondence courses, and then emigrated to the United States. While working as a laboratory assistant at an agricultural college in New Jersey, he attended Rutgers University where he obtained his Master's degree in microbiology. After completing his Ph.D. at the University of California, he returned to Rutgers as an instructor, and remained there for most of his academic life. In 1949 he became head of Rutgers' Institute of Microbiology.

Waksman's research interests centered on various aspects of soil microbiology, but he is best known for his investigation into antibiotics, particularly streptomycin, the first and one of the most effective drugs to be discovered for the treatment of tuberculosis as well as many other infectious diseases. The term "antibiotic" was itself coined by Waksman, and describes a substance produced by a micro-organism that has the capacity to destroy another micro-organism which is the cause of the disease. Waksman published an autobiography, *My Life with the Microbes,* in which he described the arduous process that led to his momentous discovery: "It was the story of the 10,000 microbes. We isolated 10,000 microbes and tested them for the ability to inhibit the growth of pathogenic (disease-causing) bacteria. We found that ten percent had that quality. We tried to grow that 1,000 microbes in cultures and found that ten percent lent themselves to the process. From that 100 we tried to extract the active substances, and we ended up with 10 chemical compounds. We tested them in animals, and one is now known as the antibiotic streptomycin."

In 1952 Waksman was awarded the Nobel Prize for Medicine and Physiology.

**WALD, LILLIAN** (1867-1940). Born to a prosperous, upper-middle-class Jewish family in Cincinnati, Ohio, Lillian Wald spent most of her years among the tattered and troubled immigrants in the teeming slums of New York's Lower East Side. Yet one could hardly call it a step down in life, for she was dedicated to the relief of suffering, the protection of the helpless, and the search for peace.

At the age of 22, she decided to become a nurse after meeting one who cared for her sister during childbirth. Her career led to contact with the poverty and disease she had never known as a child, and she resolved to bring nursing care and hygienic instruction to all who needed it.

At the turn of the 20th century, the big-city slums were bursting with social and economic problems, and government was only beginning to deal with them. Miss Wald soon realized that good health was only one of the people's requisites for finding a better life. In 1895, she and another nurse sought the financial support of several wealthy friends and established a settlement house on Rivington Street. Its services of counseling, education, recreation, health care and social work were in such demand that it expanded, moved and became famous as the Henry Street Settlement.

As an activist and liberal reformer, she campaigned for the government to create a decent and humane environment for all citizens. Among the causes she supported were improved sanitation, trade unionism, pure milk, tuberculosis control, an end to child labor and American non-involvement in World War I.

**WALES** is a country in the heart of Great Britain which forms part of the United Kingdom.

Municipalities of northern Wales in 1284 had charters that included the "liberty" to exclude Jews from their towns. Only in the 18th century did Jews begin to resettle in Wales. They were found in Swansea, now the second largest industrial city and seaport, from 1731; a community was formed there in 1768, while a community existed in Cardiff by 1840. When Russian Jews emigrated to Britain in the 1880s, some of them also went to Wales, and moved to Cardiff from the smaller mining towns. At that time, Polish Jews tried to find employment in the Welsh coal mines, but were prevented from doing so by the anti-Semitism of the native Welshmen. The miners' strike in 1911 in south Wales took an anti-Semitic turn, and Jewish shops and houses were looted and destroyed in the town of Tredegar. Troops were sent by the then home secretary, Winston Churchill, to restore order.

In the 1980s there were about 4,000 Jews in Wales, of which 3,500 lived in Cardiff and the rest in smaller towns. Numbers have declined.

**WALLACH, MOSHE**(1866-1957), medical pioneer in Ereẓ Israel. Born in Germany, Wallach received an orthodox education and also studied medicine. In 1891 he settled in Jerusalem and opened a clinic in the Old City. Soon after,he purchased land in a deserted spot outside the city walls and established a modern, yet Orthodox hospital, Sha'arei Ẓedek (Gates of Righteousness). Wallach served as director of the hospital until his retirement in 1947. The hospital served as a landmark in Jerusalem and in 1979 moved to a magnificent new building in the city.

**WALLENBERG, RAOUL** (1912-?1947), Swedish diplomat who became a legend through his efforts to save Hungarian Jews at the end of World War II. He was an architect by profession and in 1936 spent six months in Haifa where he studied management at the Holland Bank, and there he first met with Jewish refugees from Germany. Upon his return to Stockholm he became the foreign representative of a central European trading company whose president was a Hungarian Jew, K. Laur. In 1944 he was sent by the Swedish Foreign Ministry at the request of Jewish organizations on a rescue mission to Budapest, as an attache to the Swedish Embassy.

His chief operation was the distribution of Swedish certificates of protection which became known as "Wallenberg passports." He initiated the establishment of the "International Ghetto" through which some 33,000 Jews found refuge. In November 1944, thousands of Budapest Jews were forced on a death march to the Austrian border. Wallenberg followed after them with a convoy of trucks, distributing medicaments to the sick and food and clothing to the marchers. He even managed to free 500 Jews who returned to Budapest.

Shortly after the liberation of Hungary by the Russian army in January 1945, Wallenberg disappeared and was never heard of again. The Soviet authorities announced in 1952 that he had died suddenly in his cell in a labor camp in July 1947. Despite this announcement, the circumstances of his disappearance and death were regarded by many as mysterious and suspicious.

**WAR.** "When you go forth to battle against your enemies and see horses, chariots and a people more than you, do not fear them, for the Lord your God is with you."

Thus begins the biblical listing of rules concerning war. War is described here in religious terms, because in ancient times it was a religious endeavor. War was waged in honor of God, by the will of God, against the enemies of God.

The rabbis distinguished between two kinds of war: obligatory war *(milḥemet mitzvah)* and voluntary war *(milḥemet reshut)*. Obligatory wars – those which God has commanded the Israelites to fight and from which no able-bodied soldier is exempt – are: 1) the campaigns against the seven nations who inhabited Ereẓ Israel before the Israelites arrived and were to be driven from the land; 2) the battles against *Amalek, the traditional enemy of Israel; and 3) defensive wars to repulse an enemy attack on an Israelite city. In these three cases the

2

1

1. A wall relief from Medinet Habu, Egypt, showing a moated Syrian town under atack by the forces of Pharaoh Ramses III (12th century b.c.e.). Clearly represented are the military equipment and techniques in use at the time, including archers covering an assault on the city gate by a scaling party.
2. Raoul Wallenberg, Swedish diplomat who rescued hundreds of Hungarian Jews during the Holocaust.

1

2

1. Detail from a wall painting in a tomb at Bani Hasan, Egypt, dating back to the 20th century b.c.e., showing a warrior armed with the weapons that were typical in the days of the biblical patriarchs – an axe with duck-bill blade, a double-convex bow and a quiver for arrows.
2. Professor Otto Warburg (1859–1938), distinguished German research botanist and third president of the World Zionist Organization.

king could declare war without the permission of the *Sanhedrin. Voluntary wars, however, those waged merely for the expansion of territory, could be declared only by the Great Sanhedrin of 71 members.

War was not a move to be taken lightly, even in ancient times. The biblical instructions regarding war indicate that it was to be waged only after all other alternatives had failed. When nearing the enemy camp, in a voluntary war, the Jews are instructed to offer a peace treaty first, before striking. If the offer is accepted, then all the lives shall be spared and the people taken as servants. But if the enemy refuses the peace treaty, then all the males shall be killed and the women and children taken captive. Though this may sound drastic in modern times, it was considered a very humanitarian policy in ancient days, when most nations tried to totally annihilate their enemies.

In a voluntary war, any man "who has built a new house and not yet dedicated it, betrothed a wife and not yet taken her, or planted a vineyard and not yet eaten of it," was told to return home and not fight the battle, lest he be killed and someone else take the first fruits of his labors. Anyone afraid of battle was also asked to leave so as not to spread his fears to the other soldiers.

Jews were allowed to fight on the Sabbath if the enemy attacked a Jewish city and endangered lives, or if they attacked a border town. If, however, the enemy came to a non-border town only to steal goods and not take lives, then the Jews were forbidden to bear arms and desecrate the Sabbath.

Scholars have learned much about ancient weapons and warfare both from biblical descriptions and from archaeological remains. Among the favorite battle techniques of the Jews were the night attack, the surprise attack, and the ambush whereby the enemy was led into a trap and encircled by Israelite troops. Weaponry developed during biblical times from the simple bow and arrow and sword used in the days of the Patriarchs, to the more sophisticated battering rams, chariots, shields and fortified cities which persisted until the development of gunpowder in the Middle Ages.

Because wars were of a holy nature, the armies were always accompanied to the battlefield by a priest. Sometimes the holy ark was carried out to provide spiritual inspiration for the soldiers, just as the non-Jews brought their idols. Many wars were sanctioned and even suggested by the prophets, but the later prophets also spoke of the horrors of battle and prayed for peace. *Isaiah in particular longed for the time when "they shall beat their swords into plowshares and their spears into pruning hooks; Nation shall not lift up sword against nation, neither shall they learn war anymore."

Isaiah realized that war is not just a series of victories and defeats, of weapons and strategy. It is a very human experience involving bloodshed, suffering, and destruction. Unfortunately the Jewish people have been faced with the horrors of war throughout the centuries – from *Joshua's wars of conquest, through the battles against invading armies and the courageous uprisings of the *Zealots and their successors, down to the World Wars of the 20th century and the modern struggle for Israel's survival.

For more on these, see the listings for individual wars and the articles on *Bar Kokhba; *Haganah; *Hasmoneans; *History; *Irgun Ẓeva'i Le'ummi; *Jewish Brigade Group; *Military Service; *Palmaḥ; *Self-defense, Jewish.

**WARBURG**, surname of a family of German and U.S. Jews who became prominent bankers, philanthropists and scholars.

Paul Moritz Warburg (1868-1932) was born in Germany but in 1902 moved to the United States, where he made a considerable contribution to the U.S. banking system. One of the chief architects of the legislation establishing the Federal Reserve System in 1913, he served as a member of the Federal Reserve Board and later as its vice-governor. He wrote several books on the banking system and was also active in many Jewish philanthropic organizations.

Paul Warburg's son James Paul (1896-1969), also a banker, was one of the major backers of the Polaroid corporation. A liberal Democrat, he was a member of President Franklin D. *Roosevelt's "brain trust" during the early years of the New Deal. In the late 1930s he urged U.S. intervention against Nazi Germany and during World War II served as deputy director of the office of war information. He wrote several books on economics, public affairs and foreign policy.

Other outstanding members of the Warburg family included:

**Karl Johan Warburg** (1852-1918), Swedish literary historian who organized and administered the Nobel Library of the Swedish Academy and wrote an authoritative history of Swedish literature.

**Otto Warburg** (1859-1938), botanist and the third president of the World Zionist Organization who

contributed greatly to the settlement of Ereẓ Israel.
**Aby Moritz Warburg** (1866-1939), German historian of art and civilization, founder of the famous Warburg Institute, a library of classical art now located in London.
**Otto Heinrich Warburg** (1883-1970), German biochemist and Nobel Prize winner (1931) "for his discovery of the nature and mode of action of the respiratory enzyme."
**Felix Moritz Warburg** (1871-1937), active in cultural and philanthropic affairs in the United States, such as the development of the Juilliard School of Music and the Fogg Museum of Art at Harvard University.
**Gerald Warburg** (1907-1971), son of Felix Moritz, a cellist with the New York Philharmonic Orchestra, who organized the Stradivarius Society and the Brooklyn Symphony Orchestra.

**WAR OF INDEPENDENCE,** the first war waged by the Jews of the modern state of Israel for their survival and political independence. It lasted from November 1947 until July 1949 and was divided into two distinct phases. The first phase began on November 30, 1947, the day after the *United Nations General Assembly adopted the resolution on the *Partition of Palestine into two separate Jewish and Arab states. During this phase, the Jewish underground defense forces (*Haganah) fought against Arab troops living in Palestine and other irregular volunteers who came from the surrounding Arab countries.

The second phase began on the day after the British evacuated their Mandatory forces on May 15, 1948 (see *Mandate for Palestine), the day the Jewish State of Israel came into being. From that day until July 20, 1949 when the last of a series of armistice agreements was signed, the army of the newly independent State of Israel fought against the invading armies of Egypt, Iraq, Transjordan, Syria, and Lebanon, and against volunteer detachments from Saudi Arabia, Libya and Yemen. In both phases, the avowed purpose of the Arabs was to frustrate the UN partition resolution and prevent the establishment and consolidation of the Jewish state.

**Phase I.** Even prior to the UN resolution on the partition of Palestine, the Jewish settlements scattered throughout the country had been subject to frequent Arab attacks (major uprisings occurred in 1929 and in 1936-38); but when the British decided to evacuate the area and the UN agreed on partition, the *yishuv* (Jewish community in Palestine) found itself confronted with a situation of all-out war.

On the eve of the war, the state of the *yishuv* was precarious. The Haganah had a total of only 32,000 registered members, and most of these were poorly trained. It had no heavy military equipment, while in secret arsenals the Haganah had managed to gather together only some 15,000 rifles of various makes, and some "home-made" explosives manufactured in clandestine workshops. In addition to the Haganah, there were two other armed underground organizations which operated independently during the first phase, *Irgun Ẓevai Le'ummi and *Leḥi (Stern Gang), with a total of 6,000 members.

The Arabs began their campaign with the ambushes of Jewish travelers and riots within commercial centers. On June 10, a 900-man force of the volunteer Arab Liberation Army attacked a Jewish settlement, thus beginning the actual military action. Soon afterwards a platoon of 35 Jews, en route to reinforce the isolated Eẓyon bloc of settlements near Jerusalem was wiped out in a fierce engagement (see *Kefar Eẓyon). The area was later captured by the Arabs. Explosives were detonated in the Jewish areas of Haifa and Jerusalem, but most damaging of all was the Arab success in blocking some of the major roads, preventing Jewish access and leaving towns and settlements isolated and entrapped. By March, Jerusalem itself was in a state of siege. Almost no supplies or ammunition could be delivered and the civilian population was forced to ration its dwindling reserves of food and water.

In April 1948 the Jewish forces began their counter-attack, labeled "Plan D." Tiberias, several

3

1

2

1. Under almost constant attack during the many months of the War of Independence, the inhabitants of Jerusalem were often without the basic necessities of life. Shown in this photo are Jerusalemites lined up to receive fresh water which had been brought in by truck.
2. A solitary Arab in the village of Ajur waving a white flag of surrender before an approaching contingent of Israel soldiers, during the War of Independence, October 1948.
3. Karl Johan Warburg (1852–1918), Swedish literary historian.

1

1. Proclamation posted throughout Jewish Palestine on Friday, May 15, 1948, the day on which the State of Israel officially came into being, ordering the immediate conscription for military service of all males aged 26–35. The men were ordered to appear the next day, which was a Sabbath, and for this purpose a special *heter* ("dispensation") was given by the chief rabbinate. This fact was prominently indicated on the poster.
2. A barbed wire fence and an armed Arab guard block one of the main entrances to the Old City of Jerusalem (just inside the Jaffa Gate) at the outbreak of the War of Independence, 1948.

northern settlements and various vital roads were recaptured. On April 9, a combined IẒL and Leḥi force attacked Deir Yassin, an Arab village on the outskirts of Jerusalem. The Arabs claimed that 200 residents were killed, including women and children, though the Israelis asserted that the civilians were warned to leave, and the Haganah insisted that it had never ordered the attack. The incident was widely publicized as a deliberate massacre, although the Arab slaughter of Jewish civilians was played down in international reports. On April 13, for example, a convoy of medical personnel on the way to Hadassah Hospital on Mount Scopus was attacked by the Arabs and 77 civilians killed.

**Phase II.** On May 15, 1948, the day the British Mandate over Palestine ended, the regular armies of five neighboring Arab states invaded the new State of Israel. The war thus changed from a struggle between volunteer forces to a major battle between opposing nations. The invasion, heralded by an Egyptian air attack on Tel-Aviv, was vigorously resisted, but the small, ill-equipped Israel army was far outnumbered by the Arabs. The Haganah, once the Jewish underground force during British occupation, now emerged as the official Israel Defense Force and the two dissident groups – IẒL and Leḥi – agreed to disband. This small force, however, could not cover all fronts at once and often the Jewish settlements were left to hold off the invading troops on their own until help could be sent. On several border kibbutzim a handful of civilians fought off hundreds of enemy soldiers. Jerusalem and its surroundings were the scenes of continuous bitter fighting. With the regular road blocked, the Jews had to quickly establish an alternative route. This was a rough dirt track on which hundreds of elderly men worked night after night to make it fit for vehicles to use. They named it the "Burma Road," after the infamous highway the Japanese forced their Allied prisoners of war to construct during the Second World War, and this project helped Israel's forces to finally break the siege on Jerusalem. Part of the original approach, the Latrun road, however, was not recaptured and battles in this area between Jerusalem and Tel-Aviv cost Israel hundreds of casualties. On the southern front, the Israel forces managed to rout the Egyptians from the Negev and proceeded into the Sinai.

Several short-term truces were imposed by the UN during the course of the war, but it was not until July 20, 1949 that the last armistice agreement was signed and the fighting ended. Israel was forced to withdraw from several areas, including the Sinai, and the Arabs retained control of East Jerusalem, the west bank of the Jordan River, and the Gaza Strip, which they held until 1967. Israel had succeeded in greatly increasing the territory originally granted in the Partition Plan, but the war proved to be only the beginning of Israel's struggle for survival, and has been followed by a long series of wars, both of confrontation and of attrition. For more on this see *Israel; *Partition of Palestine; *Sinai Campaign; *Six-Day War, and *Yom Kippur War.

**WARREN, SIR CHARLES** (1840-1927), British army officer and archaeologist who undertook extensive archaeological excavations in various parts of Palestine and the Near East. Between 1867 and 1870, Warren conducted digs in Jerusalem, concentrating on the outer wall of the Temple Mount. He dug a series of underground tunnels, experiencing numerous problems, but he made some startling finds. Warren was a very careful worker and recorded the results of his excavations with great exactitude, so that his notes provided the main source of information concerning the outside Herodian wall of the Temple Mount until new excavations were undertaken in 1968, following the reunification of the city of Jerusalem.

Warren preserved and registered every object he uncovered – today this is a standard archaeological procedure, but then it was totally new, and this has given his work great lasting value.

Warren was among those who openly advocated Jewish settlement of Palestine (in his book *The Land of Promise,* 1875). In his opinion, the country could well absorb up to 15 million immigrants if all its resources were properly exploited.

2

**WARSAW.** "What terrible spectacles must we witness in Warsaw, the capital of our beloved Poland, on solemn holidays! Students and even adults in noisy mobs persecute the Jews and sometimes beat them with sticks. How can we look with indifference on such a survival of barbarism?"

This was the reaction of some 18th-century Poles to the maltreatment of Warsaw Jewry. Unfortunately those who raised their voices in protest against the anti-Semitic trends were few indeed, and the Jews of Warsaw suffered at the hands of their gentile neighbors for centuries.

Jewish settlement in Warsaw began in the 14th century, and records show that the hostility of the townsmen to the new inhabitants was very strong. On several occasions from the 15th century onward the Jews were expelled from the city, though their connection with this political and commercial center was never entirely broken.

By the 18th century, a Jewish bourgeoisie of businessmen and moneylenders had formed in Warsaw. After the first partition of *Poland in 1772, these Jews took an energetic part in the Polish uprising against the Russians and, as a result, a large portion of the Jewish civilian population was massacred by the advancing Russian troops.

After Warsaw became part of Prussia in 1796, Warsaw Jewry was subjected to the *Juden Reglements* – regulations restricting Jewish residence in the city. The "daily ticket" system, first used centuries before, was reinstituted, permitting the holder of a ticket to stay in Warsaw for a limited time only. Nevertheless the Jewish population of Warsaw continued to grow, and by the beginning of the 19th century there were close to 12,000 Jews living there.

In 1807 Warsaw became a duchy within the empire of Napoleon. After Napoleon's defeat in 1815, Poland was redivided by the Congress of Vienna and the Warsaw community became part of so-called "Congress Poland" under the authority of the czar of Russia. From that point there was a sharp deterioration in the status of Warsaw Jewry. Their activities were restricted and they were subjected to horrifying pogroms. Yet, by contrast, a small percentage managed to succeed in commerce and industry and even participated in political activities.

In the 19th century both Ḥasidism and Zionism became important influences on the Jewish community of Warsaw. In the 1880s the city became the center for Hebrew publishing in Poland and throughout Russia, specializing in daily and weekly newspapers and periodicals.

During World War I thousands of refugees arrived in Warsaw and by 1917 there were 343,400 Jews (41 percent of the population). The concentration of refugees and the havoc wrought by the war increased the economic distress, and yet Jewish spiritual development continued. Warsaw was the headquarters of Jewish parties and movements in Poland, and the center of Jewish cultural and educational activities. All of this ended in disaster, however, when the Germans entered the city on September 29, 1939. The German authorities issued a series of anti-Jewish measures including forced labor, the order that every Jew should wear a white armband with a blue star of David, the confiscation of Jewish real estate and other property, and a prohibition against Jews using the railways or other public transportation.

**The Warsaw Ghetto.** In April 1940, the Germans began constructing a wall to enclose the Warsaw ghetto. All the Jews of the region – four to five hundred thousand of them – were forced to live within that restricted area. The average number of persons per room was 13, while thousands remained without shelter at all. The ghetto population received a daily food allowance of 184 calories per person, while Poles received 634 and Germans 2,310 calories. The Jewish diet consisted of four pounds of bread and a half pound of sugar per month. The bread

The Warsaw Ghetto going up in flames, April, 1943.

dough was mixed with sawdust and potato peels. For their meager allotment the Jews were forced to pay 20 times as much as the Germans. Leaving the ghetto without permission was punishable by death, and from time to time the authorities rounded up able-bodied people in the streets and sent them to slave labor camps.

It is estimated that by the summer of 1942 over 100,000 Jews had died in the ghetto. Nevertheless the morale of the ghetto inhabitants was not broken, and continual efforts were made to circumvent the German decrees and organize relief. Illegal workshops were established for manufacturing goods to be smuggled out and sold. The smuggling of foodstuffs into the ghetto, carried out by Jewish children, was especially intensive. A network of schools and cultural programs operated in the ghetto, sometimes under the guise of soup kitchens, and by the end of 1940 Emanuel *Ringelblum had established a secret historical and literary society, under the code name of *Oneg Shabbat*, to set up secret archives containing the record of the life and martyrdom of the Polish Jews under the Nazis.

The Jews of Warsaw also organized an underground resistance movement and when the deportations to extermination camps began, they initiated an armed revolt. A few weapons were obtained from the Polish underground and others were made in secret workshops. A network of bunkers and underground communication channels (often through sewers) were constructed to assist in the fight against the superior German forces. For the story of the struggle of these brave fighters, led by Mordecai *Anielewicz, see the article *Ghetto.

Some Jews returned to Warsaw after the war and on April 19, 1948 (the fifth anniversary of the Warsaw Ghetto uprising) a monument designed by N. Rapaport in memory of the ghetto fighters was unveiled in the square called "The Ghetto Heroes' Square." In 1967-68 when the Polish government launched its official anti-Semitic campaign, Jewish institutions ceased to function until returning to free operation in the post-communist era from 1989 on. There are a few thousand Jews there, mostly aged.

1

2

1. A copper laver, or washing jug, used for the ritual washing of the hands. This laver bears the engraved date, 1661, but lavers of similar shape are still commonly used in many Orthodox homes even today.
2. An Italian marble "ablution niche" (with water tap and basin), dating from the 18th century, which is now located in the Italian Rite Synagogue in Jerusalem. Such niches were once found in many synagogues, and were used by the congregants to wash their hands before prayer and by the *kohanim* in particular prior to the ceremony of *birkat kohanim* ("the priestly blessing").

**WASHING THE HANDS**. The rabbis made it mandatory to perform a ceremonial washing of the hands on certain occasions. This washing is strictly ritual in nature and should not be confused with washing for the sake of cleanliness. This is evident from the fact that the hands must be clean before the ceremony is performed (see *Purity and Impurity, Ritual).

The hand-washing ritual is supposed to take place:

1. On rising from sleep;
2. After leaving the toilet;
3. After the paring of nails;
4. After touching one's shoes;
5. After the combing of hair or touching parts of the body that are usually covered;
6. After leaving a cemetery or participating in a funeral;
7. Before prayer and the recitation of the **Shema;*
8. Before eating bread;
9. Before reciting *Grace after Meals;
10. Before eating the parsley at the Passover *Seder*;
11. The Levites wash the hands of the *kohanim* before the Priestly Blessing (see *Priests and Levites).

In all these instances, the hands must be washed at least up to the third joint of the fingers. Nevertheless, the rabbis considered it preferable to wash up to the wrist. When washing before Grace, it is sufficient to wash only up to the second joint of the fingers. This particular washing is intended to remove any salt that adheres to the fingers which might cause damage to the eyes. A minimum of 1/4 *log* (approximately half a pint) of water is poured over the hands from a utensil with a wide mouth, the lip of which must be undamaged. The hands must be clean without anything adhering to them prior to the ritual washing, and no foreign object such as a ring may intervene between them and the water. Upon rising from sleep, each hand must be washed three times, but before partaking of bread, it is sufficient if they are washed once. It is customary to hold the cup in the left hand and wash the right one first, and then to reverse the procedure. A benediction is only recited after washing the hands upon rising and before eating bread. After rising, it is now recited as part of the preliminary *Shaḥarit* service, while before the meal it is recited prior to the drying of the hands. The benediction is *Barukh Attah . . . ve-ẓivanu al netilat yadayim.*

The handwashing ritual is commonly known as *netilat yadayim,* a term whose source is not entirely clear. In order to establish the practice, the rabbis warned of dire consequences for those who disregarded it, even going so far as to predict premature death. It is said that Rabbi *Akiva, who personally disapproved of the ordinance, nevertheless used the limited water allowed him in the Roman prison for this ritual rather than for drinking.

In modern times, as was mentioned, priests have their hands washed by the Levites before they perform the ceremony of the Priestly Blessing during public prayer services. The ceremonial laver has thus become the heraldic symbol for the Levites and often appears on their tombstones.

**WASHINGTON, GEORGE** (1732-1799). As the commander-in-chief of the American forces in the Revolutionary War, and first president of the United States, George Washington helped to form the young American nation and lead it to independence. History books are filled with stories of his victories against the English, and of the hard, gloomy winter of 1777-78 which his army spent at Valley Forge. Throughout this period, he was helped by prominent Jews in various fields.

Solomon Bush served under him as a captain of a Pennsylvania battalion in the Battle of Long Island. He later became a lieutenant-colonel, the highest rank held by a Jewish officer in the Revolutionary army. Philip Moses Russell served as a surgeon's mate with Virginia regiments from 1775-1778 and received a letter of commendation from General Washington. Washington's army could not have succeeded without the help of Robert Morris who imported army supplies and financed the battle at Yorktown, which ended in the surrender of the English. And the Franks family, a group of prominent Pennsylvania Jews, had much contact with the General. David Franks became secretary of a commission to the Creek Indians and in 1789 dined at Washington's table, while Isaac Franks rented his home in Germantown, Pennsylvania to the then President Washington in the fall of 1793.

Several Jewish congregations sent congratulatory letters to Washington when he was inaugurated as president. Moses *Seixas, president of the Hebrew congregation in *Newport, Rhode Island wrote in praise of the new government, "which to bigotry gives no sanction, to persecution no assistance . . . ." This phrase was later used by Washington himself, and his reply to the Hebrew congregation of Newport is a famous document of American Jewish history.

**WEAVING.** Even in ancient times when the Israelites were desert nomads, they engaged in the art of weaving to produce clothing, tents and accessories. At first they used coarse materials and simple looms, but gradually the artisans became more skilled and their tools more sophisticated.

During the biblical period the most common materials were wool (made from the coats of sheep) and linen (made from the stalks of a straw-like plant called flax). In each case the raw material had to be cleaned, spun into threads and then woven into cloth.

All ancient craftsmen wore special identifying badges and the sign of the weaver, common on the streets of Jerusalem, was a small weaving tool which he kept tucked behind his ear.

Even after their exile from Ereẓ Israel, Jews continued to follow the weaving profession. An ancient papyrus makes mention of a Jewish weaver in Upper Egypt in the second century b.c.e. Later, under Roman rule, a guild of Jewish weavers in Alexandria was registered according to Roman law as a corporation. And Pumbedita in Babylonia became a center for Jewish weavers of linen.

During talmudic times (first to fifth centuries c.e.), weaving became a popular Jewish craft, partly due to the biblical prohibition on *Sha'atnez* (mixing wool and linen; see *Mixed Species). This meant that religious Jews would trust only Jewish weavers and tailors to prepare their clothing, and thus the textile industry became an almost exclusively Jewish profession in many lands.

In the Middle Ages Jewish weavers were famous for the quality of their wool and linen. In Spain, weavers' guilds had their own synagogues. After the expulsion from Spain in 1492, Jewish weavers plied their trade in other parts of the world. In Russia Jewish weavers supplied cloth for the imperial army and in Czechoslovakia three of the first seven steam weaving factories were established by Jews. Similarly in Lodz, Poland, a celebrated textile center, 45.6 percent of the textile factories just before World War I were owned by Jews.

In modern times, with machines to do the actual

2

1

1. Moroccan Jewish women with a loom upon which carpets are woven.
2. A new immigrant to Israel (1956) learns the art of carpet weaving at a school in Or Akiva, a development town south of Haifa.

weaving, Jews have become more involved in the administrative aspects of cloth production. The textile industry is now one of the largest and most lucrative in the State of Israel. (See also *Crafts, *Silk, and *Tailoring.)

**WEIGHTS AND MEASURES.** From the earliest period of their history the Jews were alive to the necessity for an accurate system of weights and measures, and an honest handling of them. The use of false measures is denounced in several places in the Bible, which also contains legislation promoting economic honesty in general.

In very ancient periods,fixed measures and a system of weights were established for buying and selling, building, measuring areas and so on. Most of the first measures were natural or common physical attributes such as the palm of the hand, a day's journey, seeds of grain, and simple utensils. As time passed the measures were improved and made more precise,but they were still called by their ancient names.

The units of length mentioned in the Bible are derived from average measures of the length of human limbs. For example, *zeret* was the distance between the tip of the little finger *(zeret)* and the tip of the thumb with the fingers stretched apart. A handbreadth *(tefaḥ)* was the width of the four fingers. Other small measures included *kaneh* (reed), *ammah* (cubit), and *ezba* (fingerbreadth). Large measures were based on crude estimates such as the range of a bowshot, and greater distances by day's journeys. Among the instruments used for measuring small units of length mentioned in the Bible are *ḥut* (thread), *ḥevel* (rope), and *ḥevel middah* (measuring line).

1. Iron Age (12th century b.c.e.) basalt weight, with a relief of a winged lion and a Hebrew inscription.
2. The late Uriel Weinreich, for many years professor of Yiddish language and literature at Columbia University, and the author of the pioneering *Modern English-Yiddish, Yiddish-English Dictionary*

1

2

Volume was also initially measured by human limbs, e.g., *komez* (the amount that could be grasped by three fingers) and *ḥofen* (the contents of the entire palm of the hand). There are other measures mentioned, however, whose absolute values are difficult to determine, including *ephah, hin, omer,* and *log* (a liquid measure). The main area measure is *zemed* – the area which a pair *(zemed)* of oxen can plow in one day, but there was another system of measuring area which was based on the quantity of seeds sown in it.

In biblical times weights were for the most part made of stone, hence the Bible refers to weights generally as "stones" *(even).* The most important specific weights, however, were the talent, the shekel, and the *gerah.*

It is difficult today to estimate the exact values of any biblical weights and measures because by Second Temple times these had been abolished.

In talmudic times the rabbis introduced a series of "rule of thumb" measures, readily recognizable by all. Thus, for example, one was liable to be punished for eating (most) forbidden foods only after having consumed an amount equal to a medium-sized olive *(ke-zayit).* However, measures of length were still based on human limbs, bowshots, or a day's journey, while area was calculated by the amount of seed required to sow it. The basic unit of linear measure was the *ammah* (cubit) which was squared for measuring area.

Dishonest weights and measures are strongly censured in many places in the Talmud and in talmudic times the courts appointed market inspectors of weights and measures.

In modern Israel the metric system is used, while the basic unit of area measure is the *dunam* (1,000 square meters; one-quarter of an acre).

**WEINREICH, URIEL** (1925-1967), Yiddish and general linguist, editor, and teacher. The son of a Yiddish writer and linguist, Weinreich was born in Vilna and there received an excellent education. He went to the United States in 1940 and achieved immediate success as a linguist. Appointed professor of Yiddish language, literature and culture at Columbia University, New York, Weinreich was chairman of the university's department of linguistics (1957-65). He was an excellent teacher and several of his students became outstanding linguists. His books on languages, particularly Yiddish, became standard reference works and were reprinted many times. His research papers were written and published in five languages, every paper opening new paths in linguistics. Weinreich's main achievements were his *Modern English-Yiddish, Yiddish-English Dictionary* (1968), and his *Language and Culture Atlas of Ashkenazi Jewry,* a project designed to record and study Yiddish dialects.

**WEIZMAN, EZER** (1924– ), seventh president of the State of Israel, Israeli soldier and politician. Weizman was born in Tel Aviv. In 1942 he joined the RAF, trained as a fighter pilot, and then served in the Middle East and the Far East. A founder of the Israel Air Force in 1947, he was a fighter pilot in the *War of Independence. In 1949 he became commander of the first Israeli fighter squadron. As a major general, he was the Israel Air Force Commander 1958-66 and planned the strategy used in the *Six-Day War.

Retiring from the army in 1969, he entered politics. Defense minister from 1977, he played an active role in the peace process with Egypt at the Camp David talks. He left the government in 1980 over differences of opinion with Menaḥem Begin. After the 1984 elections, with his Yaḥad list gaining three seats, he joined the Alignment and was minister of science and technology, 1988–90. In 1992 he retired from the Knesset for personal reasons and was chosen president of Israel by the Knesset in 1993. He was the nephew of Chaim *Weizmann.

Ezer Weizman, seventh president of Israel.

**WEIZMANN, CHAIM** (1874-1952), first president of the State of Israel, president of the World Zionist Organization and distinguished scientist.

Weizmann was born in the village of Motol, near Pinsk in the Russian *Pale of Settlement, the third of 15 children. He received a traditional education and began to develop Zionist leanings at an early age. As it was difficult for Jews to obtain admittance to Russian universities, Weizmann left in 1892 to study biochemistry at a German university. There he joined a circle of Zionist intellectuals and soon came under the spell of the "cultural" Zionism of *Aḥad Ha-Am.

In 1896 Weizmann, in common with a great many other people, was electrified by the appearance of Theodor *Herzl and his revolutionary vision of an autonomous Jewish state (see *Zionism). Weizmann took a leading part in the Zionist movement initiated by Herzl, though differing from this great leader in his approach to Jewish nationalism. Herzl emphasized the political aspect, feeling that the main goal of the Jewish people should be the establishment of their own state, to be achieved only through diplomatic means. Weizmann, however, advocated the cultural approach, claiming that once Ereẓ Israel was provided with good schools, universities and cultural institutions, world leaders would be more inclined to grant the country statehood. So on the eve of the fifth Zionist Congress in Basle in 1901, Weizmann and his friends created the Democratic Faction within the Zionist movement, whose aim was to lessen the emphasis on the diplomatic approach.

In 1903 the Zionist movement was shaken by the introduction of the *Uganda Scheme, which proposed that the Jews settle in the East African Protectorate of Uganda rather than the disputed territory of Palestine. Weizmann was among the opponents of this plan, unwilling to agree to Zionism without Zion. By a quirk of fate this adamant stand gained him an introduction to British leader Arthur James *Balfour, who was later to play an important role in the establishment of the Jewish state. Balfour had been puzzled by the Zionist rejection of the Uganda plan and asked Weizmann to explain this step. Weizmann then asked Balfour whether, if he were offered Paris he would abandon London. Balfour answered, "No, London is the capital of my country." Weizmann replied, "Jerusalem was the capital of our country when London was a marsh."

The outbreak of World War I brought Weizmann from the margin to the center of Jewish history. He was now 40 years old, holding no executive position in the Zionist movement, but he saw the changes in international interests and power struggles as an opportunity to win political support for Zionist aims. So he found his way into political circles, winning the support of British statesmen such as Lloyd George and Herbert *Samuel. His scientific skills also helped him in this endeavor, and in 1916 he developed a chemical process for use in the production of munitions. This achievement brought him into contact with many influential members of the British government including Winston *Churchill.

The triumphant culmination of his efforts came in 1917 when Lloyd George and Lord Balfour finally agreed to an official statement of sympathy for Zionist aims being made, and the famous *Balfour Declaration was issued. The declaration was the turning point in modern Jewish history. Because of it Weizmann was thrust into the limelight and became recognized by Jews and non-Jews alike as the leading public figure in Jewish affairs. He was appointed head of the Zionist Commission and in 1918 was sent to Palestine by the British to advise on the future settlement and development of the country. In that year he also met with Emir Feisal, undisputed leader of Arab nationalism. Feisal gave Weizmann written pledges promising to recognize Zionist aims in Palestine if the Arabs were given independence in Syria and Iraq (then occupied by the British and French). Unfortunately Feisal was not given the concessions he required in the latter areas, and the Arab-Jewish alliance was therefore frustrated.

In 1919 Weizmann led the Zionist delegation to the Peace Conference at Versailles, and helped bring about the adoption of the British *Mandate for Palestine which was supposed to prepare the area for independent Jewish statehood.

In 1920 he was elected president of the Zionist

Chaim Weizmann

1

2

1. Meyer Weisgal, chief executive officer of the Weizmann Institute of Science for more than 20 years, and the man most directly responsible for the development of the institution into a world-famous research center.
2. Amos De-Shalit (1926–1969), Israel prize-winning physicist, who served as director-general of the Weizmann Institute of Science from 1966 to 1968.

organization but he was plagued by rifts within the organization. The British too were becoming increasingly cool to the Zionist cause and their attitude caused Weizmann to resign his Zionist office in 1930. Instead he worked to raise funds for Ereẓ Israel, to save Jewish refugees from Hitler's deadly grasp, and to establish a scientific institute in Ereẓ Israel – the Daniel Sieff Institute at *Reḥovot which later became the Weizmann Institute of Science.

In 1935 he resumed the presidency of the Zionist organization and two years later, appearing before the Royal Commission, delivered one of his most famous pleas for statehood for "six million people doomed to be pent up in places where they are not wanted and for whom the world is divided into places where they cannot live and places which they cannot enter."

Though his influence waned during and immediately after World War II, he made a last showing of diplomatic skill in 1947 when he appeared before the United Nations as spokesman for the Zionists. When the Jewish state was finally declared, Weizmann was the obvious choice for the presidency. Age and ill-health had now overtaken him and he could give little active service to the newly-born state. Weizmann died on November 9, 1952 and was buried in the garden of his home in Reḥovot. The area has since been designated as a national memorial and includes archives and a library devoted to his achievements.

**WEIZMANN INSTITUTE OF SCIENCE** is the foremost Israel scientific institution. It developed out of the Daniel Sieff Research Institute which was founded in Reḥovot in 1934. At that time there was a staff of ten scientists headed by Dr. Chaim Weizmann. When the Weizmann Institute of Science was formally established in 1949, it consisted of nine departments and had a scientific staff of 50. In 1990 there were over 400 full-time scientists working at the institute and 680 students, many who came from abroad. Today the institute has a score of research departments with scientists working on hundreds of different projects, such as cancer research, immunology, mathematics, nuclear physics, electronics and computer design and construction.

In 1967 the Institute built its second electronic computer which was fancifully called the Golem, after the medieval magical figure created out of clay, which was endowed with a life of its own. The Weizmann Institute's Golem is used by scientists in all departments of the Institute. In the applied mathematics department, for example, the electronic computer is used for the study of earthquakes and ocean tides.

As an adjunct to the Institute, the Yeda Research and Development Company was created to deal with the commercial offshoots of the scientific discoveries made over the years. Thus several new businesses have been started on the basis of discoveries in chemicals, electronics, pharmaceuticals and plastics. Several science-related industries have had factories built nearby. Science summer camps are held at the Institute for high school students from Israel and abroad.

The Weizmann Institute is housed on a spacious and trim campus, built and organized largely due to the ceaseless efforts of its chief executive officer (1947-77), Meyer Weisgal, Weizmann's aide for many years, who continued to build and beautify the Institute almost until his death in 1977. Chaim Weizmann and his wife as well as Meyer Weisgal are buried on the campus. The original of Weizmann's letters and writings, all of which have been published, are kept on the premises.

**WELLHAUSEN, JULIUS** (1844-1918), German orientalist and Bible critic who propounded a revolutionary theory about the origin and development of the biblical text and about the nature of the ancient Israelite religion from which it developed. The son of a Lutheran clergyman, Wellhausen at first studied theology and served as professor of theology at the University of Greifswald, but from 1882 onward, he devoted himself to biblical research and oriental studies, and served as professor of oriental studies at several German universities.

During the 19th century, great effort had been expended, particularly by German Protestant scholars, in the search for a critical, historical understanding of the biblical text; in several epoch-making studies, Wellhausen summed up the conclusions of the scholars who preceded him and based upon them a new, comprehensive view of the history of ancient Israel. By Wellhausen's time, scholars had generally come to agree that the Bible as we know it, was a composite, edited document, compiled from at least four separate literary sources that were at a later stage clumsily joined together. These sources were labeled in the scholarly literature as "J" (for "Jahwist"), "E" (for "Elohist"), "D" (for "Deuteronomy"), and "P" (for "Priestly Code"), and were deemed to be discernible from one another on the basis of differing usages of God's name, stylistic oddities and other literary features. Wellhausen's theory radically inverted the accepted order of dating these four sources. The Priestly Code, which until then had been thought to be the oldest of the four, he declared to be the latest, and he dated it from the period after the Babylonian Exile (i.e., sixth century b.c.e.). The implications of this dating, which Wellhausen fully explained in his book, *Prolegomena zur Geschichte Israels* (1882; English translation, 1885), were that major portions of the biblical text could no longer be taken as a source of information about the nature of the religion of ancient Israel; thus the laws found in Deuteronomy and the religious ideals they embodied were seen by him to reflect a much later stage in the development of the Israelite religion than the text itself proclaims, and were in fact the creation of the class of priests who lived in Ereẓ Israel in the centuries following the return from the Babylonian exile.

This theory of Wellhausen's gave powerful stimulus to furthering critical biblical scholarship, and in the first half of the 20th century, a whole generation of young scholars gave their attention to expanding, confirming and modifying many of the details of his view. In the last few decades, many aspects of Wellhausen's research which were once thought to be well-founded and confirmed, have proved to be unsound, but the "Documentary Hypothesis" and Wellhausen's view of the religion of ancient Israel still dominate biblical research at the present time.

**WESSELY, NAPHTALI HERZ** (1725-1805), Hebrew poet, linguist and biblical scholar. Born in Hamburg, Germany, Wessely began his literary career by writing translations of and commentaries on the Bible. He differed from other biblical scholars of his day in that he wrote in a lofty, biblical Hebrew, recreating the flavor and form of the ancient biblical style. His commentaries were highly praised by great contemporaries such as Moses *Mendelssohn and even the *Gaon of Vilna.

Wessely also applied this biblical form to his poetry. His major poetic work was *Shirei Tiferet* ("Poems of Glory") which is a long epic on the life of Moses and the Exodus from Egypt, filled with legends from the Talmud and Midrash.

In striving to revive biblical Hebrew, Wessely was faced with certain linguistic problems and this led him to write a number of books on the study of the Hebrew language. His pioneering work in this field laid the groundwork for future Hebrew writers and scholars.

Wessely was greatly influenced by the *Haskalah (Enlightenment) movement which called for a more worldly and modern view of Judaism. He firmly believed in the need for a general cultural education to augment Jewish religious studies. To support this view he wrote *Divrei Shalom ve-Emet,* in which he advocated that the Jewish community of Austria comply with the Edict of Tolerance issued by the Austrian emperor, by opening Jewish schools in which German and general subjects would be taught in addition to religious subjects. Wessely came to the conclusion that he who studies the Torah without acquiring common human knowledge will, when he grows up, become a burden upon society.

**WESTERN WALL** is that portion of the western supporting wall of the Temple Mount in Jerusalem which has remained intact since the destruction of the Second Temple (70 c.e.). As the only accessible remnant of all the Temple Mount structures, it became in the course of the generations, the most hallowed spot in Jewish religious consciousness and tradition.

Although in the first centuries after the destruction of the Temple the Western Wall was not a special place of Jewish worship, by the 16th century it had developed into a distinct center for the mourning over the destruction of the Temple and Israel's exile. As a result, it came to be known commonly as the "Wailing Wall." At the same time the Wall served as an enduring symbol of the hope for the restoration of the Temple and the ingathering of the exiles and, as such, the image of the Wall has been widely adopted in modern times as a popular motif in Jewish ceremonial and folkloristic art.

Over the centuries – and up until the city of Jerusalem was reunified following the *Six-Day War of June 1967 – access to the Wall for Jews was far

The narrow alleyway next to the Western Wall in Jerusalem, which served for several centuries as the only prayer area near the Wall which Jews were allowed to use. After the reunification of Jerusalem in June 1967, a massive, open plaza was cleared for the benefit of visitors and worshipers.

A recent *birkat kohanim* ceremony at the Western Wall in Jerusalem. Huddled under umbrellas for protection against the rain, many hundreds of people came to the Wall to receive the collective "priestly blessing" of several dozen *kohanim,* who can be seen standing next to the Wall covered by their white *tallitot.*

from convenient or secure. In the 12th century, the adjacent property was under the authority of Muslim religious leaders who made little effort to facilitate Jewish worship there. By the 14th century, the Wall had become so hemmed-in on its western side by a neighboring slum area that an alleyway no larger than 91 feet long and 10 feet wide was all that remained between the Wall and the surrounding buildings. In the 19th century Sir Moses *Montefiore tried to obtain permission for the placing of benches and tables for the reading of the Torah at the Wall, but the Muslim authorities refused to grant his request. Also in the latter part of the 19th century several attempts were made, by Baron Rothschild and others, to purchase the neighboring quarter,demolish the slums and provide easy access to the Wall, but all such efforts failed.

After the Balfour Declaration and the establishment of the British Mandate had won for the Jews the beginning of a recognized national status in Ereẓ Israel, the Western Wall began to take on new, national significance, and in consequence became a focus of the increasing Arab anti-Jewish belligerency. The Mufti proclaimed the Wall a sacred Muslim site, and in order to antagonize the Jews, ordered the opening of a gate at the southern end of the passageway, thus converting the area into a thoroughfare for passersby and animals. Other such acts of harassment occurred frequently, and in August 1929 a Muslim crowd rioted among the worshipers, destroying ritual objects and injuring many people. After the capitulation of the Jewish quarter of the Old City in May 1948, Jews were to be prevented for 19 years from even seeing the Wall, since the Jordanians refused to honor the ceasefire agreement which granted freedom of access to the holy places.

Since the *Six-Day War in 1967 and the liberation of Jerusalem, the Wall has become a central religious and national shrine. The entire area in front of the Wall has been leveled and converted into a large, open space with a recessed area near the Wall serving as the prayer area, and the full, open plaza as a meeting place for tens of thousands of people who gather there for important national, military and religious ceremonies. At the same time, the Wall itself has been partially excavated at its base and the buildings which stood alongside it removed. As a result, a much greater proportion of the original Wall can now be approached, and its full extent as an engineering marvel more readily appreciated. At the base rest seven layers of the earliest "Herodian" stones – huge blocks dating from the time of the Second Temple, some of which are 39 feet in length and weigh over 100 tons. Beneath them – underground – are another 19 layers of stone going down into the bedrock of the original valley. On top of these are four layers of smaller, plainer stones, of Roman or Byzantine origin (second to fourth centuries) while all the rest, making up a total height of some 72 feet, are even smaller and date from the Arab period or later. Most remarkably, the Wall was built without mortar, and yet has been strong enough to withstand the tremendous soil pressure of the earth behind it as well as the many earthquakes which occurred over the centuries. This extraordinary stability was attained through a combination of very precise cutting of the stones and an arrangement of the rows in a slightly terraced fashion, so that were the Wall to be viewed along its north-south axis, it would be seen to have a definite eastward slant, with each row of stones set back a few inches relative to the one beneath it.

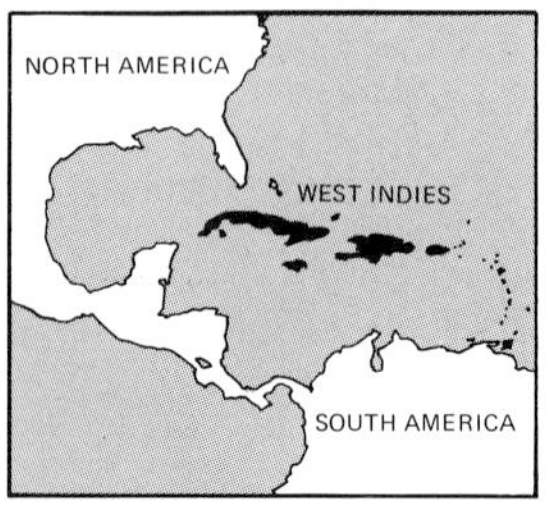


**WEST INDIES,** archipelago off Central America. The earliest Jewish settlement in the West Indies was in Curacao, Surinam, and Barbados, where Jews from Recife, *Brazil, settled in 1654. Communities were also established in the mid-17th century in Jamaica, Cuba, and Haiti. Most of these original communities declined, with new communities being established in many of these places in the 18th and 19th centuries. Puerto Rico and Trinidad were closed to Jewish settlement until 1898.

The modern Jewish communities in the West Indies began in the 1930s with the influx of immigrants from Europe. The Cuban community declined after the 1959 revolution because of the economic policies of the Castro regime which has not, however, been anti-Semitic. The significant West Indian Jewish settlements today are Puerto Rico (1,500), Cuba (700), and Jamaica (300). The development of resort facilities in Nassau and Freeport in the Bahamas led to the establishment of small communities in these places, but Bermuda never attracted Jewish settlers because of restrictive business laws.

**WHEAT**, the familiar grain which forms the basis of some of man's most essential foods including bread and cereals, is mentioned in the Bible as the first of the seven species with which the Land of Israel is

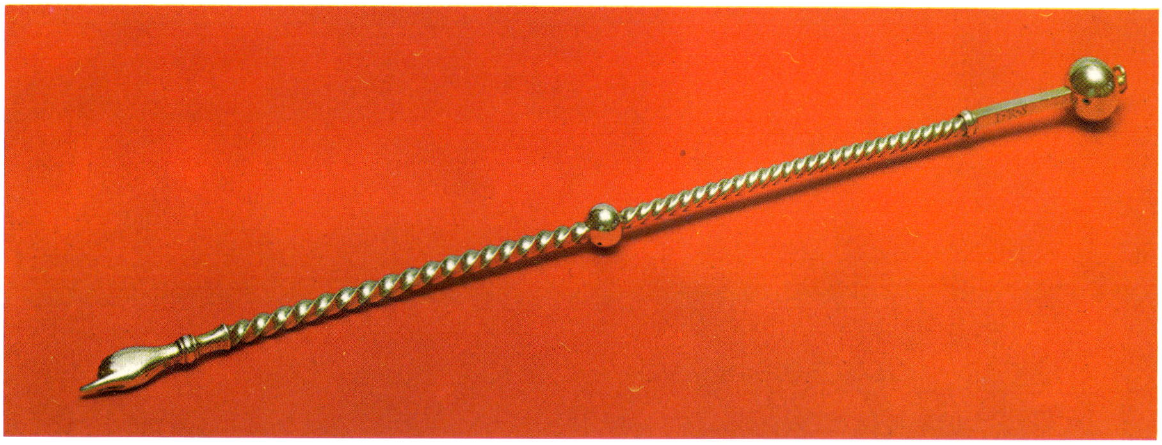

1

2

1. **Torah Ornaments.** To emphasize the sanctity of the Torah Scroll, the rabbis declared : "He who touches a naked *Sefer Torah* will be buried naked." As a result, the *yad* (pointer) is used when reading from the Torah. Pictured is a silver Torah pointer made by Abraham d'Oliveira for the Hambro Synagogue, London, about 1730.
2. **Torah Ornaments.** The Lubavicher *Rebbe,* Menaḥem Mendel Schneersohn, holds a Torah crown aloft, before placing it on the handles of the Torah scroll.

1

2

1. **Washing the Hands.** A laver and ewer used for the ritual washing of the hands, produced in France in 1768 and belonging originally to the New Synagogue of London.
2. **Synagogues.** The eastern wall of the Great Synagogue in Florence, Italy, completed in 1882. The elaborate decoration is Moorish in style.

blessed. It requires good and well-tilled soil, therefore an abundance of wheat symbolizes wellbeing and peace.

The Hebrew name given to the two species of wheat grown in Israel is *ḥittah*. It is planted at the beginning of the winter and ripens seven weeks after Passover. At this time each year, according to the Bible, the firstfruits of the *ḥittim* harvest were brought to the Temple as an offering to God.

Two other forms of wheat mentioned in the Scriptures are *kussemet* or *kusmin*, and a rare variety called *shippon*. Remnants of *kussemet* plants have been found in archaeological excavations in Israel and in Egyptian tombs. The grain is encased in a husk and to remove these husks, the wheat was moistened and then trodden by cattle, thereby releasing the grain. In 1906, an agricultural expert of Ereẓ Israel named Aaron Aaronsohn, caused a sensation in the botanical world by discovering this species of wheat still growing in modern-day Ereẓ Israel. He claimed that *kussemet* was the "mother" of all wheats, an opinion still upheld by some botanists. The general opinion, however, is that it is the forerunner of a particular variety of grain known today as *"emmer"* wheat.

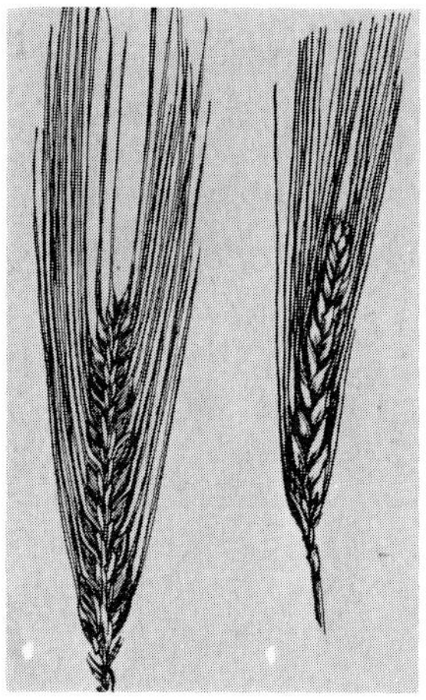

Two types of wheat grown in Ereẓ Israel: *ḥitah* (common wheat) and *kussemet* (rice wheat).

**WILLS.** When a person dies, everything he owned at the time of death passes, by way of inheritance, to his heirs. The law of inheritance specifying who the heirs are is explicitly stated in the Torah (for more details, see *Inheritance) and cannot be changed. This means that even if a person says, "I do not want my son, so-and-so, to inherit me," the stipulation is not valid and that son will still get his share in the inheritance as specified by law. However, a person can still control what happens to his belongings after his death by making a will which, in effect, means that he gives his property away as a gift with the result that there is nothing left for the heirs to inherit. Thus he can make a will dividing his belongings between all his sons except one. The dispossessed son is still an heir except that there is nothing for him to inherit. Through a will a person can give all or some of his property to somebody who is not in the line of inheritance or is not even related to him at all.

Different laws apply to wills according to the circumstances in which they were made. If a person wants to give away his property while he is healthy he can do so by drawing up a proper deed of gift with witnesses, giving the belongings to the recipient but reserving for himself the right to use that property until he dies. This is in fact a regular gift. But if he is dying, the very fact that he says (in the presence of witnesses) "I want so-and-so to get so much money or such a piece of property" is a valid will and the recipient gets the property after the giver dies. This was a special regulation made by the rabbis so that the dying man should not be disturbed by the fear that his desires may not be carried out. Should the dying man recover, the will is automatically revoked and if he wants to, he can dispose of his belongings in the regular manner. There are also certain circumstances in which a person who is not dying is considered, for the purpose of making a will, as though he is. These are: 1) if he is seriously ill even if not dying; 2) if he is about to be executed by the law of the land; 3) if he is about to embark on a long journey through the desert; or 4) by sea. This is because a man who disposes of his property in these circumstances is presumably doing so because of the chance that he might die.

Even if a will is invalid for some reason or other, it may still be recognized because the general law is that it is a *mitzvah* to carry out the wishes of the dead. However, throughout the ages some communities made special regulations limiting a person's ability to make a will in order to protect relatives who might very well become destitute.

**Ethical Wills.** The wills discussed above are means by which a person bequeaths his material belongings to another person. However there is also another kind of will by which a person passes on his moral, religious and ethical instructions. These are known as ethical wills and there are many examples of them throughout Jewish history. Some of them are indeed pearls of ethical literature. In the Middle Ages it was quite common for great rabbis or thinkers to leave a document – to be read after death – for their children in which they pointed out the correct way the children should live and even giving instructions with regard to specific ethical or religious behavior. The will of Judah he-Ḥasid, the leader of the *Ḥasidei Ashkenaz, for example, instructs his children and their offspring not to marry a woman who bears the same name as their mother. This rule was later followed by many people not in that family. The *Gaon of Vilna left a will for his children when he set out on a journey to Ereẓ Israel. He advised them not to set foot outside their homes unless absolutely necessary so as better to study Torah. He even suggested that they pray at home and not go to synagogue because the many people congregating there may prove distracting or inspire evil thoughts. In some families it became the custom for the head of each generation to leave an ethical will.

**WINE.** Although wine is drunk at many religious ceremonies, Jews have one of the lowest rates of alcoholism in the world. The same beverage that brought drunkenness and self-indulgence to other nations has been suffused with an aura of holiness, moderation, and gladness among the Jewish people and has formed an important part of their religious and social life for thousands of years. It was so favored that there are many references to it in the Bible: Wine "cheers God and man" (Judges 9:13), and is "for those that be of heavy hearts" (Proverbs 31:6). In the Book of Psalms, Israel is likened to a vine brought from Egypt and planted in the Holy Land that took root, sprouted, and prospered.

Although alcoholic drinks can be made from any fruit, including figs, dates, and pomegranates, fermented grape juice was singled out for a special blessing (*borei peri ha-gafen*). After the juice is collected and filtered, it is placed in a cool place until it ferments by action of the natural yeast in the fruit. The type of wine is determined by its age, the spices added, and the kind of grapes used.

Since wine was often used by gentiles for idol worship, Jews are forbidden to drink any unless they produce and process it themselves. Although few gentiles can be called pagans today, their wine is also prohibited to Jews in order to prevent socializing and intermarriage with them.

Because of these laws, the growing of grapes and the production and sale of wine have long been Jewish occupations. In the older settlements of Palestine, wine was pressed at home. Baron Edmond de Rothschild encouraged the growth of the wine industry and built cellars at Rishon le-Zion and Zikhron Ya'akov, and founded the Carmel Wine Growers' Cooperative in 1882. Today, Israel wine is exported throughout the world and is enjoyed by Jews and gentiles alike.

1

2

1. Woodcut from the *Prague Haggadah* (1526) of a man reciting the blessing over wine.
2. A Yemenite immigrant to Israel, working in a vineyard.

**WINGATE, CHARLES ORDE** (1903-1944), British army officer who, while serving in Palestine in 1936 to 1939, strongly supported the Jewish cause and trained Jewish soldiers, some of whom later became military leaders in the State of Israel. Wingate was born in India into a family of Christian missionaries. His Bible became his constant companion from early childhood.

In 1923 he joined the British army, and after being promoted to the rank of captain in 1936, he was sent to Palestine where he played a leading role in fighting the Arab terror campaign against the Jews. Having won the confidence of the Jewish settlers, he established contact with the *Haganah and trained its members in countering and preventing Arab attacks. The Jews expressed their appreciation of his support by calling him *"Ha-Yedid"* (The Friend). The British authorities, however, disapproved of Wingate's Zionist sympathies and unconventional military behavior, transferred him from Palestine in 1939 and forbade him to return. He was killed in Burma in World War II in a plane crash.

Although Wingate's dream of leading the army of the future Jewish state never came true, he remained devoted to the Jewish people and Ereẓ Israel until his tragic death. Israel, in turn, has not forgotten Wingate, and has named a forest, a College of Physical Education, and a children's village, Yemin Orde, after him.

During the Israel War of Independence, Wingate's widow arranged for his Bible, together with supplies, to be dropped into Yemin Orde, which was then under siege by Syrian troops. In it she wrote a dedication to the defenders of Yemin Orde: "Since Orde Wingate is with you in spirit, though he cannot lead you in the flesh, I send you the Bible he carried in all his campaigns . . . May it be a covenant between you and him, in triumph or defeat, now and always."

**WISDOM LITERATURE.** The term "wisdom" (Hebrew:*ḥokhmah*) has a wide range of meanings in different contexts, ranging from intelligence to an ethical and religious quality of life. As an historical phenomenon biblical wisdom designates a distinctive cultural tradition and scholarly activity in the history of ancient Israel, continuing in Judaism and early Christianity. It was a way of thinking and an attitude to life that emphasized experience, reasoning, morality, and the concerns of man as man rather than as Israelite. Wisdom, however, was not considered to be just intellectual ability or capacity; true wisdom had to be based on the fear of God and on a moral way of life.

The books of the Bible which fall into the category of Wisdom Literature are Proverbs, Job, and Ecclesiastes as well as several non-canonical works from pre-Christian Judaism. All these writings have in common the theme and practice of wisdom as a distinct way of life and thought, and employ certain favorite literary forms and a characteristic vocabulary.

Although the capacity to obtain wisdom might be considered a natural endowment, wisdom itself had to be learned, and could be taught. The two principal methods of teaching were *musar* (instruction or training) and *ezah* (counsel, or persuasion) according to whether the teacher's authority was imposed or freely sought. In general, the teacher's *musar* was an appeal to reason and conscience and to the pupil's own desire for knowledge and understanding. The wisdom was transmitted by a saying or proverb; a rhetorical question; a parable or allegory; and imaginative tales and anecdotes.

Despite this great emphasis on teaching and learning, however, wisdom ultimately remained a divine gift rewarding those who desired it enough to submit to its discipline.

**WISE, ISAAC MAYER** (1819-1900), U.S. rabbi and pioneer of *Reform Judaism. Born in Bohemia, he studied at various yeshivot and served for a short time as rabbi of a congregation there before moving to the United States in 1846. It was here that he began to introduce liberal reforms that were to change the face of American Judaism. As the rabbi of Congregation Beth El in Albany, New York, he was the first to have men and women sit together in the synagogue and participate jointly in choral singing and confirmations.

Wise's dream was to combine all American synagogues into one union, giving them a common prayerbook, common traditions, and a college in which to train rabbis who would follow a uniform religious policy. However,the divisiveness of the American Jewish community kept him from realizing his dream. The orthodox mistrusted him because of his liberal reforms, and the radical reformists such as Rabbi David *Einhorn, refused to join Wise because he advocated the observance of biblical and talmudic law, which they considered outmoded and irrelevant. He was reportedly ousted from his position in Albany in 1850, after which he formed his own synagogue, Anshe Emeth. In 1854 he went to Cincinnati as rabbi of Congregation B'nai Jeshurun, remaining there for the rest of his life.

Despite repeated setbacks, Wise did succeed in some of his endeavors. In 1856 he published *Minhag America,* a prayerbook for Reform congregations, and in 1873 a union of congregations in the south and west of the United States was formed, called the Union of American Hebrew Congregations.

His greatest pride, however, was the establishment by this union in 1875 of the *Hebrew Union College in Cincinnati for the training of Reform rabbis. Wise served as the first president of the college where he ordained more than 60 rabbis and was well-liked by his students. By the time of his death he had become known as the "founding father" of the Reform movement in America.

**WITTENBERG, IZHAK** (Itzig; 1907-1943). After the Nazis had murdered over 40,000 Vilna Jews, the survivors in the ghetto established a fighters' organization with Wittenberg as its commander. When he was captured by the S.S., his fellow fighters fired on them and succeeded in freeing him. The Nazis thereupon handed an ultimatum to Jacob Gens, the chief of the Jewish ghetto-police. He was ordered to turn Wittenberg over to them before 3.00 a.m., or they would destroy the ghetto and all its inhabitants. Two camps quickly emerged. The fighters insisted that under no circumstances was a man to be given over to the Nazis. Others argued that it was wrong to endanger the entire ghetto for the sake of one man. Time was running out, and the ultimatum very nearly brought the two sides to the point of fighting. But Wittenberg was not prepared to allow Jew to fight Jew while ignoring their real enemy. Full of confidence, he walked out into the deserted street, approached the ghetto gate, and turned himself over to the Germans. He was tortured to death.

**WOMAN**. In reaction to the modern Women's Liberation movement, many Jewish thinkers tended to take an apologetic stand in regard to the role of woman in Judaism. The gist of their argument was generally that woman is not inferior and that the role she plays is equal to that of the male. In action, this has been accepted to varying degrees among the various branches of Judaism, and now, among all but the Orthodox, woman are counted as part of a *minyan*, participate in public reading of the Torah, receive rabbinic ordination, and serve as cantor. There are also Orthodox women's prayer services.

Throughout the ages the woman has played many roles in Jewish life, and the attitude toward her has varied with changing conditions and circumstances.

Woman (Eve) was created primarily to serve man (Adam) as a helper, and throughout the Bible she is expected to be a good wife and mother. But in ages when many cultures regarded their women as mere chattels, the Jews did not disregard the girl's wishes

1

Isaac M. Wise

2

1. Isaac Mayer Wise, the "father" of Reform Judaism in the United States.
2. Izhak Wittenberg, first commander of the Jewish fighters' organization in the Vilna ghetto, who was brutally murdered by the Nazis.

Western Jewish women have been in the forefront of the struggle on behalf of Soviet Jewry. Shown in this photograph is a demonstration called by a London women's organization in May 1972, in indignant protest of the treatment accorded the Jewish "prisoners of conscience" in the jails of Russia. Many of these prisoners are subject to the harshest physical punishment merely for the "crime" of desiring to go to Israel.

when a marriage arrangement was made. Womanly traits, good and bad, were proverbial in the Bible. Foolishness, contentiousness and indiscretion were censured. On the other hand, graciousness, industry and generosity were lauded, particularly in the paean of praise to the woman in Proverbs, whose beginning is usually translated as "A woman of valor who shall find, and her worth is far above pearls."

The woman's legal status, as defined in the Bible, is generally the same as that of man, as is her moral responsibility but certain laws do discriminate both for and against her. For example, special attention was paid to injury suffered by a pregnant woman, and the conditions applicable to a woman sold into slavery were far better than those of a male slave. The owner was expected to marry her himself or have one of his sons marry her and he had to treat her as a daughter-in-law.

A variety of attitudes toward women are found in rabbinic literature, affected by different cultures and social backgrounds, by the special conditions which obtained in the particular age, and by the personal experiences and temperaments of the Jewish scholars who were almost exclusively men.

The wording of the benediction recited each day in which a man praises God for not having made him a woman has been the subject of much apologetic writing, the general consensus being that it is clear from the context that the thanks are for the greater opportunity a man has for carrying out the *mitzvot,* women being exempt from those positive precepts whose performance depends on a set time of the day or year. Nevertheless, a 20th-century scholar has written: "No amount of modern Jewish apologetic, endlessly poured forth, can alter the fact that the rabbinic attitude towards women was very different from our own. No amount of apologetic can get over the implications of the daily blessing which Orthodox Judaism has still lacked the courage to remove from its official prayerbook, 'Blessed art thou, O Lord our God, who has not made me a woman.' At the same time it must be readily admitted that the rabbis seemed to have loved their wives and they all, apparently, had only one wife each, and that the position of the wife was one of much influence and importance." That the rabbis themselves did not practice polygamy is a fairly well-established fact and while polygamy was legally sanctioned in biblical law and in rabbinic times, it has been convincingly argued that it was rarely practiced by Jews.

It is said that a man without a wife lives without joy, blessing and good, and that a man should love his wife as himself and respect her more than himself. Women have greater faith than men and greater powers of discernment. The Torah, the greatest joy of the rabbis, is frequently pictured as a woman and is represented as God's daughter and Israel's bride.

Nevertheless, the rabbis ascribed many negative characteristics to women. They were accused of being greedy, eavesdroppers, lazy, jealous, querulous, light-minded, and unreliable. The worst fault ascribed to women is summed up in the saying: "Ten measures of speech descended to the world; women took nine."

In the Middle Ages, thinkers like *Maimonides endorsed rabbinic teachings on man's duty to care adequately for his wife and generally treat women with kindness and compassion, but Maimonides also ruled that if a wife refused to carry out such wifely duties as washing her husband's hands and feet, or serving him at table, she is to be chastised with rods. He was possibly influenced in this ruling by contemporary Muslim practice.

In modern times the *Haskalah movement in Russia and the Reform movement sought to improve the position of the Jewish woman, particularly in the area of legal disabilities.

In modern Israel, the Declaration of Independence ensures complete equality of political and social rights to all its inhabitants, regardless of religion, race, or sex, but the real Magna Carta of the Israeli woman was the Women's Equal Rights Law of 1951, giving women equal legal status with men. The only field of law in which there remains a degree of discrimination against women is that of personal status. Matters of marriage and divorce come within the exclusive jurisdiction of the religious courts and thus, for example, a divorce must be given by the husband to the wife. On the other hand, in accordance with the *halakhah,* children take the national identity of their mother and not that of their father.

**WORLD JEWISH CONGRESS** (WJC), an association of major Jewish organizations from more than 80 countries, whose aim is to "assure the survival and to foster the unity of the Jewish people."

Edgar Bronfman was president of the World Jewish Congress from 1981.

The first World Jewish Congress was convened in Geneva, Switzerland in 1936, under the leadership of Stephen Wise and Nahum *Goldmann. The 280 delegates immediately became actively involved in one of the most tragic periods in Jewish history – that of the Holocaust – by organizing rescue attempts and relief and rehabilitation programs. The WJC played a central role in the creation of Jewish policies with regard to the peace treaties, the trial and prosecution of Nazi war criminals, reparations for war victims, and the rehabilitation of Jewish life in the years after the war.

The activities of the World Jewish Congress included working on behalf of threatened Jewish communities such as those in Arab and communist countries; representing the Jewish world community in international organizations such as the United Nations, promoting inter-religious cooperation, and preserving Jewish identity in the face of the increasing trend towards assimilation by promoting

The six main branches of the WJC are in North America, South America, Europe, Israel, Asia-Pacific, and Euro-Asia (the former Soviet Union). A research branch, the Institute of Jewish Affairs, is presently located in London.

**WORMS,** city in west Germany and an important center of Jewish learning in the 11th century. Among its most famous inhabitants was *Rashi.

During this period Worms became a flourishing Jewish center; a synagogue was inaugurated in 1034 and a cemetery established in 1077. The latter has been preserved and is the oldest Jewish cemetery in Europe.

The Jewish merchants of Worms apparently played an important role in German commerce and in 1090 were granted a special charter of privileges by the king. Their economic and social wellbeing went hand-in-hand with cultural development and the reputation of the "Sages of Worms" spread throughout Europe.

This flourishing period was interrupted by the

Drawing of the exterior and interior of "Rashi's Chapel" in Worms, Germany. The building dates back to the High Middle Ages, and it is believed that Rashi himself studied and prayed there in the 11th century.

persecutions of the First Crusade in May 1096, in which over 800 Jews from Worms were killed and the rest forced to flee or convert. But the community was reestablished a few years later and again became a successful and important center for European Jewry.

The second disaster to befall Worms struck in 1349 at the time of the *Black Death, when anti-Jewish violence broke out. The survivors fixed the anniversary of that massacre – 10th of Adar – as a perpetual fast day for the Jews of Worms.

Subsequent misfortunes took their toll and by the 18th century Worms no longer ranked among the important communities of Germany, even though it was still renowned and still adhered to its ancient customs. During the 19th century there were about 800 Jews living in the city; they were granted civic rights, and in 1848 a Jew was elected mayor of Worms.

The Nazis succeeded in destroying most of the Jewish community. After the war some Jews again settled there but an official community was not reorganized. In 1961 the German authorities rebuilt the 11th-century synagogue and *bet midrash* which were demolished during the war.

**WORMSER, SECKEL** (Isaac Loeb; 1768-1847), talmudist and kabbalist, born in Michelstadt, Germany. He received his talmudic education in Frankfort on the Main, in the yeshivah of Nathan Adler and followed in his footsteps, accepting a rigorously ascetic ḥasidic way of life and turning to kabbalistic studies. After his first marriage he returned to Michelstadt in about 1790, where he maintained a yeshivah for many years and served (at first unofficially) until 1822 as a recognized district rabbi.

For years, his ḥasidic behavior and stringent vegetarianism created considerable tension between him and the majority of his small community, but his reputation as a master of occult powers spread rapidly and Wormser became known throughout Germany as the "Ba'al Shem of Michelstadt." He denied any such supernatural power but agreed to receive people who sought his advice and guidance, giving them natural remedies and sometimes amulets. He became particularly known for his treatment of lunatics. Among the Jews of southern Germany many traditions survived regarding his miraculous cures and other feats. In 1825 his house and large library were destroyed by fire. Of his talmudic writings which were preserved by his descendants, almost nothing was published.

**WOUK, HERMAN** (1915- ), United States novelist and playwright made famous by his best-seller and Pulitzer Prize-winning novel, *The Caine Mutiny.* Born in New York City to Russian Jewish immigrant parents, Wouk worked for six years as a radio writer. He served in the United States Navy during World War II and used his wartime experiences as background material for *The Caine Mutiny* (1951), which sold three million copies, was adapted into a successful Broadway play, and was later made into a motion picture. Wouk's other novels include *The City Boy* (1948), *Marjorie Morningstar* (1955), *Don't Stop the Carnival* (1965), and more recently, *The Winds of War.*

Besides writing, Wouk also teaches English at Yeshiva University in New York. He is an Orthodox Jew who wrote about his belief in traditional Judaism in the best-seller *This is my God* (1959; translated into Hebrew in 1974). He was vice-president of the Fifth Avenue synagogue in New York and is very active for Jewish educational institutions in the United States and Israel.

**WRITING.** The ancient Near East was the scene of the earliest attempts at writing. This was where the first scripts were developed in about 3000 b.c.e., and Ereẓ Canaan in particular (later to become Ereẓ Israel) produced several writing systems. Those primitive men, making their marks over 5,000 years ago were certainly not aware that this invention called writing would, in fact, be a revolutionary influence in the world.

Early written communication consisted of drawing pictures which told a story. It took a long time to develop standardized pictures symbolizing specific subjects (the transition from representative to symbolic writing being a very important one), then to devise an "alphabet" by which individual sounds rather than subjects could be represented, and finally to combine the sounds to form words. The alphabet enabled man to communicate abstract thoughts which could never have been drawn in pictures.

The Canaanites invented the first alphabet and this Proto-Canaanite pictograph-like alphabet was used between the 17th and 12th centuries b.c.e. Another type of alphabet in use around 1500 b.c.e. was Proto-Sinaitic, which probably originated in the colonies established in the Sinai area.

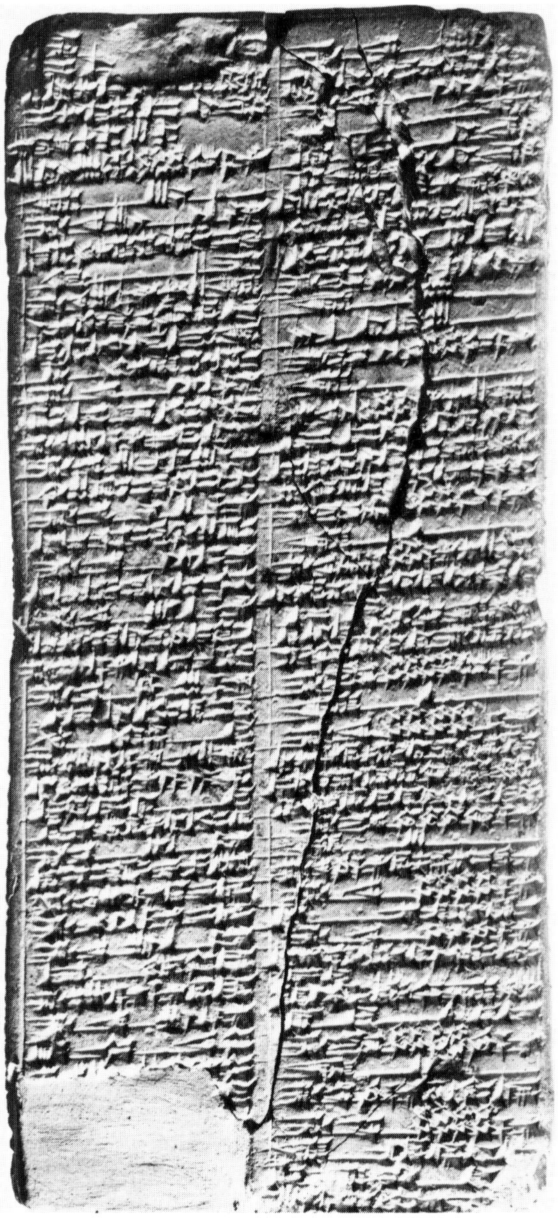

Part of the Sumerian King List, a chronological record dating from the second millennium b.c.e., written in cuneiform, the world's oldest written language. The use of cuneiform began around 3000 b.c.e., and it developed from a crude, pictographic script (in which the signs represented simple ideas) used for ordinary administrative memoranda, to become a thousand years later a flexible, phonetic system of syllabic notation which was adaptable to every kind of writing.

Eventually these picture-like symbols were refined into wedge-shaped characters called "cuneiform" and then in 1100 b.c.e. the 22-letter Phoenician script emerged. This alphabet was to be adopted by the Israelites, the Arameans and later by the Greeks.

Writing had a profound effect on Judaism. The covenant between God and the Chosen People was transformed into a written text; the central religious object became the Ten Commandments, inscribed on stone; and later the Torah scroll was to be revered. The biblical society as a whole became "book centered." In contrast to many other societies, the Israelites did not limit the acquisition of the arts of reading and writing to the nobility – any tribesman, even a non-priest, could become a literate leader. Certainly by King Hezekiah's time (eighth century b.c.e.), a great deal of literary activity was taking place. The classical prophets or their disciples wrote down their messages and many inscriptions have been found dating to the First Temple period.

**Writing Surfaces and Tools.** The earliest known writing surface is stone. Besides the Ten Commandments, some of the most important Israelite stone inscriptions date from the time of the kings and include treaties and descriptions of the monarch's victories in battle. Perhaps the most famous Hebrew inscription on stone is the Gezer Calendar. Thought to be from the tenth century b.c.e., this is the earliest Hebrew inscription found to date and cites an annual cycle of agricultural activities.

*Papyrus, a paper-like material made from a swamp plant, was used from about the third millennium b.c.e. By the fifth century b.c.e. papyrus had become the standard writing material for most of the ancient Mediterranean world and was to remain in use until replaced by true paper brought from China between the seventh and tenth centuries c.e. Of particular Jewish interest are the *Elephantine papyri (late fifth century b.c.e.) which include official letters and private papers concerning life in that period. Some of the Dead Sea Scrolls were also written on this material.

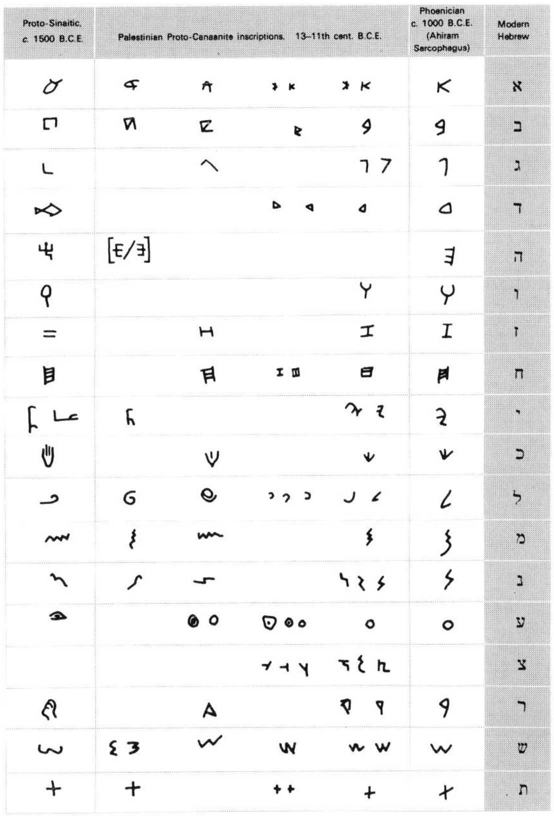


Chart showing the relationship between modern-day Hebrew script and several ancient, cognate Near Eastern forms of writing.

Other writing surfaces include animal hides (parchment), pottery, metals, ivory, wood, and wax. Writing tools include a chisel for stone or metal, stylus for clay or wax, and a brush for placing ink on papyrus. Black ink was made from carbon or a metal base while red ink was obtained from the red ocher plant.

**Writing and Jewish Law.** The talmudic sages attached tremendous importance to the art of writing. There are several important laws regarding the manner in which the *scribes should write the *Torah scroll, the **tefillin* and **mezuzot*. The sages differentiated between permanent writing (that which could not be erased) and non-permanent. The prohibition against writing on Sabbath is applied to permanent writing materials.

**XANTEN,** town in West Germany. The first documentary evidence of the presence of Jews in Xanten dates from the period of the First Crusade (see *Crusades) when Jews from *Cologne sought refuge there. On June 27, 1096, the Crusaders reached Xanten as well, and some 60 Jews were either killed or committed suicide.

The non-Jewish community remained basically anti-Semitic and records show that the market day in the 13th century was held on the Sabbath so that the Jews would not be able to participate. Many therefore turned to moneylending as a source of income. The community suffered badly during the *Black Death persecutions of 1349 when they were blamed for the fatal epidemic.

In the 17th and 18th centuries there were apparently only small numbers of Jews in Xanten. From 1690 Xanten was the meeting place for the Rhenish Jewish Diet (assembly of Jewish leaders from communities around the Rhine River), and in 1787 a special building which also contained a synagogue, was set aside for the assembly's meetings. By 1860 the Jewish community, numbering only about 80 persons, had its own elementary school.

In 1892 a butcher named Adolf Buschoff of Xanten was the victim of a *blood libel. Accused by a Catholic of murdering a Christian boy, Buschoff was arrested but then acquitted for lack of evidence. He was later re-arrested after an anti-Semitic campaign, but at his trial the jury found him not guilty (1892). The community, however, did not survive this agitation and gradually decreased to 30 persons (9.6 percent of the population) in 1916, and to 14 in 1930. The synagogue was destroyed by the Nazis in November 1938.

**XIMENES** (Jimenes) **DE CISNEROS, FRANCISCO** (originally, Gonzales; 1436-1517), Spanish churchman and ruler of Castile from 1516 to 1517. On the one hand Ximenes was active in the Inquisition and had 2,500 converted Jews burned at the stake for not maintaining their Christianity. Yet, on the other hand, he campaigned against dishonest and immoral Inquisitors. He founded a university in 1500 where, unlike other Spanish universities, Jewish converts to Christianity were admitted as students. He also encouraged the production of the first Bible to appear with parallel Hebrew, Greek, Latin and Aramaic texts, with a Hebrew glossary added at the end. This Bible, called the *Complutensian Polyglot,* appeared in six volumes. Most of the Hebrew codices used to compile this Bible, however, were later destroyed (they were apparently sold as waste to a fireworks manufacturer) and only four have survived.

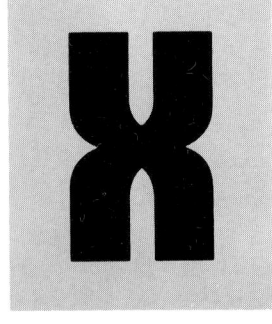

**YADIN, YIGAEL** (1917–1984), Israel archaeologist and second chief of staff of the Israel Defense Forces. He was born in Jerusalem, the son of the archaeologist Eliezer Lipa *Sukenik.

When 16 years of age, Yadin joined the Haganah, Israel's pre-State defense force. As its operations and planning officer, he was responsible for drawing up and directing the operations of the War of Independence (1948). In 1949 he was appointed chief of staff, and in three years established the standing army, compulsory military service, and particularly the system of reserves.

From 1952 Yadin devoted himself to archaeology, in 1956 receiving the Israel Prize for Jewish Studies for his research on one of the Dead Sea Scrolls. In his excavations at Hazor, a large Canaanite and Israelite city in Upper Galilee, he uncovered and explained, layer after layer, 21 levels of occupation, starting with the 27th century b.c.e., and including fortified cities mentioned in the Bible, an Assyrian citadel, and pagan temples. He decoded scrolls found in the caves of the Judean Desert, and at Masada threw new light on the second-century Bar Kokhba revolt against the Romans. He also found the rebels' *tefillin* intact and described them.

Yadin headed the Hebrew University's Institute of Archaeology from 1970 until 1977 when elected to the Knesset as representative of his newly-formed Democratic Movement for Change. He served as a deputy prime minister for the Ninth Knesset and left politics, returning to academic life, in 1981.

**YAD MORDEKHAI**, kibbutz in southern Israel, founded in 1943 by a group of refugees from Poland and named after Warsaw ghetto fighter Mordecai *Anielewicz.

Yad Mordekhai was established in an effort to spread Jewish settlement in Ereẓ Israel to the southern Negev region. But its precarious position as a lone Jewish settlement at the edge of the Gaza strip led to its being attacked by the invading Egyptian army in May, 1948, during the War of Independence. The masses of Egyptian tanks and troops were held back by a handful of Jewish settlers for six days, after which the kibbutz was overrun by the invaders. The settlement was reduced to ruins and the survivors, carrying their wounded, succeeded in slipping through the surrounding Arab lines and reaching Jewish positions miles away.

The site was retaken by the Israelis in October 1948, and the kibbutz rebuilt on a far larger scale.

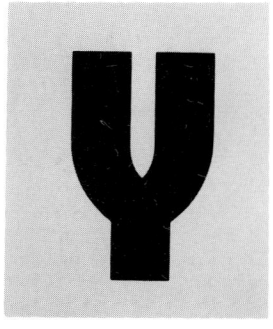

Yigael Yadin (extreme left), distinguished Israel military leader and archaeologist, shown together with the other members of the Inquiry Commission appointed by the Israel government to evaluate the actions and errors of the Israel Defense Forces during the initial days of the Yom Kippur War (October 1973). Besides Yadin, the other members of the Commission were (left to right): Supreme Court Justice Moshe Landau, Supreme Court Chief Justice Shimon Agranat, State Comptroler Yiẓhak Nebenzahl, and the former Chief of Staff of the Israel Defense Forces, Ḥayyim Laskov.

Kibbutz members have since erected two reminders of their past experiences: one, a museum of the Holocaust and ghetto resistance, and the other a lifelike outdoor reconstruction of the 1948 battle against the Arabs. Both have become popular tourist attractions.

**YAD VASHEM.** It is natural for someone who has endured a terrible disaster to want to bury his painful memories along with the dead and forget the past. But the Jews, being only a tiny minority in the world and having a long history of persecution, cannot afford to forget that *Nazism brutally murdered six million of their people. Thus in 1953 the Knesset, Israel's parliament, established Yad Vashem, the Martyrs' and Heroes' Remembrance Authority, to perpetuate their memory.

Situated on the windswept Hill of Remembrance and rising above the rugged beauty of the Jerusalem Forest, Yad Vashem is a visible reminder of the agony that *Hitler brought to the Jewish people between 1933 and 1945. Its most impressive structure is the Hall of Remembrance, a stark rectangular building of roughly-cut boulders, on whose somber gray floor are inscribed the names of the 21 largest Nazi death camps. Near an eternal light, shaped like a shattered bronze cup, is a vault containing ashes of the martyrs.

The compound also includes a synagogue, a Hall of Names of victims, a museum exhibiting the methods of persecution and the Jewish struggle against them, a 70-foot Pillar of Heroism, and a tree-lined path leading to the site in memory of the *Righteous Gentiles who risked their lives to save Jews. Ceremonies are held annually in the stone-studded plaza connecting the buildings, and throughout the State of Israel, on the 27th day of Nisan, Holocaust Memorial Day.

Two of Yad Vashem's most important tasks are

Austrian Chancellor, Dr. Bruno Kreisky (center), and the aides who accompanied him on a visit to Israel in March 1974, participating in a memorial service to the victims of the Holocaust, at Yad Vashem in Jerusalem. They are standing before the memorial flame which burns inside the Hall of Remembrance.

research and documentation. It has collected thousands of books and periodicals on the *Holocaust period and published several dozen volumes of its own. In addition, one department keeps in constant touch with legal bodies abroad and aids in bringing Nazi war criminals to trial.

**YANNAI,** one of the earliest poets to compose verses for inclusion in the prayer service *(piyyutim).* There is no exact information about the period in which Yannai lived, though many believe he was a sixth or seventh century Palestinian. He is first mentioned in a tenth-century text as a composer of Hebrew hymns and an authority on religious law. In other sources he is often referred to together with the poet Eleazar *Kallir, who apparently lived during the same period and may have been Yannai's pupil. According to one legend, Yannai's poems were not recited in Italy because he was considered to have killed Kallir by placing a scorpion in his sandal.

Yannai's works were rediscovered only in the 20th century with the finding and publication of the Cairo **Genizah* fragments. Among these ancient documents are several poems attributed to Yannai, including special poems for the Sabbath based on the *Amidah service, some hymns, and songs from the Passover *Haggadah.* He also wrote a book on religious law, called *Ḥazzarah,* which later scholars apparently relied upon for legal decisions.

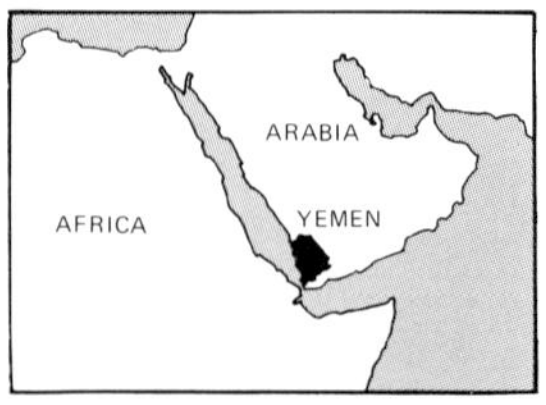


**YANNAI, ALEXANDER** (c. 126-76 b.c.e.), Hasmonean king of Judea and high priest from 103 b.c.e. until his death (see *Hasmoneans).

Yannai's brother *Aristobulus, who preceded him on the throne, apparently hated Yannai and had him imprisoned. As soon as Aristobulus died, however, Queen *Salome Alexandra released her brother-in-law and married him, thus making Yannai king and high priest of Judea.

As ruler, Yannai engaged in numerous battles with neighboring countries, conquering large portions of territory, thus annexing the entire coastal area from Mount Carmel in the north down to the Egyptian border, and territories east of the Jordan River. He was supported in these campaigns by *Cleopatra, queen of Egypt.

But this new empire was threatened by internal strife. The growing Pharisaic religious leadership (see *Pharisees and Sadducees ) objected to Yannai's assumption of the high-priesthood and rebelled against his rule and, in a civil war which lasted for six years, no less than 50,000 Jews perished in battle. The resulting weakened condition of the Jews also invited attacks from outside enemies, specifically the *Nabateans.

Nevertheless, Yannai managed to settle the internal problems and continued to expand Judean borders until the kingdom reached the largest size ever in Hasmonean times. Yannai's health, however, had been deteriorating for some years (due to heavy drinking, according to the Roman historian *Josephus) and he met his death during a battle in 76 b.c.e.

He was survived by two sons — Hyrcanus and Aristobulus — and his wife Salome, who succeeded him on the throne. Interestingly, he seems to have ironed out the differences with the Pharisees before his death and they provided him with an elaborate funeral in Jerusalem. Salome ruled for some nine years during which the country enjoyed peace and prosperity, but after her death, her two sons competed for the throne. This quarrel ultimately led to the Roman occupation of Ereẓ Israel.

**YEMEN,** country in the southwestern area of the Arabian Peninsula. Its Jewish population, though poverty-stricken and persecuted, managed more than any other Jewish community in the world to preserve the ancient customs and lifestyle of their forefathers.

According to their own traditions, the Jews of Yemen first came there after the destruction of the First Temple in 586 b.c.e. They refused to heed Ezra's call to return to Ereẓ Israel and they ascribed their sufferings to that refusal. There is no documentary or other evidence of this early settlement but it can be assumed that Jews started to live in Yemen during the period of the Second

Temple as a result of business connections between the Jews of Babylonia and Persia and between the Arabian Peninsula. Some of these merchants apparently established permanent settlements in the area, and were probably later joined by Jewish soldiers sent by Rome in 25 b.c.e. to conquer South Arabia.

As the Jewish community grew in size and strength, outsiders were drawn into its midst. There is evidence that some members of Arabian tribes converted to Judaism, the most famous case being that of Dhu Nuwas, the Himyarite king who embraced Judaism in the sixth century c.e.

In the ninth century one of the Muslim Shi'a sects known as Zaydis, conquered Yemen and ruled, with interruptions and within varying borders, until modern times. At first the Jews lived in peace under their Muslim rulers and maintained strong ties with the Jewish scholarly academies in Iraq and Egypt, but by the 12th century Muslim persecution of the Jews began. In their desperation the Jews of Yemen turned to false messiahs for salvation, and when these failed them, they appealed to the greatest scholar of the age, *Maimonides, for guidance. Maimonides' written reply to the community, called *Epistle to Yemen*, helped to bolster their spirits and renew their faith. He became a hero to Yemenite Jews and his books were revered by them for generations. His name was included in one of the *Kaddish* prayers which is still recited by Yemenite Jews today.

The invasion of the Ottoman Turks in the 16th century brought renewed disaster for the Jews who were caught between the battling Turks and Zaydis. As the only non-Muslim religious minority, they were at the bottom of the social order and were constantly subjected to discriminatory measures. In 1676 they were expelled for one year to the disease-infested area of Mawza on the southern shore of the Red Sea. Though they were subsequently allowed to return, they never achieved equal status. Even in the 19th and 20th centuries Jews were still considered as serfs. Jewish testimony against a Muslim was not accepted in the Muslim courts, and every Jew therefore had to pay a Muslim patron, called a *sayyid*, to represent him. Most of the Jews were craftsmen and the richest and most honored of the community were the silversmiths. As Islam does not allow its believers to work in gold or silver, this became the exclusive domain of the Jews. There were also those engaged in weaving, smithery and carpentry. Those living in the townlets and villages were peddlers who would wander with their packs of hardware, fancy goods and haberdashery, returning to their homes only for the Sabbath and festivals.

In 1846 the degrading duty of cleaning all sewers in the town was given to the Jewish community in the capital city of San'a. The order remained in force until 1950 and the Jewish community had to pay a ransom to allow these sanitation workers to emigrate. The Jews were forbidden to wear bright clothes or stockings; bear arms; engage in the same occupations as Muslims; use saddles; study the Torah outside the synagogue; recite prayers in a loud voice; blow the *shofar* loudly; and lend money for interest. They were also obliged to honor the Muslims and to walk on their left side. One of the most severe laws was that issued in 1921, according to which all orphans who were minors had to convert to Islam. The Jews did everything they could to rescue the orphans by adoption into families or by smuggling them over the border to Aden and from there to Ereẓ Israel.

The struggle for survival finally led many Yemenite Jews to seek refuge in Israel. The first large groups arrived in Erez Israel in 1882. In 1948 the Jews of Yemen saw the establishment of the State of Israel as the work of God and almost all those remaining decided to emigrate there. The emigrants went en masse to the British colony of Aden where they lived in a transit camp. The camp could only hold about 1,000 people at a time. The Israeli government arranged for all of them to be flown to Israel. The transfer, called "Operation Magic Carpet," which lasted until 1950, was a miraculous event for these naive Jews, many of whom had never seen an airplane before. About 2,000 more emigrated after this, leaving only a few hundred Jews still in Yemen. In 1992/93 many more left the country.

The economic and cultural adjustment of these immigrants was not easy. They were suddenly uprooted from a medieval way of life and thrust into the 20th century. The older generation clung to their ancient ways of dress, speech and traditions. The rich

2
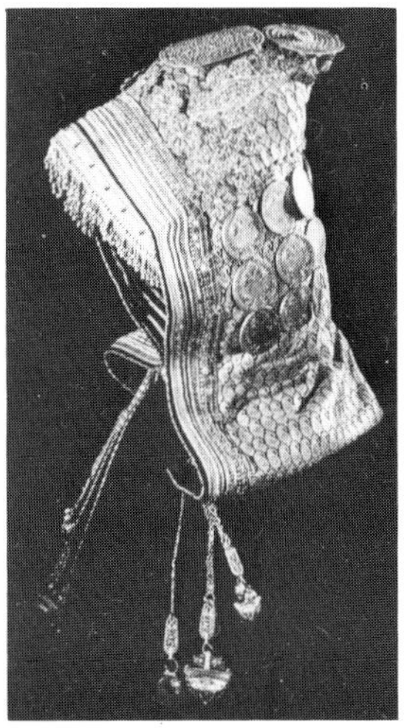

1

1. A newly-married Yemenite couple, dressed in traditional costume, are regaled and entertained by friends and relatives at a celebration following the wedding.
2. Yemenite jewelry is considered to be among the finest in the world. Shown is a *gargush* (hood worn by Yemenite women on festive occasions) from the late 19th century, made of brocade and heavily decorated with gold coins, silver and gold beads, and with pendants and filigree ornaments.

Yemenite culture thus preserved fascinated Jewish researchers. Ancient rituals which had long disappeared from other Jewish communities were still performed among the Yemenites because, for centuries, they had been isolated in Arabia far from any outside influences. Yemenite craftsmanship, folklore, music and dance have taken a special place in Israeli life. The work of Yemenite writers such as the 16th century commentator Rabbi Solomon Adani and the poet Shalem *Shabazi also contributed greatly to the wealth of Jewish culture, as did the numerous Jewish manuscripts preserved for centuries by this tradition-conscious group.

**YESHIVAH**, an institute of talmudic learning. The earliest yeshivot were the scholarly academies in Ereẓ Israel and Babylonia where the Jerusalem and Babylonian *Talmud respectively originated. After the sixth century the centers of talmudic study were transferred to the academies of Sura and Pumbedita in Babylonia, whose heads were known as *geonim* (see *Gaon).

But the local yeshivot as we know them today only began developing outside of Babylonia and Ereẓ Israel in the eighth century c.e., at first in Spain and North Africa. By the 10th and 11th centuries the idea had spread to other countries and there were yeshivot in France, Germany, Austria, Italy, and other parts of the European continent. However, between the 15th and 18th centuries, growing economic and political difficulties in western Europe forced these study centers to move to southern and eastern Europe – in particular to Italy, Bohemia, and Poland-Lithuania. In 1622 the Council of Lithuanian Jewry obliged every community with a rabbi to maintain a yeshivah. The members of the community were responsible for the material needs of the students. In the 18th century the pupils of the *Gaon of Vilna established a network of yeshivot in Lithuania and Belorussia, the most important being in *Volozhin. Soon the followers of various movements were establishing their own yeshivot and teaching their own philosophy. Thus there were *Musar yeshivot and ḥasidic yeshivot. Since married students were not accepted into regular yeshivot, they joined the **kolel*, where they could study for rabbinical ordination. Eventually, to meet pressures for broader curricula, some yeshivot began including other Jewish studies besides Talmud and some even added secular courses.

However, once again, misfortune plagued these institutions. Pogroms, poverty, and the trend towards more secular Jewish education initiated by the *Haskalah movement caused many yeshivot to close down. Finally came the Holocaust and most of these scholarly academies in Europe were totally destroyed. The new centers for yeshivah learning in modern times have been the United States and Ereẓ Israel.

Advanced students at the Yeshivah of Lomza, Poland, engrossed in the study of Talmud.

**Organization and Inner Life.** Prior to the 16th century the yeshivot of eastern Europe were semi-private institutions, and it was the responsibility of the head of the institute to find ways of financing it. Gradually, however, the yeshivot became more closely connected with the community which not only lent its support but also laid down rules and regulations for administering the school. The students in turn became the religious leaders of the community and the rabbi would consult senior members of his yeshivah regarding religious questions.

The students ranged in age from 13 to middle age. They were encouraged in independent study, with the older ones helping the younger and serving as advisers. An early method of study called *pilpul* was used by advanced students. It was a way of analyzing and debating the text, so complex that only the most sharp-witted and intellectual students could handle it. The Volozhin yeshivah introduced study in pairs or groups to replace individual study and a more straight-forward discussion of the subject matter to replace the *pilpul* method.

Today's yeshivot follow much the same methods used by their predecessors, giving the pupil an in-depth understanding of talmudic texts.

**In Ereẓ Israel.** Israel now has the greatest number of yeshivah students since talmudic times. There are several different types of yeshivot, each having its own distinct character, depending on the origin of the supporting community. Many incorporate the *kolel* where young men continue their studies after marriage and at a higher level.

A new development in the 20th century has been the founding of "minor yeshivot" designed to prepare pupils for regular yeshivah study. These yeshivot are roughly equivalent to high schools and cater to students between the ages of 13 and 18. Several of these combine half a day of talmudic studies with half a day of regular secondary school subjects.

With the establishment of the State of Israel, the heads of the yeshivot reached an agreement with the Ministry of Defense whereby their students would be exempt from army service for the duration of their studies, on the grounds that they would be helping in the spiritual rebuilding of Judaism. Nevertheless, many yeshivah students do join the armed forces and others combine studies with active service.

**In the Diaspora.** Some large yeshivot still exist outside of Israel, for example the *Gateshead on Tyne yeshivah in England and the *Ḥabad yeshivot in France, Australia and North Africa. Many yeshivot in eastern Europe transferred to the United States during World War II and others such as *Yeshiva University were established by Americans. The yeshivah brought an important change in the situation of Orthodoxy in the United States, succeeding in raising a new generation of rabbis and spiritual guides.

**YESHIVA UNIVERSITY,** institution of higher learning in New York City, known for its outstanding Jewish as well as secular educational programs. The nucleus around which Yeshiva University grew was the Rabbi Isaac Elchanan Theological Seminary, which was founded in 1897. Named after Rabbi Isaac Elchanan *Spektor, R.I.E.T.S. began as a small school for the advanced study of Talmud, the first higher yeshiva in the U.S. In 1906, the student body began pressuring for the inclusion of secular studies in the curriculum and in 1908 the administration was reorganized and secular studies added. In 1916 an accredited high school which combined talmudic and secular studies was opened. In 1922 the institution absorbed the Teachers' Institute, founded by the Mizrachi Organization of America, and in 1928 Yeshiva College accepted its first students. The high school, the teachers' institute, the college and R.I.E.T.S. were now all subdivisions of one institution which was to continue to increase its divisions as well as the number of students. In 1945 it was elevated to university status, being duly recognized by the state of New York. In addition to the divisions already mentioned, the university added a cantorial training institute, a special program for Sephardi study, the Israel Rogosin Center for Ethics and Human Values, the Bernard Revel non-denominational graduate school for Jewish and Semitic studies, and five high schools in Brooklyn and Manhattan, known as the Brooklyn and Manhattan Talmudic Academies for boys (BTA and MTA) and the Central High Schools for girls.

Of the major divisions, R.I.E.T.S. has continued to function as the advanced talmudic academy, no different from any traditional yeshivah. The course of study culminates in a three-year program to *semikhah* (rabbinic ordination) and over 1,500 rabbis have been ordained since its inception.

Yeshiva College for men and Stern College for women (opened in 1954) are the undergraduate schools of Yeshiva University which offer a dual program of Jewish and secular subjects and the faculty includes some of the outstanding rabbinic scholars of the world. All Yeshiva College students must enroll in one of three Jewish studies divisions: the James Striar School of Jewish Studies, adapted to the needs of students with little or no background in Jewish studies; the Erna Michael College of Hebraic Studies; or the undergraduate division of R.I.E.T.S.

The secular, non-sectarian divisions of Yeshiva University have undergone the greatest expansion since 1945. These divisions now include the Ferkauf Graduate School of Humanities and Social Sciences which is primarily though not exclusively a graduate school of education; the Belfer Graduate School of Science; the Wurzweiler School of Social Work; and probably best-known of all, the Albert Einstein College of Medicine and its affiliated Albert Einstein College Hospital. While these divisions include a diverse student body and a distinguished non-Jewish as well as Jewish faculty, they do in varying degrees reflect Yeshiva University's commitment to Orthodox Judaism. All divisions observe the requirements of Jewish law. The Ferkauf School has a department of religious education, and the Wurzweiler School requires all students to attend two courses in Jewish sociology and two courses in Jewish social work values.

In addition to its educational and other scholarly activities, the University plays a major role in Jewish life through its community service division which helps schools and youth and adult education groups. Together with the Rabbinic Alumni Association, the University sponsors Camp Morasha, a summer camp which opened in 1964.

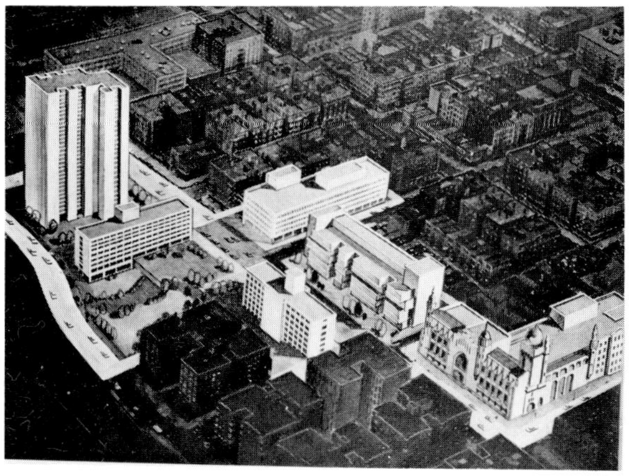

The architect's drawing of the main buildings of the Washington Heights (Manhattan) campus of Yeshiva University, showing classroom buildings, dormitories, library and science center.

**YEVSEKTSIYA,** sections within local branches of the Russian Communist Party organized from 1918

1

Forward
פארווערטס
Forward
עגיפטישע ארמיי קאפיטולירט

2

3

1. The Yiddish comedian and satirical actor Shimon Dzigan (1905–1980).
2. Front page of the June 9, 1967 issue of *Forward*, the longest surviving Yiddish daily in the United States.
3. Jacob Adler (1855–1926), one of the leading Yiddish actors and managers of the early 20th century, shown playing Shylock in Shakespeare's *Merchant of Venice*.

to 1930 to "deal" with the Jews and speed their assimilation.

Lenin, founder and leader of the Communist Party, denied that the Jews were a separate nation and believed that the sooner they were merged with the rest of the populace and stripped of their distinctive identity, the sooner the "Jewish Problem" would be solved. (See *Communism; *Lenin; and *Stalin.) In the meantime, however, he was faced with the fact that there were millions of Jews in Russia speaking their own language and maintaining their own social institutions. Therefore in 1918 he created the "Jewish Commissariat" and local *yevsektsiya* (Jewish sections) to spread communist propaganda among the Jews.

These Jewish sections used Yiddish-speaking workers, but it was strongly emphasized that Yiddish was simply a necessary means of communicating with the Jewish masses and on no account valuable in itself. Ironically, many of these workers were Jews – members of left-wing parties which supported the communist ideology. They were to work towards a "systematic destruction of Zionist and bourgeois institutions." Thus, with the help of government agencies and the police, the *Yevsektsiya* liquidated Jewish organizations, confiscated synagogue buildings, closed yeshivot and libraries, and banned Jewish books.

The destruction of the existing Jewish framework was accompanied by attempts to create a new Jewish-Communist culture. Jews were retained in "proletarian" tasks, becoming craftsmen, laborers and farmers. The territory of *Birobidzhan in the Far East was set aside for Jewish settlement so that Jews would work the land rather than engage in the hated capitalist enterprises.

However, certain elements in the Communist Party began to distrust the Jewish sections, feeling that by setting up separate Jewish territories and emphasizing Yiddish,they were making the Jews into more of a separate national unit rather than assimilating them. Therefore the *Yevsektsiya* was abolished in 1930, many of its workers imprisoned, and all achievements in Jewish autonomy gradually liquidated.

**YIDDISH**, the English form of the German word *Judisch*, is the name applied to a German dialect spoken by the Jews of Central and Eastern European origin. It is most likely that at first the German Jews employed the language of their Christian neighborhood without any changes whatever. In their communication with their fellow-Jews, they wrote the language in Hebrew characters and introduced such Hebrew words as were necessary for the observance of their Jewish religion.

### THE LANGUAGE

When the German Jews emigrated to Poland, Russia and other lands on the European continent, they were cut off from the German language. Yiddish, which was based on German vocabulary and construction, had to perpetuate itself in the form in which it was brought from their Germanic homes. This, of course, resulted in irregularities of grammar and spelling,and the Yiddish language to this day eludes strict grammatical analysis. Furthermore, the new environment subjected the Yiddish language to the influences of other languages. The loss of contact with the German language resulted in the increased absorption of biblical and talmudical words and idioms. The double influence continued throughout the years, so that the Yiddish language became a fusion of German, Hebrew, Aramaic and Slavic vocabulary and expressions.

**Vocabulary.** In vocabulary, Yiddish is predominantly German with less than a third derived from Hebrew and Slavic sources. In pronunciation the influence of Russian and Polish is minimal, while Hebrew words and expressions were themselves "yiddishized." A major difference between modern German and Yiddish is that, unlike German which continued to develop, Yiddish remained at the medieval stage of the German language. Another difference is that Yiddish vocabulary is rich in Hebrew and Slavic words which are, of course, totally absent in German.

The nature of the word absorption process makes it difficult to determine original word sources from other languages. It would also be misleading to attempt to define a "yiddishized" word from its primary source. Thus the Yiddish word *mentsh,* meaning a reliable, mature person, is lost when compared to its German source word, *mensch,* meaning simply a person.

**Writing.** The basis of Yiddish writing is the Hebrew alphabet. Most words of Hebrew or Aramaic origin retain their original spelling. The vowel system consists of the systematic use of assigned consonants to indicate vowel sounds. The silent consonant *aleph,* for example, is used as a symbol for the vowel sounds *"ah"* and *"aw"* while the consonant *ayin* is the symbol for the vowel sound *"eh."*

**Speakers.** The Yiddish language, from its beginning in

the tenth century, until the end of the 18th century was the dominant medium of oral communication among the Jews on the European continent. In Eastern Europe the number of Yiddish speakers increased rapidly as the Jewish population grew. The great migrations of Jews in the 19th and early 20th centuries caused the Yiddish-speaking community to expand throughout the world. The number of Yiddish speakers at any one time is difficult to determine. The best estimates reckon with eleven million speakers just prior to World War II. This number was drastically reduced by the Holocaust. However, among traditional Ashkenazi Jews, a knowledge of Yiddish, at least as a second language, continues to be widespread. The recent increase in the yeshivah enrolment could result in an expansion of the Yiddish community since many yeshivot still study the Talmud and biblical commentaries in Yiddish.

The historical study of Yiddish is made difficult because of the scarcity of writings and texts remaining from the earliest periods of the language. However, from 1300 to 1400 a decisive event occurred in the development of the Yiddish language when it moved into a Slavic environment. It was under Slavic influence that its grammar was restructured and its relation to German weakened. It was also in this period that a relatively uniform literary language developed. The next two hundred years were marked by a vigorous expansion of the language and a further withdrawal from its German origins. After 1700 the Yiddish language was already playing a significant role on all cultural levels: religious, ritual, communal administration, scholarship, personal correspondence and literary activity. Another factor of major importance in the development of the language was the merging of the Hebrew-Aramaic words into Yiddish. The principal sources from which Yiddish drew these words have been the Pentateuch, the daily prayers and the talmudic discourses of the yeshivot.

In Europe, at the end of the 18th century and the beginning of the 19th, Yiddish came to be seen by many thinkers as the national language of the Jews. This was particularly so among the non-Zionist circles who wanted the Jews to have an autonomous existence in Europe with Yiddish as its language. In 1908 a conference on the Yiddish language was held in Czernowitz to deal with the role of Yiddish in Jewish life. The Zionist Hebraists objected violently to Yiddish being described as the national language of the Jews. That place, they claimed, is reserved for Hebrew. In the end a compromise was reached and Yiddish was called "a national language." In the early years of the modern settlement of Ereẓ Israel, many people objected to the use of Yiddish and insisted on Hebrew.

In modern times there has been a considerable amount of academic interest in Yiddish and it is an accepted subject in many universities throughout the world including the U.S. and Israel.

## LITERATURE

It was not until the beginning of the 17th century that homiletic or sermon prose began to appear in Yiddish. This prose was a mixture of stories, tales and fables woven around the Bible and its commentaries. A very popular work belonging to this style of literature was the *Ẓe'enah u-Re'enah* which appeared in 1622 and is still being published to this day. The originality and novelty of this work lies mainly in its popular style and in the new literary form into which the scriptural stories and their moral lessons were cast. Most of the activity in prayer literature was in direct translation from the Hebrew. However, there were other areas in which Yiddish was used to express religious feelings and devotion. One example is the *tkhine*, a prayer of private supplication to meet individual needs and purposes. Written mainly in prose, *tkhines* were usually included in prayer books with Yiddish translations.

It was natural that a wealth of Yiddish literary activity should develop out of a Jewish society based on the Bible and its rules for ethical conduct. The Yiddish literature on traditional conduct instructed the Jewish community in the rules of proper behavior during synagogue worship and religious ceremonies at home. These works were written in a simple, clear style which was easily understood by the average person. *Sefer Midos* was the first comprehensive printed Yiddish ethical work translated directly from the Hebrew in 1542. This book, which is the largest Yiddish ethical work, guides the reader towards moral conduct not only by rules and commands, but also by means of stories, parables and illustrations.

The beginning of the 17th century witnessed a great demand on the part of the Jewish masses for a literature of amusement and entertainment. This demand called forth a supply of all kinds of fiction and especially of tales of *mayses* written in Yiddish prose. Some were translations but most were original works. The original works were based mainly on Jewish stories drawn either from aggadic sources or

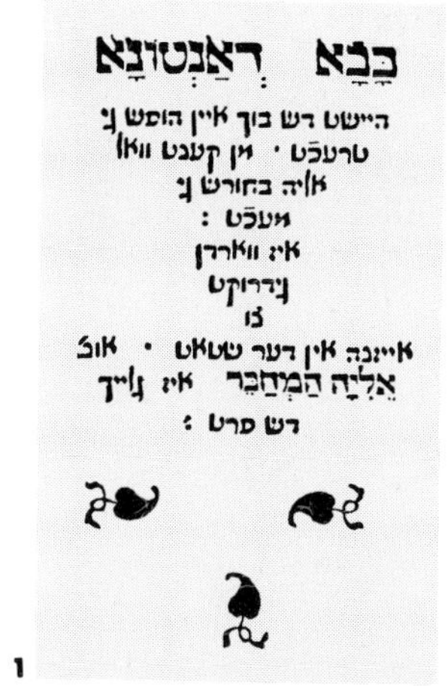

בבא דאנטונא
הייסט דש בוך איין הופש ג׳
טרעכט · מין קענט וואו
אליה בחורש ג׳
מעכט :
איז ווארדן
גדרוקט
צו
אייזנה אין דער שטאט · אונ
אליה המחבר איז גלייך
דש פרט :

1

2

1. Title page of one of the earliest Yiddish books ever written, *Bovo d'Antona,* a free translation by the 16th-century grammarian, Elijah Levita, of an Italian chivalric romance. Levita's translation was in verse form, but in the 18th century a crude prose version was published under the title *Bove Mayse,* and this eventually gave rise to the popular Yiddish expression for a fairy tale or a made-up story, *bobe mayse.*

2. Der Nister (pseudonym of Pinkhes Kahanovich; 1884–1950), one of the foremost Yiddish poets in Stalinist Russia, who died in a prison hospital after being arrested for anti-Soviet "nationalist" (i.e. Jewish) activities.

1

2

1. Poster of the Thalia Theater, New York, announcing the performance of five different Yiddish plays on the 17th and 18th September, 1898, the days on which Rosh Ha-Shanah occurred in that year.
2. Shmerl Kaczerginsky (1908–1954), Yiddish poet whose literary output serves as a chronicle of Jewish life in the Vilna ghetto and of the heroism of the Jewish partisans who chose desperate resistance rather than passive martyrdom.

from legends current at the time. This period saw an outpouring of *mayse* literature or, as it was sometimes called, secular literature, to amuse and entertain the reading public. The quality of these works was not high, yet the literature did express real feelings of the masses. To satisfy the growing desire for worldly and general knowledge, many books dealing with history, geography, travel and popular science were also published during this same period.

At the end of the 18th century Jews, especially of Western Europe, were starting to abandon the ghettos both physically and spiritually. The migration from the ghettos exposed the Jews to the danger of assimilation. The *Haskalah, or Enlightenment, movement arose with the object of stemming the tide of assimilation which was already becoming evident in the middle of the 18th century. The leaders of the movement employed literature aimed at raising the cultural level of the people, to develop a taste for beauty of nature and language and to refine their moral feelings.

The central figures in Yiddish literature at the end of the 19th century were *Mendele Mokher Seforim (1835-1917), *Shalom Aleichem (1859-1916), and Isaac *Peretz (1852-1915). These three dominated the latter part of the century. Mendele was primarily responsible for the standardization of modern literary Yiddish. His words criticize, yet they made memorable, what was characteristic and typical of Jewish life in his time. Shalom Aleichem's genius captured the essence of poor and simple people: simple folk who instinctively absorbed the Jewish faith and its affirmation of life. Sad and tragic events are treated by Shalom Aleichem with an unshakable faith that man can overcome any adversity. He satirizes but does not belittle the values of life, but rather serves to emphasize those values. Peretz's literary technique was the use of the folktale. His ḥasidic stories idealized the rabbis, painting them as the model men of the future, and helped initiate a neo-ḥasidic trend in Yiddish literature. Peretz attempted to modernize Jewish life through the use of the Yiddish language.

It was also during this same period that remarkable social progress was made. The philosophies of Zionism and socialism were heatedly debated; parties organized; and everywhere new ideas were on the march. This resulted in the development of a worldly, many-sided Yiddish literature. It supplied information and provided light reading for leisure hours, but its prime purpose was as an instrument for social progress. Although centered in Russian Jewry, there was a parallel development of this literature in America. The mass migration of Jews in the 1880s brought to America a large number of Jewish workingmen who came from the smaller towns of Eastern Europe. These immigrants turned mostly to the needle trade. Thus, within a short time there arose a large Jewish working class which struggled hard for a living. In the emerging class struggle, Yiddish was used as the medium of expression and propaganda since this was the only language the masses understood. Most of the literature was dedicated to the service of the socialist ideal and to carrying on the class struggle. It dealt mainly with scenes of poverty, the miserable conditions in the sweatshops and the tragedies in the homes of the laborers resulting from oppressive working conditions.

Much of Yiddish literature of this period had its origin in journalism. Pamphlets, brochures, daily and weekly newspapers, were published to further the cause of the laboring class. The *Forward* which began to appear in 1897 became the leading organ of the laboring masses and is still appearing today.

In the 20th century two great events took place in the life of the Jewish people, both of which affected the history of Yiddish literature: the great catastrophe which befell European Jewry during the Nazi regime and the creation of the State of Israel. The life of torture and suffering, the massacres, the death scenes in the ghettos and in the concentration camps serve as themes for numerous short stories, novels and poems. They also form the subject of many historical works, written as literary memorials to numerous Jewish communities which were scattered in the former great centers of Jewish population. Yiddish literature was also affected by the arrest and liquidation of some of its most important writers who were in the great Jewish centers of Europe behind the Iron Curtain.

At the same time, Yiddish literature developed a new and immediate tie with the State of Israel. The acquisition and rebuilding of the country are serving as central elements in Yiddish literature.

While at the beginning of the 19th century modern Yiddish literature was transferred from Western Europe to Eastern Europe, its main centers today remain those of the United States and Israel. Yiddish literature served not only as a medium for social and cultural progress but was also a definitive force for unifying the Jewish people throughout the world.

Yiddish literature was greatly honored by the award of the Nobel Prize in literature to Isaac *Bashevis Singer in 1978.

**YIVO** (Institute for Jewish Research). This organization has served as a major factor in the preservation and development of the Yiddish language and culture. The name YIVO is an abbreviation of *Yidisher Visenshaftlikher Institut* (Institute of Yiddish Scholarship). It was founded in Berlin in 1925, following the proposal of Jewish leader Nahum Shtif that the widespread research into the Yiddish language be organized and coordinated into one unified body.

The founding conference selected *Vilna as the center of the organization, with branches in various parts of the world. When Vilna was occupied by the Nazis in 1940, the American branch, earlier known as Amopteyl *(Amerikanishe Opteylung)* took over the central direction.

In the early years, research and publications were conducted in four sections: History; Literature; Economics and Statistics; and Psychology and Education. Publications were in Yiddish with summaries in English, German and Polish. A training program for young scholars was initiated and correspondents in many towns were encouraged to study the Jewish way of life around them and collect material on the local Yiddish history and culture. YIVO also did research into the problems of Jewish settlement all over the world, and variations in the Yiddish language.

Before the destruction of its headquarters during the the Nazi occupation, YIVO had amassed a specialized library of over 200,000 items which included theatrical collections, photographs and letters of famous personalities and other articles connected with Yiddish. Its present building in New York (Fifth Avenue and 86th Street) houses more than a quarter of a million books on Jewish subjects and more than two million archival items.

As the older generation died out, however, interest in Yiddish studies dwindled and membership in YIVO has greatly decreased.

**YOM KIPPUR WAR.** At 2.00 p.m. on Yom Kippur, Saturday October 6, 1973, the armed forces of Syria and Egypt attacked Israel simultaneously on her northern and southern fronts. The suddenness and magnitude of the attack presented Israel with one of the greatest threats ever to her survival as a state. And the battle of international diplomatic manoeuvres which ensued drastically changed the balance of world opinion, leaving Israel practically isolated and abandoned by both friend and foe alike.

This war, Israel's fourth major conflict in the brief 25 years of its existence, was the latest attempt on the part of the Arabs to annihilate the Jewish state. Their aim had always been to "liberate" Arab lands from Jewish control and, particularly after their defeat in the *Six-Day War of 1967, the Arabs had vowed to recapture the occupied territories.

For several weeks preceding the outbreak of the war, Israel Intelligence had noted signs of military build-up on both the Egyptian and Syrian fronts, but these were interpreted as being mere routine exercises and so, apart from minor preparations and troop reinforcements, Israel's leadership took no major precautionary action.

When at 4.00 a.m. on Yom Kippur,information was received that war was in fact imminent, Israel began a major call-up of all reserve soldiers and mobilized to meet the attack. By 10.00 a.m. on the holiest day in the Jewish calendar, military messengers began visiting homes and synagogues all over the country. Men were called out of prayer services, still wearing their *tallitot,* often without time to break their fasts, and sent off to the front. For many it would be days before they could eat a full meal and weeks before their families would hear from them again – if at all. The Israel radio, normally silent on this Sabbath of Sabbaths, broke with tradition to broadcast news of the crisis and the streets soon filled with military transports and emergency vehicles.

By attacking on Yom Kippur the Arabs had hoped to catch Israel at the worst moment when most of the soldiers would be home on leave. Ironically this turned out to be a major miscalculation on their part because Yom Kippur is the one day in the year when most of Israel's manpower is centralized either in their homes or synagogues, and thus easily available for mobilization. Israel thus saved many valuable hours in mustering her forces.

With the elements of surprise and numbers on their side, the Syrians and Egyptians easily gained the upper hand in the early stages of the fighting. On the northern front a handful of Israel's regular soldiers held off heavy Syrian air, artillery, tank and infantry divisions until reinforcements arrived. Tales of incredible bravery were to emerge from the heroic

1. A makeshift memorial for an Israel soldier who fell on October 17, 1973, during the battle on the bridgehead established across the Suez Canal by the Israel Defense Forces at the height of the Yom Kippur War.
2. Advertisement which appeared in the New York Times, February 11, 1974, appealing to the conscience of the world and asking for support in obtaining information about the Israel soldiers missing in action in the Yom Kippur War, who were believed to have been taken captive as prisoners of war by the Syrians.

1

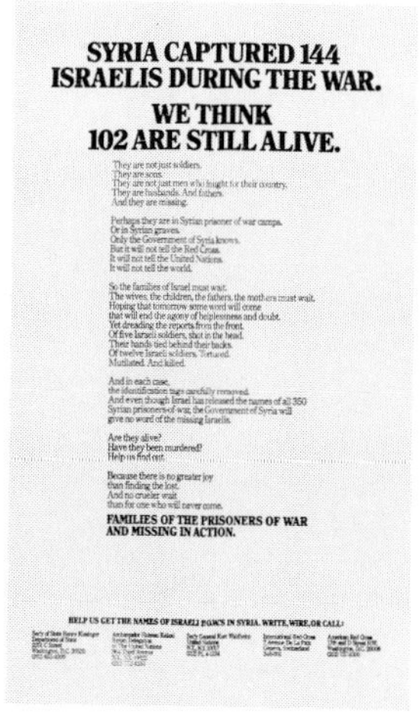

2

stand of these defenders. Syrian forces advanced to within seven miles of the Sea of Galilee and bombarded Jewish settlements in the Jezreel Valley. But by Wednesday, October 10, the Israel Northern Command, coordinated by Major-General Yiẓḥak Ḥofi and led by Generals Eitan, Laner and Peled had forced the enemy back to the 1967 cease-fire lines. Holding their own against the combined forces of Syrians, Iraqis and Jordanians, the Israelis pressed on until they were within about 20 miles of Syria's capital city of Damascus. After much heavy fighting Israel's *Golani* division also managed to capture the strategic heights of Mount Hermon, giving them control of the whole area. That was how the situation stood when the Syrian command finally agreed to a cease-fire on October 22.

The situation on the southern front also involved a complete reversal with the Israelis turning almost certain defeat into a surprise victory. On Yom Kippur the Egyptians sent more than 70,000 troops across the Suez Canal to attack the less than 500 Israelis manning the Bar-Lev line on the Israel side of the canal. Using highly effective Russian bridging equipment, the Egyptians were able to establish enough bridges across the canal to keep their forces supplied. The Israel forces then attempted to reach the units besieged in the fortifications of the Bar-Lev line, suffering very heavy casualties. Most of the line had either been captured or abandoned by the third day of fighting. A naval battle also developed at the outset of the war, pitting Egyptian and Syrian ships against the Israelis in the first missile battles in naval history. The Israeli naval operations were characterized by daring and initiative and they soon gained complete control of the marine approaches to the country.

The Israel Southern Command was organized by General Gonen and led by Major-Generals Adan, Sharon and Mandler. Through a concerted effort they managed to reach the Suez Canal and on the night of October 15/16, parachute forces followed by General Sharon's divisions crossed the canal and penetrated the Egyptian lines. Major-General Mandler was killed in action and his brigade was placed under the command of Major-General Magen, who followed Sharon across the canal. By October 22 they had reached the Cairo-Suez road, when the Egyptians considered it expedient to agree to the cease-fire engineered by Secretary of State Kissinger. By the time it came into effect, Israel had completely surrounded the Egyptian third army, but instead of making them surrender, Israel was obliged to allow supplies and medical equipment through to the besieged Egyptians. Fighting officially ended on October 24, and on November 11 the cease-fire agreement was signed in a tent erected at Kilometer 101 on the Suez-Cairo road.

The Geneva Peace Conference, convened under the auspices of the United States and the Soviet Union after much diplomatic activity, opened on December 21 with the participation of Egypt, Jordan and Israel. It proved to be ineffective in working out further agreements between the parties and all subsequent arrangements were made at the initiative of United States Secretary of State Henry *Kissinger whose jet travels back and forth between the Middle Eastern capitals and Washington became known as "shuttle diplomacy." Although the Arabs had admittedly started the war, Israel was penalized for its outcome and the agreements which Kissinger negotiated resulted in a one-sided pull-back of Israel troops from Syria and Egypt, leaving a United Nations force occupying a corridor along both the northern and southern borders.

The casualties in the Yom Kippur War were heavy on all sides: 2,522 Israelis and an estimated 15,000 Egyptians and 3,500 Syrians were killed. Egypt agreed to exchange the 240 Israeli prisoners held by them for over 8,000 Egyptians captured by Israel. But in defiance of all international law the Syrians refused to release their prisoners, resorting instead to torturing and murdering many of them. The survivors were finally released from their ordeal many months later and returned to Israel.

The Yom Kippur War had severe repercussions in many spheres. In Israel, the sudden advent of war after a period of relative peace and comparative prosperity resulted in a lowering of morale and a sharp outcry against the leadership which had failed to prepare them. The Agranat Commission was set up to investigate the circumstances surrounding the war, and the public discontent eventually led to the resignation of Prime Minister Golda Meir and Defense

The makeshift bridge thrown across the Suez Canal by the Israel Defense Forces on October 15–16, 1973, which enabled Israel troops to cross the canal and establish a strong bridgehead in Egyptian territory on the west bank of the canal.

Minister Moshe Dayan, leaving the way clear for the appointment of a new government.

This discontent should not, however, be equated with despair. The Jews both in Israel and abroad held fast more than ever to the Zionist ideal. *Am Yisrael Ḥai* – "Israel Lives !" became the rallying cry of pro-Israel demonstrators and supporters who with money, influence and sheer moral support helped Israel through the crisis.

The reaction of world governments was not as encouraging. In the aftermath of the war the Arabs began using economic pressures to force international support. They imposed an oil embargo, refusing to sell this essential commodity to any country which had supported Israel. Most countries succumbed to the blackmail. The African nations, the Eastern European bloc, and many Western European countries became either openly antagonistic or totally apathetic towards Israel. Even the supposedly impartial United Nations Organization became dominated by anti-Israel factions so that no equitable solution to the Middle East problem could be expected. One of the few steadfast supporters of Israel was Holland which, though faced with a dangerous fuel shortage, refused to be intimidated by the Arabs.

In the absence of a political solution and encouraged by the apparent success of their oil blackmail, the Arabs turned increasingly to terrorism, supporting the violent activities of the so-called Palestinian terrorist groups. The Yom Kippur War, therefore, not only failed to solve the problems of the Middle East but served only to increase tensions and adversely affect the economic and political situation all over the world. The growing involvement of the United States and the Soviet Union in Middle Eastern affairs led to widespread apprehension that the situation could develop into a serious threat to world peace.

**YORK.** Locked in the Tower, and surrounded by a mob howling for their blood, the Jews of York once made a suicide pact and perished there. York is a cathedral city in Yorkshire, and was the principal city of Northern England during the Middle Ages, when many rich Jews flocked there. The Jewish leaders were a disciple of Rabbi Jacob *Tam, Yom Tov of Joigny, and Benedict and Josce; the latter two, in 1189 went as a deputation from the Jews to the coronation of Richard I in London. During riots following the coronation Benedict was injured and later died.

In the following March Richard de Malbis (who owed great debts to Josce) and other York nobles instigated a riot against the Jews who sought refuge in Clifford's Tower of the York Castle. Realizing that they must submit either to baptism or to slaughter at the hands of the mob surrounding the Tower the Jews, led by Yom Tov and Josce, made a suicide pact on Shabbat ha-Gadol, March 16/17, 1190. The few survivors were either killed or sent to London by the sheriff of York. Joseph ben Asher of Chartres later wrote an elegy on the massacre.

In the early 13th century Jews re-settled in York; Aaron of York (Josce's son) became chief Jew of England under Henry III and chief rabbi in 1237. York was an important commercial center for Jews until the expulsion of 1290 when their property was seized by the king. In the late 19th century a few Eastern European Jews settled in York. On Oct. 31, 1978 the massacre was commemorated by the unveiling of a plaque at Clifford's Tower.

Clifford's Tower, site of the brutal massacre of the Jews of York in 1190.

**YOUNG ISRAEL**, an association of Orthodox synagogues in the United States, formed in 1912 by young American Orthodox Jews in New York's Lower East Side who wanted a more modern, Americanized religious service than those attended by their immigrant parents. And so they evolved the Young Israel idea, combining strict Orthodox practice with a modern approach. All Young Israel synagogues must have *meḥiẓot* (dividers separating men and women worshipers) and their officers must be Sabbath observers. Yet their facilities are modern as opposed to the old-fashioned *shtibls* of their parents. Young Israel also provides an attractive social program which has brought thousands of young people to the synagogue, not only for prayer but for stimulating discussions, outings and cultural activities. Because of the interest in Judaism stimulated by Young Israel, many of its members have been encouraged to enroll in intensive study courses or enter yeshivot. Young Israel has an intercollegiate program as well and sponsors kosher dining clubs on college campuses. The National Council assists new synagogues with

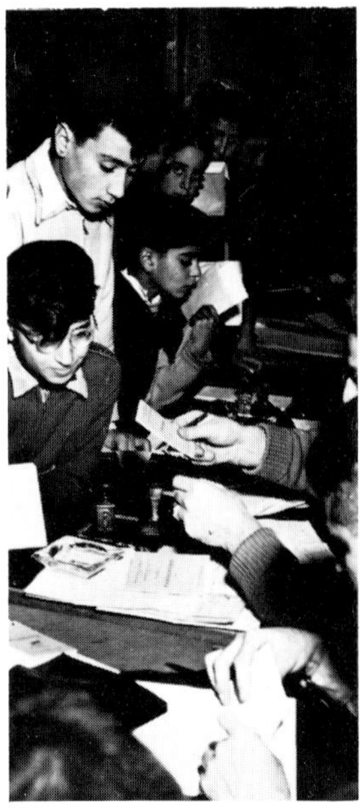

1. Children on their way to Israel under the auspices of Youth Aliyah, standing in line to receive their passports.
2. Zudioska Ulica (Jew Street) in Dubrovnik, Yugoslavia.

interest-free loans for the purpose of organization and expansion. There are several Young Israel congregations in the State of Israel.

**YOUTH ALIYAH** *(Aliyyat Yeladim ve-No'ar;* "Children and Youth Aliyah") is an organization founded in 1933 in an effort to save Jewish children from persecution and give them shelter and education in Ereẓ Israel. The first leader of Youth Aliyah was Henrietta *Szold, an American Zionist who founded Hadassah. Youth Aliyah began its activities in Germany a short while before the Nazis' rise to power and was instrumental in saving many children who had to leave their families or were orphaned by the Holocaust. Eventually Youth Aliyah became active in every European country where there was a need to rescue Jewish children. In 1941 it began caring also for children from oriental countries who were arriving in Palestine. After the war (1945) Jewish children in Europe who had survived the Holocaust, were brought to Ereẓ Israel by Youth Aliyah.

The organization did not merely concern itself with the physical welfare and instruction of young people, but provided an education which gave them individual attention and also taught them to live with others as part of a society. To attain these educational aims, the children were reared in *ḥevrot no'ar* (youth communities) by *madrikhim* (guides, counsellors or youth leaders).

Each *ḥevrat no'ar* consisted of 40 young people who stayed together for two to four years until the age of 17 or 18. The *ḥevrah* was sometimes attached to a kibbutz, or was part of a youth village or an educational institution directly managed by Youth Aliyah. The young people generally studied for four hours and worked on the farm or in the workshops for another four hours. In addition there were communal and group activities. Every *ḥevrat no'ar* had a *madrikh* and a *metappelet* (house mother) who helped the young people solve their emotional, educational and social problems as individuals and as a group.

Today Youth Aliyah is no longer a rescue organization but an educational one. It rears young newcomers orphaned, deprived or handicapped from developed as well as underdeveloped areas and gives them vocational, agricultural or academic education. There are also Youth Aliyah *ulpanim* which teach young new immigrants Hebrew and conduct special foreign language courses for those who wish to complete their secondary education in their native language.

From its founding in 1933, Youth Aliyah has cared for over 150,000 young people. Its challenge in the 1990s came, in addition to Israelis, from youth from Ethiopia, Yugoslavia, and the former U.S.S.R.

**YUGOSLAVIA,** republic in south-eastern Europe, was originally composed of six separate regions: Serbia, Slovenia, Croatia-Slavonia-Dalmatia, Bosnia-Herzegovina, Macedonia, and Vojvodna. In 1918 these regions were merged, though the Jewry of each region maintained its own distinctive cultural and social structures.

Jewish settlement in the area began in Roman times. A Greek inscription on a pillar of the church – a former synagogue – in Stobi, Macedonia, serves as evidence of Jewish settlement during the second and third centuries. By the Middle Ages Jews had settled in the major urban centers. There were sizeable communities in Belgrade, Serbia; in Zagreb, Croatia; and in Sarajevo, Bosnia. Generally, as long as the economy of the area required the presence of the Jews, they lived there without hindrance, but as soon as their usefulness declined they were persecuted and driven out.

With the establishment of the Yugoslav kingdom in 1918, about 100 Jewish communities with 70,000 members, were included in the new state. They generally belonged to the middle class, though there were some impoverished communities. The unification of these varied groups was not easy. In the southern districts the Jews were essentially *Sephardim while the other provinces were mainly inhabited by *Ashkenazim. In 1919 a "Federation of Jewish Communities" was formed and in 1923 the chief rabbinate was founded in an effort to organize and unite the differing groups.

In April 1941 Yugoslavia was occupied by German, Hungarian, Italian and Bulgarian troops and its territory divided between them. Most of the Jewish population was either exterminated or expelled, having suffered savage cruelty and terror. Yugoslav Jews took an active part in the fight against the Nazis and played a leading role among the organizers of Communist leader Tito's revolt. The most prominent Jewish resistance fighter was Mosa Pijade, and when Tito became president of Yugoslavia after the war, Pijade was chosen as one of the four vice-presidents.

The Great Synagogue in Zagreb, Yugoslavia, which was totally destroyed by the Nazis in 1941.

About 14,000 Jews returned from hiding places and prison camps to the Yugoslav cities after the liberation in 1944. But once the State of Israel was established four years later, over 8,000 of them emigrated there. The remaining six to seven thousand Jews were able to maintain their organizations and communal life within the Communist regime due to the relatively liberal Yugoslav policy and the widespread support for Judaism and Israel within the country. The official stand of the Yugoslav government towards the State of Israel was not very favorable. In 1967 Yugoslavia severed diplomatic relations with Israel and afterwards showed active support for the Arab cause. In the post-Communist era relations with Israel improved.

The civil war among the various components of Yugoslavia in the early 1990s was very unsettling for the Jewish community, particularly in Sarajevo, and resulted in some emigration and an uncertain future for the Jewish community. Many Jewish children were sent to Israel to continue their education while waiting out the war.

**ZACUTO, ABRAHAM BEN SAMUEL** (1452-c. 1515), Spanish astronomer and adviser to famous explorers, who was as much at home in the field of Jewish scholarship as he was in the world of science.

Zacuto was instructed in biblical and talmudic studies by his father and later attended the University of Salamanca where he specialized in astronomy and astrology. He thus became well-versed in both religious and secular studies. He wrote all his astronomical books in Hebrew and they were subsequently translated into several languages. His first book, *Ha-Ḥibbur ha-Gadol* (1473-78), was about the solar system and enjoyed a wide reputation. He then wrote a book on the influence of the stars and eclipses of the sun and moon.

In 1492, when the Jews were expelled from Spain, Zacuto emigrated to Portugal where he was appointed court astronomer to the king. Before sending Vasco da Gama on his sea voyage to India (1496), the king sought the advice of Zacuto. The astronomer predicted the success of the expedition and instructed the sailors in the use of his newly-perfected *astrolabe, his astronomical charts and maritime tables. These were of great value to seamen.

Columbus used Zacuto's tables on his voyage and on one occasion they may have saved his life from hostile Indians. Knowing from the Zacuto tables that a lunar eclipse was due, Columbus threatened the natives that he would deprive them of the light of the moon. The natives probably thought that this man had supernatural power to be able to cause such a phenomenon and so they refrained from attacking him.

In 1497, when all the Jews in Portugal were forced to convert, Zacuto left for North Africa. Twice he and his son Samuel were taken prisoner, but they finally reached Tunis. In 1504, during his stay there, he completed *Sefer ha-Yuḥasin,* a book intended to outline the historical development of the *Oral Law and to establish the chronology of the Jewish sages who had transmitted it. It was a thorough and scholarly work used by Jewish scholars in later generations.

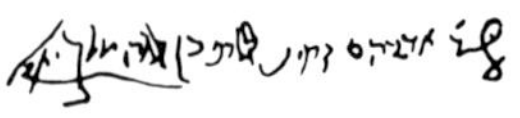

Abraham Zacuto

Zacuto eventually arrived in Ereẓ Israel where he remained for the rest of his life.

**ẒADDIK,** the title applied in the Bible and in rabbinic literature to an individual who is considered righteous in his relations with God and man. In Genesis, *Noah is described as an *ish ẓaddik,* a righteous and wholehearted man, and many of the books of the Bible, in particular Psalms and Proverbs, are replete with praise for the *ẓaddik.* Acting justly is described in Proverbs as the *ẓaddik's* greatest joy (21:15) and the author of Psalm 112 proclaims that the *ẓaddik's* righteousness will be rewarded with material prosperity and that his merit will endure forever. Even if the *ẓaddik* stumbles seven times, he will will rise up again (Proverbs 4:16) and God will not allow him to starve or be forsaken (Proverbs 10:3 and Psalms 37:25).

Nevertheless, the Bible does recognize that there are *ẓaddikim* who undergo tribulations. Prior to the destruction of the cities of *Sodom and Gomorrah, Abraham found it necessary to plead on behalf of the few potentially righteous individuals who might perish along with the wicked. And Ecclesiastes sadly noted that "there is a righteous man who perishes in his righteousness, and there is a wicked man who prolongs his years in his evil-doing." (For more on this perplexing theological problem, see *Good and Evil; *Reward and Punishment; *Suffering.)

The rabbis of the Talmud described the righteous as individuals whose behavior went beyond merely fulfilling the letter of the law, and as those who were scrupulous in monetary matters. They praised the righteousness of *ẓaddikim* as being greater than that of the ministering angels and attributed the continued existence of the world to them. According to an *aggadah* in the Babylonian Talmud, in each generation there are exactly 36 righteous men – *Lamed Vav Ẓaddikim* – who received the Divine Presence and whose righteousness sustains the world. In the folklore of the *Kabbalah and later that of *Ḥasidism, the idea of these *lamedvavniks,* as they were commonly called, assumed great significance. They were believed to be anonymous saints who remained unnoticed by other men because of their humble nature and vocations. However, in times of great peril it was believed that the *lamedvavnik* dramatically appeared and used his hidden powers to defeat the enemies of Israel. Then, as mysteriously as he came, he returned to his usual obscurity. The French author, Andre *Schwartz-Bart used this folk legend as the basis for his novel *The Last of the Just* (1959/1960).

In Ḥasidism, the religious movement that arose in central Europe during the last decades of the 18th century, the concept of the *ẓaddik* assumed a radically new connotation. It came to be applied to the charismatic leader of the ḥasidic group, a man who was endowed with great mystical power and penetrating religious insight and who functioned as confessor, moral instructor and spiritual adviser to those who considered themselves to be his followers. For more information on the nature of ḥasidic leadership, see *Ḥasidism; and for specific examples of *ẓaddikim,* see the entries on *Naḥman of Bratslav and *Levi Isaac of Berdichev in addition to the article on the *Ba'al Shem Tov.

**ZADOKITES,** priestly members of the *Qumran community (first century b.c.e. to second century c.e.). There had been a dynasty of priests serving in the Temple who were named Zadok and were known for their piety. Members of the Qumran sect considered themselves to be descendants of this line. Though they did not actually serve in the Temple, they believed that those who did were illegal priests and so the Zadokites continually prepared themselves for the day when they could take over from these usurpers and resume the full service to God in the purified Temple.

They derived the holiness of their position from a statement by the sixth century b.c.e. prophet *Ezekiel who said that the privilege of approaching God was reserved "for the priests, the Levites, the sons of Ẓadok."

Within the Qumran community, the Zadokites served as teachers of the Torah and performers of sacred rites. Newcomers to the community had to vow to place themselves "under the authority of the sons of Ẓadok, the priests, who keep the covenant."

**ZANGWILL, ISRAEL** (1864-1926), English writer on Jewish ghetto life. Born in London into a poor Russian immigrant family, Zangwill was educated at the Jews' Free School in the East End of London. In his youth he carefully noted down incidents which typified Jewish life there, and later he made use of these notes as background material for his "ghetto" novels.

Much of Zangwill's writing is concerned with the spiritual and intellectual conflicts of Jewish life in the ghetto. In *Children of the Ghetto* (1892), an internationally successful novel, his protagonist is a ghetto Jew who feels that his religion is restrictive and outdated, yet he continues to cling to the values of the Jewish past and the spiritual comfort he derives from them. In *Dreamers of the Ghetto* (1898), Zangwill presents a series of sketches based on the lives of historical personalities who resolved their conflict with Judaism by abandoning it entirely.

Zangwill also wrote several plays, only one of which, *The Melting Pot* (1909), about Jewish settlement in America, was successful.

Besides writing, Zangwill took an active part in public affairs such as women's suffrage and pacifism. *Herzl approached him in 1895 and asked for his help in rebuilding the Jewish homeland. Zangwill immediately lent his support and aided Herzl in rallying British Jewry to the Zionist cause. However, he was more committed to the idea of Jewish nationhood than to a Jewish land, and when the Seventh Zionist Congress rejected the *Uganda Scheme, he abandoned official Zionism. Zangwill then founded the Jewish Territorial Organization which was dedicated to the creation of an autonomous Jewish territory that did not necessarily have to be Palestine. (For the history of this organization, see *Territorialism.)

**ZEALOTS,** Jewish resistance fighters who revolted against the Romans in the first century c.e. The Jewish historian *Josephus reports that this was the name the rebels themselves gave to their group because of the "zealousness" of their actions.

The Zealot movement seems to have begun in 6 b.c.e. It was in that year that Judea was for the first time incorporated into the Roman empire and a tribute demanded of all Jews. A Jewish priest named Judah the Galilean then urged the Jews not to pay the tribute or to acknowledge the Roman emperor as their master. The only master over Israel, he said, is God and the Jews should rebel against these unwanted Roman rulers.

Judah and his followers encouraged their countrymen to go to battle and Josephus wrote of them that "they have a passion for liberty that is almost unconquerable, since they are convinced that God alone is their master."

Judah was apparently killed by the Romans who suppressed that first revolt, but the survivors took refuge in the deserts where they maintained a guerrilla resistance against the Romans.

The group became well-known to Jews and Romans alike. In 28 c.e., *Jesus of Nazareth chose a Zealot named Simon as one of his apostles. And at his execution, Jesus was crucified between two *lēstai* (the Greek designation for zealots) which probably indicates that the Romans viewed Jesus as a Zealot leader, though historical sources show that he probably was not.

The so-called Jewish War fought against the

Caricature by Spy of the English novelist Israel Zangwill, which appeared in *Vanity Fair,* February 25, 1897.

Israel Zangwill

Romans in 66-73 c.e. was evidently led by Menahem, son of Judah the Galilean. Menahem seized the fortress of *Masada near the Dead Sea, killed the Roman garrison and equipped his followers from the armory. He was in command of the rebel forces in Jerusalem until he was murdered. Various Zealot bands continued the struggle after Menahem's death, but in 70 c.e. the Romans finally destroyed Jerusalem and the Temple, murdering most of the Zealots and expelling the other inhabitants. A few Zealots managed to escape to Egypt and tried to organize forces there, but they were captured, tortured and executed.

The final proof of Zealot faith and fortitude was given at Masada in 73 c.e. where the last Zealot garrison under Eleazar ben Jair defied the Romans as long as possible and then, rather than surrender, killed their families and drew lots to kill themselves. For more information on this,see the article *Masada.

The spirit of courage and freedom persisted even after the death of the Zealots. Inscriptions on coins issued during the revolt proclaim their ideals "for the redemption of Zion" and "freedom of Zion." It is likely that the Zealot tradition found expression again in the *Bar Kokhba revolt against the Romans in 132-135 c.e.

**ZECHARIAH** was a prophet whose oracles are recorded in the 11th book of the Twelve Minor Prophets in the Bible. He apparently lived in the sixth century b.c.e., shortly after the destruction of the First Temple, and may have been among the first groups of Jews to return to Ereẓ Israel from the Babylonian Exile. Zechariah believed that the destruction and Exile were God's way of punishing the Jews for their sins, but he urged them to repent and rebuild the Temple with God's blessing.

Zechariah's "Vision of the Menorah," an illustration appearing in *République des Hébreux,* by Jacques Basnage (1713).

The Book of Zechariah is divided into two parts. The first eight chapters are historical in nature. They make mention of the Babylonian Exile and of contemporary figures. The second half of the book, however, makes no mention of time or place and is not as easily understood as the first. Some scholars therefore feel that the book was written by more than one person.

Both sections have one stylistic point in common: they are filled with symbolic visions, explained by an angel who speaks to Zechariah and acts as an intermediary between the prophet and God. Many of these visions concern the rebuilding of Jerusalem. For example, in the first part of the book the prophet sees four horns (like those of a ram butting against a wall), which represent the nations that destroyed Jerusalem. Zechariah them observes four craftsmen who go to cut the horns down, symbolizing the restoration of the city. The second section of the book describes the divine punishment of Israel's neighbors and the future victory of the Jews over their enemies. Jerusalem will be besieged by many nations, he predicts, but these will be struck with confusion and madness, and the "chiefs of Judah" will devour them.

Zechariah believed that the ceremonies and rituals performed in the service of God were meaningless unless accompanied by the striving for righteousness, truth and peace. He saw Jerusalem as the chosen city, protected by God.

The name Zechariah is also that of a ninth century b.c.e. priest who was stoned to death by the people of Israel for having admonished them. The tomb in the Valley of Kidron opposite the Temple Mount in Jerusalem supposedly marks his grave.

Another Zechariah, son of Jeroboam II,was king of Israel in 743 b.c.e. and was assassinated only six months after he ascended the throne.

**ZEDEKIAH** was the last king of Judah in biblical times. He was 21 years old when Nebuchadnezzar banished *Jehoiachin, his 18-year-old nephew, to Babylon and appointed him king in his place. Zedekiah became king in 597 b.c.e. and reigned for 11 years.

He inherited a small, weak, and divided kingdom. Nebuchadnezzar had destroyed many of Judah's cities and he would not allow Zedekiah to re-fortify them. Most of Judah's leaders and many craftsmen and scholars had been taken captive to Babylonia and this further weakened Judah's position. Furthermore, Zedekiah was not a strong leader: he lacked self-confidence and was indecisive.

The people still regarded Jehoiachin as their king, and they did not fully accept Zedekiah. Egypt attempted to woo Zedekiah into revolting against Babylonia and many of the people sided with Egypt against Nebuchadnezzar. The prophet * Jeremiah warned Zedekiah against revolting but other "false" prophets predicted success for those who revolted. In the ninth year of his reign, Zedekiah finally decided to revolt.

Nebuchadnezzar sent Chaldean troops to suppress the rebellion but the Egyptians came to Zedekiah's aid and the Chaldeans withdrew. When the Egyptians left, the Chaldeans returned and took the cities of Judah one by one. On the 10th of Tevet in the year 586 b.c.e., Nebuchadnezzar laid siege to Jerusalem with all his army. For half a year the city remained besieged until it fell to Nebuchadnezzar. Zedekiah attempted to flee through a cave under the city walls but he was caught. In his presence his sons were all cruelly put to death and he himself was then blinded, shackled and taken to Babylon where he died shortly thereafter.

**ZERUBBABEL,** leader of a group of Jews returning from Babylonian exile in the sixth century b.c.e. to rebuild the *Temple in Jerusalem. Zerubbabel (whose name means "scion of Babylon") was a descendant of exiled King *Jehoiachin of Judah. He and Joshua, son of Jehoẓadak the high priest, brought the first group of Jews back to the Holy Land and began the formidable task of reconstructing the Temple. Despite the harassment of neighboring peoples and the depressing barrenness and desolation of Jerusalem, they managed to set up the altar, reinstitute the sacrificial service and celebrate the Feast of Sukkot. In the second year of their return they began laying the foundations of the Temple, but their efforts were soon forced to a halt. Distrustful of the non-Jewish tribes, Zerubbabel refused their offer of help and, in retaliation, these neighboring groups blocked all further construction attempts.

For years the site remained untouched until finally the prophets Haggai and *Zechariah began exhorting the Jews to complete the unfinished task. Once more Zerubbabel and Joshua took up the challenge and this time the Temple was erected.

Zerubbabel is fondly remembered by the Jews for his accomplishment. The Second Temple is often referred to as the Temple of Zerubbabel and in the Ḥanukkah hymn *Ma'oz Ẓur,* lauding Israel's past redeemers, the "end of Babylon" is associated with Zerubbabel.

**The Book of Zerubbabel.** The name Zerubbabel is also associated with a prophet of the seventh century c.e., the last ruler of the House of David, who predicted the coming of the Messiah. The Book of Zerubbabel is found in countless medieval manuscripts and is the standard source for descriptions of the End of Days.

**ZIONISM.** The movement known as Zionism can be described as the national liberation movement of the Jews. As a formal, fully-organized movement, Zionism came into existence only in the last decades of the 19th century, at a time when nationalism had become the dominant political force throughout Europe, but the idea of Zionism – reclaiming Ereẓ Israel (Zion) as the national homeland of the Jews – was then far from being new. Ever since the destruction of the sovereign Jewish state by the Romans in 70 c.e., the Jewish people hoped and prayed for its restoration. From that time onward, the return to Zion became a central theme of Jewish prayer, and even today the Jew, no matter where he is, turns towards the Land of Israel whenever he prays.

Throughout the Middle Ages, individuals and small groups of Jews made their way to Ereẓ Israel on pilgrimages or to spend their last days there. Although there always was a permanent Jewish population in Ereẓ Israel, it remained very small, and the return to Zion, in the sense of recreating a Jewish national existence in Ereẓ Israel, was for the medieval Jew of necessity a vision and a dream, a part of the glories of the future messianic age.

**EARLY HISTORY**

In the mid-19th century, however, several active movements began to emerge in Europe which aimed at resettling large numbers of Jews in Palestine (as Ereẓ Israel was then known). The earliest of these were the Bilu and *Ḥibbat Zion movements, both of which arose in Eastern Europe in the wake of the vicious pogroms which erupted all over Russia in 1881. Earlier in the century, religious thinkers such as Judah *Alkalai and Ẓevi Hirsch *Kalischer had begun to call for Jewish resettlement of Palestine, arguing that the traditional messianic vision of the ingathering of the exiles could only be realized after the exiles themselves took the initiative in returning to the land. Other thinkers, such as Moses Hess and Leon Pinsker, who were not reared in the religious tradition but who were influenced by the waves of national fervor then sweeping Europe, and who were deeply affected by the anti-Semitic outbreaks of 1881, also wrote effective pamphlets calling for Jewish settlement of Ereẓ Israel. And in Western Europe, in the last decades of the century, many Jews became profoundly disillusioned with the results of *Emancipation and realized that in addition to civil rights for individual Jews, the Jews were also entitled to rights as a nation.

**Theodor Herzl.** The intellectual impetus provided by these thinkers and the practical, pioneering work of the Bilu'im and Ḥovevei Zion in establishing several

Plaque prepared for one of the recent Zionist Congresses held in Jerusalem, commemorating the First Zionist Congress in Basle, Switzerland, in 1897. The symbol is based on Herzl's original suggestion for the Zionist flag, a description of which he recorded and sketched in his diary.

new Jewish settlements in Ereẓ Israel (then under the rule of the Ottoman Turks), provided the background against which Theodor *Herzl rose to prominence. In 1896, he published *Der Judenstat,* and his grand vision of a vibrant, modern Jewish state created under the auspices of the great powers of the day, caught the imagination of the Ḥovevei Zion in Central and Eastern Europe, and elevated Herzl to the leadership of the return to Zion movement. Herzl sent out invitations to Ḥovevei Zion members in all parts of Europe, and in 1897 they convened in Basle, Switzerland at the First Zionist Congress. At that Congress, concerning which Herzl recorded in his diary, "Here I have created the Jewish State," the World Zionist Organization was founded as the structural framework of the Zionist movement with the officially declared goal of "establishing a home for the Jewish people in Palestine secured under public law." Herzl was elected president of the organization and several bodies were set up to implement the Zionist program. Among these was a bank to finance land purchases and support settlement, called the Jewish Colonial Trust. (Later, the Jewish National Fund for buying and afforestation of the land was also set up.) Jews throughout the world were called upon to contribute funds to these bodies and to become members of local Zionist branches. Formal organizational symbols were also adopted at the Congress, such as the movement's flag (which later became the flag of the State of Israel) and a membership fee called the shekel, after the ancient Jewish coin which used to be contributed annually to the Temple by every Jew. And from a structural point of view, it was decided that the Zionist Congress, consisting of delegates from all the local chapters spread throughout Europe, would be the supreme authority of the movement. Such Congresses at first met annually, but as the movement grew, it became standard practice to meet once every three or four years.

**Zionist Tactics.** Within the leadership circles of the Zionist Organization, there immediately arose much disagreement as to how the organization's aims should be implemented. Some thought the best way was to try, through diplomatic channels, to get the world powers of the day (Britain, France and Turkey) to grant an international charter ceding Ereẓ Israel to the Jews. Others felt that the only way was the practical, step-by-step settlement of the land. Herzl's own approach was purely political. Repeatedly he met with the German Kaiser, the Turkish Sultan and other world political leaders but his tireless efforts to win them over to his cause proved fruitless. However, while Herzl was engaged in his diplomatic maneuverings, other "practical Zionists" set about promoting and aiding pioneer settlement of the land. After Herzl's sudden and untimely death in 1904, a compromise approach, called "synthetic Zionism" was adopted by the organization. Under the leadership of A. Menaḥem *Ussishkin and later of Chaim *Weizmann, the movement declared that it "aspired to a charter" but that it realized that "our aspirations will only be achieved as a result of our practical work in Ereẓ Israel." This approach thenceforth dominated the Zionist movement.

**Uganda Scheme.** Another significant difference of opinion that arose among the early leadership of the Zionist organization centered around several proposals to settle Jews elsewhere than in Ereẓ Israel. The most famous of these was the plan proposed by the British in 1901 to settle Jews in British East Africa (the *Uganda Scheme). Herzl himself was in favor of the plan, seeing it as an immediate, humanitarian solution to the plight of the thousands of Eastern European Jews who were then fleeing Russia and had no place of refuge. However, almost all the Eastern European delegates to the Congress which discussed the issue violently opposed the plan, and the fierce controversy that ensued nearly split the Zionist Organization apart. In the end the plan was rejected, and the principle established that the Zionist organization would direct its efforts to settlement of Jews only in Ereẓ Israel.

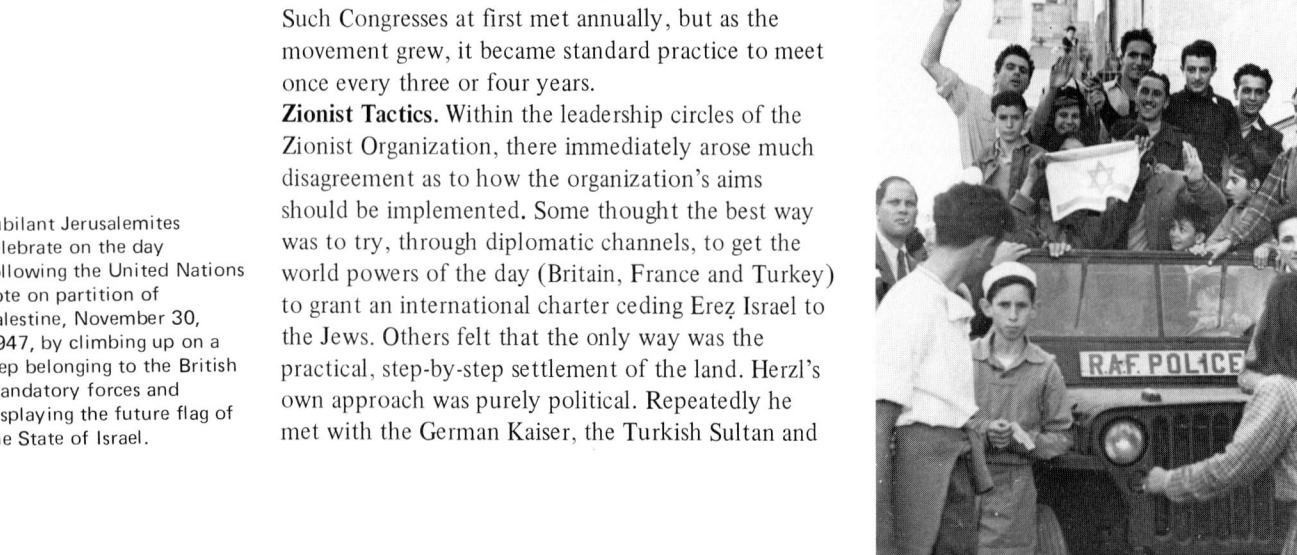

Jubilant Jerusalemites celebrate on the day following the United Nations vote on partition of Palestine, November 30, 1947, by climbing up on a jeep belonging to the British mandatory forces and displaying the future flag of the State of Israel.

**Zionist Ideologies.** The Zionist Organization's aim was thus to secure Ereẓ Israel for the Jews and to persuade the Jews to go to Ereẓ Israel. Beyond that it had no clearly defined political, social or religious platform. It was natural, therefore, that within the organization itself different Zionist groups developed, each with its own articulated ideology. Among the most prominent were the Labor-Zionists, i.e. Zionists whose political ideal was socialist and who wanted to see a Jewish socialist state in Ereẓ Israel. They were profoundly influenced by such thinkers as Ber Borochov and Naḥman Syrkin, who attempted in their writings to fuse traditional socialist and even Marxist conceptions with Zionist nationalist aspirations. Later there were – and there still are today – Communist-Zionists. There were also Zionists who wanted a free enterprise state in Ereẓ Israel, and there were religious Zionists (the *Mizrachi) who wanted the future state to be governed by religious principles and laws.

A very important aspect of Zionism was the education of Jews throughout the world towards immigration *(aliyah)* to Ereẓ Israel. For this purpose every group in the Zionist Organization set up youth movements which were described as ḥalutzic (from the word *ḥaluẓ*, which means a pioneer). These groups also provided practical training for life in Ereẓ Israel. Many even set up training farms to teach the members agriculture. For more information, see *Benei Akiva; *Betar; *Habonim; *Hashomer Ha-Ẓa'ir.

**"Cultural" Zionism.** Besides all these subgroupings there were the "cultural" or "spiritual" Zionists – those who, led by *Aḥad Ha-Am, did not see the ingathering of the exiles in Ereẓ Israel as the ultimate goal. They did not believe that a majority of the Jews of the world would emigrate to the national homeland and they therefore did not see the "Jewish problem" being solved purely by Zionist means. In Aḥad Ha-Am's view, the fundamental Jewish problem of the modern age, and the one to which Zionism could satisfactorily address itself, was the "crisis of Judaism" – the rapid disintegration of the Jews' national consciousness. His dream was that those few Jews who would in fact settle in Ereẓ Israel would serve as a "spiritual center" for the masses of Jews who would remain in the Diaspora, so that the Jewish spiritual values which would be created and developed in the Jewish land would nourish all the people and insure its continued existence and unity. These ideological differences between the various subgroupings within the Zionist organization did not, however, prevent a united commitment to the idea of creating a Jewish national existence in Palestine, and apart from occasional arguments amongst themselves as to ways and means, they worked together towards that goal.

**Non-Zionists.** There were Jews, however, who did indeed oppose Zionism. Some ultra-Orthodox circles saw the movement as an attempt to "force the end." That is, they felt that the Jews could return to Ereẓ Israel only when a sovereign Jewish state was established there under the leadership of the Messiah who would appear miraculously, and that any attempt on the part of man to bring about such a situation was heresy. At the other end of the scale were the Reform Jews who also rejected Zionism, but they did so because they understood Judaism to be a religion without nationalist implications. Thus they believed that each Jew should consider the country he lived in as his real home, and that a German Jew, for example, should regard himself as a German of the Jewish religion, or as they put it, "of the Mosaic persuasion." Still other Jews, neither ultra-Orthodox nor Reform, were apprehensive that the Zionist movement might raise doubts as to the loyalty of the Jews to the countries in which they lived, and they therefore abstained from supporting it. Even today, after the establishment of the State of Israel, such anti-Zionist views still exist, but they are held by very small groups only.

**Christian Zionism.** Although Zionism was an authentically Jewish movement, from the very beginning it received the active support of many non-Jewish groups as well. These "Christian Zionists" were for the most part strongly guided in their sympathies for Zionism by religious and theological considerations. From the time of the Protestant Reformation onward (16th century), the belief that the Jews would return to the Holy Land in accordance with biblical prophecies and as a harbinger ushering in the Second Coming and the messianic age, had become a central component of the messianic vision of many Christian groups, most notably the English Puritans. Thus, when the call for Jewish resettlement of Ereẓ Israel was sounded in the late 19th century, there were many Christians who set about aiding the Zionist cause as a practical means of hastening the fulfilment of this vision. Among the earliest and most prominent of these Christian supporters of the Zionist cause were Laurence *Oliphant, William H. Hechler and William Blackstone.

Theodor Herzl (with arms folded) at the Suez Canal, November 1903. With him are members of the El-Arish investigation commission sent to the Near East to evaluate the possibility of Jewish settlement in the region.

**Weizmann and Faisal.** Herzl once defined Zionism's aim as the "transfer of a people without a land to a land without people." This description, unfortunately, did not fit Palestine which had had a considerable Arab population since the seventh century, and almost from the very beginning of the Jewish resettlement in Palestine at the end of the 19th century, the Arabs living there began to voice strong opposition to the Zionist endeavor. Repeatedly Muslim and Christian notables of Jerusalem called upon the Ottoman administration (and later the British government) to enforce a ban on the immigration of East European Jews to Palestine and to prohibit the sale of land to them. Arabic newspapers in the country almost unanimously branded Zionism as a danger to the country. Even after the Balfour Declaration and the confirmation of the British Mandate over Palestine by the League of Nations (see below), most Arabs refused to recognize the Zionist movement as a legitimate partner in Palestine and most Arab political leaders would not negotiate with Zionist representatives. A remarkable – albeit short-lived and futile – exception to this general attitude of rejection came to the fore in 1918, during a series of meetings held between Chaim Weizmann and Emir Faisal, then the undisputed leader of Arab nationalism and the future king of Syria. Both Weizmann and Faisal agreed that there was room enough in Palestine to accommodate large Jewish and Arab populations and that, with intensive development of the land, the lot of the Arabs would be greatly improved as a result of the Zionist enterprise. In January 1919 Faisal and Weizmann signed an agreement that recommended "the closest possible collaboration in the development of the Arab State and Palestine" and mentioned measures "to encourage and facilitate the immigration of Jews to Palestine on a large scale." And in a letter he sent to Felix *Frankfurter who was a member of the American Zionist deputation at the Paris Peace Conference and who later became Justice of the United States Supreme Court, Faisal wished the Jews "a most hearty welcome home." "The two peoples," he said, were "working together for a reformed and revived Near East and our two movements complement one another." Unfortunately, Faisal who was from the Hejaz in the Arabian Peninsula, was alien to the immediate Palestinian Arab scene, and the politically active elements in the local population remained fiercely hostile to Zionism and repudiated his agreement.

**The "Arab Problem".** From the very beginning of the Zionist movement there arose a strange dichotomy among Zionist thinkers in their attitude to and treatment of the "Arab problem." Most of the early Zionists, such as Moses Hess and Herzl simply did not recognize the existence of or even the potential for such a problem; they imagined that a highly westernized element of immigrants such as the Jews would be welcomed by the Arabs because of the leadership they would provide in advancing the economy and social structure of the whole region. Only a sober realist like Aḥad Ha-Am was able to see as early as 1891 that the Arabs "will not lightly surrender the place." And after the Balfour Declaration he was in the forefront of those who believed that the only just solution would be the creation of a type of bi-national political entity in which Arabs and Jews would enjoy equal status and rights. The historical rights of the Jews to Ereẓ Israel, he then declared, did not nullify the right the Arabs of the country had acquired through generations of settlement – it was their national home as well.

In 1925, a handful of intellectuals, led by Martin *Buber and Judah Magnes (president of the Hebrew University) formed the Berit Shalom, "the Peace Association," whose aim was to seek an amicable Jewish-Arab solution for the future of Palestine. Berit Shalom advocated a bi-national state with Arabs and Jews enjoying equal rights, and although it did not see the existence of a Jewish majority as essential, it did call for the Arab acceptance of free immigration of Jews and the advancement of Hebrew culture. The Berit Shalom, however, had almost no support in the Jewish community, and its proposals found no response among the Arab leadership. At the other end of the ideological spectrum was the stand taken by Ze'ev *Jabotinsky, a stand which gained wide popular support. He declared that Palestine could not be colonized if Arab consent were required. In his view there was no "misunderstanding" between Jews and Arabs, but there was a fundamental clash of interests. The Palestinian Arabs, he believed, would accept Zionism only when they saw that they had no alternative. The moral right of the Jews to Palestine was, he declared, at least as strong, if not stronger, than that of the Arabs, especially considering that the Arabs had so much land and the Jews none. He therefore believed that there was no room for soul-searching or moral qualms about denying the Arabs something they claimed was fundamentally theirs.

**THE ROAD TO SUCCESS**

Fifty years after the convening of the First Zionist Congress in Basle in 1897, Herzl's far-reaching vision of a "Judenstat" became a concrete reality – on May May 15, 1948, the State of Israel came into being. What follows is a brief outline of the high points and the main obstacles on this seemingly miraculous road to Zionist achievement.

**The Second Aliyah.** The decade following Herzl's death in 1904 marked a period of renewed pioneering fervor among the youth of Eastern Europe. Shocked by the *Kishinev pogrom of 1903 and by the impotence of the great Russian-Jewish community in the face of similar savage mob attacks in subsequent years, close to 40,000 young Jews made their way to Palestine in the years prior to the outbreak of World War I. Although a large number left after a few years, thoroughly disillusioned by the harsh realities of life in Palestine, it was the small number who made up the hard core of this Aliyah who set the pattern of renewed Jewish life in Ereẓ Israel and who later became leaders of the *yishuv* and the future Jewish state. They were the ones who set up the first kibbutzim and the ones who established the principle of *kibbush ha-avodah* ("conquest of labor") which laid down that Jews themselves should carry out all the tasks necessary for the functioning of society no matter how lowly they were. (This ideal and that of *ḥalutziyyut* (pioneering) was the main theme of the writings of the influential Zionist thinker and member of the Second Aliyah, A.D. *Gordon.) It was also the Second Aliyah pioneers who established the basic elements of a Jewish self-defense organization known as *Ha-Shomer*, which protected Jewish settlements from Arab attacks and which served as the forerunner of the *Haganah. And it was during the period of the Second Aliyah that the Hebrew language and culture took root in the country, due largely to the tireless efforts of Eliezer *Ben-Yehuda.

**The Balfour Declaration.** World War I had a disastrous effect on the *yishuv* and brought the Second Aliyah to an end. Many thousands of Jews who were considered by the Turks to be aliens, were deported and those who were allowed to stay were penalized by heavy taxes, compulsory labor and confiscation of property. However, the war also brought an end to the Ottoman Empire and in October 1917 the English General Allenby marched into Jerusalem, signalling the beginning of a 30-year rule of the area by the British.

On November 2, 1917, Zionism realized its first and most important political achievement – the British government officially declared that it favored "the establishment in Palestine of a National Home for the Jewish People" and it proclaimed its willingness to "facilitate the achievement of this object." This declaration (which became known as the "*Balfour Declaration" because it was in the form of a letter written by Lord *Balfour, the British Foreign Secretary) was incorporated in the Mandate over Palestine conferred upon Great Britain by the League of Nations in July 1922. Thus the international charter recognizing the Jews' right to Ereẓ Israel which Herzl had so persistently and so futilely sought was finally obtained. Unfortunately turning the promise into a reality was to prove even more difficult than attaining the promise, and in fact throughout the period of the Mandate the British consistently acted to undermine the practical implementation of this promise. Already in 1920 the British High Commissioner for Palestine set out to appease the Arabs by appointing Amin al-Husseini, a man who had been sentenced to 15 years in jail for instigating riots against Jews, to the prestigious position of Grand Mufti of Jerusalem (the chief legal authority for Muslims) and al-Husseini took advantage of all the power invested in him to stir up and coordinate Arab opposition to the Zionist enterprise. In March 1921 Winston Churchill, then British colonial secretary, recognized Abdullah, the brother of Faisal, as emir of Transjordan, and soon afterward Transjordan was separated from the area to which the Balfour Declaration applied and set up as an independent state. Thus Transjordan, which in area is three times as large as western Palestine, was permanently closed to Jewish settlement.

Then in the wake of Arab riots in various parts of the country in May 1921, Churchill issued a White Paper (an official statement of government policy) which, although it reaffirmed the Balfour Declaration, also declared that the British government had no intention of allowing Palestine to become "as Jewish as England is English." The mandatory government decided, therefore, to severely restrict Jewish immigration into Palestine. Although in the next 30 years several hundreds of thousands of Jewish immigrants managed to make their way to Palestine, a large number of them were forced to enter the country illegally and under dangerous circumstances, for even in the face of the Nazi holocaust, the British stubbornly refused to relax the rigid rules they had established limiting the number of Jewish immigrants.

The British promise to maintain the security of the Jewish settlements in Ereẓ Israel also proved to be illusory. In August 1929, 70 men and women were brutally murdered in Hebron and the remainder of Hebron's Jewish inhabitants were forced to flee for their lives. Between 1936 and 1938 there were mass Arab uprisings throughout the country and the British failed to protect the Jewish settlements from Arab terrorism. Recognizing the need for an adequate self-defense organization, the *yishuv* had, in 1921, set up the Haganah. It aimed at involving the mass of the Jewish population in its own defense, and although it was looked upon by the British authorities as illegal and was subject to constant harassment by the British army, the Haganah successfully served as the defense arm of the *yishuv,* becoming the core of the Israel Defense Forces when the State came into being in 1948.

In the 1930s the British sent several commissions to Palestine to "study" the Arab-Jewish problem. The last of these, the Peel Commission, determined in the wake of the Arab riots of 1936, that the Mandate had proved unworkable. It recommended instead the division of Palestine into three geographical entities: an Arab state, A Jewish state, and a large enclave, including Jerusalem, to be administered by the British. The proposal was functionally all but unworkable, but after much heated debate within the Zionist movement, it was decided to accept it; the Arab High Command, however, rejected the proposal out of hand. In 1938 the British moved even more drastically towards a de facto abrogation of the Balfour Declaration when, in the "MacDonald White Paper" it declared its intention to close Palestine to Jewish immigration after allowing the entry of a final 75,000 persons. This change in policy was caused by the realization that a war with Nazi Germany had become unavoidable and that it was necessary for Britain to secure Arab friendship and support. Concessions to the Jews were not necessary, for their support in the struggle against the Nazis was not in the slightest doubt.

The Jewish world was practically unanimous in its opposition to this White Paper, declaring it to be utterly devoid of moral or legal validity. However the British government remained firm in its decision and with the rise of Hitler and the outbreak of the war, there began a concerted and organized effort for illegal immigration of European Jews to Palestine. The Zionist movement then set as its goal the saving of as many Jewish lives as possible, whether legally or illegally and this the wide circles of Jewish and world opinion had no alternative but to accept.

**The Biltmore Program.** During the war years the Zionist movement completely stripped away the vagueness that had previously enveloped the formulation of its ultimate aims. The Zionist organization now spoke of Palestine as "a Jewish home for the homeless" and at an exceptional Zionist conference held at the Biltmore Hotel in New York City in 1942 it announced the "Biltmore Program" – the establishment of Palestine as a Jewish commonwealth and as a sovereign Jewish state.

**The United Nations Partition Plan.** A new Labor government elected in Britain following the end of the war refused to alter the policies of its predecessor in relation to Palestine. The doors of Ereẓ Israel remained closed to Jews, leaving the hundreds of thousands of displaced persons and war refugees who were not granted asylum elsewhere in the western world, completely stranded. This callousness of the British enraged world Jewry, and the Jews of Palestine then set about establishing a Jewish Resistance Movement which aimed at wresting Ereẓ Israel from British hands. The movement was run by the Haganah in conjunction with the two other underground defense units, Irgun Ẓevai Le'ummi and Leḥi. They attacked British police posts and military installations, brought in many boat-loads of illegal immigrants and incessantly harassed and interfered with British administration of the country. The IẒL did not refrain from more violent acts of protest, most notably the bombing of British government offices located in the *King David Hotel in Jerusalem. Unable to overcome the resistance,

Drawing of Theodor Herzl addressing the Second Zionist Congress, convened in Basle, Switzerland in 1898.

Britain finally turned to the United Nations for help. A UN Special Commission on Palestine (UNSCOP) was set up and a majority of its members submitted a proposal to partition Palestine into Arab and Jewish states, with Jerusalem as an international enclave under UN trusteeship. (For more on this, see *United Nations.) On November 29, 1947, the UN General Assembly voted to adopt this plan and a half year later, on May 14, 1948, in the face of imminent invasion by the combined armies of all the surrounding Arab nations, the State of Israel was officially proclaimed by David *Ben-Gurion. Ereẓ Israel, which since the Roman conquest in the first century c.e. had never had an indigenous government (having been ruled in turn by the Romans, Arabs from the Arabian Peninsula, Ottoman Turks and the British) was once again in the hands of people who lived there.

**Zionism after the Establishment of the State.** Once the State of Israel was established, the question arose as to whether there was any further justification for a Zionist organization. Many people, including Israel's first prime minister, David Ben-Gurion, felt that Zionism had achieved its essential aim and that nothing more was left for it to do except actively to encourage all Diaspora Jewry to emigrate to the new State. However, it soon became apparent that Zionism was still valuable as an instrument of Jewish education both for the Jews of the Diaspora and for those already living within the State of Israel. Since the founding of the State, the Zionist organization has thus continued to serve an important role both in the political arena and in stimulating financial support for Israel throughout the world. And Zionism continues to act as the ideological bridge between the age-old dream of the return to Zion and the modern reality of the State of Israel.

For more detailed information on various aspects of the history of Zionism, see: *Ḥibbat Zion; Herzl, Theodor; *Weizmann, Chaim; *Aḥad Ha-Am; *Mizrachi; *Balfour Declaration; *Mandate for Palestine.

**ZODIAC,** an imaginary zone of the heavens within which lie the paths of the sun, the moon, and the planets. The zone is divided into 12 sections, each of which is designated by a sign or symbol, mostly representing animals.

The zodiac is first mentioned in Jewish texts in the ancient *Sefer Yeẓirah,* where the names given to the 12 signs are direct Hebrew translations of the Latin names. Thus Aries is called *Taleh* (ram); Taurus, *Shor* (bull); Gemini, *Te'omim* (twins); Cancer, *Sartan* (crab); Leo, *Aryeh* (lion); Virgo, *Betulah* (virgin); Libra, *Moznayim* (scales); Scorpio, *Akrav* (scorpion); Sagittarius, *Keshet* (bow); Capricorn, *Gedi* (goat); Aquarius, *Deli* (bucket); and Pisces, *Dagim* (fish).

Some Jewish astrologers believe that the twelve signs of the Zodiac correspond to the Twelve Tribes of Israel. And one rabbinical interpretation explains the signs in terms of Jewish history. Aries is the symbol of the sacrifice of Isaac, Taurus is connected with the calf which Abraham slaughtered for his angelic guests, and Gemini represents Jacob and Esau.

The signs of the zodiac figured prominently in early Jewish art, for example on the mosaic floors of ancient Palestinian synagogues as well as in prayer books and marriage certificates. A long poem based on the 12 signs of the zodiac, called *Yittaḥ Ereẓ le-Yesha* is included in old prayer books, accompanying the prayer for rain. This poem has, however, been omitted from all modern prayer books and the signs are today used in calendars and some art forms.

**ZOLA, EMILE** (1840-1902). "I Accuse!" in huge letters, was the headline of the radical Paris newspaper *The Dawn* on January 13, 1898. Under this heading the famous French writer Emile Zola accused the French government of inventing a crime of treason and falsely convicting the Jewish captain Alfred *Dreyfus. (Dreyfus was imprisoned for life on Devil's Island.) Zola's open letter to the French President Clemenceau forced the government to prosecute Zola for libel. This is exactly what Zola wanted, for it focused public attention on the Dreyfus case. He was given a jail sentence which he avoided by fleeing to England.

Emile Zola, French author and central figure in the fight to clear Alfred Dreyfus of the charge of treason.

In 1896 Zola published in a popular French journal his reasons for despising anti-Semitism: "For some years I have been following with increasing surprise and disgust the campaign which some people are trying to carry out in France against the Jews. This seems to me monstrous, by which I mean something foreign to all common sense, truth and justice, something blind and foolish, which would carry us back several centuries, and which would end in the worst of abominations – religious persecution."

In his novel *Truth,* Zola predicted the end of the Dreyfus trial: a Jew accused of using Christian blood to make *maẓẓah* was freed and his accuser was imprisoned. As a result of Zola's writing Dreyfus was given a new trial which revealed his innocence and led to his freedom. Zola, however, did not live to see the end of the trial. The chimney of his home was blocked (some say by a reactionary fanatic) and he died of carbon monoxide poisoning.

**ZUNZ, LEOPOLD** (Yom Tov Lippman; 1794-1886), historian and one of the founders of a scholarly trend known as the "Science of Judaism." The main purpose of the "Science of Judaism," formulated in Germany among the young Jewish intellectuals, was to encourage the study of Jewish subjects by means of modern scientific methods in order to give Judaism a new image in keeping with the times. By this Zunz hoped to dispel the stereotyped image of the Jew as an inferior member of society and prove instead that Judaism can and does contribute to modern life.

Leopold Zunz

Until Zunz's time, Jewish subjects had been studied strictly from a religious point of view. Zunz, however, advocated that each subject should be methodically studied from every aspect: historical, ethical, literary etc. For example, he outlined a program for studying Hebrew literature which would include the analysis of its relationship to theology, religious worship, Jewish law, and history. He also produced a comparative study of *Rashi in which he included information about the man, his work, his family and his contemporaries.

Zunz's work made a great impression on both Jewish and non-Jewish scholars. For the Jew he taught that Torah studies could be of value to any enlightened man and not just the Orthodox. For the non-Jew he provided a prime source of information on Jewish development.

After studying in the University of Berlin from 1815 to 1819, Zunz helped found the society for Jewish culture and science *(Wissenschaft des Judentums)* and edited the periodical issued by the society. He later made his living as a member of the editorial board of a Berlin daily newspaper and gave public lectures on Jewish subjects.

Zunz believed that the Jew who is familiar with his people's past will know how to reform his religious customs and thereby prepare himself for his new role in society. He therefore approved of the various reforms in German synagogues which began during his lifetime and was closely associated with members of the *Reform and *Haskalah movements.

**ZUSYA** (Meshulam Zusya) **OF HANIPOLI** (Annopol; died 1800), early ḥasidic leader and one of the best-known heroes of ḥasidic folktales. Zusya was probably born near Tarnow, Galicia. During their youth, he and his brother Elimelech wandered from place to place in the manner of ascetic kabbalists. Many folk legends tell of their wandering and present Zusya as a simple, modest, and benevolent man who despite his meager knowledge of Torah, attained merit because of his innocence and personal righteousness. Zusya's own statements, however, (few of which have survived in writing), show that he was a scholar. In addition to the close attachment to his brother, he formed a friendship with Shneur Zalman of Lyady. Apparently after the death of his teacher, the Maggid of Mezhirech, Zusya settled in Hanipoli and attracted many Ḥasidim. His oldest son, Menaḥem Ẓevi Hirsh, succeeded him in Hanipoli, while his youngest son, Israel Abraham (1772-1884) served as ḥasidic rabbi in Chernyostrov. After Israel Abraham's death, his wife led the Ḥasidim for several years. The few surviving statements of Zusya and his sons were later collected in *Menorat Zahav* (1902).

# INDEX

## HOW TO USE THE INDEX

Intelligent use of the Index enables you to make the most of *Junior Judaica*

1. In the first place, the Index gives the title of every article in bold capital letters, followed immediately by its volume and page numbers, which also appear in bold type, thus: **HISTADRUT** (Israel labor union) **3:56.**
2. More importantly, the Index lists *other* places throughout the six volumes where this subject appears in different contexts. These page references appear in plain type (though volume numbers are always printed in bold type), and follow the reference to the article itself, in numerical order. Needless to say, one should always read the first-listed reference first, since a whole article on a particular subject will obviously yield more information than may be expected from a mention of that subject in a different article.
3. You may be looking for an item which has no article of its own. Here, too, the place to start is the Index, which lists many thousands of such items and indicates where they may be found, scattered throughout the various articles on related subjects. Such items appear in plain type, thus: Lawrence of Arabia.
4. An item you need may be treated by *Junior Judaica* under a different name or with an alternative spelling. Once again, the Index is the place to start, for it will direct you to the Index entry you need, thus: Judges, *see* **COURTS**; Jerba (island off Tunisia), *see* Djerba.
5. In your reading or schooling, you may come across a puzzling term which turns out to be Hebrew, Aramaic, Yiddish, or some other language. To answer this need, the Index also serves as a glossary, and explains hundreds of such terms, including many that did not find their way into the six volumes. These non-English terms appear in italic type, unless they are relatively common in English usage, such as the word kibbutz.
6. Every reader is bothered by the fact that kings, queens, sages and scholars keep on using each other's names. The Index sorts out these namesakes for you, and tells you (in brackets) who is Maimonides (not to be confused with Naḥmanides), and who of these two scholars is known as Rambam (not to be confused with Ramban).
7. In addition, the Index includes thumbnail sketches of a great many colorful personages, places, and things. Thus, a Jew called Ai T'ien is not mentioned in the course of the six volumes (Jewish history is too long, rich, and varied for every noteworthy character to be included, even in 60 volumes), but Ai T'ien is a Jew worth reading about. In this case, too, the place to find him is the Index. And while you are browsing, you will stumble upon scores of similar items, which can make this Index enjoyable reading in its own right.
8. The Index entries are arranged alphabetically, letter by letter, up to the first comma, except that certain words like "Sir," "the," "a," and "an" are not alphabetized. *The Merchant of Venice* should therefore be sought under the letter M.
9. To summarize the main typographical conventions: **GOLEM** (bold capital letters) is the name of an article; *Golem* (italic type) is a foreign-language term, which is explained on the spot; Golem (plain type) is a different item again, which has no article of its own, but which is mentioned on the page indicated; **Bohr, Niels,** is the subject of a capsule, or mini-article, which is appended to a major article on a related subject, in this case **MATHEMATICS AND PHYSICS.** The volume and page reference which follows a capsule entry likewise appears in bold type and is first in the list of page references. Since it offers the fullest discussion of the subject, it should obviously be read before any subsequent references.
10. Finally, once you have located any desired item on the page given, skim through the next page or two within the same article in case it resurfaces.

# A


**AARON** (biblical figure; brother of Moses) **1**:1, 52; **2**:172; **4**:156; **5**:78, 174; **6**:21
Aaron, Barney (Young; sportsman) **6**:6
Aaron Ben Meir (10th-century scholar, Jerusalem) **5**:119
**AARON OF LINCOLN** (12th-century English financier) **1**:**1**; **2**:116
Aaron of York (13th-century English financier) **6**:109
Aaronsohn, Aaron (Ereẓ Israel pioneer and intelligence agent) **5**:8; **6**:91
Aaron Wolf (manuscript illuminator) **3**:81
Abarbanel, Don Isaac, *see* **ABRABANEL, ISAAC BEN JUDAH**
*Abba:* Aramaic equivalent of the Hebrew *av,* meaning father, and popularly used in modern Hebrew as a term of address corresponding to Dad.
Abba: a talmudic scholar of the late 3rd-early 4th centuries. In order not to embarrass the poor when giving charity, he would put coins in his scarf and hang it behind his back, so that the poor might take the money without being seen by their benefactor.
Abbahu (talmudic sage who lived in Caesarea at the end of the 3rd century c.e. He declined appointment as head of the academy in favor of Abba of Acre, because the latter was poor and heavily in debt. The Talmud relates that he did not disclose the true reason for his decision, preferring to ascribe it to Abba's superior scholarship) **1**:18
**ABBASIDS** (Muslim-Arabian dynasty) **1**:**2**; **4**:171; **6**:61
**ABBAYE** (3rd-4th century talmudic sage) **1**:**2**; **5**:95
**ABBREVIATIONS** **1**:3,8, 11; **4**:144, 175
Abd al-Rahman III (Spanish caliph) **3**:55
Abdihiba (ancient ruler of Jerusalem) **1**:80
**ABDULLAH IBN HUSSEIN** (king of Jordan) **1**:**4**; **3**: 178; **6**:119
Abdullah Yacoub, *see* **QUERIDO, JACOB**
Abed-Nego (biblical figure), *see* Hananiah, Mishael, and Azariah
Abel (biblical figure), *see* **CAIN AND ABEL**
**ABENATAR MELO, DAVID** (17th-century Marrano poet) **1**:**5**, 6
Abenatar Melo, Immanuel (Dutch *ḥazzan*) **1**:6
Aberdeen: Scottish seaport, northeast of Edinburgh. In 1665 it was reported that a ship with sails of white satin had put into harbor with a large party of Jews, presumably on their way to join the pseudo-messiah Shabbetai Zevi in the Levant. Today Aberdeen has a community of modest size.
Abiathar (high priest) **1**:103
Abimelech (biblical figure, Philistine king) **1**:111; **3**:97; **5**:52
Abimelech (biblical figure; son of Gideon, and ruler of Shechem) **2**:167; **5**:162
Abinadab (biblical figure) **1**:9
Abiram (biblical figure) **4**:29
Ableson, Frankie, *see* **VAUGHAN, FRANKIE**
Ablution (the washing of one's body or part of it as a religious rite), *see* **MIKVEH**, and **PURITY AND IMPURITY, RITUAL**
Abner ben Ner (biblical figure; opponent of King David) **3**:173
**ABNER OF BURGOS** (13th-century apostate) **1**:**6**, 60
Abortion **1**:151, **4**:58
**ABRABANEL, ISAAC BEN JUDAH** (15th-century statesman and scholar, Spain) **1**:**6**, 148; **4**:175
**ABRAHAM** (biblical figure; patriarch) **1**:**7**
—History: **1**:25, 111; **2**:80;**3**:41, 70, 96; **4**:131; **5**:16, 52, 162, 180
—Concepts: **1**:28, 86; **4**:165; **5**: 179
Abraham (son of Maimonides) **4**:83
Abraham, Chapman (Detroit pioneer) **2**:71
Abraham bar Ḥiyya ha-Nasi of Barcelona (12th-century scholar) **1**:87; **2**:104; **4**:108
Abraham ben David of Posquières (c. 1125-1198, talmudic authority of Provence, known both for his writings on the laws relating to women, and as a critic of Maimonides) **4**:85
**ABRAHAM BEN JACOB** (17th-century copper engraver) **1**:**8**
**ABRAHAMS** (family of English athletes) **1**:**9**
Abrahams, Sir Adolphe (English athlete) **1**:9
Abrahams, Harold Maurice (English athlete) **1**:9
Abrahams, Israel (English scholar) **3**:172
Abrahams, Sir Sidney (English athlete) **1**:**9**
Abramovitz, Max (U.S. architect) **1**:69
Abramowitsch, Shalom Jacob, *see* **MENDELE MOKHER SEFORIM**
Abrass, Osias (19th-century cantor) **3**:29
Absalom (biblical figure) **2**:57; **3**:174
**ABU GHOSH** (Arab village, Israel) **1**:**9**
Abu Isa (false messiah) **4**:126
**ABULAFIA** (Sephardi family) **1**:**9**
Abulafia, Abraham ben Samuel (13th-century kabbalist, Spain) **1**:10
Abulafia, Ḥayyim ben Jacob (17th-century talmudist, Ereẓ Israel) **1**:10
Abulafia, Ḥayyim ben Moses (17th-18th century rabbi, Ereẓ Israel and Turkey) **1**:10, 89
Abulafia, Ḥayyim Nissim (ḤANA; (19th century chief rabbi, Ereẓ Israel) **1**:10
Abulafia, Isaac ben Ḥayyim (18th-century rabbi, Ereẓ Israel) **1**:10
Abulafia, Jacob ben Solomon (16th-17th century rabbi, Damascus) **1**:10
Abulafia, Meir (12th-13th century rabbi, Spain) **1**:9
Abulafia, Samuel ben Meir ha-Levi (14th-century financier, Spain) **1**:10
Abulafia, Todros ben Joseph ha-Levi (13th-century rabbi, Spain) **1**:9
Abulafia, Todros ben Judah ha-Levi (13th-century Hebrew poet, Spain) **1**:10
Academic Council on Soviet Jewry (U.S.) **6**:68
Academies, Babylonian, *see under* **BABYLONIA**
Academy on High (Hebrew: *Yeshivah shel shel Ma'alah*): in rabbinic tradition, the academy (not identical with paradise) where Torah scholars continue their studies and debates. To this day, announcements of the death of a sage often say that on such-and-such a date he was "summoned to the Academy on High." The Creator Himself presides over its deliberations, and it is He Who teaches Torah to young children who died before they could study. On the Day of Atonement, before *Kol Nidrei,* the permission of the Academy on High is invoked to hold the service together with the "transgressors" — those who were forced to baptize.
Academy of the Hebrew Language

(Israel) **3**:34. *See also Va'ad ha-Lashon.*
**ACQUISITION** (legal term) **1:10; 3**:17; **5**:132
**ACRE** (city, Israel) **1:11**, 89, 99; **4**:172
**ACROSTICS** (poetic device) **1:11**, 4; **4**:38, 144
**ACTION FRANÇAISE** (anti-Semitic movement) **1:12**, 53
Actors, *see* **THEATER**
**ADAM AND EVE** (biblical figures) **1:12**, 103, 151, 172; **2**:175; **6**:93
Adani, Solomon (Yemenite Bible commentator) **6**:102
Adar (Hebrew month) **2**:154; **5**:86
**ADAR, THE SEVENTH OF** (minor festival) **1:13; 2**:127; **3**:52; **4**:158
Aden (city, Arabia) **1**:61
Adenauer, Konrad (chancellor of West Germany) **5**:100
Adiabene (ancient land) **3**:43
Adjima, Yeshaya (Jaffa pioneer) **6**:31
Adler, Alfred (psychologist) **5**:85
Adler, Cyrus (U.S. scholar) **3**:172
Adler, Dankmar (U.S. architect) **1**:69
**ADLER, ELKAN NATHAN** (book collector) **1:13**, 161
Adler, Nathan Marcus (chief rabbi, England) **1**:14; **3**:173
*Adloyada* (Purim festivities) **1**:28
Adonai (divine name), *see* **GOD**
Adonijah (biblical figure) **2**:57; **5**:182
*Adon Olam* (prayer) **5**:70
Adoption **2**:14
*Ado-shem* (popular substitute for one of the divine names) **2**:171
**ADRET, SOLOMON BEN ABRAHAM** (13th-century rabbinic scholar, Spain) **1:14**, 78; **4**:103
Adrianople: Turkish town near frontier with Greece, named after Hadrian (2nd century c.e.), where there has been a Jewish presence since the beginning of the Byzantine period.
Adultery **5**:153
**ADVERTISING 1:15**
Aelia Capitolina (Roman name for Jerusalem) **3**:4, 146
**AERONAUTICS, AVIATION AND ASTRONAUTICS 1:16; 2**:98
**AFGHANISTAN** (state in Central Asia) **1:17**
Afikim (kibbutz) **2**:65
*Afikoman* (part of the *seder* ritual) **5**:41
Afterlife, *see* **LIFE AND AFTERLIFE**
Agadir (city, Morocco) **4**:152
**AGE AND THE AGED 1:17**
**AGGADAH** (talmudic anecdotes, parables, ethical teachings, and poetic explanations of Scripture) **1:18**, 49; **4**:133; **5**:36; **6**:15, 22, 26
**AGNON, SHMUEL YOSEF** (modern Hebrew author) **1:19**
Agranat Commission (committee headed by Shimon Agranat, president of the Supreme Court of Israel, which investigated responsibilities and events concerning the Yom Kippur War, and reported its findings to Cabinet on 30 January, 1975) **6**:108
**AGRICULTURE 1:20; 3**:114; **4**:18, 137, 142, 159; **5**:23, 127, 160; **6**:26, 43, 91
**AGRIPPA I** (king of Judea) **1:22; 2**:25
Agrippa II (king of Judea) **2**:25
Agudat Israel (Orthodox organization and political party) **1**:130; **2**:185; **3**:1, 5, 63, 113, 123; **4**:30; **5**:30
Aguilar, Diego d' (community leader, Austria) **1**:91
**AGUILAR, GRACE** (19th-century English authoress) **1:22**
**AHAB** (biblical figure; king of Israel) **1:23**, 65, 88; **2**:100; **4**:115; **5**:24
**AḤAD HA-AM** (Hebrew writer) **1:24**, 133; **3**:36; **6**:117
*Aḥaronim* (authorities in rabbinic law from the 16th century on; compare *Rishonim*) **3**:59
Ahasuerus (biblical figure; king of Persia, and a key personage in the Purim story) **5**:86
Ahaz (biblical figure; king of Judah) **3**:98
Ahaziah (biblical figure; king of Judah) **1**:88; **3**:138
Aḥdut ha-Avodah (political party, Israel) **3**:112
Aḥer, Aḥerim (talmudic sage), *see* **ELISHA BEN AVUYA**
Ahijah the Shilonite: Israelite prophet during the reign of Solomon.
**AḤIMAAẒ BEN PALTIEL** (11th-century poet and historian, Italy) **1:25**
Airplanes, *see* **AERONAUTICS, AVIATION, AND ASTRONAUTICS**
Ai T'ien (born about 1545): Chinese Jew who gave detailed information on the Kaifeng Jewish community to an Italian Jesuit missionary, Matteo Ricci, who in turn reported this in a letter to Rome dated July 26, 1605 — the first report to reach Europe concerning the presence of Jews in China in modern times.
Akaba (Arabic name for Eilat, Israel) **2**:96
*Akademie für die Wissenschaft des Judentums* (Haskalah institution, Berlin) **3**:27
**AKAVYAH BEN MAHALALEL** (1st-century c.e. talmudic sage) **1:25**
*Akdamut* (Shavuot hymn) **5**:161
**AKEDAH** (biblical episode; the near-sacrifice of Isaac) **1:25**, 8; **3**:96, 99
Akhenaton (pharaoh) **2**:93
**AKIVA** (1st-2nd-century talmudic sage) **1:26**, 19, 106, 118, 177; **2**:101; **3**:184; **4**:36; **5**:24, 166, 185; **6**:24, 36, 84
Akkad (ancient region) **4**:124
Al-Aqsa Mosque (Temple Mount, Jerusalem) **3**:68
Albeck, H. (modern talmudic scholar) **6**:27
Albert II: Hapsburg duke of Austria 1330-1358, who gained a reputation as a "friend of the Jews." In 1338 he protected the communities of Vienna and Wiener Neustadt against massacres and requested Pope Benedict XII to investigate the validity of a libel of Desecration of the Host at Pulkau, and in 1349, following massacres in the wake of an outbreak of the Black Death, Death, he had three of the ringleaders executed.
Albert V: archduke of Austria 1411-1439, and by stages also king of Hungary, emperor of Germany and king of Bohemia. An alleged Desecration of the Host at Enns in 1420 induced Albert to institute a thoroughgoing persecution of the Jews in his realm, known in Jewish sources as the Wiener Gezerah ("the Decrees of Vienna"). The climax of this was the wholesale burning of Jews at the stake on March 12, 1421; this achievement is praised in his epitaph.
**ALBO, JOSEPH** (15th-century philosopher, Spain) **1:27**, 72, 116
**ALBRIGHT, WILLIAM FOXWELL** (biblical archaeologist) **1:28**
**ALCHEMY** (medieval mystical metallurgy) **1:28**
**ALCOHOL 1:28; 3**:25; **5**:86; **6**:92
Aleichem, Shalom (Yiddish writer), *see* **SHALOM ALEICHEM**
*Aleinu le-Shabbe'aḥ* (prayer) **5**:68, 71
Aleppo (city, Syria) **6**:19
Alexander (son of Herod) **3**:28
Alexander I (czar) **2**:131; **5**:116
Alexander II (czar) **2**:1; **3**:53; **5**:116
Alexander III (czar) **5**:8
Alexander, William (English poet) **3**:139
**ALEXANDER THE GREAT** (king of Macedonia) **1:29; 2**:94, 171; **3**:44
Alexander Yannai (king of Judea), *see* **YANNAI, ALEXANDER**
**ALEXANDRIA** (city, Egypt) **1:30; 2**:25; **5**:53
Alfandari: Spanish family claiming descent from Bezalel of the tribe of Judah, many of whose members were major scholars and communal leaders, such as Aaron ben Moses (1690-1774), who became chief rabbi in Hebron, and Solomon Eliezer ben Jacob (1826 or 1829-1930), who was chief rabbi of Damascus and Safed, and settled in Jerusalem in 1926.
**ALFASI, ISAAC BEN JACOB** (11th-century halakhic scholar; known as the Rif) **1:30; 4**:42; **6**:27
*Al Fataḥ* (Arab terrorist organization) **1**:63; **4**:47, 56
Alfonso V (king of Portugal) **1**:6
Alfonso VIII (king of Castile, Spain) **3**:168
Alfonso X (king of Castile, Spain) **1**:9, 98

**ALGERIA** (country in North Africa) **1:31,** 36
Algiers (city, North Africa) **1**:32
*Al Ha-Nissim* (Ḥanukkah prayer) **3**:20
Al-Ḥarizi, Judah (1170-1235, poet and translator, whose extensive travels helped acquaint Jewish communities in the Far East with Spanish-Hebrew culture; except for Samuel ha-Nagid was the only medieval Hebrew poet to describe battle scenes) **6**:51
*Al Ḥet* (prayer of confession) **2**:60
Al-Husseini, Hajj Amin (Grand Mufti of Jerusalem) **3**:151; **6**:119
Alignment (political party, Israel), *see Ma'arakh*
Aliturus (1st-century actor) **6**:37
*Aliyah* (Hebrew: "ascent;" the honor of being called to the Reading of the Torah during synagogue services) **6**:47
*Aliyah* (Hebrew: "ascent;" immigration to Israel) **3**:169; **4**:15, 33, 46; **6**:101, 110, 117
*Aliyah Bet, see* **ILLEGAL IMMIGRATION**
*Aliyah le-regel, see* **PILGRIMAGE**
**ALKABEZ, SOLOMON** (16th-century Safed kabbalist; author of the *Lekhah Dodi* Sabbath hymn) **1:32,** 11; **2**:38
**ALKALAI, JUDAH** (19th-century rabbi and forerunner of modern Zionism) **1:32; 6**:115
Al Kuds (Muslim name for Jerusalem) **3**:143
Allah (Muslim name for God) **4**:164
**Allen, Woody** (U.S. comedian) **6**:39
**ALLENBY, EDMUND HENRY HYNMAN, VISCOUNT** (British military leader) **1:33**
Allenby Bridge (over Jordan River) **3**:179
**ALLIANCE ISRAELITE UNIVERSELLE** (organization) **1:34; 3**:55; **4**:153; **5**:20
**ALLON, YIGAL** (statesman, Israel) **1:34**
**ALLUF** (a Hebrew title of honor or authority) **1:35**
Almudaina (fortress in Majorca) **4**:85
Alphabet, Hebrew, *see under* **HEBREW LANGUAGE**
Alroy, David (or Menahem; false messiah in 12th-century Kurdistan, whose adherents in Baghdad once stayed up all night waiting to be flown to Jerusalem by an airlift of angels) **4**:126
**ALSACE-LORRAINE** (French provinces) **1:35,** 73; **2**:143
Alshekh, Moses (16th-century): born in Adrianople; rabbi, popular Bible commentator and halakhic authority; believed to have died in Damascus. Visitors to the Old City of Safed are still shown the synagogue where he used to preach.
**ALTALENA** (ship bringing immigrants and arms to Israel in 1948) **1:36,** 113; **3**:96
**ALTAR 1:36**
Alter, Isaac Meir Rothenberg (founder of Gur ḥasidic dynasty) **2**:178
Alterman, Nathan (writer, Israel) **3**:38
*Al tikrei* (Hebrew: "do not read"): a term used by the sages to indicate that a word in Scripture should be read as if it were spelled or punctuated differently, in order to give it a significance other than its literal meaning. The latter always remains valid, since there is a rule that "a verse never loses its plain meaning;" the new interpretation is thus a means of revealing additional insights into the Scriptural text.
Altman, B. (N.Y. businessman) **2**:70
*Altneuland* (German: "Old-New Land"): Herzl's utopian Zionist novel published in 1902, which gave eloquent expression to the yearning of the Jewish people for its historic homeland.
*Altneuschul* (the imposing medieval synagogue of Prague, whose musty attic — so visitors are warned — is haunted to this day by a 16th-century *golem*) **5**:66
Altona (city, Germany) **3**:14
**AMALEK** (ancient Near Eastern people) **1:37; 3**:16; **5**:86, 126, 141, 146; **6**:79
Amasa (biblical figure) **3**:174
Amen (response in prayer) **1**:119
Amenhemet I (pharaoh) **2**:94
America, *see* **UNITED STATES OF AMERICA**
**AMERICAN COUNCIL FOR JUDAISM** (anti-Zionist organization) **1:37**
Americanization (of Jewish migrants) **6**:64
American Jewish Committee **6**:64
**AMERICAN JEWISH CONGRESS** (organization) **1:37,** 163
American Jewish Joint Distribution Committee (relief organization) **1**:127; **2**:77; **3**:171
American Joint Reconstruction Foundation **3**:171
**AM HA-AREẒ** (Hebrew term; usually means "ignoramus") **1:38**
Amharic (language) **2**:114
Amichai, Yehuda (writer, Israel) **3**:38
**AMIDAH** (Hebrew: "standing;" prayer commonly called *Shemoneh-Esreh*, and recited while standing) **1:38**
—General: **1**:119, 181; **2**:37, 153; **4**:142; **5**:68, 72
—Particular Occasions: **2**:60, 128; **3**:20; **5**:123
*Ammah* (cubit; biblical unit of measurement) **6**:86
Ammonites (biblical nation) **3**:138
**AMNON OF MAINZ** (10th-century martyr) **1:41; 5**:108
Amon (king of Judah) **3**:184
Amon, Moses (physician to Suleiman I) **6**:14
*Amora* (any sage quoted in the Gemara, 3rd-5th centuries c.e.; plural: *amora'im*) **3**:58; **5**:131; **6**:25
Amorite (ancient Middle Eastern people) **1**:182; **4**:124, 145
**AMOS** (biblical figure; prophet, 8th century b.c.e.) **1:42,** 103, 141
Am Oved (publishing house, Israel) **5**:162
Amram (biblical figure; father of Moses) **4**:154
Amram ben Sheshna, *see* **AMRAM GAON**
**AMRAM GAON** (9th-century scholar, Babylonia) **1**:42; **4**:51; **5**:74
'Amr ibn al-'As (founder of Cairo) **1**:178
**AMSTERDAM** (city, Holland) **1:43; 3**:63; **5**:2, 54, 76; **6**:45
**AMULET** (charm worn for protection) **1:44,** 47, 152; **2**:59, 104, 116, 119; **3**:17; **4**:78, 81; **6**:30
Amunhotep III (pharaoh) **2**:93
**ANAN BEN DAVID** (8th-century Karaite) **1:45,** 148; **4**:12
Ananites (sect) **1**:45
Anathoth (biblical site) **1**:103
Anatolia, *see* **ASIA MINOR**
**ANATOMY** (study of the human body) **1:45,** 93, 149; **3**:31
Anau (Italian family), *see* **ANAV**
**ANAV** (Italian family) **1:46**
Anav, Abraham (13th-century physician and talmudist) **1**:46
Anav, Abraham ben Jehiel (11th-century talmudist) **1**:46
Anav, Benjamin (13th-century physician and talmudist) **1**:46
Anav, Benjamin ben Abraham (13th-century halakhist, astronomer, and poet) **1**:46
Anav, Daniel ben Jehiel (11th-century talmudist) **1**:46
Anav, Jehiel (12th-century papal financier) **3**:128
Anav, Jehiel ben Abraham (11th-century poet) **1**:46
Anav, Jehiel ben Jekutiel (13th-century poet, copyist, and moralist) **1**:47
Anav, Judah ben Benjamin (13th-century talmudist and poet) **1**:46
Anav, Nathan ben Jehiel (11th-century talmudist) **1**:46
Anav, Paola (13th -century female copyist) **1**:47
Anav, Zedekiah ben Abraham (13th-century halakhic scholar) **1**:47
Andersen, Hans Christian (author) **3**:38
Andreas (archbishop; convert to Judaism) **5**:18
**ANGELS AND DEMONS 1**:**47,** 100; **3**:23, 134; **4**:1, 81; **5**:123; **6**:75, 114
**ANIELEWICZ, MORDECAI** (leader of Warsaw Ghetto revolt) **1:47; 3**:22; **6**:99
*An'im Zemirot:* synagogue hymn also called "Song of Glory," ascribed to Judah he-Ḥasid of Regensburg (died 1217). It is an alphabetical acrostic of

31 lines, praising God's greatness, and recited at end of Sabbath and festival *Musaf* services in the Ashkenazi rite.
**ANIMALS 1:48**
—General: **1**:12, 149; **2**:136; **3**:45, 103; **4**:52
—Laws: **2**:53, 73, 132; **4**:142; **5**:87, 129, 162; **6**:71
*Aninut* (initial period of mourning) **2**:62
**ANOINTING 1:52; 2**:40; **3**:83; **4**:24; **5**:19
*Anschluss* (Germany's annexation of Austria, 1938) **6**:74
Ant **1**:51
**ANTHROPOLOGY** (the study of man) **1:53**
Anthropomorphism (manlike descriptions of divinity) **4**:85
Antibiotic drugs **6**:78
Anti-Defamation League **1**:156
Antigonus (son of John Hyrcanus I) **1**:71
Antigonus II (Mattathias) **2**:125
Antioch (Hellenistic name for Jerusalem) **3**:146; **5**:149
Antiochus III (Seleucid ruler, 3rd century b.c.e.) **1**:83
Antiochus IV Epiphanes (Seleucid ruler during Hasmonean revolt, 2nd century b.c.e.) **2**:22, 49, 125; **3**:17, 18, 44; **4**:104, 122; **5**:148
Antipater (Idumean ruler, 1st century b.c.e.) **3**:48
**ANTI-SEMITISM 1:53**
—Medieval Manifestations: **1**:97, 152, 155; **2**:3, 36, 49, 70, 118, 164; **3**:89; **4**:97; **5**:17; **6**:53
—Post-Medieval Manifestations: **1**:96, 111, 113, 162; **2**:1, 20, 69, 82, 123, 146, 148; **3**:66; **4**:111; **5**:14, 33, 81, 163; **6**:38, 54
—Some Representative Anti-Semites: **1**:6, 161; **2**:17, 19, 95, 128; **3**:4, 62; **4**:73; **5**:49, 104; **6**:7, 50, 65
—Some Representative Movements: **1**:12, 73; **2**:125; **3**:10; **4**:182
—Attitudes to Anti-Semitism: **1**:83, 156; **2**:85, 102, 174; **3**:50; **4**:4, 49; **5**:149, 155; **6**:121
—*See also* under individual countries and cities, and under **RACIAL DISCRIMINATION.**
Antoninus (Roman personage whose friendly conversations with Judah ha-Nasi are frequently mentioned in the *aggadah,* though it is difficult to ascertain which of the powerful rulers of that name is referred to) **4**:2; **5**:104
Antoninus Caracalla (Roman emperor) **4**:2
Antwerp (city, Belgium) **1**:114
*Anusim* (Hebrew: "forced converts" to Christianity), *see* **MARRANOS**
Apartheid (separatist racial policy, South Africa) **5**:186; **6**:15
Ape **1**:51
*Apikoros:* Hebrew version of a Greek name; in common usage means atheist.
Apocalypse (ancient writings describing revelations and visions, relating especially to the End of Days) **2**:106
**APOCRYPHA** (ancient books not included in the canon of the Bible) **1:58,** 124, 135; **3**:3, 35; **4**:4, 5
**APOSTASY** (conversion from Judaism) **1:59**
—General: **1**:83, 173; **2**:20; **3**:47, 78, 87; **4**:97, 103
—Some Representative Apostates: **1**:6; **3**:43; **4**:105; **5**:33, 49, 89; **6**:52
Apostomos (Roman leader) **6**:27
Aqaba (place, Israel), *see* Akaba
Aquila, *see* **ONKELOS AND AQUILA**
**ARABIA** (peninsula in the Middle East) **1:60,** 61; **6**:100
Arabic **3**:31
**ARABS 1:61**
—Early History: **1**:2; **3**:99; **4**:13, 87, 164, 171; **5**:23; **6**:60
—20th Century: **1**:4, 60, 111, 163, 179; **2**:16, 109; **4**:16, 47, 56, 178; **5**:20, 175, 176; **6**:19, 61, 81, 107, 118
**ARAD** (city, Israel) **1:63,** 65; **3**:184
Arafat, Yasser (Arab terrorist leader) **6**:62
**ARAMAIC** (ancient Semitic language) **1:64,** 144; **3**:31, 171; **4**:101; **5**:25; **6**:26
Arameans (ancient Semitic people) **6**:18
Ararat (biblical site) **2**:137; **4**:32
Ararat (U.S. Jewish colony) **5**:10
Araunah (biblical figure) **6**:33
*Aravot* (willow sprigs; one of the "four species" of plants used in Sukkot ceremony) **6**:12
*Arba'ah minim* (Hebrew: "four species" of plants used in Sukkot ceremony) **6**:12
*Arba'ah Turim* (legal code) **3**:134; **4**:44
*Archa:* chest containing records of Jewish financial transactions, instituted in England in 1104 with the object of preserving records of Jewish assets for the Exchequer.
**ARCHAEOLOGY** (study of the material remains of the ancient past) **1:64**
—General: **1**:68; **2**:23, 140; **4**:180; **5**:34, 65, 147; **6**:32, 78
—Sites: **1**:63, 77, 80; **3**:141, 159; **4**:24, 106, 115; **5**:15, 139; **6**:32, 59
—Archaeologists: **1**:28; **2**:168; **4**:111; **6**:11, 82, 99
Archelaus (son of Herod I) **1**:103
**ARCHITECTURE 1:68,** 64; **4**:10, 115, 124; **5**:130, 181; **6**:33
**ARCHIVES** (collections of documents) **1:69**
Arch of Titus (Rome) **6**:44
Aretas (Nabatean king) **4**:171
**ARGENTINA** (country in South America) **1:70**
Ari (16th-century kabbalist), *see* **LURIA, ISAAC**
**ARISTEAS, LETTER OF** (ancient document) **1:71; 5**:153
Aristobulus (c.35 b.c.e. to 7 b.c.e., when he was put to death by order of his father, King Herod) **1**:22; **3**:28
**ARISTOBULUS I** (Judah; son of John Hyrcanus I; first Hasmonean king of Judea, 104-103 b.c.e.) **1:71; 3**:27; **5**:133; **6**:100
Aristobulus II (last independent Hasmonean king of Judea, 67 to 63 b.c.e.) **3**:69; **4**:6
**ARISTOTLE** (Greek philosopher) **1:72,** 83; **4**:64, 109; **5**:82, 91
Arkia (Israel Domestic Airlines) **3**:120
**Arkin, Alan W.** (U.S. actor) **4:161**
Ark of the Covenant (chest in the Tabernacle and Temple, housing the Tablets of the Law) **1**:9; **2**:56; **3**:185; **6**:21, 22, 33, 80
Ark of the Law (cabinet in synagogue housing Torah scrolls; in Hebrew, *aron kodesh,* "holy ark;" counterpart of the Ark of the Covenant in the Tabernacle and Temple which contained the Tablets of the Law) **6**:47
**ARLOSOROFF, CHAIM** (Zionist leader) **1:72**
Armaggedon (New Testament term) **4**:115
**ARMLEDER** (14th-century anti-Semitic gangs) **1:73,** 35, 53
Aron, Israel (17th-century communal leader, Berlin) **4**:56
*Aron kodesh* (Hebrew: "holy ark;" cabinet in synagogue housing Torah scrolls), *see* Ark of the Law
Arons, Leo (physicist) **3**:92
*Arraby Mor* (community head, Portugal) **5**:64
Arrow Cross (Nazi movement) **1**:170
**ART 1:73**
—Artists: **1**:8, 133; **2**:101, 109; **3**:127; **4**:15, 59, 130, 145; **5**:25, 54, 57, 100, 114, 155; **6**:9, 20
—Media: **1**:16, 69, 129; **2**:87; **3**:81, 130; **4**:101; **5**:35, 63, 146
—Miscellaneous: **1**:26; **2**:88, 89, 137, 141; **3**:45, 163; **4**:159
Artaxerxes I (king of Persia) **2**:120
Artaxerxes II (king of Persia) **2**:120
Artaxerxes III (king of Persia) **4**:5
Arvic (language) **3**:171
*Arvit* (evening prayer service), *see Ma'ariv*
Aryan (linguistic grouping) **5**:92
Asa: king of Judah 908-867 b.c.e., who made genuine efforts to remove pagan influences and attract to the kingdom of Israel those who were loyal to the Temple. In the Aggadah he is credited with performing many good deeds.
**ASAPH HA-ROFE** (6th-century physician) **1:76; 4**:113; **5**:84
**ASCETICISM** (rejection of physical pleasures) **1:77,** 157; **3**:23; **4**:182
Asch, Sholem (1880-1957): Polish Yiddish novelist and dramatist who

lived in the U.S., France and Poland. Though he died in London, his last years were spent in Bat Yam, a suburb of Tel Aviv, where his house was later converted into a museum.
*Aseret yemei teshuvah* (Hebrew: "ten days of penitence;" the period from Rosh Ha-Shanah to Yom Kippur) **5**:110
**ASHDOD** (city, Israel) **1:77**
Asher (biblical figure; son of Jacob; founder of the tribe named after him) **3**:45; **6**:53
**ASHER BEN JEHIEL** (13th-14th century halakhic scholar) **1:78; 3**:134; **4**:43
**ASHI** (4th-century talmudic sage) **1:79; 6**:25
**ASHKELON** (city, Israel) **1:80**
**ASHKENAZI, ASHKENAZIM** (term describing communities stemming from Europe, excluding Spain and Portugal; as opposed to Sephardim) **1:81**, 94, 174; **2**:138, 162; **3**:20, 34; **5**:131, 151
Ashkenazi, Bezalel (16th-century scholar) **4**:73
**ASHKENAZI, ẒEVI HIRSCH** (17th-18th century rabbi) **1:81; 2**:103; **3**:10
Ashman, A. (playwright, Israel) **3**:40
*Ashrei* (Psalm 145, component of daily prayer services) **5**:73, 84
**ASIA 1:82**
**ASIA MINOR** (part of Asia nearest Europe) **1:83**, 82; **3**:62; **4**:124
Asian Games (sports contest) **6**:5
Assembly of Jewish Notables (Napoleonic organization) **4**:176
Assideans (2nd-century b.c.e. pietists), *see* Hassideans
**ASSIMILATION** (losing Jewish identity) **1:83**, 166; **3**:26; **4**:49, 119, 174; **5**:6; **6**:7, 54, 104. *See also* under individual countries.
Assyria (ancient Near Eastern kingdom) **3**:52, 98, 104; **4**:5
**ASTROLABE** (astronomical instrument) **1:85**, 87; **6**:112
**ASTROLOGY 1:85; 3**:75; **5**:12; **6**:121. *See also* **ASTROLABE.**
**ASTRONOMY 1:86**, 59, 85; **3**:92 **4**:108; **6**:112
Aswan (city, Egypt) **2**:99
*Atarah* (Hebrew: "crown;" decorative collar of *tallit*) **6**:23
**ATHALIAH** (biblical figure) **1:88**
**ATHENS** (city, Greece) **1:88**
Athletics, *see* **SPORTS**
*Atlantic* (ship of "illegal" immigrants) **5**:44
Atomic energy, *see* Nuclear research
Atonement, *see* **SIN AND REPENTANCE**
**ATTAR, ḤAYYIM** (17th-18th century kabbalist) **1:88**
Attell, Abe (sportsman) **6**:6
Attlee, Clement (British statesman) **2**:22
**AUERBACH, ARNOLD JACOB** ("Red;" U.S. basketball coach) **1:89; 6**:6
*Aufrufen* (Yiddish: "calling up;" festive Reading of the Torah in the synagogue in the presence of a bridegroom who, after reciting the benedictions, is customarily showered with sweets) **4**:100
Auschwitz (concentration camp) **2**:32, 39
**AUSTRALIA AND NEW ZEALAND 1:89; 3**:97; **4**:118, 146; **6**:76
**AUSTRIA 1:91; 6**:73
Autobiographies, *see* **BIOGRAPHIES AND AUTOBIOGRAPHIES**
*Auto-da-fé* (Spanish: "act of faith;" the trial and burning of those who resisted the Inquisition) **3**:90; **5**:65
**AUTOGRAPHS 1:92**
Autonomy, *see* **SELF-GOVERNMENT, JEWISH**
**AUTOPSIES AND DISSECTION** (postmortem surgical procedures) **1:93**, 45; **3**:31; **4**:39; **6**:50;
Avadat (Nabatean king) **4**:171
*Av Bet Din* (rabbinic and judicial title) **5**:138
Averbuch, Manya, *see* Bialik, Manya
*Avinu Malkeinu* (prayer) **5**:74
Avi-Yonah, Michael (1904-1974): Professor of classical archaeology at Hebrew University; drew up specifications for scale model of the Temple and Herodian Jerusalem in the grounds of the Holyland Hotel, Jerusalem.
*Avodah Zarah* (Hebrew: "idolatry;" name of a talmudic tractate on that subject)**3**:78
**AVOT** (Hebrew: "fathers;" tractate of the Mishnah commonly known as Ethics of the Fathers, and comprising maxims on the good life) **1:93; 2**:114
Av the Fifteenth (minor festival), *see* **TU BE-AV**
Av the Ninth (fast day), *see* **TISH'AH BE-AV**
Avtinas, House of (priestly family) **3**:83
Ayllon, Solomon (Sephardi rabbi of Amsterdam) **1**:82
Ayrton, Hertha (physicist) **3**:92
Azariah (biblical figure), *see* Hananiah, Mishael, and Azariah
Azariah de Rossi (c.1511-c.1578, Hebrew scholar of Italian Ranaissance whose family, according to tradition, was brought to Rome by Titus after destruction of the Second Temple; with typical Renaissance versatility, he wrote on chronology, geography, archaeology, literature, numismatics and earthquakes) **3**:61
Azazel (sacrificial animal) **2**:59
*Aẓei ḥayyim* (Hebrew: "trees of life;" name given to the staves of a Torah scroll) **6**:48
**AZERBAIJAN** (CIS republic) **1:94**
*Aẓeret* (festival), *see* **SHAVUOT**
**AZULAI, ḤAYYIM JOSEPH DAVID** (18th-century scholar, mystic, and traveler ) **1:94**

# B

Baal (ancient idol) **1**:23, 88; **2**:100, 167; **3**:78, 138
Baalis (king of the Ammonites) **2**:157
*Ba'al koreh* (reader of the Torah in synagogue) **6**:47
Ba'al Shem of London, *see* **FALK, SAMUEL JACOB ḤAYYIM**
**BA'AL SHEM TOV** (founder of Ḥasidism) **1:95; 2**:54; **3**:9, 23, 186; **4**:31; **6**:76
*Ba'al tekiah* (blower of *shofar*) **5**:198
*Ba'al teshuvah* (Hebrew: "one who repents"), *see* **SIN AND REPENTANCE**
**BABEL, TOWER OF** (biblical episode) **1:95**, 97; **6**:1
**BABI YAR** (site in Russia of Nazi massacre) **1:96; 4**:23
Babylon (city, Babylonia) **1**:97
**BABYLONIA** (ancient state) **1:97**
—History: **1**:95, 99; **2**:51; **3**:138; **4**:13, 125, 183; **5**:157; **6**:28, 114, 115,
—Talmudic Academies: **1**:3; **2**:91, 154; **5**:95; **6**:25

Babylonian Talmud, *see* **TALMUD**
**BADGE, JEWISH** (discriminatory sign) **1:97**, 54, 158; **2**:19, 81; **3**:101; **5**:63. *See also* under individual countries.
**BADHAN** (Hebrew: "jester") **1:98**
Baer, Max (sportsman) **6**: 6
Baer, Seligmann (printer) **1**:145
Baerwald, Alexander (architect) **1:69**
"Baffy" (nickname of a celebrated non-Jewish British Zionist) *see* **DUGDALE, BLANCHE ELIZABETH CAMPBELL**
Bag Bag, Ben, *see* Ben Bag Bag
**BAGHDAD** (city, Iraq) **1:99; 3**:94
Baha Allah (founder of Bahai religion) **1**:99
**BAHA'I** (religion) **1:99; 3**:12, 68, 123
Bahai (city, Brazil) **1**:165
Bahamas (West Indies) **6**:90
Bahya ben Joseph ibn Paquda (11th century): moral philosopher, best known for his work *Hovot ha-Levavot* ("Duties of the Hearts"), written about 1080.
**BAK, ISRAEL AND NISAN** (19th-century printers, Erez Israel) **1:100**; **5**:80
Baku **1**:94
**BALAAM** (biblical figure) **1:100**, 85
Balak (biblical figure) **1**:100
**BALFOUR, ARTHUR JAMES, EARL OF** (British statesman) **1:101; 6**:87
**BALFOUR DECLARATION** (British government statement on Zionist aspirations, 1917) **1:101**, 62; **5**:179; **6**:87, 119
Balfouriyyah (settlement in Israel, named after Arthur James Balfour) **1**:101
Balsam (aromatic resin) **2**:40
**BALTIMORE** (city in Maryland, U.S.) **1:102**
*Ba-Midbar* (biblical book; Numbers), *see* **Be-Midbar**
*Bana'im* (2nd-century c.e. religious sect) **5**:148
Banias: ruined city at foot of Mount Hermon, dating from biblical times. Its name derives from the Arabic pronunciation (B for P) of the pagan god Pan, to whom its rock-carved temples were dedicated. The site was used by the Syrians from 1948 to 1967 for attacks on Israel territory.
**BANISHMENT** (form of punishment) **1:103; 2**:61
**BANKING AND BANKERS 1:104**, 1; **2**:27, 41; **3**:118, 130; **4**: 148; **5**:143; **6**:80
Bank Leumi (Israel) **4**:17
Banners, *see* **FLAGS AND BANNERS**
Baptism, forced, *see* **CONVERSION, FORCED**
**BARAK, EHUD** (military leader, Israel) **1:105**
Barak ben Avinoam (biblical figure) **2**:64; **3**:135
**BARAZANI, ASENATH** (15th-16th century female scholar) **1:105**
Barazani, Jacob (husband of Asenath) **1**:105
Barazani, Moshe (Israel freedom fighter) **4**:65
Barazani, Samuel (15th-16th century scholar) **1**:105
Barbados (West Indies) **6**:90
**BARCELONA** (city, Spain) **1:105**
Barenboim, Daniel (born 1942): pianist-conductor born in Buenos Aires, now living in Israel, whose first public appearance was made at age of seven.
**BAR GIORA, SIMEON** (first-century fighter against the Romans) **1:105**
**BAR-ILAN, MEIR** (religious Zionist leader) **1:106; 4**:143
Bar-Ilan University (Israel) **1**:106; **3**:126
**BAR KOKHBA** (leader of revolt against the Roman Empire, 132-135 c.e.) **1:106**, 27, 65; **2**:28; **3**:4; **4**:36, 126, 176; **5**:172; **6**:13, 56, 114
**BAR LEV, HAIM** (military leader, Israel) **1:107**
Bar Lev Line (military positions on Israel's side of the Suez Canal) **6**:108
**BAR MITZVAH, BAT MITZVAH 1:108; 2**:7, 14; **5**:161; **6**:30, 47
**BARON, SALO** (historian) **1:108**
Baruch (secretary of the prophet Jeremiah) **3**:140
**BARUCH, BERNARD** (U.S. financial expert and statesman) **1:109**
*Barukh she-Amar* (prayer) **5**:71
*Barukh Shem Kevod* (prayer) **5**:165
Basch, Samuel (Mexican physician) **4**:129
Baseball **6**:5
**BASHEVIS-SINGER, ISAAC** (Yiddish author) **1:109**
Basketball **6**:6
**BASLE** (city, Switzerland) **1:109**
Basloe, Frank (sportsman) **6**:6
Bassevi von Treuenberg (17th-century knight) **3**:45
Bath-Sheba (biblical figure) **2**:57; **5**:182
**BAT KOL** (heavenly voice) **1:110; 4**:40
Batsheva Ballet (Israel) **2**:55
Battle of Long Island (U.S. Revolutionary War) **6**:85
Baum, Harry (sportsman) **6**:6
Baybars (13th-century Turkish sultans) **1**:179
Bayudaya (religious group) **4**:5
Bea, Cardinal **2**:20; **5**:63
Beadle (synagogue official), *see* **SHAMMASH**
Beame, Abraham (mayor, New York) **5**:7
**BEARDS AND SHAVING 1:110; 4**:182; **5**:24
Beatitudes, Mount of (Israel) **3**:68
Beddington, Sir Edward (British soldier) **4**:138
*Bedeken* (Yiddish: "veiling the bride") **6**:72
Bedersi, Abraham (medieval Hebrew poet) **1**:12
*Bedikat hamez* (Hebrew: "search for leaven"; ceremony carried out before Passover) **5**:40
**BEDOUIN** (Middle Eastern nomadic tribesmen) **1:111; 3**:111
Be'er, Benjamin ben Elijah (15th-century physician) **4**:111
Beer, Israel (Russian spy) **2**:113
**BEERSHEBA** (city, Israel) **1:111**
**BEGGING AND BEGGARS 1:112; 2**:8
**BEGIN, MENAHEM** (Israel statesman) **1:113; 3**:96, 112
Behavior, *see* **MANNERS**
Behemoth (monster) **4**:52
Behrman, S. N. (U.S. playwright) **6**:38
**BEILIS, MENAHEM MENDEL** (victim of blood libel) **1:113**, 156; **5**:8, 116
*Bein ha-mezarim* (annual three-week period of mourning), *see* Three Weeks
Beisan (site, Erez Israel), *see* **BET SHE'AN**
*Beit Yosef* (legal commentary) **2**:5
*Bekhor* (Hebrew: "firstborn"), *see* **FIRSTBORN**
*Bel and the Dragon* (book of the Apocrypha) **1**:58
Belfast (city, Northern Ireland) **3**:95
**BELGIUM 1:114**
Belgrade (city, Yugoslavia) **6**:**110**
**BELIEF 1:115; 2**:31, 137, 168; **3**:47, 77; **4**:58, 84; **5**:70, 98, 102
*Beli neder* (disclaimer of intention to vow) **5**:18
Belloc, Hilaire (writer) **2**:108
**BELORUSSIA** (region in the west of Russia) **1:116; 4**:140; **6**:76
**BELZ** (city, Ukraine, and hasidic dynasty which originated there) **1:117; 3**:25
Belzec (concentration camp) **2**:33
**Be-Midbar** (biblical book; Numbers) **1:136**
Ben-Amotz, Dahn (writer, Israel) **3**:38
Benares (city, India) **3**:87
**BEN ASHER, MOSES AND AARON** (9th-century Hebrew linguists) **1:118; 4**:108
Ben-Avi, Ithamar (journalist and Zionist leader) **1**:125
Ben Azzai (2nd-century talmudic sage) **2**:101
Ben Bag Bag: a sage of the Mishnah period (the first centuries c.e.), though his identity is a matter of dispute. Some sources hold that he was the prospective proselyte who asked Hillel to teach him the whole Torah while he stood on one leg.
**BENE-BERAK** (city, Israel) **1:118; 6**:30, 76
**BENEDICTIONS** (blessings) **1:119**, 38, 166; **2**:37, 149; **3**:16, 20, 30; **4**:100; **5**:93, 123, 164; **6**:10, 84
Benedict of Talmont (medieval English official) **2**:116
**BENEI AKIVA** (religious Zionist youth movement) **1:120; 4**:143

**BENEI MOSHE** (Zionist movement) **1:120**
**BENE ISRAEL** (community in India) **1:121; 3:**87
**BEN-GURION, DAVID** (first prime minister of Israel) **1:121,** 36, 126; **2:**64, 97; **3:**42; **5:**44, 176
Ben-Gurion, Paula (wife of David) **1:**122
Ben Hadad (king of Aram) **2:**124
Ben He He: a first-century sage; either a pupil of Hillel, or a proselyte, or identified with Ben Bag Bag
Benjamin (biblical figure; son of Jacob) **1:**151; **3:**45; **6:**53
Benjamin, Ernest Frank (Canadian military leader) **3:**170
Benjamin, Judah P. (American statesman) **4:**138
Benjamin, Sir Benjamin (19th-century Australian statesman) **1:**90
**BENJAMIN OF TUDELA** (12th-century traveler) **1:123; 6:**51
**Benny, Jack** (U.S. comedian) **6:39**
**BEN SIRA** (2nd-century b.c.e. sage; author of Ecclesiasticus, also known as the Wisdom of Ben Sira) **1:124,** 59; **3:**44
Benveniste, Sheshet ben Isaac (medieval physician) **4:**113
Ben-Yehuda, Deborah (first wife of Eliezer Ben-Yehuda) **1:**125
**BEN-YEHUDA, ELIEZER** (Hebrew linguist) **1:124; 3:**34
Ben-Yehuda, Ḥemdah (second wife of Eliezer Ben-Yehuda) **1:**125
Ben-Yosef, Shelomo (underground fighter, Ereẓ Israel) **5:**110
Ben Zoma (2nd-century talmudic sage) **2:**101
**BEN-ZVI, IẒḤAK** (second president of Israel) **1:125,** 122; **3:**42
Ben-Zvi, Rachel Yanait (Socialist Zionist pioneer; wife of Iẓḥak Ben-Zvi) **1:**126; **2:**97
Ben-Zvi Institute (Israel; for study of Oriental communities) **1:**126
Berab, Jacob (16th-century Talmud scholar) **2:**4; **5:**28
*Beraita* (law not included in the Mishnah) **6:**25
*Berakhah* (the Hebrew word for a benediction or a blessing: plural *berakhot*), *see* **BENEDICTIONS**
Berbers (North African tribes) **4:**151
**BERDICHEV** (Ukrainian village, home of the saintly Levi Isaac) **1:126**
Berechiah ben Natronai ha-Nakdan (13th-century author) **3:**38
Berenice (wife of Hasmonean king Aristobulus) **1:**22
*Bereshit* (biblical book; Genesis) **1:135**
**Berg, Gertrude** (U.S. actress) **6:39**
Bergen-Belsen (concentration camp) **2:**32
Bergson, Henri (philosopher) **5:**54
**BERIḤAH** (underground movement for rescue of Holocaust survivors) **1:127; 4:**135
*Berit ha-Olim* (Zionist movement) **3:**3
*Berit Milah, see* **CIRCUMCISION**
Berit Shalom (organization proposing bi-national solution to the "Arab problem") **6:**118
Berkeley (University, California) **5:**1
Berkowitz, Y. D. (literary translator) **5:**156
**Berle, Milton** (U.S. actor) **6:39**
**BERLIN** (city, Germany) **1:127; 4:**56
Berlin, Daniel (banker, Germany), *see* **ITZIG, DANIEL**
Berlin, Ḥayyim (rabbi) **1;**106
Berlin, Irving (U.S. composer) **6:**39
Berlin, Sir Isaiah (born 1909): English philosopher and political scientist. He became the first Jewish Fellow of All Souls College at Oxford in 1938, and was a personal friend of Chaim Weizmann.
Berlin, Isaiah ben Judah Loeb (also known as Isaiah Pick; 1725-1799): German scholar;wrote textual commentaries on the Talmud. Late in life, he was able to entitle one of his works *She'elat Shalom* ("A Greeting of Peace"), for "all my life I have been careful not to treat my fellowmen with disrespect, even to the extent of not slighting them with faint praises."
Berlin, Judah (Court Jew), *see* **LIEBMANN, JOST**
Berlin, Naphtali Ẓevi Judah (rabbi) **1:**106
Berliner, David, *see* Hirschel, David
Berliner, Emile (inventor and aviation pioneer) **1:**16; **3:**92
Berliner, Henry Adler (aviation pioneer) **1:**16
Berlinger, Milton, *see* **Berle, Milton**
Bermuda (West Indies) **6:**90
Bernadotte, Count Folke (Swedish diplomat, and U.N. representative in Middle East) **4:**66; **6:**16, 61
Bernard, Rosine (actress), *see* **BERNHARDT, SARAH**
**Bernardi, Herschel** (U.S. actor) **6:**39
Bernback, William (U.S. advertising pioneer) **1:**15
**BERNHARDT, SARAH** (actress) **1:128**
**BERNSTEIN, LEONARD** (musician) **1:129; 6:**39
Bernstein-Namierowski, Lewis, *see* **NAMIER, SIR LEWIS**
**BERTINORO, OBADIAH** (15th-century author of classic commentary on the Mishnah) **1:129; 6:**27
**Beruryah** (wife of Rabbi Meir) **4:116; 2:**61
Besht (abbreviation of popular Hebrew name of founder of Ḥasidism), *see* **BA'AL SHEM TOV**
**Besicovitch, Abram Samoilovitch** (physicist) **4:**109
Bessarabia (region, U.S.S.R) **4:**25
Beta Israel, *see* **FALASHAS**
**BET ALFA** (ancient site, Israel) **1:129**
**BETAR** (Zionist youth movement) **1:130,** 113; **3:**95; **6:**55
*Bet din, see* **COURTS**
*Bet ha-Mikdash* (the Temple in Jerusalem), *see* **TEMPLE**
Bethar (ancient city, Ereẓ Israel) **1:**107; **2:**180
Beth-El (site in southern Ereẓ Israel, where the patriarch Jacob dreamt) **3:**133
Beth-El (town in northern Ereẓ Israel), *see* **SAFED**
Beth-Gilgal (site in Ereẓ Israel), *see* **GILGAL**
Bet Hillel (ancient Talmud academy), *see* **HILLEL**
**BETH JACOB** (religious girls' schools) **1:130**
**BETHLEHEM** (city, Israel) **1:131; 5:**91, 118
*Bet Midrash* (Hebrew: "house of study") **6:**10
Betrothal **4:**99
Bet Shammai (ancient Talmud academy), *see* **SHAMMAI**
**BET SHE'AN** (city, Israel) **1:131; 6:**32
**BET SHE'ARIM** (ancient site, Ereẓ Israel) **1:132,** 60
**BETTELHEIM, BRUNO** (psychologist) **1:132**
Bevin, Ernest (British politician) **2:**22; **3:**97
**BEZALEL** (biblical figure; chief artisan in the construction of the Tabernacle) **1:133,** 73; **2:**45, 174: **6:**21
Bezalel National Art Museum (Jerusalem) **4:**168
Bezalel School of Arts and Crafts (Jerusalem) **1:**160; **3:**171; **5:**142
**BIALIK, ḤAYYIM NAḤMAN** (Hebrew poet) **1:133; 3:**36, 38
Bialik, Manya (wife of the poet) **1:**134
Bialystok: Polish city, formerly an important Jewish center, and scene of savage pogroms in 1906. Of about 50,000 Jews at time of Holocaust only 1,085 remained there after World War II.
**BIBLE 1:134**
—Books of the Bible:
**Bereshit 1:135**
**Shemot 1:135**
**Va-Yikra 1:136**
**Be-Midbar 1:136**
**Devarim 1:136**
**JOSHUA 3:82; 1:137**
**Judges 1:137**
**Samuel I & II 1:138**
**Kings I & II 1:138**
**ISAIAH 3:98; 1:139**
**JEREMIAH 3:139; 1:140**
**EZEKIEL 2:119; 1:140**
**HOSEA3:70; 1:141**
**JOEL 1:141**
**AMOS 1:42; 1:141**

**Obadiah 1:141**
**JONAH 3:177; 1:141**
**Micah 1:141**
**Nahum 1:141**
**HABAKKUK 3:2; 1:142**
**Zephaniah 1:142**
**Haggai 1:142**
**Zechariah 6:144; 1:142**
**Malachi 1:142**
**PSALMS 5:83; 1:143**
**PROVERBS 5:82; 1:143**
**JOB 3:174; 1:143**
**SONG OF SONGS 5:184; 1:143**
**RUTH 5:118; 1:143**
**LAMENTATIONS 4:37; 1:143**
**ECCLESIASTES 2:90; 1:143**
**Esther 1:143**
**DANIEL 2:55; 1:143**
**EZRA & NEHEMIAH 2:120; 1:144**
**Chronicles 1:144**
*See also* the individual alphabetical entries.
—Commentators: **1**:7, 14, 146; **3**:75; **4**:15, 87, 119, 132, 172; **5**:94; **6**:3, 88
—Law and Concepts: **1**:18; **2**:46, 169, 177; **4**:40; **5**:35; **6**:10, 24, 46
—Text and Editions: **1**:73, 118, 158, 159; **4**:12, 107; **5**:79, 135, 153; **6**:98
—Miscellaneous: **1**:4, 48, 53, 65; **3**:35, 58; **5**:16; **6**:35, 92
Bible Contest, *see* International Bible Contest for Jewish Youth
**Bikel, Theodore Meir** (actor and folk singer) **6:39**
Bigamy **2**:164
*Bikkur ḥolim* (Hebrew "visiting the sick") **5**:170
*Bikkurim* (Temple ceremony), *see* **FIRST FRUITS**
Bildad (biblical figure; friend of Job) **3**:174
Biltmore Program (U.S. Zionist forum, 1942) **6**:120
Bilu (pioneering Zionist movement) **5**:48; **6**:115
*Bimah* (platform in synagogue for Torah reading) **6**:18
**BIOGRAPHIES AND AUTOBIOGRAPHIES 1:148,** 171; **3**:45; **5**:18
**BIOLOGY 1:149; 4**:115; **5**:132; **6**:78
Biow, Milton H. (U.S. advertising pioneer) **1**:15
**BIRDS 1:149** 51; **2**:73
*Birds' Head Haggadah* (13th-century German illuminated manuscript) **3**:8, 81
Birkenau (concentration camp) **2**:32
Birkenhead, Lord Cohen of (British medical figure) **4**:63, 115
**BIROBIDZHAN** (Jewish autonomous region in Russia) **1:150; 5**:117; **6**:104
**BIRTH 1:151; 2**:116; **5**:87
Birthright (privileges of firstborn son) **3**:133; **5**:16
*Biur ḥameẓ* (Hebrew: "removal of leaven"; ceremony on the eve of Passover) **5**:40
*Bittul ha-Tamid:* literally the suspension of the daily sacrifice, but more commonly used to mean the right of an aggrieved plaintiff to disrupt the synagogue service, and not to allow the Reading of the Torah to begin, until given a promise by the communal leaders that justice would be dispensed or that a wrong would be righted. This European custom has lately fallen into disuse.
Black Dragon Society (Japan) **6**:52
**BLACK DEATH** (bubonic plague) **1:152**
—General: **1**:54; **2**:32, 118; **4**:104
—Some Instances: **1**:35, 109; **2**:29, 141; **3**:63; **6**:16, 95. *See also* under individual countries and cities.
Black Jews (natives of India) **3**:86. *See also* **BENE ISRAEL.**
**BLACK JEWS IN AMERICA 1:153; 4**:5
Blackman, P. (translator of Mishnah) **6**:27
Black Muslims (U.S. organization) **4**:185
**BLAKE, WILLIAM** (English poet) **1:153**
**BLASPHEMY** (misusing God's name) **1:154; 2**:171
Blau, Amram (leader of Neturei Karta) **4**:186
Blessing of children **2**:14
Blessings, *see* **BENEDICTIONS**
**BLINDNESS 1:154,** 168; **2**:43
*Blintses* (pancakes filled with cheese and sour cream; customarily served on certain festivals) **2**:140
Bloch, Elijah Meyer (head of Telz yeshivah) **6**:32
**Bloch, Felix** (physicist) **4:109**
Bloch, Joseph Leib (Lithuanian scholar) **6**:32
Bloch, Marcel (Marcel Dassault; aviation pioneer) **1**:16
Bloch, René (aviation pioneer) **1**:16
Block, Marcus Eliezer (18th-century biologist) **1**:149
**BLOOD 1:155;2**:74
**BLOOD LIBEL** (allegations of ritual murder) **1:155**
—General: **1**:53; 155; **2**:20, 144; **3**:90; **6**:121
—Some Instances: **1**:113, 158; **2**:11, 39, 54, 141; **3**:10; **6**:53, 98. *See also* under individual countries and cities.
Blum, Léon (prime minister, France) **2**:143
Bluwstein, Raḥel (Hebrew poetess), *see* **RAḤEL**
**B'NAI B'RITH** (service organization) **1:156; 3**:54; **6**:64
Bnei Akiva (youth movement), *see* **BENEI AKIVA**
Bnei-Berak (city, Israel), *see* **BENE-BERAK**
Bnei Israel (community in India), *see* **BENE ISRAEL**
Board of Deputies of British Jews (communal organization) **2**:107
Boaz (biblical figure) **5**:118
*Bobe mayse* (Yiddish: "old wives' tale") **1**:162
Bodleian Library (at Oxford University, named after Sir Thomas Bodley (1544/45-1613) who was instrumental in restoring it, and regarded as having most important collection of Hebraica in the world) **4**:55
**BODY AND SOUL 1:157,** 77, 93, 151; **3**:73; **4**:58
**BOHEMIA** (region in Czechoslovakia) **1:157; 5**:66
Bohr, Harald (mathematician and soccer player) **6**:5
**Bohr, Niels Henrik David** (physicist) **4:109; 6**:5
Boleslav the Pious (king, Poland) **5**:59
Bombay (city, India) **3**:87
**BOMBERG, DANIEL** (Hebrew printer) **1:158,** 145; **4**:108; **5**:80
Bonafida, Honoratus de, *see* **DURAN, PROFIAT**
**Bondi, Hermann** (mathematician) **4:110**
**BONDS, STATE OF ISRAEL 1:159**
Bonet de Lattes (physician) **4**:114
Bonjorn, David Bonet (14th-15th century apostate) **2**:87
Bookplates (labels) **1**:161
**BOOKS 1:159**
—Writing and Printing: **1**:8, 100; **3**:80; **4**:52; **5**:79, 183; **6**:97
—Miscellaneous: **1**:4, 13, 61, 69, 135; **2**:5, 15; **3**:8, 129; **4**:54; **5**:75. *See also* **PRAYER BOOKS.**
Borach, Fanny, *see* **Brice (Borach), Fanny**
**Borge, Victor** (comedian) **6:39**
**BORMANN, MARTIN** (Nazi) **1:161**
Borochov, Ber (Socialist Zionist) **6**:117
*Borsht* (a soup made from beetroot; originated in Russia) **2**:140
**BOSTON** (city, U.S.) **1:162**
Botvinnik, Mikhail (chess player) **2**:11
**Bouwmeester, Louis Frederick Johannes** (Dutch actor) **6:39**
**BOVE-BUKH** (Yiddish book) **1:162; 4**:53
Boxing **4**:120; **6**:6
**BOYCOTT 1:162,** 62; **2**:69; **4**:178; **5**:20, 80
Brafman, Jacob (Russian apostate) **3**:88
Brahm, Otto (German theater director) **6**:38
Braille **1**:154
**BRAND, JOEL JENÖ** (rescue worker for War victims) **1:163**
**BRANDEIS, LOUIS DEMBITZ** (U.S. Supreme Court justice) **1:164; 2**:145
Brandeis University (Massachusetts) **1**:162; **6**:69
**BRATISLAVA** (Pressburg; city, Czechoslovakia) **1:164; 5**:181
Bratslaver Ḥasidim **4**:173
**BRAZIL 1:165**
**BREAD 1:166; 2**:116, 180; **3**:12; **5**:160, 167; **6**:21, 84, 90

**BRENNER, JOSEPH ḤAYYIM** (Hebrew novelist) **1:166**
**BREST-LITOVSK** (Brisk; city, Lithuania) **1:167**
Breton, Tomas (Spanish composer) 3:169
Breuer, Isaac (1883-1946): a Hungarian-born leader of German Orthodoxy who settled in Jerusalem in 1936, and became president of the Po'alei Agudat Israel movement.
**BRIBERY** **1:167**; 2:42
**Brice (Borach), Fanny** (U.S. actress and singer) **6:39**
Bride, *see* **MARRIAGE**
Bridegrooms of the Law, *see Ḥatan Bereshit* and *Ḥatan Torah.*
Bridge (card game) 2:153
Briscoe, Abraham (British soldier) 4:138
**BRISCOE, ROBERT** (Irish statesman) **1:168**; 3:95
Brisk (city, Lithuania), *see* **BREST-LITOVSK**
Britain, *see* entries on **ENGLAND, IRELAND, SCOTLAND** and **WALES**
British Mandate, *see* **MANDATE FOR PALESTINE**
Brit Milah, *see* **CIRCUMCISION**
Brod, Max (German writer) 4:9
Broder Singers (theatrical group) 2:173; 6:38
Brodie, Israel (former British chief rabbi) 4:118
Bronfman, Edgar 6:95
Bronstein, Lev Davidovich, *see* **TROTSKY, LEV DAVIDOVICH**
Bronze 4:128
Browning, Robert (English poet) 3:76
**Bruce, Lenny** (U.S. comedian) **6:39**
**BUBER, MARTIN** (philosopher) **1:168**; 2:78, 117, 145; 3:51; 5:97; 102, 107
Buber, Solomon (19th-century scholar) 1:168
Bucer, M. (16th-century Protestant Reformation leader) 3:150
Buchenwald (concentration camp) 2:32
Buchner, Abraham (19th-century Haskalah scholar) 3:26
Bucky, Gustav (radiologist) 4:114
**BUDAPEST** (city, Hungary) **1:169**
Buenos Aires (city, Argentina) 1:70
**BUKHARA** (region in Central Asia) **1:170**; 2:82, 140
Bulan (Khazar king) 4:18
**BULGARIA** (country in Eastern Europe) **1:171**
Bull (papal pronouncement) 5:63
Bund (Jewish Socialist organization) 4:49; 5:117
*Burekas* (pastries filled with pine nuts, meat and onion or cheese, and topped with sesame seeds) 2:140
**BURIAL** **1:171**, 93, 132; 2:48, 62; 3:52; 4:27 6:24, 50
Burla, Yehuda (writer, Israel) 3:38
Burlesque (form of theatrical entertainment) 6:38
"Burma Road" (built in Israel's War of Independence) 6:82
**BURNING BUSH** (biblical episode) **1:175**; 4:156
Bursa (city, Turkey) 5:31
**BUSH, GEORGE WALKER HERBERT** (U.S. president), **1:175**
**Burstein** (family of Yiddish actors) **6:39**
Buschoff, Adolf (victim of blood libel) 6:98
Bush, Solomon (American patriot) 6:85
Business ethics 2:114; 6:86
**BUSTANAI BEN ḤANINAI** (7th-century Babylonian leader) **1:175**
**Buttons, Red** (U.S. actor) **4:161**
**BUXTORF, JOHANNES** (Christian Hebraist) **1:176**
Byron, George Gordon, Lord (English poet) 3:139
**BYZANTINE EMPIRE** (region in Asia Minor and Near East, from 4th to 15th century) **1:176**; 2:35; 5:133

# C

Caesar Augustus (Roman emperor) 2:94
Caesar, Julius 2:26
Caesar, Sid (U.S. entertainer) 6:39
**CAESAREA** (city, Israel) **1:177**; 2:167
Cahan, Abraham (Yiddish journalist) 5:4
**CAIN AND ABEL** (biblical figures) **1:178**, 103, 172; 2:44; 5:128
**CAIRO** (city, Egypt) **1:178**; 2:95
Cairo Genizah (ancient archive), *see* **GENIZAH**
Caleb (biblical figure; partner of Joshua) 1:136; 2:111; 4:157
**CALENDAR** **1:179**, 87; 2:46, 20, 58, 129; 4:1, 2, 13, 150; 5:107, 119, 135; 6:42
Calendar, Muslim 5:23
Caligula (Roman emperor) 2:94; 5:53
Calixtus II (pope) 5:63
**CAMBRIDGE** (town, England) **1:181**
Cameri Theater (Israel) 3:40; 4:123
**CANAAN, LAND OF** **1:182**, 7, 63, 68, 138; 2:24; 3:62
**CANADA** **1:182**; 3:21; 4:150; 5:130; 6:49
**CANDLES** **1:183**; 2:62; 3:20, 46; 5:122; 6:13
Cantillation (traditional melody for the Reading of the Torah; known in Yiddish as *trop*) 4:107, 170
**CANTONISTS** (Jewish boys drafted into the Russian army in the 19th century) **2:1**, 132; 4:138; 5:8, 179
Cantor, *see* **ḤAZZAN**
**Cantor, Eddie** (U.S. comedian) **4:161**
Capelus, Ludovicus (Christian Hebraist) 1:176
**CAPERNAUM** (ancient village, Ereẓ Israel) **2:2**; 3:68, 165
Cape Town (city, South Africa) 5:185
Capitalism (economic system) 2:177
**CAPP, AL** (U.S. cartoonist) **2:2**
Cardiff (city, Wales) 6:79
Cardozo, Abraham (Shabbatean) 4:56
**CARDOZO, BENJAMIN NATHAN** (U.S. Supreme Court judge) **2:3**, 146
Cardplaying 2:153
**CARICATURES** **2:3**
Carmel, Mount 3:10
"Carmelit" (Haifa subway) 3:12
**CARO, JOSEPH** (author of the *Shulḥan Arukh,* the Code of Jewish Law) **2:4**; 1:32; 2:38; 4:44; 5:28; 6:76. *See also Shulḥan Arukh*
Carobs 2:140
Carol, Prince (19th-century Rumanian ruler) 5:115
**CARTER, JAMES EARL (Jimmy)** (U.S. president) **3:5**
Cartography of Israel, *see* **MAPS OF EREẒ ISRAEL**
Cartoons 2:155. *See also* **CARICATURES**
Casablanca (city, Morocco) 4:152
Casimir the Great (king, Poland) 5:59
**Castelnuova, G. (It. math.)** **3:129**
Catalanic (language) 3:171
Catholicism, *see under* **CHRISTIANITY**
Cattavi, Jacob (Egyptian government official) 1:179
Cattavi, Joseph (Egyptian government official) 1:179
**Caucasus (mt. region, Russ.)** **4:17**
Cave of Machpelah, (ancient site, Hebron), *see* Machpelah, Cave of
Celibacy 4:98

*Celqa* (Falasha beverage) **5**:43
Cemeteries **1**:173
**CENSORSHIP 2:5;** **1**:161; **3**:81; **4**:103; **5**:49, 63
**CEREMONIAL OBJECTS 2:6;** **1**:73, 132, 183; **3**:20; **4**:27, 130, 144, 168; **5**:168; **6**:18, 30, 48
**CHAGALL, MARC** (artist) **2:7;** **1**:76; **2**:168
Chagy, Berele (cantor) **3**:29
Chaldeans (ancient people) **3**:2; **4**:125
Chamberlain, Joseph (British statesman) **1**:101
Chamber of Hewn Stone (courtroom in Temple) **6**:35
Chao Kung (Hungarian Jewish adventurer), *see* **TREBITSCH-LINCOLN, IGNATIUS TIMOTHY**
Chapbooks (unbound pamphlets) **1**:161
**CHARITY** 2:8
—The Needy: **1**:18, 112; **4**:122, 147; **5**:66, 118, 170, 179
—Means of Distribution: **1**:21, 156; **3**:13, 52, 55; **4**:28; **6**:43
**CHARLEMAGNE** (medieval ruler) **2:10**
Charles II (king of England) **2**:107
Charles IV (king of Bohemia) **1**:158
Charles VI (king of Hungary) **2**:123
**CHARLESTON, S.C. 2:10**
**CHAUCER, GEOFFREY** (English poet) **2:11;** **1**:155
Chelmno (concentration camp) **2**:32
Chemosh (Moabite god) **4**:145
Cherubim (angelic figures) **6**:21, 33
**CHESS 2:11,** 153
Chesterton, G. K. (writer) **2**:108
**CHICAGO** (city, Illinois) **2:13**
**CHILDREN 2:13;** **1**:108, 151; **2**:123; **4**:19, 30, 102; **5**:78; **6**:110
Children's Hebrew literature **3**:37
**CHILE 2:15;** **4**:5
**CHINA 2:16;** **1**:124
**CHMIELNICKI, BOGDAN** (Ukrainian leader of the Cossack uprising and pogroms of 1648) **2:17;** **1**:53, 113; **3**:10; **4**:76; **5**:59, 154
Choirs (in synagogue) **3**:29
*Cholent* (Sabbath dish) **2**:139; **5**:123
**CHOSEN PEOPLE 2:17,** 20
Chosroes II (king of Persia) **1**:176
Choynski, Joe (sportsman) **6**:6
Christian IV (17th-century king of Denmark) **2**:68
Christian X (20th-century king of Denmark) **1**:98; **2**:68
**CHRISTIAN HEBRAISTS 2:18;** **1**:176; **2**:54; **5**:49
**CHRISTIANI, PABLO** (13th-century apostate) **2:19**
**CHRISTIANITY 2:19**
—Places: **1**:131, 176; **2**:96; **3**:68, 122, 162; **4**:181; **6**:71. *See also* under individual countries
—Anti-Semitism: **1**:54, 155; **2**:5, 70, 89; **3**:89; **4**:4, 73, 103; **5**:17, 18; **6**:1, 50, 53
—Miscellaneous: **1**:83, 135, 147; **2**:124, 144, 171; **3**:164, 79; **4**:5, 158; **5**:53, 62, 152
Christian Zionism **6**:117
Christmas **2**:153
Chronicles (biblical book) **1:144**
**CHRONOLOGY 2:20;** **1**:179
Chrysostom, John (4th-century Christian patriarch) **3**:89
**CHURCHILL, SIR WINSTON** (British statesman) **2:21;** **1**:5; **6**:119
Church of the Holy Sepulcher (Jerusalem) **3**:68
Church of the Nativity (Bethlehem) **1**:131; **3**:68
Cinema, *see* **MOTION PICTURES**
**CIRCUMCISION 2:22;** **1**:8, 28, 151; **2**:37, 100, 138, 167, 181; **3**:96; **4**:4
**CIRCUSES (ANCIENT) 2:23**
**CITIES 2:23;** **1**:64, 68, 78; **2**:25; **4**:115
**CITIES OF REFUGE** (levitical cities offering protection to accidental manslaughterer) **2:25;** **1**:103; **3**:82
Civil rights (U.S.) **4**:184
Claims Conference (post-World War II), *see* Conference on Jewish Material Claims against Germany
**CLAUDIUS** (Roman emperor) **2:25**
**CLEOPATRA** (Egyptian queens) **2:25**
Clermont-Ferrand (city, France) **2**:36
Clifford's Tower (York, England) **6**:109
**CLINTON, WILLIAM JEFFERSON (Bill) 2:26;** **3**:110
**Cobb, Lee J.** (U.S. actor) **4:161**
**COCHIN** (region, India) **2:26;** **3**:86
Code of Jewish Law, *see Shulḥan Arukh*
Coffin **1**:173
Cohen, Baron Henry, *see* Birkenhead, Lord Cohen of
Cohen, David (20th-century Nazirite) **4**:182
**COHEN, ELI 2:27,** 112; **6**:19
Cohen, Gerson W. (U.S. scholar) **3**:173
Cohen, Henry (U.S. rabbi) **2**:152
Cohen, Judith (wife of Sir Moses Montefiore) **4**:149
Cohen, Samuel (composer of *Ha-Tikvah* melody) **3**:28
Cohn, Ferdinand Julius (19th-century biologist) **1**:149
Cohn-Bendit, Daniel (radical French student leader) **5**:1
**COINS AND CURRENCY 2:27;** **1**:3, 11, 132; **4**:100, 111, 128; **5**:163; **6**:114
Collectivism (theory of collective living) **2**:113; **4**:18
**COLOGNE** (city, West Germany) **2:29**
Colophon: either an identifying printers' mark, or a page at the end of a book or manuscript containing information about its production.
Colossus of Rhodes (statue) **5**:102
Columbia University (New York) **5**:1
**COLUMBUS, CHRISTOPHER 2:29;** **1**:87; **2**:127; **3**:92; **6**:44, 112
Columbus Platform (statement of policy of Reform Judaism, 1937) **5**:99
**COMMANDMENTS 2:30**
—General: **1**:77, 108; **2**:36, 59, 113; **3**:24, 73, 81, 84; **4**:1, 40, 112; **5**:10, 98, 102; **6**:9, 22, 23, 35
—Some Examples: **1**:119; **2**:22, 62, 63, 73, 132; **3**:7, 12, 16, 19, 70, 91, 186; **5**:173. *See also* entries on individual commandments
**COMMONWEALTH OF INDEPENDENT STATES** (CIS) **2**:68; **3**:111
**COMMUNISM 2:31,** 125; **4**:49, 74, 105; **6**:7, 54, 103
**COMMUNITY OF ISRAEL 2:31**
**COMMUNITY RECORDS 2:32**
Compassion, *see* **MERCY**
*Complutensian Polyglot* (multi-language edition of the Bible) **6**:98
Comtino, Mordecai (15th-century mathematician) **4**:109
**CONCENTRATION CAMPS 2:32;** **1**:53, 76, 91, 133; **2**:29; **3**:66; **4**:33
Conduct, *see* **MANNERS**
Conference on Jewish Material Claims against Germany **5**:100
Confession of sins **2**:60, 62; **5**:174
Congratulations, *see* **GREETINGS**
Congressional Medal of Honor (military decoration) **4**:138
Congress of Vienna (international conference, 1815) **4**:176
**CONSERVATIVE JUDAISM 2:34,** 131, 144, 167; **3**:30, 137, 172; **5**:29, 68, 75, 142
**CONSISTORY** (French communal organization) **2:34**, 142: **4**:176
Constantine (Roman emperor) **2**:35, 49, 182; **3**:146; **4**:5
**CONSTANTINOPLE** (city, Turkey; also known as Istanbul) **2:35;** **3**:13; **5**:31
*Constitutio pro Judeis* (papal bulls) **5**:63
Contradiction (in testimony; legal concept) **5:46**
**CONVERSION, FORCED** (baptism under threat or torture) **2:36;** **1**:41, 53, 59, 83, 170; **2**:127; **3**:76; **4**:60, 83, 97, 153; **5**:155; **6**:1
**CONVERSION TO JUDAISM 2:36;** **1**:8, 59; **4**:4, 17, 46, 151; **5**:18, 25, 118; **5**:64; **6**:53, 98, 101
*Conversos* (forced converts to Christianity), *see* **MARRANOS**
Cooking, *see* **FOOD**
**COPLAND, AARON** (U.S. composer) **2**:38
Copper **4**:128
**COPPER SERPENT** (biblical episode) **2**:38
**CORDOVERO, MOSES BEN JACOB** (16th-century Kabbalist) **2:38;** **4:8**
**CORFU** (island off the coast of Greece) **2:39,** 183
**COSMETICS 2:40**
Cossacks (Ukrainian peasants) **2**:17; **5**:59
**COSTA, URIEL DA** (17th-century heretical philosopher) **2**:40
Coughlin, Father Charles E. (Detroit

anti-Semite) **2**:71
Council of the Four Lands (institution of Jewish self-government in Poland) **2**:32; **4**:96; **5**:59, 150
Counting of the Omer (seven-week period from Passover to Shavuot), *see* **OMER**
**Courant, Richard** (mathematician) **4:110**
**COURT JEWS** (influential lobbyists and financiers in royal courts) **2:41; 1**:83, 104; **3**:26, 130, 179; **5**:25; **6**:14
**COURTS 2:42**, 37; **3**:46, 87, 113; **4**:6, 22; **5**:17, 28, 46, 138, 150, 171. *See also* **OATH MORE JUDAICO**
Covenant (Hebrew: *"berit;"* bond of mutual obligations between two parties, e.g. between the Jews and God) **1**:8, 22; **4**:1
**COWEN, ZELMAN 2**:44
Cozbi (Midianite princess) **4**:132
**CRACOW** (city, Poland) **2:44**
**CRAFTS 2:44; 1**:73, 133; **2**:186; **4**:127; **6**:22, 85
**CREATION 2:46; 1**:12, 149, 179; **2**:21, 58, 135, 169; **4**:141, 180; **5**:120; **6**:14
Cremation **1**:175
**CRESCAS, ḤASDAI** (or Ḥisdai; 14th-century philosopher, Spain) **2:48; 4**:109
Cresson, Warder (proselyte; 19th-century U.S. consul to Jerusalem) **2**:38
Crime **1**:167; **2**:25, 42; **4**:22; **5**:46, 85, 174; **6**:41. *See also* Murder
Crimea (peninsula in the Ukraine, Russia) **4**:13, 17-18
**CROMWELL, OLIVER** (17th-century, Lord Protector of England) **2:48**, 107; **4**:89
**CRUCIFIXION 2:48; 3**:165
**CRUSADES** (medieval Christian military expeditions) **2:49; 1**:54; **2**:29, 98, 141, 163; **3**:22, 41, 59, 68, 105, 146; **4**:104; **5**:131
Crypto-Jews, *see* **MARRANOS**
Cuba (West Indies) **6**:90
Cubit (biblical unit of measurement), *see Ammah*
Cukierman, Yiẓḥak (Zionist leader) **1**:127
*Cum nimis absurdum* (papal bull) **5**:63
Cuneiform script (ancient mode of writing) **6**:97
Curacao (West Indies) **6**:90
**Curtis, Tony** (U.S. actor) **4:161**
**CUSTOM** (Hebrew: *minhag*) **2:50**
—General: **1**:81; **4**:44; **5**:152
—Examples: **1**:13, 152; **2**:137; **3**:30; **4**:164, 175; **5**:24, 35, 86; **6**:12, 49
Cybernetics (branch of applied mathematics) **4**:111
**CYPRUS** (Mediterranean island) **2:51; 3**:80
Cyrenaica (region, North Africa) **4**:55
Cyrene (region, North Africa) **2**:51; **4**:55
Cyril (5th-century Christian patriarch) **2**:94
**CYRUS** (6th-century b.c.e. Persian king) **2:51; 1**:57; **2**:120; **3**:90; **5**:46
Czaczkes, Shmuel Yosef (Hebrew writer), *see* **AGNON, SHMUEL YOSEF**
**CZECHOSLOVAKIA 2:52; 1**:164; **5**:67

# D

Dachau (concentration camp) **2**:32
Dacia (ancient land, now Rumania) **9**:114
**DAMAGES** (legal concept) **2:53**
**DAMASCUS** (city, Syria) **2:53; 6**:19
Damascus Affair (blood libel) **1**:156; **2**:54, 142; **3**:43
Da Modena, Leone, *see* **MODENA, LEONE**
Dan (biblical figure; son of Jacob, and founder of one of the Twelve Tribes) **3**:45; **6**:53
**DANBY, HERBERT** (Anglican translator of the Mishnah) **2:54; 6**:27
**DANCE 2:54; 3**:25, 82; **6**:13
Danglow, Jacob (Australian rabbi) **4**:118
**DANIEL** (biblical figure) **2:55; 1**:29, 58, 143; **3**:3; **4**:184
Daniel Sieff Research Institute (Israel) **5**:171
Danilovich, Issur, *see* **Douglas, Kirk**
**DANTE ALIGHIERI** (medieval Italian poet) **2:55; 3**:82, 132
*Darkhei ha-Emori* (Hebrew: "the ways of the Amorites"): term used by the rabbis to describe those gentile customs and lifestyles that were considered undesirable and not to be imitated.
*Darmstadt Haggadah* (15th-century illuminated manuscript) **3**:8
*Darshan* (synagogue preacher), *see* **PREACHING**
Dassault, Marcel (aviation pioneer), *see* Bloch, Marcel
Dathan (biblical figure) **4**:29
*Davar* (newspaper, Israel) **3**:57; **4**:14; **5**:161
*Davar li-Yeladim* (children's magazine) **5**:78
**DAVID** (biblical figure; second king of Israel) **2:56**
—Biblical Episodes: **1**:131; **2**:53, 54, 90, 93, 106, 166; **3**:41, 144, 173; **4**:24, 51, 70, 169; **5**:52, 142, 182; **6**:33
—Miscellaneous: **1**:1, 53; **2**:116, 159; **4**:78, 126; **5**:83, 118
David ben Zakkai (10th-century leader, Babylonia) **5**:119
**DAVIS, SAMMY JR.** (U.S. entertainer) **2:57**
**DAYAN, MOSHE** (Israel military leader and statesman) **2:58; 1**:11; **5**:176, **6**:109
**DAY AND NIGHT 2:58; 1**:181
**DAY OF ATONEMENT** (Yom Kippur) **2:59**
—Laws and Customs: **1**:77, 172; **2**:126, 130; **4**:27; **5**:127, 165, 169; **6**:24, 48
—Miscellaneous: **2**:160; **4**:1, 60, 128; **5**:174; **6**:14, 21, 36
Day of Judgment (New Year), *see* **ROSH HA-SHANAH**
Day of Judgment (at the End of Days) **2**:171
Day of the Lord (at the End of Days) **2**:105
*Dayyan* (Hebrew: "judge"): member of a rabbinical court, or *Bet Din.*
Dead Sea (Israel) **2**:106; **5**:134
Dead Sea Scrolls (major archaeological find), *see* **DEAD SEA SECTS**
**DEAD SEA SECTS 2:60; 1**:69, 107, 159; **2**:113; **3**:22, 34, 35; **5**:88; **6**:11, 99
Dead Sea Works (Israel) **5**:180
Deafness **2**:43
*Dearborn Independent* (anti-Semitic U.S. newspaper) **6**:65
**DEATH AND MOURNING 2:61**
—Laws and Customs: **1**:110, 157, 171, 184; **2**:40, 138, 181; **3**:52; **6**:18, 43, 91
—Miscellaneous: **1**:13, 93; **2**:48; **4**:57, 116; **6**:50
**DEBORAH** (biblical figure; judge and prophetess) **2:64; 1**:137; **3**:135
Decalogue (from the Greek word for ten), *see* **TEN COMMANDMENTS**
Decimal system **4**:109

**DECLARATION OF INDEPENDENCE, ISRAEL 2:64; 3**:121
Deedes, Sir Wyndham (1883-1956): British Christian Zionist who while chief secretary to Sir Herbert Samuel, High Commissioner for Palestine, unofficially recognized the Haganah and introduced Jews into the Palestine Police Force.
**DEGANYAH** (name of two kibbutzim) **2:65**; 111, 176; **4**:18
Deir Yassin (Arab village, Israel) **3**:96; **4**:65; **6**:82
Delilah (biblical figure) **5**:136
Delmedigo, Joseph Solomon (1591-1655 , rabbi, philosopher, mathematician, astronomer; born in Crete, where he also practiced medicine) **4**:109
De Luna, Beatrice, *see* **NASI, GRACIA**
**DEMOCRACY 2:65; 1**:133; **2**:125; **4**:118; **5**:1; **6**:18
Democratic Fraction (early opposition group in the Zionist movement) **6**:87
Democratic Party (U.S.) **6**:65
Democritus (ancient Greek thinker) **4**:109
**DEMOGRAPHY** (the study of the distribution of population) **2:66; 3**:155
Demons, *see* **ANGELS AND DEMONS**
**DENMARK 2:68**
**DEPARTMENT STORES 2:69; 5**:3
Depression (economic crisis beginning 1929) **6**:65
*Deputy, The* (play by Rolf Hochhuth) **3**:62
*Derashah* (Hebrew: "sermon"), *see* **PREACHING**
*Derekh Ereẓ, see* **MANNERS**
*Der Judenstadt* (German: "The Jewish State;" book published by Herzl in 1896) **3**:50
**DESECRATION OF THE HOST** (Christian anti-Semitic allegation) **2:70; 1**:53; **2**:20
**De-Shalit, Amos** (physicist) **4**:**110**
**DESSLER, ELIJAH ELIEZER** (exponent of *musar* movement, in Russia, England and Israel) **2:71**
**DETROIT** (city, Michigan) **2:71**
Deuteronomy (biblical book), *see* **Devarim**
**Devarim** (biblical book; Deuteronomy) **1:136; 3**:184; **6**:14
*Devekut* (cleaving to God; ḥasidic concept) **2**:100; **3**:24; **5**:69
Devil's Island (off South America) **2**:82
*Devir* (the Holy of Holies; the inner sanctuary of the Temple, housing the Ark of the Covenant) **6**:33
Dew, *see* **RAIN AND DEW**
*Dhimmi* (Arabic: "protected ones;" term describing the status of Jews in Muslim lands as a tolerated minority) **3**:101
Dhu Nuwas (6th-century convert to Judaism) **6**:101
Diamante, Juan Buatista (17th-century Spanish playwright) **3**:169
Diamonds, *see* **PRECIOUS STONES**
**DIASPORA** (collective term for the lands of Jewish dispersion outside Ereẓ Israel) **2:72; 1**:82; **2**:146; **3**:13; **4**:12, 14, 133; **5**:149
**DIBBUK** (evil spirit) **2:72; 4**:9, 81
**DICKENS, CHARLES** (19th-century English novelist) **2:74**
Diego Deza (Spanish inquisitor) **3**:91
**DIETARY LAWS 2:73; 1**:48, 76, 81, 150, 155, 166; **2**:50, 135, 138, 149; **5**:40, 134, 162; **6**:71
Digestive organs **1**:45
Dimonah (town, Israel) **5**:180
*Dina de-Malkhuta Dina* (Aramaic: "the law of the kingdom is the law"): the halakhic rule that the law of the country is binding in certain clearly-defined cases with which Jewish law also deals.
Dinah (biblical figure) **5**:162
Dinur, Jehiel, *see* **K. ZETNIK**
**DISKIN, MOSES JOSHUA JUDAH LEIB** (rabbi, Jerusalem) **2:75**
Dispersion, *see* **DIASPORA**
**DISPLACED PERSONS** (the homeless of World War II) **2:76**, 51, 117; **3**:22; **6**:120
**DISPUTATIONS** (the theological debates in defense of Judaism) **2:77; 1**:53; **2**:18, 19, 20; **3**:180; **4**:68, 103, 172
**DISRAELI, BENJAMIN** (19th-century British prime minister and novelist) **2:78; 1**:60; **2**:51, 108
Disraeli, Isaac (father of Benjamin) **2**:78
Distinguished Service Cross (military decoration) **4**:138
Divekar, Samuel E. (Bene Israel leader, India) **3**:87
Divorce, **4**:101
*Divrei ha-Yamim* (biblical book), *see* **Chronicles**
**DIZENGOFF, MEIR** (a founder and the first mayor of Tel Aviv) **2:79; 6**:31
**DJERBA** (island off coast of Tunisia) **2:79**
Doctors, *see* **MEDICINE**
Doctors' Plot (Stalinist anti-Semitic libel, 1952) **4**:136; **6**:7
*Doctor Zhivago* (novel by Pasternak) **5**:44
Doenmeh (Shabbatean Muslim Judaizers) **5**:89
Dogma, *see* **BELIEF**
Dome of the Rock (also known as the Mosque of Omar, atop Temple Mount, Jerusalem) **3**:68; **5**:23
**DOMICILE** (legal concept) **2:79**
Dominicans (order of the Catholic Church) **3**:90
Donnolo, Shabbetai (10th-century physician and philosopher) **5**:84
Don Zag (medieval scholar), *see* Ibn Sid, Isaac
Dosh (cartoonist, Israel), *see* **GARDOSH, KARIEL**
**Douglas, Kirk** (U.S. actor) **4:161**
Dov Baer of Mezhirech (the Maggid, or preacher of a Ukrainian village called Mezhirech; 18th-century ḥasidic *ẓaddik;* disciple of the Ba'al Shem Tov) **3**:1, 23
Dove **2**:137
Dowry **3**:89; **4**:102
D.P.'s, *see* **DISPLACED PERSONS**
Drama, *see* **THEATER**
Drawing, *see* **ART**
**DREAMS 2:80; 1**:175; **2**:127; **3**:133, 181; **4**:184; **6**:75
*Dreidl* (Yiddish: "spinning top" used in traditional Ḥanukkah games) **3**:20
**DRESS 2:81; 1**:97; **2**:160; **3**:23, 30, 79; **4**:27, 74, 93; **5**:90; **6**:22, 23, 72
**DREYFUS, ALFRED** (French army officer, whose false conviction for treason unleashed a wave of anti-Semitism that threw France into turmoil at the turn of the century) **2:82; 6**:121
Dreyfuss, Barney (sportsman) **6**:5
**DROPSIE, MOSES AARON** (U.S. philanthropist) **2:83**
Dropsie College (Philadelphia, U.S.) **2**:83; **5**:52
**DRUG ADDICTION 2:83**
**DRUZE** (members of an Arabic-speaking Middle Eastern community with its own religion) **2:83; 3**:68, 111, 123, 166
Dubcek, Alexander (20th-century Czechoslovakian statesman) **2**:52
Dublin (city, Ireland) **1**:168; **3**:95
**DUBNO** (city, in Ukraine) **2:84**
Dubno, Solomon (Russian *maskil*) **3**:26
Dubno Maggid, *see* **KRANZ, JACOB**
**DUBNOW, SIMON** (historian) **2:84**
**DUGDALE, BLANCHE ELIZABETH CAMPBELL** (non-Jewish British Zionist) **2:85; 1**:101
*Dukhenen* (Yiddish for "delivering the priestly blessing" as performed by the *kohanim;* from the Hebrew word *dukhan,* meaning the platform on which this used to take place), *see* Priestly Blessing
**DUMA** (Imperial Russian legislature) **2:85**
*Dunam* (unit of area measure) **6**:86
**DUNASH BEN LABRAT** (10th-century Hebrew linguist and poet) **2:86**
**DURA-EUROPOS** (ancient city in Iraq, site of a spectacular archaeological discovery in 1932) **2:86; 6**:17
**DURAN, PROFIAT** (medieval Spanish scholar and physician) **2:87**
Durban (port in Natal, and third largest city in Republic of South Africa, one of whose founders was Nathaniel Isaacs) **5:186**
**DURKHEIM, EMILE** (French sociologist) **2:88**

Dutch East India Company 5:185
Dutch Sam (boxer), *see* Elias, Samuel
**DUVEEN, JOSEPH, LORD** (English art dealer) **2:88**
*Dybbuk* (evil spirit), *see* **DIBBUK**
Dylan, Bob (Robert Zimmerman): born in 1941 in Duluth, Minnesota; well-known as a singer and composer, and prominent in the folk music revival and protest song movement of the 1960s.
**Dzigan, Shimon** (Yiddish satirical actor) **6:39**

# E

**EARTHQUAKE 2:89**
**EBAN, ABBA** (Israel statesman and diplomat) **2:89**
**ECCLESIA ET SYNAGOGA** (form of anti-Semitic Christian symbolism) **2:89**; 1:53
**ECCLESIASTES** (biblical book; one of the five *Megillot,* known in Hebrew as Kohelet) **2:90**; 1:143; 5:183; 6:92
Ecclesiasticus (Apocryphal wisdom book), *see* Wisdom of Ben Sira
**ECOLOGY** (the study and protection of man's natural environment) **2:90**
Ecumenical Council (Vatican conference) 2:20
Eden, Garden of, *see* Garden of Eden
Edinburgh (city, Scotland) 5:145
**EDOM** (ancient land south of the Dead Sea) **2:90**; 1:141; 3:48; 4:171
**EDUCATION 2:91**
–Concepts: 2:14, 123; 3:26; 4:30; 5:75, 90, 107; 6:9, 122
–Varieties: 1:34, 130; 3:40, 42, 123, 173; 4:54; 5:5, 29; 6:64, 68, 102, 103
Educational Alliance (New York welfare organization) 5:4
*Eduyyot* (Talmud tractate) 3:131
Edward I (king of England) 1:98, 181; 2:107
Edward VII (king of England) 2:108
**EGER, AKIVA** (talmudic scholar) **2:92**
Eger, Solomon (talmudic scholar) 2:93
Egged (Israel bus cooperative) 3:119
Eggs 1:150
Eglon (biblical figure; king of Moab) 2:95
**EGYPT 2:93**; 1:30, 178
–Ancient: 2:99, 124, 167; 4:13, 24, 154; 5:8, 57, 85; 6:32
–Modern: 1:62; 4:56, 178; 5:175; 6:107
Ehrlich, Paul (German biochemist) 2:145; 4:114
**EHUD** (biblical figure) **2:95**
**EICHMANN, ADOLF OTTO** (Nazi master-mind of the "Final Solution") **2:95**; 1:70, 164, 170; 3:66,114; 4:33; 5:67, 85
Eiger (rabbinic family, Lublin) 4:72
*Eikhah* (Book of Lamentations chanted on the fast of Tish'ah be-Av), *see* **LAMENTATIONS, BOOK OF**
**EILAT** (city, Israel) **2:96**; 5:159
Ein Fashḥah: an oasis (today a seaside resort) on the west shore of the Dead Sea, about 2½ miles south of Qumran.
Ein Gev (settlement, Israel) 4:25
Ein ha-Shofet (settlement, Israel) 1:164
**EINHORN, DAVID** (Reform theologian) **2:96**; 4:184; 5:5, 98
**EIN KEREM** (vill. near Jerusalem) **2:96**
**EINSTEIN, ALBERT** (physicist; Nobel Laureate) **2:97**; 3:27; 4:109
Eisenstein, Ira (U.S. Reconstructionist leader) 4:12
Eisenstein, Judah David (scholar) 2:104
Eisenstein, Sergei (film producer) 4:161
**EITAN, RAPHAEL** (Raful; Israel military leader) **2:97**
El (divine name), *see* **GOD**
Elah (king of Israel) 5:24
**EL AL** (Israel national airline) **2:98**; 4:17, 76
El-Arish: town on Mediterranean coast of Sinai Peninsula; its main center through most historic periods because of its good soil and plentiful rainfall.
Elath (site, Israel) *see* **EILAT**
Elazar, David (Israel military leader) 1:108
El Berit (divine name), *see* **GOD**
**ELDAD HA-DANI** (9th-century traveler) **2:98**
Eleanor of Provence (mother of Edward I of England) 1:181
Eleazar (biblical figure; son of Aaron) 1:1, 71; 6:70
Eleazar (son of the Talmud sage Simeon bar Yoḥai) 5:172
Eleazar ben Azariah (talmud sage) 3:131
**ELEAZAR BEN JUDAH OF WORMS** (medieval scholar; leader of Ḥasidei Ashkenaz) **2:98**; 3:9
Eleazar ben Yair (Jair; 1st-century resistance fighter against Roman rule) 4:106; 6:114
Eleazar of Modi'in (2nd-century figure) 1:107
Electricity 5:125
El Elyon (divine name), *see* **GOD**
**ELEPHANTINE** (ancient Egyptian island-city) **2:99**; 6:97
**ELI** (biblical figure; high priest) **2:99**; 1:154; 3:17; 5:137, 168
Elias (12th-century English financier) 1:2
Elias, Henry Hart (sportsman) 6:6
Elias, Samuel (Dutch Sam; sportsman) 6:6
Eliezer (biblical figure; servant of Abraham) 1:8
Eliezer (sage of the Mishnah) 6:24
Eliezer ben Hyrcanus (talmudic sage) 2:153; 4:40
**ELIEZER BEN JOEL HALEVI BONN** (known as Ravyah; medieval German rabbinic scholar) **2:99**
**ELIJAH** (biblical figure; prophet) **2:100**; 1:23, 27; 2:23, 101; 5:24, 42; 6:75
Elijah ben Solomon Zalman, *see* **GAON OF VILNA**
Elijah ha-Baḥur, *see* **LEVITA, ELIJAH**
Elijah Mizraḥi (scholar) 4:109
Elijah of Montalto (French court physician) 5:36
Elimelech (biblical figure) 5:118
**ELIMELECH OF LYZHANSK** (ḥasidic *ẓaddik;* brother of Zusya of Hanipoli) 2:100; 6:122
Eliot, George (British writer) 4:46
Eliot, John (Bible translator) 1:146
Eliphaz (biblical figure; friend of Job) 3:174
**ELISHA** (biblical figure; prophet, disciple of Elijah) **2:101**; 3:138; 4:4, 169; 5:24
**ELISHA BEN AVUYA** (2nd-century sage and apostate) **2:101**; 1:17, 59; 4:116
Elisheba (biblical figure) 1:1
Elizabeth (mother of John the Baptist) 2:96
Elizabeth I (queen of England) 2:107; 4:67
Elizaphan ben Uzziel (biblical figure) 4:29
**ELKAN, BENNO** (sculptor) **2:101**
Elkanah (biblical figure) 3:17
Ellis Island (New York) 5:3
Elohei Ẓeva'ot (divine name), *see* **GOD**
Elohim (divine name), *see* **GOD**

El Olam (divine name), *see* **GOD**
EL Shaddai (divine name), *see* **GOD**
Elul (Hebrew month) **2**:154; **5**:169
**EMANCIPATION 2:102; 1**:83; **2**:44, 147, 165; **3**:63; **4**:77, 119; **5**:150, 180; **6**:15, 16
**EMDEN, JACOB** (18th-century German rabbi) **2:103; 1**:81; **2**:118; **3**:14; **4**:39
*Encyclopaedia Hebraica* (Israel) **4**:27
*Encyclopaedia Britannica* **2**:105
*Encyclopaedia Judaica* **2**:104, 174
**ENCYCLOPEDIAS 2:104**
**END OF DAYS 2:105,** 171; **3**:88
**EN-GEDI** (oasis on western shore of Dead Sea) **2:106**
Engels, Friederich (Communist theorist) **4**:105
Engineers, *see* **INVENTORS AND ENGINEERS**
**ENGLAND 2:107**
—People: **1**:1; **2**:48, 78; **3**:49, 55; **4**:39, 67, 89; **5**:111
—Places: **1**:84, 181; **4**:47, 62, 66, 90; **5**:32; **6**:78, 109
—Miscellaneous: **2**:118; **4**:138; **5**:175
Enheduanna (Mesopotamian priestess) **4**:124
Enlightenment (movement), *see* **HASKALAH**
Enoch (biblical figure; son of Cain) **2**:24
Enoch (figure in the Apocrypha) **1**:59
Enoch, Book of (Apocryphal work) **1**:86
Entertainment, *see* **THEATER, MOTION PICTURES,** and other relevant entries
*Ephah* (biblical unit of measurement) **6**:86
Ephraim (biblical figure; son of Joseph, and founder of one of the Twelve Tribes) **3**:45; **6**:53
Ephraim ben al-Zafran (11th-century physician) **4**:113
Ephraim ben Jacob ha-Kohen (17th-century scholar) **1**:81
Ephron (biblical figure) **3**:41
Epitaphs (inscriptions on tombstones) **1**:174
**Epstein, Brian** (Beatles' manager) **6:40**
Epstein, Isidore (1864-1962; English rabbi and educator; translator of the Soncino English edition of the Babylonian Talmud) **6**:27
**EPSTEIN, SIR JACOB** (English sculptor) **2:109; 1**:76; **5**:146
Epstein, Moses Henry (sportsman) **6**:6
*Ereẓ ha-Damim* ("the Bloodstained Land"), *see* **AUSTRIA**
**ERUV** (concept in the law of Sabbath and festivals) **2:110,** 128; **5**:125
Esau (biblical figure; twin brother of Jacob) **2**:90; **3**:132; **5**:16
Eschatology (the mystical doctrine of the End of Days), *see* **END OF DAYS**
*Eshet Ḥayil* (Hebrew: "a woman of valor;" opening words of an alphabetical passage from the last chapter of the Book of Proverbs, which is sung in praise of the wife and mother of the household on Friday evening before *Kiddush*) **5**:123
**ESHKOL, LEVI** (Israel prime minister) **2:111; 1**:123; **2**:58; **3**:176; **5**:176
**ESPIONAGE 2:111; 4**:157
**ESSENES** (religious sect toward end of Second Temple period) **2:113,** 61; **3**:44; **4**:1; **5**:88
Esterhazy, Ferdinand Walsin (French army officer) **2**:82
Esther (biblical figure; heroine of Purim story) **1**:143; **5**:86
Esther, Fast of (eve of Purim) **2**:126
Estori ha-Parḥi (medieval traveler) **6**:51
Eternal Light (in synagogue), *see Ner tamid*
**ETHICS** (principles of proper relations between man and man) **2:113; 1**:93, 168; **3**:4, 17, 22, 54, 70; **4**:166; **5**:96; **6**:91
Ethics of the Fathers (tractate of the Mishnah), *see* **AVOT**
**ETHIOPIA 2:114**; 121; **3**:110
Etiquette, *see* **MANNERS**
*Etrog* (citron used on Sukkot) **3**:12; **6**:12
Euchel, Isaac (author) **1**:148
**EUPHRATES** (longest river in western Asia) **2:115**
**EUTHANASIA** ("mercy killing") **2**:115; **4**:58
Eve (biblical figure), *see* **ADAM AND EVE**
Evidence, *see* Testimony
*Ever min ha-ḥai* ("a limb from a living animal"): the biblical prohibition against the removal of a limb or a piece of flesh from a living animal, in the manner common in pagan times.
Evil, *see* **GOOD AND EVIL**
**EVIL EYE 2:115;1**:44; **4**:81
Evolution **2**:47
**EXCHEQUER OF THE JEWS** (medieval English government department for Jewish affairs) **2:116**
**EXILARCH** (governor of exiled Babylonian Jewish community) **2:116; 1**:45, 97, 99, 175; **4**:171; **5**:119
Exile (from the land of Israel)
—Babylonian: **1**:97; **2**:72, 120; **4**:38, 184
—General: **1**:42, 82, 103; **3**:88; **4**:133; **6**:36, 114
**EXISTENTIALISM** (modern philosophical movement) **2:117**
Exodus (biblical book), *see* **Shemot**
Exodus from Egypt **1**:1, 136, 179; **2**:38, 93, 146; **3**:7; **4**:92, 154; **5**:39, 97, 174; **6**:11, 21
**EXODUS 1947** ("illegal" immigrant ship) **2:117; 3**:6, 80
Exorcism (procedure to neutralize evil spirit) **2**:72
Explorers, *see* **TRAVELERS AND EXPLORERS**
**EXPULSIONS 2:118; 1**:53; **2**:29, 107, 141; **3**:91, 181; **4**:23; **6**:2
Extermination Camps, *see* **CONCENTRATION CAMPS**
**EYBESCHUETZ, JONATHAN** (18th-century talmudist and kabbalist) **2:118,** 103; **3**:14; **4**:39
Eybeschuetz, Wolf (son of Jonathan Eybeschuetz) **2**:119
*Eẓba* (biblical unit of measurement) **6**:86
**EZEKIEL** (biblical figure; prophet) **2:119; 1**:140; **4**:184; **5**:161
Ezekiel of Alexandria (1st-century b.c.e. playwright) **6**:37
*Eẓ ḥayyim* (Hebrew: "tree of life;" name given to either of the staves of a Torah scroll), *see Aẓei ḥayyim*
Eẓ Ḥayyim (yeshivah, Belorussia) **6**:76
Ezion-Geber (biblical site near Eilat) **2**:168
**EZRA** (biblical figure; leader of the Return after Babylonian exile) **2:120; 1**:97, 144; **3**:46; **4**:185; **5**:50; **6**:24
Ezra (Zionist youth group) **1**:121
Ezra (religious youth movement) **3**:126
Ezra, Abraham Ibn, *see* **IBN EZRA, ABRAHAM**
Eẓyon, Kefar, *see* **KEFAR EẒYON**
Eẓyon Bloc (group of settlements, Ereẓ Israel), *see* **KEFAR EẒYON**

# F


Faisal I (king of Iraq) **1**:5; **2**:146; **6**:87, 118
**FALAQUERA, SHEM TOV BEN JOSEPH** (philosophical author and translator) **2:121**
**FALASHAS** (Ethiopian Judaizers) **2:121**; **1**:125; **2**:114; **3**:110; **4**:1; **5**:43
Falk, Aryeh Leib (18th-century scholar) **2**:122
Falk, Issachar Dov (18th-century scholar) **2**:122
**FALK, JACOB JOSHUA BEN ẒEVI HIRSCH** (Polish halakhic authority) **2:122**
**FALK, SAMUEL JACOB ḤAYYIM** (mystic and adventurer) **2:122**
False messiahs, *see* **MESSIANIC MOVEMENTS**
**FAMILIANTS LAW** (18th-century law limiting Jewish marriages and families) **2:123**
**FAMILY 2:123**; **1**:151; **2**:158; **4**:93; **5**:169
**FAMINE 2:124**, 126
Farming, *see* **AGRICULTURE**
Farouk (king, Egypt) **4**:178
**FASCISM** (European political movement) **2:125**; **1**:12; **2**:108
Fasi, Isaac, *see* **ALFASI, ISAAC BEN JACOB**
**FASTING AND FAST DAYS 2:126**; **1**:13, 39, 77; **2**:59; **4**:100; **5**:42, 86; **6**:27, 42, 48, 95
Fast of Gedaliah **2**:126, 157
Fast of the Firstborn **2**:134
Fataḥ, *see* Al Fataḥ.
Fataḥland (Arab terrorist bases in southern Lebanon) **4**:47
Father **2**:13, 123
Fatima (daughter of Muhammad) **4**:164
**FATIMIDS** (Muslim dynasty from 10th to 12th centuries) **2:127**, 94
Fear of God, *see* **LOVE AND FEAR OF GOD**
Feast of Booths, *see* **SUKKOT**
Feast of Weeks, *see* **SHAVUOT**
Fedayeen (Arab suicide squads) **5**:175
Federation of Jewish Philanthropies (U.S.) **5**:5
Federation of Labor in Israel, *see* **HISTADRUT**
Feiner, Jehiel (Holocaust writer), *see* **K. ZETNIK**
Feinstein, Meir (Israel freedom fighter) **4**:65
Feisal, *see* Faisal
Felix, Judah (biologist) **1**:149
Ferber, Herbert (U.S. sculptor) **5**:146
Ferdinand I (Italy) **4**:48
Ferdinand I (Portugal) **4**:60
**FERDINAND AND ISABELLA** (15th-16th century Spanish monarchs) **2:127**; **1**:7; **3**:90; **6**:2, 50
Ferdinand, Philip (16th-century teacher) **1**:181
Fernandez, Simon (16-century seaman) **5**:168
**FERRER, VICENTE** (anti-Semite, declared a saint by the Catholic Church) **2:127**
**FESTIVALS 2:128**
—General: **1**:29, 39, 172; **2**:80, 110, 130, 139; **3**:121, 186; **4**:21, 22; **5**:121; **6**:48
—Examples: **3**:18; **4**:36; **5**:43, 86, 107, 159; **6**:11, 52, 56
**FESTIVE MEAL** (feast connected with religious occasion) **2:130**, 128; **3**:85; **4**:74, 100; **5**:41, 55; **6**:12, 72
Feuchtwanger, Leon (German author) **3**:169; **5**:26
Fezzan (region, North Africa) **4**:55
Fichmann, Jacob (writer, Israel) **3**:38
*Fiddler on the Roof* (musical play) **5**:156; **6**:45
Fifteenth of Av (minor festival), *see* **TU BE'AV**
Fifteenth of Shevat (New Year of Trees), *see* **TU BI-SHEVAT**
Films, *see* **MOTION PICTURES**
Filosof, Joseph (Shabbatean) **5**:89
"Final Solution" (Hitler's plan to destroy European Jewry) **2**:33, 95; **3**:62, 66, 129. *See also* **HOLOCAUST.**
Financier, *see* **BANKING AND BANKERS**
Fine, Sylvia (U.S. writer) **4**:15
Finials (ornaments atop Torah scroll) **6**:49
**FINKELSTEIN, LOUIS** (U.S. Conservative rabbi, scholar and educator) **2:131**; **3**:173; **5**:50
**FINLAND 2:131**
Fire (in civil law) **2**:53
**FIRKOVICH, ABRAHAM** (Karaite community leader) **2:132**
First Aliyah (1882-1903): the earliest wave of migration in the modern return to Ereẓ Israel, comprising members of the Bilu. Their longstanding desire to return to the ancestral homeland was activated by the Russian and Rumanian pogroms, and by disillusionment with the hopes of the Haskalah, that through education and enlightenment the position of Diaspora Jewry would be normalized. *See* **3**:106.
**FIRSTBORN 2:132**, 127; **4**:112; **5**:42, 79
**FIRST FRUITS** (*Bikkurim;* thanksgiving offering in Temple times) **2:134**, 133; **5**:24, 160
**Fischer, Robert** (chess-player) **2**:12
**FISH AND FISHING 2:135**; **1**:51, 80, 155; **2**:73, 138, 139; **3**:177; **4**:52
Five Books of Moses (Pentateuch), *see* **BIBLE**
Five Scrolls (series of biblical books), *see* Scrolls, the Five
Five Species: the varieties of grain (including wheat and barley) to which the *halakhot* concerning the agricultural produce of Ereẓ Israel apply, and which are subject to the laws relating to Grace after Meals.
**FLAGS AND BANNERS 2:135**; **4**:79
Flavius Claudius Julianus, *see* **JULIAN THE APOSTATE**
Flavius Silva (Roman general) **4**:106
**FLESH** (biblical term for mortal man) **2:136**
**FLOOD, THE** (deluge described in Genesis) **2:136**; **4**:1; **5**:9, 93
**FOLKLORE 2:137**; **1**:44, 152; **2**:59, 62, 72, 115; **4**:33, 80
**FOOD 2:138**
—Laws and Customs: **1**:155, 166; **2**:73, 110, 131, 149; **3**:74; **4**:93; **5**:19, 39, 122, 134, 161, 162; **6**:71
—Miscellaneous: **3**:17; **4**:92; **6**:90
Football **6**:6
Forbidden Fruit (in the Garden of Eden), *see* **ADAM AND EVE**
Forced Conversion (baptism under threat or torture), *see* **CONVERSION, FORCED**
Ford, Gerald (U.S. pres.) **6**:68
Ford, Henry (U.S. auto man.) **2**:71; **6**:65
**FORGERY 2:140**; **1**:92, 104
*Forward* (Yiddish newspaper) **5**:5, 78; **6**:106
Fostat, *see* **CAIRO**
**FOUR CAPTIVES, THE** (story from medieval Spain) **2:141**; **3**:15, 75; **4**:10

Four Questions (part of the *seder* service on Passover), *see Mah Nishtanah*
Four Sacred Cities (in Ereẓ Israel: Jerusalem, Hebron, Safed and Tiberias) **5**:130
Four Species (Sukkot ceremony), *see Arba'ah minim*
Fox, Jacob Samuel (British educator) **4**:63
**FRANCE 2:141**; **1**:12, 35; **2**:34, 39, 118, 147; **3**:49; **4**:139, 176; **5**:36, 175; **6**:121
Franciscans (order of the Catholic Church) **2**:97; **3**:90
Franco, Francisco (Spanish ruler) **1**:105
**FRANK, ANNE** (teenage Dutch diarist during Holocaust) **2:143**; **1**:148
**FRANK, JACOB** (adventurer and false messiah) **2:143**; **4**:127
Frank, Moses (sportsman) **6**:5
Frank, Sydney (sportsman) **6**:5
**FRANKEL, ZACHARIAS** (Haskalah scholar) **2:144**; **3**:27, 55
Frankfort, Jacob (Los Angeles pioneer) **4**:68
**FRANKFORT ON THE MAIN** (city, Germany) **2:144**
Frankfurter, Akiva (German scholar) **2**:145
**FRANKFURTER, FELIX** (U.S. Supreme Court justice) **2:145**; **5**:106
Franks, Bobby (U.S. murder victim) **4**:64
Franks, David (U.S. colonial merchant and patriot) **5**:2; **6**:85
Franks, Isaac (U.S. patriot) **6**:85
Franks, Jacob (U.S. colonial merchant) **5**:2
Franz Josef (Emperor of Austro-Hungary) **4**:15
Fraud **2**:140; **5**:132
Frederick the Great (Frederick II, Emperor of Prussia) **1**:155; **2**:162; **3**:130; **5**:67
Frederick William III **2**:92
**FREEDOM 2:146**; **3**:7, 20, 28, 45; **5**:39
**FREEMASONS** (fraternal society begun in 17th century) **2:146**
**FREE WILL 2:147**, 169, 177; **3**:84; **5**:82
*Freischule* (German: "free school;" the first Haskalah school, in Berlin) **3**:26
French (language) **5**:94
**FRENCH REVOLUTION, THE 2:147**, 103, 142, 163; **3**:63
**FREUD, SIGMUND** (founder of psychoanalysis) **2:148**, 80; **5**:85
Friedman, Benny (sportsman) **6**:6
Friedman, Max (sportsman) **6**:6
Friedmann, Israel (ḥasidic *ẓaddik*), *see* **RUZHIN, ISRAEL**
**FRIENDSHIP 2:148**
**FRISCHMANN, DAVID** (Hebrew writer) **2:149**
**FRUITS AND VEGETABLES 2:149**; **1**:12; **2**:75; **4**:137; **5**:127, 160; **6**:52, 56
**FRUMKIN, GAD** (Supreme Court judge, Israel) **2:150**
**Fubini, Guido** (mathematician) **4:110**
Funeral, *see* **BURIAL**
Funk, Casimir (biochemist) **4**:114
**FUR TRADE 2:150**
Fu-Yong (pianist) **4**:122

# G

*Gabbai* (community official) **6**:18
**GABIROL, SOLOMON IBN** (philosopher and poet) **2:151**; **1**:87
Gabriel (angel) **1**:7, 47
Gad (biblical figure; son of Jacob, and founder of one of the Twelve Tribes) **2**:56; **3**:45; **6**:53
Gaddafi, Muhamar (ruler of Libya) **4**:56
**GADNA** (youth movement, Israel) **2:151**
Gaḥal (Israel coalition party) **3**:112
Gainsborough, Thomas (18th-century English painter) **5**:64
*Galei Ẓahal*: Hebrew for "Ẓahal (Army) Waves:" Israel's radio station for army servicemen.
*Gal ha-kal:* Hebrew for "Light Wave;" Israel's radio station for lowbrow listeners.
**GALICIA** (region overlapping Poland and the Ukraine) **2:151**
Galilee: the northernmost region of Ereẓ Israel whose most important Jewish centers are Safed and Tiberias, although the inhabitants are mostly non-Jewish, with Druze predominating. Its picturesque hills and historic sites make it a foremost attraction for tourists and Israelis alike.
Galilee, Sea of, *see* **KINNERET, LAKE**
Gallipoli: port on south coast of Europian Turkey, where Jews have lived since the 12th century, and in whose vicinity the pseudo-messiah Shabbetai Ẓevi was imprisoned in 1666.
*Galut* (Hebrew: "exile;" its Yiddish form, *goles,* is popularly used in a phrase describing something — such as a speech — that drags on interminably: "as long as the *goles* of the Jews"), *see* **EXILE**
**GALVESTON PLAN** (Texas settlement project for East European refugees, 1907) **2:152**
**GAMALIEL II** (1st-century Talmud sage; president of Jabneh Sanhedrin) **2:153**; **1**:41, 110; **4**:2; **5**:171
Gambling **2**:153; **4**:145
**GAMES 2:153**, 130
*Gan Eden, see* Garden of Eden
**GANS, DAVID BEN SOLOMON** (historian) **2:154**; **1**:158
Ganzfried, Solomon (19th-century halakhic scholar) **4**:44
**GAON** (head of medieval Babylonian academy) **2:154**; **1**:42; **4**:13, 42; **5**:119, 167; **6**:102
**GAON OF VILNA** (Elijah ben Solomon Zalman; outstanding 18th-century spiritual and rabbinic leader) **2:154**; **1**:3; **3**:24; **4**:31, 32, 61; **6**:27, 75, 91
Garcia de Orta (physician) **4**:114
Garden of Eden **1**:12, 103, 151; **2**:115; **3**:162; **4**:58
**GARDOSH, KARIEL** (better known as Dosh; Israel cartoonist) **2:155**
**GATESHEAD ON TYNE** (city, England) **2:156**, 71
Gath (town, Ereẓ Israel) **5**:93
Gath-Rimmon (town, Ereẓ Israel) **5**:93
**GAZA** (ancient city, Israel) **2:156**; **5**:52
Gaza Strip (territory on Israel's southwestern coast) **2**:157; **5**:175
**GEDALIAH** (governor of Jerusalem in 586 b.c.e.) **2:157**; **1**:131; **2**:126
*Gedud ha-Avodah, see* Trumpeldor Labor Battalion
Ge'ez (language of Ethiopia) **2**:114
*Gefilte fish* (traditionally part of the Sabbath eve meal) **2**:139
*Gehinnom, see* Hell
**GEIGER, ABRAHAM** (German leader of Reform Judaism) **2:157**, 144; **3**:27, 55; **5**:98
Geldern, Simon von (18th-century scholar) **2**:159

*Gelilah* (Hebrew: "rolling up;" the ceremonial rolling up and clothing of the Torah scroll at the conclusion of its public reading in synagogue service) **6**:47
Geller, Sandor (soccer player) **6**:5
*Gemara, see* **TALMUD**
**GEMATRIA** (mystical interpretation of biblical words through calculating the numerical value of their component letters; the letter *alef* = 1, the letter *bet* = 2, and so on) **2:157; 3**:32; **4**:108
Gems, *see* **PRECIOUS STONES**
**GENEALOGY** (the study of a person's ancestry) **2:158; 1**:69; **2**:124; **3**:164; **5**:78
General Mortgage Bank (Israel) **4**:17
Genesis (biblical book), *see* **Bereshit**
Geneva Peace Conference (after Yom Kippur War) **4**:27; **6**:108
**GENIZAH** (storehouse for sacred books and ritual objects, the most famous being the ancient archive discovered in Old Cairo in 1753) **2:159; 1**:14, 70, 124, 179; **3**:81; **4**:55; **5**:142; **6**:100
Gennesareth, Sea of, *see* **KINNERET, LAKE**
Gens, Jacob (Jewish ghetto leader, Vilna) **6**:93
**GENTILE** (non-Jew) **2:159**
Geography (of Israel) **3**:102
*Geonim, see* **GAON**
George V (king of England) **1**:102
**GEORGIA** (CIS republic) **2**:161, 82
Gera (biblical figure) **2**:95
*Gerah* (biblical unit of weight) **6**:86
Gerar (Philistine city-state) **5**:52
Gerer Ḥasidim (Gur Ḥasidim), *see* **GORA KALWARIA**
*Gerim* (Hebrew: "Proselytes"), *see* **CONVERSION TO JUDAISM**
Gerizim, Mount (biblical site) **3**:68; **5**:135, 162
**GERMANY 2:162**
—Cities: **1**:127; **2**:29; **3**:13; **4**:165; **5**:14; **6**:95, 98
—General: **1**:35, 73, 81, 163; **2**:69, 118; **3**:62, 65; **4**:139, 182; **5**:98, 100; **6**:104
Géronimo de Santa Fé, *see* **LORKI, JOSHUA**
**GERSHOM BEN JUDAH** (medieval German talmudic scholar) **2:164**, 163; **3**:47; **4**:98
**GERSHWIN, GEORGE** (U.S. composer) **2:164; 6**:39
Gersonides (known as Ralbag; 14th-century scholar), *see* Levi ben Gershom
*Ger Ẓedek* (Hebrew: "righteous proselyte"), *see* **CONVERSION TO JUDAISM**
Gesenius, Heinrich (Christian Hebraist) **2**:19
*Geshem* (prayer for rain) **6**:14
*Get* (bill of divorce), *see* Divorce
*Gezerah shavah* (term used in biblical interpretation), *see* **HERMENEUTICS**
Gezer Calendar (earliest Hebrew inscription found to date) **3**:34; **6**:97
*Gezerot taḥ ve-tat:* Hebrew term for the "decrees" (i.e., the Chmielnicki massacres) of 1648 and 1649, the dates being expressed by Hebrew letters.
*Gezerot tatnav:* Hebrew term for the "decrees" of 1096, i.e., the massacres of the Jews of the Rhine Valley in Germany, as part of the First Crusade.
**GHETTO 2:164; 1**:47, 53, 127; **2**:39; **3**:66; **4**:63; **5**:63; **6**:38, 73, 83, 93, 113
Ghetto Fighters Museum (Israel) **4**:168
**GIBEON, GIBEONITES** (ancient city and people) **2:166; 3:46**
Gibraltar: strategic area south of Spain, which shared its facilities as an important military outpost with Great Britain. There has been a Jewish community there since the 14th century.
**GIDEON** (biblical figure) **2:166; 4**:131; **5**:162
Gifter, Mordecai (head of Telz yeshivah) **6**:33
Giges (king of Lydia) **2**:171
Gihon (spring, Jerusalem) **3**:160; **5**:171
Gilead (territory near Canaan) **3**:138
**GILGAL** (ancient sites) **2:167**
Gilgamesh (Mesopotamian warrior) **4**:124
*Gilgamesh, Epic of* **2**:137
Gillman, Sidney (sportsman) **6**:6
Gimbel, Adam (U.S. businessman) **2**:69
Ginsberg, Asher Hirsch (Hebrew writer and thinker), *see* **AḤAD HA-AM**
**Ginsberg, Jekuthiel** (mathematician and writer) **4:110**
**Ginzberg, Eli** (economist) **2**:167
**GINZBERG, LOUIS** (talmudic scholar) **2:167; 4**:12; **6**:20, 27,
Givatayim (town, Israel) **6**:31
Giv'at Brenner (kibbutz) **3**:3
Giv'at Ḥayyim (kibbutz) **1**:73
Givens, Philip G. (mayor, Toronto, Canada) **6**:50
**GLADIATORS 2:167,** 23
Glanz, Leib (cantor) **3**:29
**Glaser, Donald Arthur** (physicist) **4:110**
Glasgow (city, Scotland) **5**:145
**GLASS 2:167**
Glubb, John G. (Glubb Pasha; soldier) **1**:5
**GLUECK, NELSON** (Reform leader and archaeologist) **2:168;** 40
**GLUECKEL OF HAMELN** (17th-18th century diarist) **2:168**
**GOD 2:168**
—Belief and Disbelief: **1**:7, 25, 77, 115, 154, 157, 169; **3**:47, 52, 77, 135; **4**:70, 174; **5**:108, 164; **6**:3, 75
—In History: **2**:17, 30, 171, 172; **3**:174, 177; **4**:154; **6**:21, 33, 46
—In the Universe: **2**:46, 136; **4**:6, 98, 122, 141, 180; **5**:45, 82, 97; **6**:41, 42
—Miscellaneous: **1**:4, 47, 138; **2**:176; **3**:16; **4**:80
Godfrey of Bouillon (Crusader leader) **3**:105
Godowsky, Leo (violinist and photographer) **3**:93
Goetz, Benjamin (18th-century British engraver) **4**:62
**GOG AND MAGOG** (antagonists of Israel in the pre-Messianic battle at the End of Days) **2:171**
Gogo (king of Lydia), *see* Giges
Golan Heights (area bordering Israel and Syria) **5**:176
Gold, *see* **GOLDSMITHS AND SILVERSMITHS**
Gold, Max (sportsman) **6**:6
**GOLDBERG, ARTHUR JOSEPH** (U.S. Supreme Court justice and U.S. ambassador to the U.N.) **2:171**
Goldberg, Leah (writer, Israel) **3**:39
Goldberg, Marshall (sportsman) **6**:6
Goldberger, Joseph (biochemist) **4**:114
Goldbloom, Victor (Canadian politician) **4**:150
Goldbogen, Avrom Hirsch, *see* **Todd, Mike**
**GOLDEN, HARRY LEWIS** (U.S. author) **2:173; 5**:4
**GOLDEN CALF 2:172; 1**:1; **2**:174; **4**:151, 157; **5**:174; **6**:22
*Golden Haggadah* (earliest illuminated Sephardi *Haggadah*) **3**:9
**GOLDFADEN, ABRAHAM** (poet and composer) **2::173; 6**:38
Goldman, (Judge) Harry (sportsman) **6**:15
**GOLDMANN, NAHUM** (Zionist leader) **2:173; 5**:100
Goldschmidt, Hans (chemist) **3**:93
**GOLDSMITHS AND SILVERSMITHS 2:174; 1**:28, 73; **2**:172, 186; **4**:86, 127; **6**:101
—Gold: **2**:167; **4**:127, 152; **5**:183, 185
**GOLDWATER** (U.S. family) **2**:175
Goldwater, Baron (U.S. businessman, senator) **2**:175
Goldwater, Barry W. (U.S. senator) **2**:175
Goldwater, Joseph (U.S. businessman) **2**:175
Goldwater, Michael (U.S. businessman) **2**:175
Goldwater, Morris (U.S. businessman) **2**:175
**GOLEM** (mystically animated figure of clay) **2:175; 4**:82
*Golem* (Yiddish: *goilem*): uncomplimentary slang term for a witless clod.
Golem (Weizmann Institute's electronic computer) **6**:88
Goliath (biblical figure) **2**:56; **5**:52
**GOLOMB, ELIYAHU** (Ereẓ Israel military leader) **2:176**
Gomer (biblical figure) **2**:171
Gomorrah (biblical site) **1**:8; **5**:180
**GOMPERS, SAMUEL** (U.S. trade unionist) **2:176**
Gomulka, Wladyslaw (Polish premier) **5**:62

**GOOD AND EVIL** (philosophical concept) **2**:177; **1**:12; **2**:147; **3**:2, 76, 83, 174; **4**:8; **5**:102; **6**:112. *See also* **JUSTICE**
Goodman, Tobias (British preacher) **4**:62
**GORA KALWARIA** (Polish town where Gur-Gerer Hasidim originated) **2:177**
Gorbachev, Mikhail **4**:154; **5**:117
Gordimer, Nadine (author; Nobel Laureate) **5**:11, 186
**GORDON, AHARON DAVID** (Hebrew writer and labor ideologist) **2:178**; **5**:92; **6**:119
Gordon, Eliezer (founder of the Telz yeshivah) **6**:32
**GORDON, JUDAH LEIB** (poet, critic and journalist) **2:178**
**GOREN, SHLOMO** (chief rabbi of Israel) **2:179**
Gottlieb, Edward (sportsman) **6**:6
Gottschalk, Alfred (U.S. Reform leader) **3**:40
Gouri,Haim (writer, Israel) **3**:39
**GRACE BEFORE AND AFTER MEALS 2:179**; **1**:119, 166; **2**:131, 138, 149; **3**:20; **5**:123; **6**:84
**GRADE, CHAIM** (Yiddish poet and novelist) **2:181**; **6**:67
**GRAETZ, HEINRICH** (historian) **2:182**
*Grager* (Purim noisemaker), *see Greger*
Grammar, Hebrew,*see* **HEBREW LANGUAGE**
Granada (city, Spain) **5**:137; **6**:2
Granovsky, Alexander (drama teacher) **4**:135
Grant, Ulysses S. (U.S. general and president) **4**:59
Grapheus, Benvenutus (medieval oculist) **4**:113
Gratz College (Philadelphia) **5**:52; **6**:68
Graves, Philip (journalist) **5**:82
Great Britain, *see* entries on **ENGLAND, IRELAND, SCOTLAND** and **WALES**
Great Universal Stores (U.K.) **2:70**
**GREECE 2:182**; **1**:29, 88; **2**:23, 39; **3**:18, 27; **5**:133. *See also* **HELLENISM.**
Greek (language) **3**:44; **5**:25, 53, 153
Green, Monroe (U.S. advertising pioneer) **1**:16
Greenberg, Henry (Hank; sportsman) **6**:5
Greenberg, Uri Ẓevi (writer, Israel) **3**:39
**GREETINGS 2:183**, 130; **5**:45
*Greger* (Purim noisemaker) **5**:86
Gregory I (pope) **5**:62
Gregory IX (pope) **3**:90, **5**:63
**Grey, Joel** (U.S. actor) **6:40**
Grillparzer, Franz (Austrian playwright) **3**:169
**GRODNO** (city, Belorussia) **2:184**
**GRODZINSKI, ḤAYYIM OZER** (Lithuanian talmudic scholar) **2:185**
Groom, *see* **MARRIAGE**
Gross, Naphtali (Yiddish author) **1**:49
Gruen, David, *see* **BEN-GURION, DAVID**
Gruen, Victor (U.S. architect) **1**:69
**GRUENBAUM, YIẒḤAK** (Zionist leader) **2:185**
**GRYNSZPAN, HERSCHEL** (assassin of German diplomat) **2:185**
Guenzburg, Joseph (Russian communal leader) **2**:178
*Guide to the Perplexed*(philosophic work by Maimonides) **4**:84
**GUILDS 2:186**, 44
Gulf War **3**:95
Gumplowicz, Ludwig (sociologist) **5**:180
Gunzenhausen, Joseph ben Jacob (15th-century printer) **4**:175
Gur (Hebrew name for the dynasty of Gerer *rebbes* and their Ḥasidim) **2**:177; **3**:25
Gustav III (Sweden) **6**:15
Guttman, Beta (sportsman) **6**:5
Guttmann, Julius (German scholar) **3**:27
*Gut Yom-Tov* (Yiddish and Hebrew): greeting: "Have a happy festival."

# H

**HAAN, JACOB ISRAËL DE** (anti-Zionist) **3:1**
*Ha-apalah, see* **ILLEGAL IMMIGRATION**
*Ha-Aretz* (Israel newspaper) **5**:144
Ha-Ari (16th-century kabbalist), *see* **LURIA, ISAAC**
**ḤABAD** (intellectual trend in Hasidism) **3:1**, 25, 41; **5**:143, 161; **6**:67
**HABAKKUK** (biblical figure; prophet) **3:2**; **1**:142; **2**:170; **5**:161; **6**:10
Ḥabban: South Arabian town, whose Jews (before their *aliyah* in 1950) were desert dwellers of distinctive appearance —tall with delicate features, long hair, but no sidelocks or moustache, which they plucked. They are all descendants of one family, have a distinctive folklore of their own, and still live in a closely-knit community.
Ḥabib, Jacob ibn, *see* Ibn Ḥabib, Jacob
Habimah (theatrical company, Israel) **3**:40; **5**:114
Habiru (ancient warrior race) **1**:132; **4**:124
**HABONIM** (Zionist youth movement) **3:3**
**Hackett, Buddy** (Leonard Hacker; U.S. comedian) **6:40**
Hadad (biblical figure) **2**:91
*Ḥadash* (Hebrew: "new grain") **2**:135
*Hadasim* (myrtle twigs used on Sukkot) **6**:12
Hadassah (U.S. women's Zionist organization, and name of hospitals in Israel) **3**:71, 127; **6**:20
**ḤADERAH** (town, Israel) **3:3**
*Hadith* (Muslim oral tradition) **3**:100
**HADRIAN, PUBLIUS AELIUS** (Roman emperor, 2nd century c.e.) **3:4**; **1**:107; **3**:15, 184; **5**:25; **6**:36
**ḤAFEẒ ḤAYYIM** (Israel Meir Ha-Kohen Kagan; talmudic scholar and ethical writer) **3:4**; **2**:114; **4**:44
*Ḥafez Ḥayyim* (book on slander) **3**:4; **5**:178
Ḥafeẓ Ḥayyim (kibbutz) **4**:5; **5**:128
**HAFFKINE, WALDEMAR MORDECAI** (bacteriologist) **3:5**, 87
*Haftarah* (passage from the Prophets chanted after the public reading from the Torah scroll during synagogue service) **1**:147; **6**:48
**HAGANAH** (underground defense organization in Ereẓ Israel during the British Mandate) **3:5**
—General: **1**:11; **3**:1, 80, 95; **4**:16, 21, 79; **5**:34; **6**:81, 120
—Leaders: **1**:34; **2**:58, 176; **3**:132; **4**:39, 96; **5**:99, 130; **6**:19, 92
Hagar (biblical figure) **1**:7; **3**:99; **5**:16
*Hagbahah* (Hebrew: "lifting;" the ceremonial holding aloft of the Torah scroll before or after it is read in the synagogue) **6**:47
Hager, Menaḥem Mendel ben Ḥayyim (founder of Vizhnitz ḥasidic dynasty) **6**:76
**HAGGADAH** (book relating the events of the Exodus from Egypt, recited at the *seder* service on Passover eve) **3:7**; **1**:4, 8, 73, 118; **5**:41

Haggai (biblical figure; prophet) **1**:142; **6**:115
*Ḥag ha-Bikkurim* (Hebrew: "festival of the First Fruits;" one of the names for the festival of Shavuot), *see* **SHAVUOT**
Hagiographa (third section of the Bible; the *Ketuvim*, or Writings) **1**:137, 142
**HAGIOGRAPHY** (stories of saints and great men) **3:9**
**ḤAGIZ** (Sephardi family) **3:9**
Ḥagiz, Abraham (Moroccan scholar) **3**:9
Ḥagiz, Jacob (opponent of Shabbetai Ẓevi) **3**:10
Ḥagiz, Moses (18th-century kabbalist) **1**:82; **3**:10
Ḥagiz, Samuel (I; 16-century scholar) **3**:10
Ḥagiz, Samuel (II; 16th-century scholar) **3**:10
*Ha-Golel* (congregant who rolls up and clothes the Torah scroll at the conclusion of its public reading in synagogue service) **6**:47
*Ḥag Same'aḥ:* Hebrew greeting meaning: "Have a happy festival! "
Haham (from Hebrew *ḥakham,* meaning "sage"): title of head of Anglo-Sephardi community.
*Ḥai* (the number 18) **5**:14
**HAIDAMACKS** (18th-century Ukrainian terrorists) **3:10; 1**:53,**5**:59
**HAIFA** (port city, Israel) **3:10; 1**:99; **6**:29
Hai Gaon (10th-11th century Babylonian scholar and leader) **1**:30; **5**:147, 167
Haile Selassie (emperor of Ethiopia) **2**:114, 122
Haiti (West Indies) **6**:90
*Ha-Kadosh Barukh Hu* (Hebrew: "the Holy One, blessed be He"): one of the divine names.
*Ḥakham* (Hebrew: "sage;" title of Sephardi rabbi and community leader) **4**:33; **5**:131
*Ḥakham Bashi* (Hebrew and Turkish; title of chief rabbi in Ottoman lands) **5**:32
Ḥakham Zevi, *see* **ASHKENAZI, ẒEVI HIRSCH**
*Ḥakhmei Yisrael* (collective name for the Pharisees) **5**:50
**HAKKAFOT** (ceremonial circular processions, especially in the synagogue) **3**:**12**; **1**:174; **6**:14
*Ḥalaf* (ritual slaughter's knife) **5**:163
*Ḥalah* (bread), *see* **ḤALLAH**
*Halakhah, see* **LAW, JEWISH**
*Ha-Lamed-He* (Hebrew: "the 35;" unit of 35 soldiers killed in 1948) **4**:16
*Halizah:* ceremony exempting a man from marrying his childless brother's widow. *See* Levirate marriage.
**ḤALLAH** (a form of bread baked for festive occasions) **3:12; 1**:166; **2**:139; **4**:22; **5**:109, 123
*Ḥallah* (Talmud tractate dealing with the tithe of dough) **3**:12
*Hallel* (cycle of thanksgiving Psalms recited on festive occasions) **2**:128; **3**:20, 85; **5**:72, 84
**ḤALUKKAH** (system of support for poor scholars in Ereẓ Israel) **3:13; 1**:125, 167; **4**:28
*Ḥalutz* (Hebrew: "pioneer"): in the Bible used to describe the vanguard of an army; in modern Zionist history signifies the pioneers who reclaimed the neglected soil of Ereẓ Israel.
Ham (biblical figure; son of Noah) **5**:10
*Ha-Magbe'ah* (or *Ha-Magbi'ah;* congregant who raises the Torah scroll during the synagogue service) **6**:47
*Ha-Makom* (Hebrew: "the Place"): one of the divine names, signifying that God is present everywhere.
Haman (biblical figure; villain of the Purim story) **1**:37; **5**:86
Hamashbir (consumer cooperative in Israel) **4**:14
**HAMBURG** (city, Germany) **3:13**
*Ḥameẓ* (food forbidden on Passover) **5**:40
*Ḥamin* (Hebrew: "hot;" Sephardi name for *cholent*), *see Cholent*
Hammerstein, Oscar (composer) **6**:39
Hammurapi (ancient Babylonian ruler) **4**:124
Hamon, Joseph (physician) **4**:114
*Ha-moẓi* (key word of the benediction made before eating bread, which concludes with the words *ha-moẓi leḥem min ha-areẓ)* **2**:166
**ḤANANEL BEN ḤUSHI'EL** (11th-century Talmud scholar) **3:15; 1**:115
Hananiah, Mishael, and Azariah (biblical figures) **2**:55, **4**:104
**HANANIAH BEN TERADYON** (2nd-century C.E. sage of the Mishnah) **3:15; 6**:36
Handball **6**:6
**HANDS 3**:**15**; **5**:28
**ḤANINA BEN DOSA** (1st-century sage) **3:17**
Haninai (6th-7th century leader) **1**:175
**HANNAH** (biblical figure; mother of prophet Samuel) **3:17; 1**:29, 39; **2**:64; **5**:136, 168
**HANNAH AND HER SEVEN SONS** (Apocryphal figures, martyred at the hands of Antiochus IV Epiphanes) **3:17; 1**:59
**HANNOVER, NATHAN NATA** (17th-century Polish chronicler) **3:18**
Ha-No'ar ha-Dati ha-Oved (Hebrew: "religious working youth;" Israel youth movement) **3**:126
Ha-No'ar ha-Oved ha-Le'ummi (Hebrew: "national working youth;" Israel youth movement) **3**:126
Ha-No'ar ha-Ẓiyyoni (Israel youth movement) **3**:127
**ḤANUKKAH** (festival of lights) **3:18; 1**:183; **2**:6,130, 140, 181; **4**:13, 40, 142; **5**:20; **6**: 5, 19. *See also* **JUDAH MACCABEE**
*Ḥanukkiyyah* (Hebrew: Ḥanukkah lamp) **3**:20
Ha-Poel Ha-Mizrachi (religious labor Zionists), *see* **MIZRACHI**
Ha-Poel (Israel sports organization) **3**:57
Hapsburg (European dynasty) **3**:72
*Ha-Raḥaman* (Hebrew: "the Merciful One"): one of the divine names.
*Haram al-Sharif* (Muslim holy site on the Temple Mount in Jerusalem) **3**:68
*Haran* (biblical site) **1:8; 5**:16
*Ḥaroset* (relish used in Passover *seder*) **5**:41
Harris, Harry ("The Human Hairpin;" sportsman) **6**:6
Harris, Sam (U.S. theater producer) **6**:38
Harris, Ted (U.S. theater producer) **6**:38
**HART, AARON** (18th-century settler in Canada) **3:21; 1**:182
Hart, Joel (American educator) **6**:69
Hart, Lorenz (composer) **6**:39
Hart, Moss (U.S. playwright) **4**:15
**HARZFELD, AVRAHAM** (labor leader, Israel) **3:21**
*Ha-Shaḥar (*pioneering Hebrew journal) **5**:179
*Ha-Shem*:common way of referring to God without mentioning one of the actual divine names.
Hashemite Kingdom of Jordan, *see* **JORDAN, HASHEMITE KINGDOM OF**
*Hashgaḥah* (Hebrew: "supervision"): when used in connexion with kosher food products, signifies rabbinic supervision by a *mashgi'aḥ* to ensure conformity with the dietary laws.
*Hashgaḥah* (divine surveillance of mortal affairs), *see* **PROVIDENCE, DIVINE**
Ha-Shomer (Hebrew: "the watchman;" defense organization in pre-Mandate Ereẓ Israel) **3**:5
Ha-Shomer (youth movement) **1**:126; **3**:21
**HASHOMER HA-ẒA'IR** (Zionist youth movement) **3:21; 1**:48; **3**:126
Ḥasid (pious man), *see* **PIETY** (the religious and ethical ideal); **ḤASIDEI ASHKENAZ** (medieval pietists); **ḤASIDISM** (modern movement)
**ḤASIDEI ASHKENAZ** (12th-13th century German pietists) **3:22; 1**:81; **2**:98, 163, 176; **4**:7, 12, 81, 175; **5**:55
*Ḥasidei ummot ha-Olam, see* **RIGHTEOUS GENTILES**
**ḤASIDISM** (religious movement) **3:23**
—Leaders: **1**:95;**3**:134; **4**:31, 52, 72, 173; **5**:118, 143; **6**:122
—Dynasties and Centers: **1**:116, 117; **2**:44, 152, 178; **3**:1; **6**:76
—Lifestyle and ideas: **2**:54, 82; **3**:186; **4**:8, 170; **5**:55, 69; **6**:18, 112
—Miscellaneous: **1**:81, 168; **2**:155; **5**:161; **6**:75
**HASKALAH** (18th-19th century

movement known as the Enlightenment) **3:26;** **1**:83; **2**:92, 104, 155; **3**:35, 40; **4**:32, 39, 119; **5**:116; **6**:75, 106
**HASMONEANS** (ruling family in Ereẓ Israel in 3rd-1st centuries b.c.e.) **3:27**
–Rulers: **1**:71; **3**:49; **5**:133; **6**:100
–History: **1**:11, 59; **2**:21, 27, 91, 158; **3**:17, 18, 44, 146; **4**:171; **5**:121, 149. *See also* **JUDAH MACCABEE.**
Hassideans (or Assideans: 2nd-century b.c.e. pietists) **3**:44
Hat, *see* **HEAD, COVERING OF THE**
*Ḥatam Sofer, see* **SOFER, MOSES**
*Ḥatan Bereshit* (Hebrew: "bridegroom of Genesis;" congregant called to the reading of the opening passage of the Torah) **6**:14
*Ḥatan Torah* (Hebrew: "bridegroom of the Torah;" congregant called to the reading of the last passage of the Torah) **6**:14
**HA-TIKVAH** (Israel's national anthem) **3:28;** **2**:146
*Havdalah* (ceremony ending Sabbath and festivals) **3**:13; **5**:124
*Ḥaver:* Hebrew for "friend," but sometimes signifying an associate of the Pharisaic community, or used as a title of honor for a prominent scholar. In Socialist circles, used to mean "comrade."
*Ḥavurah* (plural: *ḥavurot;* group for mutual ethical and spiritual improvement) 5:50
Ḥayon, Nehemiah (emissary of Shabbetai Ẓevi) **1**:82
Ḥayyim Aharon ben David (artist), *see* **STRUCK, HERMANN**
Ḥayyim of Hameln (husband of Glueckel, the diarist) **2**:168
*Ḥazal* (abbreviation for the Hebrew words *ḥakhameinu zikhronam li-verakhah,* meaning "our sages of blessed memory;" common term for the sages of the Talmud), *see* **SAGES**
Hazaz, Ḥayyim (Israel writer) **3**:39
*Hazkarat Neshamot* (memorial service), *see Yizkor*
Ḥazon Ish (talmudic scholar), *see* Karelitz, Avraham Yeshayahu
Hazor (biblical site, Ereẓ Israel) **6**:99
**ḤAZZAN** (synagogue cantor) **3:28;** **1**:38, 110; **4**:27, 170; **5**:45, 106; **6**:47, 93
**HEAD, COVERING OF THE 3:30;** **2**:81
**HEART 3:31;** **1**:46
Heber the Kenite (biblical figure) **3**:135
Hebrea, Maria (1st-century chemist) **3**:92
**HEBREW LANGUAGE 3:31**
–Linguists: **1**:118, 124, 134; **2**:18, 86; **3**:75, 76; **4**:27, 53; **6**:41
–General: **1**:4, 11, 64, 82, 144, 154; **3**:31; **4**:51, 64, 107; **5**:69; **6**:24, 29, 60, 96, 104
**HEBREW LITERATURE 3:35**
–Miscellaneous: **1**:11, 18; **3**:40; **4**:1; **5**:137, 153
–19th-20th Century Writers: **1**:19, 24, 133, 166; **2**:149, 178; **4**:26, 33, 118; **5**:92, 156, 179, 181; **6**:19, 29, 89
Hebrew Teachers College (Boston, U.S.) **1**:162
**HEBREW THEATER 3:40;** **6**:37
**HEBREW UNION COLLEGE – JEWISH INSTITUTE OF RELIGION** (U.S. Reform Seminary) **3:40;** **2**:168; **4**:28; **6**:93
Hebrew University of Jerusalem **2**:167; **3**:27, 126; **4**:27
**HEBRON** (city, Israel) **3:41;** **6**:120
Hébuterne, Jeanne (wife of the artist Modigliani) **4**:146
**ḤEDER** (traditional elementary Hebrew school) **3:42;** **2**:92
*Hefker* (legal term, meaning ownerless property) **1**:10
Hegel, Georg W. F. (German philosopher) **4**:105
**HE-ḤALUTZ** (Zionist youth movement) **3:42;** **1**:126
He He, Ben, *see* Ben He He
*Heikhal* (room in Jerusalem Temple) **6**:33
**HEINE, HEINRICH** (19th-century German writer) **3:43;** **1**:60, 83; **5**:91
Hejaz (region, southern Arabia) **1**:60
**HELENA OF ADIABENE** (1st-century convert to Judaism) **3:43**
Hell **4**:58
**HELLENISM** (imitation of Greek culture in the 3rd-1st centuries b.c.e.) **3:44;** **1**:59, 68, 71, 72, 83; **3**:69; **4**:3, 104; **5**:53
**HELLER, YOM TOV LIPMANN** (17th-century Talmud scholar) **3:45**
Hellman, I. W. (U.S. banker) **4**:68
Helsinki (city, Finland) **2**:132
Hemerobaptists (1st-century c.e. religious sect) **5**:148
Henle, Friedrich Gustav David (19th-century anatomist) **1**:46
Henna: a plant whose dye is widely used in the East for coloring the hair, palms of the hands, and nails. In Yemenite communities, the hands of the bridal party are rubbed with henna.
Henry, H. J. (French army officer) **2**:82
Henry VIII (king of England) **2**:107
*Hep! Hep!* : a rallying-cry against the Jews, common in Germany and, more specifically, the name given to the series of anti-Jewish riots in August 1819, in Germany and in several neighboring countries.
Heraclius (7th-century Roman emperor) **2**:182
**HERALDRY** (emblems and coats of arms) **3:45;** **1**:161; **4**:79
Herberg, Will (U.S. sociologist) **5**:180
Heredity **1**:149
**ḤEREM** (Hebrew: "ban or excommunication") **3:46;** **1**:25, 103, 162; **2**:164; **3**:25, 47, 78, 88; **5**:85; **6**:3
**HERESY 3:47;** 89
**HERMENEUTICS** (traditional mode of interpreting the Torah) **3:47;** **1**:27, 146; **4**:40, 132
Hermon, Mount (biblical site) **6**:108
**HEROD I** (also known as Herod the Great, 73 to 4 b.c.e.; king of Judea) **3:48;** **1**:22, 69, 177; **2**:26, 125, 159; **3**:28, 44; **4**:106; **6**:34
Herod Agrippa II (1st century c.e.) **2**:28
Herod Antipas (son of Herod I) **6**:42
Hershkowitz, Victor (sportsman) **6**:6
**HERTZ, JOSEPH HERMAN** (British chief rabbi) **3:49,** 173; **5**:144
Ḥerut (political party, Israel) **3**:112
Herzfeld, Jacob (19th-century German actor) **6**:38
**HERZL, THEODOR** (founder of the Zionist Organization) **3:49;** **1**:91, 98, 101; **2**:51, 83; **3**:53; **5**:11; **6**:59, 87, 115
Herzl, Mount (Jerusalem) **3**:84
Herzlia (town, Israel) **6**:31
**HERZOG, CHAIM** (6th president of Israel) **3:51**, 95
**HERZOG, ISAAC HALEVI** (second chief rabbi of Israel) **3:51;** **1**:93; **3**:95
Herzog, Jacob (Israel diplomat) **3**:51
Herzog, Sarah (head of Mizrachi religious Zionist women's organization) **3**:51
**HESCHEL, ABRAHAM JOSHUA** (U.S. philosopher) **3:51;** **4**:184; **5**:69
*Ḥesed* (Hebrew: "lovingkindness"), *see* **CHARITY**
Ḥeshvan (Hebrew month) **1**:180
Heas, Alfred (biochemist) **4**:114
Hess, Moses (Zionist theorist) **6**:115
**HESS, DAME MYRA** (British pianist) **3:52**
*Heter Iska* (legal procedure relating to interest on loans) **5**:38
**ḤEVRA KADDISHA** (group that prepares the dead for burial) **3:52;** **1**:13, 172; **2**:131
**HEZEKIAH** (king of Judah) **3:52;** **1**:143; **2:38;** 3:**98**, 144, **5**:171
HIAS (Hebrew Immigrant Aid Society) **1**:22; **5**:4
**ḤIBBAT ZION** (19th-century movement for Jewish resettlement of Ereẓ Israel) **3:53;** **1**:24, 120; **3**:3, 50; **4**:14; **5**:19; **6**:115
Ḥida (18th-century scholar, mystic, and traveler), *see* **AZULAI, ḤAYYIM JOSEPH DAVID**
Hiel the Bethelite (biblical figure) **3**:141
High priest, *see* **PRIESTS AND LEVITES**
**HILLEL** (1st-century Talmud sage) **3:53;** **1**:110, 180; **3**:47, 68, 73; **5**:51, 157
**HILLEL FOUNDATION** (organization for Jewish university students) **3:54;** **1**:156
*Ḥillul ha-Shem:* Hebrew phrase meaning "desecration of the Name [of God]"

applied to an ignoble act done in the name of religion which brings shame and disgrace; in opposition to *Kiddush ha-Shem,* "sanctification of the Name [of God]."
*Hin* (biblical unit of measurement) **6**:86
Hippocratic Oath (medical ethics) **4**:113
Hiram (Phoenician king) **5**:54, 168, 182; **6**:33, 58
**HIRSCH, BARON MAURICE DE** (19th-century philanthropist) **3:54; 1**:22, 70; **3**:170
Hirsch, Emil G. (sportsman) **6**:6
**HIRSCH, SAMSON (BEN) RAPHAEL** (19th-century German rabbinic leader) **3:55; 5**:30
Hirschel, David (murder victim; son of Solomon Hirschel) **3**:56
**HIRSCHEL, SOLOMON** (English chief rabbi) **3:55**
**ḤISDAI IBN SHAPRUT** (10th-century leader of Spanish Jewry) **3:56; 4**:18
**HISTADRUT** (Israel labor union) **3:56; 1**:122; **2**:70; **3**:21; **4**:14; **5**:181
Historical Judaism, *see* **CONSERVATIVE JUDAISM**
**HISTORY, JEWISH 3:57; 1**:148; **5**:111, 167; **6**:46
*Hitlahavut:* Hebrew word usually signifying the ecstasy of worship, and enthusiasm in carrying out the *mitzvot,* or Commandments.
**HITLER, ADOLF** (Nazi leader) **3:62; 2**:32, 125; **3**:64; **4**:182
**HITTITES** (ancient people of the Near East) **3:62; 4**:124
Ḥiyya (3rd-century c.e. Talmud sage) **5**:95
Hizbullah (Arab terrorist organization) **4**:47
**HOCHHUTH, ROLF** (German playwright) **3:62**
Hod, Mordekhai (Israel military leader) **5**:177
*Ḥofen* (biblical unit of measurement) **6**:86
**HOFFMANN, DAVID ẒEVI** (biblical and Talmud scholar) **3:63**
**Hoffmann, Dustin** (U.S. actor) **4:162**
Holdheim, Samuel (19th-century religious reformer) **5**:98
*Ḥol ha-moed* (the semi-festive intermediate days of the festivals of Passover and Sukkot) **2**:129
Holidays, *see* **FESTIVALS**
**HOLLAND 3:63; 2**:26
**Holliday, Judy**(U.S. actress) **4:162**
Hollywood (U.S. city) **4**:160
Holman, Nat (sportsman) **6**:6
**HOLOCAUST, THE** (destruction of European Jewry by the Nazis in World War II) **3:64**
—The "Final Solution": **1**:55, 98, 161; **2**:32, 95, 165; **3**:62; **4**:134, 182
—Countries and Cities: **1**:92, 96, 114; **2**:162, 183; **3**:64, 73, 129; **4**:23, 61, 166; **5**:12, 19, 58, 67, 141; **6**:15, 16, 74. *See also* other countries and cities.
—Rescue and Resistance: **1**:47, 127, 164; **2**:143; **3**:170; **4**:30, 33, 97, 104; **5**:149; **6**:79, 93, 95
—Miscellaneous: **1**:84; **2**:181; **3**:62; **4**:13; **5**:100, 170; **6**:99
Holofernes (Assyrian general) **4**:5
Holtzman, Kenneth (Ken; sportsman) **6**:5
Holtzman, William (Red; sportsman) **6**:6
Holy ark (cabinet in synagogue housing Torah scrolls), *see* Ark of the Law
Holy of Holies (inner sanctuary of the Tabernacle and the Temple) **6**:21, 33
**HOLY PLACES IN ISRAEL 3:67,** 100; **6**:89
Holzmann, S. Z. (Ereẓ Israel pioneer) **4**:16
**HOMER** (ancient Greek epic poet)**3:69**, 45
Homicide, *see* Murder
Honesty **3**:17; **6**:55, 86
Honey **2**:74
**ḤONI HA-ME'AGGEL** (1st-century b.c.e. miracle-worker) **3:69**
**HONG KONG** (city, British colony in South China) **3:69; 2**:16
Honorius III (pope) **1**:98
Hor, Mount (biblical site) **1**:1
Horeb, Mt. (biblical site), *see* **SINAI, MOUNT**
**HOROWITZ, ISAIAH HA-LEVI** (17th-century kabbalist) **3:70; 2**:84
Horowitz, Phinehas Elijah ben Meir (18th-century scholar) **2**:104
**HOSEA** (biblical figure; prophet) **3**:70; **1**:141; **3**:139
Hoshana Rabbah (7th day of festival of Sukkot) **3**:12; **6**:14
*Hoshanot* (Sukkot ceremony) **3**:12
*Ḥoshen* (high priest's breastplate) **5**:76
**HOSPITALITY 3:70; 6**:12
**HOSPITALS 3:71,** 127; **4**:80, 113; **5**:3, 170; **6**:79
Host, Desecration of (Christian anti-Semitic libel), *see* **DESECRATION OF THE HOST**
**HOUDINI, HARRY** (magician and escape artist) **3:72**
*Hoyche Schul* (synagogue and museum in Cracow, Poland) **2:44**
Hovav (biblical figure), *see* **JETHRO**
*Ḥovevei Zion* (members of pioneering Zionist group), *see* **ḤIBBAT ZION**
Huberman, Bronislaw (1882–1947): violinist who, at the age of ten, played before the emperor Franz-Josef in Vienna, and at 14 played the Brahms violin concerto in the presence of the composer. In Nazi Germany in 1933 he refused the invitation of the prestigious German conductor Furtwaengler to appear with him. In 1936 he founded the Palestine Orchestra, now called the Israel Philharmonic Orchestra.
Huessy, Eugene Rosenstock (Christian philosopher) **2**:78
Hugh of Lincoln (victim of medieval English blood libel) **1**:155
*Ḥukkat ha-goi* (the prohibition of imitating undesirable gentile customs) **2**:160; **3**:179
Hulda (biblical figure; prophetess) **3**:184
Huleh Valley: region in upper eastern Galilee, to the north of Lake Kinneret. Since ancient times it has been notorious for its malarial swamps, which covered 11 square miles in the 1940s, and which took their toll of the early *ḥalutzim.* These swamps were finally drained by the J.N.F. in a massive project (1951–1958), and now constitute a thriving agricultural region.
Humility **5**:157, 175
*Ḥummash* (the Five Books of Moses; from the Hebrew word for five; corresponding to the name Pentateuch, from the Latin word for five, which derives in turn from the Greek word for five), *see* **BIBLE**
Humor **2**:155; **3**:8, 37; **4**:26
Huna (talmudic sage) **1**:166
**HUNGARY 3:72; 1**:164, 169; **2**:123; **6**:79
Huns (ancient people) **4**:17
Hunsche, Otto (Nazi) **1**:164
*Ḥuppah* (wedding canopy) **4**:99
Hur (biblical figure) **1**:37
**Hurok, Solomon** (U.S. impressario) **6:40**
Hurrians (ancient Near Eastern people) **5**:16
Ḥurva (famous synagogue, now in ruins, in Jerusalem) **3**:77
Hurwitz, Judah (19th-century Russian *maskil*) **3**:26
Ḥushiel ben Elhanan (10th-century rabbi in North Africa) **3**:15; **4**:10
Hussein (king of Jordan) **3**:178; **5**:177
Hussein ibn Ali (Hashemite ruler) **1**:4
Husseini, Amin al- (Arab Muslim leader), *see* Al-Husseini, Ḥajj Amin
Hyatt, Abraham (aviation expert) **1**:17
Hydroponics (growing plants in water) **5**:128
**HYGIENE 3:73; 2**:23; **3**:16; **4**:112; **5**:88
Hyksos (ancient people) **2**:93; **4**:115
Hypsistarians (ancient religious sect) **5**:148
Hyram (Phoenician king), *see* Hiram
Hyrcanus, John (2nd-century b.c.e. Hasmonean ruler and high priest), *see* John Hyrcanus I
Hyrcanus II (1st-century b.c.e. Hasmonean ruler and high priest) **3**:28, 48, 69; **4**:6; **5**:133; **6**:100
Hymn, *see* *Piyyut*

# I

**IBN DAUD, ABRAHAM BEN DAVID HALEVI** (12th-century Spanish historian and philosopher) **3:75; 4:**43
**IBN EZRA, ABRAHAM** (12th-century Spanish Bible scholar) **3:75; 1:**85, 86; **3:**9, 92; **4:**109
Ibn Ḥabib, Jacob (15th-century scholar) **3:**38
**IBN JANAH, JONAH** (11th-century Hebrew grammarian, Spain) **3:76**
Ibn Labrat, Dunash (10th-century Hebrew linguist and poet), *see* **DUNASH BEN LABRAT**
Ibn Pulgar, Isaac ben Joseph (13th-century scholar) **1:**6
Ibn Sid, Isaac (Don Zag; 13th-century scientist) **1:**85
Ibn Tibbon (family of translators), *see* **TIBBON, IBN**
**IBN VERGA, SOLOMON** (17th-century Spanish historian) **3:76**
**IBRAHIM PASHA** (19th-century ruler of Ereẓ Israel) **3:76**
**ICA,** *see* **JEWISH COLONIZATION ASSOCIATION**
**IDELSOHN, ABRAHAM ẒVI** (musicologist) **3:77**
**IDOLATRY** (worship of images and false gods) **3:77**
—Biblical Period: **1:**7, 23, 88, 96, 138; **2:**100, 172; **3:**46, 52, 142, 184; **4:**80; **6:**14
—General: **1:**54, 59, 73, 80; **2:**160, 169; **3:**69, 100; **4:**5, 103; **5:**174; **6:**16
Idumeans (ancient people), *see* **EDOM**
Ifra Hormizd (4th-century Persian queen) **5:**158
*Iggeret ha-Shemad* (Maimonides' epistle on forced conversion) **4:**83
Iglesia Israelita (religious group) **4:**5
Iḥud Habonim (Zionist youth organization), *see* **HABONIM**
ILAN (Israel foundation for handicapped children) **3:**127
**ILLEGAL IMMIGRATION** (immigration to Ereẓ Israel prior to the establishment of the State in defiance of the instructions imposed by the Turks and later by the British mandatory government) **3:79; 1:**122, 130; **2:**117; **3:**6, 22, 169, 170; **4:**14, 135; **5:**44; **6:**119
**ILLUMINATED MANUSCRIPTS, HEBREW 3:80; 4:**101
Imber, Naphtali Herz (composer of *Ha-Tikvah)* **3:**28
**IMMANUEL OF ROME** (medieval poet) **3:81**
Immigration, "Illegal," *see* **ILLEGAL IMMIGRATION**
Impressionism (painting style) **5:**57
**IMPRISONMENT 3:82,** 45
Impurity, Ritual, *see* **PURITY AND IMPURITY, RITUAL**
**INBAL** (Israel Dance theater) **3:82; 2:**55
**INCENSE AND PERFUMES 3:83; 1:**36
Incest (forbidden relationships) **4:**102
**INCLINATION, GOOD AND EVIL 3:83; 1:**47; **2:**177; **3:**79; **5:**140, 174
Incunabula (early printed books) **5:**79
**INDEPENDENCE DAY, ISRAEL 3:84; 2:**130
*Index Expurgatorius* (medieval papal listing of Hebrew books to be censored) **2:**5
**INDIA 3:86; 1:**121; **2:**26
Indians, American **1:**146
**INFORMERS 3:87; 1:**103
**INGATHERING OF THE EXILES** (the end of the Diaspora in Messianic times) **3:88; 1:**40; **3:**85; **6:**115
**INHERITANCE 3:89; 2:**134; **6:**91
Injury (in civil law) **2:**53
Innocent II (pope) **5:**36
Innocent III (pope) **5:**63
Innocent IV (pope) **3:**90
**INQUISITION** (institution of the Catholic church which sought out heresy, and tortured and burned non-Catholics) **3:89**
—The Persecutors: **1:**54; **2:**20, 127; **5:**63; **6:**50, 98
—The Persecuted: **4:**4, 60, 97; **5:**48, 64; **6:**2
Insects **2:**74
**INSULT 3:91**
Interest (on loans), *see* **MONEYLENDING AND USURY**
Intermarriage **1:**84; **4:**102, 185; **5:**106; **6:**92
International Bible Contest for Jewish Youth **1:**147; **3:**85
"International Ghetto" (refugee rescue organization) **6:**79
International Military Tribunal, *see* War Crimes Trials, Nuremberg
**INVENTORS AND ENGINEERS 3:92; 1:**85, 87; **6:**29
Iran, *see* **PERSIA**
**IRAQ 3:93; 1:**97, 99; **4:**32
*Ir David* (Hebrew: "City of David;" biblical name for Jerusalem) **3:**143
**IRELAND 3:95; 1:**168; **3:**51
**IRGUN ẒEVA'I LE'UMMI** (underground military defense organization in Ereẓ Israel) **3:95; 1:**36, 113, 130, 168; **3:**6, 131; **4:**24, 65; **5:**96; **6:**81, 120
*Ir ha-Niddaḥat* (idolatrous city), **3:**78
Iron **4:**128
Iron Guard (Rumanian right-wing anti-Semitic movement and party) **5:**115
Irrigation (in Israel) **3:**115
**ISAAC** (biblical figure; patriarch) **3:96; 1:**8, 25, 111, 154; **3:**41, 132; **4:**174; **5:**16
Isaac, Aaron (Swedish settler) **6:**15
Isaac ben Joseph Israeli (14th-century astronomer) **4:**109
Isaac ben Mordecai (physician) **4:**114
Isaac ben Moses ha-Levi (14th-15th century philosopher and physician), *see* **DURAN, PROFIAT**
Isaac ben Moses of Vienna (14th-century scholar) **6:**74
Isaac Elchanan Theological Seminary (N.Y.), *see* **YESHIVA UNIVERSITY**
Isaacs, Daniel (governor-general of India) **3:**87
**ISAACS, SIR ISAAC ALFRED** (Australian jurist and governor-general) **3:97**
Isaacs, Samuel (19th-century U.S. rabbi) **5:**5
Isabella (queen of Spain, wife of Ferdinand), *see* **FERDINAND AND ISABELLA**
Isabella (Spanish princess, wife of Manuel of Portugal) **5:**64
**ISAIAH** (biblical figure; prophet) **3:97; 1:**139; **3:**53; **4:**89
Ish-Bosheth (biblical figure) **2:**56, 166
**ISHMAEL** (biblical figure; son of Abraham) **3:99; 1:**7, 61; **3:**96
Ishmael (sage of the Mishnah) **3:**47
*Iska* (legal procedure) **5:**38
Iskowitch, Isidor, *see* **Cantor, Eddie**
**ISLAM** (religion of Muslims) **3:99; 1:**54, 60, 61; **3:**68, 79, 99, 122, 162; **4:**158, 164; **5:**23; **6:**2
Ismailism (10th-century religious-political movement) **2:**83
**ISRAEL 3:101**
The article is divided into the following sections:

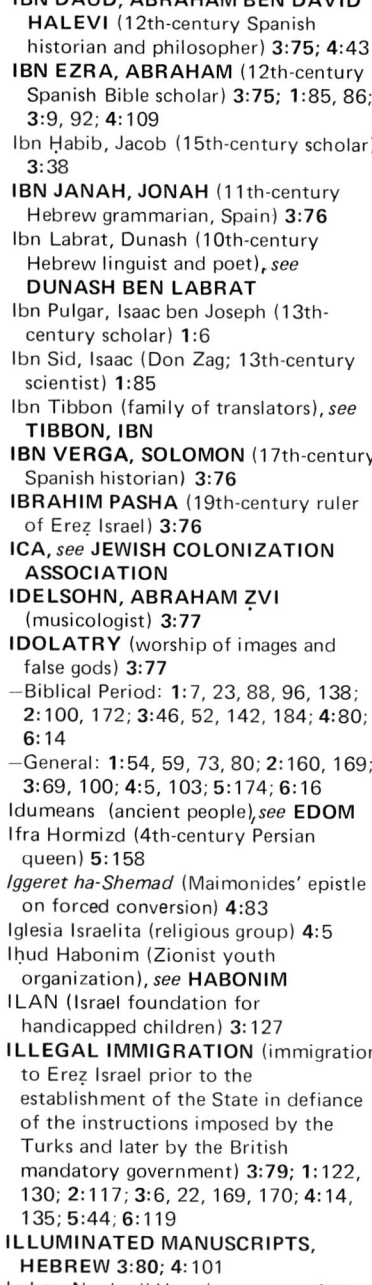

—Names **3**:101
—Geography **3**:102
—Climate **3**:102
—Flora and Fauna **3**:103
—History **3**:103
—Population **3**:110
—Government **3**:111
—Judicial System **3**:113
—Defense Forces **3**:114
—Economic Affairs **3**:114
—Religious Life **3**:121
—Education **3**:123
—Health and Welfare **3**:127
For further information, see the following references to Israel in *other* articles, set out below according to subject matter:
—History: **1**:4, 101, 182; **2**:64, 95, 143, 164; **3**:13, 27, 76, 79; **4**:35, 45, 47, 65, 90, 93, 135, 149; **5**:175, 176; **6**:8, 18, 53, 61, 71, 81, 107, 115
—Government: **1**:34, 113, 123; **3**:112, 113; **4**:117, 143; **5**:90
—Economic Life: **1**:20, 69, 159; **2**:29, 167; **3**:56, 120, 136; **4**:17, 25, 35, 76; **5**:77, 181; **6**:29
—Defense Forces: **1**:35, 107, 161; **2**:84, 176; **4**:22, 39, 137; **5**:90; **6**:55, 82, 99, 102
—Society and Religion: **1**:18, 63, 99, 111; **3**:21, 67; **4**:18, 186; **5**:32, 185
—Culture, Education, and Health: **1**:106; **3**:34, 71, 123, 126; **4**:27, 55, 80, 143, 168; **6**:5, 29, 60, 79, 110
—Miscellaneous: **1**:48, 121; **3**:82, 84; **4**:120, 179; **5**:182; **6**:7, 52, 78, 88
*See also* under individual places, and *Aliyah.*
Israel, Michael Cresson Boaz, *see* Cresson, Warder
Israel Aircraft Industries **4**:76
Israel ben Eliezer Ba'al Shem Tov (founder of Ḥasidism), *see* **BA'AL SHEM TOV**
Israel Declaration of Independence, *see* **DECLARATION OF INDEPENDENCE, ISRAEL**
Israel Electric Corporation **4**:17
Israel Labor Party **1**:123; **3**:112
Israel Land Development Corporation **4**:17
Israel Liberal Party **3**:112
Israel Meir Ha-Kohen,*see* **ḤAFEẒ ḤAYYIM**
Israel Museum (Jerusalem) **4**:168
Israel Philharmonic Orchestra: founded by the violinist Bronislaw Huberman in 1936, who envisaged a Jewish orchestra in Ereẓ Israel as a rescue operation for musicians persecuted by the Nazis, as well as a contribution to the cultural life of the country. Arturo Toscanini, the eminent Italian conductor, gave the orchestra international standing by conducting the first concerts. This status has been enhanced by numerous international tours, and recording for Columbia and Decca.
Issachar (biblical figure; son of Jacob, and founder of one of the Twelve Tribes) **3**:45; **6**:53
Issachar Dov (Belzer *rebbe*) **1**:117
Isserles, Moses (16th-century halakhic authority, Poland) **1**:81; **4**:44
Istanbul, *see* **CONSTANTINOPLE**
**ITALIA, SHALOM** (17th-century engraver) **3**:127
Italiaander, Isak (Dutch tobacco dealer) **6:45**
Italkian (language) **3**:171
**ITALY 3:128; 2**:118; **4**:48, 175; **5**:105, 171; **6**:38, 68, 71, 73
**ITINERARIES OF EREẒ ISRAEL 3:129; 1**:123; **4**:94; **6**:51
Itureans (ancient tribe in Erez Israel) **1**:71
**ITZIG, DANIEL** (18th-century German banker) **3**:130
Itzig, Isaac Daniel (18th-century educator, son of the banker) **3**:130
**IVORY 3:130**
Iyyar, 28th of (the 28th day of the Hebrew month of Iyyar; the anniversary of the liberation of Jerusalem on the third day of the Six-Day War, 1967), *see* Jerusalem Day
Izates (son of Helena, queen of Adiabene) **3**:43
Izdundad (early medieval figure; Persian wife of Bustanai) **1:176**
IẒL (underground resistance movement in mandatory Palestine), *see* **IRGUN ẒEVA'I LE'UMMI**
Izmir (city, Turkey), *see* **SMYRNA**


# J


Jabali (language) **3**:171
Jabin (biblical figure; king of Canaan) **2**:64; **3**:135
**JABNEH** (ancient city, Ereẓ Israel) **3:131; 2**:153; **3**:176
**JABOTINSKY, VLADIMIR (ZE'EV)** (Zionist leader) **3:131; 1**:11, 130; **3**:96; **6**:118
Jackson, Henry: U.S. senator and presidential candidate, known for the so-called Jackson Amendment to U.S.-Soviet agreement linking emigration of Soviet Jews to trade concessions.
**JACKSON, SOLOMON HENRY** (19th-century printer) **3:132**
**JACOB** (biblical figure; patriarch) **3:132;** 93, 149; **3**:9, 41, 180; **4**:174; **5**:16, 91, 162, 165, **6**:53
**JACOB BEN ASHER** (known from the title of his major halakhic work as the Tur; 14th-century Talmud scholar) **3::134; 1**:78; **4**:43
Jacob ben Ḥayyim ibn Adonijah (16th-century Bible scholar) **1**:145; **4**:108
Jacob Berab (16th-century Talmud scholar), *see* Berab, Jacob
Jacob Isaac (the Seer of Lublin; Polish ḥasidic *ẓaddik*) **4**:72
**JACOB JOSEPH OF POLONNOYE** (early ḥasidic leader) **3:134,** 23
Jacobs, Jimmy (sportsman) **6**:6
Jacobson, Eddie (friend of U.S. President Truman) **6**:55
Jacobstahl, E. (19th-century architect) **1**:69
Jaddua (high priest) **1**:29
**JAEL** (biblical heroine) **3:135; 2**:64
Jaffe, Daniel (18th-century German banker and communal leader), *see* **ITZIG, DANIEL DANIEL**
Jaffe, Leonard (aviation expert) **1**:17
Jaffe, Mordecai ben Abraham (16th-century rabbi) **4**:72
Jakobovits, Immanuel (British chief rabbi) **2**:109; **6**:51
Jamaica (West Indies) **6**:90
James (brother of Jesus) **3**:165
Janaḥ, Jonah ibn (grammarian), *see* **IBN JANAḤ, JONAH**
**JAPAN 3:135; 4**:5
Japhet (biblical figure; son of Noah) **5**:10
Jason (2nd-century b.c.e. high priest) **3**:44; **5**:148
Jassy (city in N.E. Rumania, once a thriving spiritual center, whose

community, the oldest in Moldavia, was decimated in the Holocaust) **3**:18
Jastrow, Joseph (psychologist) **3**:137
**JASTROW, MARCUS MORDECAI** (19th-century German lexicographer) **3:137**
Jastrow, Morris (orientalist) **3**:137
**JAVITS, JACOB KOPPEL** (U.S. senator) **3:137**
Jawitz, Ze'ev (19th-century historian) **3**:61
**JEALOUSY 3:137; 1**:178; **4**:29
Jebel Musa (mountain in Sinai Peninsula) **5**:175
Jebusites (ancient Canaanite people) **3**:143
Jedidiah, *see* **SOLOMON**
Jeḥiel ben Joseph (13th-century rabbi) **1**:11
Jehoahaz (king of Israel) **3**:138
**JEHOIACHIN** (king of Judah) **3:138; 4**:183; **6**:114, 115
Jehoiakim (king of Judah) **3**:140
Jehoiada (biblical figure; high priest) **1**:88
Jehoram (biblical figure; king of Judah, 9th century b.c.e.; husband of Athaliah) **1**:88
Jehoram (biblical figure; king of Israel, 9th century b.c.e.; son of Ahab) **2**:101; **3**:138
**JEHU** (biblical figure; king of Israel, 9th century b.c.e.) **3:138; 1**:88
**JEPHTHAH** (biblical figure; judge and warrior) **3:138; 2**:54
Jerba (island off Tunisia), *see* **DJERBA**
**JEREMIAH** (biblical figure, prophet) **3:139; 1**:140; **4**:38, 184; **5**:81; **6**:43
Jeremiah (talmudic sage) **1:18**
**JERICHO** (ancient city, Ereẓ Israel) **3:140; 1**:64; **2**:23, 167; **3**:12, 183
**JEROBOAM** (king of Israel) **3:141; 1**:138; **2**:173; **5**:162
Jerome (4th-5th century Christian Bible scholar) **1**:145
Jerubaal (biblical figure; judge), *see* **GIDEON**
**JERUSALEM 3:142, 4**:144
—Ancient Period & Archaeology: **1:65; 2**:124; **3**:4; **4**:6, 78; **5**:55, 151, 171, 183; **6**:13, 33, 44, 82
—Middle Ages: **1**:80; **2**:49; **4**:172; **5**:23; **6**:14
—Modern Period: **1**:100, 166; **3**:5, 85; **4**:23, 28, 149; **5**:132, 135, 177, 185; **6**:82, 89
Jerusalem Day (commemorating liberation of the Old City on 28th of Iyyar, 1967) **2**:130; **3**:85
Jerusalem of gold (medallion or brooch) **2**:174
"Jerusalem of Gold" (song of the Six-Day War), *see Yerushalayim shel Zahav*
"Jerusalem of Lithuania" (affectionate name for the city which before the Holocaust served as the spiritual and scholarly pivot of the surrounding provinces), *see* **VILNA**
*Jerusalem Post* (newspaper) **5**:78
Jessner, Leopold (German theater director) **6**:38
Jerusalem Talmud, *see* **TALMUD**
**JESSEL, SIR GEORGE** (19th-century English jurist) **3:164**
**JESUS** (founder of Christianity) **3:164; 1**:131; **2**:2, 19, 21, 48; **3**:44; **4**:25, 26, 126, 158, 181; **5**:65, 97; **6**:113
**JETHRO** (biblical figure; Moses' father-in-law) **3:165; 2**:42, 66, 83; **3**:68, 135; **4**:156
**JEW 3:166**
—General **1**:83; **2**:17, 19, 32, 36; **4**:45
—Sects: **1**:53, 121, 152; **2**:121; **4**:97, 164
*Jew, The* (periodical) **5**:77
**JEWESS OF TOLEDO, THE** (legendary Spanish heroine) **3:168**
**JEWISH AGENCY** (official Zionist organization) **3:169; 1**:72, 122, 164; **2**:77; **4**:17, 92, 175; **5**:158
Jewish Anti-Fascist League (Russian anti-Nazi group) **4**:135; **6**:7
*Jewish Antiquities* (book by Josephus) **3**:182
**JEWISH BRIGADE GROUP** (military unit in World War II) **3:170; 1**:127; **3**:6, 96; **4**:39
*Jewish Chronicle* (English newspaper) **2**:109; **5**:77
Jewish Colonial Trust (early Zionist settlement fund) **6**:115
**JEWISH COLONIZATION ASSOCIATION (ICA)** (organization for resettlement of European Jewry) **3:170; 1**:21, 70; **3**:54
*Jewish Daily Forward, see Forward*
Jewish Defense League (U.S.) **4**:185; **5**:149; **6**:67
*Jewish Encyclopaedia* (published 1901-06) **2**:104, 167; **3**:137; **4**:28; **6**:20
Jewish Exchequer (medieval English authority), *see* **EXCHEQUER OF THE JEWS**
Jewish Institute of Religion, *see* **HEBREW UNION COLLEGE – JEWISH INSTITUTE OF RELIGION**
Jewish Labor Committee (U.S.) **1:37**
**JEWISH LANGUAGES** (languages spoken by Jews, which are modified forms of the languages of the host environment) **3:171; 1**:17, 64, 145; **4**:33, 164; **6**:104
Jewish law, *see* **LAW, JEWISH**
Jewish Legion (World War I fighting force) **1**:122, 126; **2**:176; **3**:131
Jewish Museum (London) **4**:67
Jewish Museum (New York) **3**:173
Jewish National and University Library (Jerusalem) **4**:55
**JEWISH NATIONAL FUND** (organization for purchase and development of land in Ereẓ Israel) **3:171; 4**:17; **6**:8, 70, 116
Jewish Publication Society (U.S.) **5**:52
Jewish Quarter, *see* **GHETTO**
**JEWISH QUARTERLY REVIEW** (scholarly periodical) **3:172**
Jewish Star, *see* **MAGEN DAVID**
Jewish Studies **6**:69
Jewish Theological Seminary (Breslau) **2**:182
**JEWISH THEOLOGICAL SEMINARY OF AMERICA** (U.S. Conservative rabbinical seminary) **3:172; 2**:34, 131, 167; **3**:49; **5**:5, 142; **6**:64
Jewish War (rebellion against Roman rule of Ereẓ Israel) **6**:113
*Jewish War, The* (by Josephus) **3**:182
**JEWS' COLLEGE** (London) **3:173**, 164; **4**:67; **6**:69
"Jew Suess" (German Court Jew), *see* **OPPENHEIMER, JOSEPH BEN ISSACHAR SUESSKIND**
Jezebel (biblical figure; wife of Ahab) **1**:23, 88; **2**:100; **5**:54
*Jihad* (Islamic holy war to conquer the infidel) **3**:100
Jimenes de Cisneros, Francisco, *see* **XIMENES de CISNEROS, FRANCISCO**
**JOAB** (biblical figure; military leader) **3:173; 2**:57
Joao Micas, *see* Nasi, Joseph
Joash (biblical figure) **1**:88
**JOB, BOOK OF** (biblical book) **3:174; 1**:143; **3**:70; **4**:6; **6**:10, 92
Jochebed (biblical figure; mother of Moses) **4**:154
Joel (biblical figure; prophet) **1**:141
Johanan (talmudic sage) **1**:17; **5**:173
**JOHANAN BEN ZAKKAI** (1st-century c.e. sage) **3:175**, 17, 131, 184
Johannesburg (city, South Africa) **5**:185
John (king of England) **2**:107
John XXIII (pope) **5**:63
John Hyrcanus I (2nd-century b.c.e. Hasmonean ruler and high priest) **1**:71; **2**:91; **3**:27, 48; **6**:75
John of Giscala (1st-century Zealot) **1**:106
**JOHNSON, LYNDON BAINES** (U.S. president) **3:176; 5**:111
Johnson Act (U.S. legislation restricting immigration) **6**:65
John the Baptist (Apostle) **2**:96; **3**:164, 179
Joint (relief organization) , *see* American Jewish Joint Distribution Committee
Joint Boycott Council (U.S. anti-Nazi organization) **1**:37
**JOLSON, AL** (U.S. film star) **3:176; 5**:106; **6**:38
**JONAH, BOOK OF** (biblical book) **3:177; 1**:141; 2:60; **4**:69; **5**:81, 168
Jonah ibn Bikhlarish (medieval physician) **4**:113
Jonas, Abraham (U.S., 19th-century) **4**:59
Jonas, Deborah, *see* Ben-Yehuda, Deborah

Jonathan (biblical figure) **2**:56
Jonathan ben Mattathias (Hasmonean; brother of Judah Maccabee) **3**:27
Jonathan the Weaver (Zealot, 1st century) **4**:55
**JORDAN, HASHEMITE KINGDOM OF 3:177**; **1**:4, 62; **3**:102; **5**:176; **6**:119
**JORDAN RIVER 3:178**; **2**:167; **4**:24
**JOSELMANN OF ROSHEIM** (16th-century German Court Jew) **3:179**
**JOSEPH** (biblical figure; son of Jacob) **3:180**; **1**:53, 93, 136; **2**:80, 124; **3**:68, 134; **5**:162; **6**:14
Joseph (3rd-century talmudic sage) **1**:3
Joseph (Khazar king) **4**:18
Joseph, Dov (born 1899): Canadian-born lawyer and political leader in mandatory Palestine, who in April 1948 became military governor of Jerusalem. His energy and determination played a vital part in the successful defense of the city despite the critical siege during Israel's War of Independence.
Joseph, Jacob (19th-century Lithuanian and U.S. rabbi) **5**:5
Joseph II (18th-century emperor of Austria) **1**:91; **2**:123, 151; **5**:67; **6**:74
**JOSEPH HA-KOHEN** (16th-century historian) **3:181**
Joseph ibn Sham'un (student of Maimonides) **4**:84
Joseph of Rossheim, *see* **JOSELMANN OF ROSSHEIM**
**JOSEPHUS FLAVIUS** (1st-century historian) **3:182**, **44**; **6**:44
**JOSHUA** (biblical figure; conqueror of the land of Canaan) **3:182**; **1**:37, 137; **2**:111, 166, 167; **3**:141; **4**:157; **6**:14, 70
Joshua (1st-century talmudic sage) **2**:153; **4**:40; **6**:24
Joshua ben Gamla (high priest) **2:91**
**JOSHUA BEN ḤANANIA** (2nd-century c.e. talmudic sage) **3:184**; **1**:86, 149
Joshua ben Jehozadak (high priest who helped build the Second Temple) **6**:115
**JOSIAH** (king of Judah) **3:184**; **2**:93; **4**:38
Journalism, *see* **PRESS**
Jousting (medieval sport) **6**:3
**JOY 3:185**; **1**:77, 95; **3**:23; **5**:121
Juan I (king of Arragon) **2**:88
Juan Carlos (king of Spain) **6**:2
Jubal (biblical figure) **4**:169
Jubilee (fiftieth year), *see* **SABBATICAL YEAR AND JUBILEE**
**JUBILEES, BOOK OF** (Jewish sectarian work, Second Temple period) **4:1**; **1**:86
Judah (biblical figure; son of Jacob) **3**:45; **6**:53
Judah ben Kalonymus ben Moses of Mainz (12th-century scholar) **2**:99
Judah ben Samuel he-Hasid ("Judah the Pious;" main ethical teacher of the medieval German Ḥasidei Ashkenaz movement) **2**:99; **3**:22
Judah ben Tabbai (Pharisaic leader) **5**:133
Judah Hadassi (12th-century Karaite) **1**:115
Judah ha-Kohen ibn Susan (12th-century scholar) **4**:83
**JUDAH HALEVI** (12th-century Spanish poet and philosopher) **4:1**; **3**:75, 76; **4**:18, 109; **5**:53, 101, 167; **6**:43, 51
**JUDAH HA-NASI** (2nd-3rd century c.e.; editor of the Mishnah) **4:2**; **1**:132, 173; **4**:41, 176; **5**:27, 152; **6**:24
Judah he-Ḥasid (main ethical teacher of the medieval German Hasidei Ashkenaz movement), *see* Judah ben Samuel he-Ḥasid
Judah Leone ben Isaac (17th-century Hebrew playwright) **3**:40
Judah Loew ben Bezalel, *see* **MAHARAL OF PRAGUE**
**JUDAH MACCABEE** (2nd-century b.c.e. Hasmonean leader of the rebellion against Seleucid tyranny) **4:3**; **1**:58; **3**:18, 27; **4**:122; **5**:149
Judah the Galilean (1st-century priest, and fighter against the Roman regime) **6**:113
**JUDAIZERS** (non-Jews who claim to be Jews or follow Jewish practices) **4:4**; **1**:83; **3**:90; **5**:64
Judas Iscariot (betrayer of Jesus) **3**:165
*Judenstaat, Der* (book by Herzl) **3**:50
*Judenrat* (Jewish council during Nazi occupation) **3**:67
*Judenrein* (German: "cleansed of Jews:" term used by the Nazis to describe areas in which the "Final Solution" had been efficiently pursued) **3**:65
Judeznio (language) **3**:171
Judges, *see* **COURTS**
Judges (rulers and military leaders of Ereẓ Israel in the early centuries after the conquest of Canaan by Joshua and before the establishment of the monarchy, such as Ehud, Gideon, Deborah and Samson; also the biblical book which tells their story) **1**:137; **2**:64, 95, 166; **3**:103, 138; **5**:135, 141
**JUDITH, BOOK OF** (Apocryphal historical narrative, Second Temple period) **4:5**; **3**:44
Judith Lady Montefiore College (England) **4**:149
**JULIAN THE APOSTATE** (4th-century Roman emperor) **4:5**; **1**:176
Julius III (pope) **3**:128
**JULIUS CAESAR** (1st-century b.c.e. Roman emperor) **4:6**; **3**:48; **5**:128
**JUSTICE 4:6**; **1**:167; **2**:42; **3**:98, 133, 174; **4**:123; **5**:45, 85, 102, 183. *See also Bittul ha-Tamid*


# K


Ka'aba (Muslim shrine) **3**:100
**KABBALAH** (the mystical tradition) **4:7**
–Scholars: **1**:32, 95; **2**:4, 38; **4**:73, 173; **5**:158, 172; **6**:23, 59
–Concepts: **1**:28; **2**:31, 80; **4**:181; **5**:54; **6**:76
–Miscellaneous: **5**:130, 154
*Kabbalat Shabbat* (Friday evening service welcoming the Sabbath) **5**:122
Kadesh, Operation (1956 war), *see* **SINAI CAMPAIGN**
*Kaddish* (prayer) **2**:63; **4**:84; **5**:68, 72; **6**:47
Kadimah (Zionist youth movement) **3**:3
Kadman, Gurit (choreographer, Israel) **2**:55
Kadovic (family) **3**:69
**KAFKA, FRANZ** (German novelist) **4:9**
Kagan, Israel Meir Ha-Kohen, *see* **ḤAFEZ ḤAYYIM**
**KAHANEMAN, JOSEPH** (known as the Ponevezher Rav; rabbi in Lithuania and Ereẓ Israel) **4:9**
**KAHN, LOUIS I.** (U.S. architect) **4:10**; **1**:69
**KAIROUAN** (city in Tunisia, North Africa) **4:10**
Kalba Savua (1st-century merchant, Ereẓ Israel) **1**:27
Kaleb (Ethiopian king) **2**:121
**KALISCHER, ZEVI HIRSCH** (19th-century Polish rabbi and Zionist thinker) **4:10**; **6**:115

Kalish, Bertha (U.S. actress) **6**:38
Kalish, Sophie, *see* **TUCKER, SOPHIE**
Kalley, Miklos (Hungarian regent) **3**:73
**KALLIR, ELEAZAR** (medieval liturgical poet, Erez Israel) **4:11; 5**:108; **6**:100
**KALONYMUS** (German family, 9th-13th century) **4:11; 2**:98
Kalonymus ben Kalonymus (physician) **4**:114
Kalonymus ben Meshullam (10th-century rabbi) **1**:42
*Kal va-homer* (a rule of logic used in legal discussions), *see* **HERMENEUTICS**
**Kaminska, Ida** (Polish actress) **6:40**
Kaminski, Daniel, *see* **KAYE, DANNY**
*Kaneh* (biblical unit of measurement) **6**:86
Kaplan, Fanya (Russian activist) **4**:50
**KAPLAN, MORDECAI MENAHEM** (Reconstructionist theologian) **4:12; 5**:96, 102
*Kapote* (Yiddish: "long coat") **3**:25
*Kapporet* (gold cover of the Ark of the Covenant) **6**:21
**KARAITES** (Jewish sect, established in the 8th century, which rejects the authority of the Oral Law) **4:12; 1**:45, 115, 178; **2**:132; **3**:75; **4**:18, 84; **5**:43, 51, 80, 119
Karelitz, Avraham Yeshayahu (20th-century Talmud scholar, known as the "Hazon Ish" after the title of his influential halakhic work. During the last 20 years of his life he lived in Bene Berak, Israel, and although he held no official position, had a profound impact on many aspects of Orthodox Jewish life, through the force of his personality and intellect) **2**:181
Kaskel, Cesar (U.S., 19th century) **4**:59
*"Kashering"* (Hebrew plus English: making vessels ritually fit for use) **5**:40
*Kasher le-Pesah* (Hebrew: "ritually fit for Passover use") **5**:40
*Kashrut, see* **DIETARY LAWS**
Katchalski, *see* **KATZIR**
Kattowitz (German/Polish city) **3**:53
**KATZIR, AHARON** (Israel scientist) **4**:13
**KATZIR, EPHRAIM** (4th president of Israel) **4**:14
**KATZNELSON, BERL** (leader of the labor Zionist movement) **4:14**,122
Kauffmann, Richard (architect) **4**:171
Kaufman, Denis (film producer), *see* Vertov, Dziga
Kaufman, George S. (composer) **6**:39
Kaufman, Irving R. (U.S. judge) **5**:106
**KAUFMANN, ISIDOR** (or Philip; Hungarian painter) **4:15**
**KAUFMANN, YEHEZKEL** (biblical scholar) **4:15**
Kaunas, *see* **KOVNO**
*Kavvanah* (devout concentration) **5**:68, 71
*Kavvanot* (meditative preludes to prayer) **5**:68
**KAYE, DANNY** (U.S. actor) **4:15; 6**:39
Kazimierz (city, Poland) **2**:44
*Kedushah* (prayer) **5**:72
*Kefar:* the Hebrew word for village; appears before the name of many kibbutzim and townships in Israel.
Kefar Blum (kibbutz) **3**:3
**KEFAR EZYON** (kibbutz) **4:16; 6**:81
Kefar Habad (village, Israel) **3**:2; **5**:144
Kefar Hasidim (township, Israel) **2**:179
Kefar Hayyim (settlement, Israel) **1**:73
Kefar Hittin (village, Israel) **2**:84; **3**:166, 171
Kefar Monash (village, Israel **4**:147
Kefar Nahum, *see* **CAPERNAUM**
*Kehillah* (East European semi-autonomous community) **5**:59, 150
Kehillah (New York community roof organization) **5**:5
Keneset Yisrael (community organization, Erez Israel) **6**:71
Kenesset (Israel's parliament), *see* Knesset
**KENNEDY, JOHN FITZGERALD** (U.S. president) **4:16; 3**:176
Kennedy, Robert F. (U.S. senator) **4**:17
Kenya (Africa) **6**:59
Kenyon, Kathleen (English archaeologist) **3**:160
**KEREN HAYESOD** (Palestine Foundation Fund) **4:17**
*Keren Kayemeth le-Israel, see* **JEWISH NATIONAL FUND**
*Keri'ah* (tearing of garments as a sign of mourning) **2**:63
*Keri'at Shema* (prayer), *see* **SHEMA, READING OF**
Kern, Jerome (U.S. composer) **6**:39
**Kessler, David** (Yiddish actor) **6:40**
*Kest* (maintenance arrangement for newlyweds) **4**:102
*Ketubbah* (Hebrew: "marriage contract;" a document that is often ornately inscribed and illuminated) **3**:89; **4**:99
Keturah (biblical figure) **1**:8
*Ketuvim* (third section of the Bible; also known as the Writings, or Hagiographa, and including Psalms, Proverbs, Job, and other books), *see* Hagiographa
*Ke-zayit* (talmudic unit of measurement) **6**:86
*Kfar* (Hebrew: "village;" part of hundreds of place-names in Israel), *see Kefar*
Khadija (wife of Muhammad) **4**:164
*Khapers* (Yiddish: "catchers;" the dreaded agents of Czar Nicholas I, whose task it was to kidnap Jewish children for 25 years' conscription in the Russian army), *see* **CANTONISTS**
Khawarij (sect in Islam) **3**:100
**KHAZARS** (seventh-tenth century people, southeast Europe) **4:17; 2**:150; **4**:2
**KIBBUTZ** (collective settlement in Israel) **4:18; 2**:65, 82, 107; **3**:3; **4**:16, 143, 159; **6**:8
Kibbutz Arzi Ha-Shomer Ha-Zair (kibbutz organization) **3**:21
Kibbutz Society (Japanese Zionist group) **3**:137
**KIDDUSH** (sanctification over wine, recited on Sabbath and festivals) **4:22; 1**:166; **2**:131; **3**:13; **5**:121
*Kiddush ha-Shem, see* **MARTYRDOM**
*Kiddushin* (part of marriage ceremony) **4**:98
*Kiddush levanah* (prayer after New Moon) **4**:151
**KIDNAPPING 4:22; 2**:1; **6**:40
Kidron (valley and brook, Jerusalem) **5**:121
**KIEV** (city, Ukraine) **4:23; 1**:96
*Kilayim* (the mixing of crops), *see* **MIXED SPECIES**
Killing, *see* Murder
Kilometer 101 (a point on the Cairo-Suez road; location of cease-fire negotiations between Israel and Egypt after Yom Kippur War) **6**:108
King, Phil (sportsman) **6**:6
**KING DAVID HOTEL** (Jerusalem) **4:23**
King James Bible **1**:146
Kings, Book of (biblical book) **1**:138
King's Highway (ancient trade route) **4**:145; **5**:182
**KINGSHIP 4:24; 1**:1; 52, 138; **5**:137; **6**:28
Kings of Israel and Judah **1**:22, 23, 88, 138; **3**:48, 52, 138, 141, 184; **4**:88; **5**:24, 142, 182; **6**:100, 114
**KINNERET, LAKE** (Israel) **4:24; 3**:179; **6**:41
*Kinot, see* **LAMENTATIONS, BOOK OF**
*Kinyan* (legal term concerning contracts), *see* **ACQUISITION**
Kipling, Rudyard (English writer) **2**:108
*Kippah* (Hebrew: "skullcap"), *see Yarmulka*
Kiriath-Arba (biblical town), *see* **HEBRON**
Kiriath-Jearim (biblical town) **1**:9
*Kiryah:* poetic biblical Hebrew word meaning "town;" in modern usage sometimes means a housing development project or neighborhood in Israel, built for a specific group of people.
Kiryat Anavim (kibbutz) **1**:9
Kiryat Gat (town, Israel) **4**:36
Kiryat Hayyim (settlement, Israel) **1**:73
Kiryat Ponevezh (yeshivah campus, Bene Berak, Israel) **4**:10
**KISHINEV** (city in Bessarabia) **4:25; 1**:134
*Kishke* (a traditional delicacy prepared on Friday for the Sabbath meals) **2**:140
**KISHON, EPHRAIM** (writer, Israel) **4:26; 3**:37, 40
Kishont, Ferenc, *see* **KISHON, EPHRAIM**

Kislev (Hebrew month) **1**:180; **3**:18
**KISSINGER, HENRY** (U.S. statesman) **4**:26; **5**:9; **6**:108
**KITEL** (Yiddish, "gown;" white ceremonial garment) **4:27**
*Kiẓẓur Shulḥan Arukh* (abbreviated Code of Jewish Law) **4**:44
Klarsfeld, Beate: courageous German woman dedicated to righting wrongs against Jewish people by Nazis and others.
*Klaus* (small, informal ḥasidic prayer-house), *see Shtibl*
**KLAUSNER, JOSEPH GEDALIAH** (historian) **4**:27; **2**:105
Klein, Philip (U.S. rabbi) **5**:5
Klein, S. (U.S. department store) **2**:70
**KLEMPERER, OTTO** (conductor) **4**:27
*Kloyz* (small, informal hasidic prayer-house), *see Shtibl*
Knesset (Israel's parliament) **2**:66; **3**:111; **4**:22
Knights Hospitalers of St. John of Jerusalem (medieval Christian group) **5**:102
Knowledge, Tree of, *see* Tree of Knowledge
Kobe (city, Japan) **3**:136
Kohelet (biblical book; one of the five *Megillot*), *see* **ECCLESIASTES**
*Kohen, Kohanim, see* **PRIESTS AND LEVITES**
Kohen, Solomon (16th-century printer) **5**:80
Kol-Bo Shalom (department store, Israel) **2**:70
**KOLEL** (system of funding in Israel; post-graduate yeshivah for married men) **4:28**; **3**:13; **6**:102
KOLLEK, THEODORE (Teddy) (mayor of Jerusalem), **4:28**
*Kol Nidrei* (opening service of Day of Atonement) **2**:60
*Komeẓ* (biblical unit of measurement) **6**:86
Konigsberg, Allen Stewart, *see* **Allen, Woody**
**KOOK, ABRAHAM ISAAC** (Israel's first chief rabbi) **4:29**; **1**:93; **3**:51; **4**:82, 181; **5**:97, 185
Kook, Ẓevi Judah (rabbi, Israel) **4**:29
**KORAH** (biblical figure) **4:29**, 157
Koran (holy book of Islam) **1**:148; **3**:100; **4**:164
*Korban, see* **SACRIFICES**
**KORCZAK, JANUSZ** (Polish educator and ghetto hero ) **4:30**
Korn, Arthur (inventor) **3**:92
Korvette, E. J. (U.S. department store) **2**:70
Kosher food, *see* **DIETARY LAWS**
*Kosher le-Pesaḥ, see Kasher le-Pesaḥ*
*Kotel Ma'aravi, see* **WESTERN WALL**
**KOTLER, RABBI AARON** (scholar and spokesman for Orthodoxy) **4:30**
**KOTSK, MENAḤEM MENDEL OF** (ḥasidic leader) **4:31**
**KOUFAX, SANFORD** (Sandy; U.S. sportsman) **4:31**; **6**:5
Koussevitsky, David (cantor) **3**:29
Koussevitsky, Jacob (cantor) **3**:29
Koussevitsky, Moshe (cantor) **3**:29
Koussevitzky, Serge (conductor) **2**:38
Koussevitsky, Simcha (cantor) **3**:29
*Kova tembel:* floppy cloth hat that genuine *sabras* wear occasionally, and that genuine American tourists in Israel wear almost universally.
Kovner, Abba (Zionist leader and writer) **1**:127; **3**:39
**KOVNO** (city, U.S.S.R.) **4:31**
Kozinets, Isaac Pavlovish (Russian resistance fighter) **4**:141
Kramer, Louis (sportsman) **6**:5
Kranz, Isaac (son of Maggid of Dubno) **4**:32
**KRANZ, JACOB** (known as the Dubno *Maggid;* 18th-century preacher) **4:32**; **5**:76
Krause, Eliyahu (agronomist, Israel) **4**:137
Kreisky, Bruno (Austrian statesman) **1**:92
*Kreplakh* (traditional Ashkenazi delicacy prepared for festival meals) **2**:140
*Kristallnacht* (German: "night of [shattered] glass;" the night of November 10, 1938, marked by mass desecration and looting of synagogues and other Jewish buildings by the Nazis) **2**:69, 185; **3**:65
**KROCHMAL, NACHMAN** (19th-century philosopher) **4:32**; **5**:102
Kronenberg, Leopold (Polish industrialist) **6**:45
Krumey, Hermann (Nazi) **1**:164
Kubelsky, Benny, *see* **Benny, Jack**
*Kugel* (traditional Sabbath delicacy) **2**:140
Ku Klux Klan (U.S. organization) **6**:65
Kuppat Ḥolim (sick fund in Israel) **3**:56, 127; **4**:14
**KURDISTAN** (region in the Middle East) **4:32**; **1**:64; **2**:82
Kuwait (country in Middle East) **1**:61
*Kuzari* (book by Judah Halevi) **4**:2, 18
*Kvatter:* person honored with carrying the baby to the room where the circumcision is to take place. This word is the Yiddish form of the German word for "godfather."
*Kvitl* (written petition to a ḥasidic *rebbe*) **3**:26
Kwartin, Zavel (cantor) **3**:29
**K. ZETNIK** (Holocaust writer) **4:33**

# L

Laban (biblical figure) **3**:133; **5**:91
**LABOR 4:35**; **3**:56, 120; **4**:14, 20, 35, 105; **5**:29, 120, 178; **6**:23, 64, 119
**LACHISH** (region, Israel) **4:35**
Lachish Letters (6th century b.c.e.) **4**:51
Ladino (language; a Sephardi equivalent of Yiddish) **1**:145; **2**:36; **3**:171
**LAG BA-OMER** (festival) **4:36**; **2**:130, 153; **4**:123; **5**:24, 173
**LA GUARDIA, FIORELLO HENRY** (U.S. statesman) **4:37**; **5**:6
*Lamedvavnik* (one of 36 hidden saints in each generation) **6**:112
*Lamed-vav Ẓaddikim* (the 36 hidden saints) **3**:9
**LAMENTATIONS, BOOK OF** (biblical book) **4:37**; **1**:143; **5**:75; **6**:43
**LANDAU, EZEKIEL BEN JUDAH** (18th-century scholar) **4:38**; **1**:93
*Landsmannschaften* (social and mutual-help societies founded in the New World by migrants hailing from the same European hometown) **6**:64
Landynski, N. (talmudic scholar) **2**:156
Lang, Fritz (film director) **4**:161
Language, Hebrew, *see* **HEBREW LANGUAGE**
Lansdowne, Lord (British statesman) **1**:101
Lappidoth (biblical figure) **2**:64
*Lashon ha-ra* (Hebrew: "the evil tongue"), *see* **SLANDER**
Lasker, Albert D. (U.S. advertising pioneer) **1**:15
Lasker, Emanuel (chess-player) **2**:12
**LASKI, HAROLD** (British statesman)

**4:39**
Laski, Margharita (novelist) **4**:39
Laski, Neville Jonas (British judge) **4**:39
Laskin, Bora (Canada) **1**:183
**LASKOV, ḤAYYIM** (military leader, Israel) **4:39**; **3**:170
*Last of the Just, The* (novel by André Schwarz-Bart) **5**:145
Lateran Council (church conference) **5**:63
*Latkes* (Yiddish: "potato pancakes") **3**:20
Latrun (site of battles in Israel's War of Independence) **6**:82
Lavater, John (Swiss clergyman) **4**:119
Lavi, Simeon (16th-century rabbi) **4**:56
Lavon Affair (Israel political crisis) **1**:123
**LAW, JEWISH 4:39**
—Sources: **1**:18, 110, 135; **2**:42, 50, 154; **3**:47; **4**:51, 132; **5**:26, 28; **6**:24
—Scholars: **1**:30, 79; **2**:5; **3**:4, 54, 55, 134; **4**:2, 39, 117, 84; **5**:157, 167
—Subjects: **1**:10, 168; **2**:36, 53, 65, 79, 110, 115, 128, 134; **3**:46; **4**:6, 21, 22, 69, 148; **5**:85, 121, 132
—Sects: **4**:12, 18; **5**:134
**LAW OF RETURN** (grant of Israel citizenship to Jews) **4:45**; **2**:37; **3**:88
Lawrence of Arabia (T. E. Lawrence; British military leader) **2**:146; **3**:178
Lawyers **2**:43
**LAZARUS, EMMA** (U.S. poetess) **4:46**; **2**:15; **5**:3
Lazarus, Harry (sportsman) **6**:6
Lazarus, Johnny (sportsman) **6**:6
Lazarus, Mark (sportsman) **6**:5
League of Nations (forerunner of the United Nations) **4**:92
League of Nations Permanent Mandates Commission **6**:71
Leah (biblical figure; wife of Jacob) **3**:133; **5**:91
**LEBANON** (country in the Middle East) **4:46**; **1**:62; **6**:18, 58
**LEEDS** (city, England) **4:47**
Leeser, Isaac (U.S. rabbi) **5**:52; **6**:63
*Legends of the Jews* (book by Louis Ginzberg) **2**:67
**LEGHORN** (city, Italy) **4**:48
*Leḥem ha-Panim* (bread used in Temple service), *see* **SHEWBREAD**
Leḥi (Ereẓ Israel underground organization), *see* **LOḤAMEI ḤERUT ISRAEL**
Lehman (U.S. banking family) **5**:3
**LEHMAN, HERBERT HENRY** (U.S. statesman) **4:49**
*Lehrhaus* (Frankfort on the Main "House of Learning") **5**:107
**LEIVICK, HALPERN** (Yiddish writer) **4:49**
*Leket* (Hebrew: "gleaning;" the ears of grain which the reapers had dropped, and which by biblical law was not to be picked up, but left for the widow, the orphan, and the foreigner) **2**:8
*Lekhah Dodi* (Friday evening hymn of welcome to the Sabbath) **1**:32; **5**:84, 122
Lellever, Heinrich (sportsman) **4**:77
Lemberg (city, Ukraine), *see* **LVOV**
**LENIN, VLADIMIR ILYICH ULYANOV** (Soviet leader) **4:49**; **2**:31; **5**:117; **6**:54, 104
**LENINGRAD** (city, Russia) **4:50**
Leningrad Trial (anti-Semitic episode, 1970) **5**:117
Leo III (emperor) **2**:182
Leo X (pope) **1**:159; **5**:63
Leon, David de (American surgeon-general) **4**:138
Leonard, Benny (sportsman) **6**:6
Leontopolis (city, ancient Egypt) **5**:24
Leopold, Isaiah Edwin, *see* **Wynn, Ed**
Leopold, Nathan Freuenthal, *see* **LOEB-LEOPOLD CASE**
Leopold-Loeb Case, *see* **LOEB-LEOPOLD CASE**
**LEPROSY** (disease) **4:50**; **1**:52; **3**:73; **5**:50, 87, 178; **6**:72
Lerner, Alan Jay (composer) **6**:39
*Le-shanah tovah tikatevu* (New Year greeting) **5**:110
Lessing, G. E. (German playwright) **6**:38
Letter of Aristeas (ancient document), *see* **ARISTEAS, LETTER OF**
**LETTERS AND LETTER-WRITERS 4:51**; **1**:69, 71, 148; **3**:56; **4**:18; **6**:32
**Levenson, Samuel** (U.S. humorist) **6:40**; **5**:4
Levi (biblical figure; son of Jacob, and founder of one of the Twelve Tribes; the ancestor of *kohanim* and levites) **3**:45; **6**:53
Levi, Benjamin (18th-century engraver) **1**:161
*Levi, Levi'im, see* **PRIESTS AND LEVITES**
**LEVIATHAN** (huge sea animal) **4:52**
Levi ben Gershom (1288-1344; known also as Ralbag, from the initials of his Hebrew name, or as Gersonides, a Greek form meaning "son of Gershom;" astronomer, philosopher, biblical commentator, and mathematician, whose treatise on trigonometry calculates sine tables correct to the fifth decimal; inventor of the Jacob Staff, an important astronomical and navigational instrument) **1**:87; **3**:92; **4**:109
**LEVI ISAAC OF BERDICHEV** (hasidic *rebbe*) **4**:52; **1**:126; **3**:24, 70; **5**:56
**LEVIN, ARYEH** (20th-century saint) **4:52**, 51
**LEVIN, MEYER** (U.S. novelist) **4**:53, 64
**Levine, Joseph E.** (U.S. film producer) **4:162**
Levinsky, Battling (sportsman) **6**:6
Levinsohn, Benjamin (Israel advertising pioneer) **1**:16
Levirate marriage (Hebrew: *yibum;* the biblical law obliging a man to marry his childless brother's widow in order that the name of the deceased be perpetuated by the children of the second marriage. The ceremony granting exemption from this obligation is called *ḥaliẓah)* **5**:133
**LEVITA, ELIJAH** (Hebrew grammarian) **4:53**; **1**:162
Levitan, Isaac (19th-century artist) **1**:76
Levi-Tannai, Sarah (dancer) **3:82**
Levitch, Joseph, *see* **Lewis, Jerry**
Levites, *see* **PRIESTS AND LEVITES**
Leviticus (biblical book), *see* **Va-Yikra**
Levy, Jonas (U.S. naval officer) **4**:54
**LEVY, URIAH PHILLIPS** (U.S. naval officer) **4:54**, 138
**Lewis, Jerry** (U.S. comedian) **4:162**
Lewis, Ted (Kid; sportsman) **6**:6
Lewis Stores (U.K. department store) **2**:70
Lewit, Tanya (wife of Joseph Dov Soloveitchik) **5**:183
Liberal Judaism, *see* **REFORM JUDAISM**
Liberberg, Joseph (Russian leader) **1**:150
**LIBRARIES 4:54**; **1**:13, 34; 69, 92, 161; **3**:173; **5**:19
**LIBYA** (country, North Africa) **4:55**
Lieban, Robert von (inventor) **3**:93
Liebermann, Max (artist) **1**:76
Lieberman, Saul (modern Talmud commentator) **6**:27
Liebman, Charles S. (sociologist) **5**:180
**LIEBMANN, JOST** (17th-century Court Jew) **4:56**
**LIFE AND AFTERLIFE 4:57**; **1**:93, 157, 171; **2**:115, 177; **3**:31; **4**:84; **5**:50
**LIFSHITZ, NEḤAMAH** (folksinger) **4**:58
Lightning, *see* **THUNDER AND LIGHTNING**
Likud (coalition political party, Israel) **3**:112
Li'l Abner (cartoon character) **2**:2
**LINCOLN, ABRAHAM** (U.S. president) **4:59**
Lindbergh, Charles A. (aviation pioneer) **6**:65
Lindo, Moses (17th-century U.S. businessman) **2**:10
Lindsay, John (mayor, New York) **5**:6
Linen **4**:142; **6**:85
Lion **1**:51; **2**:55
**LIPCHITZ, JACQUES** (U.S. sculptor) **4:59**; **1**:76; **5**:146
**LIPKIN, ISRAEL BEN ZE'EV WOLF** (19th-century founder of Musar Movement) **4:59**; **2**:114; **4**:116
Lipkin, Yom Tov Lipman (scientist) **4**:60
Lipski, Abraham (engineer) **3**:93
Lipton, Seymour (U.S. sculptor) **5**:146
*Lira* (monetary unit, Israel) **5**:164
**LISBON** (city, Portugal) **4:60**
Lishansky, Yosef (1890–1917): member of Nili, the intelligence organization which aided the British in the First

World War. He was caught in an attempt to reach Egypt, sentenced to death by the Turkish authorities in Damascus, and hanged together with his Nili comrade Na'aman Belkind in 1917.
Literature (writers in languages other than than Hebrew) **1**:22, 109, 153; **2**:56, 73, 168; **3**:43, 69; **4**:46, 53; **5**:44, 155; **6**:96, 113. *See also* under names of various authors. For drama, *see* **THEATER**, and for children's literature, *see* **CHILDREN**.
**LITHUANIA** (country, N.E. Europe) **4:61; 1**:104, 167; **4**:31; **5**:56, 169; **6**:2, 74
Littauer, Lucius (sportsman) **6**:6
*Litvaks* (Yiddish: "Lithuanian Jews;" in the opinion of Lithuanian Jews, *Litvaks* are the intellectual elite of world Jewry) **4**:61
Litwack, Harry (sportsman) **6**:6
**LIVERPOOL** (city, England) **4:62**
Lloyd-George, David (British statesman) **1**:102; **6**:87
Lockspeiser, Sir Ben (aviation pioneer) **1**:16
Locusts **2**:74, 124
Lod (airport and town, Israel), *see* **LYDDA**
**LODZ** (city, Poland) **4:63**
**LOEB-LEOPOLD CASE** (U.S. murder case) **4:64,** 53
Loesser, Frank (composer) **6**:39
**Loew, Marcus** (U.S. movie executive) **4:162**
Loewe, Frederick (composer) **6**:39
Loewe, Isidor (German industrialist) **3**:93
**LOGIC 4:64**
**LOḤAMEI ḤERUT ISRAEL** (known by its Hebrew initials as Leḥi; the name of this pre-state underground force means "Fighters for Israel's Freedom") **4:65; 3**:6; **6**:81, 120
**LOKSHEN** (Yiddish: "noodles") **2**:140
**LONDON 4:66; 2**:165; **3**:76; **5**:76
London, Meyer (U.S. lawyer and Congressman) **5**:5
Londonderry (county, Northern Ireland) **3**:95
**LOPEZ , RODERIGO** 16th-century Marrano physician) **4:67; 2**:107
**LORKI, JOSHUA** (16th-century apostate) **4:68; 5**:33
**Lorre, Peter** (U.S. actor) **4:162**
**LOS ANGELES** (city, U.S.) **4:68**
Loshinsky, Mikhail (sportsman) **6:5**
**LOST PROPERTY 4:69**
Lot (biblical figure) **1**:7; **4**:145; **5**:134, 180
**LOTS** (lotteries) **4:69; 3**:177; **4**:106
Lotz, Wolfgang (Israel secret agent) **2**:112
Louis VII (king of France) **2**:141
Louis Bonaparte (19th-century French ruler) **3**:63
**LOVE 4:70; 1**:95; **4**:29; **5**:184
**LOVE AND FEAR OF GOD 2**:168; **3**:22; **4**:70; **5**:164, 174, 185
Love of Zion (desire of Diaspora Jews to return to Ereẓ Israel) **4**:1, 10, 13
Lower East Side (New York) **5**:3; **6**:64
Lubavich (ḥasidic movement, originating in a Russian village of that name), *see* **ḤABAD**
Lubavicher *Rebbe, see* Schneersohn, Menaḥem Mendel
**LUBLIN** (city, Poland) **4:72**
Lublin, Meir ben Gedaliah (16th-century rabbi) **4**:72
Luckman, Sydney (sportsman) **6**:6
**LUDOMIR, MAID OF** (19th-century ḥasidic *ẓaddik*) **4:72**
Lueger, Karl (Austrian anti-Semite) **6**:74
Luna, Beatrice de, *see* **NASI, GRACIA**
Lugal-zaggi-si (ancient Mesopotamian ruler) **4**:124
Luke (Apostle) **3**:164
Lukuan (rebel, 2nd century) **4**:56
**Lulav** (palm branch used on Sukkot) **3**:12; **6**:12
**LURIA, ISAAC** (the Ari; 16th-century kabbalist) **4:73; 1**:81; **2**:39; **3**:9; **4**:8; **5**:75
Luria, Solomon ben Jehiel (16th-century rabbi) **4**:72
Lusitanus, Amatus (16th-century doctor) **1**:46; **4**:114
**LUTHER, MARTIN** (German Christian reformer) **4:73; 1**:55; **2**:78, 163; **5**:94
**LUXEMBURG, ROSA** (German revolutionary) **4:74**
**LUXURY LAWS** (limitations on lavish lifestyles) **4:74**
Luzzatti, Luigi (Italian prime minister **3**:129
**LUZZATTO, MOSES ḤAYYIM** (18th-century scholar) **4:75; 3**:40
**LVOV** (Lemberg; city, Ukraine) **4:75**
**LYDDA** (Lod; town Israel) **4:76; 2**:98; **4**:14
Lydia (ancient kingdom) **5**:139
Lyon, Morton Sahl, *see* **Sahl, Mort**
Lyons, Jacques Judah (19th-century U.S. rabbi) **5:5**

# m

*Ma'abarah:* temporary transit camp of tents, later huts or tin shacks, devised in 1950 to cope with the sudden flood of refugee immigration to Israel.
Ma'aleh ha-Ḥamishah (settlement, Israel) **1:9**
*Ma'arakh* (labor coalition party, Israel) **3**:112
*Ma'ariv* (or *Arvit:* daily evening prayer service) **5**:74
*Ma'aser* (tax of agricultural produce), *see* **TITHES**
Macalister, R. A. S. (archaeologist) **5**:34
**MACAULAY, THOMAS BABINGTON** (British statesman) **4:77**
Maccabee, Judah, *see* **JUDAH MACCABEE**
Maccabees (leaders of the Judean uprising in the 2nd century b.c.e. against the rule of the Seleucids), *see* **HASMONEANS**
Maccabees, Books of (Apocryphal works telling the Ḥanukkah story) **3**:17, 18; **4**:104
Maccabiah Games (Jewish Olympics) **4**:77
Maccabi ha-Ẓair (youth movement, Israel) **3**:127
**MACCABI WORLD UNION** (sports organization) **4:77; 6**:4
MacDonald White Paper (British statement in 1938 which resulted in the closing of Ereẓ Israel to Jewish refugees throughout the Holocaust years) **3**:96; **6**:120
Machaut, Denis de (14th-century apostate) **5**:36
Machpelah, Cave of (tomb of the Patriarchs at Hebron) **1**:8, 171; **3**:41, 68
Macy's (U.S. department store) **2**:69
**MADABA MAP** (6th-century mosaic) **4:77, 93**
Madai (biblical figure) **2**:171
*Madrikh:* Hebrew word for guide, and used especially for group leaders in Youth Aliyah projects, youth movements, and the like. In Israel it is

also used to mean a tourist guide, and a guide-book.
Madrid (city, Spain) **6**:2
Madrid Peace Conference (1991) **3**:110
Mafdal (National Religious Party, Israel) **3**:112; **4**:143
*Maftir* (final passage of Torah read in synagogue service) **6**:47
**MAGEN DAVID** (6-pointed star) **4:78;** **1**:28, 98; **2**:136; **5**:67
**MAGEN DAVID ADOM** (Israel first aid society) **4:79**
*Maggid* (divine voice described in kabbalistic writings) **6**:23
*Maggid* (a synagogue preacher), *see* **PREACHING**
*Maggid* of Dubno, *see* **KRANZ, JACOB**
Maggid of Mezhirech (ḥasidic *ẓaddik;* disciple of the Ba'al Shem Tov), *see* Dov Baer of Mezhirech
*Maghariya* (1st-century b.c.e. religious sect) **5**:148
**MAGIC 4:80;** **1**:44, 47, 86, 100; **2**:175; **3**:12, 69, 74; **4**:70, 78, 112
Magic Carpet, *see* Operation Magic Carpet
Magnes, Judah (U.S. rabbi and Zionist leader) **5**:5
Magog (biblical name, *see* **GOG AND MAGOG**
*Mahallah* (Persian ghetto) **5**:47
**MAHARAL OF PRAGUE** (16th-century scholar) **4:81;** **3**:52; **5**:67
Maharam, Schiff, *see* **SCHIFF, MEIR BEN JACOB**
**MAHLER, GUSTAV** (composer and conductor) **4:82**
Mahlon (biblical figure) **5**:118
*Mah Nishtanah* (the opening words of the Four Questions asked by small children at the beginning of the *seder* service on Passover eve) **5**:41
Maḥoza (Babylonian town and Talmud academy) **5**:95; **6**:25
*Maḥzor* (festival prayer book) **5**:75
*Maḥzor Vitry* (an early prayer book) **5**:75, 94
Maierzuk, Hanna, *see* **MERON, HANNA**
**MAIMONIDES, MOSES** (Rambam; 12th-century scholar) **4:82**
–Views: **1**:72, 116; **2**:8, 170; **4**:42, 58, 64, 113; **5**:53, 82, 84, 101
–Misc: **1**:148; **3**:76; **6**:27, 42, 101
*Maimuna* (Moroccan holiday) **5**:43
Majdanek (concentration camp) **2**:33
**MAJORCA** (Mediterranean island) **4:85**
Majority rule, *see* **DEMOCRACY**
Maki (political party, Israel) **3**:113
Makleff, Mordecai (military leader, Israel) **3**:170
Malachi (biblical figure; prophet) **1**:142
**MALAKH, ḤAYYIM BEN SOLOMON** (17th-century Shabbatean scholar) **4:86**
Malamud, Bernard (U.S. author) **1**:114
Malaria (in Ereẓ Israel pioneering period) **3**:127; **5**:48
Malavsky, Samuel (cantor) **3**:29
Malben (Israel institutions for the handicapped) **3**:127
**MALBIM, MEIR LOEB** (19th-century scholar) **4:87**
*Malkhuyyot* (Rosh Ha-Shanah prayer) **5**:108
Malta (Mediterranean island) **2**:79
**MAMLUKS** (Muslim warrior group) **4:87;** **3**:106
*Mamme-loshen* (Yiddish: "mother tongue"): affectionate nickname for the Yiddish language.
Manasseh (biblical figure; son of Joseph, and founder of one of the Twelve Tribes) **3**:45; **6**:53
**MANASSEH** (king of Judah) **4:88;** **6**:14
**MANASSEH BEN ISRAEL** (17th-century scholar) **4:89;** **1**:43; **2**:48; **5**:80, 100
**MANCHESTER** (city, England) **4:90**
**MANDATE FOR PALESTINE** (British administration ending 1948) **4:90**
–General: **1**:62, 101; **2**:108; **3**:102, 178; **4**:21, 135; **5**:8, 38; **6**:61, 71, 81, 119
–Personalities: **1**:5, 33, 72, 113, 121; **4**:116; **5**:96, 137; **6**:87
–Resistance: **3**:5, 80, 96; **4**:24, 44, 65
Manduzio, Donato (convert from the Italian village of San Nicandro) **2**:38
Manin, Daniele (Venetian public figure) **6**:73
**MANNA** (miraculous food) **4:92;** **1**:166; **2**:139; **3**:13; **4**:157; **5**:120; **6**:21
**MANNERS 4:93**
Mannes, Leopold (pianist and photographer) **3**:93
Manslaughter, *see* **CITIES OF REFUGE**
Mantle (of Torah scroll) **6**:49
Mantua (city, Italy) **6**:38
Manuel (king, Portugal) **3**:1; **4**:97; **5**:64
Manuscripts, *see* **BOOKS**
*Ma'oz Ẓur* (Ḥanukkah humn) **3**:20
*Mapah* (halakhic work by Isserles) **4**:44
Mapai (political party, Israel) **1**:72, 123; **3**:112
Mapam (political party, Israel) **3**:112
**MAPS OF EREẒ ISRAEL 4:93,**77
Mar bar Rav Ashi (5th-century sage) **1**:80
**MARCUS, DAVID** (Mickey; U.S. soldier, a hero of War of Independence) **4:96,** 162
Marcus, Siegfried (German inventor) **3**:93
Marcus Aurelius (Roman emperor) **4**:2
Marcuse, Herbert (philosopher) **5**:1
Margolies, Moses (18th-century Talmud commentator) **6**:27
Margolis, Moses Z. (U.S. rabbi) **5**:5
Maria de Molina (14th-century Castillian queen) **1**:79
Maria Theresa (empress of Austria) **1**:111; **5**:67
Mariamne (Hasmonean princess, wife of Herod I) **1**:22; **3**:28, 48
Mark (Apostle) **3**:164
Mark Antony (Roman ruler) **2**:26; **3**:48
**MARKET DAYS AND FAIRS 4:96;** 72
Marks, Alexander (19th-century businessman) **3**:135
Marks, Simon (English businessman) **2**:70; **5**:170
Marks and Spencer Ltd. (British department stores) **2**:70; **5**:170
*Maror* (bitter herb used in Passover *seder*) **5**:41
**MARRANOS** (forced converts to Christianity in Spain and Portugal; known in Hebrew as *Anusim*) **4:97**
–Personalities: **1**:5, 23; **2**:29; **4**:89, 177
–Places: **1**: 32, 43; **2**:15, 107; **3**:63; **4**:86, 129; **5**:64; **6**:1
–General: **1**:55, 60, 83, 165; **2**:36; **3**:45; **4**:127; **6**:44
**MARRIAGE 4:98**
–Concepts: **2**:15, 124; **4**:70; **5**:153; **6**:94
–Laws: **2**:37, 80, 160, 164
–Wedding Laws & Customs: **1**:28, 98, 174, 184; **2**:7, 51, 126, 130, 138, 181; **3**:12; **4**:27, 74; **5**:152; **6**:18, 52, 72
–Miscellaneous: **2**:123; **3**:70; **4**:13, 97; **5**:183
Mar Samuel (Talmud sage) **1**:86
Marshall, Louis (U.S. communal leader) **4**:184; **6**:64
**MARTINI, RAYMOND** (13th-century missionary) **4:103**
Martyr, Justin (2nd-century Christian polemicist) **2**:77
**MARTYRDOM** (sacrificing one's life for the faith) **4:103;** **1**:41, 59, 96, 152; **2**:32, 36, 49, 163; **3**:15, 17, 22, 45; **4**:30, 57, 97, 106; **5**:166; **6**:36
Mark, Alexander (U.S. scholar) **4**:12
**MARX BROTHERS** (U.S. comedians) **4:105**
**MARX, KARL HEINRICH** (Communist theorist) **4:104;** **2**:31
Mary (mother of Jesus) **2**:97; **3**:165
Mary (16th-century queen of England) **2**:107
**MASADA** (historic site, Israel) **4**:106; **1**:65, 68; **3**:35, 49; **4**:69, 136; **6**:114
Masha Allah (medieval scholar) **1**:85; **4**:108
*Mashgiaḥ* (supervisor of the processing of kosher food), *see* **DIETARY LAWS**
*Mashgiaḥ* (yeshivah supervisor and teacher of ethics) **4**:167
*Maskil* (adherent of the Haskalah movement) **3**:26
**MASORAH** (textual apparatus of the Bible) **4:107;** **1**:118, 144; **4**:170; **6**:42
Masoretes (ancient scholars of Bible text), *see* **MASORAH**
Masquerade **5**:86
Massachusetts (city, U.S.) **1**:162
Mata Meḥasya (site of talmudic academy in Babylonia) **6**:25
*Matanot le'evyonim* (Hebrew: "alms for the poor;" Purim rite) **5**:86

**MATHEMATICS, AND PHYSICS 4:108; 1**:86; **2**:97; **5**:26
Matriarch: feminine of patriarch; title of honor given to the Mothers of the Jewish people: Sarah, Rebekah, Leah and Rachel.
Mattathias (Hasmonean priest, 2nd century b.c.e.; father of Judah Maccabee) **1**:59; **3**:27; **4**:3
Mattathias Antigonus (last Hasmonean ruler, 1st century c.e.) **3**:28, 48
Matthew (Apostle) **3**:164
*Matzah* (unleavened Passover bread), *see Mazzah*
Mauritius (Mediterranean island) **5**:44
Maximillian (emperor, Mexico) **4**:129
May Day (labor holiday) **4**:37
**Mayer, Louis B.** (U.S. movie executive) **4**:162
"May Laws" (anti-Semitic edicts, Russia, 1881) **5**:34
*Mayses* (Yiddish stories) **6**:105
Mazal Tov (Hebrew: literally "good luck;" all-purpose form of congratulation) **1**:86; **3**:184
**MAZAR, BENJAMIN** (Israel archaeologist) **4:111; 3**:160
*Mazzah* (unleavened Passover bread) **3**:13; **4**:23; **5**:39
*Mazzah shemurah: mazzah* which has been very carefully guarded from contact with moisture (which causes leavening), either from the moment the flour is ground, or even from the time of reaping.
Me'ah She'arim (quarter, Jerusalem) **3**:150; **5**:185
Measurement, *see* **WEIGHTS AND MEASURES**
Meat **2**:139, 140
Meat and milk (dietary laws), *see* Milk and meat
Mecca (city, Arabian Peninsula) **1**:4, 60; **3**:100; **4**:164
**MEDALS 4:111**
Medici (Italian family) **5**:63
**MEDICINE 4:112**
—Personalities: **1**:76; **3**:5; **4**:67, 83; **5**:132; **6**:78;
—General: **1**:45, 155; **3**:31, 93, 149, 71, 127; **4**:50, 57, 79; **5**:84, 170; **6**:50, 68
Medicine, psychosomatic **5**:85
Medina (city, Arabia) **1**:60; **4**:165
Meged, Aharon (writer, Israel) **3**:39
**MEGIDDO** (ancient site, Israel) **4:115; 2**:24; **3**:185
*Megillah* (biblical scroll; common name for the Book of Esther, read on Purim) **5**:86
*Megillot* (biblical books), *see* Scrolls, the Five
*Mehizah* (partition in synagogue) **6**:18, 34, 109
**MEIR** (scholar prominent in the Mishnah) **4:116; 1**:59; **2**:101; **6**:25
Meir Ba'al ha-Nes, *see* **MEIR**
**MEIR BEN BARUCH OF ROTHENBURG** (13th-century rabbi) **4:117; 1**:78; **3**:81
Meir ben Isaac of Orleans (11th-century poet) **5**:161
**MEIR, GOLDA** (Israel prime minister) **4:116; 1**:5; **4**:153; **6**:108
Meir of Rothenburg, *see* **MEIR BEN BARUCH OF ROTHENBURG**
*Mekhirat hamez* (Hebrew: "the sale of *hamez*;" Passover ritual) **5**:40
Mekorot Water Company (Israel) **4**:17
*Melamed:* Hebrew for teacher in a *heder*, or traditional elementary religious school; also a teacher giving private tuition. The modern Hebrew term for both is *moreh.*
*Melaveh Malkah* (festive meal ushering out the Sabbath Queen) **2**:131; **5**:124
**MELBOURNE** (city, Australia) **4:118; 1**:89
Melitzer, Samuel (sportsman) **6**:6
*Mellah* (North African ghetto) **4**:152
Meltzer, Isser Zalman (rabbi) **4**:30
*Memorbuch, see* **COMMUNITY RECORDS**
Memorial Service, *see Yizkor*
Menahem ben Judah (1st-century fighter against Roman rule) **6**:114
Menahem Mendel of Kotsk (hasidic *rebbe*) **3**:24
Menahem of Merseburg (14th-century rabbi) **1**:103
Menahem Zevi Hirsch (son of Zusya of Hanipoli, hasidic leader) **6**:122
**MENDELE MOKHER SEFORIM** (Hebrew and Yiddish writer) **4:118; 6**:106
Mendelssohn, Felix (composer) **4**:119
**MENDELSSOHN, MOSES** (Haskalah philosopher) **4:119; 1**:116; **3**:26
Mendes, Diego (16th-century banker) **4**:177
Mendes, Francisco (16th-century banker) **4**:177
Mendes, Isaac (18th-century rabbi and international merchant) **1**:161
Mendoza, Cardinal (inquisitor, Spain) **6**:50
**MENDOZA, DANIEL** (boxer) **4:120; 6**:6
Menelaus (Hellenistic high priest) **3**:44
Menelik (founder of the Ethiopian dynasty) **2**:114, 121
**MENORAH** (candelabrum) **4:120; 2**:102; **3**:19; **5**:19; **6**:18
Mental illness **5**:84
Menuhin, Hephzibah (pianist) **4**:122
Menuhin, Jeremy (pianist) **4**:122
Menuhin, Yalta (pianist) **4**:122
**MENUHIN, YEHUDI** (violinist) **4:122**
Me'or ha-Golah, *see* **GERSHOM BEN JUDAH**
*Merchant of Venice, The* (Shakespearean play) **5**:155
**MERCY 4:122; 1**:26; **2**:171; **3**:177
Meretz (pol. party, Israel). **3**:112
Merhavyah (kibbutz) **4**:117
*Merkaz ha-Rav* (yeshivah, Israel) **4**:29
Merneptah (pharaoh) **2**:93
**MERON** (town, Israel) **4:123; 5**:173
**MERON, HANNA** (actress, Israel) **4:123**
Meroth (ancient city), *see* **MERON**
Mesha (king of Moab) **4**:145
Meshach (biblical figure), *see* Hananiah, Mishael, and Azariah
*Meshal ha-Kadmoni* (book) **3**:38
*Meshummad:* Hebrew word meaning one who has voluntarily converted from Judaism. *See* **APOSTASY.**
**Meskin, Aharon** (actor, Israel) **6:40**
**MESOPOTAMIA** (region in ancient Near East, including the area of modern Iraq) **4:123; 1**:82; **2**:115, 167; **4**:88; **5**:15, 151
Messahalla (early medieval mathematician), *see* Masha Allah
Messel, Alfred (German architect) **1**:69
**MESSIAH 4:125**
—Opinions of Scholars: **4**:10, 29, 73, 89
—General: **1**:53, 107, 116; **2**:56, 100, 105, 171; **3**:88; **4**:1; **5**:45; **6**:117
**MESSIANIC MOVEMENTS** (belief in false messiahs) **4:126; 2**:143; **4**:75, 86, 125, 146; **5**:154; **6**:76
**METALS AND MINING 4:127; 1**:8, 28, 73; **2**:174; **4**:124
Metchnikoff, Eli (bacteriologist) **3**:5
Mexican Indians (religious group) **4**:5
**MEXICO 4:129**
Mezhirech (Ukrainian village), *see* Dov Baer of Mezhirech
*Mezumman* (quorum for the Grace after Meals), *see Zimmun*
**MEZUZAH** (tiny parchment scroll inscribed with the Shema, affixed to doorposts) **4:130; 1**:44; **2**:137; **4**:30
Michaelis, Sir Archie (Australian statesman) **1**:90
Micah (biblical figure; prophet) **1**:141; **2**:174
Michael (angel) **1**:47
Michal (biblical figure) **2**:56
**MICHELANGELO BUONARROTI** (Renaissance artist) **4:130**
**Michelson, Albert Abraham** (physicist) **4:110**
**MIDIAN** (ancient biblical people) **4:131**, 156
**MIDRASH** (mode of biblical interpretation, and the body of literature in which it is found) **4:132; 1**:18, 146; **3**:35; **5**:76, 172; **6**:24
Mifal ha-Payis (Israel lottery) **4**:70
Migdal Shalom (Tel Aviv skyscraper) **6**:31
**MIGRATION 4:133, 1**:70, 82, 127; **2**:66; **3**:170; **4**:16
Migresse, Sarah la (13th-century physician) **4**:113
*Mikdash* (portable sanctuary), *see* **TABERNACLE**
**MIKHOELS, SOLOMON** (Russian Yiddish actor) **4:135**
*Mikra'ot Gedolot:* a standard edition of

the Bible with rabbinic commentaries
**MIKVEH** (pool for ritual purification) **4:136**; **2**:37; **3**:73; **5**:88
**MIKVEH ISRAEL** (agricultural school, Israel) **4:137**
**MILITARY SERVICE 4:137**; **6**:79
—Ereẓ Israel: **1**:4; **2**:58, 179; **3**:5, 95, 114, 170; **4**:3, 65, 96; **5**:129; **6**:55, 92, 102, 113
—Diaspora: **2**:1; **4**:4, 54, 147, 178; **5**:149; **6**:19, 62, 65
Milk and meat (dietary laws) **2**:74
**Miller, Arthur** (U.S. playwright) **6:40**
Milton, John (17th-century English poet) **5**:136
*Minhag, see* **CUSTOMS**
*Minḥah* (daily afternoon prayer service) **5**:73
**MINORITY RIGHTS 4:139**; **1**:53
Minor Prophets (group of 12 biblical books) **1**: **141**
**MINSK** (city, U.S.S.R.) **4:140**; **1**:116
Minyan (quorum of ten for prayer) **5**:68; **6**:93
**MIRACLES 4:141**; **1**:1; **2**:101, 169; **3**:16, 19, 69, 183; **4**:58, 81, 92, 156, 180; **5**:58; **6**:70, 95
Mirage (fighter plane) **1**:16
Mirat, Eugénie (wife of Heine) **3**:43
Miriam (biblical figure; sister of Moses and Aaron) **2**:54; **4**:50, 154
Mirza Ali Muhammad (Bahai leader) **3**:68
Mishael (biblical figure), *see* Hananiah, Mishael and Azariah
*Mi she-berakh* (prayer) **5**:170
*Mishkan* (portable sanctuary), *see* **TABERNACLE**
*Mishkan ha-Edut* (portable sanctuary), *see* **TABERNACLE**
*Mishlei, see* **PROVERBS, BOOK OF**
Mishloaḥ Manot (Hebrew: "sending of food gifts;" Purim rite) **5**:86
*Mishmar* (rostered watch of priests and levites) **5**:79
Mishmar David (settlement, Israel) **4**:96
Mishnah, *see* **TALMUD**
*Mishnah Berurah* (halakhic work by Ḥafeẓ Ḥayyim) **3**:4; **4**:44
*Mishneh Torah* (Maimonides' legal code) **4**:42; 84
*Mitnaggedim* (opponents of Ḥasidism) **3**:24; **4**:61; **6**:75
*Mitzvah* (plural: *mitzvot*), *see* **COMMANDMENTS**
**MIXED SPECIES** (the prohibitions against mixing certain species of fibers and grains) **4:142**
Mizpah (ancient site, Israel) **2**:157
**MIZRACHI** (religious Zionist movement) **4:143**; **1**:106; **3**:51, 113; **5**:30
**MIZRAḤ** (east; direction of prayer) **4:144**; **5**:35
**MNEMONICS** (memory aids) **4:144**; **1**:3; **2**:158; **4**:108
**MOAB** (biblical land) **4:144**; **1**:100; **2**:95; **5**:118
Mocatta, David (19th-century architect) **1**:69
*Modeh Ani* (a morning prayer) **5**:70
Modell, Art (sportsman) **6**:6
**MODENA, LEONE** (16th-17th century scholar) **4:145**; **1**:148
Modern Orthodoxy, *see* **ORTHODOXY**
Modesty **2**:81; *see also* Humility
**MODIGLIANI, AMADEO** (painter) **4:145**; **1**:76
Mohammedanism (religion), *see* **ISLAM**
*Mohel* (ritual circumcisor) **2**:22
**MOLCHO, SOLOMON** (false messiah) **4:146**, 127; **6**:23
Moldavia, *see* **RUMANIA**
Molinari, Bernardo (conductor, Italy) **3**:28
Moloch (Canaanite cult of child sacrifice) **3**:184
Molokans (Russian Judaizing sect) **4**:4
**MONASH, SIR JOHN** (Australian soldier) **4:146**, 118, 138
Monastery of St. Catherine (Sinai Peninsula) **5**:175
**MONEYLENDING AND USURY 4:147**; **1**:1, 54, 104; **2**:116; **3**:128, 168, 180; **5**:38, 66, 127, 155; **6**:16
Monobaz of Adiabene (king of Parthia; 1st-century convert to Judaism) **3**:43
Monogamy (marriage with one wife) **4**:98
Monotheism (belief in one God) **2**:160; **4**:15
Montagu, Edwin (British statesman) **1**:102; **3**:87
Montalto, Philatheus (physician) **4:114**
Montefiore, C.G. (English scholar) **3**:172
**MONTEFIORE, SIR MOSES** (19th-century philanthropist) **4:149**; **3**:45, 149; **5**:56, 131
Montevideo (city, Uruguay) **6**:70
Months (Hebrew) **1**:181
**MONTREAL** (city, Canada) **4:150**; **1**:182
**MOON 4:150**; **1**:87, 179; **2**:46, 129, 173; **4**:13
Morais, Sabato (U.S. rabbi and scholar) **3**:173
Moravia, Alberto (Italian novelist) **3**:129
Mordecai (biblical figure; key character in the Purim story) **5**:86
*More Judaico* (medieval anti-Semitic oath), *see* **OATH MORE JUDAICO**
Morgenthau, Henry, Jr. (U.S. Secretary of the Treasury) **6**:66
Moriah, Mount (site, Israel) **1**:8, 25; **3**:143; **5**:135; **6**:33
Morning Benedictions **5**:70
**MOROCCO** (country, North Africa) **4:151**; **2**:81
Morris, Robert (U.S. patriot) **6**:85
Morrison-Grady Scheme (Palestine partition plan, 1946) **5**:38
Morse, Jacob C. (Jake; sportsman) **6**:5
**MORTARA CASE** (19th-century kidnapping) **4:153**; **2**:142
Mosaics (ancient) **1**:130, 132; **4**:77, 93
**MOSCOW** (city, Russia) **4:153**; **3**:53
**MOSES** (biblical figure) **4:154**
—Biblical Episodes: **1**:1, 37, 53, 175; **2**:38, 42, 172; **3**:16, 165, 182; **4**:29, 81, 120, 132; **5**:174; **6**:22, 72
—General: **1**:13, 135, 110; **2**:66; **3**:7; **4**:70; **5**:81; **6**:46
Moses, Raphael J. (politician, South Carolina) **6**:63
Moses ben Ḥanokh (medieval Talmud scholar; one of the heroes of the story of the Four Captives) **2**:141; **3**:56
Moses ben Joshua of Narbonne (13th-century scholar) **1**:6
Moses ben Maimon, *see* **MAIMONIDES**
Moses ben Naḥman, *see* **NAḤMANIDES**
Moses Cohen of Metz (physician) **4:114**
Moses de Leon (13th-century Spanish mystic) **4**:8
Moses Sephardi (10th-century mathematician) **4**:108
**MOSHAV** (agricultural settlement, Israel) **4:159**, 171
Moslem religion, *see* **ISLAM**
Mosley, Sir Oswald (English fascist leader) **2**:108
Mosque of Omar (Temple Mount, Jerusalem), *see* Dome of the Rock
**Mostel, Zero** (Samuel Joel; U.S. actor) **4:162**; **6**:39
Mother **2**:13, 123
**MOTION PICTURES 4:160**; **3**:176; **4**:15, 53, 105, 123; **6**:9, 39, 45
**MOUNTAIN JEWS** (Russian tribe) **4:164**; **1**:91; **4**:18
Mount Gerizim (biblical site), *see* Gerizim, Mount
Mount Hermon (biblical site), *see* Hermon, Mount
Mount Hor (biblical site), *see* Hor, Mount
Mount Moriah (biblical site), *see* Moriah, Mount
Mount Sinai (biblical site), *see* **SINAI, MOUNT**
Mount Sinai (New York hospital and medical school) **5**:3
Mourning, *see* **DEATH AND MOURNING**
Movies, *see* **MOTION PICTURES**
Moyne, Lord (British minister) **4**:65
**MUHAMMAD** (founder of Islam) **4:164**; **1**:60, 61; **3**:99
Muhammad II (sultan) **2**:35; **5**:31
Muhammad Ali (19th-century ruler of Egypt) **2**:94; **3**:76
Muhammad Riza (Shah, Iran) **5**:47
*Mukẓeh* (that which it is forbidden to touch on Sabbath) **5**:121
*Mumar:* Hebrew word for apostate.
**Muni, Paul** (U.S. actor) **4:163**
**MUNICH** (city, Germany) **4:165**
Munweis, Paula, *see* Ben-Gurion, Paula
Murder **1**:178; **2**:25, 115, 124; **4**:58, 103; **5**:149, 174
*Musaf* (additional prayer service for

Sabbath and festivals) 5:72
**MUSAR MOVEMENT** (a school of ethical teachings) **4:166;** 2:71, 114, 181; 3:4; 4:59; 5:54; 6:32
**MUSEUMS 4:167;** 3:173
**MUSIC 4:169**
—Musicians: 1:129; 2:164; 4:27, 58, 82, 122; 5:18, 45, 106, 114, 166; 6:8
—Miscellaneous: 3:25, 28, 77, 85; 4:159; 5:168; 6:38
Musical comedy 6:38
Muslim religion, *see* **ISLAM**
Mussolini, Benito (Italian dictator) 2:125; 3:129
Myer, Charles Solomon (Buddy; sportsman) 6:5
Myer, Sidney (Australian businessman, founder of Myer Emporium) 2:70
Myerson, Morris (husband of Golda Meir) 4:117
Mystère (fighter plane) 1:16
Mysticism, *see* **KABBALAH**

# n

Naaman (biblical figure; minister to king of Syria, c.850 b.c.e.) 4:4
**NABATEANS** (ancient semitic people) **4:171;** 2:168
Nablus (city, Israel), *see* **SHECHEM**
Naboth (biblical figure) 1:23
Nadir Shah (Persian ruler) 5:47
Nagasaki (Japanese city) 3:136
**NAGID** (title of medieval communal leader) **4:171;** 5:137
Naguib, Mohammed (Egyptian head of state) 4:178
Naḥal (unit of Israel Defense Forces) 3:114
**NAHALAL** (settlement, Israel) **4:171,** 159
**NAḤMANIDES**(Ramban; 13th-century scholar) **4:172;** 1:14; 2:19, 77; 4:7, 103
**NAḤMAN OF BRATSLAV** (ḥasidic *ẓaddik)* 4:173
Nahshon (biblical figure) 1:1
Nahum (biblical figure; prophet) 1:141
**NAHUM OF GIMZO** (or Gamzu; sage of Mishnah period) **4:174**
**NAMES 4:174;** 1:3, 8, 24, 95, 154; 3:101; 6:91
Names of God, *see* **GOD**
**NAMIER, SIR LEWIS** (English historian and Zionist) **4:175**
Naomi (biblical figure) 5:118
Naphtali (biblical figure; son of Jacob, and founder of one of the Twelve Tribes) 3:45; 6:53
**NAPLES** (city, Italy) **4:175;** 3:128
**NAPOLEON BONAPARTE** (French emperor) **4:176;** 1:11, 35; 2:34, 142, 148; 4:88
Narmer (pharaoh) 2:93
NASA (National Aeronautics and Space Administration, U.S.) 1:16
Nash, William M. (Billy :sportsman) 6:5
*Nashim ẓadkaniyyot* (Hebrew: "righteous women "): name of many charitable societies
**NASI** (title of exalted communal head) **4:176;** 3:54; 4:33; 5:138; 6:42
**NASI, GRACIA** (Portuguese stateswoman) **4:177**
Nasi, Joseph (16th-century philanthropist) 4:177; 6:14, 42
Nasi, Reyna (14th-century Marrano) 4:177
Nasir-i Khussau (11th-century Persian traveller) 3:12
Nasr-ed-Din (shah, Persia) 5:47
**NASSER, GAMAL ABDUL** (Egyptian president) **4:178;** 1:62; 2:95, 96; 4:17; 5:82, 159, 176
Nathan (biblical figure; prophet) 2:56; 5:35, 182; 6:33
Nathan of Gaza (Shabbatean publicist) 2:156; 5:154
**NATIONAL JEWISH WELFARE BOARD** (U.S. service organization) **4:178**
**NATIONAL PARKS OF ISRAEL 4:179;** 1:81
National Water Carrier (Israel irrigation system) 3:179; 4:24
**NATURE 4:180;** 2:90; 4:141; 5:10; 6:41
Navarro, Abraham (17th-cen. dipl.) 3:87
**NAVON, ITZHAK** (5th president of Israel) **4:181**
**NAZARETH** (city, Israel) **4:181;** 1:52
**NAZIRITE** (ascetic bound by vow) **4:182;** 1:29, 77; 5:135
**NAZISM 4:182**
—Leading Figures: 1:161; 2:95; 3:62
—General: 1:55, 163; 2:3, 5, 33, 162; 3:64; 5:14, 92; 6:65. *See also* the Index entry headed **HOLOCAUST, THE**
NBC (U.S. television network) 5:139
**NEBUCHADNEZZAR** (king, Babylon) **4:183;** 1:59, 97; 2:52, 55, 124; 4:5, 51, 125; 6:114
Neco II (pharaoh) 2:93
*Neder* (Hebrew: "vow"), *see* **OATHS AND VOWS**
**NEGRO-JEWISH RELATIONS** (U.S.) **4:184;** 1:38, 84, 153; 5:1; 6:67
Nehardea (town and site of talmudic academy in Babylonia) 1:97; 2:87; 5:95; 6:25
**NEHEMIAH** (biblical figure; governor of Judea , *circa* 400 b.c.e.) **4:185;** 1:78, 97, 144, 148; 2:120; 4:54; 6:12
Neḥunyah ben Hakanah (*tanna,* 1st century) 4:7
*Ne'ilah* (closing prayer service of Yom Kippur) 2:60; 5:74
Nemirov (town, Ukraine) 2:17
Neo-Orthodoxy (19th-century religious movement, Germany) 5:30
*Ner tamid* (lamp burning continuously in synagogue) 1:183; 6:18
*Nesi'at kappayim* (Hebrew: "the raising of the hands"), *see* Priestly Blessing
Netherlands, *see* Holland
Nethinim (ancient people) 2:166
*Netilat yadayim, see* **WASHING THE HANDS**
Netter, Charles (educator, Israel) 4:137
**NETUREI KARTA** (radical religious group) **4:185;** 5:185
*Nevi'im* (second section of the Bible; the Prophets) 1:137
New Amsterdam, *see* **NEW YORK, CITY OF**
New Christians (Jews forced to convert) 4:60; 5:64
**NEW LEFT** (movement of political radicals of the 1960s) **5:1;** 1:84
**Newman, Paul** (U.S. actor) 4:163
Newmark, Joseph (Los Angeles communal leader) 4:68
New Moon (Hebrew: *Rosh Ḥodesh;* first day of the month) 1:180; 4:150; 5:126
**NEWPORT** (city, Rhode Island) **5:1;** 6:50, 85
Newspapers, *see* **PRESS**
New Testament 1:135; 2:19; 4:112
New Year of Trees (minor festival), *see* **TU BI-SHEVAT**
**NEW YORK, CITY OF 5:2;** 4:37, 46; 6:38, 64, 78

New Zealand, *see* **AUSTRALIA AND NEW ZEALAND**
Nezaḥ Israel (Zionist movement) **1**:134
Nicanor (ancient Syrian officer) **1**:30
Nicanor Gates (Temple, Jerusalem) **4**:128
**NICHOLAS I** (czar) **5:8; 1**:111; **2**:1; **3**:26; **4**:23, 50; **5**:179
Nicolas II (czar) **3**:30; **5**:8, 116
**Nichols, Mike** (U.S. actor and director) **4:163**
Nicolas de Lyre (French Bible commentator) **5**:94
*Niddah* (a woman during her menstrual period) **5**:87
*Niddui* (form of excommunication), *see* **ḤEREM**
*Niggun* (Hebrew: "melody;" refers especially to a religious theme) **3**:25
Night and day, *see* **DAY AND NIGHT**
Night Prayer **5**:166
**NILE** (river, Egypt) **5:8**
**NILI** (espionage group during World War I) **5:8**
Nimrod (biblical figure) **1**:7
Nineveh (biblical city in Assyria) **1**:142; **3**:177; **5**:151
Ninth of Av (fast day), *see* **TISH'AH BE-AV**
*Nishmat Kol Ḥai* (opening words of an ancient prayer of gratitude) **5**:71
Nissim ben Jacob ibn Shahin (11th-century rabbi in North Africa) **4**:10
*Nissu'in* (part of marriage ceremony) **4**:98
**NIXON, RICHARD MILHAUS** (U.S. president) **5:9; 4**:27
Noachide Laws (seven laws given to all of humanity) **1**:154; **2**:160; **4**:104; **5**:10, 103
**NOAH** (biblical figure) **5:9; 2**:136; **5**:93, 168; **6**:41, 112
**NOAH, MORDECAI MANUEL** (founder of the U.S. Jewish colony of Ararat) **5:10; 1**:22
Nobel, Alfred (Swedish philanthropist) **5**:10
**NOBEL PRIZES 5:10; 1**:149; **4**:109, 112
Nod (biblical site) **1**:178
*Nodah bi-Yehudah* (name of a book and its author), *see* **LANDAU, EZEKIEL BEN JUDAH**
Nodel, Sol (artist) **3**:81
Non-Jews, *see* **GENTILE**
**NORDAU, MAX** (Zionist leader) **5:11**
Norman, Norman B. (U.S. advertiser) **1**:16
Norsa, Hanna (British actor) **6**:38
Northern Ireland **3**:95
**NORWAY 5:12**
**NOSTRADAMUS** (16th-century French astrologer) **5:12**
Nuclear research **2**:97; **4**:109; **5**:26
Numbers (biblical book), *see* **Be-Midbar**
**NUMBERS 5:13; 2**:46, 158; **3**:32; **4**:108; **5**:42
**NUMERUS CLAUSUS** (academic quota system involving racial discrimination) **5:14; 1**:53; **4**:114; **6**:67, 68
**NUREMBERG** (city, Germany) **5:14; 1**:162
Nuremberg Laws (Nazi restrictions) **3**:62; **4**:183; **5**:14
*Nusaḥ Ashkenaz* (prayer rite) **5**:75
*Nusaḥ Sepharad* (prayer rite) **5**:75
**NUZI** (ancient city, Mesopotamia) **5:15**

# O

**OATH MORE JUDAICO** (medieval anti-Semitic courtroom procedure) **5:17; 1**:53; **2**:141
**OATHS AND VOWS 5:17; 3**:139
Obadiah (Khazar king) **4**:18
Obadiah, Book of (biblical book) **1**:141
**OBADIAH, THE NORMAN PROSELYTE** (11th-12th century) **5:18; 4**:170
*Obadiah Scroll* (medieval autobiography) **5**:18
*Occident* (newspaper) **5**:52
Occult, *see* **MAGIC**
**ODESSA** (city, U.S.S.R.) **5:18; 3**:38
Odessa Committee (Zionist organization) **5**:19
Odets, Clifford (U.S. playwright) **6**:38
Og (biblical figure) **4**:158
Ohel (theater group) **3**:40
*Ohel Mo'ed* (portable sanctuary), *see* **TABERNACLE**
Oholiab (biblical figure) **1**:133; **2**:174; **6**:21
Ohrbach (U.S. department store) **2**:70
**OIL 5:19;**
—Mineral: **3**:118; **6**:109
—Vegetable: **1**:52, 184; **2**:40; **3**:19, 83, 185
*Olam ha-ba* (Hebrew:" the World to Come") **5**:102
*Olam Ḥadash* (Hebrew: "a new world;" children's magazine) **5**:78
*Olam Katan* (Hebrew: "a small world;" children's newspaper) **3**:38
Olam Katan (publishing house, Odessa) **3**:38
*Oleh:* a Hebrew word meaning "one who ascends," and thus used in connection with either of the meanings of the word *aliyah* — in the context of the Reading of the Torah, or of migration to Israel.
**OLIPHANT, LAURENCE** (Christian Zionist) **5:20**
Olives, Mount of (Jerusalem) **3**:68, 155
**OLYMPIC GAMES 5:20; 4**:166; **6**:2,4
**OMAR IBN AL- KHATTAB** (7th-century caliph) **5:23; 1**:97
*Omer* (biblical unit of measurement) **6**:86
**OMER** (the name of the barley offering of the volume of an *omer,* brought to the Temple on the second day of Passover; also the period of seven weeks of semi-mourning between that day and Shavu'ot, each day being counted during the Evening Service) **5:23; 1**:111; **4**:36; **5**:43, 159
**OMRI** (king of Israel) **5:24; 1**:23
*Oneg Shabbat:* literally, "the delight of the Sabbath;" often used to describe a social-cultural gathering on the Sabbath.
*Oneg Shabbat* (code name for Warsaw historical organization) **5**:104
Onias (priest, 2nd century b.c.e.) **5**:24, 148
**ONIAS, TEMPLE OF** (ancient sanctuary, Egypt) **5:24**
**ONKELOS AND AQUILA** (translators of the Bible) **5:24; 1**:64, 145; **5**:153
Operation Ezra and Nehemiah (Iraqi *aliyah* program) **4**:33
Operation Kadesh, *see* **SINAI CAMPAIGN**
Operation Magic Carpet (Yemenite airlift-*aliyah* to Israel) **6**:101
Oppenheim, David (17th-century rabbi) **1**:161
**OPPENHEIM, MORITZ DANIEL** (19th-century artist) **5:25; 1**:76
**OPPENHEIMER, JOSEPH BEN ISSACHAR SUESSKIND** (known as "Jew Suess;" German Court Jew) **5:25; 2**:41

**OPPENHEIMER, J. ROBERT** (U.S. nuclear physicist) **5:26**
**ORAL LAW** (authoritative interpretation of the Torah) **5:26**; 1:94, 146; 2:43; 3:47; 4:12, 40, 144; 5:50; 6:24, 46
Orban, Arpad (soccer player) 6:5
**ORDINATION** (certification for rabbinic leadership) **5:28**; 1:52; 5:90
Ordraonaux, John (American Revolution hero) 4:138
*Orlah* (the prohibited fruit of young trees) 2:135
Orpa (biblical figure) 5:118
**ORT** (vocational training organization) **5:29**
**ORTHODOXY** (traditional Judaism) **5:29**; 1:119; 2:34; 3:31, 55, 121; 4:30, 87, 143; 5:181; 6:109
Oslo (city, Norway) 5:12
**OTTOMAN EMPIRE** (area ruled by the Turks) **5:30**; 1:82; 2:28, 35, 94, 182; 3:72, 94, 106; 5:8; 6:14, 58
**OUZIEL, BEN-ZION MEIR ḤAI** (Sephardi chief rabbi of Israel) **5:32**
Oved (biblical figure) 5:118
Ownership (legal concept), *see* **ACQUISITION**
**OXFORD** (university town, England) **5:32**
Oysher, Moishe (cantor) 3:28

# P

**PABLO DE SANTA MARIA** (15th-century apostate, Christian Spain) **5:33**
Paganism, *see* **IDOLATRY**
Pahlevi dynasty (Persia) 5:47
Painting, *see* **ART**
Palavir (Haganah airborne commando unit), *see* **PALMAḤ**
**PALE OF SETTLEMENT** (restricted region of Jewish settlement in Russia) **5:33**; 1:54; 2:165; 4:97; 5:116, 169; 6:22
Palestine, *see* **ISRAEL**
Palestine Conciliation Committee (United Nations body) 6:61
Palestine Land Development Corporation 5:116
Palestine Liberation Organization (PLO) **5:34**; 1:63; 2:26; 3:110; 6:62
Palestinian refugees 6:61
**PALMAḤ** (Haganah commando group) **5:34**; 1:34, 36, 107; 2:176; 3:6; 4:16, 21; 5:90, 129
Palyam (Haganah naval commando force), *see* **PALMAḤ**
Papa (Babylonian Talmud scholar) 1:29, 79
**PAPER-CUTS** (folk art form) **5:35**
**PAPYRI** (ancient writing material) **5:35**; 6:97
**PARABLE** (moral tale or fable) **5:35**; 3:37. *See also* **KRANZ, JACOB** (*maggid* of Dubno)
Paradise, *see* Garden of Eden
*Parashah* (weekly portion of the Torah as read in synagogue) 6:47
Parents 2:14, 123
**PARIS 5:36**; 2:34
*Parnas* (community head) 6:18
*Parokhet* (curtain in front of ark in synagogue) 6:18
**PARTISANS** (anti-Nazi guerrilla fighters) **5:37**; 3:67; 4:139, 141; 5:149; 6:20, 93
**PARTITIONS OF PALESTINE** (international proposals) **5:38**; 6:61, 81, 120
**PARTNERSHIP** (commercial relationship) **5:38**
Pascin, Jules (artist) 1:76
**PASSOVER** (the festival of *Pesaḥ*) **5:39**
—Laws and Customs: 1:28, 111, 184; 2:6, 100; 3:7, 13; 4:27, 36; 5:23, 126, 152, 185
—Miscellaneous: 1:118, 155; 2:128, 134, 167; 4:157; 5:135, 159
**PASTERNAK, BORIS LEONIDOVICH** (Russian author) **5:44**
**PATRIA** (ship of "illegal" immigrants, sunk in November, 1940) **5:44**
Patriarchs: title of honor given to the Fathers of the Jewish people — Abraham, Isaac and Jacob.
**PAUKER, ANA** (Rumanian politician) **5:44**
Paul of Tarsus (Apostle) 1:83; 2:19
Paul IV (pope) 5:63
Paul VI (pope) 2:131; 3:62; 5:63
**PEACE** (Hebrew: *shalom*) **5:44**; 6:80
"Peace for Galilee" War (1982 against Lebanon) 3:110; 4:47
*Pe'ah* (the corner of the field which the Torah obliges each farmer to leave unharvested, for the benefit of the widow, the orphan and the stranger) 2:8
Pearl Harbor (critical turning-point in World War II) 6:65
Pecherski, Gedaliah (chairman of Leningrad) 4:50
Pedro the Cruel (14th-century king of Spain) 1:10
Peel Commission (British investigation into the Arab-Jewish problem after the riots of 1936) 5:38; 6:120
**PEERCE, JAN** (cantor and operatic tenor) **5:45**; 3:29
**Pekeris, Chaim Leib** (mathematician) **4:110**
Pelty, Barney (sportsman) 6:5
Peninah (biblical figure) 3:17
Penitence, *see* **SIN AND REPENTANCE REPENTANCE**
Pentateuch (Five Books of Moses), *see* **BIBLE** and **TORAH**
Pentecost, *see* **SHAVUOT**
People's Front for the Liberation of Palestine (Arab terrorist organization) 2:98
*Pe'ot* (sidelocks of men and boys) 1:111
Péreire, Jacob Rodrigues (1715-1780): the first French educator of congenital deaf-mutes, teaching communication by articulating sounds and lipreading rather than by the use of signs. For this pioneering work he was awarded a grant by King Louis XV. Was also a leader of the Sephardi community in Paris.
Perelman, Eliezer Yiẓhak, *see* **BEN-YEHUDA, ELIEZER**
Perelmann, Judah Leib (Russian rabbi) 4:140
**PERES, SHIMON** (Israel statesman and prime minister) **5:44**
**PERETZ, ISAAC LEIB** (Yiddish author) **5:45**; 6:106
Perfumes, *see* **COSMETICS**
**PERJURY** (false sworn testimony) **5:46**
Peron, Juan (Argentinian statesman) 1:70
**PERSIA (Iran) 5:46**; 1:97; 4:185; 5:157
**PERU** (country, South America) **5:47**
*Perushim, see* **PHARISEES**
*Pesaḥ, see* **PASSOVER**
Peschowsky, Michael Igor, *see* **Nichols, Mike**
Pest (city, Hungary), *see* **BUDAPEST**

*Pesukei de-Zimra* (cycle of Psalms in *Shaharit* prayer service) **5**:71, 84
**PETAH TIKVAH** (city, Israel) **5:48; 2**:111; **6**:31
**PETHAHIAH OF REGENSBURG** (12th-century traveller) **5:48; 6**:51
Petra (ancient city, Jordan) **4**:171
Petrie, W. M. F. (archaeologist) **5**:34
Petrograd, *see* **LENINGRAD**
Petrus Alfonsi (10th-century mathematician), *see* Moses Sephardi
Petticoat Lane, London **4**:97
**PFEFFERKORN, JOHANNES** (16th-century apostate) **5:49**
**PHARAOH** (ruler, ancient Egypt) **5:49; 1**:1, 7; **2**:80; **4**:123, 154; **5**:8, 57
**PHARISEES** (ancient scholarly community) **5:50; 1**:38; **3**:165, 175; **5**:131, 133; **6**:100
Phasael (brother of Herod the Great) **3**:48
**PHILADELPHIA** (city, Pennsylvania) **5:51**
Philanthropy, *see* **CHARITY**
Philately, *see* **STAMPS**
Philip the Fair (king of France) **1**:98
**PHILISTINES** (ancient Near East people) **5:52; 1**:77; **2**:156, 166; **5**:135
Philip IV (king of Spain) **3**:91
Phillips, Nathan (mayor, Toronto) **6**:50
Phillipson, Joseph (U.S. pioneer) **5**:131
**PHILO JUDAEUS** (1st-century philosopher) **5:53; 1**:30; **3**:44
**PHILOSOPHY, JEWISH 5:53**
—Concepts: **1**:115, 157; **2**:117, 147, 168; **4**:64, 142, 180; **5**:82, 101; **6**:42
—Ancient and Medieval Thinkers: **1**:27, 72, 79; **2**:48, 121; **3**:35, 75, 76; **4**:1, 81, 84; **5**:53; **6**:2
—The Modern Period: **1**:168; **3**:51; **4**:32, 119; **5**:107
Phinehas (biblical figure) **4**:132
**PHINEHAS BEN JAIR** (2nd-century sage and saint) **5:54**
**PHOENICIANS** (ancient Near Eastern people) **5:54; 4**:47; **5**:168; **6**:58
Phylacteries, *see* **TEFILLIN**
Physicians, *see* **MEDICINE**
Physics, *see* **MATHEMATICS AND PHYSICS**
**PICART, BERNARD** (18th-century French artist) **5:54**
Picon, Molly (U.S. actress) **6**:38
Picquart, Georges (French army officer involved in the Dreyfus Case) **2**:82
*Pidyon ha-Ben* (redemption of firstborn son) **2**:133
**PIETY 5:55; 3**:17, 22, 70; **6**:122
Pig **1**:52
Pijade, Mosa (Yugoslav resistance fighter) **6**:111
Pike, Lipman (Lip; sportsman) **6**:5
*Pikkuah nefesh* (Hebrew: "saving a life") **4**:57; **6**:51
**PILGRIMAGE** (to Jerusalem) **5:55; 3**:129; **5**:49, 135; **6**:11, 34
Pilgrim festivals (Passover, Shavuot and Sukkot) **2**:128. *See also* each individual entry.
*Pilpul* (method of talmudic study) **6**:102
Pinchik, Pierre (cantor) **3**:29
Pines, Shneur Zalman (rabbi) **4**:30
*Pinkas, see* **COMMUNITY RECORDS**
**PINSK** (city, U.S.S.R.) **5:56; 1**:116
Pinsker, Leon (Zionist thinker) **3**:53; **6**:115
**Pinter, Harold** (English playwright) **6:40**
Pires, Diogo (false messiah), *see* **MOLCHO, SOLOMON**
*Pirkei Avot* (Hebrew: "Chapters of the Fathers;" tractate of the Mishnah, dealing with ethics), *see* **AVOT**
**PISSARRO, CAMILLE** (French painter) **5:57; 1**:76
Pittsburgh Platform (program of Reform Judaism, 1885) **2**:96; **4**:28; **5**:99
Pius IX (pope) **4**:153
Pius XI (pope) **5**:63
Pius XII (pope) **3**:62; **5**:63
*Piyyut* (liturgical poem, or hymn) **1**:11, 41; **2**:98; **3**:35; **4**:1, 11, 170; **5**:73; **6**:100
**PLAGUES OF EGYPT** (biblical episode) **5:57; 1**:1; **4**:157; **5**:39
Plahm, Baer (pupil of Jacob Kranz, the preacher of Dubno) **4**:32
Plays, *see* **THEATER**
Playwrights, *see* **THEATER**
PLO (Arab terrorist group), *see* Palestine Liberation Organization
Po'alei Zion (Zionist group) **1**:121, 126
Podolia (region of Poland) **3**:23
Poetry **1**:11; **3**:35, 82. *See also* the entries on **HEBREW LITERATURE** and (for hymns) *Piyyut.*
Pogroms (anti-Semitic riots and massacres) **1**:54, 133; **2**:17; **4**:23, 25; **5**:149
Polak, J.E. (Austrian physician) **5**:47
**POLAND 5:58; 1**:116; **2**:44, 151, 185; **3**:10, 23; **4**:63, 76; **5**:169; **6**:83
Polemics, *see* **DISPUTATIONS**
Poliomyelitis **5**:132
Pollack, Jacob (15th-century talmudic scholar, Poland) **2**:44
Polygamy (multiple marriage) **4**:98; **5**:152
Polyglots (multilingual editions of the Bible) **1**:145
Pommer, Erich (film director) **4**:161
Pompey (Roman emperor) **3**:28; **4**:6
Ponevezh (town in Lithuania whose yeshivah, the largest in Lithuania, was transferred to Bene Berak, Israel) **4**:9
Ponevezher Rav (rabbi and educator in Lithuania and Erez Israel), *see* **KAHANEMAN, JOSEPH**
**PONTIUS PILATE** (Roman ruler of Erez Israel) **5:62; 3**:160
**POPES 5:62; 2**:19, 49; **3**:89, 128; **4**:153; **5**:105; **6**:53, 71
Popper, Joseph (philosopher and inventor) **3**:93
Population, *see* **DEMOGRAPHY**
**PORTRAITS OF JEWS 5:63 3**:128; **4**:111, 146
**PORTUGAL 5:64; 2**:118; **3**:90; **4**:60, 97; **5**:151
Portuguesic (language) **3**:171
Postmortem examination, *see* **AUTOPSIES AND DISSECTION**
Potash (mineral) **5**:180
Potok, Chaim (U.S. author) **3:2**
**POTTERY 5:65; 1**:65
**POVERTY 5:65; 1**:27, 112; **2**:8; **5**:45, 169
Praag, Jaap van (sportsman) **6**:5
**PRAGUE** (city, Czechoslovakia) **5:66; 1**:158; **4**:81
Pratensis, Felix (16th-century apostate) **1**:158
**PRAYER 5:67**
—Specific Prayers: **1**:26, 38, 108, 119, 147, 174; **5**:84, 93, 164, 170; **6**:15, 47
—Sabbath, Festivals and Fasts: **2**:59, 126, 128; **3**:20, 85; **4**:22; **5**:86, 107, 122, 160
—Authors: **1**:32, 42; **2**:151; **4**:1, 11, 73
—Sanctuaries and Synagogues: **1**:37; **3**:28; **4**:170; **5**:129; **6**:17, 21, 34
—Accessories of Prayer: **3**:30; **4**:27; **5**:169; **6**:23, 30
—Miscellaneous: **1**:12, 47, 64; **2**:51; **3**:23, 177; **4**:72; **5**:152
**PRAYER BOOKS 5:74; 1**:42, 81; **4**:12; **5**:79; **6**:93
**PREACHING 5:75; 4**:32, 62
**PRECIOUS STONES 5:76; 1**:11, 114; **3**:63; **4**:56, 129; **5**:185; **6**:70
**Preminger, Otto Ludwig** (U.S. film director and producer) **4:163**
Presidents of Israel, *see* **entries on WEIZMANN, CHAIM; BEN-ZVI, IZHAK; SHAZAR, SHNEUR ZALMAN; KATZIR, EPHRAIM**
**PRESS 5:77; 1**:16, 100; **3**:26, 172; **4**:53, 62; **5**:161, 179, 181; **6**:59, 106
Pressburg, *see* **BRATISLAVA**
Priestly Blessing **1**:39; **3**:16
**PRIESTS AND LEVITES 5:78**
—History: **1**:1, 136; **2**:158, 167, 172; **6**:13, 53, 69, 113
—Duties and Privileges: **1**:36, 52; **2**:25, 133, 134; **3**:12, 16; **4**:50, 112, 169; **5**:129; **6**:21, 34, 43, 47
—Other Laws: **1**:110, 171; **2**:37, 59; **4**:103; **5**:87; **6**:84
—Miscellaneous: **1**:60; **2**:79, 124; **4**:1; **5**:135
Prime ministers of Israel, *see* **BEN-GURION, DAVID; SHARETT, MOSHE; MEIR, GOLDA; RABIN, YIZHAK**
**PRINTING, HEBREW 5:79**
—Printers: **1**:100, 158; **3**:132; **4**:89; **5**:183
—Centers: **1**:43, 110; **2**:79; **3**:14; **4**:175
—Books: **1**:145; **3**:8, 81; **4**:54; **5**:94; **6**:27
Prisoners of Zion (Russian Jews arrested for "Zionist" activities) **4**:23, 50

*Privilegium* (charter of rights) **5:150**
**PROFITEERING 5:80**
Progressive Judaism, *see* **REFORM JUDAISM**
Prokezz, Anton (19th-century Austrian inventor) **3:**92
**PROPHECY 5:81**
—The Concept: **1:**110, 135; **2:**105; **3:**78; **5:**101; **6:**34, 69, 75
—Representative Prophets: **1:**42; **2:**100, 119; **3:**2, 70, 97, 139, 177; **4:**154; **6:**114
Prophets (second section of the Bible; the *Nevi'im*) **1:**137
Prophets, Minor, *see* Minor Prophets
*Prosbul* (Hillel's ordinance on collection of debts) **5:**128
Proselytes, *see* **CONVERSION TO JUDAISM**
Protestantism, *see* **CHRISTIANITY**
Protestant Reformation **1:**54; **2:**20; **4:**73; **5:**49, 63
**PROTOCOLS OF THE LEARNED ELDERS OF ZION** (anti-Semitic book) **5:81; 1:**55; **4:**183
Provençal, David (Italian educator) **6:**68
**PROVERBS, BOOK OF** (biblical book) **5:82; 1:**124, 143; **5:**183; **6:**92
**PROVIDENCE, DIVINE 5:82; 3:**133; **5:**102
Prussia **6:**83
**PSALMS** (biblical book) **5:83; 1:**5, 152, 143, 174; **2:**57; **3:**7, 85; **4:**169; **5:**122
Pseudepigrapha (ancient non-biblical books) **1:**59
Pseudo-messiahs, *see* **MESSIANIC MOVEMENTS**
Psychiatry, *see* **PSYCHOLOGY**
**PSYCHOLOGY 5:84; 1:**132; **2:**148
**PTOLEMY** (rulers of Egypt, 4th-1st centuries b.c.e.) **5:85; 2:**21; **5:**148
Ptolemy II Philadelphus (3rd century b.c.e.) **1:**71
Ptolemy V Epiphanes (2nd century b.c.e.) **2:**26
Ptolemy VI (2nd century b.c.e.) **2:**26
Ptolemy VII (Euergetes II; 2nd century b.c.e.) **2:**26; **4:**55
Ptolemy Lagus (4th century b.c.e.) **4:**55
Public health, *see* **MEDICINE**
Puerto Rico (West Indies) **6:**90
Pumbedita (Babylonian town and Talmud academy) **5:**95; **1:**3, 97, 99; **5:**119, 167; **6:**102
**PUNISHMENT 5:85; 1:**103, 154; **2:**40, 43; **3:**46,78, 82, 87, 98; **4:**22, 50; **6:**40, 72
*Pur* (Persian: "lots"): the word from which the festival of Purim takes its name.
**PURIM** (minor festival) **5:86; 1:**28; **2:**7, 126, 130, 140, 153, 181; **4:**70, 112; **5:**126; **6:**37
Puritanism (movement in Christianity) **4:**4
**PURITY AND IMPURITY, RITUAL 5:87; 1:**151, 171; **3:**16, 73; **4:**27, 50, 136; **5:**50, 98; **6:**84
**PYTHAGORAS** (ancient Greek philosopher) **5:88; 3:**44

# Q · R

Quebec (province of Canada) **1:**183
**QUEEN OF SHEBA** (biblical figure) **5:89,** 183
**QUERIDO, JACOB** (17th-century Shabbatean) **5:89**
**QUIETUS, LUSIUS** (Roman general) **5:89**
Quintilius Varus (Roman leader) **2:**49
Quota (for academic enrollments as a form of racial discrimination), *see* **NUMERUS CLAUSES**
Qumran (site of the caves in the Judean Desert where the Dead Sea Scrolls were discovered, and the name of the sectarian community who lived there in ancient times) **2:**60; **4:**1; **6:**113
Rabad (12th-century talmudic authority), *see* Abraham ben David of Posquières
Rabban, Joseph (Indian Jew) **3:**86
Rabban, Zeev (artist) **3:**81
Rabbana (Talmud sage), *see* **ASHI**
Rabbanites (the traditionalist opponents of Karaism), *see* **KARAITES**
Rabbenu Gershom, *see* **GERSHOM BEN JUDAH**
Rabbenu Tam (tosafist; commentator on Talmud), *see* **TAM, JACOB BEN MEIR**
**RABBI 5:90; 1:**81; **2:**42, 179; **3:**40, 41, 49, 51, 173; **5:**28; **6:**93
Rabbi (2nd-century editor of the Mishnah), *see* **JUDAH HA-NASI**
Rabbi Isaac Elchanan Theological Seminary, *see* **YESHIVA UNIVERSITY**
**Rabi, Isidor Isaac** (physicist) **4:110**
**RABIN, YIẒḤAK** (military leader and prime minister, Israel) **5:90,** 176
Rabinovitz, Shalom, *see* **SHALOM ALEICHEM**
Rabinowitz, Ḥayyim (Lithuanian scholar) **6:**32
Rabinowitz, Samuel Jacob (rabbi, Liverpool) **4:**63
**RACHEL** (biblical figure; matriarch **5:91; 1:**131, 151, 173; **3:**133; **5:**16
Rachel (wife of Rabbi Akiva; 2nd century c.e.) **1:**27
**RACIAL DISCRIMINATION 5:91; 1:**12, 53, 54, 84, 97; **3:**62; **4:**139, 182; **5:**14, 17, 33, 149, 186; **6:**7, 15, 16, 19, 101. *See also* **ANTI-SEMITISM** and under individual countries and cities.
*Radaniya* (medieval traders) **6:**51
Radio **1:**15; **3:**120; **4:**161; **5:**139
**RADOSHKOVICHI** (town, Russia) **5:92**
Radun (or Radin; town, Poland) **3:**4
Rafi (Israel political party) **1:**123; **3:**112
Rahab (biblical figure) **3:**141, 183
**RAḤEL** (Hebrew poetess) **5:92**
**RAIN AND DEW 5:92; 1:**21, 41, 181; **2:**136; **3:**102; **5:**42, 102; **6:**14, 41
**RAINBOW 5:93; 4:**37; **5:**9
Rakkath (biblical city) **6:**42
Ralbag (or Gersonides; 14th-century scholar), *see* Levi ben Gershom
Ramadan (Muslim month) **3:**100
*Ramah:* Hebrew for "a high place," or "plateau," and accordingly used (in the form *Ramat* or *Ramot*) as the first part of many place-names in Israel.
Ramat Gan (city, Israel) **6:**31
*Ramat ha-Golan,* see Golan Heights
Ramathaim-Zophim (town, Ereẓ Israel) **5:**93
Ramat Raziel (moshav, Israel) **5:**96
Ramat Yoḥanan (settlement, Israel) **5:**179
Rambam, *see* **MAIMONIDES, MOSES**
Ramban, *see* **NAḤMANIDES**
Ramḥal (18th-century scholar), *see* **LUZZATTO, MOSES ḤAYYIM**
**RAMLEH** (city, Israel) **5:93**
Ramot Eshkol: Post-Six-Day War

neighborhood in northern Jerusalem, between the tombs of the Sanhedrin and Ammunition Hill, and named after prime minister Levi Eshkol.
Ramses II (Egyptian pharaoh) **2**:93; **4**:123
Raphaelson, Samson (U.S. playwright) **6**:38
Rapoport, S. J. C. (Galician scholar) **3**:27
Rashba (13th-century scholar), *see* **ADRET, SOLOMON BEN ABRAHAM**
*Rashei tevot, see* **ABBREVIATIONS**
**RASHI** (11th-century Bible and Talmud commentator) **5:94; 2**:142; 159; **3**:32; **6**:27, 30
Ra's Nusrani (cape, southern Sinai Peninsula) **5**:159, 176
Rath, Ernst von (German official) **2**:186
Rathenau, Emil (German industrialist and engineer) **3**:93
**RATHENAU, WALTER** (German industrialist and statesman) **5:95**
Rattner, Sarah (Sonia; *rebbetzin* of Moses Diskin) **2**:76
**RAV** (3rd-century c.e. Talmud sage) **5:95; 1**:97; **6**:25
Rav (rabbinic title) **5**:28, 90
**RAVA** (3rd-century c.e. Talmud sage) **5:95; 1**:3; **5**:158
Ravina ben Huna (5th-century sage) **1**:79; **6**:25
Ravyah (medieval German rabbinic scholar), *see* **ELIEZER BEN JOEL HALEVI BONN**
Rawnitzki, Yehoshua Ḥana (editor) **1**:134
**RAZIEL, DAVID** (underground military leader, Ereẓ Israel) **5:95**
Razinsky, Boris (soccer player) **6**:5
RCA (U.S. electronics corporation) **5**:139
**REAGAN, RONALD WILSON** (U.S. president) **5:96**
Reason **4**:84
Reb Aryeh (20th-century Jerusalem saint), *see* **LEVIN, ARYEH**
*Rebbe:* Yiddish form of the Hebrew title Rabbi (which literally means "my teacher or master"). It means either a teacher in a traditional religious school, or the leader of a ḥasidic group, often coupled with the name of the town from which the sect originated.
*Rebbetzin* (Yiddish) for the wife of a traditional rabbi.
Rebekah (biblical figure; matriarch) **3**:70, 97, 132
**REBUKE 5:96; 3**:78, 98
Recife (city, Brazil) **1**:165
**RECONSTRUCTIONISM** (religious movement) **5:96; 4**:12; **5**:29, 69, 75
Red Cross, International **4**:80
Red Cross, Jewish, *see* **MAGEN DAVID ADOM**
"Red Danny," *see* Cohn-Bendit, Daniel
**REDEMPTION 5:97; 1**:33, 42; **3**:7, 85, 88; **4**:11, 29, 125, 126, 151; **5**:39, 154
Redemption of Firstborn, *see Pidyon ha-Ben*
**RED HEIFER** (animal used for ritual purification) **5:98,** 88, 126, 172
Red Sea (south of Sinai Peninsula) **4**:141, 157; **5**:159
Reformation, Protestant, *see* Protestant Reformation
**REFORM JUDAISM** (religious movement) **5:98**
—Concepts: **1**:175; **3**:30; **4**:22, 170; **5**:68, 75, 90; **6**:18, 117
—History: **1**:37; **2**:10, 34, 157, 168; **3**:26, 40, 55; **4**:28, 87; **5**:29, 181; **6**:63, 93
Refugees **4**:16. *See also* **DISPLACED PERSONS.**
*Regalim* (Hebrew for "pilgrim festivals"), *see* **FESTIVALS** and **PILGRIMAGE**
Rehaviah (quarter of Jerusalem) **3**:150
Rehoboam (king of Judah) **1**:138; **3**:141
**REḤOVOT** (city, Israel) **5:99; 1**:121; **6**:31, 88
Reḥovot Conferences (scientific forum, Israel) **6**:88
Reich, the Third (Nazi regime) **5**:14
**REIK, ḤAVIVAH** (Haganah secret agent) **5:99**
Reilly, Sidney (spy), *see* Rosenblum, Sigmund Georgievich
Reines, Isaac (leader of religious Zionism) **4**:143
**REINHARDT, MAX** (German theatrical innovator) **5:99; 6**:38
Rejoicing of the Law (festival), *see* Simḥat Torah
Remak, Robert (biologist) **1:149**
**REMBRANDT VAN RIJN** (17th-century Dutch artist) **5:100; 1**:26; **4**:89; **5**:64
Remembrance Day (Israel) **3**:85
**REPARATIONS, GERMAN** (damages paid to Holocaust victims) **5:100; 2**:174
Repentance, *see* **SIN AND REPENTANCE**
Republican Party (U.S.) **6**:65
*Representative, The* (play by Rolf Hochhuth) **3**:62
Reshevsky, Samuel (chess-player) **2**:12
*Resh galuta* (communal head of the exiles in Babylonia), *see* **EXILARCH**
Resh Lakish, *see* **SIMEON BEN LAKISH**
Residence (legal concept), *see* **DOMICILE**
Respiratory organs **1**:46
Responsa literature (post-talmudic law) **4**:42
Resurrection **2**:171; **4**:58
Reuben (biblical figure; firstborn son of Jacob, and founder of one of the Twelve Tribes) **3**:45, 180; **6**:53
Reuchlin, Johannes (Christian Hebraist) **5**:49
Reuel (biblical figure; father-in-law of Moses) *see* **JETHRO**
**REUTER, PAUL JULIUS, BARON VON** (journalist, founder of news agency) **5:101**
Reuters (news agency) **5**:101
Reuveni, David (false messiah) **4**:127, 146
**REVELATION** (God communicating with man) **5:101; 1**:1, 110, 175; **2**:169; **4**:75, 157; **5**:53, 81, 174; **6**:22, 35, 75
Revisionism (a trend within the Zionist movement) **3**:95
*Revue des Etudes Juives* (journal) **5**:77
**REWARD AND PUNISHMENT** (doctrine of divine justice) **5:102; 1**:12, 103; **2**:147, 177; **3**:2, 175; **4**:6, 58; **5**:9, 83, 92, 164, 178; **6**:10, 112
Reynolds, Joshua (18th-century English painter) **5**:64
Rhenish Jewish Diet (assembly of German community representatives) **6**:98
**RHODES** (Greek island and city) **5:102**
**RIBICOFF, ABRAHAM** (U.S. senator) **5:103**
*Ribono shel Olam* (Hebrew: "Master of the Universe"): form of addressing the Almighty.
Rice, Elmer (U.S. playwright) **6**:38
Richard the Lion-hearted (Richard I, king of England) **2**:107; **4**:83
Rif (halakhic authority), *see* **ALFASI, ISAAC BEN JACOB**
**RIGHTEOUS GENTILES 5:103; 2**:160; **5**:10; **6**:79, 99
Righteousness, *see* **ẒADDIK**
*Rimmonim* (finials which decorate top of Torah scroll) **6**:49
**RINDFLEISCH** (13th-century German anti-Semitic knight) **5:104; 1**:53, 78
Ring, wedding **4**:98
**RINGELBLUM, EMMANUEL** (historian, martyr of the Warsaw Ghetto) **5:104; 6**:84
Rio de Janeiro (city, Brazil) **1**:165
*Rishonim* (Hebrew: "the first ones;" authorities in rabbinic law from approximately 1000 c.e. to the 16th century; compare *Aḥaronim*) **3**:59
**RISHON LE-ZION** (town, Israel) **5:104; 4**:137
*Rishon le-Zion* (title of Sephardi chief rabbi of Israel) **5:104**
Ritual objects, *see* **CEREMONIAL OBJECTS**
Ritz Brothers (U.S. performers) **6**:39
Roach, Hal (film producer) **4**:160
Robbery, *see* **THEFT AND ROBBERY**
Robert of Anjou (14th-century ruler) **4**:175
Robinson, Edward (U.S. archaeologist) **3**:160
**Robinson, Edward G.** (U.S. actor) **4:163**
Rockefeller Museum (Jerusalem) **4**:168
Rogers, Richard (composer) **6**:39
Roitman, David (cantor) **3**:29

Roke'aḥ (dynasty of Belzer rabbis) **1**:117
Roman Catholicism, *see under* **CHRISTIANITY**
Roman Empire
—Emperors: **2**:25; **3**:4; **4**:2, 6; **5**:104; **6**:44
—General: **1**:106, 176; **2**:23, 28, 49, 167; **3**:28, 44, 48, 128, 182; **4**:2; **5**:89; **6**:113
Romaniots (sect) **1**:171, 176; **2**:39
**ROME** (city, Italy) **5:105; 2**:165; **3**:128, 184; **6**:44, 71
Romm, Mikhail (sportsman) **6**:5
Roosevelt, Eleanor (wife of U.S. president) **5**:106
**ROOSEVELT, FRANKLIN DELANO** (U.S. president) **5:105; 6**:65
**Rose, Billy** (U.S. showman) **6:40**, 38
Roseman, James T. (Chief; sportsman) **6**:5
Rosen, Al (sportsman) **6**:5
Rosen, Moses (Rumanian chief rabbi) **5**:115
Rosenbaum, Borge, *see* **BORGE, VICTOR**
Rosenberg, Aaron (sportsman) **6**:6
**ROSENBERG CASE** (U.S. espionage trial) **5:106; 2**:112
Rosenberg, William Samuel, *see* **Rose, Billy**
**ROSENBLATT, JOSEF** (known as Yossele; cantor and liturgical composer) **5:106; 3**:29
Rosenblum, Sigmund Georgievich (British secret agent) **2**:112
Rosenthal, Erich (sociologist) **5**:180
Rosenwald, Julius (U.S. philanthropist) **4**:184; **6**:63
**ROSENZWEIG, FRANZ** (German philosopher) **5:107; 1**:168; **2**:78, 117; **5**:97
Rosh (medieval halakhic authority), *see* **ASHER BEN JEHIEL**
**ROSH HA-SHANAH** (New Year) **5:107; 1**:26, 39, 41, 166, 179; **2**:128, 140; **3**:13; **4**:27; **5**:168
*Rosh Ḥodesh* (first day of the month), *see* New Moon
*Rosh kneset* (community official) **6**:18
**ROSH PINNAH** (settlement, Israel) **5:110**
Ross, Barney (sportsman) **6**:6
Rossi, Azariah de (Renaissance Hebrew scholar), *see* Azariah de Rossi
Rossi, Giovanni Bernardo de (Catholic priest) **1**:161
**ROSTOW, EUGENE VICTOR** (U.S. lawyer and government official) **5:111**
**ROTH, CECIL** (20th century historian) **5:111**
Rothenberg Alter, Isaac, *see* Alter, Isaac Meir Rothenberg
Rothenburg, Moses (17th-century scholar) **1**:81
Rothenstein, Sir William (1872-1945): British impressionist painter, and principal of the Royal College of Art, London. His work includes sensitive studies of synagogue interiors.
Rottenberg, Henri (French soldier) **4**:139
**ROVINA, HANNA** (actress, Israel) **5: 113**
*Ruaḥ ha-Kodesh* (holy spirit) **5**:81
Rubashov, Shneur Zalman, *see* **SHAZAR, SHNEUR ZALMAN**
Rubin, Jerry (U.S. political radical) **5**:1
**RUBIN, REUVEN** (painter, Israel) **5:114**
Rubinstein, Akiva (chess player) **2**:12
**RUBINSTEIN, ARTUR** (pianist) **5:114**
Rudd, Mark (U.S. student radical) **5**:1
Rudolf II (ruler of Bohemia) **1**:158; **5**:67
Rudolph I (emperor of Germany) **4**:118
Rufeisen, Oswald (convert to Christianity; case involving Jewish identity) **4**:46
**RUMANIA 5:114,** 44
**RUPPIN, ARTHUR** (economist and Zionist leader) **5:115**
Russell, Philip Moses (U.S. patriot) **6**:85
**ROTHSCHILD** (family of financiers and philanthropists) **5:111; 1**:104; **2**:142; **3**:50; **5**:25
Rothschild, Edmond de, Baron ("Father of the *Yishuv;*" 1845-1934, France) **2**:79; **3**:4, 53, 171; **5**:48, 99, 104, 113; **6**:92
Rothschild, Edmond (20th century, England; grandson of his famous French namesake) **5**:113
Rothschild, Eugene de (20th century, France) **5**:113
Rothschild, James Armand (20th century, France) **5**:113
Rothschild, James Jacob (19th century, France) **5**:113
Rothschild, Lionel Nathan (19th century, England) **5**:113
Rothschild, Lionel Walter (England; recipient of the Balfour Declaration) **1**:101
Rothschild, Mayer Amschel (18th century, Germany) **5**:111
Rothschild, Mayer Karl (19th century, Prussia) **5**:111
Rothschild, Nathan Mayer (19th century, England) **4**:149; **5**:111
Rothschild, Nathaniel Mayer (19th-20th centuries, England) **5**:113
**RUSSIA** (country, Europe) **5**:116
—Pre-1917: **1**:156; **2**:1, 118; **3**:26, 42, 53, 88; **4**:4, 13, 17, 138, 164; **5**:8, 33, 169
—Post-1917: **1**:84; **2**:31; **4**:49, 59, 139; **5**:176; **6**:7, 54, 62, 103
—Places: **1**:96, 116, 126, 150, 170; **2**:161; **4**:23, 25, 153; **5**:18, 56
**RUTH** (biblical figure, and biblical book) **5:118; 1**:131, 143; **4**:70, 145; **5**:160
**RUZHIN, ISRAEL** (ḥasidic *ẓaddik*) **5:118**
Ryskind, Morrie (composer) **6**:39

# S

**SAADIAH GAON** (leading 10th-century scholar) **5:119; 1**:148; **2**:86; **4**:13; **5**:53, 74, 101
**SABBATH 5:119**
—Prayers and Benedictions: **1**:39; **2**:181; **4**:22; **5**;185; **6**:47
—Laws and Customs: **1**:28, 48, 151, 166, 172, 183; **2**:6, 11, 40, 82, 110, 128, 135, 139, 153; **3**:13, 20; **4**:113; **6**:97
—History and Concepts: **1**:73, 157; **2**:59, 160; **3**:48, 121, 186; **4**:92, 96; **5**:135; **6**:80
Sabbath Observers (religious group) **4**:4
**SABBATICAL YEAR AND JUBILEE** (seventh and fiftieth year) **5:127: 1**:20; **2**:8, 125, 146; **4**:1; **5**:168, 178; **6**:2, 43
*Sabra:* modern Hebrew slang word for a native-born Israeli, taken from the Arabic name for the fruit of the cactus, which Israelis are said to resemble — tough and prickly, perhaps, on the outside, but very sweet beneath the

skin.
Sachs, Curt (musicologist) **4**:169
Sachs, Leonard D. (sportsman) **6**:6
Sacks, Jonathan (British chief rabbi) **2**:109
**SACRIFICES 5:128**
–Laws: **1**:36, 49, 155; **4**:182; **5**:19, 39, 121, 134
–History: **1**:25, 178; **2**:59, 100; **5**:55, 135; **6**:27
–General: **5**:68, 72, 167; **6**:17, 21, 33
**SADAT, MUHAMMED ANWAR AL-** (Egyptian president) **5:129; 4**:178
Sadducees (ancient priestly sect) **5**:50
**SADEH, YIẒḤAK** (military leader, Israel) **5:129**
**SAFDIE, MOSHE** (architect) **5:130**
**SAFED** (town, Israel) **5:130; 1**:32; **2**:4, 89; **3**:68; **4**:8, 73
**SAGES 5:131; 3**:175; **5**:28, 50, 54
**Sahl, Mort** (U.S. satirist) **6:40**
Sahula, Isaac ibn (13th-century kabbalist) **3**:37
Said, Nuri (Iraqi prime minister) **2**:109
**ST. LOUIS** (U.S. city) **5:131**
St. Petersburg, *see* **LENINGRAD**
Sak, Jacob (17th-century scholar) **1**:81
Saks (U.S. department store) **2**:70
**SALADIN** (12th-century Kurdish conqueror of Ereẓ Israel) **5:131**
Salama ibn Ramhamum (11th-century physician) **4**:113
Salomons, David (British public figure) **4**:67
**SALANT, SAMUEL** (chief rabbi, Jerusalem) **5:131**
Salanter, Israel (founder of the *Musar* movement), *see* **LIPKIN, ISRAEL BEN ZE'EV WOLF**
**SALE** (legal concept) **5:132; 1**:10
Sale of *ḥameẓ* (Passover ritual), *see Mekhirat ḥameẓ*
**SALK, JONAS** (immunologist) **5:132**
**SALOME ALEXANDRA** (Hasmonean queen) **5:133; 1**:72; **3**:28; **6**:100
Salomon, Ḥaym (18th-century U.S. patriot) **2**:112; **5**:2; **6**:62
**SALONIKA** (city, Greece) **5:133**
**SALT 5:134; 1**:166; **2**:116; **5**:180
Salt water (in Passover *seder*) **5**:42
Salvador, Francis (early U.S. patriot) **2**:10
Samaria (ancient city, Ereẓ Israel) **1**:71; **5**:24
**SAMARITANS** (religious sect, Israel) **5:134; 3**:68; **5**:43, 162
**SAMBATYON** (legendary river) **5:135; 2**:114; **4**:127; **6**:36
**SAMSON** (biblical figure) **5:135; 1**:154; **2**:156; **4**:182; **5**:52
*Samson Agonistes* (poem by John Milton) **5**:136
**SAMUEL** (biblical figure; prophet) **5:136; 1**:138; **2**:80, 167; **3:17; 4**:81, 182; **5**:81, 137, 141, 168
Samuel (third-century c.e. talmudic sage) **1**:97; **5**:95; **6**:25
Samuel, Edwin (British political scientist) **5**:137
**SAMUEL, HERBERT LOUIS** (British high commissioner for Palestine) **5:137**
Samuel ben Abba ha-Kohen (ancient physician) **4**:113
Samuel ben Samson (13th-century traveller) **3**:129
**SAMUEL HA-NAGID** (11th-century Spanish poet and military leader) **5:137**
San'a (city, Yemen) **6**:101
Sanchez, Antonio (physician) **4**:114
*Sandak* (or *Sandek:* person honored with holding the child during the circumcision; the word is of Greek derivation) **2**:23
**SANHEDRIN** (supreme political, religious and judicial body in Ereẓ Israel) **5:138; 1**:29, 69, 132; **2**:43, 153; **4**:41, 116, 176; **5**:152; **6**:35, 42, 80
Sanhedrin, the French (convened by Napoleon in 1807) **2**:142; **4**:176
San Nicandro (town, Italy ) **2**:38
Santiago (city, Chile) **2**:16
Sao Paolo (city, Brazil) **1**:165
Saperstein, Abe (sportsman) **6**:6
**SAPHIR, JACOB** (19th-century traveller) **5:138; 2**:159
Saphir, Naomi, *see* **SHEMER, NAOMI**
**SAPIR, PINḤAS** (political leader, Israel) **5:139**
Sarah (biblical figure; matriarch) **1:7; 3**:96; **5**:16
Sarajevo (city, Yugoslavia) **6**:110
*Sarajevo Haggadah* (medieval illuminated manuscript) **3**:9
**SARDIS** (ancient city in Asia Minor) **5:139; 1**:83
Sargon (ancient Mesopotamian ruler) **4**:124
**SARNOFF, DAVID** (U.S. electronics executive) **5:139**
Sartre, Jean-Paul (philosopher) **5**:1
**SASSOON** (family of merchants, scholars and philanthropists) **5:139; 3**:69, 87
Sassoon, Abdulla (philanthropis and England) **5**:140
Sassoon, Albert, *see* Sassoon, Abdulla
Sassoon, David Solomon (scholar and bibliophile) **5**:140
Sassoon, David S. (philanthropist, India) **5**:140
Sassoon, Elias (businessman) **5**:140
Sassoon, Flora (scholar, India) **5**:140
Sassoon, Siegfried Lorraine (poet) **5**:140
Sassoon, Solomon (19th century, China) **5**:140
Sassoon ben Salah (Baghdad community leader) **5**:140
**SATAN 5:140; 1**:47; **2**:172; **3**:84
**SATMAR** (ḥasidic sect) **5:141; 3**:25; **4**:186
Saudi Arabia **1**:61
**SAUL** (biblical figure; first king of Israel) **5:141; 1**:53; **2**:56, 166, 167; **4**:24, 81, 169; **5**:137; **6**:70
*Savora* (legal scholar of the 6th century, following the *amora'im* of the talmud, and preceding the *geonim;* plural: *savora'im*) **6**:26
Sayyid Ali Muhammed (founder of Bahai religion) **1**:99
Schacht, Alexander (Al; sportsman) **6**:6
Schapp, Milton (U.S. politician) **5**:52
**SCHATZ, BORIS** (artist, Israel) **5:142; 1**:133
Schayes, Adolphe (sportsman) **6**:6
**SCHECHTER, SOLOMON** (U.S. scholar) **5:142; 2**:159; **3**:27, 172, 173
Scheurer-Kestner, August (French senator, supporter of Dreyfus) **2**:82
**SCHIFF, DAVID TEVELE** (18th-century English rabbi) **5:142**
**SCHIFF, JACOB HENRY** (U.S. financier) **5:143**
**SCHIFF, MEIR BEN JACOB** (17th-century Talmud scholar) **5:143**
Schildkraut, Rudolph (U.S. actor) **6**:38
Schloezer, A. L. (18th-century linguist) **3**:31
**SCHMIDT, JOSEPH** (operetta singer) **5:143**
Schmidt, Karl Ludwig (polemicist) **2**:78
Schmieles, Jacob Batsheba, *see* Bassevi von Treuenberg
**SCHNEERSOHN, JOSEPH ISAAC** (former Lubavitcher *Rebbe;* leader of Ḥabad Ḥasidism) **5:143; 6**:67
Schneersohn, Menahem Mendel (Lubavitcher Rebbe; leader of Ḥabad Hasidism) **3**:2; **5**:144; **6**:67
Schneider, Leonard Alfred, *see* **Bruce, Lenny**
Schnirer, Sara (religious educator) **1**:130
**SCHOCKEN, SALMAN** (German publisher and bibliophile) **5:144; 1**:20
Scholem, Gershom (scholar of mysticism, Israel) **4:9**
**SCHONFELD, VICTOR** (English rabbi) **5:144**
Schonfeld, Solomon (English rabbi) **5**:144
Schorr, Joshua (19th-century *maskil*) **3**:43
Schorsch, Ismar (U.S. scholar) **3**:173
Schulhoff, Esther (court jeweler, Berlin) **4**:56
Schumacher, Gottlieb (archaeologist) **4**:115
Schumacher, Israel (Yiddish satirical actor) **6**:39
Schwadron, Avraham (collector), *see* Sharon, Avraham
Schwaner, Wilhelm (German anti-Semite) **5**:95
Schwartz, Bernard, *see* **Curtis, Tony**
**Schwarz, David** (aviation pioneer) **3:93; 1**:16
**SCHWARZ-BART, ANDRE** (French novelist) **5:145; 6**:112
Science of Judaism (Haskalah

movement), *see* Wissenschaft des Judentums
Scopus, Mount (Jerusalem) **3**:154
**SCOTLAND 5:145**
**SCRIBE 5:145; 1**:81, 159; **4**:51, 107; **6**:30, 48, 97
Scroll of the Torah, *see* **TORAH**
Scrolls, the Five (series of biblical books, known as the *Megillot,* comprising the Song of Songs, Ruth, Lamentations, Ecclesiastes, and Esther, each of which may be separately found in this Index) **1**:143
**SCULPTURE 5:146; 1**:73; **4**:59
SDS, *see* Students for a Democratic Society
**SEALS 5:147; 3**:45; **4**:51, 79
Seasons **1**:181
Second Aliyah (wave of immigration to Ereẓ Israel prior to World War I) **6**:31, 119
Second Passover (minor festival) **5**:43
Second Vatican Council **5**:63
**SECTS, JEWISH 5:147; 1**:45, 77; **5**:50; **6**:113
Sedeh Boker (kibbutz) **1**:123
*Seder* (Passover ritual meal) **3**:7; **4**:27; **5**:41
*Seder Rav Amram* (prayer book) **1**:42; **5**:74
Sedran, Barney (sportsman) **6**:6
*Sefatenu Ittanu* (pioneering Hebrew-speaking society) **4**:27
*Sefer ha-Bahir* (mystical work) **4**:7
*Sefer Ḥasidim* (ethical work) **3**:22; **5**:55
*Sefer ha-Yezirah* (mystical work) **4**:7
*Sefer Torah* (scroll), *see* **TORAH**
*Sefirat ha-Omer* (counting of the days between Passover and Shavuot), *see* **OMER**
*Sefirot* (mystical term meaning creative powers emanating from God) **4**:8
**Segre, Beniamino** (mathematician) **4:111**
Segre, E. (physicist) **3**:129
**SEIXAS** (family of U.S. communal leaders) **5:148**
Seixas, Benjamin (18th-century financier) **5**:148
Seixas, David (19th-century inventor) **5**:148
Seixas, Gershom Mendes (U.S. rabbi) **5**:5, 148
Seixas, Moses (18th-century U.S. banker) **5**:148; **6**:85
*Sekhakh* (leafy roof of *Sukkah*) **6**:12
**SELEUCIDS** (ancient Middle Eastern dynasty) **5:148; 1**:59; **2**:21, 26; **3**:17, 58; **4**:3
Seleucus I Nicator (Assyrian ruler) **2**:86
**SELF-DEFENSE 5:149; 1**:47, 125, 130; **3**:22, 67, 95; **4**:26, 139; **5**:37; **6**:55, 79, 120
**SELF-GOVERNMENT, JEWISH 5:149; 1**:103, 150; **2**:32, 34, 42, 116; **3**:26, 45, 46, 82, 87, 111, 180; **4**:176; **5**:180; **6**:28, 37
*Seliḥot* (prayers for forgiveness) **5**:109
Selim I (Ottoman sultan) **3**:149; **5**:31
**Sellers, Peter** (English actor) **4**:163
Selznick, David (film producer) **4**:160
*Semikhah* (granting of rabbinical status), *see* **ORDINATION**
**SENNACHERIB** (king of Assyria, 705-681 b.c.e.) **5:151; 1**:37; **3**:52, 98
**SEPHARDI, SEPHARDIM** (Jews of Spanish or Oriental origin) **5:151**
—Distinctive Religious Practices: **1**:13, 94, 174; **5**:75; **6**:48
—Folkways and Culture: **2**:45, 81, 138; **3**:34; **4**:168
—Centers: **1**:43, 179; **3**:63, 111; **6**:2, 62
**SEPPHORIS** (ancient city, Ereẓ Israel) **5:152**
Septimus Severus (Roman emperor) **4**:2
**SEPTUAGINT** (Greek translation of the Bible) **5:153; 1**:71, 120, 124; **3**:44, 81
Sepulveda, Lorenzo de (Spanish poet) **3**:168
Serpent, Copper, *see* **COPPER SERPENT**
*Se'udah Mafseket* (Hebrew): last meal before a fast.
*Se'udah Shelishit* (third Sabbath meal) **5**:124
*Se'udat Mitzvah, see* **FESTIVE MEAL**
Seventeenth of Tammuz (communal fast), *see* **TAMMUZ, FAST OF**
Seventh Day Adventists (Christian sect) **4**:4
Severus, Julius (Roman leader) **1**:107
Seville (city, Spain) **6**:2
*Sevivon* (Hebrew:"spinning-top"), *see Dreidl*
**SEX 5:153; 1**:77, 151; **3**:84; **4**:98
Sexton (synagogue official), *see* **SHAMMASH**
Sforno, Obadiah (16th-century scholar) **3**:129
*Sha'arei Ẓedek* (Orthodox hospital, Jerusalem) **6**:79
*Sha'atnez* (the biblical prohibition against the interweaving of wool and linen), *see* **MIXED SPECIES**
*Sha'atnez* laboratories (textile analysis) **2**:156; **4**:143
**SHABAZI, SHALEM** (Yemenite poet) **5:153**
Shabbat, *see* **SABBATH**
"Shabbat clock" (automatic time-switch) **5**:125
Shabbateanism (messianic movement), *see* **SHABBETAI ẒEVI**
Shabbat ha-Gadol (special Sabbath, preceding Passover) **5**:127
Shabbat ha-Ḥodesh (special Sabbath, preceding beginning of month of Nisan) **5**:127
Shabbat Ḥazon (Sabbath preceding Tish'ah be-Av) **5**:127
Shabbat Mevarekhim (Sabbath preceding New Moon) **5**:126
Shabbat Naḥamu (Sabbath following Tish'ah be-Av) **5**:127
Shabbat Parah (special Sabbath) **5**:126
Shabbat Rosh Ḥodesh (Sabbath coinciding with New Moon) **5**:126
Shabbat Shekalim (special Sabbath) **5**:126
Shabbat Shirah (Sabbath on which Moses' Song of the Sea is read) **5**:127
Shabbat Shuvah (special Sabbath, preceding Day of Atonement) **5**:110, 127
Shabbat Zakhor (special Sabbath, preceding Purim) **5**:126
**SHABBETAI ẒEVI** (false messiah) **5:154; 1**:82; **2**:35, 103, 119, 144; **3**:10, 14; **4**:8, 86, 125; **5**:89, 133, 135
*Shaddai* (divine name) **4**:130
Shadrach (biblical figure, *see* Hananiah, Mishael, and Azariah
*Shaḥarit* (daily morning prayer service) **5**:69
**SHAHN, BEN** (artist) **5:155**
**SHAKESPEARE, WILLIAM 5:155; 3**:37; **4**:67
*Shaleshudes* (Yiddish: "third Sabbath meal"), *see Se'udah Shelishit*
Shalit case (Israel legal question involving Jewish identity) **4**:46
Shalmanesser (king of Assyria) **1**:139; **2**:161; **3**:138; **4**:125
*Shalom, see* **PEACE**
**SHALOM ALEICHEM** (Yiddish writer) **5:156; 3**:36; **6**:106
*Shalom Aleikhem* (Hebrew greeting: "Peace unto you") **2**:184
*Shalom Aleikhem:* hymn of welcome sung by the family to the ministering angels who, in the words of the *aggadah,* accompany each worshiper home from synagogue on Friday evening, anxious to see whether his home and family have set aside their workaday cares in readiness for the Sabbath Queen.
*Shalom Zakhar* (festive gathering on the Friday evening before a circumcision) **2**:138
*Shalosh regalim* (the three pilgrim festivals),*see* **FESTIVALS** and **PILGRIMAGE**
Shamir, Moshe (Israel writer) **3**:39
**SHAMIR, YIZḤHAK** (Israel statemsan) **5:157**
**SHAMMAI** (1st-century Talmud sage) **5:157; 3**:54, 68; **5**:51, 121
**SHAMMASH** (synagogue official) **5:157; 6**:18
Shamsky, Arthur (Art; sportsman) **6**:5
Shanghai (city, China) **2**:16
Shapira, M. W. (19th-century forger) **2**:140
**SHAPUR** (Persian dynasty) **5:157**
**SHARABI, SHALOM** (Jerusalem kabbalist) **5:158**
**SHARETT, MOSHE** (Israel statesman) **5:158; 1**:164; **5**:100
**SHARM EL-SHEIKH** (bay, southern Sinai Peninsula) **5:159; 2**:95; **5**:176
Sharon, Ariel: military and political

leader in Israel, who commanded the force which crossed the Suez Canal at a decisive point in the Yom Kippur War of October, 1973.
Sharon, Avraham (Schwadron; collector) **1**:92
*Shas* (name for Talmud) **6**:25
Shas (political party, Israel) **3**:112
Shaving, *see* **BEARDS AND SHAVING**
**SHAVUOT** (festival) **5:159; 1**:32; **2**:128, 134, 140; **3**:121; **4**:1; **5**:23, 118; **6**:53
**SHAZAR, SHNEUR ZALMAN** (third president of Israel) **5:161; 1**:4
**SHECHEM** (ancient city, Ereẓ Israel) **5:162**, 135
*She-heḥeyanu* (blessing) **1**:119; **3**:20
**SHEḤITAH** (ritual slaughter of animals) **5:162; 2**:74; **3**:25; **6**:16, 72
**SHEKEL** (unit of weight, coinage and tax in ancient Ereẓ Israel) **5:163; 4**:112, 128; **6**:25, 86, 116, 126
*Shekhinah* (Heb.): Divine Presence
Shelomẓiyyon (Hasmonean queen), *see* **SALOME ALEXANDRA**
*Sheloshim* (period of mourning) **2**:63
*Shalosh Se'udot* (third Sabbath meal), *see Se'udah Shelishit*
Shem (biblical figure; son of Noah) **5**:10
**SHEMA, READING OF** (prayer) **5:164; 1**:27, 119; **2**:55, 171; **4**:72, 103; **6**:10, 24
Shemed (biblical figure) **4**:76
**SHEMER, NAOMI** (composer and folksinger, Israel) **5:166**
Shemini Aẓeret (8th day Sukkot) **6**:14
*Shemittah* (sanctified seventh year), *see* **SABBATICAL YEAR AND JUBILEE**
*Shemoneh-Esreh* (Hebrew: "eighteen;" prayer originally comprising 18 blessings), *see* **AMIDAH**
**Shemot** (biblical book; Exodus) **1:135**
**SHERIRA GAON** (10th-century scholar) **5:167**
Sherry, Larry (sportsman) **6**:5
Shertok, Moshe, *see* **SHARETT, MOSHE**
Sheshonk (pharaoh), *see* Shishak
*Shetar* (legal document) **1**:10
*Sheva Berakhot* (Hebrew: the seven benedictions recited at the wedding ceremony, and repeated during the festive meals of the week following the wedding) **4**:100
*Shevarim* (*shofar* note) **5**:108
**SHEWBREAD** (bread used in Temple service) **5:167; 1**:166
Shield of David, *see* **MAGEN DAVID**
Shi'ite (Muslim dynasty) **2**:127; **3**:100
*Shikheḥah* (Hebrew: a forgotten sheaf, which the Torah obliges the reaper to leave in the field for the widow, the orphan, and the stranger) **2**:8
*Shiloaḥ* (pool, Jerusalem), *see* **SILOAM**
**SHILOH** (ancient city, Ereẓ Israel) **5:167; 1**:65; **6**:22
Shilumim Corporation (for German Reparations) **5**:101
Shimoni, David (writer, Israel) **3**:39
*Shin Bet* (Israel secret service) **2**:112
**SHIPS AND SAILING 5:168; 1**:85, 87; **3**:10; **4**:94; **6**:58
*Shirat ha-Yam, see* Song of the Sea
*Shir Shel Yom* (Daily Psalm, in morning service) **5**:72
Shishak (pharaoh)**2**:93
*Shivah* (week of mourning) **2**:63
*Shiv'ah-asar be-Tammuz, see* **TAMMUZ, FAST OF**
Shkop, Simeon (Lithuanian scholar) **6**:32
Shlomowitz, Marcus (English Jew who sued the publisher of the Oxford English Dictionary) **3**:168
Shlonsky, Abraham (writer, Israel) **3**:39
Shneour, Zalman (Hebrew writer) **3**:39
Shneur Zalman of Lyady (founder of Ḥabad Ḥasidism) **2**:112; **3**:1, **4**:50
**SHOFAR** (horn for ritual use) **5:168; 1**:26; **2**:60; **3**:46; **4**:128, 169; **5**:108, 128
*Shofarot* (Rosh Ha-Shanah prayer) **5**:108
*Shoḥet* (ritual slaughterer), *see* **SHEḤITAH**
*Sholem Zokhor* (festive gathering), *see Shalom Zakhar*
**Shore, Dinah** (Francis Rose; U.S. singer) **6:40**
Shostakovich, Dmitri (Russian composer) **1**:96
Shrine of the Book (museum housing the Dead Sea Scrolls, Jerusalem) **2**:61; **4**:168
*Shtadlan, see* **COURT JEWS**
**SHTETL** (townlet in Eastern Europe) **5:169; 4**:15, 97; **5**:45, 92, 157; **6**:23
*Shtibl* (Yiddish: small informal hasidic prayer-house) **3**:25
Shtreimel (Yiddish: "fur hat") **2**:81; **3**:25
Shuadit (language) **3**:171
**Shubert** (U.S. theater family) **6:40**, 39
*Shulḥan Arukh* (the Code of Jewish Law, compiled by Caro in the 16th century) **1**:81; **2**:5; **3**:134; **4**:44, 118; **5**:181
*Shulklapper* (East European town-crier) **5**:157
Shunami, Shlomo (bibliographer) **1**:161
Shushan (ancient city, Persia; setting of the Purim story) **5**:86
Shylock (Shakespearian character) **5**:155
Sicily (island off Italy) **6**:68
**SICK, THE 5:170; 1**:40, 44, 95; **3**:71; **4**:60, 112; **5**:125
*Sicut Judeis* (papal bull) **5**:62
*Siddur, see* **PRAYER BOOKS**
Sidon (ancient city, Lebanon) **4**:47 **5**:54
*Sidrah* (weekly portion of the Torah as read in synagogue) **6**:47
**SIEFF, ISRAEL MOSES** (British industrialist and Zionist) **5:170; 2**:70
Sieff, Rebecca (British Zionist) **5**:171
*Sifrei* (midrashic compilation) **5**:172
Sihon (biblical figure) **4**:158
Sikhnin (town, Israel) **3**:15
**SILBERG, MOSHE** (judge, Israel) **5:171**
**SILK 5:171; 2**:186
**SILOAM** (historic pool and tunnel, Jerusalem) **5:171; 3**:160; **6**:13
Silva, Jean Baptiste (physician) **4**:114
Silver, *see* **GOLDSMITHS AND SILVERSMITHS**
**SILVER, ABBA HILLEL** (Zionist leader) **5:172**
Silverstein, Abe (aviation expert) **1**:16
Silwan (village near Jerusalem), *see* **SILOAM**
Simeon (biblical figure; son of Jacob, and founder of one of the Twelve Tribes) **3**:45; **6**:53
**SIMEON BAR YOḤAI** (second-century Talmud sage) **5:172; 4**:8, 37, 123
Simeon ben Gamaliel (head of Sanhedrin) **4**:116
Simeon ben Jesua ben Eleazar, *see* **BEN SIRA**
**SIMEON BEN LAKISH** (third-century Talmud scholar) **5:173; 2**:167; **6**:3
Simeon ben Mattathias (Hasmonean leader) **3**:27
Simeon ben Shetaḥ (1st century b.c.e.; leader of Pharisees) **2**:91; **5**:133
**SIMEON THE JUST** (Second Temple high priest) **5:173; 1**:29
Simḥah ben Samuel of Vitry (12th-century scholar) **5**:94
*Simḥah shel Mitzvah* (Hebrew: "joy in fulfilling a Commandment"), *see* **JOY**
*Simḥat Bet ha-Sho'evah* (Sukkot celebration) **6**:13
Simḥat Torah (last day of the festival of Sukkot) **2**:140; **3**:12; **6**:14
Simmel, George (sociologist) **5:180**
**Simon, Neil** (U.S. playwright) **6:40**
Simson, Sampson (U.S. religious leader) **5**:5
Sinafir Island (off southern Sinai Peninsula) **5**:159
**SINAI,MOUNT** (biblical site) **5:174; 1**:175; **2**:100; **4**:157; **6**:22
**SINAI CAMPAIGN** (Israel-Egypt war, 1956) **5:145; 1**:123; **2**:58; **5**:159, 176
Sinai Peninsula (Middle East) **5**:159, 175
**SIN AND REPENTANCE 5:173**
—In the Bible: **1**:12, 141; **2**:59; **3**:70, 79, 177; **4**:38; **5**:129, 180
—General: **1**:157; **2**:126, 169; **3**:84; **4**:27; **6**:72
Sinatra, Frank (American entertainer) **2**:58
Singer, Isidore (editor) **2**:104
Sington, Fred (sportsman) **6**:6
Sirota, Gershon (cantor) **3**:30
Sisera (biblical figure; Canaanite general) **2**:64; **3**:135
**SIX-DAY WAR** (between Israel and Arab neighbors, 1967) **5:176; 1**:37; **2**:58, 157, 172; **3**:42, 69, 85, 154; **4**:16, 17, 24, 25, 80, 178; **5**:159, 176;

**6:**19, 62, 67
Sixtus IV (pope) **3:**90
*Siyyum* (completion of studying a tractate of Talmud, often marked by a festive meal) **2:**131
Skeleton (anatomy) **1:**45
Sklare, Marshall (sociologist) **5:**180
**SLANDER 5:177; 3:**4, 87, 91; **4:**50
Slaughter, ritual, *see* **SHEḤITAH**
**SLAVERY 5:178; 2:**33, 43, 146; **4:**156, 184; **5:**120, 128; **6:**28, 41, 94. *See also* **KIDNAPPING**
**Slovakia,** *see* **CZECHOSLOVAKIA**
**SMOLENSKIN, PEREZ** (Hebrew writer) **5:179**
**SMUTS, JAN CHRISTIAAN** (South African statesman) **5:179**
**SMYRNA** (city, Turkey) **5:179**
Sobell, Morton (convicted U.S. spy) **5:**106
Sobibor (concentration camp) **2:**33
Soccer **6:**5
Socialism (economic system) **2:**31; **3:**56; **4:**39, 74, 104
Society for the Advancement of Judaism (U.S. Reconstructionist organization) **4:**12
**SOCIOLOGY 5:179; 1:**53; **4:**35
**SODOM** (biblical town) **5:180; 1:**8; **5:**179
**SOFER, MOSES** (rabbi and communal leader, Hungary) **5:180; 1:**165; **2:**93
*Soferim* (ancient scholars of Bible text) **4:**107
**SOKOLOW, NAHUM** (Zionist leader) **5:181**
**SOLEL BONEH** (construction firm, Israel) **5:181**
**SOLOMON** (biblical figure; third king of Israel) **5:182; 1:**17, 65, 103; **2:**53, 57, 90, 96; **3:**141, 174; **4:**78; **5:**54, 82, 89, 168; **6:**33
Solomon, Nahum (19th-century English inventor) **3:**92
Solomon ben Isaac, *see* **RASHI**
Solomon ben Samuel of Wuerzburg (13th-century scribe and artist) **3:**81
Solomon Halevi (Spanish apostate), *see* **PABLO DE SANTA MARIA**
Solomons, Levi (Detroit pioneer) **2:**71
**SOLOVEITCHIK, JOSEPH DOV** (U.S. rabbinic scholar) **5:183,** 97; **6:**67
Sommi, Leone Portaleone (16th-century theater promoter) **6:**38
**SONCINO** (family of Hebrew printers) **5:183; 1:**145; **5:**79
Soncino, Gershom ben Moses (printer) **5:**184
Soncino, Joshua Solomon (printer) **5:**183
**SONG OF SONGS** (biblical book) **5:184; 1:**143; **4:**70; **5:**43, 183
Song of the Sea (Moses' exultant song of thanksgiving at the Red Sea) **3:**85; **4:**157
**SONNENFELD, JOSEPH ḤAYYIM** (rabbi, Jerusalem) **5:185; 3:**1; **4:**186
Soul, *see* **BODY AND SOUL**
**SOUTH AFRICA 5:185; 3:**49; **5:**77, 179; **6:**15
*Sovetish Heymland* (journal) **5:**77
Soviet Jewry (the struggle for their emigration) **1:**92; **2:**111, 174; **6:**68. *See also* **RUSSIA.**
**SPACE EXPLORATION 6:1; 1:**16
**SPAIN 6:1; 1:**7, 9, 105; **2:**118, 127; 90; **4:**97; **5:**64, 137, 151; **6:**45, 50
Spassky, Boris (chess player) **2:**12
Special Night Squads (Haganah defense units) **3:**6
**SPEKTOR, ISAAC ELCHANAN** (Lithuanian rabbi) **6:2; 5:**128
Speyer (city, Germany) **4:**175
Spices, *see* **INCENSE AND PERFUMES**
Spiegel, Sam (film producer) **4:**160
Spies, *see* **ESPIONAGE**
Spingarn, Arthur (U.S. activist) **4:**184
**SPINOZA, BARUCH** (17th-century philosopher) **6:2; 3:** 47
Spitz, Mark (sportsman) **6:**7
*Spodik* (Yiddish): high fur hat worn by Gerer Hasidim on festive occasions.
**SPORTS 6:3; 1:**9, 89; **2:**153; **4:**31, 77, 120; **5:**20
St. (abbreviation): alphabetized as Saint.
**STALIN, JOSEF VISSARIONOVICH** (ruler of U.S.S.R.) **6:7; 2:**31; **4:**136; **5:**117; **6:**54
**STAMPS 6:7**
Star of David, *see* **MAGEN DAVID**
Statute of Kalisz (Polish charter) **5:**59
Statutes of Blood Purity (Portugal) **5:**65
Stearns, Daniel E. (sportsman) **6:**5
Stein, Theodore de (European nobleman) **2:**123
Steinberg, Paul (Twister; sportsman) **6:**6
**STEINER, HANNAH** (WIZO leader, Czechoslovakia) **6:8**
Steinitz, Wilhelm (chess player) **2:**12
Steinmetz, Charles Protens (electrical engineer) **3:**93
Steinsalz, Adin (modern Talmud commentator) **6:**27
Steinschneider, Moritz (bibliographer) **3:**27
Stern, Abraham (inventor) **3:**92
Stern, Avraham (Ereẓ Israel underground fighter) **4:**65
Stern, Grigori (Russian soldier) **4:**139
**STERN, ISAAC** (U.S. violinist) **6:8**
**Stern, Otto** (physicist) **4:111**
Stern College (New York) **6:**103
Stern Gang, *see* **LOḤAMEI ḤERUT ISRAEL**
Stern's (U.S. department store) **2:**70
Stilling, Benedikt (anatomist) **1:**46
**STOCKADE AND WATCHTOWER** (fortified settlement, Israel) **6:8; 4:**21; **5:**182
Stockholm (city, Sweden) **6:**15
Stone, Mickey, *see* **MARCUS, DAVID**
Strabo (ancient Greek geographer) **2:**72
Straits of Tiran, *see* Tiran Straits
Strand, Oscar (Austrian architect) **1:**69
**Strasberg, Lee** (U.S. theatrical director) **6:40**
Strasbourg (city, Alsace) **1:**35, 73
Straton (4th-century ruler) **1:**177
Straus, Isidore (U.S. businessman) **2:**69
Straus, Lazarus (U.S. businessman) **2:**70
Straus, Nathan (U.S. businessman) **2:**69
Stravinsky, Igor (Russian composer) **1:**26
Streicher, Julius (Nazi) **2:**3; **5:**14
**STREISAND, BARBARA** (U.S. performer) **6:9**
Strikes (industrial) **4:**35
**STRUCK, HERMANN** (artist) **6:9**
*Struma* (ship of "illegal" immigrants to Ereẓ Israel) **3:**80
Student press (U.S., Canada) **5:**78
Students for a Democratic Society (U.S. radical political organization) **5:**1
Student Struggle for Soviet Jewry (U.S.) **6:**68
**STUDY 6:9; 1:**27; **2:**91, **3:**13, 15, 24, 26, 42; **4:**61; **5:**165; **6:**24, 68, 77, 102
Stuyvesant, Peter (colonial governor of New York) **5:**2
Suess, Joseph (Court Jew), *see* **OPPENHEIMER, JOSEPH BEN ISSACHAR SUESSKIND**
Suez Canal (Egypt) **1:**104; **2:**95; **5:**175
**SUFFERING 6:10; 3:**76, 173; **5:**102. *See also* **JUSTICE**
*Sufganiyyot* (Hebrew: "doughnuts") **3:**20
Suicide **1:**173; **4:**104
**SUKENIK, ELIEZER LIPA** (archaeologist, Israel) **6:11,** 99
*Sukkah, see* **SUKKOT**
**SUKKOT** (festival) **6:11; 2:**54, 128, 134, 140; **3:**12, 19; **4:**27, 52
**SULEIMAN I** (16th-century Ottoman sultan) **6:14; 5:**31
Sumer (ancient region) **4:**123
**SUN 6:14; 1:**87, 179; **2:**47; **4:**150
Sunnite (member of dominant sect within Islam) **3:**150
Sura (Babylonian town and Talmud academy) **1:**79, 97, 99; **5:**95, 119; **6:**25, 102
Surat (city, India) **3:**87
Surgery, *see* **MEDICINE**
Surinam (West Indies) **6:**90
Susannah and the Elders (book of the Apocrypha) **1:**58
**SUZMAN, HELEN** (South African stateswoman) **6:15**
Swansea (city, Wales) **6:**79
Swart, Jack (sportsman) **6:**5
Swastika (Nazi symbol) **4:**183
Sweat shops (U.S. garment factories at turn of the century) **6:**23
**SWEDEN 6:15; 2:**131; **5:**12; **6:**79
**SWITZERLAND 6:16; 1:**109
Sydney (city, Australia) **1:**90
**SYMBOLISM 6:16; 1:**44, 49, 52, 175, 183; **3:**130; **4:**78, 102, 122; **5:**13, 41, 93, 134; **6:**13, 22, 23, 89, 121
**SYNAGOGUE 6:17**

—Localities: **1**:30, 43, 78, 100, 129, 170; **2**:2, 86, 107; **3**:87; **5**:2, 52, 66, 139
—General: **1**:69, 183; **2**:34; **3**:25, 145; **4**:22, 168; **5**:50, 157; **6**:22, 91, 93, 109
**SYRIA 6**:18; **1**:62; **4**:16; **5**:176; **6**:59, 107
Syrkin, Naḥman (Socialist Zionist) **6**:117
**SZENES, HANNAH** (freedom fighter, World War II) **6:19**
**Szilard, Leo** (physicist) **4:111**
**SZOLD, HENRIETTA** (Zionist leader) **6:20**; **1**;103; **6**:110
**SZYK, ARTHUR** (artist) **6:20**; **3**:81

# T

**TABERNACLE** (portable sanctuary constructed after Exodus from Egypt) **6:21**; **1**:36, 63, 133; **2**:166, 173; **4**:122; **5**:120, 129, 168; **6**:17, 33
Tabernacles (festival), *see* **SUKKOT**
**TABLETS OF THE LAW** (given to Moses on Mount Sinai) **6:22**; **4**:157; **5**:174; **6**:21, 27, 33, 35
*Taḥanun* (prayer) **5**:71
*Taharat ha-Mishpaḥah* (Hebrew: "family purity"; marital laws), *see Tohorat ha-Mishpaḥah.*
**TAILORING 6:22**;**4**:90, 142; **5**:5; **6**:85
**TAITAZAK, JOSEPH** (16th-century kabbalist) **6:23**
*Takkanot* (rulings by a governing communal or rabbinic body) **2**:164
*Tal* (Hebrew: "dew"), *see* **RAIN AND DEW**
Talal (Hashemite ruler) **1**:5
**TALLIT AND ẒIẒIT** (ritual garb; prayer shawl and its fringes) **6:23**; **1**:173; **2**:60, 81, 158; **4**:102; **5**:70; **6**:43, 47
*Tallit katan* (small *tallit* worn under upper garments) **6**:24
**TALMUD** (written record of the Oral Law taught by the Sages, comprising the Mishnah, which states the laws, and the Gemara, which discusses them, as well as topics ranging through biblical interpretation, *aggadah,* history, ethics and customs) **6:24**;
—Scholars: **1**:2, 79, 97, 129; **3**:45; **4**:2, 83, 116; **5**:94, 95, 131, 167; **6**:10, 102
—Languages and Editions: **1**:64, 159; **3**:34; **5**:79, 183
—Component Elements: **1**:18, 134; **3**:48; **4**:41, 132; **5**:28
Talmud Torah (part-time religious Hebrew school) **2**:92
**TAM, JACOB BEN MEIR** (leading 12th-century author of *tosafot* commentaries on Talmud) **6:27**; **5**:94; **6**:30
Tamerlane (14th-century conqueror) **5**:46
Tammany Hall (New York Democratic Club) **5**:5
**TAMMUZ, FAST OF** (public fast) **6:27**; **1**:111; **2**:127; **6**:43
*Tanakh* (Hebrew abbreviation), *see* **BIBLE**
Tangier (city, Morocco) **4**:152
*Tanna* (sage whose legal opinions are quoted in the Mishnah; plural: *tanna'im*) **5**:131; **6**:24
*Tanya* (central text of Ḥabad Ḥasidism) **3**:1
Targum (Aramaic translation of the Bible) **5**:25
Tashima, J. (Japanese Bible scholar) **3**:136
*Tashlikh* (Rosh Ha-Shanah ceremony) **5:110**
**TATTOO 6:28**
Tats (tribe), *see* **MOUNTAIN JEWS**
Tauber, E. (German scholar) **3**:27
**TAXATION 6:28**; **1**:184; **2**:42, 152; **4**:2, 6; **5**:128, 150; **6**:35
**TCHERNICHOWSKY, SAUL** (Hebrew poet) **6:29**
*Te'atron Ereẓ Yisre'eli* (theater group) **3**:40
**TECHNION** (Israel Institute of Technology) **6:29**
*Tefaḥ* (biblical unit of measurement) **6**:86
*Tefillah* (Hebrew: "prayer"), *see* **PRAYER**
*Tefillah* (singular of *tefillin*), *see* **TEFILLIN**
**TEFILLIN** (pair of small leather boxes containing parchment scrolls inscribed with scriptural passages, and worn on the head and arm during the morning prayers) **6:30**; **1**:44, 108; **5**:70; **6**:43
Teheran (city, Persia) **5**:47
*Tehillim, see* **PSALMS**
Teitelbaum, Joel (Satmar *rebbe*) **4**:186; **5**:141
Teixeira, Pedro (17th-century Portuguese Marrano traveller) **1**:99; **6**:51
*Tekhelet* (blue dye) **6**:23
*Tekiah* (*shofar* note) **5**:108
**TEL AVIV-JAFFA** (city, Israel) **6:30**; **1**:118; **2**:79; **3**:11; **4**:6
Television **1**:15; **3**:120; **4**:161; **6**:39
Tel Ḥai (settlement, Israel) **2**:176; **6**:55
**TELL** (archaeological mound) **6:32**; **4**:115
**TELL EL-AMARNA LETTERS** (ancient Egyptian tablets) **6:32**
Tell el-Kheleifeh (ancient site), *see* Ezion-Geber
**Teller, Edward** (physicist) **4:111**
**TELZ** (Telshi or Telsiai; Lithuanian city, and name of the U.S. yeshivah which was first founded there) **6: 32**
Templars (medieval Christian military group) **3**:11
**TEMPLE** (ancient sanctuary in Jerusalem) **6:33**
The entries listed below refer sometimes to the First Temple (destroyed in 586 b.c.e.), sometimes to the Second Temple (destroyed 70 c.e.), and often to both.
—Structure and Contents: **1**:36, 68; **2**:43; **3**:49; **4**:54, 122; **5**:182; **6**:22
—The Service: **3**:83; **4**:169; **5**:78, 87, 129, 167; **6**:11
—Destruction: **3**:140; **4**:37, 100, 184; **6**:27, 43, 44, 89
—Historical Episodes:**1**:30; **2**:52, 79; **3**:18, 44, 184; **6**:115
—Other Sanctuaries: **1**:63; **5**:24; **6**:17, 22
"Temporary Laws" (Russia, 1881) **5**:34
*Tena'im* (conditions of betrothal) **4**:102
*Tenakh* (Hebrew abbreviation), *see* **BIBLE**
**TEN COMMANDMENTS 6:35**; **2**:172; **3**:138; **4**:22, 157; **5**:120, 160, 174; **6**:21, 22, 33, 40, 97
Ten Days of Penitence (between Rosh Ha-Shanah and the Day of Atonement), *see Aseret yemei teshuvah*
Tendler, Lew (sportsman) **6**:6
**TEN LOST TRIBES** (inhabitants of the Northern Kingdom of ancient Israel, whose movements have remained untraced since their exile by the Assyrians in 722 b.c.e.) **6:36**; **1**:17, 170; **4**:33, 126, 164; **5**:135; **6**:53
**TEN MARTYRS** (2nd-century sages

killed by Romans) **6:36; 3:**9, 15
Tentori, Abraham ben Ḥayyim di, (printer) **1:**145
Terah (biblical figure; father of Abraham) **1:**7
*Terefah* (Hebrew): opposite of kosher; i.e., ritually unfit for use as food.
**TERRITORIALISM** (movements for Jewish settlement, especially outside Ereẓ Israel) **6:36; 1:**150; **6:**59, 113
Terrorism, Arab **1:**63; **3:**136; **4:**14, 47, 123, 166; **6:**19, 62, 109
*Teru'ah* (*shofar* note) **5:**108
*Terumah* (tax of agricultural produce), *see* **TITHES**
*Teshuvah* (Hebrew: "repentance"), *see* **SIN AND REPENTANCE**
*Testament of Joseph* (ancient book) **3:**44
Testimony (evidence given in court) **2:**43; **5:**17, 46
Tetragrammaton, *see* **GOD**
Tevet, 10th of (fast day) **2:**126
Textiles **4:**63; **5:**171; **6:**23, 85
Tezuka, N. (Japanese Judeophile) **3:**137
**THEATER 6:37**
—Performers: **1:**128; **2:**58; **3:**176; **4:**15, 105, 123, 135; **5:**113; **6:**9, 45, 56
—Miscellaneous: **1:**98, 129; **2:**173; **3:**62; **4:**9, 160; **5:**99, 155
Theater, Hebrew, *see* **HEBREW THEATER**
**THEFT AND ROBBERY 6:40**
Theodicy (justification of God's actions), *see* **JUSTICE**
Theodor Duces Angelus (13th-century Greek despot) **2:**182
Theology, *see* **GOD**
Third Aliyah (1919–1923): a wave of 35,000 migrants to Ereẓ Israel, mainly *halutzim* who, with their predecessors, founded the Histadrut organization, and many kibbutzim and moshavim.
"Third World" (term for the nations of Asia and Africa) **6:**62
Thirteen (number) **5:**14
Thirteen Principles of Faith (Maimonides' formulation) **4:**84; **5:**70
**Thomashefsky, Boris** (U.S. Yiddish actor and director) **6:40**
Three Weeks (annual period of mourning) **6:**28, 43
**THUNDER AND LIGHTNING 6:41**
Thuthotep (ancient Egyptian official) **4:**115
Thutmose I (pharaoh) **2:**93
Thutmose III (or Thutmosis) III (pharaoh) **2:**94, 111, 156; **4:**115, 123
**TIBBON, IBN** (medieval family of translators and authors) **6:41; 3:**35
Tibbon, Jacob ben Machir Ibn **6:**41
Tibbon, Judah ben Saul Ibn **6:**41; **1:**159
Tibbon, Moses ben Samuel Ibn **4:**109; **6:**41
Tibbon, Samuel Ibn **1:**72; **4:**83; **6:**41
**TIBERIAS** (city, Israel) **6:41; 1:**10; **3:**68; **4:**25, 108, 178; **6:**14
Tiberias, Sea of, *see* **KINNERET, LAKE**
Tiberius (Roman emperor) **6:**42
Tiglath-Pileser III (king of Assyria) **3:**98; **4:**125
Tigris (river in Mesopotamia) **2:**115
*Tikkun leil Shavuot* (all-night vigil) **5:**161
*Tikkun Soferim* (scribes' Torah text) **5:**145
**TIME 6:42; 1:**181
Timna (mining town in Israel) **3:**118
Tiran Island (off southern Sinai Peninsula) **5:**159
Tiran, Straits of (off southern Sinai Peninsula) **2:**95, 96; **5:**159, 176
**TISH'AH BE-AV** (Hebrew: "the ninth day of the month of Av;" fast day commemorating the destruction of both Temples) **6:**42; **1:**77, 107, 111; **2:**30, 126; **4:**37; **6:**24, 27, 30, 34, 36
Tishrei (Hebrew month) **5:**107
**TITHES** (tax of agricultural produce) **6:43; 2:**135; **5:**66, 79; **6:**28
**TITUS, FLAVIUS VESPASIANUS** (Roman emperor) **6:44; 1:**106; **4:**122
Titus' Arch (Rome) **6:**44
*Tkhine* (informal or spontaneous prayer of private supplication, such as those offered by women while lighting the candles on Friday before sunset) **6:**105
Tlemcen (city, Algeria) **1:**31
Tnuva (agricultural co-operative, Israel) **6:**44
**TOBACCO 6:44; 3:**25
Tobey, David (sportsman) **6:**6
Tobit, Book of **3:44**
Toch, Hermon (19th-century Austrian inventor) **3:**92
**Todd, Mike** U.S. film producer) **4:163**
*Tohorah, see* **PURITY AND IMPURITY, RITUAL**
*Tohorat ha-Mishpahah* (Hebrew: "family purity;" laws concerning sexual relations between husband and wife) **5:**87, 153
*Toite* Ḥasidim, *see* Bratslaver Ḥasidim
Tokyo (city, Japan) **3:**136
**TOLEDO** (city, Spain) **6:45; 1:**9; **4:**168
Toleranzpatent (edict of tolerance issued by Austrian Emperor Joseph II) **6:**74
Tombs of the Kings (archaeological discovery, Jerusalem) **3:**43
Tombstones **1:**173
**TOPOL, CHAIM** (actor, Israel) **6:45**
**TORAH 6:46**
In the context of this entry, "Torah" is used not in its broader meaning of the whole body of religious law, ethics and philosophy, but in its narrower sense — the Five Books of Moses.
—Revelation and Commandments: **2:**30; **4:**30, 98; **5:**102, 159, 174; **6:**22, 35, 94
—Study and Interpretation: **1:**134; **2:**91; **3:**47, 55; **4:**40, 142; **5:**26; **6:**9, 24
—The Scroll and its Public Reading: **1:**108, 154, 159, 184; **2:**6, 60, 129; **4:**107, 170; **5:**122; **6:**14, 97
Torah, Reading of the, *see* **TORAH**
Torah Scroll, *see* **TORAH**
**TORONTO** (city, Canada) **6:49; 1:**183
**TORQUEMADA, TOMAS DE** (organizer of the Spanish Inquisition) **6:50; 3:**91
Tortosa, Disputation of (Spain, 1413) **2:**128
*Tosafot* (Talmud commentaries) **5:**94; **6:**27
*Tosefta* (book of laws not included in the Mishnah) **6:**25
**TOURO, JUDAH** (U.S. philanthropist) **6:50; 5:**2
Toynbee, Arnold (historian) **3:**51
Trade **2:**186; **4:**96; **6:**51
Trajan (Roman emperor) **5:**89; **6:**36
Trani, Moses di (16th-century Talmud scholar) **5:**28
Transjordan, *see* **JORDAN, HASHEMITE KINGDOM OF**
Translations of the Bible, *see* **BIBLE**
Transmigration of souls, *see* **DIBBUK**
**TRANSPLANTS** (surgical) **6:**50; **3:**31
**TRAVELERS AND EXPLORERS 6:51; 1:**85, 123; **2:**98; **3:**75, 129; **5:**48, 138, 185; **6:**1, 112
Trebitsch, Moses Leib (illuminator of manuscripts) **3:**81
**TREBITSCH-LINCOLN, IGNATIUS TIMOTHY** (international adventurer) **6:52; 2:**112
Treblinka (concentration camp) **2:**32 **3:**67
Tredegar (town, Wales) **6:**79
Tree of Knowledge (biblical Garden of Eden) **1:**12
Tree of Life (biblical Garden of Eden) **1:**13
**TREES AND PLANTS 6:52; 1:**149; **2:**90, 150; **3:**103, 172; **4:**46, 93, 102, 142; **5:**127, 161; **6:**12, 56
Tremellius, John Immanuel (16th-century scholar) **1:**181
Trent (city, Italy) **6:**53
**TRENT, SIMON OF** (subject of a medieval blood libel) **6:53**
**Treves, Eliezer** (German scholar) **2:**145
Triangle Shirtwaist Company (New York) **6:**64
**TRIBES, TWELVE** (of ancient Israel) **6:53; 2:**135; **3:**13, 45, 133; **6:**36, 70
Tripoli (city, Libya) **4:**56
Tripolitania (region, North Africa) **4:**55
Trois Rivières (city, Canada) **3:**21
Troitsky, Professor (Russian defender of Beilis) **1:**114
*Trop* (Yiddish: "cantillation;" the traditional melody for the Reading of the Torah, and its musical notation, expressed in small symbols printed immediately above and below the consonants, like the vowel signs), *see* Cantillation
**TROTSKY, LEV DAVIDOVICH** (Soviet revolutionary leader) **6:54; 2:**31
**TRUMAN, HARRY S.** (U.S. president)

6:54; 2:77
**TRUMPELDOR, JOSEPH** (pioneer, Ereẓ Israel) **6:55; 1:**130; **3:**42, 132
Trumpeldor Labor Battalion (Ereẓ Israel) **5:**129
**TRUTH 6:55; 4:**31; **5:**53
Tryphon (2nd-century Jewish polemicist) **2:**77
Tubal-Cain (biblical figure) **4:**127
**TU BE-AV** (Hebrew: "fifteenth day of the month of Av;" minor festival) **6:56**
**TU BI-SHEVAT** (Hebrew: "fifteenth day of the month of Shevat"; New Year of Trees) **6:56; 2:**130, 140
**Tucker, Richard** (opera star) **3:30**
**TUCKER, SOPHIE** (U.S. actress and singer) **6:56,** 38
*Tumah, see* **PURITY AND IMPURITY, RITUAL**
**TUNISIA** (country, N. Africa) **6:57; 4:**10
*Tur, see* **JACOB BEN ASHER** and *Arba'ah Turim*
**TURKEY** (country, Asia Minor) **6:58; 1:**83, 123; **2:**81, 115; **4:**13, 17; **5:**30, 179
Tutenkhamun (pharaoh) **2:**93
Tuvim, Judith, *see* **Holliday, Judy**
Twelve Tribes, *see* **TRIBES, TWELVE**
Tyndale, William (16th-century Bible scholar) **1:**146
**TYRE** (city, Lebanon) **6:58; 4:**46; **5:**54, 182; **6:**33
Tzomet (political party, Israel) **2:**97

# U

**UCEDA, SAMUEL BEN ISAAC** (16th-century scholar) **6:59**
Uganda (African state) **4:**5
**UGANDA SCHEME** (plan for Jewish colonization in British East Africa) **6:59; 6:**36, 87, 116
**UGARIT** (ancient city, Syria) **6:59**
Ugaritic (ancient Semitic language) **3:**31
Ukraine (CIS republic) **2:**17; **3:**10
*Ulam* (porch in Jerusalem Temple) **6:**33
**ULLSTEIN** (family of German publishers) **6:59**
Ullstein, Leopold (19th-century publisher) **6:**59
**ULPAN** (intensive Hebrew language course) **6:60; 3:**34
Ulster, *see* Northern Ireland
**UMAYYADS** (7th-8th century Arab dynasty) **6:60; 3:**101
Umm Rashrash, *see* **EILAT**
U.N., *see* **UNITED NATIONS**
Underground resistance (in mandatory Palestine) **3:**95; **4:**65; **6:**120
UNEF, *see* United Nations Emergency Force
UNESCO, *see* United Nations Educational, Scientific and Cultural Organization
*U-Netannah Tokef* (prayer) **5:**108
Union of American Hebrew Congregations (Reform organization) **2:**168
United Jewish Appeal **4:**17
**UNITED NATIONS 6:61; 1:**4; **2:**157, 172; **3:**151, 154; **5:**38, 176; **6:**54, 109
United Nations Educational, Scientific and Cultural Organization (UNESCO; became a center of controversy following its adoption of anti-Israel resolutions in 1974) **6:**62
United Nations Emergency Force **6:**62
United Nations International Children's Emergency Fund **4:**16
United Nations Relief and Works Agency **6:**61
United Palestine Appeal **4:**17
**UNITED STATES OF AMERICA 6:62;**
—Personalities: **3:**176; **4:**16, 26, 37, 49, 54, 59; **5:**10; **6:**50, 54, 80, 85
—Places: **1:**102, 162; **2:**10, 13, 71; **4:**68; **5:** 1, 51, 131
—Miscellaneous: **1:**84, 152; **2:**66, 152; **4:** 114, 137, 184; **5:**176, 178; **6:**5, 38, 45, 68. *See also* under names of various organizations and communal bodies.
United Synagogue of America (Conservative organization) **2:**34; **3:**173
Universal Jewish Encyclopedia **2:**105
**UNIVERSITIES 6:68; 1:**157, 181; **3:**54, 126; **4:**54; **5:**32; **6:**29, 98, 103
U.N.O., *see* **UNITED NATIONS**
UNRRA (United Nations Relief and Rehabilitation Administration) **2:**77
UNRWA, *see* United Nations Relief and Works Agency
UNSCOP (United Nations Special Committee on Palestine) **5:**38; **6:**61, 71, 120
Unterman, Isser (third Ashkenazi chief rabbi of Israel) **2:**179; **3:**31; **4:**63; **6:**51
Ur (ancient city, Mesopotamia) **1:**7, 97; **4:**124
Urban II (pope) **2:**49; **3:**105
Uriah the Hittite (biblical figure) **2:**57; **5:**35
Uri ben Joel ha-Levi (12th-century martyr) **2:**99
**URIM AND THUMMIM** (part of breastplate worn by high priest) **6:69**
**URUGUAY** (country, South America) **6:70**
U.S.A., *see* **UNITED STATES OF AMERICA**
Usha (city in Asia Minor) **4:**116
*Ushpizin* (Sukkot tradition) **6:**12
**USSISHKIN, ABRAHAM MENAHEM MENDEL** (Zionist leader) **6:70; 3:**42; **6:**116
Usury (exorbitant interest on loans), *see* **MONEYLENDING AND USURY**
U.S.S.R., *see* **RUSSIA**
U Thant (secretary-general of the UN) **5:**176; **6:**62
'Uthman (Turkish sultan) **5:**30
Utnapishtim (Mesopotamian literary figure) **2:**137
Uziel, Ben-Zion Meir Ḥai, *see* **OUZIEL, BEN-ZION MEIR ḤAI**
Uzziah (biblical figure; king of Judah) **1:**77, 139; **2:**89; **3:**144; **4:**50

# V


Va'ad (organization of CIS Jews) **5**:117
Va'ad ha-Lashon (forerunner of Academy of the Hebrew Language) **4**:27
Va'ad Hazzalah (Orthodox rescue organization, World War II) **6**:66
**VA'AD LE'UMMI** (National Council of the Jews of Palestine, 1920-1948) **6:71**
*Vakhnacht* (Yiddish: all-night vigil before a circumcision) **2**:23
Valenstein, Lawrence (advertising executive) **1**:15
Valera, Eamon de (Irish prime minister) **3**:51
Valley of Dry Bones : scene of a vision of Ezekiel in which the prophet brought hope to the downhearted Babylonian exiles, comparing their fate with that of an assemblage of dry bones which, responding to the divine command, became clothed in flesh and sinew, and were revived. And, in fact, some few years later, the exiles were enabled to return to Erez Israel. *See* **2**:119
Van Praag, Jaap (sportsman), *see* Praag, Jaap van
Vasco da Gama (explorer) **5**:185; **6**:112
**VATICAN** (headquarters of the Roman Catholic Church) **6:71**; **4**:131; **5**:63. *See also* **CHRISTIANITY** and **POPES.**
*Vatikin* (especially pious people) **5**:70
Vaudeville (entertainment form) **4**:160; **6**:38
**Vaughan, Frankie** (English entertainer) **6:40**
*Va-Yikra* (biblical book; Leviticus) **1:136**
Vecinho, Joseph (15th-century physician) **1**:85
Vega, Lope de (Spanish poet) **3**:168
Vegetables, *see* **FRUIT AND VEGETABLES**
**VEGETARIANISM 6:71**; 95
**VEIL 6:72**; **3**:30; **4**:99
**VENGEANCE 6:72**; **3**:84
**VENICE** (city, Italy) **6:73**; **2**:164; **3**:129
Versailles Peace Conference (post-World War I) **4**:140
Vertov, Dziga (film producer) **4**:161
Vespasian (Roman emperor) **3**:176; **5**:24
*Via Maris* (ancient highway, Israel) **4**:25; **5**:182
Victoria (queen of England) **2**:79; **3**:5, 45
Victoria Cross (military decoration) **4**:138
**VIENNA** (city, Austria) **6**:73; **1**:91
Vietnam War **3**:176; **4**:27, 138
Vigil (all-night watch) **2**:23; **5**:161; **6**:14
**VILNA** (city, Lithuania) **6:74**, 93
Vilna Gaon (Elijah ben Solomon Zalman; 18th-century rabbinic leader), *see* **GAON OF VILNA**
Visigoths (ancient peoples) **6**:1
**VISIONS 6:75**; **1**:59, 100, 110, 140, 175; **4**:72, 75, 164; **5**:81, 101
Visiting the sick, *see* **SICK,THE**
Vital, Hayyim (16th-century kabbalist) **3**:9; **4**:8, 73
**VIZHNITZ** (hasidic dynasty) **6:76**
Vocational training **5**:29; **6**:110
**VOGEL, SIR JULIUS** (prime minister of New Zealand) **6:76**; **1**:91
Volhynia (region of Poland) **3**:23
**VOLOZHIN** (city, Belorussia) **6:76**; **1**:133; **6**:102
**VOLOZHINER, HAYYIM BEN ISAAC** (Lithuanian talmudist) **6:77**; **2**:155; **6**:76
Volynov, Boris (Russian cosmonaut) **1**:17
Von Schnoerer, Georg (Austrian anti-Semite) **6**:74
Vowel signs (Hebrew) **4**:108
Vows, *see* **OATHS AND VOWS**
Vulgate (Latin version of the Bible) **1**:145


# W


**WADI** (Arabic: "Dry stream bed") **6:78**
Wadi al-Nattuf (archaeological site, Israel) **6**:78
Wadi Qilt (or Kelt; archaeological site, Israel) **6**:78
Wadi Qumran (archaeological site, Israel) **6**:78. *See also* Qumran.
Wahl, Saul (1541-c. 1617): merchant and community leader of Brest-Litovsk who, according to legend, acted as king for a day before the final election of King Sigismund III of Poland.
Wailing Wall, *see* **WESTERN WALL**
**WAKSMAN, SELMAN ABRAHAM** (U.S. microbiologist) **6:78**
Walachia, *see* **RUMANIA**
**WALD, LILLIAN** (U.S. social worker) **6:78**
**Waldman, Leibele** (cantor) **3:30**
*Wall, The* (novel by John Hersey) **5**:104
**WALES** (country in Great Britain) **6:78**
**WALLACH, MOSHE** (Orthodox medical pioneer, founder of Sha'arei Zedek Hospital, Jerusalem) **6:79**; **3**:71
**WALLENBERG, RAOUL** (Swedish diplomat; rescuer of Holocaust victims) **6:79**
Wandsbeck (city, Germany) **3**:14
**WAR 6:79**; **3**:98; **4**:137; **5**:45
—Ancient: **1**:37, 106; **2**:95; **3**:27, 78; **4**:3, 106, 169; **6**:72, 113
—Modern: **1**:33; **3**:5, 170; **4**:80; **5**:175, 176; **6**:81, 107
**WARBURG** (family of scholars and philanthropists) **6:80**
Warburg, Aby Moritz (German historian) **6**:81
Warburg, Felix Mortiz (U.S. philanthropist) **6**:81

Warburg, Gerald (U.S. musician) 6:81
Warburg, James Paul (U.S. statesman) 6:80
Warburg, Karl Johan (Swedish historian) 6:80
Warburg, Otto (botanist and Zionist leader) 6:80
Warburg, Otto Heinrich (German biochemist) 6:81
Warburg, Paul Moritz (U.S. banker) 6:80
Warburg Institute (art library, London) 6:81
War Crimes Trials, Nuremberg 5:15
**WAR OF INDEPENDENCE** (Israel) **6:81**; 1:34, 36, 62, 78, 81, 112, 122; 2:157; 3:6, 11, 69, 151; 4:16, 65, 96; 5:103; 6:61, 92, 99
War Refugee Board (U.S. organization) 5:106; 6:66
**WARREN, SIR CHARLES** (British archaeologist) **6:82**
**WARSAW** (city, Poland) **6:83**; 1:47; 2:166, 178; 3:7, 67; 5:42, 104
**WASHING THE HANDS 6:84**; 1:166; 2:131, 180; 3:16, 74
**WASHINGTON, GEORGE** (first president of the U.S.) **6:85**; 2:10
Wasserman, August von (physician) 4:114
Watchman Society, *see* **HASHOMER HA-ẔA'IR**
Water 4:136; 5:88; 6:84
Water-Drawing Celebration (Sukkot) 6:13
Watergate Affair (U.S. politics) 5:9
**WEAVING 6:85**; 4:63
Wedding, *see* **MARRIAGE**
**WEIGHTS AND MEASURES 6:86**; 5:80, 163; 6:40
Weilerstein, Sadie Rose (author) 2:15
Weimar Republic (Germany) 2:164
**WEINREICH, URIEL** (Yiddish linguist) **6:86**
Weisenfreund, Muni, *see* **Muni, Paul**
Weisgal, Meyer (Zionist leader and head of Weizmann Institute of Science) 6:88
Weiss, J. (Talmud scholar) 3:31
**WEIZMAN, EZER** (7th president of Israel) **6:86**
**WEIZMANN, CHAIM** (first president of Israel) **6:86**; 1:72, 101, 122; 2:85, 97, 108, 174; 5:99; 6:116
**WEIZMANN INSTITUTE OF SCIENCE** (Israel) **6:88**; 5:99, 171
**WELLHAUSEN, JULIUS** (Bible critic) **6:88**; 1:146
Wenceslaus I (ruler, Bohemia) 5:66
Werbermacher, Hannah Rachel (ḥasidic *rebbe*), *see* **LUDOMIR, MAID OF**
Wergeland, Henrik (Norwegian writer) 5:12
**WESSELY, NAPHTALI HERZ** (Haskalah scholar) **6:89**; 3:26
West Bank (of the Jordan River; the regions of Judea and Samaria) 5:176
**WESTERN WALL** (remaining wall of the Temple Mount, Jerusalem) **6:89**; 1:68, 152; 3:68; 5:177; 6:34, 43
**WEST INDIES** (archipelago off the coast of Central America) **6:90**
**WHEAT 6:90**; 5:160
"White lies," *see* **TRUTH**
White Papers (British government policy statements on Ereẓ Israel) 1:122; 6:119
"Who is a Jew? " (Israel legal question) 4:45; 5:171
Widowhood 2:8, 123
**Wiener, Norbert** (mathematician) **4:111**
*Wiener Gezerah* (Austrian massacres of 1421), *see* Albert V
Wiesenthal, Simon (Holocaust historian) 6:74
Wilhelm II (German kaiser) 3:50
**WILLS 6:91**; 1:10; 3:89
Wilson, Woodrow (U.S. president) 1:164
**WINE 6:92**; 1:28; 2:74, 180; 3:79; 4:22, 182; 5:10, 104
**WINGATE, CHARLES ORDE** (British army officer and Christian Zionist) **6:92**; 2:114; 3:6
**Winters, Shelley** (U.S. actress) **4:163**
Wisdom 1:17; 5:53
**WISDOM LITERATURE** (biblical and other ancient books of ethical counsel) **6:92**; 1:124; 2:90; 5:82, 183
Wisdom of Ben Sira (ancient Apocryphal book) 1:124
**WISE, ISAAC MAYER** (pioneer of U.S. Reform Judaism) **6:93**; 2:96; 3:40; 4:184; 5:98; 6:63
Wise, Stephen (U.S. Reform Rabbi) 3:40; 4:184; 6:95
Wisliceny, Dieter (Nazi official) 2:52
Wissenschaft des Judentums (19th-century German movement for the scientific study of Judaism) 3:26; 4:32; 5:98; 6:122
Wissotzky, Kalonymus (tea merchant and philanthropist) 6:29
Witness, *see* Testimony
**WITTENBERG, IZḤAK** (Vilna ghetto fighter) **6:93**, 75
WIZO (Women's International Zionist Organization) 4:171; 5:171; 6:7
Wolfsohn, David (designer of the Zionist flag) 2:136
Wolfson, Sir Isaac (English philanthropist) 2:70
**WOMAN 6:93**
—Nature and Status: 1:12, 151; 2:43; 3:25; 4:20; 5:153; 6:41
—Laws and Customs: 1:166, 172, 184; 2:81; 3:30; 4:113, 151; 5:122; 6:34, 47
—Some Famous Women: 1:23, 105; 3:52, 135; 4:72, 116, 177; 6:8
Women's Liberation 6:93
Woodhead Commission (British investigation in Palestine, 1938) 5:38
Wool 4:142; 6:85
Work, *see* **LABOR**
Workmen's Circle (U.S. Yiddish cultural foundation) 5:5
World Federation of Ha-Shomer Ha-Ẓair, *see* **HA-SHOMER HA-ẒAIR**
**WORLD JEWISH CONGRESS 6:95**
*World Over* (children's magazine) 5:78
World War II 2:95; 3:66, 170; 4:182; 5:37, 105; 6:65
World Zionist Organization 4:17; 5:181; 6:116. *See also* **ZIONISM.**
**WORMS** (city, Germany) **6:95**; 1:84
**WORMSER, SECKEL** (German kabbalist) **6:95**
**WOUK, HERMAN** (U.S. writer) **6:96**
**WRITING 6:96**; 1:3, 64, 69, 82, 92, 159; 4:108, 123; 5:35, 145; 6:28, 32, 48, 59
Written Law, *see* **TORAH** and **ORAL LAW**
**Wynn, Ed** (U.S. actor) **4:164**
**Wynn, Keenan** (U.S. actor) **4:164**


# X-Y


**XANTEN** (town, Germany) **6:98**
**XIMENES DE CISNEROS, FRANCISCO** (Spanish churchman) **6:98**
*Ya'aleh ve-Yavo:* name of a short prayer which is added to the Amidah and to the Grace after Meals on major festivals and on the New Moon.
*Yad* (pointer used during Torah reading in synagogue) 6:49

*Yad ha-Ḥazakah* (Maimonides' legal code), *see Mishneh Torah*
**YAD MORDEKHAI** (kibbutz) **6:99; 1:**48
**YAD VASHEM** (Israel memorial to the Holocaust victims) **6:99; 1:**70, 76; **3:**67; **5:**104
**YADIN, YIGAEL** (archaeologist, Israel) **6:99; 4:**106, 115; **6:**11
Yaffo, *see* **TEL AVIV-JAFFA**
*Yahrzeit* (Yiddish: "anniversary of a death") **2:**63, 126
Yale University (U.S.) **6:**70
Yalta: the wife of Nahman ben Jacob, a prominent Talmud scholar in the 4th century c.e., and the daughter of the contemporary exilarch of the Babylonian community. Several of her sharp-tongued comments have been preserved among the aggadic anecdotes found in the Babylonian Talmud. These reveal her to have been possessed of a demanding and fiery-tempered personality.
Yanait, Raḥel, *see* Ben-Ẓvi, Raḥel
**YANNAI** (early medieval religious poet) **6:100; 4:**11
**YANNAI, ALEXANDER** (first-century b.c.e. king of Judea) **6:100; 1:**72, 132, 177; **3:**27, 48; **4:**171; **5:**133; **6:**13
*Yarḥei Kallah* (Hebrew: "the months of the academy): ancient Babylonian tradition whereby adult laymen would spend a month, twice a year, during the agricultural off-season, refreshing their acquaintance with the Torah. This may be seen as the original of the extension courses which are offered today by many universities for adults in the general community. The practice of *Yarḥei Kallah* has been revived in modern Israel.
*Yarmulka* (Yiddish: "skullcap") **2:**82; **3:**30
Yarmuk: tributary of the Jordan River rising in the Moab mountains, which has been used by both Israel and Jordan for irrigation purposes.
Yates, Benjamin, *see* Goetz, Benjamin
Yavneh (kibbutz) **3:**131
Yavneh Teachers' Seminary (Cleveland, Ohio) **6:**33
*Yaẓi'a* (building adjacent to Jerusalem Temple) **6:**33
Yehoash (pseudonym of Yehoash Solomon Bloomgarden; 1872–1927): Yiddish poet, whose translation of the Bible into Yiddish became a best-seller.
*Yekke:* Yiddish slang for a Jew of German extraction; also used to describe a person who is exasperatingly thorough, over-organized, and utterly lacking in humor. According to non-*yekkes*, the above two categories are identical.
Yekutieli, Joseph (sportsman) **4:**77
**YEMEN** (country in the Arabian Peninsula) **6:100; 1:**60; **3:**34, 83; **4:**84; **5:**154; **6:**22
Yemin Orde (settlement, Israel) **6:**92
*Ye'or, see* **NILE**
*Yerushalayim shel Zahav* (song) **5:**166
**YESHIVAH** (institute of talmudic learning) **6:102; 1:**119; **3:**42; **4:**9, 28, 29, 30, 61, 143, 167; **6:**32, 76, 77, 103, 105
*Yeshivah shel Ma'lah, see* Academy on High.
**YESHIVA UNIVERSITY** (New York) **6:103; 5:**6, 183; **6:**2
Yevanic (language) **3:**171
**YEVSEKTSIYA** (Jewish sections of Russian Communist Party) **6:103**
Yevtushenko, Yevgeni (Russian poet) **1:**96
*Yeẓer ha-Ra* (Hebrew: "the evil inclination") **5:**174, and *see* **INCLINATION, GOOD AND EVIL.**
*Yeẓer ha-Tov* (Hebrew: "the good inclination") **5:**174, and *see* **INCLINATION, GOOD AND EVIL.**
Y-H-W-H (divine name), *see* **GOD.**
*Yibum, see* Levirate marriage
**YIDDISH** (language) **6:104**
–Writers: **1:**19,109; **2:**168, 179, 181; **4:**49, 53, 118; **5:**45, 156
–Miscellaneous: **1:**38, 71, 81, 146, 162; **2:**147; **3:**26, 171; **4:**161; **6:**38, 64, 86, 104, 107
*Yigdal* (hymn) **1:**116; **5:**70
*Yiḥus* (impressive genealogy) **2:**159
*Yishtabbaḥ* (prayer) **5:**71
*Yishuv:* Hebrew term for the Jewish community of Ereẓ Israel prior to the establishment of the State
*Yissurim shel ahavah* (Hebrew: "afflictions of love"; doctrine on suffering) **5:**102
**YIVO** (institute for Yiddish scholarship and Jewish research) **6:107**
Yizhar, S. (writer, Israel) **3:**39
*Yizkor* (memorial service) **6:**14
YMHA (social organization) **4:**178
Yokohama (city, Japan) **3:**135
*Yom ha-Aẓma'ut, see* **INDEPENDENCE DAY, ISRAEL**
*Yom ha-Zikkaron, see* Remembrance Day
Yom Kippur, *see* **DAY OF ATONEMENT**
*Yom Kippur Katan* (fast on eve of New Moon) **4:**151
**YOM KIPPUR WAR** (1973; between Israel, and Syria and Egypt) **6:107; 2:**58, 95, 183; **4:**27, 117; **5:**177; **6:**8, 19
*Yom Tov, see* **FESTIVALS**
*Yom-tov Sheni shel Galuyot* (Hebrew: "the second festival-day observed in the Diaspora") **2:**129.
*Yom Yerushalayim, see* Jerusalem Day
**YORK** (city, England) **6:109**
Yosef, Ovadiah (Sephardi chief rabbi of Israel) **5:**105
Yose ha-Gelili: 2nd-century sage of the Mishnah, who lived in the Galilee – hence his name. He was first a disciple and later a colleague of Rabbi Akiva. His marriage was unhappy and he was persuaded by his colleagues to divorce his wife, but after the divorce he generously supported her and her second husband, who became blind. According to a medieval tradition, his tomb is located near Safed in the Galilee.
**YOUNG ISRAEL** (association of U.S. orthodox synagogues) **6:109; 5:**6
*Young Israel* (children's magazine) **5:**78
Young Men's Hebrew Association, *see* YMHA
**YOUTH ALIYAH** (rescue and welfare organization) **6:110; 4:**21, 172; **6:**20
*Yovel* (Hebrew word for the sanctified 50th year, from which the English word "jubilee" stems), *see* **SABBATICAL YEAR AND JUBILEE**
**YUGOSLAVIA** (country, Europe) **6:110**
Yushchinsky, Andrei (victim of the Beilis blood libel case) **1:**113.

# Z

*Za'ar ba'alei hayyim* (avoidance of cruelty to animals) **1**:48; **5**:163
**ZACUTO, ABRAHAM BEN SAMUEL** (Spanish astronomer) **6:112; 1**:87; **4**:114; **5**:168
Zadkine, Ossip (1890–1967): Russian-born sculptor who became famous with his sculpture – "The Destroyed City" – which represents a mutilated giant 20 feet high, arms upheld in agony, symbolizing the Dutch port city of Rotterdam, which was ruthlessly bombarded by German planes in 1940.
**ZADDIK** (righteous man) **6:112; 1**:92, 95; **2**:100, 177; **3**:1, 26, 135; **4**:6, 52, 72, 173; **5**:145
Zadok (high priest) **5**:50
**ZADOKITES** (ancient priestly sect) **6:113**
Zagreb (city, Yugoslavia) **6**:110
Zahal (Israel Defense Forces) **3**:114
Zalmanson, Silva (Russian Zionist activist) **5**:117
Zamenhof, Ludwik Lazar (1859–1917): Polish philologist who invented the international language called Esperanto, into which he translated works from German, English and Russian, as well as part of the Bible. His language comprised only 900 root words, and a grammar with only 16 rules.
Zamosc, Israel (19th-century Russian *maskil*) **3**:26
**ZANGWILL, ISRAEL** (English writer) **6:113** **1**:113; **6**:37, 38
Zarchin, Alexander (inventor of desalination process) **3**:93
Zarphatic (language) **3**:171
**ZEALOTS** (resistance fighters against Roman domination of Erez Israel in the first century) **6:113; 1**:65, 105, 177; **2**:61, 146; **4**:106
Zebulun (biblical figure; son of Jacob and founder of one of the Twelve Tribes) **2**:135; **3**:45; **6**:53
**ZECHARIAH** (biblical figure; prophet) **6:114; 1**:142; **6**:115
Zechariah (9th-century b.c.e. priest) **6**:114
Zechariah (8th-century b.c.e. king of Israel) **6**:114
*Zedakah* (Hebrew term) **4**:6. *See also* **CHARITY**
**ZEDEKIAH** (6th-century b.c.e. king of Israel) **6:114; 4**:183
*Zedukim,* see Sadducees
*Ze'enah u-Re'enah:* a simple Yiddish interpretation of the Pentateuch, the *haftarot* and the Five Scrolls, written at the end of the 16th century by Jacob ben Isaac Ashkenazi and primarily used by women for Sabbath reading. It has run through 210 editions in several languages.
Zefat, *see***SAFED**
Ze'irei Zion (Galician youth movement) **3**:21
Zeitlin, Solomon (U.S. scholar) **3**:172
*Zekhut Avot* (Hebrew: "the merit of one's fathers"): the teaching that the virtuous deeds of one's forefathers stand him in good stead, helping to tip the heavenly balance in his favor, in times of trial or peril.
Zelophehad, daughters of (biblical figures) **3**:89
*Zemed* (biblical unit of measurement) **6**:86
*Zemirot* (Shabbath table hymns) **5**:123
*Zephaniah* (biblical book) **1**:142
Zeppelin (airship) **1**:16
Zeresh: biblical figure; wife of Haman, and chief villainess of the Purim story.
*Zeret* (biblical unit of measurement) **6**:86
Zerlin, Rebekah (15th-century oculist) **4**:114
**ZERUBBABEL** (leader of Return to Zion from Babylonian exile, 6th-century b.c.e.) **6:115; 3**:138
Zerubbabel (7th-century b.c.e. prophet) **6**:115
Zetnik, K. (Holocaust writer), *see* **K. ZETNIK**
Zhidovin, Skhariya (15th-century Russian personage) **4**:4
Zhitlowsky, Chaim (1865–1943): Yiddish philosopher and writer who favored Territorialism rather than Zionism, advocating Yiddish-speaking socialist nationalism in various parts of the Diaspora.
Ziegfeld, Florenz (musical comedy promoter) **6**:39
Ziegfield Follies (entertainment group) **4**:161
*Zikhronot* (Rosh Ha-Shanah prayer) **5**:108
*Zimmun* : the Hebrew word for preparation or readiness. It is most commonly used, however, to describe a responsorial thanksgiving formula: the introduction to the Grace after Meals which may only be recited with a quorum of three, who together are called a *mezumman. See* **2**:181.
Zim Navigation Company (Israel) **4**:17
Zion: the name of a hill and fortress in Jerusalem, whose exact location has been understood differently in various generations. It sometimes meant the hill which is today called Mt. Zion, and included the site of the Citadel (the "Tower of David"); sometimes the Temple Mount; and poetically Zion often means the whole city of Jerusalem, or even the whole of Judea.
Zion, Mount (Jerusalem) **3**:68
**ZIONISM 6:115; 1**:55, 62, 100, 101, 110, 127, 130, 150, 171; **2**:21, 109, 136; **3**:3, 21, 28, 42, 53, 55, 79; **4**:12, 17, 77, 92, 143; **5**:20, 38, 97; **6**:36, 59, 74
Zion Mule Corps (Jewish military unit, World War I) **1**:30; **4**:138; **6**:55
Zipporah (biblical figure; wife of Moses) **2**:22; **3**:165; **4**:156
*Zizit, see* **TALLIT AND ZIZIT**
**ZODIAC** (heavenly zones and symbols representing them) **6:121; 1**:85
Zofim (Israel scouts organization) **3**:126
Zohar (central book of Jewish mysticism) **2**:138; **4**:7; **5**:80, 172
**ZOLA, EMILE** (French writer who fought anti-Semitism) **6:121; 2**:82
Zom Gedaliah (fast day), *see* Fast of Gedaliah
Zophar (biblical figure; friend of Job) **3**:174
Zorach, William (sculptor) **1**:76
Zoroastrianism (Oriental religion) **4**:7
Zosima (15th-century Russian cleric) **4**:4
Zuckerman, Solly, Lord (born 1904): British anatomist who became famous for his studies of baboons as well as for his studies of society in relation to science and to military affairs. He was scientific adviser to the British armed forces during World War II, and later chief scientific adviser to the British government.
**ZUNZ, LEOPOLD** (historian, and a pioneer of the *Wissenschaft* movement for the study of the "Science of Judaism") **6:122**
**ZUSYA OF HANIPOLI** (hasidic leader, bore his sufferings with uncomplaining optimism) **6:122; 2**:100

# HUNDRED-YEAR JEWISH CALENDAR 1920-2020

# HUNDRED-YEAR JEWISH CALENDAR, 1920–2020

**Introduction.** This calendar gives the Jewish calendar and its Gregorian equivalent for a period of a century. It also marks festivals and the weekly portions of the Torah reading. Two modifications should be noted for use in Israel. The first is that Second Days of Festivals (except Rosh Ha-Shanah) are not holidays in Israel. Such days are indicated by vertical stripes. The other is that when the Second Day of a festival in the Diaspora falls on a Sabbath (in which case a special portion of the Law replaces the regular Sabbath reading), there will be a discrepancy during the following weeks between the reading in Israel and the reading outside Israel. Eventually this is compensated by having two portions read in one week in the Diaspora but not in Israel. Such variations can occur during the readings of the Books of Exodus, Leviticus, and Numbers. An Israel calendar should be consulted to discover where such discrepancies occur.

**Notes.** The Gregorian and the Jewish years are given at the top of each half page. The Jewish New Year (Tishri 1) falls in September/October.

The names of the Hebrew months are printed in bold type in the relevant columns. The beginning of the month (Rosh Ḥodesh) is indicated by the letters R.Ḥ.

The figures 1–31 at the extreme left of the page are the days of the Gregorian month. The corresponding days of the Hebrew months are printed in light type in the columns for each of the twelve months. The figures in heavy type in these columns indicate the Sabbath, with the appropriate weekly portion of the Law in italics in the box to the right. The major holy days are boxed on a dark background, the second day observed in the Diaspora appearing on a striped background below.

The postponement of a fast falling on the Sabbath is indicated by an arrow.

The word Omer indicates the day on which the Counting of the Omer starts.

## 1920

5680/81 תר״פ / תרפ״א

| | January | February | March | April | May | June | July | August | September | October | November | December |
|---|---|---|---|---|---|---|---|---|---|---|---|---|
| 1 | 10 **Tevet** Fast | 12 | 11 | 13 | **13** *Aḥarei Mot Kedoshim* | 15 | 15 | 17 | 18 | 19 Ḥol ha- | 20 | 20 |
| 2 | 11 | 13 | 12 | 14 | 14 | 16 | 16 | 18 | 19 | **20** Mo'ed | 21 | 21 |
| 3 | **12** *Va-Yeḥi* | 14 | 13 Ta'anit Esther | **15** Pesaḥ | 15 | 17 | **17** ↓ *Balak* | 19 | 20 | 21 Hoshana Rabba | 22 | 22 |
| 4 | 13 | 15 | 14 Purim | 16 Omer | 16 | 18 | 18 Fast | 20 | **21** *Ki Tavo* | 22 Shemini Aẓeret | 23 | **23** *Va-Yeshev* |
| 5 | 14 | 16 | 15 Shushan Purim | 17 Ḥol ha-Mo'ed | 17 | **19** *Be-Ha'alotkha* | 19 | 21 | 22 | 23 Simḥat Torah *Ve-Zot Ha-Berakhah* | 24 | 24 |
| 6 | 15 | 17 | **16** *Ki Tissa* | 18 | 18 Lag ba-Omer | 20 | 20 | 22 | 23 | 24 | **25** *Ḥayyei Sarah* | 25 Ḥanukkah 1 |
| 7 | 16 | **18** *Yitro* | 17 | 19 | 19 | 21 | 21 | **23** *Ekev* | 24 | 25 | 26 | 26 2 |
| 8 | 17 | 19 | 18 | 20 | **20** *Emor* | 22 | 22 | 24 | 25 | 26 | 27 | 27 3 |
| 9 | 18 | 20 | 19 | 21 Pesaḥ | 21 | 23 | 23 | 25 | 26 | **27** *Bereshit* | 28 | 28 4 |
| 10 | **19** *Shemot* | 21 | 20 | **22** | 22 | 24 | **24** *Pinhas* | 26 | 27 | 28 | 29 | 29 5 |
| 11 | 20 | 22 | 21 | 23 | 23 | 25 | 25 | 27 | **28** *Niẓẓavim* | 29 | 30 R. Ḥ. | **30** R. Ḥ. *Mi-Keẓ* 6 |
| 12 | 21 | 23 | 22 | 24 | 24 | **26** *Shelaḥ* | 26 | 28 | 29 | 30 R. Ḥ. | 1 **Kislev** R. Ḥ. | 1 **Tevet** R. Ḥ. 7 |
| 13 | 22 | 24 | **23** *Va-Yakhel Pekudei* Parah | 25 | 25 | 27 | 27 | 29 | 1 **Tishri** Rosh Ha-Shanah | 1 **Ḥeshvan** R. Ḥ. | **2** *Toledot* | 2 8 |
| 14 | 23 | **25** *Mishpatim* Shekalim | 24 | 26 | 26 | 28 | 28 | **30** R. Ḥ. *Re'eh* | 2 | 2 | 3 | 3 |
| 15 | 24 | 26 | 25 | 27 | **27** *Be-Har Be-Ḥukkotai* | 29 | 29 | 1 **Elul** R. Ḥ. | 3 Fast | 3 | 4 | 4 |
| 16 | 25 | 27 | 26 | 28 | 28 | 30 R. Ḥ. | 1 **Av** R. Ḥ. | 2 | 4 | **4** *No'aḥ* | 5 | 5 |
| 17 | **26** *Va-Era* | 28 | 27 | **29** *Shemini* | 29 | 1 **Tammuz** R. Ḥ. | **2** *Mattot Masei* | 3 | 5 | 5 | 6 | 6 |
| 18 | 27 | 29 | 28 | 30 R. Ḥ. | 1 **Sivan** R. Ḥ. | 2 | 3 | 4 | **6** *Va-Yelekh* Shabbat Shuvah | 6 | 7 | **7** *Va-Yiggash* |
| 19 | 28 | 30 R. Ḥ. | 29 | 1 **Iyyar** R. Ḥ. | 2 | **3** *Koraḥ* | 4 | 5 | 7 | 7 | 8 | 8 |
| 20 | 29 | 1 **Adar** R. Ḥ. | **1** R. Ḥ. *Va-Yikra* **Nisan** Ha-Ḥodesh | 2 | 3 | 4 | 5 | 6 | 8 | 8 | **9** *Va-Yeẓe* | 9 |
| 21 | 1 **Shevat** R. Ḥ. | **2** *Terumah* | 2 | 3 | 4 | 5 | 6 | **7** *Shofetim* | 9 | 9 | 10 | 10 Fast |
| 22 | 2 | 3 | 3 | 4 | **5** *Be-Midbar* | 6 | 7 | 8 | 10 Yom Kippur | 10 | 11 | 11 |
| 23 | 3 | 4 | 4 | 5 | 6 Shavu'ot | 7 | 8 | 9 | 11 | **11** *Lekh Lekha* | 12 | 12 |
| 24 | **4** *Bo* | 5 | 5 | **6** *Tazri'a Meẓora* | 7 | 8 | **9** ↓ *Devarim* Tishah be-Av | 10 | 12 | 12 | 13 | 13 |
| 25 | 5 | 6 | 6 | 7 | 8 | 9 | 10 Fast | 11 | **13** *Ha'azinu* | 13 | 14 | **14** *Va-Yeḥi* |
| 26 | 6 | 7 | 7 | 8 | 9 | **10** *Ḥukkat* | 11 | 12 | 14 | 14 | 15 | 15 |
| 27 | 7 | 8 | **8** *Ẓav* Shabbat ha-Gadol | 9 | 10 | 11 | 12 | 13 | 15 Sukkot | 15 | **16** *Va-Yishlaḥ* | 16 |
| 28 | 8 | **9** *Teẓavveh* Zakhor | 9 | 10 | 11 | 12 | 13 | **14** *Ki Teẓe* | 16 | 16 | 17 | 17 |
| 29 | 9 | 10 | 10 | 11 | **12** *Naso* | 13 | 14 | 15 | 17 Ḥol ha- | 17 | 18 | 18 |
| 30 | 10 | | 11 | 12 | 13 | 14 | 15 | 16 | 18 Mo'ed | **18** *Va-Yera* | 19 | 19 |
| 31 | **11** *Be-Shallaḥ* | | 12 | | 14 | | **16** *Va-Etḥannan* | 17 | | 19 | | 20 |

# 1921

**5681/82** תרפ״א / תרפ״ב

| | January | February | March | April | May | June | July | August | September | October | November | December |
|---|---|---|---|---|---|---|---|---|---|---|---|---|
| 1 | **21** Tevet *Shemot* | 23 | 21 | 22 | 23 | 24 | 25 | 26 | 28 | **28** *Nizzavim* | 30 R. H. | 30 R. H. |
| 2 | 22 | 24 | 22 | **23** *Shemini Parah* | 24 | 25 | **26** *Shelah* | 27 | 29 | 29 | 1 **Heshvan** R. H. | 1 **Kislev** R. H. |
| 3 | 23 | 25 | 23 | 24 | 25 | 26 | 27 | 28 | **30** R. H. *Re'eh* | **1 Tishri** Rosh Ha-Shanah | 2 | **2** *Toledot* |
| 4 | 24 | 26 | 24 | 25 | 26 | **27** *Be-Hukkotai* | 28 | 29 | 1 **Elul** R. H. | 2 | 3 | 3 |
| 5 | 25 | **27** *Mishpatim* | **25** *Va-Yakhel* Shekalim | 26 | 27 | 28 | 29 | **1 Av** R. H. | 2 | 3 Fast | **4** *No'ah* | 4 |
| 6 | 26 | 28 | 26 | 27 | 28 | 29 | 30 R. H. | **2** *Mattot Masei* | 3 | 4 | 5 | 5 |
| 7 | 27 | 29 | 27 | 28 | **29** *Aharei Mot* | 1 **Sivan** R. H. | 1 **Tammuz** R. H. | 3 | 4 | 5 | 6 | 6 |
| 8 | **28** *Va-Era* | 30 R. H. | 28 | 29 | 30 R. H. | 2 | 2 | 4 | 5 | **6** *Va-Yelekh* Shabbat Shuvah | 7 | 7 |
| 9 | 29 | 1 **Adar I** R. H. | 29 | **1** R. H. **Nisan** *Tazri'a* Ha-Hodesh | 1 **Iyyar** R. H. | 3 | **3** *Korah* | 5 | 6 | 7 | 8 | 8 |
| 10 | 1 **Shevat** R. H. | 2 | 30 R. H. | 2 | 2 | 4 | 4 | 6 | **7** *Shofetim* | 8 | 9 | **9** *Va-Yeze* |
| 11 | 2 | 3 | 1 **Adar II** R. H. | 3 | 3 | **5** *Be-Midbar* | 5 | 7 | 8 | 9 | 10 | 10 |
| 12 | 3 | **4** *Terumah* | **2** *Pekudei* | 4 | 4 | 6 Shavuot | 6 | 8 | 9 | 10 Yom Kippur | **11** *Lekh Lekha* | 11 |
| 13 | 4 | 5 | 3 | 5 | 5 | 7 | 7 | **9** *Devarim* Tishah be-Av | 10 | 11 | 12 | 12 |
| 14 | 5 | 6 | 4 | 6 | **6** *Kedoshim* | 8 | 8 | 10 Fast | 11 | 12 | 13 | 13 |
| 15 | **6** *Bo* | 7 | 5 | 7 | 7 | 9 | 9 | 11 | 12 | **13** *Ha'azinu* | 14 | 14 |
| 16 | 7 | 8 | 6 | **8** *Mezora* Shabbat ha-Gadol | 8 | 10 | **10** *Hukkat* | 12 | 13 | 14 | 15 | 15 |
| 17 | 8 | 9 | 7 | 9 | 9 | 11 | 11 | 13 | **14** *Ki Teze* | 15 Sukkot | 16 | **16** *Va-Yishlah* |
| 18 | 9 | 10 | 8 | 10 | 10 | **12** *Naso* | 12 | 14 | 15 | 16 | 17 | 17 |
| 19 | 10 | **11** *Tezavveh* | **9** *Va-Yikra* Zakhor | 11 | 11 | 13 | 13 | 15 | 16 | 17 | **18** *Va-Yera* | 18 |
| 20 | 11 | 12 | 10 | 12 | 12 | 14 | 14 | **16** *Va-Ethannan* | 17 | 18 Hol ha-Mo'ed | 19 | 19 |
| 21 | 12 | 13 | 11 | 13 | **13** *Emor* | 15 | 15 | 17 | 18 | 19 | 20 | 20 |
| 22 | **13** *Be-Shallah* | 14 | 12 | 14 | 14 | 16 | 16 | 18 | 19 | **20** | 21 | 21 |
| 23 | 14 | 15 | 13 Ta'anit Esther | **15** Pesah | 15 | 17 | **17** *Balak* | 19 | 20 | 21 Hoshana Rabba | 22 | 22 |
| 24 | 15 | 16 | 14 Purim | 16 Omer | 16 | 18 | 18 Fast | 20 | **21** *Ki Tavo* | 22 Shemini Azeret | 23 | **23** *Va-Yeshev* |
| 25 | 16 | 17 | 15 Shushan Purim | 17 | 17 | **19** *Be-Ha'alotkha* | 19 | 21 | 22 | 23 Simhat Torah *Ve-Zot Ha-Berakhah* | 24 | 24 |
| 26 | 17 | **18** *Ki Tissa* | **16** *Zav* | 18 Hol ha-Mo'ed | 18 Lag ba-Omer | 20 | 20 | 22 | 23 | 24 | **25** *Hayyei Sarah* | 25 Hanukkah 1 |
| 27 | 18 | 19 | 17 | 19 | 19 | 21 | 21 | **23** *Ekev* | 24 | 25 | 26 | 26 2 |
| 28 | 19 | 20 | 18 | 20 | **20** *Be-Har* | 22 | 22 | 24 | 25 | 26 | 27 | 27 3 |
| 29 | **20** *Yitro* | | 19 | 21 Pesah | 21 | 23 | 23 | 25 | 26 | **27** *Bereshit* | 28 | 28 4 |
| 30 | 21 | | 20 | 22 | 22 | 24 | **24** *Pinhas* | 26 | 27 | 28 | 29 | 29 5 |
| 31 | 22 | | 21 | | 23 | | 25 | 27 | | 29 | | **30** R. H. *Mi-Kez* 6 |

# 1922

**5682/83** תרפ״ב / תרפ״ג

| | January | February | March | April | May | June | July | August | September | October | November | December |
|---|---|---|---|---|---|---|---|---|---|---|---|---|
| 1 | 1 **Tevet** R. H. 7 | 3 | 1 **Adar** R. H. | **3** *Va-Yikra* | 3 | 5 | **5** *Korah* | 7 | 8 | 9 | 10 | 11 |
| 2 | 2 8 | 4 | 2 | 4 | 4 | 6 Shavuot | 6 | 8 | **9** *Ki Teze* | 10 Yom Kippur | 11 | **12** *Va-Yeze* |
| 3 | 3 | 5 | 3 | 5 | 5 | 7 | 7 | 9 Tishah be-Av | 10 | 11 | 12 | 13 |
| 4 | 4 | **6** *Bo* | **4** *Terumah* | 6 | 6 | 8 | 8 | 10 | 11 | 12 | **13** *Lekh Lekha* | 14 |
| 5 | 5 | 7 | 5 | 7 | 7 | 9 | 9 | **11** *Va-Ethannan* | 12 | 13 | 14 | 15 |
| 6 | 6 | 8 | 6 | 8 | **8** *Aharei Mot Kedoshim* | 10 | 10 | 12 | 13 | 14 | 15 | 16 |
| 7 | **7** *Va-Yiggash* | 9 | 7 | 9 | 9 | 11 | 11 | 13 | 14 | **15** Sukkot | 16 | 17 |
| 8 | 8 | 10 | 8 | **10** *Zav* Shabbat ha-Gadol | 10 | 12 | **12** *Hukkat Balak* | 14 | 15 | 16 | 17 | 18 |
| 9 | 9 | 11 | 9 | 11 | 11 | 13 | 13 | 15 | **16** *Ki Tavo* | 17 | 18 | **19** *Va-Yishlah* |
| 10 | 10 Fast | 12 | 10 | 12 | 12 | **14** *Naso* | 14 | 16 | 17 | 18 Hol ha-Mo'ed | 19 | 20 |
| 11 | 11 | **13** *Be-Shallah* | **11** *Tezavveh* Zakhor | 13 | 13 | 15 | 15 | 17 | 18 | 19 | **20** *Va-Yera* | 21 |
| 12 | 12 | 14 | 12 | 14 | 14 | 16 | 16 | **18** *Ekev* | 19 | 20 | 21 | 22 |
| 13 | 13 | 15 | 13 Ta'anit Esther | 15 Pesah | **15** *Emor* | 17 | 17 Fast | 19 | 20 | 21 Hoshana Rabba | 22 | 23 |
| 14 | **14** *Va-Yehi* | 16 | 14 Purim | 16 Omer | 16 | 18 | 18 | 20 | 21 | **22** Shemini Azeret | 23 | 24 |
| 15 | 15 | 17 | 15 Shushan Purim | **17** | 17 | 19 | **19** *Pinhas* | 21 | 22 | 23 Simhat Torah *Ve-Zot Ha-Berakhah* | 24 | 25 Hanukkah 1 |
| 16 | 16 | 18 | 16 | 18 Hol ha-Mo'ed | 18 Lag ba-Omer | 20 | 20 | 22 | **23** *Nizzavim Va-Yelekh* | 24 | 25 | **26** *Va-Yeshev* 2 |
| 17 | 17 | 19 | 17 | 19 | 19 | **21** *Be-Ha'alotkha* | 21 | 23 | 24 | 25 | 26 | 27 3 |
| 18 | 18 | **20** *Yitro* | **18** *Ki Tissa* Parah | 20 | 20 | 22 | 22 | 24 | 25 | 26 | **27** *Hayyei Sarah* | 28 4 |
| 19 | 19 | 21 | 19 | 21 Pesah | 21 | 23 | 23 | **25** *Re'eh* | 26 | 27 | 28 | 29 5 |
| 20 | 20 | 22 | 20 | 22 | **22** *Be-Har Be-Hukkotai* | 24 | 24 | 26 | 27 | 28 | 29 | 1 **Tevet** R. H. 6 |
| 21 | **21** *Shemot* | 23 | 21 | 23 | 23 | 25 | 25 | 27 | 28 | **29** *Bereshit* | 1 **Kislev** R. H. | 2 7 |
| 22 | 22 | 24 | 22 | **24** *Shemini* | 24 | 26 | **26** *Mattot Masei* | 28 | 29 | 30 R. H. | 2 | 3 8 |
| 23 | 23 | 25 | 23 | 25 | 25 | 27 | 27 | 29 | **1 Tishri** Rosh Ha-Shanah | 1 **Heshvan** R. H. | 3 | **4** *Mi-Kez* |
| 24 | 24 | 26 | 24 | 26 | 26 | **28** *Shelah* | 28 | 30 R. H. | 2 | 2 | 4 | 5 |
| 25 | 25 | **27** *Mishpatim* Shekalim | **25** *Va-Yakhel Pekudei* Ha-Hodesh | 27 | 27 | 29 | 29 | 1 **Elul** R. H. | 3 Fast | 3 | **5** *Toledot* | 6 |
| 26 | 26 | 28 | 26 | 28 | 28 | 30 R. H. | 1 **Av** R. H. | **2** *Shofetim* | 4 | 4 | 6 | 7 |
| 27 | 27 | 29 | 27 | 29 | **29** *Be-Midbar* | 1 **Tammuz** R. H. | 2 | 3 | 5 | 5 | 7 | 8 |
| 28 | **28** *Va-Era* | 30 R. H. | 28 | 30 R. H. | 1 **Sivan** R. H. | 2 | 3 | 4 | 6 | **6** *No'ah* | 8 | 9 |
| 29 | 29 | | 29 | **1** R. H. **Iyyar** *Tazri'a Mezora* | 2 | 3 | **4** *Devarim* | 5 | 7 | 7 | 9 | 10 Fast |
| 30 | 1 **Shevat** R. H. | | 1 **Nisan** R. H. | 2 | 3 | 4 | 5 | 6 | **8** *Ha'azinu* Shabbat Shuvah | 8 | 10 | **11** *Va-Yiggash* |
| 31 | 2 | | 2 | | 4 | | 6 | 7 | | 9 | | 12 |

# 1923

**5683/84** תרפ"ג / תרפ"ד

| | January | February | March | April | May | June | July | August | September | October | November | December |
|---|---|---|---|---|---|---|---|---|---|---|---|---|
| 1 | 13 **Tevet** | 15 | 13 Ta'anit Esther | 15 Pesaḥ | 15 | 17 | 17 Fast | 19 | **20** *Ki Tavo* | 21 Hoshana Rabba | 22 | **23** *Va-Yeshev* |
| 2 | 14 | 16 | 14 Purim | 16 Omer | 16 | **18** *Be-Ha'alotkha* | 18 | 20 | 21 | 22 Shemini Aẓeret | 23 | 24 |
| 3 | 15 | **17** *Be-Shallaḥ* | **15** *Teẓavveh* Shushan Purim | 17 Ḥol ha-Mo'ed | 17 | 19 | 19 | 21 | 22 | 23 Simḥat Torah *Ve-Zot Ha-Berakhah* | **24** *Ḥayyei Sarah* | 25 Ḥanukkah 1 |
| 4 | 16 | 18 | 16 | 18 | 18 Lag ba-Omer | 20 | 20 | **22** *Ekev* | 23 | 24 | 25 | 26 2 |
| 5 | 17 | 19 | 17 | 19 | **19** *Emor* | 21 | 21 | 23 | 24 | 25 | 26 | 27 3 |
| 6 | **18** *Va-Yeḥi* | 20 | 18 | 20 | 20 | 22 | 22 | 24 | 25 | **26** *Bereshit* | 27 | 28 4 |
| 7 | 19 | 21 | 19 | **21** Pesaḥ | 21 | 23 | **23** *Pinḥas* | 25 | 26 | 27 | 28 | 29 5 |
| 8 | 20 | 22 | 20 | 22 | 22 | 24 | 24 | 26 | **27** *Niẓẓavim* | 28 | 29 | **30** *Mi-Keẓ* R. Ḥ. 6 |
| 9 | 21 | 23 | 21 | 23 | 23 | **25** *Shelaḥ* | 25 | 27 | 28 | 29 | 1 **Kislev** R. Ḥ. | 1 **Tevet** R. Ḥ. 7 |
| 10 | 22 | **24** *Yitro* | **22** *Ki Tissa* Parah | 24 | 24 | 26 | 26 | 28 | 29 | 30 R. Ḥ. | **2** *Toledot* | 2 8 |
| 11 | 23 | 25 | 23 | 25 | 25 | 27 | 27 | **29** *Re'eh* | 1 **Tishri** Rosh Ha-Shanah | 1 **Ḥeshvan** R. Ḥ. | 3 | 3 |
| 12 | 24 | 26 | 24 | 26 | **26** *Be-Har Be-Ḥukkotai* | 28 | 28 | 30 R. Ḥ. | 2 | 2 | 4 | 4 |
| 13 | **25** *Shemot* | 27 | 25 | 27 | 27 | 29 | 29 | 1 **Elul** R. Ḥ. | 3 Fast | **3** *No'aḥ* | 5 | 5 |
| 14 | 26 | 28 | 26 | **28** *Shemini* | 28 | 30 R. Ḥ. | **1** R. Ḥ. **Av** *Mattot Masei* | 2 | 4 | 4 | 6 | 6 |
| 15 | 27 | 29 | 27 | 29 | 29 | 1 **Tammuz** R. Ḥ. | 2 | 3 | **5** *Va-Yelekh* Shabbat Shuvah | 5 | 7 | **7** *Va-Yiggash* |
| 16 | 28 | 30 R. Ḥ. | 28 | 30 R. Ḥ. | 1 **Sivan** R. Ḥ. | **2** *Koraḥ* | 3 | 4 | 6 | 6 | 8 | 8 |
| 17 | 29 | **1** R. Ḥ. **Adar** *Mishpatim* Shekalim | **29** *Va-Yakhel Pekudei* Ha-Ḥodesh | 1 **Iyyar** R. Ḥ. | 2 | 3 | 4 | 5 | 7 | 7 | **9** *Va-Yeẓe* | 9 |
| 18 | 1 **Shevat** R. Ḥ. | 2 | 1 **Nisan** R. Ḥ. | 2 | 3 | 4 | 5 | **6** *Shofetim* | 8 | 8 | 10 | 10 Fast |
| 19 | 2 | 3 | 2 | 3 | **4** *Be-Midbar* | 5 | 6 | 7 | 9 | 9 | 11 | 11 |
| 20 | **3** *Va-Era* | 4 | 3 | 4 | 5 | 6 | 7 | 8 | 10 Yom Kippur | **10** *Lekh Lekha* | 12 | 12 |
| 21 | 4 | 5 | 4 | **5** *Tazri'a Meẓora* | 6 Shavuot | 7 | **8** *Devarim* | 9 | 11 | 11 | 13 | 13 |
| 22 | 5 | 6 | 5 | 6 | 7 | 8 | 9 Tishah be-Av | 10 | **12** *Ha'azinu* | 12 | 14 | **14** *Va-Yeḥi* |
| 23 | 6 | 7 | 6 | 7 | 8 | **9** *Ḥukkat* | 10 | 11 | 13 | 13 | 15 | 15 |
| 24 | 7 | **8** *Terumah* Zakhor | **7** *Va-Yikra* | 8 | 9 | 10 | 11 | 12 | 14 | 14 | **16** *Va-Yishlaḥ* | 16 |
| 25 | 8 | 9 | 8 | 9 | 10 | 11 | 12 | **13** *Ki Teẓe* | 15 Sukkot | 15 | 17 | 17 |
| 26 | 9 | 10 | 9 | 10 | **11** *Naso* | 12 | 13 | 14 | 16 | 16 | 18 | 18 |
| 27 | **10** *Bo* | 11 | 10 | 11 | 12 | 13 | 14 | 15 | 17 Ḥol ha-Mo'ed | **17** *Va-Yera* | 19 | 19 |
| 28 | 11 | 12 | 11 | **12** *Aḥarei Mot Kedoshim* | 13 | 14 | **15** *Va-Etḥannan* | 16 | 18 | 18 | 20 | 20 |
| 29 | 12 | | 12 | 13 | 14 | 15 | 16 | 17 | **19** | 19 | 21 | **21** *Shemot* |
| 30 | 13 | | 13 | 14 | 15 | **16** *Balak* | 17 | 18 | 20 | 20 | 22 | 22 |
| 31 | 14 | | **14** *Ẓav* Shabbat ha-Gadol | | 16 | | 18 | 19 | | 21 | | 23 |

# 1924

**5684/85** תרפ"ד / תרפ"ה

| | January | February | March | April | May | June | July | August | September | October | November | December |
|---|---|---|---|---|---|---|---|---|---|---|---|---|
| 1 | 24 **Tevet** | 26 | **25** *Va-Yakhel* Shekalim | 26 | 27 | 28 | 29 | 1 **Av** R. Ḥ. | 2 | 3 Fast | **4** *No'aḥ* | 4 |
| 2 | 25 | **27** *Mishpatim* | 26 | 27 | 28 | 29 | 30 R. Ḥ. | **2** *Mattot Masei* | 3 | 4 | 5 | 5 |
| 3 | 26 | 28 | 27 | 28 | **29** *Aḥarei Mot* | 1 **Sivan** R. Ḥ. | 1 **Tammuz** R. Ḥ. | 3 | 4 | 5 | 6 | 6 |
| 4 | 27 | 29 | 28 | 29 | 30 R. Ḥ. | 2 | 2 | 4 | 5 | **6** *Va-Yelekh* Shabbat Shuvah | 7 | 7 |
| 5 | **28** *Va-Era* | 30 R. Ḥ. | 29 | **1** R. Ḥ. **Nisan** *Tazri'a* Ha-Ḥodesh | 1 **Iyyar** R. Ḥ. | 3 | **3** *Koraḥ* | 5 | 6 | 7 | 8 | 8 |
| 6 | 29 | 1 **Adar I** R. Ḥ. | 30 R. Ḥ. | 2 | 2 | 4 | 4 | 6 | **7** *Shofetim* | 8 | 9 | **9** *Va-Yeẓe* |
| 7 | 1 **Shevat** R. Ḥ. | 2 | 1 **Adar II** R. Ḥ. | 3 | 3 | **5** *Be-Midbar* | 5 | 7 | 8 | 9 | 10 | 10 |
| 8 | 2 | 3 | **2** *Pekudei* | 4 | 4 | 6 Shavuot | 6 | 8 | 9 | 10 Yom Kippur | **11** *Lekh Lekha* | 11 |
| 9 | 3 | **4** *Terumah* | 3 | 5 | 5 | 7 | 7 | **9** *Devarim* Tishah be-Av | 10 | 11 | 12 | 12 |
| 10 | 4 | 5 | 4 | 6 | **6** *Kedoshim* | 8 | 8 | 10 Fast | 11 | 12 | 13 | 13 |
| 11 | 5 | 6 | 5 | 7 | 7 | 9 | 9 | 11 | 12 | **13** *Ha'azinu* | 14 | 14 |
| 12 | **6** *Bo* | 7 | 6 | **8** *Meẓora* Shabbat ha-Gadol | 8 | 10 | **10** *Ḥukkat* | 12 | 13 | 14 | 15 | 15 |
| 13 | 7 | 8 | 7 | 9 | 9 | 11 | 11 | 13 | **14** *Ki Teẓe* | 15 Sukkot | 16 | **16** *Va-Yishlaḥ* |
| 14 | 8 | 9 | 8 | 10 | 10 | **12** *Naso* | 12 | 14 | 15 | 16 | 17 | 17 |
| 15 | 9 | 10 | **9** *Va-Yikra* Zakhor | 11 | 11 | 13 | 13 | 15 | 16 | 17 Ḥol ha-Mo'ed | **18** *Va-Yera* | 18 |
| 16 | 10 | **11** *Teẓavveh* | 10 | 12 | 12 | 14 | 14 | **16** *Va-Etḥannan* | 17 | 18 | 19 | 19 |
| 17 | 11 | 12 | 11 | 13 | **13** *Emor* | 15 | 15 | 17 | 18 | 19 | 20 | 20 |
| 18 | 12 | 13 | 12 | 14 | 14 | 16 | 16 | 18 | 19 | **20** | 21 | 21 |
| 19 | **13** *Be-Shallaḥ* | 14 | 13 Ta'anit Esther | **15** Pesaḥ | 15 | 17 | **17** *Balak* | 19 | 20 | 21 Hoshana Rabba | 22 | 22 |
| 20 | 14 | 15 | 14 Purim | 16 Omer | 16 | 18 | 18 Fast | 20 | **21** *Ki Tavo* | 22 Shemini Aẓeret | 23 | **23** *Va-Yeshev* |
| 21 | 15 | 16 | 15 Shushan Purim | 17 Ḥol ha-Mo'ed | 17 | **19** *Be-Ha'alotkha* | 19 | 21 | 22 | 23 Simḥat Torah *Ve-Zot Ha-Berakhah* | 24 | 24 |
| 22 | 16 | 17 | **16** *Ẓav* | 18 | 18 Lag ba-Omer | 20 | 20 | 22 | 23 | 24 | **25** *Ḥayyei Sarah* | 25 Ḥanukkah 1 |
| 23 | 17 | **18** *Ki Tissa* | 17 | 19 | 19 | 21 | 21 | **23** *Ekev* | 24 | 25 | 26 | 26 2 |
| 24 | 18 | 19 | 18 | 20 | **20** *Be-Har* | 22 | 22 | 24 | 25 | 26 | 27 | 27 3 |
| 25 | 19 | 20 | 19 | 21 Pesaḥ | 21 | 23 | 23 | 25 | 26 | **27** *Bereshit* | 28 | 28 4 |
| 26 | **20** *Yitro* | 21 | 20 | **22** | 22 | 24 | **24** *Pinḥas* | 26 | 27 | 28 | 29 | 29 5 |
| 27 | 21 | 22 | 21 | 23 | 23 | 25 | 25 | 27 | **28** *Niẓẓavim* | 29 | 30 R. Ḥ. | **30** *Mi-Keẓ* R. Ḥ. 6 |
| 28 | 22 | 23 | 22 | 24 | 24 | **26** *Shelaḥ* | 26 | 28 | 29 | 30 R. Ḥ. | 1 **Kislev** R. Ḥ. | 1 **Tevet** R. Ḥ. 7 |
| 29 | 23 | 24 | **23** *Shemini* Parah | 25 | 25 | 27 | 27 | 29 | 1 **Tishri** Rosh Ha-Shanah | 1 **Ḥeshvan** R. Ḥ. | **2** *Toledot* | 2 8 |
| 30 | 24 | | 24 | 26 | 26 | 28 | 28 | **30** R. Ḥ. *Re'eh* | 2 | 2 | 3 | 3 |
| 31 | 25 | | 25 | | **27** *Be-Ḥukkotai* | | 29 | 1 **Elul** R. Ḥ. | | 3 | | 4 |

## 1925

**5685/86** — תרפ״ה / תרפ״ו

| | January | February | March | April | May | June | July | August | September | October | November | December |
|---|---|---|---|---|---|---|---|---|---|---|---|---|
| 1 | 5 Tevet | 7 | 5 | 7 | 7 | 9 | 9 | 11 *Va-Ethannan* | 12 | 13 | 14 | 14 |
| 2 | 6 | 8 | 6 | 8 | 8 *Aharei Mot Kedoshim* | 10 | 10 | 12 | 13 | 14 | 15 | 15 |
| 3 | 7 *Va-Yiggash* | 9 | 7 | 9 | 9 | 11 | 11 | 13 | 14 | 15 Sukkot | 16 | 16 |
| 4 | 8 | 10 | 8 | 10 *Zav* Shabbat ha-Gadol | 10 | 12 | 12 *Hukkat Balak* | 14 | 15 | 16 | 17 | 17 |
| 5 | 9 | 11 | 9 | 11 | 11 | 13 | 13 | 15 | 16 *Ki Tavo* | 17 | 18 | 18 *Va-Yishlah* |
| 6 | 10 Fast | 12 | 10 | 12 | 12 | 14 *Naso* | 14 | 16 | 17 | 18 Hol ha-Mo'ed | 19 | 19 |
| 7 | 11 | 13 *Be-Shallah* | 11 *Tezavveh* Zakhor | 13 | 13 | 15 | 15 | 17 | 18 | 19 | 20 *Va-Yera* | 20 |
| 8 | 12 | 14 | 12 | 14 | 14 | 16 | 16 | 18 *Ekev* | 19 | 20 | 21 | 21 |
| 9 | 13 | 15 | 13 Ta'anit Esther | 15 Pesah | 15 *Emor* | 17 | 17 Fast | 19 | 20 | 21 Hoshana Rabba | 22 | 22 |
| 10 | 14 *Va-Yehi* | 16 | 14 Purim | 16 Omer | 16 | 18 | 18 | 20 | 21 | 22 Shemini Azeret | 23 | 23 |
| 11 | 15 | 17 | 15 Shushan Purim | 17 | 17 | 19 | 19 *Pinhas* | 21 | 22 | 23 Simhat Torah *Ve-Zot Ha-Berakhah* | 24 | 24 |
| 12 | 16 | 18 | 16 | 18 Hol ha-Mo'ed | 18 Lag ba-Omer | 20 | 20 | 22 | 23 *Nizzavim Va-Yelekh* | 24 | 25 | 25 *Va-Yeshev* Hanukkah 1 |
| 13 | 17 | 19 | 17 | 19 | 19 | 21 *Be-Ha'alotkha* | 21 | 23 | 24 | 25 | 26 | 26 2 |
| 14 | 18 | 20 *Yitro* | 18 *Ki Tissa* Parah | 20 | 20 | 22 | 22 | 24 | 25 | 26 | 27 *Hayyei Sarah* | 27 3 |
| 15 | 19 | 21 | 19 | 21 Pesah | 21 | 23 | 23 | 25 *Re'eh* | 26 | 27 | 28 | 28 4 |
| 16 | 20 | 22 | 20 | 22 | 22 *Be-Har Be-Hukkotai* | 24 | 24 | 26 | 27 | 28 | 29 | 29 5 |
| 17 | 21 *Shemot* | 23 | 21 | 23 | 23 | 25 | 25 | 27 | 28 | 29 *Bereshit* | 30 R. H. | 30 R. H. 6 |
| 18 | 22 | 24 | 22 | 24 *Shemini* | 24 | 26 | 26 *Mattot Masei* | 28 | 29 | 30 R. H. | 1 Kislev R. H. | 1 Tevet R. H. 7 |
| 19 | 23 | 25 | 23 | 25 | 25 | 27 | 27 | 29 | 1 Tishri Rosh Ha-Shanah | 1 Heshvan R. H. | 2 | 2 *Mi-Kez* 8 |
| 20 | 24 | 26 | 24 | 26 | 26 | 28 *Shelah* | 28 | 30 R. H. | 2 | 2 | 3 | 3 |
| 21 | 25 | 27 *Mishpatim* Shekalim | 25 *Va-Yakhel Pekudei* Ha-Hodesh | 27 | 27 | 29 | 29 | 1 Elul R. H. | 3 Fast | 3 | 4 *Toledot* | 4 |
| 22 | 26 | 28 | 26 | 28 | 28 | 30 R. H. | 1 Av R. H. | 2 *Shofetim* | 4 | 4 | 5 | 5 |
| 23 | 27 | 29 | 27 | 29 | 29 *Be-Midbar* | 1 Tammuz R. H. | 2 | 3 | 5 | 5 | 6 | 6 |
| 24 | 28 *Va-Era* | 30 R. H. | 28 | 30 R. H. | 1 Sivan R. H. | 2 | 3 | 4 | 6 | 6 *No'ah* | 7 | 7 |
| 25 | 29 | 1 Adar R. H. | 29 | 1 Iyyar R. H. *Tazri'a Mezora* | 2 | 3 | 4 *Devarim* | 5 | 7 | 7 | 8 | 8 |
| 26 | 1 Shevat R. H. | 2 | 1 Nisan R. H. | 2 | 3 | 4 | 5 | 6 | 8 *Ha'azinu* Shabbat Shuvah | 8 | 9 | 9 *Va-Yiggash* |
| 27 | 2 | 3 | 2 | 3 | 4 | 5 *Korah* | 6 | 7 | 9 | 9 | 10 | 10 Fast |
| 28 | 3 | 4 *Terumah* | 3 *Va-Yikra* | 4 | 5 | 6 | 7 | 8 | 10 Yom Kippur | 10 | 11 *Va-Yeze* | 11 |
| 29 | 4 | | 4 | 5 | 6 Shavuot | 7 | 8 | 9 *Ki Teze* | 11 | 11 | 12 | 12 |
| 30 | 5 | | 5 | 6 | 7 | 8 | 9 Tishah be-Av | 10 | 12 | 12 | 13 | 13 |
| 31 | 6 *Bo* | | 6 | | 8 | | 10 | 11 | | 13 *Lekh Lekha* | | 14 |

## 1926

**5686/87** — תרפ״ו / תרפ״ז

| | January | February | March | April | May | June | July | August | September | October | November | December |
|---|---|---|---|---|---|---|---|---|---|---|---|---|
| 1 | 15 Tevet | 17 | 15 Shushan Purim | 17 | 17 *Emor* | 19 | 19 | 21 | 22 | 23 Simhat Torah *Ve-Zot Ha-Berakhah* | 24 | 25 Hanukkah 1 |
| 2 | 16 *Va-Yehi* | 18 | 16 | 18 Hol ha-Mo'ed | 18 Lag ba-Omer | 20 | 20 | 22 | 23 | 24 *Bereshit* | 25 | 26 2 |
| 3 | 17 | 19 | 17 | 19 | 19 | 21 | 21 *Pinhas* | 23 | 24 | 25 | 26 | 27 3 |
| 4 | 18 | 20 | 18 | 20 | 20 | 22 | 22 | 24 | 25 *Nizzavim Va-Yelekh* | 26 | 27 | 28 *Mi-Kez* 4 |
| 5 | 19 | 21 | 19 | 21 Pesah | 21 | 23 *Shelah* | 23 | 25 | 26 | 27 | 28 | 29 5 |
| 6 | 20 | 22 *Yitro* | 20 *Ki Tissa* Parah | 22 | 22 | 24 | 24 | 26 | 27 | 28 | 29 *Toledot* | 1 Tevet R. H. 6 |
| 7 | 21 | 23 | 21 | 23 | 23 | 25 | 25 | 27 *Re'eh* | 28 | 29 | 1 Kislev R. H. | 2 7 |
| 8 | 22 | 24 | 22 | 24 | 24 *Be-Har Be-Hukkotai* | 26 | 26 | 28 | 29 | 30 R. H. | 2 | 3 8 |
| 9 | 23 *Shemot* | 25 | 23 | 25 | 25 | 27 | 27 | 29 | 1 Tishri Rosh Ha-Shanah | 1 R. H. Heshvan *No'ah* | 3 | 4 |
| 10 | 24 | 26 | 24 | 26 *Shemini* | 26 | 28 | 28 *Mattot Masei* | 30 R. H. | 2 | 2 | 4 | 5 |
| 11 | 25 | 27 | 25 | 27 | 27 | 29 | 29 | 1 Elul R. H. | 3 *Ha'azinu* Shabbat Shuvah | 3 | 5 | 6 *Va-Yiggash* |
| 12 | 26 | 28 | 26 | 28 | 28 | 30 R. H. *Korah* | 1 Av R. H. | 2 | 4 Fast | 4 | 6 | 7 |
| 13 | 27 | 29 *Mishpatim* Shekalim | 27 *Va-Yakhel Pekudei* Ha-Hodesh | 29 | 29 | 1 Tammuz R. H. | 2 | 3 | 5 | 5 | 7 *Va-Yeze* | 8 |
| 14 | 28 | 30 R. H. | 28 | 30 R. H. | 1 Sivan R. H. | 2 | 3 | 4 *Shofetim* | 6 | 6 | 8 | 9 |
| 15 | 29 | 1 Adar R. H. | 29 | 1 Iyyar R. H. | 2 *Be-Midbar* | 3 | 4 | 5 | 7 | 7 | 9 | 10 Fast |
| 16 | 1 Shevat R. H. *Va-Era* | 2 | 1 Nisan R. H. | 2 | 3 | 4 | 5 | 6 | 8 | 8 *Lekh Lekha* | 10 | 11 |
| 17 | 2 | 3 | 2 | 3 *Tazri'a Mezora* | 4 | 5 | 6 *Devarim* | 7 | 9 | 9 | 11 | 12 |
| 18 | 3 | 4 | 3 | 4 | 5 | 6 | 7 | 8 | 10 Yom Kippur | 10 | 12 | 13 *Va-Yehi* |
| 19 | 4 | 5 | 4 | 5 | 6 Shavuot | 7 *Hukkat* | 8 | 9 | 11 | 11 | 13 | 14 |
| 20 | 5 | 6 *Terumah* | 5 *Va-Yikra* | 6 | 7 | 8 | 9 Tishah be-Av | 10 | 12 | 12 | 14 *Va-Yishlah* | 15 |
| 21 | 6 | 7 | 6 | 7 | 8 | 9 | 10 | 11 *Ki Teze* | 13 | 13 | 15 | 16 |
| 22 | 7 | 8 | 7 | 8 | 9 *Naso* | 10 | 11 | 12 | 14 | 14 | 16 | 17 |
| 23 | 8 *Bo* | 9 | 8 | 9 | 10 | 11 | 12 | 13 | 15 Sukkot | 15 *Va-Yera* | 17 | 18 |
| 24 | 9 | 10 | 9 | 10 *Aharei Mot Kedoshim* | 11 | 12 | 13 *Va-Ethannan* | 14 | 16 | 16 | 18 | 19 |
| 25 | 10 | 11 Ta'anit Esther | 10 | 11 | 12 | 13 | 14 | 15 | 17 | 17 | 19 | 20 *Shemot* |
| 26 | 11 | 12 | 11 | 12 | 13 | 14 *Balak* | 15 | 16 | 18 Hol ha-Mo'ed | 18 | 20 | 21 |
| 27 | 12 | 13 *Tezavveh* Zakhor | 12 *Zav* Shabbat ha-Gadol | 13 | 14 | 15 | 16 | 17 | 19 | 19 | 21 *Va-Yeshev* | 22 |
| 28 | 13 | 14 Purim | 13 | 14 | 15 | 16 | 17 | 18 *Ki Tavo* | 20 | 20 | 22 | 23 |
| 29 | 14 | | 14 | 15 | 16 *Be-Ha'alotkha* | 17 Fast | 18 | 19 | 21 Hoshana Rabba | 21 | 23 | 24 |
| 30 | 15 *Be-Shallah* | | 15 Pesah | 16 | 17 | 18 | 19 | 20 | 22 Shemini Azeret | 22 *Hayyei Sarah* | 24 | 25 |
| 31 | 16 | | 16 Omer | | 18 | | 20 *Ekev* | 21 | | 23 | | 26 |

## 1927

**5687/88** תרפ״ז / תרפ״ח

| | January | February | March | April | May | June | July | August | September | October | November | December |
|---|---|---|---|---|---|---|---|---|---|---|---|---|
| 1 | 27 Tevet Va-Era | 29 | 27 | 28 | 29 | 1 Sivan R. H. | 1 Tammuz R. H. | 3 | 4 | 5 Va-Yelekh Shabbat Shuvah | 6 | 7 |
| 2 | 28 | 30 R. H. | 28 | 29 Tazri'a Ha-Ḥodesh | 30 R. H. | 2 | 2 Ḥukkat | 4 | 5 | 6 | 7 | 8 |
| 3 | 29 | 1 Adar I R. H. | 29 | 1 Nisan R. H. | 1 Iyyar R. H. | 3 | 3 | 5 | 6 Shofetim | 7 | 8 | 9 Va-Yeẓe |
| 4 | 1 Shevat R. H. | 2 | 30 R. H. | 2 | 2 | 4 Naso | 4 | 6 | 7 | 8 | 9 | 10 |
| 5 | 2 | 3 Terumah | 1 R. H. Adar II Pekudei Shekalim | 3 | 3 | 5 | 5 | 7 | 8 | 9 | 10 Lekh Lekha | 11 |
| 6 | 3 | 4 | 2 | 4 | 4 | 6 Shavuot | 6 | 8 Devarim | 9 | 10 Yom Kippur | 11 | 12 |
| 7 | 4 | 5 | 3 | 5 | 5 Emor | 7 | 7 | 9 Tishah be-Av | 10 | 11 | 12 | 13 |
| 8 | 5 Bo | 6 | 4 | 6 | 6 | 8 | 8 | 10 | 11 | 12 Ha'azinu | 13 | 14 |
| 9 | 6 | 7 | 5 | 7 Meẓora | 7 | 9 | 9 Balak | 11 | 12 | 13 | 14 | 15 |
| 10 | 7 | 8 | 6 | 8 | 8 | 10 | 10 | 12 | 13 Ki Teẓe | 14 | 15 | 16 Va-Yishlaḥ |
| 11 | 8 | 9 | 7 | 9 | 9 | 11 Be-Ha'alotkha | 11 | 13 | 14 | 15 Sukkot | 16 | 17 |
| 12 | 9 | 10 Teẓavveh | 8 Va-Yikra Zakhor | 10 | 10 | 12 | 12 | 14 | 15 | 16 | 17 Va-Yera | 18 |
| 13 | 10 | 11 | 9 | 11 | 11 | 13 | 13 | 15 Va-Etḥannan | 16 | 17 Ḥol ha-Mo'ed | 18 | 19 |
| 14 | 11 | 12 | 10 | 12 | 12 Be-Har | 14 | 14 | 16 | 17 | 18 | 19 | 20 |
| 15 | 12 Be-Shallaḥ | 13 | 11 | 13 | 13 | 15 | 15 | 17 | 18 | 19 | 20 | 21 |
| 16 | 13 | 14 | 12 | 14 Aḥarei Mot Shabbat ha-Gadol | 14 | 16 | 16 Pinḥas | 18 | 19 | 20 | 21 | 22 |
| 17 | 14 | 15 | 13 Ta'anit Esther | 15 Pesaḥ | 15 | 17 | 17 Fast | 19 | 20 Ki Tavo | 21 Hoshana Rabba | 22 | 23 Va-Yeshev |
| 18 | 15 | 16 | 14 Purim | 16 Omer | 16 | 18 Shelaḥ | 18 | 20 | 21 | 22 Shemini Aẓeret | 23 | 24 |
| 19 | 16 | 17 Ki Tissa | 15 Ẓav Shushan Purim | 17 Ḥol ha-Mo'ed | 17 | 19 | 19 | 21 | 22 | 23 Simḥat Torah Ve-Zot Ha-Berakhah | 24 Ḥayyei Sarah | 25 Ḥanukkah 1 |
| 20 | 17 | 18 | 16 | 18 | 18 Lag ba-Omer | 20 | 20 | 22 Ekev | 23 | 24 | 25 | 26 2 |
| 21 | 18 | 19 | 17 | 19 | 19 Be-Ḥukkotai | 21 | 21 | 23 | 24 | 25 | 26 | 27 3 |
| 22 | 19 Yitro | 20 | 18 | 20 | 20 | 22 | 22 | 24 | 25 | 26 Bereshit | 27 | 28 4 |
| 23 | 20 | 21 | 19 | 21 Pesaḥ | 21 | 23 | 23 Mattot | 25 | 26 | 27 | 28 | 29 5 |
| 24 | 21 | 22 | 20 | 22 | 22 | 24 | 24 | 26 | 27 Niẓẓavim | 28 | 29 | 30 R. H. Mi-Keẓ 6 |
| 25 | 22 | 23 | 21 | 23 | 23 | 25 Koraḥ | 25 | 27 | 28 | 29 | 1 Kislev R. H. | 1 Tevet R. H. 7 |
| 26 | 23 | 24 Va-Yakhel | 22 Shemini Parah | 24 | 24 | 26 | 26 | 28 | 29 | 30 R. H. | 2 Toledot | 2 8 |
| 27 | 24 | 25 | 23 | 25 | 25 | 27 | 27 | 29 Re'eh | 1 Tishri Rosh Ha-Shanah | 1 Ḥeshvan R. H. | 3 | 3 |
| 28 | 25 | 26 | 24 | 26 | 26 Be-Midbar | 28 | 28 | 30 R. H. | 2 | 2 | 4 | 4 |
| 29 | 26 Mishpatim | | 25 | 27 | 27 | 29 | 29 | 1 Elul R. H. | 3 Fast | 3 No'aḥ | 5 | 5 |
| 30 | 27 | | 26 | 28 Kedoshim | 28 | 30 R. H. | 1 R. H. Av Masei | 2 | 4 | 4 | 6 | 6 |
| 31 | 28 | | 27 | | 29 | | 2 | 3 | | 5 | | 7 Va-Yiggash |

## 1928

**5688/89** תרפ״ח / תרפ״ט

| | January | February | March | April | May | June | July | August | September | October | November | December |
|---|---|---|---|---|---|---|---|---|---|---|---|---|
| 1 | 8 Tevet | 10 | 9 | 11 | 11 | 13 | 13 | 15 | 16 Ki Tavo | 17 | 18 | 18 Va-Yishlaḥ |
| 2 | 9 | 11 | 10 | 12 | 12 | 14 Naso | 14 | 16 | 17 | 18 | 19 | 19 |
| 3 | 10 Fast | 12 | 11 Teẓavveh Zakhor | 13 | 13 | 15 | 15 | 17 | 18 | 19 Ḥol ha-Mo'ed | 20 Va-Yera | 20 |
| 4 | 11 | 13 Be-Shallaḥ | 12 | 14 | 14 | 16 | 16 | 18 Ekev | 19 | 20 | 21 | 21 |
| 5 | 12 | 14 | 13 Ta'anit Esther | 15 Pesaḥ | 15 Emor | 17 | 17 Fast | 19 | 20 | 21 Hoshana Rabba | 22 | 22 |
| 6 | 13 | 15 | 14 Purim | 16 Omer | 16 | 18 | 18 | 20 | 21 | 22 Shemini Aẓeret | 23 | 23 |
| 7 | 14 Va-Yeḥi | 16 | 15 Shushan Purim | 17 Ḥol ha-Mo'ed | 17 | 19 | 19 Pinḥas | 21 | 22 | 23 Simḥat Torah Ve-Zot Ha-Berakhah | 24 | 24 |
| 8 | 15 | 17 | 16 | 18 | 18 Lag ba-Omer | 20 | 20 | 22 | 23 Niẓẓavim Va-Yelekh | 24 | 25 | 25 Va-Yeshev Ḥanukkah 1 |
| 9 | 16 | 18 | 17 | 19 | 19 | 21 Be-Ha'alotkha | 21 | 23 | 24 | 25 | 26 | 26 2 |
| 10 | 17 | 19 | 18 Ki Tissa Parah | 20 | 20 | 22 | 22 | 24 | 25 | 26 | 27 Ḥayyei Sarah | 27 3 |
| 11 | 18 | 20 Yitro | 19 | 21 Pesaḥ | 21 | 23 | 23 | 25 Re'eh | 26 | 27 | 28 | 28 4 |
| 12 | 19 | 21 | 20 | 22 | 22 Be-Har Be-Ḥukkotai | 24 | 24 | 26 | 27 | 28 | 29 | 29 5 |
| 13 | 20 | 22 | 21 | 23 | 23 | 25 | 25 | 27 | 28 | 29 Bereshit | 30 R. H. | 30 R. H. 6 |
| 14 | 21 Shemot | 23 | 22 | 24 Shemini | 24 | 26 | 26 Mattot Masei | 28 | 29 | 30 R. H. | 1 Kislev R. H. | 1 Tevet R. H. 7 |
| 15 | 22 | 24 | 23 | 25 | 25 | 27 | 27 | 29 | 1 Tishri Rosh Ha-Shanah | 1 Ḥeshvan R. H. | 2 | 2 Mi-Keẓ 8 |
| 16 | 23 | 25 | 24 | 26 | 26 | 28 Shelaḥ | 28 | 30 R. H. | 2 | 2 | 3 | 3 |
| 17 | 24 | 26 | 25 Va-Yakhel Pekudei Ha-Ḥodesh | 27 | 27 | 29 | 29 | 1 Elul R. H. | 3 Fast | 3 | 4 Toledot | 4 |
| 18 | 25 | 27 Mishpatim Shekalim | 26 | 28 | 28 | 30 R. H. | 1 Av R. H. | 2 Shofetim | 4 | 4 | 5 | 5 |
| 19 | 26 | 28 | 27 | 29 | 29 Be-Midbar | 1 Tammuz R. H. | 2 | 3 | 5 | 5 | 6 | 6 |
| 20 | 27 | 29 | 28 | 30 R. H. | 1 Sivan R. H. | 2 | 3 | 4 | 6 | 6 No'aḥ | 7 | 7 |
| 21 | 28 Va-Era | 30 R. H. | 29 | 1 R. H. Iyyar Tazri'a Meẓora | 2 | 3 | 4 Devarim | 5 | 7 | 7 | 8 | 8 |
| 22 | 29 | 1 Adar R. H. | 1 Nisan R. H. | 2 | 3 | 4 | 5 | 6 | 8 Ha'azinu Shabbat Shuvah | 8 | 9 | 9 Va-Yiggash |
| 23 | 1 Shevat R. H. | 2 | 2 | 3 | 4 | 5 Koraḥ | 6 | 7 | 9 | 9 | 10 | 10 Fast |
| 24 | 2 | 3 | 3 Va-Yikra | 4 | 5 | 6 | 7 | 8 | 10 Yom Kippur | 10 | 11 Va-Yeẓe | 11 |
| 25 | 3 | 4 Terumah | 4 | 5 | 6 Shavuot | 7 | 8 | 9 Ki Teẓe | 11 | 11 | 12 | 12 |
| 26 | 4 | 5 | 5 | 6 | 7 | 8 | 9 Tishah be-Av | 10 | 12 | 12 | 13 | 13 |
| 27 | 5 | 6 | 6 | 7 | 8 | 9 | 10 | 11 | 13 | 13 Lekh Lekha | 14 | 14 |
| 28 | 6 Bo | 7 | 7 | 8 Aḥarei Mot Kedoshim | 9 | 10 | 11 Va-Etḥannan | 12 | 14 | 14 | 15 | 15 |
| 29 | 7 | 8 | 8 | 9 | 10 | 11 | 12 | 13 | 15 Sukkot | 15 | 16 | 16 Va-Yeḥi |
| 30 | 8 | | 9 | 10 | 11 | 12 Ḥukkat Balak | 13 | 14 | 16 | 16 | 17 | 17 |
| 31 | 9 | | 10 Ẓav Shabbat ha-Gadol | | 12 | | 14 | 15 | | 17 | | 18 |

# 1929

**5689/90** תרפ״ט / תר״צ

| | January | February | March | April | May | June | July | August | September | October | November | December |
|---|---|---|---|---|---|---|---|---|---|---|---|---|
| 1 | 19 Tevet | 21 | 19 | 20 | 21 Pesah | 22 Be-Hukkotai | 23 | 24 | 26 | 26 | 28 | 28 |
| 2 | 20 | 22 Yitro | 20 Ki Tissa | 21 | 22 | 23 | 24 | 25 | 27 | 27 | 29 Bereshit | 29 |
| 3 | 21 | 23 | 21 | 22 | 23 | 24 | 25 | 26 Mattot Masei | 28 | 28 | 30 R. H. | 1 Kislev R. H. |
| 4 | 22 | 24 | 22 | 23 | 24 Aharei Mot | 25 | 26 | 27 | 29 | 29 | 1 Heshvan R. H. | 2 |
| 5 | 23 Shemot | 25 | 23 | 24 | 25 | 26 | 27 | 28 | 30 R. H. | 1 Tishri Rosh Ha-Shanah | 2 | 3 |
| 6 | 24 | 26 | 24 | 25 Shemini Ha-Hodesh | 26 | 27 | 28 Shelah | 29 | 1 Elul R. H. | 2 | 3 | 4 |
| 7 | 25 | 27 | 25 | 26 | 27 | 28 | 29 | 1 Av R. H. | 2 Shofetim | 3 Fast | 4 | 5 Toledot |
| 8 | 26 | 28 | 26 | 27 | 28 | 29 Be-Midbar | 30 R. H. | 2 | 3 | 4 | 5 | 6 |
| 9 | 27 | 29 Mishpatim | 27 Va-Yakhel Shekalim | 28 | 29 | 1 Sivan R. H. | 1 Tammuz R. H. | 3 | 4 | 5 | 6 No'ah | 7 |
| 10 | 28 | 30 R. H. | 28 | 29 | 30 R. H. | 2 | 2 | 4 Devarim | 5 | 6 | 7 | 8 |
| 11 | 29 | 1 Adar I R. H. | 29 | 1 Nisan R. H. | 1 Iyyar R. H. Kedoshim | 3 | 3 | 5 | 6 | 7 | 8 | 9 |
| 12 | 1 Shevat R. H. Va-Era | 2 | 30 R. H. | 2 | 2 | 4 | 4 | 6 | 7 | 8 Ha'azinu Shabbat Shuvah | 9 | 10 |
| 13 | 2 | 3 | 1 Adar II R. H. | 3 Tazri'a | 3 | 5 | 5 Korah | 7 | 8 | 9 | 10 | 11 |
| 14 | 3 | 4 | 2 | 4 | 4 | 6 Shavuot | 6 | 8 | 9 Ki Teze | 10 Yom Kippur | 11 | 12 Va-Yeze |
| 15 | 4 | 5 | 3 | 5 | 5 | 7 | 7 | 9 Tishah be-Av | 10 | 11 | 12 | 13 |
| 16 | 5 | 6 Terumah | 4 Pekudei | 6 | 6 | 8 | 8 | 10 | 11 | 12 | 13 Lekh Lekha | 14 |
| 17 | 6 | 7 | 5 | 7 | 7 | 9 | 9 | 11 Va-Ethannan | 12 | 13 | 14 | 15 |
| 18 | 7 | 8 | 6 | 8 | 8 Emor | 10 | 10 | 12 | 13 | 14 | 15 | 16 |
| 19 | 8 Bo | 9 | 7 | 9 | 9 | 11 | 11 | 13 | 14 | 15 Sukkot | 16 | 17 |
| 20 | 9 | 10 | 8 | 10 Mezora Shabbat ha-Gadol | 10 | 12 | 12 Hukkat Balak | 14 | 15 | 16 | 17 | 18 |
| 21 | 10 | 11 | 9 | 11 | 11 | 13 | 13 | 15 | 16 Ki Tavo | 17 Hol ha-Mo'ed | 18 | 19 Va-Yishlah |
| 22 | 11 | 12 | 10 | 12 | 12 | 14 Naso | 14 | 16 | 17 | 18 | 19 | 20 |
| 23 | 12 | 13 Tezavveh | 11 Va-Yikra Zakhor | 13 | 13 | 15 | 15 | 17 | 18 | 19 | 20 Va-Yera | 21 |
| 24 | 13 | 14 | 12 | 14 | 14 | 16 | 16 | 18 Ekev | 19 | 20 | 21 | 22 |
| 25 | 14 | 15 | 13 Ta'anit Esther | 15 Pesah | 15 Be-Har | 17 | 17 Fast | 19 | 20 | 21 Hoshana Rabba | 22 | 23 |
| 26 | 15 Be-Shallah | 16 | 14 Purim | 16 Omer | 16 | 18 | 18 | 20 | 21 | 22 Shemini Azeret | 23 | 24 |
| 27 | 16 | 17 | 15 Shushan Purim | 17 Hol ha-Mo'ed | 17 | 19 | 19 Pinhas | 21 | 22 | 23 Simhat Torah Ve-Zot Ha-Berakhah | 24 | 25 Hanukkah 1 |
| 28 | 17 | 18 | 16 | 18 | 18 Lag ba-Omer | 20 | 20 | 22 | 23 Nizzavim Va-Yelekh | 24 | 25 | 26 Va-Yeshev 2 |
| 29 | 18 | | 17 | 19 | 19 | 21 Be-Ha'alotkha | 21 | 23 | 24 | 25 | 26 | 27 3 |
| 30 | 19 | | 18 Zav Parah | 20 | 20 | 22 | 22 | 24 | 25 | 26 | 27 Hayyei Sarah | 28 4 |
| 31 | 20 | | 19 | | 21 | | 23 | 25 Re'eh | | 27 | | 29 5 |

# 1930

**5690/91** תר״צ / תרצ״א

| | January | February | March | April | May | June | July | August | September | October | November | December |
|---|---|---|---|---|---|---|---|---|---|---|---|---|
| 1 | 1 Tevet R. H. Hanukkah 6 | 3 Va-Era | 1 Adar R. H. Mishpatim Shekalim | 3 | 3 | 5 | 5 | 7 | 8 | 9 | 10 Lekh Lekha | 11 |
| 2 | 2 7 | 4 | 2 | 4 | 4 | 6 Shavuot | 6 | 8 Devarim | 9 | 10 Yom Kippur | 11 | 12 |
| 3 | 3 8 | 5 | 3 | 5 | 5 Tazri'a Mezora | 7 | 7 | 9 Tishah be-Av | 10 | 11 | 12 | 13 |
| 4 | 4 Mi-Kez | 6 | 4 | 6 | 6 | 8 | 8 | 10 | 11 | 12 Ha'azinu | 13 | 14 |
| 5 | 5 | 7 | 5 | 7 Va-Yikra | 7 | 9 | 9 Hukkat | 11 | 12 | 13 | 14 | 15 |
| 6 | 6 | 8 | 6 | 8 | 8 | 10 | 10 | 12 | 13 Ki Teze | 14 | 15 | 16 Va-Yishlah |
| 7 | 7 | 9 | 7 | 9 | 9 | 11 Naso | 11 | 13 | 14 | 15 Sukkot | 16 | 17 |
| 8 | 8 | 10 Bo | 8 Terumah Zakhor | 10 | 10 | 12 | 12 | 14 | 15 | 16 | 17 Va-Yera | 18 |
| 9 | 9 | 11 | 9 | 11 | 11 | 13 | 13 | 15 Va-Ethannan | 16 | 17 Hol ha-Mo'ed | 18 | 19 |
| 10 | 10 Fast | 12 | 10 | 12 | 12 Aharei Mot Kedoshim | 14 | 14 | 16 | 17 | 18 | 19 | 20 |
| 11 | 11 Va-Yiggash | 13 | 11 | 13 | 13 | 15 | 15 | 17 | 18 | 19 | 20 | 21 |
| 12 | 12 | 14 | 12 | 14 Zav Shabbat ha-Gadol | 14 | 16 | 16 Balak | 18 | 19 | 20 | 21 | 22 |
| 13 | 13 | 15 | 13 Ta'anit Esther | 15 Pesah | 15 | 17 | 17 Fast | 19 | 20 Ki Tavo | 21 Hoshana Rabba | 22 | 23 Va-Yeshev |
| 14 | 14 | 16 | 14 Purim | 16 Omer | 16 | 18 Be-Ha'alotkha | 18 | 20 | 21 | 22 Shemini Azeret | 23 | 24 |
| 15 | 15 | 17 Be-Shallah | 15 Shushan Purim Tezavveh | 17 Hol ha-Mo'ed | 17 | 19 | 19 | 21 | 22 | 23 Simhat Torah Ve-Zot Ha-Berakhah | 24 Hayyei Sarah | 25 Hanukkah 1 |
| 16 | 16 | 18 | 16 | 18 | 18 Lag ba-Omer | 20 | 20 | 22 Ekev | 23 | 24 | 25 | 26 2 |
| 17 | 17 | 19 | 17 | 19 | 19 Emor | 21 | 21 | 23 | 24 | 25 | 26 | 27 3 |
| 18 | 18 Va-Yehi | 20 | 18 | 20 | 20 | 22 | 22 | 24 | 25 | 26 Bereshit | 27 | 28 4 |
| 19 | 19 | 21 | 19 | 21 Pesah | 21 | 23 | 23 Pinhas | 25 | 26 | 27 | 28 | 29 5 |
| 20 | 20 | 22 | 20 | 22 | 22 | 24 | 24 | 26 | 27 Nizzavim | 28 | 29 | 30 R. H. Mi-Kez 6 |
| 21 | 21 | 23 | 21 | 23 | 23 | 25 Shelah | 25 | 27 | 28 | 29 | 1 Kislev R. H. | 1 Tevet R. H. 7 |
| 22 | 22 | 24 Yitro | 22 Ki Tissa Parah | 24 | 24 | 26 | 26 | 28 | 29 | 30 R. H. | 2 Toledot | 2 8 |
| 23 | 23 | 25 | 23 | 25 | 25 | 27 | 27 | 29 Re'eh | 1 Tishri Rosh Ha-Shanah | 1 Heshvan R. H. | 3 | 3 |
| 24 | 24 | 26 | 24 | 26 | 26 Be-Har Be-Hukkotai | 28 | 28 | 30 R. H. | 2 | 2 | 4 | 4 |
| 25 | 25 Shemot | 27 | 25 | 27 | 27 | 29 | 29 | 1 Elul R. H. | 3 Fast | 3 No'ah | 5 | 5 |
| 26 | 26 | 28 | 26 | 28 Shemini | 28 | 30 R. H. | 1 Av R. H. Mattot Masei | 2 | 4 | 4 | 6 | 6 |
| 27 | 27 | 29 | 27 | 29 | 29 | 1 Tammuz R. H. | 2 | 3 | 5 Va-Yelekh Shabbat Shuvah | 5 | 7 | 7 Va-Yiggash |
| 28 | 28 | 30 R. H. | 28 | 30 R. H. | 1 Sivan R. H. | 2 Korah | 3 | 4 | 6 | 6 | 8 | 8 |
| 29 | 29 | | 29 Va-Yakhel Pekudei Ha-Hodesh | 1 Iyyar R. H. | 2 | 3 | 4 | 5 | 7 | 7 | 9 Va-Yeze | 9 |
| 30 | 1 Shevat R. H. | | 1 Nisan R. H. | 2 | 3 | 4 | 5 | 6 Shofetim | 8 | 8 | 10 | 10 Fast |
| 31 | 2 | | 2 | | 4 Be-Midbar | | 6 | 7 | | 9 | | 11 |

# 1931

**5691/92** תרצ״א / תרצ״ב

| | January | February | March | April | May | June | July | August | September | October | November | December |
|---|---|---|---|---|---|---|---|---|---|---|---|---|
| 1 | 12 Tevet | 14 | 12 | 14 | 14 | 16 | 16 | 18 Ekev | 19 | 20 Ḥol ha-Mo'ed | 21 | 21 |
| 2 | 13 | 15 | 13 Ta'anit Esther | 15 Pesaḥ | 15 Emor | 17 | 17 Fast | 19 | 20 | 21 Hoshana Rabba | 22 | 22 |
| 3 | 14 Va-Yeḥi | 16 | 14 Purim | 16 Omer | 16 | 18 | 18 | 20 | 21 | 22 Shemini Aẓeret | 23 | 23 |
| 4 | 15 | 17 | 15 Shushan Purim | 17 Ḥol ha-Mo'ed | 17 | 19 | 19 Pinḥas | 21 | 22 | 23 Simḥat Torah Ve-Ẓot Ha-Berakhah | 24 | 24 |
| 5 | 16 | 18 | 16 | 18 | 18 Lag ba-Omer | 20 | 20 | 22 | 23 Niẓẓavim Va-Yelekh | 24 | 25 | 25 Va-Yeshev Ḥanukkah 1 |
| 6 | 17 | 19 | 17 | 19 | 19 | 21 Be-Ha'alotkha | 21 | 23 | 24 | 25 | 26 | 26 2 |
| 7 | 18 | 20 Yitro | 18 Ki Tissa Parah | 20 | 20 | 22 | 22 | 24 | 25 | 26 | 27 Ḥayyei Sarah | 27 3 |
| 8 | 19 | 21 | 19 | 21 Pesaḥ | 21 | 23 | 23 | 25 Re'eh | 26 | 27 | 28 | 28 4 |
| 9 | 20 | 22 | 20 | 22 | 22 Be-Har Be-Ḥukkotai | 24 | 24 | 26 | 27 | 28 | 29 | 29 5 |
| 10 | 21 Shemot | 23 | 21 | 23 | 23 | 25 | 25 | 27 | 28 | 29 Bereshit | 30 R. Ḥ. | 30 R. Ḥ. 6 |
| 11 | 22 | 24 | 22 | 24 Shemini | 24 | 26 | 26 Mattot Masei | 28 | 29 | 30 R. Ḥ. | 1 Kislev R. Ḥ. | 1 Tevet R. Ḥ. 7 |
| 12 | 23 | 25 | 23 | 25 | 25 | 27 | 27 | 29 | 1 Tishri Rosh Ha-Shanah | 1 Heshvan R. Ḥ. | 2 | 2 Mi-Keẓ 8 |
| 13 | 24 | 26 | 24 | 26 | 26 | 28 Shelaḥ | 28 | 30 R. Ḥ. | 2 | 2 | 3 | 3 |
| 14 | 25 | 27 Mishpatim Shekalim | 25 Va-Yakhel Pekudei Ha-Ḥodesh | 27 | 27 | 29 | 29 | 1 Elul R. Ḥ. | 3 Fast | 3 | 4 Toledot | 4 |
| 15 | 26 | 28 | 26 | 28 | 28 | 30 R. Ḥ. | 1 Av R. Ḥ. | 2 Shofetim | 4 | 4 | 5 | 5 |
| 16 | 27 | 29 | 27 | 29 | 29 Be-Midbar | 1 Tammuz R. Ḥ. | 2 | 3 | 5 | 5 | 6 | 6 |
| 17 | 28 Va-Era | 30 R. Ḥ. | 28 | 30 R. Ḥ. | 1 Sivan R. Ḥ. | 2 | 3 | 4 | 6 | 6 No'aḥ | 7 | 7 |
| 18 | 29 | 1 Adar R. Ḥ. | 29 | 1 Iyyar R. Ḥ. Tazri'a Mezora | 2 | 3 | 4 Devarim | 5 | 7 | 7 | 8 | 8 |
| 19 | 1 Shevat R. Ḥ. | 2 | 1 Nisan R. Ḥ. | 2 | 3 | 4 | 5 | 6 | 8 Ha'azinu Shabbat Shuvah | 8 | 9 | 9 Va-Yiggash |
| 20 | 2 | 3 | 2 | 3 | 4 | 5 Koraḥ | 6 | 7 | 9 | 9 | 10 | 10 Fast |
| 21 | 3 | 4 Terumah | 3 Va-Yikra | 4 | 5 | 6 | 7 | 8 | 10 Yom Kippur | 10 | 11 Va-Yeẓe | 11 |
| 22 | 4 | 5 | 4 | 5 | 6 Shavuot | 7 | 8 | 9 Ki Teẓe | 11 | 11 | 12 | 12 |
| 23 | 5 | 6 | 5 | 6 | 7 | 8 | 9 Tishah be-Av | 10 | 12 | 12 | 13 | 13 |
| 24 | 6 Bo | 7 | 6 | 7 | 8 | 9 | 10 | 11 | 13 | 13 Lekh Lekha | 14 | 14 |
| 25 | 7 | 8 | 7 | 8 Aḥarei Mot Kedoshim | 9 | 10 | 11 Va-Etḥannan | 12 | 14 | 14 | 15 | 15 |
| 26 | 8 | 9 | 8 | 9 | 10 | 11 | 12 | 13 | 15 Sukkot | 15 | 16 | 16 Va-Yeḥi |
| 27 | 9 | 10 | 9 | 10 | 11 | 12 Ḥukkat Balak | 13 | 14 | 16 | 16 | 17 | 17 |
| 28 | 10 | 11 Teẓavveh Zakhor | 10 Ẓav Shabbat ha-Gadol | 11 | 12 | 13 | 14 | 15 | 17 Ḥol ha-Mo'ed | 17 | 18 Va-Yishlaḥ | 18 |
| 29 | 11 | | 11 | 12 | 13 | 14 | 15 | 16 Ki Tavo | 18 | 18 | 19 | 19 |
| 30 | 12 | | 12 | 13 | 14 Naso | 15 | 16 | 17 | 19 | 19 | 20 | 20 |
| 31 | 13 Be-Shallaḥ | | 13 | | 15 | | 17 | 18 | | 20 Va-Yera | | 21 |

# 1932

**5692/93** תרצ״ב תרצ״ג

| | January | February | March | April | May | June | July | August | September | October | November | December |
|---|---|---|---|---|---|---|---|---|---|---|---|---|
| 1 | 22 Tevet | 24 | 23 | 24 | 25 | 26 | 27 | 28 | 30 R. Ḥ. | 1 Tishri Rosh Ha-Shanah | 2 | 2 |
| 2 | 23 Shemot | 25 | 24 | 25 Shemini Ha-Ḥodesh | 26 | 27 | 28 Shelaḥ | 29 | 1 Elul R. Ḥ. | 2 | 3 | 3 |
| 3 | 24 | 26 | 25 | 26 | 27 | 28 | 29 | 1 Av R. Ḥ. | 2 Shofetim | 3 Fast | 4 | 4 Toledot |
| 4 | 25 | 27 | 26 | 27 | 28 | 29 Be-Midbar | 30 R. Ḥ. | 2 | 3 | 4 | 5 | 5 |
| 5 | 26 | 28 | 27 Va-Yakhel Shekalim | 28 | 29 | 1 Sivan R. Ḥ. | 1 Tammuz R. Ḥ. | 3 | 4 | 5 | 6 No'aḥ | 6 |
| 6 | 27 | 29 Mishpatim | 28 | 29 | 30 R. Ḥ. | 2 | 2 | 4 Devarim | 5 | 6 | 7 | 7 |
| 7 | 28 | 30 R. Ḥ. | 29 | 1 Nisan R. Ḥ. | 1 Iyyar R. Ḥ. Kedoshim | 3 | 3 | 5 | 6 | 7 | 8 | 8 |
| 8 | 29 | 1 Adar I R. Ḥ. | 30 R. Ḥ. | 2 | 2 | 4 | 4 | 6 | 7 | 8 Ha'azinu Shabbat Shuvah | 9 | 9 |
| 9 | 1 Shevat R. Ḥ. Va-Era | 2 | 1 Adar II R. Ḥ. | 3 Tazri'a | 3 | 5 | 5 Koraḥ | 7 | 8 | 9 | 10 | 10 |
| 10 | 2 | 3 | 2 | 4 | 4 | 6 Shavuot | 6 | 8 | 9 Ki Teẓe | 10 Yom Kippur | 11 | 11 Va-Yeẓe |
| 11 | 3 | 4 | 3 | 5 | 5 | 7 | 7 | 9 Tishah be-Av | 10 | 11 | 12 | 12 |
| 12 | 4 | 5 | 4 Pekudei | 6 | 6 | 8 | 8 | 10 | 11 | 12 | 13 Lekh Lekha | 13 |
| 13 | 5 | 6 Terumah | 5 | 7 | 7 | 9 | 9 | 11 Va-Etḥannan | 12 | 13 | 14 | 14 |
| 14 | 6 | 7 | 6 | 8 | 8 Emor | 10 | 10 | 12 | 13 | 14 | 15 | 15 |
| 15 | 7 | 8 | 7 | 9 | 9 | 11 | 11 | 13 | 14 | 15 Sukkot | 16 | 16 |
| 16 | 8 Bo | 9 | 8 | 10 Mezora Shabbat ha-Gadol | 10 | 12 | 12 Ḥukkat Balak | 14 | 15 | 16 | 17 | 17 |
| 17 | 9 | 10 | 9 | 11 | 11 | 13 | 13 | 15 | 16 Ki Tavo | 17 Ḥol ha-Mo'ed | 18 | 18 Va-Yishlaḥ |
| 18 | 10 | 11 | 10 | 12 | 12 | 14 Naso | 14 | 16 | 17 | 18 | 19 | 19 |
| 19 | 11 | 12 | 11 Va-Yikra Zakhor | 13 | 13 | 15 | 15 | 17 | 18 | 19 | 20 Va-Yera | 20 |
| 20 | 12 | 13 Teẓavveh | 12 | 14 | 14 | 16 | 16 | 18 Ekev | 19 | 20 | 21 | 21 |
| 21 | 13 | 14 | 13 Ta'anit Esther | 15 Pesaḥ | 15 Be-Har | 17 | 17 Fast | 19 | 20 | 21 Hoshana Rabba | 22 | 22 |
| 22 | 14 | 15 | 14 Purim | 16 Omer | 16 | 18 | 18 | 20 | 21 | 22 Shemini Aẓeret | 23 | 23 |
| 23 | 15 Be-Shallaḥ | 16 | 15 Shushan Purim | 17 Ḥol ha-Mo'ed | 17 | 19 | 19 Pinḥas | 21 | 22 | 23 Simḥat Torah Ve-Ẓot Ha-Berakhah | 24 | 24 |
| 24 | 16 | 17 | 16 | 18 | 18 Lag ba-Omer | 20 | 20 | 22 | 23 Niẓẓavim Va-Yelekh | 24 | 25 | 25 Va-Yeshev Ḥanukkah 1 |
| 25 | 17 | 18 | 17 | 19 | 19 | 21 Be-Ha'alotkha | 21 | 23 | 24 | 25 | 26 | 26 2 |
| 26 | 18 | 19 | 18 Ẓav Parah | 20 | 20 | 22 | 22 | 24 | 25 | 26 | 27 Ḥayyei Sarah | 27 3 |
| 27 | 19 | 20 Ki Tissa | 19 | 21 Pesaḥ | 21 | 23 | 23 | 25 Re'eh | 26 | 27 | 28 | 28 4 |
| 28 | 20 | 21 | 20 | 22 | 22 Be-Ḥukkotai | 24 | 24 | 26 | 27 | 28 | 29 | 29 5 |
| 29 | 21 | 22 | 21 | 23 | 23 | 25 | 25 | 27 | 28 | 29 Bereshit | 30 R. Ḥ. | 30 R. Ḥ. 6 |
| 30 | 22 Yitro | | 22 | 24 Aḥarei Mot | 24 | 26 | 26 Mattot Masei | 28 | 29 | 30 R. Ḥ. | 1 Kislev R. Ḥ. | 1 Tevet R. Ḥ. 7 |
| 31 | 23 | | 23 | | 25 | | 27 | 29 | | 1 Heshvan R. Ḥ. | | 2 Mi-Keẓ 8 |

## 1933

**5693/94** — תרצ״ג / תרצ״ד

| | January | February | March | April | May | June | July | August | September | October | November | December |
|---|---|---|---|---|---|---|---|---|---|---|---|---|
| 1 | 3 Tevet | 5 | 3 | **5** Va-Yikra | 5 | 7 | **7** Ḥukkat | 9 Tishah be-Av | 10 | 11 | 12 | 13 |
| 2 | 4 | 6 | 4 | 6 | 6 | 8 | 8 | 10 | **11** Ki Teẓe | 12 | 13 | **14** Va-Yishlaḥ |
| 3 | 5 | 7 | 5 | 7 | 7 | **9** Naso | 9 | 11 | 12 | 13 | 14 | 15 |
| 4 | 6 | **8** Bo | **6** Terumah | 8 | 8 | 10 | 10 | 12 | 13 | 14 | **15** Va-Yera | 16 |
| 5 | 7 | 9 | 7 | 9 | 9 | 11 | 11 | **13** Va-Etḥannan | 14 | 15 Sukkot | 16 | 17 |
| 6 | 8 | 10 | 8 | 10 | **10** Aḥarei Mot Kedoshim | 12 | 12 | 14 | 15 | 16 | 17 | 18 |
| 7 | **9** Va-Yiggash | 11 | 9 | 11 | 11 | 13 | 13 | 15 | 16 | **17** | 18 | 19 |
| 8 | 10 Fast | 12 | 10 | **12** Ẓav Shabbat ha-Gadol | 12 | 14 | **14** Balak | 16 | 17 | 18 Ḥol ha-Mo'ed | 19 | 20 |
| 9 | 11 | 13 | 11 Ta'anit Esther | 13 | 13 | 15 | 15 | 17 | **18** Ki Tavo | 19 | 20 | **21** Va-Yeshev |
| 10 | 12 | 14 | 12 | 14 | 14 | **16** Be-Ha'alotkha | 16 | 18 | 19 | 20 | 21 | 22 |
| 11 | 13 | **15** Be-Shallaḥ | **13** Teẓavveh Zakhor | 15 Pesaḥ | 15 | 17 | 17 Fast | 19 | 20 | 21 Hoshana Rabba | **22** Ḥayyei Sarah | 23 |
| 12 | 14 | 16 | 14 Purim | 16 Omer | 16 | 18 | 18 | **20** Ekev | 21 | 22 Shemini Aẓeret | 23 | 24 |
| 13 | 15 | 17 | 15 Shushan Purim | 17 | **17** Emor | 19 | 19 | 21 | 22 | 23 Simḥat Torah Ve-Zot Ha-Berakhah | 24 | 25 Ḥanukkah 1 |
| 14 | **16** Va-Yeḥi | 18 | 16 | 18 Ḥol ha-Mo'ed | 18 Lag ba-Omer | 20 | 20 | 22 | 23 | **24** Bereshit | 25 | 26 2 |
| 15 | 17 | 19 | 17 | **19** | 19 | 21 | **21** Pinḥas | 23 | 24 | 25 | 26 | 27 3 |
| 16 | 18 | 20 | 18 | 20 | 20 | 22 | 22 | 24 | **25** Niẓẓavim Va-Yelekh | 26 | 27 | **28** Mi-Keẓ 4 |
| 17 | 19 | 21 | 19 | 21 Pesaḥ | 21 | **23** Shelaḥ | 23 | 25 | 26 | 27 | 28 | 29 5 |
| 18 | 20 | **22** Yitro | **20** Ki Tissa Parah | 22 | 22 | 24 | 24 | 26 | 27 | 28 | **29** Toledot | 30 R. H. 6 |
| 19 | 21 | 23 | 21 | 23 | 23 | 25 | 25 | **27** Re'eh | 28 | 29 | 1 Kislev R. H. | 1 Tevet R. H. 7 |
| 20 | 22 | 24 | 22 | 24 | **24** Be-Har Be-Ḥukkotai | 26 | 26 | 28 | 29 | 30 R. H. | 2 | 2 8 |
| 21 | **23** Shemot | 25 | 23 | 25 | 25 | 27 | 27 | 29 | 1 Tishri Rosh Ha-Shanah | 1 Ḥeshvan R. H. No'aḥ | 3 | 3 |
| 22 | 24 | 26 | 24 | **26** Shemini | 26 | 28 | **28** Mattot Masei | 30 R. H. | 2 | 2 | 4 | 4 |
| 23 | 25 | 27 | 25 | 27 | 27 | 29 | 29 | 1 Elul R. H. | **3** Ha'azinu Shabbat Shuvah | 3 | 5 | **5** Va-Yiggash |
| 24 | 26 | 28 | 26 | 28 | 28 | **30** R. H. Koraḥ | 1 Av R. H. | 2 | 4 Fast | 4 | 6 | 6 |
| 25 | 27 | **29** Mishpatim Shekalim | **27** Va-Yakhel Pekudei Ha-Ḥodesh | 29 | 29 | 1 Tammuz R. H. | 2 | 3 | 5 | 5 | **7** Va-Yeẓe | 7 |
| 26 | 28 | 30 R. H. | 28 | 30 R. H. | 1 Sivan R. H. | 2 | 3 | **4** Shofetim | 6 | 6 | 8 | 8 |
| 27 | 29 | 1 Adar R. H. | 29 | 1 Iyyar R. H. | **2** Be-Midbar | 3 | 4 | 5 | 7 | 7 | 9 | 9 |
| 28 | **1** Shevat R. H. Va-Era | 2 | 1 Nisan R. H. | 2 | 3 | 4 | 5 | 6 | 8 | **8** Lekh Lekha | 10 | 10 Fast |
| 29 | 2 | | 2 | **3** Tazri'a Meẓora | 4 | 5 | **6** Devarim | 7 | 9 | 9 | 11 | 11 |
| 30 | 3 | | 3 | 4 | 5 | 6 | 7 | 8 | **10** Yom Kippur | 10 | 12 | **12** Va-Yeḥi |
| 31 | 4 | | 4 | | 6 Shavuot | | 8 | 9 | | 11 | | 13 |

## 1934

**5694/95** — תרצ״ד / תרצ״ה

| | January | February | March | April | May | June | July | August | September | October | November | December |
|---|---|---|---|---|---|---|---|---|---|---|---|---|
| 1 | 14 Tevet | 16 | 14 Purim | 16 Omer | 16 | 18 | 18 Fast | 20 | **21** Ki Tavo | 22 Shemini Aẓeret | 23 | **24** Va-Yeshev |
| 2 | 15 | 17 | 15 Shushan Purim | 17 | 17 | **19** Be-Ha'alotkha | 19 | 21 | 22 | 23 Simḥat Torah Ve-Zot Ha-Berakhah | 24 | 25 Ḥanukkah 1 |
| 3 | 16 | **18** Yitro | **16** Ki Tissa | 18 Ḥol ha-Mo'ed | 18 Lag ba-Omer | 20 | 20 | 22 | 23 | 24 | **25** Ḥayyei Sarah | 26 2 |
| 4 | 17 | 19 | 17 | 19 | 19 | 21 | 21 | **23** Ekev | 24 | 25 | 26 | 27 3 |
| 5 | 18 | 20 | 18 | 20 | **20** Emor | 22 | 22 | 24 | 25 | 26 | 27 | 28 4 |
| 6 | **19** Shemot | 21 | 19 | 21 Pesaḥ | 21 | 23 | 23 | 25 | 26 | **27** Bereshit | 28 | 29 5 |
| 7 | 20 | 22 | 20 | **22** | 22 | 24 | **24** Pinḥas | 26 | 27 | 28 | 29 | 1 Tevet R. H. 6 |
| 8 | 21 | 23 | 21 | 23 | 23 | 25 | 25 | 27 | **28** Niẓẓavim | 29 | 1 Kislev R. H. | **2** Mi-Keẓ 7 |
| 9 | 22 | 24 | 22 | 24 | 24 | **26** Shelaḥ | 26 | 28 | 29 | 30 R. H. | 2 | 3 8 |
| 10 | 23 | **25** Mishpatim Shekalim | **23** Va-Yakhel Pekudei Parah | 25 | 25 | 27 | 27 | 29 | 1 Tishri Rosh Ha-Shanah | 1 Ḥeshvan R. H. | **3** Toledot | 4 |
| 11 | 24 | 26 | 24 | 26 | 26 | 28 | 28 | **30** R. H. Re'eh | 2 | 2 | 4 | 5 |
| 12 | 25 | 27 | 25 | 27 | **27** Be-Har Be-Ḥukkotai | 29 | 29 | 1 Elul R. H. | 3 Fast | 3 | 5 | 6 |
| 13 | **26** Va-Era | 28 | 26 | 28 | 28 | 30 R. H. | 1 Av R. H. | 2 | 4 | **4** No'aḥ | 6 | 7 |
| 14 | 27 | 29 | 27 | **29** Shemini | 29 | 1 Tammuz R. H. | **2** Mattot Masei | 3 | 5 | 5 | 7 | 8 |
| 15 | 28 | 30 R. H. | 28 | 30 R. H. | 1 Sivan R. H. | 2 | 3 | 4 | **6** Va-Yelekh Shabbat Shuvah | 6 | 8 | **9** Va-Yiggash |
| 16 | 29 | 1 Adar R. H. | 29 | 1 Iyyar R. H. | 2 | **3** Koraḥ | 4 | 5 | 7 | 7 | 9 | 10 Fast |
| 17 | 1 Shevat R. H. | **2** Terumah | **1** R. H. Nisan Va-Yikra Ha-Ḥodesh | 2 | 3 | 4 | 5 | 6 | 8 | 8 | **10** Va-Yeẓe | 11 |
| 18 | 2 | 3 | 2 | 3 | 4 | 5 | 6 | **7** Shofetim | 9 | 9 | 11 | 12 |
| 19 | 3 | 4 | 3 | 4 | **5** Be-Midbar | 6 | 7 | 8 | 10 Yom Kippur | 10 | 12 | 13 |
| 20 | **4** Bo | 5 | 4 | 5 | 6 Shavuot | 7 | 8 | 9 | 11 | **11** Lekh Lekha | 13 | 14 |
| 21 | 5 | 6 | 5 | **6** Tazri'a Meẓora | 7 | 8 | **9** Devarim Tishah be-Av | 10 | 12 | 12 | 14 | 15 |
| 22 | 6 | 7 | 6 | 7 | 8 | 9 | 10 Fast | 11 | **13** Ha'azinu | 13 | 15 | **16** Va-Yeḥi |
| 23 | 7 | 8 | 7 | 8 | 9 | **10** Ḥukkat | 11 | 12 | 14 | 14 | 16 | 17 |
| 24 | 8 | **9** Teẓavveh Zakhor | **8** Ẓav Shabbat ha-Gadol | 9 | 10 | 11 | 12 | 13 | 15 Sukkot | 15 | **17** Va-Yishlaḥ | 18 |
| 25 | 9 | 10 | 9 | 10 | 11 | 12 | 13 | **14** Ki Teẓe | 16 | 16 | 18 | 19 |
| 26 | 10 | 11 | 10 | 11 | **12** Naso | 13 | 14 | 15 | 17 | 17 | 19 | 20 |
| 27 | **11** Be-Shallaḥ | 12 | 11 | 12 | 13 | 14 | 15 | 16 | 18 Ḥol ha-Mo'ed | **18** Va-Yera | 20 | 21 |
| 28 | 12 | 13 Ta'anit Esther | 12 | **13** Aḥarei Mot Kedoshim | 14 | 15 | **16** Va-Etḥannan | 17 | 19 | 19 | 21 | 22 |
| 29 | 13 | | 13 | 14 | 15 | 16 | 17 | 18 | **20** | 20 | 22 | **23** Shemot |
| 30 | 14 | | 14 | 15 | 16 | **17** Balak | 18 | 19 | 21 Hoshana Rabba | 21 | 23 | 24 |
| 31 | 15 | | **15** Pesaḥ | | 17 | | 19 | 20 | | 22 | | 25 |

# 1935

**5695/96** תרצ״ה / תרצ״ו

| | January | February | March | April | May | June | July | August | September | October | November | December |
|---|---|---|---|---|---|---|---|---|---|---|---|---|
| 1 | 26 Tevet | 28 | 26 | 27 | 28 | 29 Be-Midbar | 30 R. Ḥ. | 2 | 3 | 4 | 5 | 5 |
| 2 | 27 | 29 Mishpatim | 27 Va-Yakhel Shekalim | 28 | 29 | 1 Sivan R. Ḥ. | 1 Tammuz R. Ḥ. | 3 | 4 | 5 | 6 No'aḥ | 6 |
| 3 | 28 | 30 R. Ḥ. | 28 | 29 | 30 R. Ḥ. | 2 | 2 | 4 Devarim | 5 | 6 | 7 | 7 |
| 4 | 29 | 1 Adar I R. Ḥ. | 29 | 1 Nisan R. Ḥ. | 1 Iyyar R. Ḥ. Kedoshim | 3 | 3 | 5 | 6 | 7 | 8 | 8 |
| 5 | 1 Shevat R. Ḥ. Va-Era | 2 | 30 R. Ḥ. | 2 | 2 | 4 | 4 | 6 | 7 | 8 Ha'azinu Shabbat Shuvah | 9 | 9 |
| 6 | 2 | 3 | 1 Adar II R. Ḥ. | 3 Tazri'a | 3 | 5 | 5 Koraḥ | 7 | 8 | 9 | 10 | 10 |
| 7 | 3 | 4 | 2 | 4 | 4 | 6 Shavuot | 6 | 8 | 9 Ki Teẓe | 10 Yom Kippur | 11 | 11 Va-Yeẓe |
| 8 | 4 | 5 | 3 | 5 | 5 | 7 | 7 | 9 Tishah be-Av | 10 | 11 | 12 | 12 |
| 9 | 5 | 6 Terumah | 4 Pekudei | 6 | 6 | 8 | 8 | 10 | 11 | 12 | 13 Lekh Lekha | 13 |
| 10 | 6 | 7 | 5 | 7 | 7 | 9 | 9 | 11 Va-Etḥannan | 12 | 13 | 14 | 14 |
| 11 | 7 | 8 | 6 | 8 | 8 Emor | 10 | 10 | 12 | 13 | 14 | 15 | 15 |
| 12 | 8 Bo | 9 | 7 | 9 | 9 | 11 | 11 | 13 | 14 | 15 Sukkot | 16 | 16 |
| 13 | 9 | 10 | 8 | 10 Meẓora Shabbat ha-Gadol | 10 | 12 | 12 Ḥukkat Balak | 14 | 15 | 16 | 17 | 17 |
| 14 | 10 | 11 | 9 | 11 | 11 | 13 | 13 | 15 | 16 Ki Tavo | 17 Ḥol ha-Mo'ed | 18 | 18 Va-Yishlaḥ |
| 15 | 11 | 12 | 10 | 12 | 12 | 14 Naso | 14 | 16 | 17 | 18 | 19 | 19 |
| 16 | 12 | 13 Teẓavveh | 11 Va-Yikra Zakhor | 13 | 13 | 15 | 15 | 17 | 18 | 19 | 20 Va-Yera | 20 |
| 17 | 13 | 14 | 12 | 14 | 14 | 16 | 16 | 18 Ekev | 19 | 20 | 21 | 21 |
| 18 | 14 | 15 | 13 Ta'anit Esther | 15 Pesaḥ | 15 Be-Har | 17 | 17 Fast | 19 | 20 | 21 Hoshana Rabba | 22 | 22 |
| 19 | 15 Be-Shallaḥ | 16 | 14 Purim | 16 Omer | 16 | 18 | 18 | 20 | 21 | 22 Shemini Aẓeret | 23 | 23 |
| 20 | 16 | 17 | 15 Shushan Purim | 17 Ḥol ha-Mo'ed | 17 | 19 | 19 Pinḥas | 21 | 22 | 23 Simḥat Torah Ve-Zot ha-Berakhah | 24 | 24 |
| 21 | 17 | 18 | 16 | 18 | 18 Lag ba-Omer | 20 | 20 | 22 | 23 Niẓẓavim Va-Yelekh | 24 | 25 | 25 Va-Yeshev Ḥanukkah 1 |
| 22 | 18 | 19 | 17 | 19 | 19 | 21 Be-Ha'alotkha | 21 | 23 | 24 | 25 | 26 | 26 2 |
| 23 | 19 | 20 Ki Tissa | 18 Ẓav Parah | 20 | 20 | 22 | 22 | 24 | 25 | 26 | 27 Ḥayyei Sarah | 27 3 |
| 24 | 20 | 21 | 19 | 21 Pesaḥ | 21 | 23 | 23 | 25 Re'eh | 26 | 27 | 28 | 28 4 |
| 25 | 21 | 22 | 20 | 22 | 22 Be-Ḥukkotai | 24 | 24 | 26 | 27 | 28 | 29 | 29 5 |
| 26 | 22 Yitro | 23 | 21 | 23 | 23 | 25 | 25 | 27 | 28 | 29 Bereshit | 30 R. Ḥ. | 30 R. Ḥ. 6 |
| 27 | 23 | 24 | 22 | 24 Aḥarei Mot | 24 | 26 | 26 Mattot Masei | 28 | 29 | 30 R. Ḥ. | 1 Kislev R. Ḥ. | 1 Tevet R. Ḥ. 7 |
| 28 | 24 | 25 | 23 | 25 | 25 | 27 | 27 | 29 | 1 Tishri Rosh Ha-Shanah | 1 Ḥeshvan R. Ḥ. | 2 | 2 Mi-Keẓ 8 |
| 29 | 25 | | 24 | 26 | 26 | 28 Shelaḥ | 28 | 30 R. Ḥ. | 2 | 2 | 3 | 3 |
| 30 | 26 | | 25 Shemini Ha-Ḥodesh | 27 | 27 | 29 | 29 | 1 Elul R. Ḥ. | 3 Fast | 3 | 4 Toledot | 4 |
| 31 | 27 | | 26 | | 28 | | 1 Av R. Ḥ. | 2 Shofetim | | 4 | | 5 |

# 1936

**5696/97** תרצ״ו / תרצ״ז

| | January | February | March | April | May | June | July | August | September | October | November | December |
|---|---|---|---|---|---|---|---|---|---|---|---|---|
| 1 | 6 Tevet | 8 Bo | 7 | 9 | 9 | 11 | 11 | 13 Va-Etḥannan | 14 | 15 Sukkot | 16 | 17 |
| 2 | 7 | 9 | 8 | 10 | 10 Aḥarei Mot Kedoshim | 12 | 12 | 14 | 15 | 16 | 17 | 18 |
| 3 | 8 | 10 | 9 | 11 | 11 | 13 | 13 | 15 | 16 | 17 Ḥol ha-Mo'ed | 18 | 19 |
| 4 | 9 Va-Yiggash | 11 | 10 | 12 Ẓav Shabbat ha-Gadol | 12 | 14 | 14 Balak | 16 | 17 | 18 | 19 | 20 |
| 5 | 10 Fast | 12 | 11 Ta'anit Esther | 13 | 13 | 15 | 15 | 17 | 18 Ki Tavo | 19 | 20 | 21 Va-Yeshev |
| 6 | 11 | 13 | 12 | 14 | 14 | 16 Be-Ha'alotkha | 16 | 18 | 19 | 20 | 21 | 22 |
| 7 | 12 | 14 | 13 Teẓavveh Zakhor | 15 Pesaḥ | 15 | 17 | 17 Fast | 19 | 20 | 21 Hoshana Rabba | 22 Ḥayyei Sarah | 23 |
| 8 | 13 | 15 Be-Shallaḥ | 14 Purim | 16 Omer | 16 | 18 | 18 | 20 Ekev | 21 | 22 Shemini Aẓeret | 23 | 24 |
| 9 | 14 | 16 | 15 Shushan Purim | 17 Ḥol ha-Mo'ed | 17 Emor | 19 | 19 | 21 | 22 | 23 Simḥat Torah Ve-Zot Ha-Berakhah | 24 | 25 Ḥanukkah 1 |
| 10 | 15 | 17 | 16 | 18 | 18 Lag ba-Omer | 20 | 20 | 22 | 23 | 24 Bereshit | 25 | 26 2 |
| 11 | 16 Va-Yeḥi | 18 | 17 | 19 | 19 | 21 | 21 Pinḥas | 23 | 24 | 25 | 26 | 27 3 |
| 12 | 17 | 19 | 18 | 20 | 20 | 22 | 22 | 24 | 25 Niẓẓavim Va-Yelekh | 26 | 27 | 28 Mi-Keẓ 4 |
| 13 | 18 | 20 | 19 | 21 Pesaḥ | 21 | 23 Shelaḥ | 23 | 25 | 26 | 27 | 28 | 29 5 |
| 14 | 19 | 21 | 20 Ki Tissa Parah | 22 | 22 | 24 | 24 | 26 | 27 | 28 | 29 Toledot | 30 R. Ḥ. 6 |
| 15 | 20 | 22 Yitro | 21 | 23 | 23 | 25 | 25 | 27 Re'eh | 28 | 29 | 1 Kislev R. Ḥ. | 1 Tevet R. Ḥ. 7 |
| 16 | 21 | 23 | 22 | 24 | 24 Be-Har Be-Ḥukkotai | 26 | 26 | 28 | 29 | 30 R. Ḥ. | 2 | 2 8 |
| 17 | 22 | 24 | 23 | 25 | 25 | 27 | 27 | 29 | 1 Tishri Rosh Ha-Shanah | 1 Ḥeshvan R. Ḥ. No'aḥ | 3 | 3 |
| 18 | 23 Shemot | 25 | 24 | 26 Shemini | 26 | 28 | 28 Mattot Masei | 30 R. Ḥ. | 2 | 2 | 4 | 4 |
| 19 | 24 | 26 | 25 | 27 | 27 | 29 | 29 | 1 Elul R. Ḥ. | 3 Ha'azinu Shabbat Shuvah | 3 | 5 | 5 Va-Yiggash |
| 20 | 25 | 27 | 26 | 28 | 28 | 30 R. Ḥ. Koraḥ | 1 Av R. Ḥ. | 2 | 4 Fast | 4 | 6 | 6 |
| 21 | 26 | 28 | 27 Va-Yakhel Pekudei Ha-Ḥodesh | 29 | 29 | 1 Tammuz R. Ḥ. | 2 | 3 | 5 | 5 | 7 Va-Yeẓe | 7 |
| 22 | 27 | 29 Mishpatim Shekalim | 28 | 30 R. Ḥ. | 1 Sivan R. Ḥ. | 2 | 3 | 4 Shofetim | 6 | 6 | 8 | 8 |
| 23 | 28 | 30 R. Ḥ. | 29 | 1 Iyyar R. Ḥ. | 2 Be-Midbar | 3 | 4 | 5 | 7 | 7 | 9 | 9 |
| 24 | 29 | 1 Adar R. Ḥ. | 1 Nisan R. Ḥ. | 2 | 3 | 4 | 5 | 6 | 8 | 8 Lekh Lekha | 10 | 10 Fast |
| 25 | 1 Shevat R. Ḥ. Va-Era | 2 | 2 | 3 Tazri'a Meẓora | 4 | 5 | 6 Devarim | 7 | 9 | 9 | 11 | 11 |
| 26 | 2 | 3 | 3 | 4 | 5 | 6 | 7 | 8 | 10 Yom Kippur | 10 | 12 | 12 Va-Yeḥi |
| 27 | 3 | 4 | 4 | 5 | 6 Shavuot | 7 Ḥukkat | 8 | 9 | 11 | 11 | 13 | 13 |
| 28 | 4 | 5 | 5 Va-Yikra | 6 | 7 | 8 | 9 Tishah be-Av | 10 | 12 | 12 | 14 Va-Yishlaḥ | 14 |
| 29 | 5 | 6 Terumah | 6 | 7 | 8 | 9 | 10 | 11 Ki Teẓe | 13 | 13 | 15 | 15 |
| 30 | 6 | | 7 | 8 | 9 Naso | 10 | 11 | 12 | 14 | 14 | 16 | 16 |
| 31 | 7 | | 8 | | 10 | | 12 | 13 | | 15 Va-Yera | | 17 |

# 1937

**5697/98** תרצ״ז / תרצ״ח

| | January | February | March | April | May | June | July | August | September | October | November | December |
|---|---|---|---|---|---|---|---|---|---|---|---|---|
| 1 | 18 Tevet | 20 | 18 | 20 Ḥol ha-Mo'ed | 20 *Emor* | 22 | 22 | 24 | 25 | 26 | 27 | 27 3 |
| 2 | 19 *Shemot* | 21 | 19 | 21 Pesaḥ | 21 | 23 | 23 | 25 | 26 | 27 *Bereshit* | 28 | 28 4 |
| 3 | 20 | 22 | 20 | 22 | 22 | 24 | 24 *Pinḥas* | 26 | 27 | 28 | 29 | 29 5 |
| 4 | 21 | 23 | 21 | 23 | 23 | 25 | 25 | 27 | 28 *Niẓẓavim* | 29 | 30 R. Ḥ. | 30 R. Ḥ. *Mi-Keẓ* 6 |
| 5 | 22 | 24 | 22 | 24 | 24 | 26 *Shelaḥ* | 26 | 28 | 29 | 30 R. Ḥ. | 1 Kislev R. Ḥ. | 1 Tevet R. Ḥ. 7 |
| 6 | 23 | 25 *Mishpatim* Shekalim | 23 *Va-Yakhel Pekudei* Parah | 25 | 25 | 27 | 27 | 29 | 1 Tishri Rosh Ha-Shanah | 1 Ḥeshvan R. Ḥ. | 2 *Toledot* | 2 8 |
| 7 | 24 | 26 | 24 | 26 | 26 | 28 | 28 | 30 R. Ḥ. *Re'eh* | 2 | 2 | 3 | 3 |
| 8 | 25 | 27 | 25 | 27 | 27 *Be-Har Be-Ḥukkotai* | 29 | 29 | 1 Elul R. Ḥ. | 3 Fast | 3 | 4 | 4 |
| 9 | 26 *Va-Era* | 28 | 26 | 28 | 28 | 30 R. Ḥ. | 1 Av R. Ḥ. | 2 | 4 | 4 *No'aḥ* | 5 | 5 |
| 10 | 27 | 29 | 27 | 29 *Shemini* | 29 | 1 Tammuz R. Ḥ. | 2 *Mattot Masei* | 3 | 5 | 5 | 6 | 6 |
| 11 | 28 | 30 R. Ḥ. | 28 | 30 R. Ḥ. | 1 Sivan R. Ḥ. | 2 | 3 | 4 | 6 *Va-Yelekh* Shabbat Shuvah | 6 | 7 | 7 *Va-Yiggash* |
| 12 | 29 | 1 Adar R. Ḥ. | 29 | 1 Iyyar R. Ḥ. | 2 | 3 *Koraḥ* | 4 | 5 | 7 | 7 | 8 | 8 |
| 13 | 1 Shevat R. Ḥ. | 2 *Terumah* | 1 Nisan R. Ḥ. *Va-Yikra* Ha-Ḥodesh | 2 | 3 | 4 | 5 | 6 | 8 | 8 | 9 *Va-Yeẓe* | 9 |
| 14 | 2 | 3 | 2 | 3 | 4 | 5 | 6 | 7 *Shofetim* | 9 | 9 | 10 | 10 Fast |
| 15 | 3 | 4 | 3 | 4 | 5 *Be-Midbar* | 6 | 7 | 8 | 10 Yom Kippur | 10 | 11 | 11 |
| 16 | 4 *Bo* | 5 | 4 | 5 | 6 Shavuot | 7 | 8 | 9 | 11 | 11 *Lekh Lekha* | 12 | 12 |
| 17 | 5 | 6 | 5 | 6 *Tazri'a Meẓora* | 7 | 8 | 9 *Devarim* Tishah be-Av | 10 | 12 | 12 | 13 | 13 |
| 18 | 6 | 7 | 6 | 7 | 8 | 9 | 10 Fast | 11 | 13 *Ha'azinu* | 13 | 14 | 14 *Va-Yeḥi* |
| 19 | 7 | 8 | 7 | 8 | 9 | 10 *Ḥukkat* | 11 | 12 | 14 | 14 | 15 | 15 |
| 20 | 8 | 9 *Teẓavveh* Zakhor | 8 *Ẓav* Shabbat ha-Gadol | 9 | 10 | 11 | 12 | 13 | 15 Sukkot | 15 | 16 *Va-Yishlaḥ* | 16 |
| 21 | 9 | 10 | 9 | 10 | 11 | 12 | 13 | 14 *Ki Teẓe* | 16 | 16 | 17 | 17 |
| 22 | 10 | 11 | 10 | 11 | 12 *Naso* | 13 | 14 | 15 | 17 Ḥol ha-Mo'ed | 17 | 18 | 18 |
| 23 | 11 *Be-Shallaḥ* | 12 | 11 | 12 | 13 | 14 | 15 | 16 | 18 | 18 *Va-Yera* | 19 | 19 |
| 24 | 12 | 13 Ta'anit Esther | 12 | 13 *Aḥarei Mot Kedoshim* | 14 | 15 | 16 *Va-Etḥannan* | 17 | 19 | 19 | 20 | 20 |
| 25 | 13 | 14 Purim | 13 | 14 | 15 | 16 | 17 | 18 | 20 | 20 | 21 | 21 *Shemot* |
| 26 | 14 | 15 Shushan Purim | 14 | 15 | 16 | 17 *Balak* | 18 | 19 | 21 Hoshana Rabba | 21 | 22 | 22 |
| 27 | 15 | 16 *Ki Tissa* | 15 Pesaḥ | 16 | 17 | 18 Fast | 19 | 20 | 22 Shemini Aẓeret | 22 | 23 *Va-Yeshev* | 23 |
| 28 | 16 | 17 | 16 Omer | 17 | 18 | 19 | 20 | 21 *Ki Tavo* | 23 Simḥat Torah *Ve-Zot Ha-Berakhah* | 23 | 24 | 24 |
| 29 | 17 | | 17 | 18 Lag ba-Omer | 19 *Be-Ha'alotkha* | 20 | 21 | 22 | 24 | 24 | 25 Ḥanukkah 1 | 25 |
| 30 | 18 *Yitro* | | 18 Ḥol ha-Mo'ed | 19 | 20 | 21 | 22 | 23 | 25 | 25 *Ḥayyei Sarah* | 26 2 | 26 |
| 31 | 19 | | 19 | | 21 | | 23 *Ekev* | 24 | | 26 | | 27 |

# 1938

**5698/99** תרצ״ח / תרצ״ט

| | January | February | March | April | May | June | July | August | September | October | November | December |
|---|---|---|---|---|---|---|---|---|---|---|---|---|
| 1 | 28 Tevet *Va-Era* | 30 R. Ḥ. | 28 | 29 | 30 R. Ḥ. | 2 | 2 | 4 | 5 | 6 *Va-Yelekh* Shabbat Shuvah | 7 | 8 |
| 2 | 29 | 1 Adar I R. Ḥ. | 29 | 1 Nisan R. Ḥ. *Tazri'a* Ha-Ḥodesh | 1 Iyyar R. Ḥ. | 3 | 3 *Koraḥ* | 5 | 6 | 7 | 8 | 9 |
| 3 | 1 Shevat R. Ḥ. | 2 | 30 R. Ḥ. | 2 | 2 | 4 | 4 | 6 | 7 *Shofetim* | 8 | 9 | 10 *Va-Yeẓe* |
| 4 | 2 | 3 | 1 Adar II R. Ḥ. | 3 | 3 | 5 *Be-Midbar* | 5 | 7 | 8 | 9 | 10 | 11 |
| 5 | 3 | 4 *Terumah* | 2 *Pekudei* | 4 | 4 | 6 Shavuot | 6 | 8 | 9 | 10 Yom Kippur | 11 *Lekh Lekha* | 12 |
| 6 | 4 | 5 | 3 | 5 | 5 | 7 | 7 | 9 *Devarim* Tishah be-Av | 10 | 11 | 12 | 13 |
| 7 | 5 | 6 | 4 | 6 | 6 *Kedoshim* | 8 | 8 | 10 Fast | 11 | 12 | 13 | 14 |
| 8 | 6 *Bo* | 7 | 5 | 7 | 7 | 9 | 9 | 11 | 12 | 13 *Ha'azinu* | 14 | 15 |
| 9 | 7 | 8 | 6 | 8 *Meẓora* Shabbat ha-Gadol | 8 | 10 | 10 *Ḥukkat* | 12 | 13 | 14 | 15 | 16 |
| 10 | 8 | 9 | 7 | 9 | 9 | 11 | 11 | 13 | 14 *Ki Teẓe* | 15 Sukkot | 16 | 17 *Va-Yishlaḥ* |
| 11 | 9 | 10 | 8 | 10 | 10 | 12 *Naso* | 12 | 14 | 15 | 16 | 17 | 18 |
| 12 | 10 | 11 *Teẓavveh* | 9 *Va-Yikra* Zakhor | 11 | 11 | 13 | 13 | 15 | 16 | 17 Ḥol ha-Mo'ed | 18 *Va-Yera* | 19 |
| 13 | 11 | 12 | 10 | 12 | 12 | 14 | 14 | 16 *Va-Etḥannan* | 17 | 18 | 19 | 20 |
| 14 | 12 | 13 | 11 | 13 | 13 *Emor* | 15 | 15 | 17 | 18 | 19 | 20 | 21 |
| 15 | 13 *Be-Shallaḥ* | 14 | 12 | 14 | 14 | 16 | 16 | 18 | 19 | 20 | 21 | 22 |
| 16 | 14 | 15 | 13 Ta'anit Esther | 15 Pesaḥ | 15 | 17 | 17 *Balak* | 19 | 20 | 21 Hoshana Rabba | 22 | 23 |
| 17 | 15 | 16 | 14 Purim | 16 Omer | 16 | 18 | 18 Fast | 20 | 21 *Ki Tavo* | 22 Shemini Aẓeret | 23 | 24 *Va-Yeshev* |
| 18 | 16 | 17 | 15 Shushan Purim | 17 Ḥol ha-Mo'ed | 17 | 19 *Be-Ha'alotkha* | 19 | 21 | 22 | 23 Simḥat Torah *Ve-Zot Ha-Berakhah* | 24 | 25 Ḥanukkah 1 |
| 19 | 17 | 18 *Ki Tissa* | 16 *Ẓav* | 18 | 18 Lag ba-Omer | 20 | 20 | 22 | 23 | 24 | 25 *Ḥayyei Sarah* | 26 2 |
| 20 | 18 | 19 | 17 | 19 | 19 | 21 | 21 | 23 *Ekev* | 24 | 25 | 26 | 27 3 |
| 21 | 19 | 20 | 18 | 20 | 20 *Be-Har* | 22 | 22 | 24 | 25 | 26 | 27 | 28 4 |
| 22 | 20 *Yitro* | 21 | 19 | 21 Pesaḥ | 21 | 23 | 23 | 25 | 26 | 27 *Bereshit* | 28 | 29 5 |
| 23 | 21 | 22 | 20 | 22 | 22 | 24 | 24 *Pinḥas* | 26 | 27 | 28 | 29 | 1 Tevet R. Ḥ. 6 |
| 24 | 22 | 23 | 21 | 23 | 23 | 25 | 25 | 27 | 28 *Niẓẓavim* | 29 | 1 Kislev R. Ḥ. | 2 *Mi-Keẓ* 7 |
| 25 | 23 | 24 | 22 | 24 | 24 | 26 *Shelaḥ* | 26 | 28 | 29 | 30 R. Ḥ. | 2 | 3 8 |
| 26 | 24 | 25 *Va-Yakhel* Shekalim | 23 *Shemini* Parah | 25 | 25 | 27 | 27 | 29 | 1 Tishri Rosh Ha-Shanah | 1 Ḥeshvan R. Ḥ. | 3 *Toledot* | 4 |
| 27 | 25 | 26 | 24 | 26 | 26 | 28 | 28 | 30 R. Ḥ. *Re'eh* | 2 | 2 | 4 | 5 |
| 28 | 26 | 27 | 25 | 27 | 27 *Be-Ḥukkotai* | 29 | 29 | 1 Elul R. Ḥ. | 3 Fast | 3 | 5 | 6 |
| 29 | 27 *Mishpatim* | | 26 | 28 | 28 | 30 R. Ḥ. | 1 Av R. Ḥ. | 2 | 4 | 4 *No'aḥ* | 6 | 7 |
| 30 | 28 | | 27 | 29 *Aḥarei Mot* | 29 | 1 Tammuz R. Ḥ. | 2 *Mattot Masei* | 3 | 5 | 5 | 7 | 8 |
| 31 | 29 | | 28 | | 1 Sivan R. Ḥ. | | 3 | 4 | | 6 | | 9 *Va-Yiggash* |

# 1939

**5699/5700** תרצ״ט ׀ ת״ש

| | January | February | March | April | May | June | July | August | September | October | November | December |
|---|---|---|---|---|---|---|---|---|---|---|---|---|
| 1 | 10 Tevet Fast | 12 | 10 | 12 Ẓav Shabbat ha-Gadol | 12 | 14 | 14 Balak | 16 | 17 | 18 Ḥol ha-Mo'ed | 19 | 19 |
| 2 | 11 | 13 | 11 Ta'anit Esther | 13 | 13 | 15 | 15 | 17 | 18 Ki Tavo | 19 | 20 | 20 Va-Yeshev |
| 3 | 12 | 14 | 12 | 14 | 14 | 16 Be-Ha'alotkha | 16 | 18 | 19 | 20 | 21 | 21 |
| 4 | 13 | 15 Be-Shallaḥ | 13 Teẓavveh Ẓakhor | 15 Pesaḥ | 15 | 17 | 17 Fast | 19 | 20 | 21 Hoshana Rabba | 22 Ḥayyei Sarah | 22 |
| 5 | 14 | 16 | 14 Purim | 16 Omer | 16 | 18 | 18 | 20 Ekev | 21 | 22 Shemini Aẓeret | 23 | 23 |
| 6 | 15 | 17 | 15 Shushan Purim | 17 Ḥol ha-Mo'ed | 17 Emor | 19 | 19 | 21 | 22 | 23 Simḥat Torah Ve-Zot Ha-Berakhah | 24 | 24 |
| 7 | 16 Va-Yeḥi | 18 | 16 | 18 | 18 Lag ba-Omer | 20 | 20 | 22 | 23 | 24 Bereshit | 25 | 25 Ḥanukkah 1 |
| 8 | 17 | 19 | 17 | 19 | 19 | 21 | 21 Pinḥas | 23 | 24 | 25 | 26 | 26 2 |
| 9 | 18 | 20 | 18 | 20 | 20 | 22 | 22 | 24 | 25 Niẓẓavim Va-Yelekh | 26 | 27 | 27 Mi-Keẓ 3 |
| 10 | 19 | 21 | 19 | 21 Pesaḥ | 21 | 23 Shelaḥ | 23 | 25 | 26 | 27 | 28 | 28 4 |
| 11 | 20 | 22 Yitro | 20 Ki Tissa Parah | 22 | 22 | 24 | 24 | 26 | 27 | 28 | 29 Toledot | 29 5 |
| 12 | 21 | 23 | 21 | 23 | 23 | 25 | 25 | 27 Re'eh | 28 | 29 | 30 R. Ḥ. | 30 R. Ḥ. 6 |
| 13 | 22 | 24 | 22 | 24 | 24 Be-Har Be-Ḥukkotai | 26 | 26 | 28 | 29 | 30 R. Ḥ. | 1 Kislev R. Ḥ. | 1 Tevet R. Ḥ. 7 |
| 14 | 23 Shemot | 25 | 23 | 25 | 25 | 27 | 27 | 29 | 1 Tishri Rosh Ha-Shanah | 1 Ḥeshvan R. Ḥ. No'aḥ | 2 | 2 8 |
| 15 | 24 | 26 | 24 | 26 Shemini | 26 | 28 | 28 Mattot Masei | 30 R. Ḥ. | 2 | 2 | 3 | 3 |
| 16 | 25 | 27 | 25 | 27 | 27 | 29 | 29 | 1 Elul R. Ḥ. | 3 Ha'azinu Shabbat Shuvah | 3 | 4 | 4 Va-Yiggash |
| 17 | 26 | 28 | 26 | 28 | 28 | 30 R. Ḥ. Koraḥ | 1 Av R. Ḥ. | 2 | 4 Fast | 4 | 5 | 5 |
| 18 | 27 | 29 Mishpatim Shekalim | 27 Va-Yakhel Pekudei Ha-Ḥodesh | 29 | 29 | 1 Tammuz R. Ḥ. | 2 | 3 | 5 | 5 | 6 Va-Yeẓe | 6 |
| 19 | 28 | 30 R. Ḥ. | 28 | 30 R. Ḥ. | 1 Sivan R. Ḥ. | 2 | 3 | 4 Shofetim | 6 | 6 | 7 | 7 |
| 20 | 29 | 1 Adar R. Ḥ. | 29 | 1 Iyyar R. Ḥ. | 2 Be-Midbar | 3 | 4 | 5 | 7 | 7 | 8 | 8 |
| 21 | 1 Shevat R. Ḥ. Va-Era | 2 | 1 Nisan R. Ḥ. | 2 | 3 | 4 | 5 | 6 | 8 | 8 Lekh Lekha | 9 | 9 |
| 22 | 2 | 3 | 2 | 3 Tazri'a Meẓora | 4 | 5 | 6 Devarim | 7 | 9 | 9 | 10 | 10 Fast |
| 23 | 3 | 4 | 3 | 4 | 5 | 6 | 7 | 8 | 10 Yom Kippur | 10 | 11 | 11 Va-Yeḥi |
| 24 | 4 | 5 | 4 | 5 | 6 Shavuot | 7 Ḥukkat | 8 | 9 | 11 | 11 | 12 | 12 |
| 25 | 5 | 6 Terumah | 5 Va-Yikra | 6 | 7 | 8 | 9 Tishah be-Av | 10 | 12 | 12 | 13 Va-Yishlaḥ | 13 |
| 26 | 6 | 7 | 6 | 7 | 8 | 9 | 10 | 11 Ki Teẓe | 13 | 13 | 14 | 14 |
| 27 | 7 | 8 | 7 | 8 | 9 Naso | 10 | 11 | 12 | 14 | 14 | 15 | 15 |
| 28 | 8 Bo | 9 | 8 | 9 | 10 | 11 | 12 | 13 | 15 Sukkot | 15 Va-Yera | 16 | 16 |
| 29 | 9 | | 9 | 10 Aḥarei Mot Kedoshim | 11 | 12 | 13 Va-Etḥannan | 14 | 16 | 16 | 17 | 17 |
| 30 | 10 | | 10 | 11 | 12 | 13 | 14 | 15 | 17 Ḥol ha-Moed | 17 | 18 | 18 Shemot |
| 31 | 11 | | 11 | | 13 | | 15 | 16 | | 18 | | 19 |

# 1940

**5700/01** ת״ש ׀ תש״א

| | January | February | March | April | May | June | July | August | September | October | November | December |
|---|---|---|---|---|---|---|---|---|---|---|---|---|
| 1 | 20 Tevet | 22 | 21 | 22 | 23 | 24 Be-Midbar | 25 | 26 | 28 | 28 | 30 R. Ḥ. | 1 Kislev R. Ḥ. |
| 2 | 21 | 23 | 22 Va-Yakhel | 23 | 24 | 25 | 26 | 27 | 29 | 29 | 1 Ḥeshvan R. Ḥ. No'aḥ | 2 |
| 3 | 22 | 24 Mishpatim | 23 | 24 | 25 | 26 | 27 | 28 Masei | 30 R. Ḥ. | 1 Tishri Rosh Ha-Shanah | 2 | 3 |
| 4 | 23 | 25 | 24 | 25 | 26 Kedoshim | 27 | 28 | 29 | 1 Elul R. Ḥ. | 2 | 3 | 4 |
| 5 | 24 | 26 | 25 | 26 | 27 | 28 | 29 | 1 Av R. Ḥ. | 2 | 3 Ha'azinu Shabbat Shuvah | 4 | 5 |
| 6 | 25 Va-Era | 27 | 26 | 27 Tazri'a Ha-Ḥodesh | 28 | 29 | 30 R. Ḥ. Ḥukkat | 2 | 3 | 4 Fast | 5 | 6 |
| 7 | 26 | 28 | 27 | 28 | 29 | 1 Sivan R. Ḥ. | 1 Tammuz R. Ḥ. | 3 | 4 Shofetim | 5 | 6 | 7 Va-Yeẓe |
| 8 | 27 | 29 | 28 | 29 | 30 R. Ḥ. | 2 Naso | 2 | 4 | 5 | 6 | 7 | 8 |
| 9 | 28 | 30 R. Ḥ. | 29 Pekudei Shekalim | 1 Nisan R. Ḥ. | 1 Iyyar R. Ḥ. | 3 | 3 | 5 | 6 | 7 | 8 Lekh Lekha | 9 |
| 10 | 29 | 1 Adar I R. Ḥ. Terumah | 30 R. Ḥ. | 2 | 2 | 4 | 4 | 6 Devarim | 7 | 8 | 9 | 10 |
| 11 | 1 Shevat R. Ḥ. | 2 | 1 Adar II R. Ḥ. | 3 | 3 Emor | 5 | 5 | 7 | 8 | 9 | 10 | 11 |
| 12 | 2 | 3 | 2 | 4 | 4 | 6 Shavuot | 6 | 8 | 9 | 10 Yom Kippur | 11 | 12 |
| 13 | 3 Bo | 4 | 3 | 5 Meẓora | 5 | 7 | 7 Balak | 9 Tishah be-Av | 10 | 11 | 12 | 13 |
| 14 | 4 | 5 | 4 | 6 | 6 | 8 | 8 | 10 | 11 Ki Teẓe | 12 | 13 | 14 Va-Yishlaḥ |
| 15 | 5 | 6 | 5 | 7 | 7 | 9 Be-Ha'alotkha | 9 | 11 | 12 | 13 | 14 | 15 |
| 16 | 6 | 7 | 6 Va-Yikra | 8 | 8 | 10 | 10 | 12 | 13 | 14 | 15 Va-Yera | 16 |
| 17 | 7 | 8 Teẓavveh | 7 | 9 | 9 | 11 | 11 | 13 Va-Etḥannan | 14 | 15 Sukkot | 16 | 17 |
| 18 | 8 | 9 | 8 | 10 | 10 Be-Har | 12 | 12 | 14 | 15 | 16 | 17 | 18 |
| 19 | 9 | 10 | 9 | 11 | 11 | 13 | 13 | 15 | 16 | 17 Ḥol ha-Mo'ed | 18 | 19 |
| 20 | 10 Be-Shallaḥ | 11 | 10 | 12 Aḥarei Mot Shabbat ha-Gadol | 12 | 14 | 14 Pinḥas | 16 | 17 | 18 | 19 | 20 |
| 21 | 11 | 12 | 11 Ta'anit Esther | 13 | 13 | 15 | 15 | 17 | 18 Ki Tavo | 19 | 20 | 21 Va-Yeshev |
| 22 | 12 | 13 | 12 | 14 | 14 | 16 Shelaḥ | 16 | 18 | 19 | 20 | 21 | 22 |
| 23 | 13 | 14 | 13 Ẓav Ẓakhor | 15 Pesaḥ | 15 | 17 | 17 Fast | 19 | 20 | 21 Hoshana Rabba | 22 Ḥayyei Sarah | 23 |
| 24 | 14 | 15 Ki Tissa | 14 Purim | 16 Omer | 16 | 18 | 18 | 20 Ekev | 21 | 22 Shemini Aẓeret | 23 | 24 |
| 25 | 15 | 16 | 15 Shushan Purim | 17 Ḥol ha-Mo'ed | 17 Be-Ḥukkotai | 19 | 19 | 21 | 22 | 23 Simḥat Torah Ve-Zot Ha-Berakhah | 24 | 25 Ḥanukkah 1 |
| 26 | 16 | 17 | 16 | 18 | 18 Lag ba-Omer | 20 | 20 | 22 | 23 | 24 Bereshit | 25 | 26 2 |
| 27 | 17 Yitro | 18 | 17 | 19 | 19 | 21 | 21 Mattot | 23 | 24 | 25 | 26 | 27 3 |
| 28 | 18 | 19 | 18 | 20 | 20 | 22 | 22 | 24 | 25 Niẓẓavim Va-Yelekh | 26 | 27 | 28 Mi-Keẓ 4 |
| 29 | 19 | 20 | 19 | 21 Pesaḥ | 21 | 23 Koraḥ | 23 | 25 | 26 | 27 | 28 | 29 5 |
| 30 | 20 | | 20 Shemini Parah | 22 | 22 | 24 | 24 | 26 | 27 | 28 | 29 Toledot | 30 R. Ḥ. 6 |
| 31 | 21 | | 21 | | 23 | | 25 | 27 Re'eh | | 29 | | 1 Tevet R. Ḥ. 7 |

# 1941

5701/02 תש״א / תש״ב

| | January | February | March | April | May | June | July | August | September | October | November | December |
|---|---|---|---|---|---|---|---|---|---|---|---|---|
| 1 | 2 Tevet Ḥanukkah 8 | 4 Bo | 2 Terumah | 4 | 4 | 6 Shavuot | 6 | 8 | 9 | 10 Yom Kippur | 11 Lekh Lekha | 11 |
| 2 | 3 | 5 | 3 | 5 | 5 | 7 | 7 | 9 Devarim Tishah be-Av | 10 | 11 | 12 | 12 |
| 3 | 4 | 6 | 4 | 6 | 6 Tazri'a Meẓora | 8 | 8 | 10 Fast | 11 | 12 | 13 | 13 |
| 4 | 5 Va-Yiggash | 7 | 5 | 7 | 7 | 9 | 9 | 11 | 12 | 13 Ha'azinu | 14 | 14 |
| 5 | 6 | 8 | 6 | 8 Ẓav Shabbat ha-Gadol | 8 | 10 | 10 Ḥukkat | 12 | 13 | 14 | 15 | 15 |
| 6 | 7 | 9 | 7 | 9 | 9 | 11 | 11 | 13 | 14 Ki Teẓe | 15 Sukkot | 16 | 16 Va-Yishlaḥ |
| 7 | 8 | 10 | 8 | 10 | 10 | 12 Naso | 12 | 14 | 15 | 16 | 17 | 17 |
| 8 | 9 | 11 Be-Shallaḥ | 9 Teẓavveh Zakhor | 11 | 11 | 13 | 13 | 15 | 16 | 17 | 18 Va-Yera | 18 |
| 9 | 10 Fast | 12 | 10 | 12 | 12 | 14 | 14 | 16 Va-Etḥannan | 17 | 18 Ḥol ha-Mo'ed | 19 | 19 |
| 10 | 11 | 13 | 11 | 13 | 13 Aḥarei Mot Kedoshim | 15 | 15 | 17 | 18 | 19 | 20 | 20 |
| 11 | 12 Va-Yeḥi | 14 | 12 | 14 | 14 | 16 | 16 | 18 | 19 | 20 | 21 | 21 |
| 12 | 13 | 15 | 13 Ta'anit Esther | 15 Pesaḥ | 15 | 17 | 17 Balak | 19 | 20 | 21 Hoshana Rabba | 22 | 22 |
| 13 | 14 | 16 | 14 Purim | 16 Omer | 16 | 18 | 18 Fast | 20 | 21 Ki Tavo | 22 Shemini Aẓeret | 23 | 23 Va-Yeshev |
| 14 | 15 | 17 | 15 Shushan Purim | 17 | 17 | 19 Be-Ha'alotkha | 19 | 21 | 22 | 23 Simḥat Torah Ve-Ẓot Ha-Berakhah | 24 | 24 |
| 15 | 16 | 18 Yitro | 16 Ki Tissa | 18 Ḥol ha-Mo'ed | 18 Lag ba-Omer | 20 | 20 | 22 | 23 | 24 | 25 Ḥayyei Sarah | 25 Ḥanukkah 1 |
| 16 | 17 | 19 | 17 | 19 | 19 | 21 | 21 | 23 Ekev | 24 | 25 | 26 | 26 2 |
| 17 | 18 | 20 | 18 | 20 | 20 Emor | 22 | 22 | 24 | 25 | 26 | 27 | 27 3 |
| 18 | 19 Shemot | 21 | 19 | 21 Pesaḥ | 21 | 23 | 23 | 25 | 26 | 27 Bereshit | 28 | 28 4 |
| 19 | 20 | 22 | 20 | 22 | 22 | 24 | 24 Pinḥas | 26 | 27 | 28 | 29 | 29 5 |
| 20 | 21 | 23 | 21 | 23 | 23 | 25 | 25 | 27 | 28 Niẓẓavim | 29 | 30 R. H. | 30 R. H. Mi-Keẓ 6 |
| 21 | 22 | 24 | 22 | 24 | 24 | 26 Shelaḥ | 26 | 28 | 29 | 30 R. H. | 1 Kislev R. H. | 1 Tevet R. H. 7 |
| 22 | 23 | 25 Mishpatim Shekalim | 23 Va-Yakhel Pekudei Parah | 25 | 25 | 27 | 27 | 29 | 1 Tishri Rosh Ha-Shanah | 1 Ḥeshvan R. H. | 2 Toledot | 2 8 |
| 23 | 24 | 26 | 24 | 26 | 26 | 28 | 28 | 30 R. H. Re'eh | 2 | 2 | 3 | 3 |
| 24 | 25 | 27 | 25 | 27 | 27 Be-Har Be-Ḥukkotai | 29 | 29 | 1 Elul R. H. | 3 Fast | 3 | 4 | 4 |
| 25 | 26 Va-Era | 28 | 26 | 28 | 28 | 30 R. H. | 1 Av R. H. | 2 | 4 | 4 No'aḥ | 5 | 5 |
| 26 | 27 | 29 | 27 | 29 Shemini | 29 | 1 Tammuz R. H. | 2 Mattot Masei | 3 | 5 | 5 | 6 | 6 |
| 27 | 28 | 30 R. H. | 28 | 30 R. H. | 1 Sivan R. H. | 2 | 3 | 4 | 6 Va-Yelekh Shabbat Shuvah | 6 | 7 | 7 Va-Yiggash |
| 28 | 29 | 1 Adar R. H. | 29 | 1 Iyyar R. H. | 2 | 3 Koraḥ | 4 | 5 | 7 | 7 | 8 | 8 |
| 29 | 1 Shevat R. H. | | 1 Nisan R. H. Va-Yikra Ha-Ḥodesh | 2 | 3 | 4 | 5 | 6 | 8 | 8 | 9 Va-Yeẓe | 9 |
| 30 | 2 | | 2 | 3 | 4 | 5 | 6 | 7 Shofetim | 9 | 9 | 10 | 10 Fast |
| 31 | 3 | | 3 | | 5 Be-Midbar | | 7 | 8 | | 10 | | 11 |

# 1942

5702/03 תש״ב / תש״ג

| | January | February | March | April | May | June | July | August | September | October | November | December |
|---|---|---|---|---|---|---|---|---|---|---|---|---|
| 1 | 12 Tevet | 14 | 12 | 14 | 14 | 16 | 16 | 18 Ekev | 19 | 20 Ḥol ha-Mo'ed | 21 | 22 |
| 2 | 13 | 15 | 13 Ta'anit Esther | 15 Pesaḥ | 15 Emor | 17 | 17 Fast | 19 | 20 | 21 Hoshana Rabba | 22 | 23 |
| 3 | 14 Va-Yeḥi | 16 | 14 Purim | 16 Omer | 16 | 18 | 18 | 20 | 21 | 22 Shemini Aẓeret | 23 | 24 |
| 4 | 15 | 17 | 15 Shushan Purim | 17 | 17 | 19 | 19 Pinḥas | 21 | 22 | 23 Simḥat Torah Ve-Ẓot Ha-Berakhah | 24 | 25 Ḥanukkah 1 |
| 5 | 16 | 18 | 16 | 18 Ḥol ha-Mo'ed | 18 Lag ba-Omer | 20 | 20 | 22 | 23 Niẓẓavim Va-Yelekh | 24 | 25 | 26 Va-Yeshev 2 |
| 6 | 17 | 19 | 17 | 19 | 19 | 21 Be-Ha'alotkha | 21 | 23 | 24 | 25 | 26 | 27 3 |
| 7 | 18 | 20 Yitro | 18 Ki Tissa Parah | 20 | 20 | 22 | 22 | 24 | 25 | 26 | 27 Ḥayyei Sarah | 28 4 |
| 8 | 19 | 21 | 19 | 21 Pesaḥ | 21 | 23 | 23 | 25 Re'eh | 26 | 27 | 28 | 29 5 |
| 9 | 20 | 22 | 20 | 22 | 22 Be-Har Be-Ḥukkotai | 24 | 24 | 26 | 27 | 28 | 29 | 1 Tevet R. H. 6 |
| 10 | 21 Shemot | 23 | 21 | 23 | 23 | 25 | 25 | 27 | 28 | 29 Bereshit | 1 Kislev R. H. | 2 7 |
| 11 | 22 | 24 | 22 | 24 Shemini | 24 | 26 | 26 Mattot Masei | 28 | 29 | 30 R. H. | 2 | 3 8 |
| 12 | 23 | 25 | 23 | 25 | 25 | 27 | 27 | 29 | 1 Tishri Rosh Ha-Shanah | 1 Ḥeshvan R. H. | 3 | 4 Mi-Keẓ |
| 13 | 24 | 26 | 24 | 26 | 26 | 28 Shelaḥ | 28 | 30 R. H. | 2 | 2 | 4 | 5 |
| 14 | 25 | 27 Mishpatim Shekalim | 25 Va-Yakhel Pekudei Ha-Ḥodesh | 27 | 27 | 29 | 29 | 1 Elul R. H. | 3 Fast | 3 | 5 Toledot | 6 |
| 15 | 26 | 28 | 26 | 28 | 28 | 30 R. H. | 1 Av R. H. | 2 Shofetim | 4 | 4 | 6 | 7 |
| 16 | 27 | 29 | 27 | 29 | 29 Be-Midbar | 1 Tammuz R. H. | 2 | 3 | 5 | 5 | 7 | 8 |
| 17 | 28 Va-Era | 30 R. H. | 28 | 30 R. H. | 1 Sivan R. H. | 2 | 3 | 4 | 6 | 6 No'aḥ | 8 | 9 |
| 18 | 29 | 1 Adar R. H. | 29 | 1 Iyyar R. H. Tazri'a Meẓora | 2 | 3 | 4 Devarim | 5 | 7 | 7 | 9 | 10 Fast |
| 19 | 1 Shevat R. H. | 2 | 1 Nisan R. H. | 2 | 3 | 4 | 5 | 6 | 8 Ha'azinu Shabbat Shuvah | 8 | 10 | 11 Va-Yiggash |
| 20 | 2 | 3 | 2 | 3 | 4 | 5 Koraḥ | 6 | 7 | 9 | 9 | 11 | 12 |
| 21 | 3 | 4 Terumah | 3 Va-Yikra | 4 | 5 | 6 | 7 | 8 | 10 Yom Kippur | 10 | 12 Va-Yeẓe | 13 |
| 22 | 4 | 5 | 4 | 5 | 6 Shavuot | 7 | 8 | 9 Ki Teẓe | 11 | 11 | 13 | 14 |
| 23 | 5 | 6 | 5 | 6 | 7 | 8 | 9 Tishah be-Av | 10 | 12 | 12 | 14 | 15 |
| 24 | 6 Bo | 7 | 6 | 7 | 8 | 9 | 10 | 11 | 13 | 13 Lekh Lekha | 15 | 16 |
| 25 | 7 | 8 | 7 | 8 Aḥarei Mot Kedoshim | 9 | 10 | 11 Va-Etḥannan | 12 | 14 | 14 | 16 | 17 |
| 26 | 8 | 9 | 8 | 9 | 10 | 11 | 12 | 13 | 15 Sukkot | 15 | 17 | 18 Va-Yeḥi |
| 27 | 9 | 10 | 9 | 10 | 11 | 12 Ḥukkat Balak | 13 | 14 | 16 | 16 | 18 | 19 |
| 28 | 10 | 11 Teẓavveh Zakhor | 10 Ẓav Shabbat ha-Gadol | 11 | 12 | 13 | 14 | 15 | 17 Ḥol ha-Mo'ed | 17 | 19 Va-Yishlaḥ | 20 |
| 29 | 11 | | 11 | 12 | 13 | 14 | 15 | 16 Ki Tavo | 18 | 18 | 20 | 21 |
| 30 | 12 | | 12 | 13 | 14 Naso | 15 | 16 | 17 | 19 | 19 | 21 | 22 |
| 31 | 13 Be-Shallaḥ | | 13 | | 15 | | 17 | 18 | | 20 Va-Yera | | 23 |

# 1943

**5703/04** תש״ג / תש״ד

| | January | February | March | April | May | June | July | August | September | October | November | December |
|---|---|---|---|---|---|---|---|---|---|---|---|---|
| 1 | 24 Tevet | 26 | 24 | 25 | 26 Aḥarei Mot | 27 | 28 | 29 | 1 Elul R. Ḥ. | 2 Rosh Ha-Shanah | 3 | 4 |
| 2 | 25 Shemot | 27 | 25 | 26 | 27 | 28 | 29 | 1 Av R. Ḥ. | 2 | 3 Ha'azinu Shabbat Shuvah | 4 | 5 |
| 3 | 26 | 28 | 26 | 27 Shemini Ha-Hodesh | 28 | 29 | 30 R. Ḥ. Koraḥ | 2 | 3 | 4 Fast | 5 | 6 |
| 4 | 27 | 29 | 27 | 28 | 29 | 1 Sivan R. Ḥ. | 1 Tammuz R. Ḥ. | 3 | 4 Shofetim | 5 | 6 | 7 Va-Yeẓe |
| 5 | 28 | 30 R. Ḥ. | 28 | 29 | 30 R. Ḥ. | 2 Be-Midbar | 2 | 4 | 5 | 6 | 7 | 8 |
| 6 | 29 | 1 Adar I R. Ḥ. Mishpatim | 29 Va-Yakhel Shekalim | 1 Nisan R. Ḥ. | 1 Iyyar R. Ḥ. | 3 | 3 | 5 | 6 | 7 | 8 Lekh Lekha | 9 |
| 7 | 1 Shevat R. Ḥ. | 2 | 30 R. Ḥ. | 2 | 2 | 4 | 4 | 6 Devarim | 7 | 8 | 9 | 10 |
| 8 | 2 | 3 | 1 Adar II R. Ḥ. | 3 | 3 Kedoshim | 5 | 5 | 7 | 8 | 9 | 10 | 11 |
| 9 | 3 Va-Era | 4 | 2 | 4 | 4 | 6 Shavuot | 6 | 8 | 9 | 10 Yom Kippur | 11 | 12 |
| 10 | 4 | 5 | 3 | 5 Tazri'a | 5 | 7 | 7 Ḥukkat | 9 Tishah be-Av | 10 | 11 | 12 | 13 |
| 11 | 5 | 6 | 4 | 6 | 6 | 8 | 8 | 10 | 11 Ki Teẓe | 12 | 13 | 14 Va-Yishlaḥ |
| 12 | 6 | 7 | 5 | 7 | 7 | 9 Naso | 9 | 11 | 12 | 13 | 14 | 15 |
| 13 | 7 | 8 Terumah | 6 Pekudei | 8 | 8 | 10 | 10 | 12 | 13 | 14 | 15 Va-Yera | 16 |
| 14 | 8 | 9 | 7 | 9 | 9 | 11 | 11 | 13 Va-Etḥannan | 14 | 15 Sukkot | 16 | 17 |
| 15 | 9 | 10 | 8 | 10 | 10 Emor | 12 | 12 | 14 | 15 | 16 | 17 | 18 |
| 16 | 10 Bo | 11 | 9 | 11 | 11 | 13 | 13 | 15 | 16 | 17 Ḥol ha-Mo'ed | 18 | 19 |
| 17 | 11 | 12 | 10 | 12 Meẓora Shabbat ha-Gadol | 12 | 14 | 14 Balak | 16 | 17 | 18 | 19 | 20 |
| 18 | 12 | 13 | 11 Ta'anit Esther | 13 | 13 | 15 | 15 | 17 | 18 Ki Tavo | 19 | 20 | 21 Va-Yeshev |
| 19 | 13 | 14 | 12 | 14 | 14 | 16 Be-Ha'alotkha | 16 | 18 | 19 | 20 | 21 | 22 |
| 20 | 14 | 15 Teẓavveh | 13 Va-Yikra Zakhor | 15 Pesaḥ | 15 | 17 | 17 Fast | 19 | 20 | 21 Hoshana Rabba | 22 Ḥayyei Sarah | 23 |
| 21 | 15 | 16 | 14 Purim | 16 Omer | 16 | 18 | 18 | 20 Ekev | 21 | 22 Shemini Aẓeret | 23 | 24 |
| 22 | 16 | 17 | 15 Shushan Purim | 17 Ḥol ha-Mo'ed | 17 Be-Har | 19 | 19 | 21 | 22 | 23 Simḥat Torah Ve-Zot Ha-Berakhah | 24 | 25 Ḥanukkah 1 |
| 23 | 17 Be-Shallaḥ | 18 | 16 | 18 | 18 Lag ba-Omer | 20 | 20 | 22 | 23 | 24 Bereshit | 25 | 26 2 |
| 24 | 18 | 19 | 17 | 19 | 19 | 21 | 21 Pinḥas | 23 | 24 | 25 | 26 | 27 3 |
| 25 | 19 | 20 | 18 | 20 | 20 | 22 | 22 | 24 | 25 Niẓẓavim Va-Yelekh | 26 | 27 | 28 Mi-Keẓ 4 |
| 26 | 20 | 21 | 19 | 21 Pesaḥ | 21 | 23 Shelaḥ | 23 | 25 | 26 | 27 | 28 | 29 5 |
| 27 | 21 | 22 Ki Tissa | 20 Ẓav Parah | 22 | 22 | 24 | 24 | 26 | 27 | 28 | 29 Toledot | 30 R. Ḥ. 6 |
| 28 | 22 | 23 | 21 | 23 | 23 | 25 | 25 | 27 Re'eh | 28 | 29 | 1 Kislev R. Ḥ. | 1 Tevet R. Ḥ. 7 |
| 29 | 23 | | 22 | 24 | 24 Be-Hukkotai | 26 | 26 | 28 | 29 | 30 R. Ḥ. | 2 | 2 8 |
| 30 | 24 Yitro | | 23 | 25 | 25 | 27 | 27 | 29 | 1 Tishri Rosh Ha-Shanah | 1 Ḥeshvan R. Ḥ. No'aḥ | 3 | 3 |
| 31 | 25 | | 24 | | 26 | | 28 Mattot Masei | 30 R. Ḥ. | | 2 | | 4 |

# 1944

**5704/05** תש״ד / תש״ה

| | January | February | March | April | May | June | July | August | September | October | November | December |
|---|---|---|---|---|---|---|---|---|---|---|---|---|
| 1 | 5 Tevet Va-Yiggash | 7 | 6 | 8 Ẓav Shabbat ha-Gadol | 8 | 10 | 10 Ḥukkat | 12 | 13 | 14 | 15 | 15 |
| 2 | 6 | 8 | 7 | 9 | 9 | 11 | 11 | 13 | 14 Ki Teẓe | 15 Sukkot | 16 | 16 Va-Yishlaḥ |
| 3 | 7 | 9 | 8 | 10 | 10 | 12 Naso | 12 | 14 | 15 | 16 | 17 | 17 |
| 4 | 8 | 10 | 9 Teẓavveh Zakhor | 11 | 11 | 13 | 13 | 15 | 16 | 17 Ḥol ha-Mo'ed | 18 Va-Yera | 18 |
| 5 | 9 | 11 Be-Shallaḥ | 10 | 12 | 12 | 14 | 14 | 16 Va-Etḥannan | 17 | 18 | 19 | 19 |
| 6 | 10 Fast | 12 | 11 | 13 | 13 Aḥarei Mot Kedoshim | 15 | 15 | 17 | 18 | 19 | 20 | 20 |
| 7 | 11 | 13 | 12 | 14 | 14 | 16 | 16 | 18 | 19 | 20 | 21 | 21 |
| 8 | 12 Va-Yeḥi | 14 | 13 Ta'anit Esther | 15 Pesaḥ | 15 | 17 | 17 Balak | 19 | 20 | 21 Hoshana Rabba | 22 | 22 |
| 9 | 13 | 15 | 14 Purim | 16 Omer | 16 | 18 | 18 Fast | 20 | 21 Ki Tavo | 22 Shemini Aẓeret | 23 | 23 Va-Yeshev |
| 10 | 14 | 16 | 15 Shushan Purim | 17 Ḥol ha-Mo'ed | 17 | 19 Be-Ha'alotkha | 19 | 21 | 22 | 23 Simḥat Torah Ve-Zot Ha-Berakhah | 24 | 24 |
| 11 | 15 | 17 | 16 Ki Tissa | 18 | 18 Lag ba-Omer | 20 | 20 | 22 | 23 | 24 | 25 Ḥayyei Sarah | 25 Ḥanukkah 1 |
| 12 | 16 | 18 Yitro | 17 | 19 | 19 | 21 | 21 | 23 Ekev | 24 | 25 | 26 | 26 2 |
| 13 | 17 | 19 | 18 | 20 | 20 Emor | 22 | 22 | 24 | 25 | 26 | 27 | 27 3 |
| 14 | 18 | 20 | 19 | 21 Pesaḥ | 21 | 23 | 23 | 25 | 26 | 27 Bereshit | 28 | 28 4 |
| 15 | 19 Shemot | 21 | 20 | 22 | 22 | 24 | 24 Pinḥas | 26 | 27 | 28 | 29 | 29 5 |
| 16 | 20 | 22 | 21 | 23 | 23 | 25 | 25 | 27 | 28 Niẓẓavim | 29 | 30 R. Ḥ. | 30 R. Ḥ. Mi-Keẓ 6 |
| 17 | 21 | 23 | 22 | 24 | 24 | 26 Shelaḥ | 26 | 28 | 29 | 30 R. Ḥ. | 1 Kislev R. Ḥ. | 1 Tevet R. Ḥ. 7 |
| 18 | 22 | 24 | 23 Va-Yakhel Pekudei Parah | 25 | 25 | 27 | 27 | 29 | 1 Tishri Rosh Ha-Shanah | 1 Ḥeshvan R. Ḥ. | 2 Toledot | 2 8 |
| 19 | 23 | 25 Mishpatim Shekalim | 24 | 26 | 26 | 28 | 28 | 30 R. Ḥ. Re'eh | 2 | 2 | 3 | 3 |
| 20 | 24 | 26 | 25 | 27 | 27 Be-Har Be-Hukkotai | 29 | 29 | 1 Elul R. Ḥ. | 3 Fast | 3 | 4 | 4 |
| 21 | 25 | 27 | 26 | 28 | 28 | 30 R. Ḥ. | 1 Av R. Ḥ. | 2 | 4 | 4 No'aḥ | 5 | 5 |
| 22 | 26 Va-Era | 28 | 27 | 29 Shemini | 29 | 1 Tammuz R. Ḥ. | 2 Mattot Masei | 3 | 5 | 5 | 6 | 6 |
| 23 | 27 | 29 | 28 | 30 R. Ḥ. | 1 Sivan R. Ḥ. | 2 | 3 | 4 | 6 Va-Yelekh Shabbat Shuvah | 6 | 7 | 7 Va-Yiggash |
| 24 | 28 | 30 R. Ḥ. | 29 | 1 Iyyar R. Ḥ. | 2 | 3 Koraḥ | 4 | 5 | 7 | 7 | 8 | 8 |
| 25 | 29 | 1 Adar R. Ḥ. | 1 Nisan R. Ḥ. Va-Yikra Ha-Hodesh | 2 | 3 | 4 | 5 | 6 | 8 | 8 | 9 Va-Yeẓe | 9 |
| 26 | 1 Shevat R. Ḥ. | 2 Terumah | 2 | 3 | 4 | 5 | 6 | 7 Shofetim | 9 | 9 | 10 | 10 Fast |
| 27 | 2 | 3 | 3 | 4 | 5 Be-Midbar | 6 | 7 | 8 | 10 Yom Kippur | 10 | 11 | 11 |
| 28 | 3 | 4 | 4 | 5 | 6 Shavuot | 7 | 8 | 9 | 11 | 11 Lekh Lekha | 12 | 12 |
| 29 | 4 Bo | 5 | 5 | 6 Tazri'a Meẓora | 7 | 8 | 9 Devarim Tishah be-Av | 10 | 12 | 12 | 13 | 13 |
| 30 | 5 | | 6 | 7 | 8 | 9 | 10 Fast | 11 | 13 Ha'azinu | 13 | 14 | 14 Va-Yeḥi |
| 31 | 6 | | 7 | | 9 | | 11 | 12 | | 14 | | 15 |

## 1945

**5705/06** תש״ה / תש״ו

| | January | February | March | April | May | June | July | August | September | October | November | December |
|---|---|---|---|---|---|---|---|---|---|---|---|---|
| 1 | 16 **Tevet** | 18 | 16 | 18 Hol ha-Mo'ed | 18 Lag ba-Omer | 20 | 20 | 22 | **23** *Nizzavim Va-Yelekh* | 24 | 25 | **26** *Va-Yeshev* 2 |
| 2 | 17 | 19 | 17 | 19 | 19 | **21** *Be-Ha'alotkha* | 21 | 23 | 24 | 25 | 26 | 27 3 |
| 3 | 18 | **20** *Yitro* | **18** *Ki Tissa* Parah | 20 | 20 | 22 | 22 | 24 | 25 | 26 | **27** *Hayyei Sarah* | 28 4 |
| 4 | 19 | 21 | 19 | 21 Pesah | 21 | 23 | 23 | **25** *Re'eh* | 26 | 27 | 28 | 29 5 |
| 5 | 20 | 22 | 20 | 22 | **22** *Be-Har Be-Hukkotai* | 24 | 24 | 26 | 27 | 28 | 29 | 1 **Tevet** R. H. 6 |
| 6 | **21** *Shemot* | 23 | 21 | 23 | 23 | 25 | 25 | 27 | 28 | **29** *Bereshit* | 1 **Kislev** R. H. | 2 7 |
| 7 | 22 | 24 | 22 | **24** *Shemini* | 24 | 26 | **26** *Mattot Masei* | 28 | 29 | 30 R. H. | 2 | 3 8 |
| 8 | 23 | 25 | 23 | 25 | 25 | 27 | 27 | 29 | **1 Tishri** Rosh Ha-Shanah | 1 **Heshvan** R. H. | 3 | **4** *Mi-Kez* |
| 9 | 24 | 26 | 24 | 26 | 26 | **28** *Shelah* | 28 | 30 R. H. | 2 | 2 | 4 | 5 |
| 10 | 25 | **27** *Mishpatim* Shekalim | *Va-Yakhel Pekudei* **25** Ha-Hodesh | 27 | 27 | 29 | 29 | 1 **Elul** R. H. | 3 Fast | 3 | **5** *Toledot* | 6 |
| 11 | 26 | 28 | 26 | 28 | 28 | 30 R. H. | 1 **Av** R. H. | **2** *Shofetim* | 4 | 4 | 6 | 7 |
| 12 | 27 | 29 | 27 | 29 | **29** *Be-Midbar* | 1 **Tammuz** R. H. | 2 | 3 | 5 | 5 | 7 | 8 |
| 13 | **28** *Va-Era* | 30 R. H. | 28 | 30 R. H. | 1 **Sivan** R. H. | 2 | 3 | 4 | 6 | **6** *No'ah* | 8 | 9 |
| 14 | 29 | 1 **Adar** R. H. | 29 | **1** R. H. **Iyyar** *Tazri'a Mezora* | 2 | 3 | **4** *Devarim* | 5 | 7 | 7 | 9 | 10 Fast |
| 15 | 1 **Shevat** R. H. | 2 | 1 **Nisan** R. H. | 2 | 3 | 4 | 5 | 6 | **8** *Ha'azinu* Shabbat Shuvah | 8 | 10 | **11** *Va-Yiggash* |
| 16 | 2 | 3 | 2 | 3 | 4 | **5** *Korah* | 6 | 7 | 9 | 9 | 11 | 12 |
| 17 | 3 | **4** *Terumah* | **3** *Va-Yikra* | 4 | 5 | 6 | 7 | 8 | 10 Yom Kippur | 10 | **12** *Va-Yeze* | 13 |
| 18 | 4 | 5 | 4 | 5 | 6 Shavuot | 7 | 8 | **9** *Ki Teze* | 11 | 11 | 13 | 14 |
| 19 | 5 | 6 | 5 | 6 | **7** | 8 | 9 Tishah be-Av | 10 | 12 | 12 | 14 | 15 |
| 20 | **6** *Bo* | 7 | 6 | 7 | 8 | 9 | 10 | 11 | 13 | **13** *Lekh Lekha* | 15 | 16 |
| 21 | 7 | 8 | 7 | **8** *Aharei Mot Kedoshim* | 9 | 10 | **11** *Va-Ethannan* | 12 | 14 | 14 | 16 | 17 |
| 22 | 8 | 9 | 8 | 9 | 10 | 11 | 12 | 13 | **15** Sukkot | 15 | 17 | **18** *Va-Yehi* |
| 23 | 9 | 10 | 9 | 10 | 11 | **12** *Hukkat Balak* | 13 | 14 | 16 | 16 | 18 | 19 |
| 24 | 10 | **11** *Tezavveh* Zakhor | **10** *Zav* Shabbat ha-Gadol | 11 | 12 | 13 | 14 | 15 | 17 | 17 | **19** *Va-Yishlah* | 20 |
| 25 | 11 | 12 | 11 | 12 | 13 | 14 | 15 | **16** *Ki Tavo* | 18 Hol ha-Mo'ed | 18 | 20 | 21 |
| 26 | 12 | 13 Ta'anit Esther | 12 | 13 | **14** *Naso* | 15 | 16 | 17 | 19 | 19 | 21 | 22 |
| 27 | **13** *Be-Shallah* | 14 Purim | 13 | 14 | 15 | 16 | 17 | 18 | 20 | **20** *Va-Yera* | 22 | 23 |
| 28 | 14 | 15 Shushan Purim | 14 | **15** *Emor* | 16 | 17 Fast | **18** *Ekev* | 19 | 21 Hoshana Rabba | 21 | 23 | 24 |
| 29 | 15 | | 15 Pesah | 16 | 17 | 18 | 19 | 20 | **22** Shemini Azeret | 22 | 24 | **25** *Shemot* |
| 30 | 16 | | 16 Omer | 17 | 18 | **19** *Pinhas* | 20 | 21 | 23 Simhat Torah *Ve-Zot Ha-Berakhah* | 23 | 25 Hanukkah 1 | 26 |
| 31 | 17 | | **17** Hol ha-Mo'ed | | 19 | | 21 | 22 | | 24 | | 27 |

## 1946

**5706/07** תש״ו / תש״ז

| | January | February | March | April | May | June | July | August | September | October | November | December |
|---|---|---|---|---|---|---|---|---|---|---|---|---|
| 1 | 28 **Tevet** | 30 R. H. | 28 | 29 | 30 R. H. | **2** *Be-Midbar* | 2 | 4 | 5 | 6 | 7 | 8 |
| 2 | 29 | **1** *Mishpatim* **Adar I** R. H. | **29** *Va-Yakhel* Shekalim | 1 **Nisan** R. H. | 1 **Iyyar** R. H. | 3 | 3 | 5 | 6 | 7 | **8** *Lekh Lekha* | 9 |
| 3 | 1 **Shevat** R. H. | 2 | 30 R. H. | 2 | 2 | 4 | 4 | **6** *Devarim* | 7 | 8 | 9 | 10 |
| 4 | 2 | 3 | 1 **Adar II** R. H. | 3 | **3** *Kedoshim* | 5 | 5 | 7 | 8 | 9 | 10 | 11 |
| 5 | **3** *Va-Era* | 4 | 2 | 4 | 4 | 6 Shavuot | 6 | 8 | 9 | **10** Yom Kippur | 11 | 12 |
| 6 | 4 | 5 | 3 | **5** *Tazri'a* | 5 | 7 | **7** *Hukkat* | 9 Tishah be-Av | 10 | 11 | 12 | 13 |
| 7 | 5 | 6 | 4 | 6 | 6 | 8 | 8 | 10 | **11** *Ki Teze* | 12 | 13 | **14** *Va-Yishlah* |
| 8 | 6 | 7 | 5 | 7 | 7 | **9** *Naso* | 9 | 11 | 12 | 13 | 14 | 15 |
| 9 | 7 | **8** *Terumah* | **6** *Pekudei* | 8 | 8 | 10 | 10 | 12 | 13 | 14 | **15** *Va-Yera* | 16 |
| 10 | 8 | 9 | 7 | 9 | 9 | 11 | 11 | **13** *Va-Ethannan* | 14 | 15 Sukkot | 16 | 17 |
| 11 | 9 | 10 | 8 | 10 | **10** *Emor* | 12 | 12 | 14 | 15 | 16 | 17 | 18 |
| 12 | **10** *Bo* | 11 | 9 | 11 | 11 | 13 | 13 | 15 | 16 | **17** Hol ha-Mo'ed | 18 | 19 |
| 13 | 11 | 12 | 10 | **12** *Mezora* Shabbat ha-Gadol | 12 | 14 | **14** *Balak* | 16 | 17 | 18 | 19 | 20 |
| 14 | 12 | 13 | 11 Ta'anit Esther | 13 | 13 | 15 | 15 | 17 | **18** *Ki Tavo* | 19 | 20 | **21** *Va-Yeshev* |
| 15 | 13 | 14 | 12 | 14 | 14 | **16** *Be-Ha'alotkha* | 16 | 18 | 19 | 20 | 21 | 22 |
| 16 | 14 | **15** *Tezavveh* | **13** *Va-Yikra* Zakhor | 15 Pesah | 15 | 17 | 17 Fast | 19 | 20 | 21 Hoshana Rabba | **22** *Hayyei Sarah* | 23 |
| 17 | 15 | 16 | 14 Purim | 16 Omer | 16 | 18 | 18 | **20** *Ekev* | 21 | 22 Shemini Azeret | 23 | 24 |
| 18 | 16 | 17 | 15 Shushan Purim | 17 Hol ha-Mo'ed | **17** *Be-Har* | 19 | 19 | 21 | 22 | 23 Simhat Torah *Ve-Zot Ha-Berakhah* | 24 | 25 Hanukkah 1 |
| 19 | **17** *Be-Shallah* | 18 | 16 | 18 | 18 Lag ba-Omer | 20 | 20 | 22 | 23 | **24** *Bereshit* | 25 | 26 2 |
| 20 | 18 | 19 | 17 | **19** | 19 | 21 | **21** *Pinhas* | 23 | 24 | 25 | 26 | 27 3 |
| 21 | 19 | 20 | 18 | 20 | 20 | 22 | 22 | 24 | **25** *Nizzavim Va-Yelekh* | 26 | 27 | **28** *Mi-Kez* 4 |
| 22 | 20 | 21 | 19 | 21 Pesah | 21 | **23** *Shelah* | 23 | 25 | 26 | 27 | 28 | 29 5 |
| 23 | 21 | **22** *Ki Tissa* | **20** *Zav* Parah | 22 | 22 | 24 | 24 | 26 | 27 | 28 | **29** *Toledot* | 30 R. H. 6 |
| 24 | 22 | 23 | 21 | 23 | 23 | 25 | 25 | **27** *Re'eh* | 28 | 29 | 1 **Kislev** R. H. | 1 **Tevet** R. H. 7 |
| 25 | 23 | 24 | 22 | 24 | **24** *Be-Hukkotai* | 26 | 26 | 28 | 29 | 30 R. H. | 2 | 2 8 |
| 26 | **24** *Yitro* | 25 | 23 | 25 | 25 | 27 | 27 | 29 | **1 Tishri** Rosh Ha-Shanah | **1** R. H. *No'ah* **Heshvan** | 3 | 3 |
| 27 | 25 | 26 | 24 | **26** *Aharei Mot* | 26 | 28 | **28** *Mattot Masei* | 30 R. H. | 2 | 2 | 4 | 4 |
| 28 | 26 | 27 | 25 | 27 | 27 | 29 | 29 | 1 **Elul** R. H. | **3** *Ha'azinu* Shabbat Shuvah | 3 | 5 | **5** *Va-Yiggash* |
| 29 | 27 | | 26 | 28 | 28 | **30** R. H. *Korah* | 1 **Av** R. H. | 2 | 4 Fast | 4 | 6 | 6 |
| 30 | 28 | | **27** *Shemini* Ha-Hodesh | 29 | 29 | 1 **Tammuz** R. H. | 2 | 3 | 5 | 5 | **7** *Va-Yeze* | 7 |
| 31 | 29 | | 28 | | 1 **Sivan** R. H. | | 3 | **4** *Shofetim* | | 6 | | 8 |

# 1947

**5707/08** תש״ז / תש״ח

| | January | February | March | April | May | June | July | August | September | October | November | December |
|---|---|---|---|---|---|---|---|---|---|---|---|---|
| 1 | 9 Tevet | 11 Be-Shallaḥ | 9 Teẓavveh Zakhor | 11 | 11 | 13 | 13 | 15 | 16 | 17 | 18 Va-Yera | 18 |
| 2 | 10 Fast | 12 | 10 | 12 | 12 | 14 | 14 | 16 Va-Ethannan | 17 | 18 Ḥol ha-Mo'ed | 19 | 19 |
| 3 | 11 | 13 | 11 | 13 | 13 Aḥarei Mot Kedoshim | 15 | 15 | 17 | 18 | 19 | 20 | 20 |
| 4 | 12 Va-Yeḥi | 14 | 12 | 14 | 14 | 16 | 16 | 18 | 19 | 20 | 21 | 21 |
| 5 | 13 | 15 | 13 Ta'anit Esther | 15 Pesaḥ | 15 | 17 | 17 Balak | 19 | 20 | 21 Hoshana Rabba | 22 | 22 |
| 6 | 14 | 16 | 14 Purim | 16 Omer | 16 | 18 | 18 Fast | 20 | 21 Ki Tavo | 22 Shemini Aẓeret | 23 | 23 Va-Yeshev |
| 7 | 15 | 17 | 15 Shushan Purim | 17 | 17 | 19 Be-Ha'alotkha | 19 | 21 | 22 | 23 Simḥat Torah Ve-Zot Ha-Berakhah | 24 | 24 |
| 8 | 16 | 18 Yitro | 16 Ki Tissa | 18 Ḥol ha-Mo'ed | 18 Lag ba-Omer | 20 | 20 | 22 | 23 | 24 | 25 Ḥayyei Sarah | 25 Ḥanukkah 1 |
| 9 | 17 | 19 | 17 | 19 | 19 | 21 | 21 | 23 Ekev | 24 | 25 | 26 | 26 2 |
| 10 | 18 | 20 | 18 | 20 | 20 Emor | 22 | 22 | 24 | 25 | 26 | 27 | 27 3 |
| 11 | 19 Shemot | 21 | 19 | 21 Pesaḥ | 21 | 23 | 23 | 25 | 26 | 27 Bereshit | 28 | 28 4 |
| 12 | 20 | 22 | 20 | 22 | 22 | 24 | 24 Pinḥas | 26 | 27 | 28 | 29 | 29 5 |
| 13 | 21 | 23 | 21 | 23 | 23 | 25 | 25 | 27 | 28 Niẓẓavim | 29 | 30 R. Ḥ. | 30 R. Ḥ. Mi-Keẓ 6 |
| 14 | 22 | 24 | 22 | 24 | 24 | 26 Shelaḥ | 26 | 28 | 29 | 30 R. Ḥ. | 1 Kislev R. Ḥ. | 1 Tevet R. Ḥ. 7 |
| 15 | 23 | 25 Mishpatim Shekalim | 23 Va-Yakhel Pekudei Parah | 25 | 25 | 27 | 27 | 29 | 1 Tishri Rosh Ha-Shanah | 1 Ḥeshvan R. Ḥ. | 2 Toledot | 2 8 |
| 16 | 24 | 26 | 24 | 26 | 26 | 28 | 28 | 30 Re'eh R. Ḥ. | 2 | 2 | 3 | 3 |
| 17 | 25 | 27 | 25 | 27 | 27 Be-Har Be-Ḥukkotai | 29 | 29 | 1 Elul R. Ḥ. | 3 Fast | 3 | 4 | 4 |
| 18 | 26 Va-Era | 28 | 26 | 28 | 28 | 30 R. Ḥ. | 1 Av R. Ḥ. | 2 | 4 | 4 No'aḥ | 5 | 5 |
| 19 | 27 | 29 | 27 | 29 Shemini | 29 | 1 Tammuz R. Ḥ. | 2 Mattot Masei | 3 | 5 | 5 | 6 | 6 |
| 20 | 28 | 30 R. Ḥ. | 28 | 30 R. Ḥ. | 1 Sivan R. Ḥ. | 2 | 3 | 4 | 6 Va-Yelekh Shabbat Shuvah | 6 | 7 | 7 Va-Yiggash |
| 21 | 29 | 1 Adar R. Ḥ. | 29 | 1 Iyyar R. Ḥ. | 2 | 3 Koraḥ | 4 | 5 | 7 | 7 | 8 | 8 |
| 22 | 1 Shevat R. Ḥ. | 2 Terumah | 1 Nisan R. Ḥ. Va-Yikra Ha-Ḥodesh | 2 | 3 | 4 | 5 | 6 | 8 | 8 | 9 Va-Yeẓe | 9 |
| 23 | 2 | 3 | 2 | 3 | 4 | 5 | 6 | 7 Shofetim | 9 | 9 | 10 | 10 Fast |
| 24 | 3 | 4 | 3 | 4 | 5 Be-Midbar | 6 | 7 | 8 | 10 Yom Kippur | 10 | 11 | 11 |
| 25 | 4 Bo | 5 | 4 | 5 | 6 Shavuot | 7 | 8 | 9 | 11 | 11 Lekh Lekha | 12 | 12 |
| 26 | 5 | 6 | 5 | 6 Tazri'a Meẓora | 7 | 8 | 9 Devarim Tishah be-Av | 10 | 12 | 12 | 13 | 13 |
| 27 | 6 | 7 | 6 | 7 | 8 | 9 | 10 Fast | 11 | 13 Ha'azinu | 13 | 14 | 14 Va-Yeḥi |
| 28 | 7 | 8 | 7 | 8 | 9 | 10 Ḥukkat | 11 | 12 | 14 | 14 | 15 | 15 |
| 29 | 8 | | 8 Ẓav Shabbat ha-Gadol | 9 | 10 | 11 | 12 | 13 | 15 Sukkot | 15 | 16 Va-Yishlaḥ | 16 |
| 30 | 9 | | 9 | 10 | 11 | 12 | 13 | 14 Ki Teẓe | 16 | 16 | 17 | 17 |
| 31 | 10 | | 10 | | 12 Naso | | 14 | 15 | | 17 | | 18 |

# 1948

**5708/09** תש״ח / תש״ט

| | January | February | March | April | May | June | July | August | September | October | November | December |
|---|---|---|---|---|---|---|---|---|---|---|---|---|
| 1 | 19 Tevet | 21 | 20 | 21 | 22 | 23 | 24 | 25 | 27 | 27 | 29 | 29 |
| 2 | 20 | 22 | 21 | 22 | 23 | 24 | 25 | 26 | 28 | 28 Niẓẓavim | 30 R. Ḥ. | 30 R. Ḥ. |
| 3 | 21 Shemot | 23 | 22 | 23 Shemini Parah | 24 | 25 | 26 Shelaḥ | 27 | 29 | 29 | 1 Ḥeshvan R. Ḥ. | 1 Kislev R. Ḥ. |
| 4 | 22 | 24 | 23 | 24 | 25 | 26 | 27 | 28 | 30 R. Ḥ. Re'eh | 1 Tishri Rosh Ha-Shanah | 2 | 2 Toledot |
| 5 | 23 | 25 | 24 | 25 | 26 | 27 Be-Ḥukkotai | 28 | 29 | 1 Elul R. Ḥ. | 2 | 3 | 3 |
| 6 | 24 | 26 | 25 Va-Yakhel Shekalim | 26 | 27 | 28 | 29 | 1 Av R. Ḥ. | 2 | 3 Fast | 4 No'aḥ | 4 |
| 7 | 25 | 27 Mishpatim | 26 | 27 | 28 | 29 | 30 R. Ḥ. | 2 Mattot Masei | 3 | 4 | 5 | 5 |
| 8 | 26 | 28 | 27 | 28 | 29 Aḥarei Mot | 1 Sivan R. Ḥ. | 1 Tammuz R. Ḥ. | 3 | 4 | 5 | 6 | 6 |
| 9 | 27 | 29 | 28 | 29 | 30 R. Ḥ. | 2 | 2 | 4 | 5 | 6 Va-Yelekh Shabbat Shuvah | 7 | 7 |
| 10 | 28 Va-Era | 30 R. Ḥ. | 29 | 1 Nisan R. Ḥ. Tazri'a Ha-Ḥodesh | 1 Iyyar R. Ḥ. | 3 | 3 Koraḥ | 5 | 6 | 7 | 8 | 8 |
| 11 | 29 | 1 Adar I R. Ḥ. | 30 R. Ḥ. | 2 | 2 | 4 | 4 | 6 | 7 Shofetim | 8 | 9 | 9 Va-Yeẓe |
| 12 | 1 Shevat R. Ḥ. | 2 | 1 Adar II R. Ḥ. | 3 | 3 | 5 Be-Midbar | 5 | 7 | 8 | 9 | 10 | 10 |
| 13 | 2 | 3 | 2 Pekudei | 4 | 4 | 6 Shavuot | 6 | 8 | 9 | 10 Yom Kippur | 11 Lekh Lekha | 11 |
| 14 | 3 | 4 Terumah | 3 | 5 | 5 | 7 | 7 | 9 Devarim Tishah be-Av | 10 | 11 | 12 | 12 |
| 15 | 4 | 5 | 4 | 6 | 6 Kedoshim | 8 | 8 | 10 Fast | 11 | 12 | 13 | 13 |
| 16 | 5 | 6 | 5 | 7 | 7 | 9 | 9 | 11 | 12 | 13 Ha'azinu | 14 | 14 |
| 17 | 6 Bo | 7 | 6 | 8 Meẓora Shabbat ha-Gadol | 8 | 10 | 10 Ḥukkat | 12 | 13 | 14 | 15 | 15 |
| 18 | 7 | 8 | 7 | 9 | 9 | 11 | 11 | 13 | 14 Ki Teẓe | 15 Sukkot | 16 | 16 Va-Yishlaḥ |
| 19 | 8 | 9 | 8 | 10 | 10 | 12 Naso | 12 | 14 | 15 | 16 | 17 | 17 |
| 20 | 9 | 10 | 9 Va-Yikra Zakhor | 11 | 11 | 13 | 13 | 15 | 16 | 17 | 18 Va-Yera | 18 |
| 21 | 10 | 11 Teẓavveh | 10 | 12 | 12 | 14 | 14 | 16 Va-Ethannan | 17 | 18 Ḥol ha-Mo'ed | 19 | 19 |
| 22 | 11 | 12 | 11 | 13 | 13 Emor | 15 | 15 | 17 | 18 | 19 | 20 | 20 |
| 23 | 12 | 13 | 12 | 14 | 14 | 16 | 16 | 18 | 19 | 20 | 21 | 21 |
| 24 | 13 Be-Shallaḥ | 14 | 13 Ta'anit Esther | 15 Pesaḥ | 15 | 17 | 17 Balak | 19 | 20 | 21 Hoshana Rabba | 22 | 22 |
| 25 | 14 | 15 | 14 Purim | 16 Omer | 16 | 18 | 18 Fast | 20 | 21 Ki Tavo | 22 Shemini Aẓeret | 23 | 23 Va-Yeshev |
| 26 | 15 | 16 | 15 Shushan Purim | 17 | 17 | 19 Be-Ha'alotkha | 19 | 21 | 22 | 23 Simḥat Torah Ve-Zot Ha-Berakhah | 24 | 24 |
| 27 | 16 | 17 | 16 Ẓav | 18 Ḥol ha-Mo'ed | 18 Lag ba-Omer | 20 | 20 | 22 | 23 | 24 | 25 Ḥayyei Sarah | 25 Ḥanukkah 1 |
| 28 | 17 | 18 Ki Tissa | 17 | 19 | 19 | 21 | 21 | 23 Ekev | 24 | 25 | 26 | 26 2 |
| 29 | 18 | 19 | 18 | 20 | 20 Be-Har | 22 | 22 | 24 | 25 | 26 | 27 | 27 3 |
| 30 | 19 | | 19 | 21 Pesaḥ | 21 | 23 | 23 | 25 | 26 | 27 Bereshit | 28 | 28 4 |
| 31 | 20 Yitro | | 20 | | 22 | | 24 Pinḥas | 26 | | 28 | | 29 5 |

# 1949

**5709/10** תש״ט / תש״י

| | January | February | March | April | May | June | July | August | September | October | November | December |
|---|---|---|---|---|---|---|---|---|---|---|---|---|
| 1 | 30 Kislev R. Ḥ. 6 Ḥanukkah *Mi-Keẓ* | 2 | 30 R. Ḥ. | 2 | 2 | 4 | 4 | 6 | 7 | 8 *Ha'azinu* Shabbat Shuvah | 9 | 10 |
| 2 | 1 Tevet R. Ḥ. 7 | 3 | 1 Adar R. Ḥ. | 3 *Va-Yikra* | 3 | 5 | 5 *Koraḥ* | 7 | 8 | 9 | 10 | 11 |
| 3 | 2 8 | 4 | 2 | 4 | 4 | 6 Shavuot | 6 | 8 | 9 *Ki Teẓe* | 10 Yom Kippur | 11 | 12 *Va-Yeẓe* |
| 4 | 3 | 5 | 3 | 5 | 5 Yom ha-Aẓma'ut | 7 | 7 | 9 Tishah be-Av | 10 | 11 | 12 | 13 |
| 5 | 4 | 6 *Bo* | 4 *Terumah* | 6 | 6 | 8 | 8 | 10 | 11 | 12 | 13 *Lekh Lekha* | 14 |
| 6 | 5 | 7 | 5 | 7 | 7 | 9 | 9 | 11 *Va-Etḥannan* | 12 | 13 | 14 | 15 |
| 7 | 6 | 8 | 6 | 8 | 8 *Aḥarei Mot Kedoshim* | 10 | 10 | 12 | 13 | 14 | 15 | 16 |
| 8 | 7 *Va-Yiggash* | 9 | 7 | 9 | 9 | 11 | 11 | 13 | 14 | 15 Sukkot | 16 | 17 |
| 9 | 8 | 10 | 8 | 10 *Ẓav* Shabbat ha-Gadol | 10 | 12 | 12 *Ḥukkat Balak* | 14 | 15 | 16 | 17 | 18 |
| 10 | 9 | 11 | 9 | 11 | 11 | 13 | 13 | 15 | 16 *Ki Tavo* | 17 Ḥol ha-Mo'ed | 18 | 19 *Va-Yishlaḥ* |
| 11 | 10 Fast | 12 | 10 | 12 | 12 | 14 *Naso* | 14 | 16 | 17 | 18 | 19 | 20 |
| 12 | 11 | 13 *Be-Shallaḥ* | 11 *Teẓavveh Zakhor* | 13 | 13 | 15 | 15 | 17 | 18 | 19 | 20 *Va-Yera* | 21 |
| 13 | 12 | 14 | 12 | 14 | 14 | 16 | 16 | 18 *Ekev* | 19 | 20 | 21 | 22 |
| 14 | 13 | 15 | 13 Ta'anit Esther | 15 Pesaḥ | 15 *Emor* | 17 | 17 Fast | 19 | 20 | 21 Hoshana Rabba | 22 | 23 |
| 15 | 14 *Va-Yeḥi* | 16 | 14 Purim | 16 Omer | 16 | 18 | 18 | 20 | 21 | 22 Shemini Aẓeret | 23 | 24 |
| 16 | 15 | 17 | 15 Shushan Purim | 17 Ḥol ha-Mo'ed | 17 | 19 | 19 *Pinḥas* | 21 | 22 | 23 Simḥat Torah *Ve-Zot Ha-Berakhah* | 24 | 25 Ḥanukkah 1 |
| 17 | 16 | 18 | 16 | 18 | 18 Lag ba-Omer | 20 | 20 | 22 | 23 *Niẓẓavim Va-Yelekh* | 24 | 25 | 26 *Va-Yeshev* 2 |
| 18 | 17 | 19 | 17 | 19 | 19 | 21 *Be-Ha'alotkha* | 21 | 23 | 24 | 25 | 26 | 27 3 |
| 19 | 18 | 20 *Yitro* | 18 *Ki Tissa* Parah | 20 | 20 | 22 | 22 | 24 | 25 | 26 | 27 *Ḥayyei Sarah* | 28 4 |
| 20 | 19 | 21 | 19 | 21 Pesaḥ | 21 | 23 | 23 | 25 *Re'eh* | 26 | 27 | 28 | 29 5 |
| 21 | 20 | 22 | 20 | 22 | 22 *Be-Har Be-Ḥukkotai* | 24 | 24 | 26 | 27 | 28 | 29 | 1 Tevet R. Ḥ. 6 |
| 22 | 21 *Shemot* | 23 | 21 | 23 | 23 | 25 | 25 | 27 | 28 | 29 *Bereshit* | 1 Kislev R. Ḥ. | 2 7 |
| 23 | 22 | 24 | 22 | 24 *Shemini* | 24 | 26 | 26 *Mattot Masei* | 28 | 29 | 30 R. Ḥ. | 2 | 3 8 |
| 24 | 23 | 25 | 23 | 25 | 25 | 27 | 27 | 29 | 1 Tishri Rosh Ha-Shanah | 1 Ḥeshvan R. Ḥ. | 3 | 4 *Mi-Keẓ* |
| 25 | 24 | 26 | 24 | 26 | 26 | 28 *Shelaḥ* | 28 | 30 R. Ḥ. | 2 | 2 | 4 | 5 |
| 26 | 25 | 27 *Mishpatim* Shekalim | 25 *Va-Yakhel Pekudei* Ha-Ḥodesh | 27 | 27 | 29 | 29 | 1 Elul R. Ḥ. | 3 Fast | 3 | 5 *Toledot* | 6 |
| 27 | 26 | 28 | 26 | 28 | 28 | 30 R. Ḥ. | 1 Av R. Ḥ. | 2 *Shofetim* | 4 | 4 | 6 | 7 |
| 28 | 27 | 29 | 27 | 29 | 29 *Be-Midbar* | 1 Tammuz R. Ḥ. | 2 | 3 | 5 | 5 | 7 | 8 |
| 29 | 28 *Va-Era* | | 28 | 30 R. Ḥ. | 1 Sivan R. Ḥ. | 2 | 3 | 4 | 6 | 6 *No'ah* | 8 | 9 |
| 30 | 29 | | 29 | 1 Iyyar R. Ḥ. *Tazri'a Meẓora* | 2 | 3 | 4 *Devarim* | 5 | 7 | 7 | 9 | 10 Fast |
| 31 | 1 Shevat R. Ḥ. | | 1 Nisan R. Ḥ. | | 3 | | 5 | 6 | | 8 | | 11 *Va-Yiggash* |

# 1950

**5710/11** תש״י / תשי״א

| | January | February | March | April | May | June | July | August | September | October | November | December |
|---|---|---|---|---|---|---|---|---|---|---|---|---|
| 1 | 12 Tevet | 14 | 12 | 14 *Ẓav* Shabbat ha-Gadol | 14 | 16 | 16 *Balak* | 18 | 19 | 20 Ḥol ha-Mo'ed | 21 | 22 |
| 2 | 13 | 15 | 13 Ta'anit Esther | 15 Pesaḥ | 15 | 17 | 17 Fast | 19 | 20 *Ki Tavo* | 21 Hoshana Rabba | 22 | 23 *Va-Yeshev* |
| 3 | 14 | 16 | 14 Purim | 16 Omer | 16 | 18 *Be-Ha'alotkha* | 18 | 20 | 21 | 22 Shemini Aẓeret | 23 | 24 |
| 4 | 15 | 17 *Be-Shallaḥ* | 15 Shushan Purim *Teẓavveh* | 17 Ḥol ha-Mo'ed | 17 | 19 | 19 | 21 | 22 | 23 Simḥat Torah *Ve-Zot Ha-Berakhah* | 24 *Ḥayyei Sarah* | 25 Ḥanukkah 1 |
| 5 | 16 | 18 | 16 | 18 | 18 Lag ba-Omer | 20 | 20 | 22 *Ekev* | 23 | 24 | 25 | 26 2 |
| 6 | 17 | 19 | 17 | 19 | 19 *Emor* | 21 | 21 | 23 | 24 | 25 | 26 | 27 3 |
| 7 | 18 *Va-Yeḥi* | 20 | 18 | 20 | 20 | 22 | 22 | 24 | 25 | 26 *Bereshit* | 27 | 28 4 |
| 8 | 19 | 21 | 19 | 21 Pesaḥ | 21 | 23 | 23 *Pinḥas* | 25 | 26 | 27 | 28 | 29 5 |
| 9 | 20 | 22 | 20 | 22 | 22 | 24 | 24 | 26 | 27 *Niẓẓavim* | 28 | 29 | 30 R. Ḥ. *Mi-Keẓ* 6 |
| 10 | 21 | 23 | 21 | 23 | 23 | 25 *Shelaḥ* | 25 | 27 | 28 | 29 | 1 Kislev R. Ḥ. | 1 Tevet R. Ḥ. 7 |
| 11 | 22 | 24 *Yitro* | 22 *Ki Tissa* Parah | 24 | 24 | 26 | 26 | 28 | 29 | 30 R. Ḥ. | 2 *Toledot* | 2 8 |
| 12 | 23 | 25 | 23 | 25 | 25 | 27 | 27 | 29 *Re'eh* | 1 Tishri Rosh Ha-Shanah | 1 Ḥeshvan R. Ḥ. | 3 | 3 |
| 13 | 24 | 26 | 24 | 26 | 26 *Be-Har Be-Ḥukkotai* | 28 | 28 | 30 R. Ḥ. | 2 | 2 | 4 | 4 |
| 14 | 25 *Shemot* | 27 | 25 | 27 | 27 | 29 | 29 | 1 Elul R. Ḥ. | 3 Fast | 3 *No'ah* | 5 | 5 |
| 15 | 26 | 28 | 26 | 28 *Shemini* | 28 | 30 R. Ḥ. | 1 Av R. Ḥ. *Mattot Masei* | 2 | 4 | 4 | 6 | 6 |
| 16 | 27 | 29 | 27 | 29 | 29 | 1 Tammuz R. Ḥ. | 2 | 3 | 5 *Va-Yelekh* Shabbat Shuvah | 5 | 7 | 7 *Va-Yiggash* |
| 17 | 28 | 30 R. Ḥ. | 28 | 30 R. Ḥ. | 1 Sivan R. Ḥ. | 2 *Koraḥ* | 3 | 4 | 6 | 6 | 8 | 8 |
| 18 | 29 | 1 Adar R. Ḥ. *Mishpatim* Shekalim | 29 *Va-Yakhel Pekudei* Ha-Ḥodesh | 1 Iyyar R. Ḥ. | 2 | 3 | 4 | 5 | 7 | 7 | 9 *Va-Yeẓe* | 9 |
| 19 | 1 Shevat R. Ḥ. | 2 | 1 Nisan R. Ḥ. | 2 | 3 | 4 | 5 | 6 *Shofetim* | 8 | 8 | 10 | 10 Fast |
| 20 | 2 | 3 | 2 | 3 Yom ha-Aẓma'ut | 4 *Be-Midbar* | 5 | 6 | 7 | 9 | 9 | 11 | 11 |
| 21 | 3 *Va-Era* | 4 | 3 | 4 | 5 | 6 | 7 | 8 | 10 Yom Kippur | 10 *Lekh Lekha* | 12 | 12 |
| 22 | 4 | 5 | 4 | 5 *Tazri'a Meẓora* | 6 Shavuot | 7 | 8 *Devarim* | 9 | 11 | 11 | 13 | 13 |
| 23 | 5 | 6 | 5 | 6 | 7 | 8 | 9 Tishah be-Av | 10 | 12 *Ha'azinu* | 12 | 14 | 14 *Va-Yeḥi* |
| 24 | 6 | 7 | 6 | 7 | 8 | 9 *Ḥukkat* | 10 | 11 | 13 | 13 | 15 | 15 |
| 25 | 7 | 8 *Terumah Zakhor* | 7 *Va-Yikra* | 8 | 9 | 10 | 11 | 12 | 14 | 14 | 16 *Va-Yishlaḥ* | 16 |
| 26 | 8 | 9 | 8 | 9 | 10 | 11 | 12 | 13 *Ki Teẓe* | 15 Sukkot | 15 | 17 | 17 |
| 27 | 9 | 10 | 9 | 10 | 11 *Naso* | 12 | 13 | 14 | 16 | 16 | 18 | 18 |
| 28 | 10 *Bo* | 11 | 10 | 11 | 12 | 13 | 14 | 15 | 17 Ḥol ha-Mo'ed | 17 *Va-Yera* | 19 | 19 |
| 29 | 11 | | 11 | 12 *Aḥarei Mot Kedoshim* | 13 | 14 | 15 *Va-Etḥannan* | 16 | 18 | 18 | 20 | 20 |
| 30 | 12 | | 12 | 13 | 14 | 15 | 16 | 17 | 19 | 19 | 21 | 21 *Shemot* |
| 31 | 13 | | 13 | | 15 | | 17 | 18 | | 20 | | 22 |

# 1951

**5711/12** תשי״א / תשי״ב

| | January | February | March | April | May | June | July | August | September | October | November | December |
|---|---|---|---|---|---|---|---|---|---|---|---|---|
| 1 | 23 Tevet | 25 | 23 | 24 | 25 | 26 | 27 | 28 | 30 R. H. *Re'eh* | 1 Tishri Rosh Ha-Shanah | 2 | **2** *Toledot* |
| 2 | 24 | 26 | 24 | 25 | 26 | **27** *Be-Ḥukkotai* | 28 | 29 | 1 Elul R. H. | 2 | 3 | 3 |
| 3 | 25 | **27** *Mishpatim* | **25** *Va-Yakhel Shekalim* | 26 | 27 | 28 | 29 | 1 Av R. H. | 2 | 3 Fast | **4** *No'aḥ* | 4 |
| 4 | 26 | 28 | 26 | 27 | 28 | 29 | 30 R. H. | **2** *Mattot Masei* | 3 | 4 | 5 | 5 |
| 5 | 27 | 29 | 27 | 28 | **29** *Aḥarei Mot* | 1 Sivan R. H. | 1 Tammuz R. H. | 3 | 4 | 5 | 6 | 6 |
| 6 | **28** *Va-Era* | 30 R. H. | 28 | 29 | 30 R. H. | 2 | 2 | 4 | 5 | **6** *Va-Yelekh* Shabbat Shuvah | 7 | 7 |
| 7 | 29 | 1 Adar I R. H. | 29 | **1** R. H. *Tazri'a* Nisan Ha-Hodesh | 1 Iyyar R. H. | 3 | **3** *Koraḥ* | 5 | 6 | 7 | 8 | 8 |
| 8 | 1 Shevat R. H. | 2 | 30 R. H. | 2 | 2 | 4 | 4 | 6 | **7** *Shofetim* | 8 | 9 | **9** *Va-Yeze* |
| 9 | 2 | 3 | 1 Adar II R. H. | 3 | 3 | **5** *Be-Midbar* | 5 | 7 | 8 | 9 | 10 | 10 |
| 10 | 3 | **4** *Terumah* | **2** *Pekudei* | 4 | 4 Yom ha-Azma'ut | 6 Shavuot | 6 | 8 | 9 | 10 Yom Kippur | **11** *Lekh Lekha* | 11 |
| 11 | 4 | 5 | 3 | 5 | 5 | 7 | 7 | **9** *Devarim* Tishah be-Av | 10 | 11 | 12 | 12 |
| 12 | 5 | 6 | 4 | 6 | **6** *Kedoshim* | 8 | 8 | 10 Fast | 11 | 12 | 13 | 13 |
| 13 | **6** *Bo* | 7 | 5 | 7 | 7 | 9 | 9 | 11 | 12 | **13** *Ha'azinu* | 14 | 14 |
| 14 | 7 | 8 | 6 | **8** *Mezora* Shabbat ha-Gadol | 8 | 10 | **10** *Ḥukkat* | 12 | 13 | 14 | 15 | 15 |
| 15 | 8 | 9 | 7 | 9 | 9 | 11 | 11 | 13 | **14** *Ki Teze* | 15 Sukkot | 16 | **16** *Va-Yishlaḥ* |
| 16 | 9 | 10 | 8 | 10 | 10 | **12** *Naso* | 12 | 14 | 15 | 16 | 17 | 17 |
| 17 | 10 | **11** *Tezavveh* | **9** *Va-Yikra* Zakhor | 11 | 11 | 13 | 13 | 15 | 16 | 17 | **18** *Va-Yera* | 18 |
| 18 | 11 | 12 | 10 | 12 | 12 | 14 | 14 | **16** *Va-Ethannan* | 17 | 18 Hol ha-Mo'ed | 19 | 19 |
| 19 | 12 | 13 | 11 | 13 | **13** *Emor* | 15 | 15 | 17 | 18 | 19 | 20 | 20 |
| 20 | **13** *Be-Shallaḥ* | 14 | 12 | 14 | 14 | 16 | 16 | 18 | 19 | **20** | 21 | 21 |
| 21 | 14 | 15 | 13 Ta'anit Esther | **15** Pesaḥ | 15 | 17 | **17** *Balak* | 19 | 20 | 21 Hoshana Rabba | 22 | 22 |
| 22 | 15 | 16 | 14 Purim | 16 Omer | 16 | 18 | 18 Fast | 20 | **21** *Ki Tavo* | 22 Shemini Azeret | 23 | **23** *Va-Yeshev* |
| 23 | 16 | 17 | 15 Shushan Purim | 17 | 17 | **19** *Be-Ha'alotkha* | 19 | 21 | 22 | 23 Simḥat Torah *Ve-Zot Ha-Berakhah* | 24 | 24 |
| 24 | 17 | **18** *Ki Tissa* | **16** *Zav* | 18 | 18 Lag ba-Omer | 20 | 20 | 22 | 23 | 24 | **25** *Ḥayyei Sarah* | 25 Ḥanukkah 1 |
| 25 | 18 | 19 | 17 | 19 Hol ha-Mo'ed | 19 | 21 | 21 | **23** *Ekev* | 24 | 25 | 26 | 26 2 |
| 26 | 19 | 20 | 18 | 20 | **20** *Be-Har* | 22 | 22 | 24 | 25 | 26 | 27 | 27 3 |
| 27 | **20** *Yitro* | 21 | 19 | 21 Pesaḥ | 21 | 23 | 23 | 25 | 26 | **27** *Bereshit* | 28 | 28 4 |
| 28 | 21 | 22 | 20 | **22** | 22 | 24 | **24** *Pinḥas* | 26 | 27 | 28 | 29 | 29 5 |
| 29 | 22 | | 21 | 23 | 23 | 25 | 25 | 27 | **28** *Nizzavim* | 29 | 30 R. H. | **30** R. H. *Mi-Kez* 6 |
| 30 | 23 | | 22 | 24 | 24 | **26** *Shelaḥ* | 26 | 28 | 29 | 30 R. H. | 1 Kislev R. H. | 1 Tevet R. H. 7 |
| 31 | 24 | | **23** *Shemini Parah* | | 25 | | 27 | 29 | | 1 Heshvan R. H. | | 2 8 |

# 1952

**5712/13** תשי״ב / תשי״ג

| | January | February | March | April | May | June | July | August | September | October | November | December |
|---|---|---|---|---|---|---|---|---|---|---|---|---|
| 1 | 3 Tevet | 5 | **4** *Terumah* | 6 | 6 | 8 | 8 | 10 | 11 | 12 | **13** *Lekh Lekha* | 13 |
| 2 | 4 | **6** *Bo* | 5 | 7 | 7 | 9 | 9 | **11** *Va-Ethannan* | 12 | 13 | 14 | 14 |
| 3 | 5 | 7 | 6 | 8 | **8** *Aḥarei Mot Kedoshim* | 10 | 10 | 12 | 13 | 14 | 15 | 15 |
| 4 | 6 | 8 | 7 | 9 | 9 | 11 | 11 | 13 | 14 | **15** Sukkot | 16 | 16 |
| 5 | **7** *Va-Yiggash* | 9 | 8 | **10** *Zav* Shabbat ha-Gadol | 10 | 12 | **12** *Ḥukkat Balak* | 14 | 15 | 16 | 17 | 17 |
| 6 | 8 | 10 | 9 | 11 | 11 | 13 | 13 | 15 | **16** *Ki Tavo* | 17 | 18 | **18** *Va-Yishlaḥ* |
| 7 | 9 | 11 | 10 | 12 | 12 | **14** *Naso* | 14 | 16 | 17 | 18 Hol ha-Mo'ed | 19 | 19 |
| 8 | 10 Fast | 12 | **11** *Tezavveh* Zakhor | 13 | 13 | 15 | 15 | 17 | 18 | 19 | **20** *Va-Yera* | 20 |
| 9 | 11 | **13** *Be-Shallaḥ* | 12 | 14 | 14 | 16 | 16 | **18** *Ekev* | 19 | 20 | 21 | 21 |
| 10 | 12 | 14 | 13 Ta'anit Esther | 15 Pesaḥ | **15** *Emor* | 17 | 17 Fast | 19 | 20 | 21 Hoshana Rabba | 22 | 22 |
| 11 | 13 | 15 | 14 Purim | 16 Omer | 16 | 18 | 18 | 20 | 21 | **22** Shemini Azeret | 23 | 23 |
| 12 | **14** *Va-Yeḥi* | 16 | 15 Shushan Purim | **17** | 17 | 19 | **19** *Pinḥas* | 21 | 22 | 23 Simḥat Torah *Ve-Zot Ha-Berakhah* | 24 | 24 |
| 13 | 15 | 17 | 16 | 18 | 18 Lag ba-Omer | 20 | 20 | 22 | **23** *Nizzavim Va-Yelekh* | 24 | 25 | **25** Hanukkah *Va-Yeshev* 1 |
| 14 | 16 | 18 | 17 | 19 Hol ha-Mo'ed | 19 | **21** *Be-Ha'alotkha* | 21 | 23 | 24 | 25 | 26 | 26 2 |
| 15 | 17 | 19 | **18** *Ki Tissa* Parah | 20 | 20 | 22 | 22 | 24 | 25 | 26 | **27** *Ḥayyei Sarah* | 27 3 |
| 16 | 18 | **20** *Yitro* | 19 | 21 Pesaḥ | 21 | 23 | 23 | **25** *Re'eh* | 26 | 27 | 28 | 28 4 |
| 17 | 19 | 21 | 20 | 22 | **22** *Be-Har Be-Ḥukkotai* | 24 | 24 | 26 | 27 | 28 | 29 | 29 5 |
| 18 | 20 | 22 | 21 | 23 | 23 | 25 | 25 | 27 | 28 | **29** *Bereshit* | 30 R. H. | 30 R. H. 6 |
| 19 | **21** *Shemot* | 23 | 22 | **24** *Shemini* | 24 | 26 | **26** *Mattot Masei* | 28 | 29 | 30 R. H. | 1 Kislev R. H. | 1 Tevet R. H. 7 |
| 20 | 22 | 24 | 23 | 25 | 25 | 27 | 27 | 29 | 1 Tishri Rosh Ha-Shanah | 1 Heshvan R. H. | 2 | **2** *Mi-Kez* 8 |
| 21 | 23 | 25 | 24 | 26 | 26 | **28** *Shelaḥ* | 28 | 30 R. H. | 2 | 2 | 3 | 3 |
| 22 | 24 | 26 | **25** *Va-Yakhel Pekudei* Ha-Hodesh | 27 | 27 | 29 | 29 | 1 Elul R. H. | 3 Fast | 3 | **4** *Toledot* | 4 |
| 23 | 25 | **27** *Mishpatim* Shekalim | 26 | 28 | 28 | 30 R. H. | 1 Av R. H. | **2** *Shofetim* | 4 | 4 | 5 | 5 |
| 24 | 26 | 28 | 27 | 29 | **29** *Be-Midbar* | 1 Tammuz R. H. | 2 | 3 | 5 | 5 | 6 | 6 |
| 25 | 27 | 29 | 28 | 30 R. H. | 1 Sivan R. H. | 2 | 3 | 4 | 6 | **6** *No'aḥ* | 7 | 7 |
| 26 | **28** *Va-Era* | 30 R. H. | 29 | **1** Iyyar R. H. *Tazri'a Mezora* | 2 | 3 | **4** *Devarim* | 5 | 7 | 7 | 8 | 8 |
| 27 | 29 | 1 Adar R. H. | 1 Nisan R. H. | 2 | 3 | 4 | 5 | 6 | **8** *Ha'azinu* Shabbat Shuvah | 8 | 9 | **9** *Va-Yiggash* |
| 28 | 1 Shevat R. H. | 2 | 2 | 3 | 4 | **5** *Koraḥ* | 6 | 7 | 9 | 9 | 10 | 10 Fast |
| 29 | 2 | 3 | **3** *Va-Yikra* | 4 | 5 | 6 | 7 | 8 | 10 Yom Kippur | 10 | **11** *Va-Yeze* | 11 |
| 30 | 3 | | 4 | 5 Yom ha-Azma'ut | 6 Shavuot | 7 | 8 | **9** *Ki Teze* | 11 | 11 | 12 | 12 |
| 31 | 4 | | 5 | | **7** | | 9 Tishah be-Av | 10 | | 12 | | 13 |

## 1953

**5713/14** תשי״ג / תשי״ד

| | January | February | March | April | May | June | July | August | September | October | November | December |
|---|---|---|---|---|---|---|---|---|---|---|---|---|
| 1 | 14 **Tevet** | 16 | 14 Purim | 16 Omer | 16 | 18 | 18 | **20** *Ekev* | 21 | 22 Shemini Aẓeret | 23 | 24 |
| 2 | 15 | 17 | 15 Shushan Purim | 17 | **17** *Emor* | 19 | 19 | 21 | 22 | 23 Simḥat Torah *Ve-Zot Ha-Berakhah* | 24 | 25 Ḥanukkah 1 |
| 3 | **16** *Va-Yeḥi* | 18 | 16 | 18 Ḥol ha-Mo'ed | 18 Lag ba-Omer | 20 | 20 | 22 | 23 | **24** *Bereshit* | 25 | 26 2 |
| 4 | 17 | 19 | 17 | **19** | 19 | 21 | **21** *Pinḥas* | 23 | 24 | 25 | 26 | 27 3 |
| 5 | 18 | 20 | 18 | 20 | 20 | 22 | 22 | 24 | **25** *Niẓẓavim Va-Yelekh* | 26 | 27 | **28** *Mi-Keẓ* 4 |
| 6 | 19 | 21 | 19 | 21 Pesaḥ | 21 | **23** *Shelaḥ* | 23 | 25 | 26 | 27 | 28 | 29 5 |
| 7 | 20 | **22** *Yitro* | **20** *Ki Tissa* Parah | 22 | 22 | 24 | 24 | 26 | 27 | 28 | **29** *Toledot* | 1 **Tevet** R. Ḥ. 6 |
| 8 | 21 | 23 | 21 | 23 | 23 | 25 | 25 | **27** *Re'eh* | 28 | 29 | 1 **Kislev** R. Ḥ. | 2 7 |
| 9 | 22 | 24 | 22 | 24 | **24** *Be-Har Be-Ḥukkotai* | 26 | 26 | 28 | 29 | 30 R. Ḥ. | 2 | 3 8 |
| 10 | **23** *Shemot* | 25 | 23 | 25 | 25 | 27 | 27 | 29 | 1 **Tishri** Rosh Ha-Shanah | 1 **Ḥeshvan** R. Ḥ. *No'aḥ* | 3 | 4 |
| 11 | 24 | 26 | 24 | **26** *Shemini* | 26 | 28 | **28** *Mattot Masei* | 30 R. Ḥ. | 2 | 2 | 4 | 5 |
| 12 | 25 | 27 | 25 | 27 | 27 | 29 | 29 | 1 **Elul** R. Ḥ. | **3** *Ha'azinu* Shabbat Shuvah | 3 | 5 | **6** *Va-Yiggash* |
| 13 | 26 | 28 | 26 | 28 | 28 | **30** R. Ḥ. *Koraḥ* | 1 **Av** R. Ḥ. | 2 | 4 Fast | 4 | 6 | 7 |
| 14 | 27 | **29** *Mishpatim* Shekalim | **27** *Va-Yakhel Pekudei* Ha-Ḥodesh | 29 | 29 | 1 **Tammuz** R. Ḥ. | 2 | 3 | 5 | 5 | **7** *Va-Yeẓe* | 8 |
| 15 | 28 | 30 R. Ḥ. | 28 | 30 R. Ḥ. | 1 **Sivan** R. Ḥ. | 2 | 3 | **4** *Shofetim* | 6 | 6 | 8 | 9 |
| 16 | 29 | 1 **Adar** R. Ḥ. | 29 | 1 **Iyyar** R. Ḥ. | **2** *Be-Midbar* | 3 | 4 | 5 | 7 | 7 | 9 | 10 Fast |
| 17 | **1 Shevat** R. Ḥ. *Va-Era* | 2 | 1 **Nisan** R. Ḥ. | 2 | 3 | 4 | 5 | 6 | 8 | **8** *Lekh Lekha* | 10 | 11 |
| 18 | 2 | 3 | 2 | **3** *Tazri'a Meẓora* | 4 | 5 | **6** *Devarim* | 7 | 9 | 9 | 11 | 12 |
| 19 | 3 | 4 | 3 | 4 | 5 | 6 | 7 | 8 | **10** Yom Kippur | 10 | 12 | **13** *Va-Yeḥi* |
| 20 | 4 | 5 | 4 | 5 Yom ha-Aẓma'ut | 6 Shavuot | **7** *Ḥukkat* | 8 | 9 | 11 | 11 | 13 | 14 |
| 21 | 5 | **6** *Terumah* | **5** *Va-Yikra* | 6 | 7 | 8 | 9 Tishah be-Av | 10 | 12 | 12 | **14** *Va-Yishlaḥ* | 15 |
| 22 | 6 | 7 | 6 | 7 | 8 | 9 | 10 | **11** *Ki Teẓe* | 13 | 13 | 15 | 16 |
| 23 | 7 | 8 | 7 | 8 | **9** *Naso* | 10 | 11 | 12 | 14 | 14 | 16 | 17 |
| 24 | **8** *Bo* | 9 | 8 | 9 | 10 | 11 | 12 | 13 | 15 Sukkot | **15** *Va-Yera* | 17 | 18 |
| 25 | 9 | 10 | 9 | **10** *Aḥarei Mot Kedoshim* | 11 | 12 | **13** *Va-Etḥannan* | 14 | 16 | 16 | 18 | 19 |
| 26 | 10 | 11 Ta'anit Esther | 10 | 11 | 12 | 13 | 14 | 15 | **17** | 17 | 19 | **20** *Shemot* |
| 27 | 11 | 12 | 11 | 12 | 13 | **14** *Balak* | 15 | 16 | 18 | 18 | 20 | 21 |
| 28 | 12 | **13** *Teẓavveh* Zakhor | **12** *Ẓav* Shabbat ha-Gadol | 13 | 14 | 15 | 16 | 17 | 19 Ḥol ha-Mo'ed | 19 | **21** *Va-Yeshev* | 22 |
| 29 | 13 | | 13 | 14 | 15 | 16 | 17 | **18** *Ki Tavo* | 20 | 20 | 22 | 23 |
| 30 | 14 | | 14 | 15 | **16** *Be-Ha'alotkha* | 17 Fast | 18 | 19 | 21 Hoshana Rabba | 21 | 23 | 24 |
| 31 | **15** *Be-Shallaḥ* | | 15 Pesaḥ | | 17 | | 19 | 20 | | **22** *Ḥayyei Sarah* | | 25 |

## 1954

**5714/15** תשי״ד / תשט״ו

| | January | February | March | April | May | June | July | August | September | October | November | December |
|---|---|---|---|---|---|---|---|---|---|---|---|---|
| 1 | 26 **Tevet** | 28 | 26 | 27 | **28** *Kedoshim* | 29 | 30 R. Ḥ. | 2 | 3 | 4 | 5 | 6 |
| 2 | **27** *Va-Era* | 29 | 27 | 28 | 29 | 1 **Sivan** R. Ḥ. | 1 **Tammuz** R. Ḥ. | 3 | 4 | **5** *Va-Yelekh* Shabbat Shuvah | 6 | 7 |
| 3 | 28 | 30 R. Ḥ. | 28 | **29** *Tazri'a* Ha-Ḥodesh | 30 R. Ḥ. | 2 | **2** *Ḥukkat* | 4 | 5 | 6 | 7 | 8 |
| 4 | 29 | 1 **Adar I** R. Ḥ. | 29 | 1 **Nisan** R. Ḥ. | 1 **Iyyar** R. Ḥ. | 3 | 3 | 5 | **6** *Shofetim* | 7 | 8 | **9** *Va-Yeẓe* |
| 5 | 1 **Shevat** R. Ḥ. | 2 | 30 R. Ḥ. | 2 | 2 | **4** *Naso* | 4 | 6 | 7 | 8 | 9 | 10 |
| 6 | 2 | **3** *Terumah* | **1 Adar II** R. Ḥ. Shekalim *Pekudei* | 3 | 3 Yom ha-Aẓma'ut | 5 | 5 | 7 | 8 | 9 | **10** *Lekh Lekha* | 11 |
| 7 | 3 | 4 | 2 | 4 | 4 | 6 Shavuot | 6 | **8** *Devarim* | 9 | 10 Yom Kippur | 11 | 12 |
| 8 | 4 | 5 | 3 | 5 | **5** *Emor* | 7 | 7 | 9 Tishah be-Av | 10 | 11 | 12 | 13 |
| 9 | **5** *Bo* | 6 | 4 | 6 | 6 | 8 | 8 | 10 | 11 | **12** *Ha'azinu* | 13 | 14 |
| 10 | 6 | 7 | 5 | **7** *Meẓora* | 7 | 9 | **9** *Balak* | 11 | 12 | 13 | 14 | 15 |
| 11 | 7 | 8 | 6 | 8 | 8 | 10 | 10 | 12 | **13** *Ki Teẓe* | 14 | 15 | **16** *Va-Yishlaḥ* |
| 12 | 8 | 9 | 7 | 9 | 9 | **11** *Be-Ha'alotkha* | 11 | 13 | 14 | 15 Sukkot | 16 | 17 |
| 13 | 9 | **10** *Teẓavveh* | **8** *Va-Yikra* Zakhor | 10 | 10 | 12 | 12 | 14 | 15 | 16 | **17** *Va-Yera* | 18 |
| 14 | 10 | 11 | 9 | 11 | 11 | 13 | 13 | **15** *Va-Etḥannan* | 16 | 17 | 18 | 19 |
| 15 | 11 | 12 | 10 | 12 | **12** *Be-Har* | 14 | 14 | 16 | 17 | 18 Ḥol ha-Mo'ed | 19 | 20 |
| 16 | **12** *Be-Shallaḥ* | 13 | 11 | 13 | 13 | 15 | 15 | 17 | 18 | **19** | 20 | 21 |
| 17 | 13 | 14 | 12 | **14** *Aḥarei Mot* Shabbat ha-Gadol | 14 | 16 | **16** *Pinḥas* | 18 | 19 | 20 | 21 | 22 |
| 18 | 14 | 15 | 13 Ta'anit Esther | 15 Pesaḥ | 15 | 17 | 17 Fast | 19 | **20** *Ki Tavo* | 21 Hoshana Rabba | 22 | **23** *Va-Yeshev* |
| 19 | 15 | 16 | 14 Purim | 16 Omer | 16 | **18** *Shelaḥ* | 18 | 20 | 21 | 22 Shemini Aẓeret | 23 | 24 |
| 20 | 16 | **17** *Ki Tissa* | **15** *Ẓav* Shushan Purim | 17 | 17 | 19 | 19 | 21 | 22 | 23 Simḥat Torah *Ve-Zot Ha-Berakhah* | **24** *Ḥayyei Sarah* | 25 Ḥanukkah 1 |
| 21 | 17 | 18 | 16 | 18 Ḥol ha-Mo'ed | 18 Lag ba-Omer | 20 | 20 | **22** *Ekev* | 23 | 24 | 25 | 26 2 |
| 22 | 18 | 19 | 17 | 19 | **19** *Be-Ḥukkotai* | 21 | 21 | 23 | 24 | 25 | 26 | 27 3 |
| 23 | **19** *Yitro* | 20 | 18 | 20 | 20 | 22 | 22 | 24 | 25 | **26** *Bereshit* | 27 | 28 4 |
| 24 | 20 | 21 | 19 | **21** Pesaḥ | 21 | 23 | **23** *Mattot* | 25 | 26 | 27 | 28 | 29 5 |
| 25 | 21 | 22 | 20 | 22 | 22 | 24 | 24 | 26 | **27** *Niẓẓavim* | 28 | 29 | **30** R. Ḥ. *Mi-Keẓ* 6 |
| 26 | 22 | 23 | 21 | 23 | 23 | **25** *Koraḥ* | 25 | 27 | 28 | 29 | 1 **Kislev** R. Ḥ. | 1 **Tevet** R. Ḥ. 7 |
| 27 | 23 | **24** *Va-Yakhel* | **22** *Shemini* Parah | 24 | 24 | 26 | 26 | 28 | 29 | 30 R. Ḥ. | **2** *Toledot* | 2 8 |
| 28 | 24 | 25 | 23 | 25 | 25 | 27 | 27 | **29** *Re'eh* | 1 **Tishri** Rosh Ha-Shanah | 1 **Ḥeshvan** R. Ḥ. | 3 | 3 |
| 29 | 25 | | 24 | 26 | **26** *Be-Midbar* | 28 | 28 | 30 R. Ḥ. | 2 | 2 | 4 | 4 |
| 30 | **26** *Mishpatim* | | 25 | 27 | 27 | 29 | 29 | 1 **Elul** R. Ḥ. | 3 Fast | **3** *No'aḥ* | 5 | 5 |
| 31 | 27 | | 26 | | 28 | | **1 Av** R. Ḥ. *Masei* | 2 | | 4 | | 6 |

# 1955

**5715/16** תשט״ו / תשט״ז

| | January | February | March | April | May | June | July | August | September | October | November | December |
|---|---|---|---|---|---|---|---|---|---|---|---|---|
| 1 | 7 Tevet Va-Yiggash | 9 | 7 | 9 | 9 | 11 | 11 | 13 | 14 | 15 Sukkot | 16 | 16 |
| 2 | 8 | 10 | 8 | 10 Ẓav Shabbat ha-Gadol | 10 | 12 | 12 Ḥukkat Balak | 14 | 15 | 16 | 17 | 17 |
| 3 | 9 | 11 | 9 | 11 | 11 | 13 | 13 | 15 | 16 Ki Tavo | 17 Ḥol ha-Mo'ed | 18 | 18 Va-Yishlaḥ |
| 4 | 10 Fast | 12 | 10 | 12 | 12 | 14 Naso | 14 | 16 | 17 | 18 | 19 | 19 |
| 5 | 11 | 13 Be-Shallaḥ | 11 Teẓavveh Zakhor | 13 | 13 | 15 | 15 | 17 | 18 | 19 | 20 Va-Yera | 20 |
| 6 | 12 | 14 | 12 | 14 | 14 | 16 | 16 | 18 Ekev | 19 | 20 | 21 | 21 |
| 7 | 13 | 15 | 13 Ta'anit Esther | 15 Pesaḥ | 15 Emor | 17 | 17 Fast | 19 | 20 | 21 Hoshana Rabba | 22 | 22 |
| 8 | 14 Va-Yeḥi | 16 | 14 Purim | 16 Omer | 16 | 18 | 18 | 20 | 21 | 22 Shemini Aẓeret | 23 | 23 |
| 9 | 15 | 17 | 15 Shushan Purim | 17 Ḥol ha-Mo'ed | 17 | 19 | 19 Pinḥas | 21 | 22 | 23 Simḥat Torah Ve-Zot Ha-Berakhah | 24 | 24 |
| 10 | 16 | 18 | 16 | 18 | 18 Lag ba-Omer | 20 | 20 | 22 | 23 Niẓẓavim Va-Yelekh | 24 | 25 | 25 Ḥanukkah 1 Va-Yeshev |
| 11 | 17 | 19 | 17 | 19 | 19 | 21 Be-Ha'alotkha | 21 | 23 | 24 | 25 | 26 | 26 2 |
| 12 | 18 | 20 Yitro | 18 Ki Tissa Parah | 20 | 20 | 22 | 22 | 24 | 25 | 26 | 27 Ḥayyei Sarah | 27 3 |
| 13 | 19 | 21 | 19 | 21 Pesaḥ | 21 | 23 | 23 | 25 Re'eh | 26 | 27 | 28 | 28 4 |
| 14 | 20 | 22 | 20 | 22 | 22 Be-Har Be-Ḥukkotai | 24 | 24 | 26 | 27 | 28 | 29 | 29 5 |
| 15 | 21 Shemot | 23 | 21 | 23 | 23 | 25 | 25 | 27 | 28 | 29 Bereshit | 30 R. Ḥ. | 30 R. Ḥ. 6 |
| 16 | 22 | 24 | 22 | 24 Shemini | 24 | 26 | 26 Mattot Masei | 28 | 29 | 30 R. Ḥ. | 1 Kislev R. Ḥ. | 1 Tevet R. Ḥ. 7 |
| 17 | 23 | 25 | 23 | 25 | 25 | 27 | 27 | 29 | 1 Tishri Rosh Ha-Shanah | 1 Ḥeshvan R. Ḥ. | 2 | 2 Mi-Keẓ 8 |
| 18 | 24 | 26 | 24 | 26 | 26 | 28 Shelaḥ | 28 | 30 R. Ḥ. | 2 | 2 | 3 | 3 |
| 19 | 25 | 27 Mishpatim Shekalim | 25 Va-Yakhel Pekudei Ha-Ḥodesh | 27 | 27 | 29 | 29 | 1 Elul R. Ḥ. | 3 Fast | 3 | 4 Toledot | 4 |
| 20 | 26 | 28 | 26 | 28 | 28 | 30 R. Ḥ. | 1 Av R. Ḥ. | 2 Shofetim | 4 | 4 | 5 | 5 |
| 21 | 27 | 29 | 27 | 29 | 29 Be-Midbar | 1 Tammuz R. Ḥ. | 2 | 3 | 5 | 5 | 6 | 6 |
| 22 | 28 Va-Era | 30 R. Ḥ. | 28 | 30 R. Ḥ. | 1 Sivan R. Ḥ. | 2 | 3 | 4 | 6 | 6 No'aḥ | 7 | 7 |
| 23 | 29 | 1 Adar R. Ḥ. | 29 | 1 Iyyar R. Ḥ. Tazri'a Meẓora | 2 | 3 | 4 Devarim | 5 | 7 | 7 | 8 | 8 |
| 24 | 1 Shevat R. Ḥ. | 2 | 1 Nisan R. Ḥ. | 2 | 3 | 4 | 5 | 6 | 8 Ha'azinu Shabbat Shuvah | 8 | 9 | 9 Va-Yiggash |
| 25 | 2 | 3 | 2 | 3 | 4 | 5 Koraḥ | 6 | 7 | 9 | 9 | 10 | 10 Fast |
| 26 | 3 | 4 Terumah | 3 Va-Yikra | 4 | 5 | 6 | 7 | 8 | 10 Yom Kippur | 10 | 11 Va-Yeẓe | 11 |
| 27 | 4 | 5 | 4 | 5 Yom ha-Aẓma'ut | 6 Shavuot | 7 | 8 | 9 Ki Teẓe | 11 | 11 | 12 | 12 |
| 28 | 5 | 6 | 5 | 6 | 7 | 8 | 9 Tishah be-Av | 10 | 12 | 12 | 13 | 13 |
| 29 | 6 Bo | | 6 | 7 | 8 | 9 | 10 | 11 | 13 | 13 Lekh Lekha | 14 | 14 |
| 30 | 7 | | 7 | 8 Aḥarei Mot Kedoshim | 9 | 10 | 11 Va-Etḥannan | 12 | 14 | 14 | 15 | 15 |
| 31 | 8 | | 8 | | 10 | | 12 | 13 | | 15 | | 16 Va-Yeḥi |

# 1956

**5716/17** תשט״ז / תשי״ז

| | January | February | March | April | May | June | July | August | September | October | November | December |
|---|---|---|---|---|---|---|---|---|---|---|---|---|
| 1 | 17 Tevet | 19 | 18 | 20 Ḥol ha-Mo'ed | 20 | 22 | 22 | 24 | 25 Niẓẓavim Va-Yelekh | 26 | 27 | 27 Mi-Keẓ 3 |
| 2 | 18 | 20 | 19 | 21 Pesaḥ | 21 | 23 Shelaḥ | 23 | 25 | 26 | 27 | 28 | 28 4 |
| 3 | 19 | 21 | 20 Ki Tissa Parah | 22 | 22 | 24 | 24 | 26 | 27 | 28 | 29 Toledot | 29 5 |
| 4 | 20 | 22 Yitro | 21 | 23 | 23 | 25 | 25 | 27 Re'eh | 28 | 29 | 30 R. Ḥ. | 30 R. Ḥ. 6 |
| 5 | 21 | 23 | 22 | 24 | 24 Be-Har Be-Ḥukkotai | 26 | 26 | 28 | 29 | 30 R. Ḥ. | 1 Kislev R. Ḥ. | 1 Tevet R. Ḥ. 7 |
| 6 | 22 | 24 | 23 | 25 | 25 | 27 | 27 | 29 | 1 Tishri Rosh Ha-Shanah | 1 Ḥeshvan R. Ḥ. No'aḥ | 2 | 2 8 |
| 7 | 23 Shemot | 25 | 24 | 26 Shemini | 26 | 28 | 28 Mattot Masei | 30 R. Ḥ. | 2 | 2 | 3 | 3 |
| 8 | 24 | 26 | 25 | 27 | 27 | 29 | 29 | 1 Elul R. Ḥ. | 3 Ha'azinu Shabbat Shuvah | 3 | 4 | 4 Va-Yiggash |
| 9 | 25 | 27 | 26 | 28 | 28 | 30 R. Ḥ. Koraḥ | 1 Av R. Ḥ. | 2 | 4 Fast | 4 | 5 | 5 |
| 10 | 26 | 28 | 27 Va-Yakhel Pekudei Ha-Ḥodesh | 29 | 29 | 1 Tammuz R. Ḥ. | 2 | 3 | 5 | 5 | 6 Va-Yeẓe | 6 |
| 11 | 27 | 29 Mishpatim Shekalim | 28 | 30 R. Ḥ. | 1 Sivan R. Ḥ. | 2 | 3 | 4 Shofetim | 6 | 6 | 7 | 7 |
| 12 | 28 | 30 R. Ḥ. | 29 | 1 Iyyar R. Ḥ. | 2 Be-Midbar | 3 | 4 | 5 | 7 | 7 | 8 | 8 |
| 13 | 29 | 1 Adar R. Ḥ. | 1 Nisan R. Ḥ. | 2 | 3 | 4 | 5 | 6 | 8 | 8 Lekh Lekha | 9 | 9 |
| 14 | 1 Shevat R. Ḥ. Va-Era | 2 | 2 | 3 Tazri'a Meẓora | 4 | 5 | 6 Devarim | 7 | 9 | 9 | 10 | 10 Fast |
| 15 | 2 | 3 | 3 | 4 | 5 | 6 | 7 | 8 | 10 Yom Kippur | 10 | 11 | 11 Va-Yeḥi |
| 16 | 3 | 4 | 4 | 5 Yom ha-Aẓma'ut | 6 Shavuot | 7 Ḥukkat | 8 | 9 | 11 | 11 | 12 | 12 |
| 17 | 4 | 5 | 5 Va-Yikra | 6 | 7 | 8 | 9 Tishah be-Av | 10 | 12 | 12 | 13 Va-Yishlaḥ | 13 |
| 18 | 5 | 6 Terumah | 6 | 7 | 8 | 9 | 10 | 11 Ki Teẓe | 13 | 13 | 14 | 14 |
| 19 | 6 | 7 | 7 | 8 | 9 Naso | 10 | 11 | 12 | 14 | 14 | 15 | 15 |
| 20 | 7 | 8 | 8 | 9 | 10 | 11 | 12 | 13 | 15 Sukkot | 15 Va-Yera | 16 | 16 |
| 21 | 8 Bo | 9 | 9 | 10 Aḥarei Mot Kedoshim | 11 | 12 | 13 Va-Etḥannan | 14 | 16 | 16 | 17 | 17 |
| 22 | 9 | 10 | 10 | 11 | 12 | 13 | 14 | 15 | 17 Ḥol ha-Mo'ed | 17 | 18 | 18 Shemot |
| 23 | 10 | 11 Ta'anit Esther | 11 | 12 | 13 | 14 Balak | 15 | 16 | 18 | 18 | 19 | 19 |
| 24 | 11 | 12 | 12 Ẓav Shabbat ha-Gadol | 13 | 14 | 15 | 16 | 17 | 19 | 19 | 20 Va-Yeshev | 20 |
| 25 | 12 | 13 Teẓavveh Zakhor | 13 | 14 | 15 | 16 | 17 | 18 Ki Tavo | 20 | 20 | 21 | 21 |
| 26 | 13 | 14 Purim | 14 | 15 | 16 Be-Ha'alotkha | 17 Fast | 18 | 19 | 21 Hoshana Rabba | 21 | 22 | 22 |
| 27 | 14 | 15 Shushan Purim | 15 Pesaḥ | 16 | 17 | 18 | 19 | 20 | 22 Shemini Aẓeret | 22 Ḥayyei Sarah | 23 | 23 |
| 28 | 15 Be-Shallaḥ | 16 | 16 Omer | 17 Emor | 18 | 19 | 20 Ekev | 21 | 23 Simḥat Torah Ve-Zot Ha-Berakhah | 23 | 24 | 24 |
| 29 | 16 | 17 | 17 Ḥol ha-Mo'ed | 18 Lag ba-Omer | 19 | 20 | 21 | 22 | 24 Bereshit | 24 | 25 Ḥanukkah 1 | 25 Va-Era |
| 30 | 17 | | 18 | 19 | 20 | 21 Pinḥas | 22 | 23 | 25 | 25 | 26 2 | 26 |
| 31 | 18 | | 19 | | 21 | | 23 | 24 | | 26 | | 27 |

# 1957

**5717/18** תשי״ז / תשי״ח

| | January | February | March | April | May | June | July | August | September | October | November | December |
|---|---|---|---|---|---|---|---|---|---|---|---|---|
| 1 | 28 Tevet | 30 R. H. | 28 | 29 | 30 R. H. | 2 Naso | 2 | 4 | 5 | 6 | 7 | 8 |
| 2 | 29 | 1 Adar I R. H. Terumah | 29 Pekudei Shekalim | 1 Nisan R. H. | 1 Iyyar R. H. | 3 | 3 | 5 | 6 | 7 | 8 Lekh Lekha | 9 |
| 3 | 1 Shevat R. H. | 2 | 30 R. H. | 2 | 2 | 4 | 4 | 6 Devarim | 7 | 8 | 9 | 10 |
| 4 | 2 | 3 | 1 Adar II R. H. | 3 | 3 Emor | 5 | 5 | 7 | 8 | 9 | 10 | 11 |
| 5 | 3 Bo | 4 | 2 | 4 | 4 | 6 Shavuot | 6 | 8 | 9 | 10 Yom Kippur | 11 | 12 |
| 6 | 4 | 5 | 3 | 5 Mezora | 5 Yom ha-Azma'ut | 7 | 7 Balak | 9 Tishah be-Av | 10 | 11 | 12 | 13 |
| 7 | 5 | 6 | 4 | 6 | 6 | 8 | 8 | 10 | 11 Ki Teze | 12 | 13 | 14 Va-Yishlah |
| 8 | 6 | 7 | 5 | 7 | 7 | 9 Be-Ha'alotkha | 9 | 11 | 12 | 13 | 14 | 15 |
| 9 | 7 | 8 Tezavveh | 6 Va-Yikra | 8 | 8 | 10 | 10 | 12 | 13 | 14 | 15 Va-Yera | 16 |
| 10 | 8 | 9 | 7 | 9 | 9 | 11 | 11 | 13 Va-Ethannan | 14 | 15 Sukkot | 16 | 17 |
| 11 | 9 | 10 | 8 | 10 | 10 Be-Har | 12 | 12 | 14 | 15 | 16 | 17 | 18 |
| 12 | 10 Be-Shallah | 11 | 9 | 11 | 11 | 13 | 13 | 15 | 16 | 17 Hol ha-Mo'ed | 18 | 19 |
| 13 | 11 | 12 | 10 | 12 Aharei Mot Shabbat ha-Gadol | 12 | 14 | 14 Pinhas | 16 | 17 | 18 | 19 | 20 |
| 14 | 12 | 13 | 11 Ta'anit Esther | 13 | 13 | 15 | 15 | 17 | 18 Ki Tavo | 19 | 20 | 21 Va-Yeshev |
| 15 | 13 | 14 | 12 | 14 | 14 | 16 Shelah | 16 | 18 | 19 | 20 | 21 | 22 |
| 16 | 14 | 15 Ki Tissa | 13 Zav Zakhor | 15 Pesah | 15 | 17 | 17 Fast | 19 | 20 | 21 Hoshana Rabba | 22 Hayyei Sarah | 23 |
| 17 | 15 | 16 | 14 Purim | 16 Omer | 16 | 18 | 18 | 20 Ekev | 21 | 22 Shemini Azeret | 23 | 24 |
| 18 | 16 | 17 | 15 Shushan Purim | 17 | 17 Be-Hukkotai | 19 | 19 | 21 | 22 | 23 Simhat Torah Ve-Zot Ha-Berakhah | 24 | 25 Hanukkah 1 |
| 19 | 17 Yitro | 18 | 16 | 18 Hol ha-Mo'ed | 18 Lag ba-Omer | 20 | 20 | 22 | 23 | 24 Bereshit | 25 | 26 2 |
| 20 | 18 | 19 | 17 | 19 | 19 | 21 | 21 Mattot | 23 | 24 | 25 | 26 | 27 3 |
| 21 | 19 | 20 | 18 | 20 | 20 | 22 | 22 | 24 | 25 Nizzavim Va-Yelekh | 26 | 27 | 28 Mi-Kez 4 |
| 22 | 20 | 21 | 19 | 21 Pesah | 21 | 23 Korah | 23 | 25 | 26 | 27 | 28 | 29 5 |
| 23 | 21 | 22 Va-Yakhel | 20 Shemini Parah | 22 | 22 | 24 | 24 | 26 | 27 | 28 | 29 Toledot | 30 R. H. 6 |
| 24 | 22 | 23 | 21 | 23 | 23 | 25 | 25 | 27 Re'eh | 28 | 29 | 1 Kislev R. H. | 1 Tevet R. H. 7 |
| 25 | 23 | 24 | 22 | 24 | 24 Be-Midbar | 26 | 26 | 28 | 29 | 30 R. H. | 2 | 2 8 |
| 26 | 24 Mishpatim | 25 | 23 | 25 | 25 | 27 | 27 | 29 | 1 Tishri Rosh Ha-Shanah | 1 R. H. No'ah Heshvan | 3 | 3 |
| 27 | 25 | 26 | 24 | 26 Kedoshim | 26 | 28 | 28 Masei | 30 R. H. | 2 | 2 | 4 | 4 |
| 28 | 26 | 27 | 25 | 27 | 27 | 29 | 29 | 1 Elul R. H. | 3 Ha'azinu Shabbat Shuvah | 3 | 5 | 5 Va-Yiggash |
| 29 | 27 | | 26 | 28 | 28 | 30 R. H. Hukkat | 1 Av R. H. | 2 | 4 Fast | 4 | 6 | 6 |
| 30 | 28 | | 27 Tazri'a Ha-Hodesh | 29 | 29 | 1 Tammuz R. H. | 2 | 3 | 5 | 5 | 7 Va-Yeze | 7 |
| 31 | 29 | | 28 | | 1 Sivan R. H. | | 3 | 4 Shofetim | | 6 | | 8 |

# 1958

**5718/19** תשי״ח / תשי״ט

| | January | February | March | April | May | June | July | August | September | October | November | December |
|---|---|---|---|---|---|---|---|---|---|---|---|---|
| 1 | 9 Tevet | 11 Be-Shallah | 9 Tezavveh Zakhor | 11 | 11 | 13 | 13 | 15 | 16 | 17 | 18 Va-Yera | 19 |
| 2 | 10 Fast | 12 | 10 | 12 | 12 | 14 | 14 | 16 Va-Ethannan | 17 | 18 Hol ha-Mo'ed | 19 | 20 |
| 3 | 11 | 13 | 11 | 13 | 13 Aharei Mot Kedoshim | 15 | 15 | 17 | 18 | 19 | 20 | 21 |
| 4 | 12 Va-Yehi | 14 | 12 | 14 | 14 | 16 | 16 | 18 | 19 | 20 | 21 | 22 |
| 5 | 13 | 15 | 13 Ta'anit Esther | 15 Pesah | 15 | 17 | 17 Balak | 19 | 20 | 21 Hoshana Rabba | 22 | 23 |
| 6 | 14 | 16 | 14 Purim | 16 Omer | 16 | 18 | 18 Fast | 20 | 21 Ki Tavo | 22 Shemini Azeret | 23 | 24 Va-Yeshev |
| 7 | 15 | 17 | 15 Shushan Purim | 17 | 17 | 19 Be-Ha'alotkha | 19 | 21 | 22 | 23 Simhat Torah Ve-Zot Ha-Berakhah | 24 | 25 Hanukkah 1 |
| 8 | 16 | 18 Yitro | 16 Ki Tissa | 18 Hol ha-Mo'ed | 18 Lag ba-Omer | 20 | 20 | 22 | 23 | 24 | 25 Hayyei Sarah | 26 2 |
| 9 | 17 | 19 | 17 | 19 | 19 | 21 | 21 | 23 Ekev | 24 | 25 | 26 | 27 3 |
| 10 | 18 | 20 | 18 | 20 | 20 Emor | 22 | 22 | 24 | 25 | 26 | 27 | 28 4 |
| 11 | 19 Shemot | 21 | 19 | 21 Pesah | 21 | 23 | 23 | 25 | 26 | 27 Bereshit | 28 | 29 5 |
| 12 | 20 | 22 | 20 | 22 | 22 | 24 | 24 Pinhas | 26 | 27 | 28 | 29 | 1 Tevet R. H. 6 |
| 13 | 21 | 23 | 21 | 23 | 23 | 25 | 25 | 27 | 28 Nizzavim | 29 | 1 Kislev R. H. | 2 Mi-Kez 7 |
| 14 | 22 | 24 | 22 | 24 | 24 | 26 Shelah | 26 | 28 | 29 | 30 R. H. | 2 | 3 8 |
| 15 | 23 | 25 Mishpatim Shekalim | 23 Va-Yakhel Pekudei Parah | 25 | 25 | 27 | 27 | 29 | 1 Tishri Rosh Ha-Shanah | 1 Heshvan R. H. | 3 Toledot | 4 |
| 16 | 24 | 26 | 24 | 26 | 26 | 28 | 28 | 30 R. H. Re'eh | 2 | 2 | 4 | 5 |
| 17 | 25 | 27 | 25 | 27 | 27 Be-Har Be-Hukkotai | 29 | 29 | 1 Elul R. H. | 3 Fast | 3 | 5 | 6 |
| 18 | 26 Va-Era | 28 | 26 | 28 | 28 | 30 R. H. | 1 Av R. H. | 2 | 4 | 4 No'ah | 6 | 7 |
| 19 | 27 | 29 | 27 | 29 Shemini | 29 | 1 Tammuz R. H. | 2 Mattot Masei | 3 | 5 | 5 | 7 | 8 |
| 20 | 28 | 30 R. H. | 28 | 30 R. H. | 1 Sivan R. H. | 2 | 3 | 4 | 6 Va-Yelekh Shabbat Shuvah | 6 | 8 | 9 Va-Yiggash |
| 21 | 29 | 1 Adar R. H. | 29 | 1 Iyyar R. H. | 2 | 3 Korah | 4 | 5 | 7 | 7 | 9 | 10 Fast |
| 22 | 1 Shevat R. H. | 2 Terumah | 1 Nisan Va-Yikra R. H. Ha-Hodesh | 2 | 3 | 4 | 5 | 6 | 8 | 8 | 10 Va-Yeze | 11 |
| 23 | 2 | 3 | 2 | 3 | 4 | 5 | 6 | 7 Shofetim | 9 | 9 | 11 | 12 |
| 24 | 3 | 4 | 3 | 4 Yom ha-Azma'ut | 5 Be-Midbar | 6 | 7 | 8 | 10 Yom Kippur | 10 | 12 | 13 |
| 25 | 4 Bo | 5 | 4 | 5 | 6 Shavuot | 7 | 8 | 9 | 11 | 11 Lekh Lekha | 13 | 14 |
| 26 | 5 | 6 | 5 | 6 Tazri'a Mezora | 7 | 8 | 9 Devarim Tishah be-Av | 10 | 12 | 12 | 14 | 15 |
| 27 | 6 | 7 | 6 | 7 | 8 | 9 | 10 Fast | 11 | 13 Ha'azinu | 13 | 15 | 16 Va-Yehi |
| 28 | 7 | 8 | 7 | 8 | 9 | 10 Hukkat | 11 | 12 | 14 | 14 | 16 | 17 |
| 29 | 8 | | 8 Zav Shabbat ha-Gadol | 9 | 10 | 11 | 12 | 13 | 15 Sukkot | 15 | 17 Va-Yishlah | 18 |
| 30 | 9 | | 9 | 10 | 11 | 12 | 13 | 14 Ki Teze | 16 | 16 | 18 | 19 |
| 31 | 10 | | 10 | | 12 Naso | | 14 | 15 | | 17 | | 20 |

# 1959

**5719/20** תשי״ט / תש״כ

| | January | February | March | April | May | June | July | August | September | October | November | December |
|---|---|---|---|---|---|---|---|---|---|---|---|---|
| 1 | 21 Tevet | 23 | 21 | 22 | 23 | 24 | 25 | 26 Mattot Masei | 28 | 28 | 30 R. Ḥ. | 30 R. Ḥ. |
| 2 | 22 | 24 | 22 | 23 | 24 Aḥarei Mot | 25 | 26 | 27 | 29 | 29 | 1 Ḥeshvan R. Ḥ. | 1 Kislev R. Ḥ. |
| 3 | 23 Shemot | 25 | 23 | 24 | 25 | 26 | 27 | 28 | 30 R. Ḥ. | 1 Tishri Rosh Ha-Shanah | 2 | 2 |
| 4 | 24 | 26 | 24 | 25 Shemini Ha-Ḥodesh | 26 | 27 | 28 Shelaḥ | 29 | 1 Elul R. Ḥ. | 2 | 3 | 3 |
| 5 | 25 | 27 | 25 | 26 | 27 | 28 | 29 | 1 Av R. Ḥ. | 2 Shofetim | 3 Fast | 4 | 4 Toledot |
| 6 | 26 | 28 | 26 | 27 | 28 | 29 Be-Midbar | 30 R. Ḥ. | 2 | 3 | 4 | 5 | 5 |
| 7 | 27 | 29 Mishpatim | 27 Va-Yakhel Shekalim | 28 | 29 | 1 Sivan R. Ḥ. | 1 Tammuz R. Ḥ. | 3 | 4 | 5 | 6 No'aḥ | 6 |
| 8 | 28 | 30 R. Ḥ. | 28 | 29 | 30 R. Ḥ. | 2 | 2 | 4 Devarim | 5 | 6 | 7 | 7 |
| 9 | 29 | 1 Adar I R. Ḥ. | 29 | 1 Nisan R. Ḥ. | 1 Iyyar R. Ḥ. Kedoshim | 3 | 3 | 5 | 6 | 7 | 8 | 8 |
| 10 | 1 Shevat R. Ḥ. Va-Era | 2 | 30 R. Ḥ. | 2 | 2 | 4 | 4 | 6 | 7 | 8 Ha'azinu Shabbat Shuvah | 9 | 9 |
| 11 | 2 | 3 | 1 Adar II R. Ḥ. | 3 Tazri'a | 3 | 5 | 5 Koraḥ | 7 | 8 | 9 | 10 | 10 |
| 12 | 3 | 4 | 2 | 4 | 4 | 6 Shavuot | 6 | 8 | 9 Ki Teẓe | 10 Yom Kippur | 11 | 11 Va-Yeẓe |
| 13 | 4 | 5 | 3 | 5 | 5 Yom ha-Aẓma'ut | 7 | 7 | 9 Tishah be-Av | 10 | 11 | 12 | 12 |
| 14 | 5 | 6 Terumah | 4 Pekudei | 6 | 6 | 8 | 8 | 10 | 11 | 12 | 13 Lekh Lekha | 13 |
| 15 | 6 | 7 | 5 | 7 | 7 | 9 | 9 | 11 Va-Etḥannan | 12 | 13 | 14 | 14 |
| 16 | 7 | 8 | 6 | 8 | 8 Emor | 10 | 10 | 12 | 13 | 14 | 15 | 15 |
| 17 | 8 Bo | 9 | 7 | 9 | 9 | 11 | 11 | 13 | 14 | 15 Sukkot | 16 | 16 |
| 18 | 9 | 10 | 8 | 10 Meẓora Shabbat ha-Gadol | 10 | 12 | 12 Ḥukkat Balak | 14 | 15 | 16 | 17 | 17 |
| 19 | 10 | 11 | 9 | 11 | 11 | 13 | 13 | 15 | 16 Ki Tavo | 17 Ḥol ha-Mo'ed | 18 | 18 Va-Yishlaḥ |
| 20 | 11 | 12 | 10 | 12 | 12 | 14 Naso | 14 | 16 | 17 | 18 | 19 | 19 |
| 21 | 12 | 13 Teẓavveh | 11 Va-Yikra Zakhor | 13 | 13 | 15 | 15 | 17 | 18 | 19 | 20 Va-Yera | 20 |
| 22 | 13 | 14 | 12 | 14 | 14 | 16 | 16 | 18 Ekev | 19 | 20 | 21 | 21 |
| 23 | 14 | 15 | 13 Ta'anit Esther | 15 Pesaḥ | 15 Be-Har | 17 | 17 Fast | 19 | 20 | 21 Hoshana Rabba | 22 | 22 |
| 24 | 15 Be-Shallaḥ | 16 | 14 Purim | 16 Omer | 16 | 18 | 18 | 20 | 21 | 22 Shemini Aẓeret | 23 | 23 |
| 25 | 16 | 17 | 15 Shushan Purim | 17 Ḥol ha-Mo'ed | 17 | 19 | 19 Pinḥas | 21 | 22 | 23 Simḥat Torah Ve-Ẓot Ha-Berakhah | 24 | 24 |
| 26 | 17 | 18 | 16 | 18 | 18 Lag ba-Omer | 20 | 20 | 22 | 23 Niẓẓavim Va-Yelekh | 24 | 25 | 25 Ḥanukkah Va-Yeshev 1 |
| 27 | 18 | 19 | 17 | 19 | 19 | 21 Be-Ha'alotkha | 21 | 23 | 24 | 25 | 26 | 26 2 |
| 28 | 19 | 20 Ki Tissa | 18 Ẓav Parah | 20 | 20 | 22 | 22 | 24 | 25 | 26 | 27 Ḥayyei Sarah | 27 3 |
| 29 | 20 | | 19 | 21 Pesaḥ | 21 | 23 | 23 | 25 Re'eh | 26 | 27 | 28 | 28 4 |
| 30 | 21 | | 20 | 22 | 22 Be-Ḥukkotai | 24 | 24 | 26 | 27 | 28 | 29 | 29 5 |
| 31 | 22 Yitro | | 21 | | 23 | | 25 | 27 | | 29 Bereshit | | 30 R. Ḥ. 6 |

# 1960

**5720/21** תש״כ / תשכ״א

| | January | February | March | April | May | June | July | August | September | October | November | December |
|---|---|---|---|---|---|---|---|---|---|---|---|---|
| 1 | 1 Tevet R. Ḥ. 7 Ḥanukkah | 3 | 2 | 4 | 4 | 6 Shavuot | 6 | 8 | 9 | 10 Yom Kippur | 11 | 12 |
| 2 | 2 Mi-Keẓ 8 | 4 | 3 | 5 Va-Yikra | 5 Yom ha-Aẓma'ut | 7 | 7 Ḥukkat | 9 Tishah be-Av | 10 | 11 | 12 | 13 |
| 3 | 3 | 5 | 4 | 6 | 6 | 8 | 8 | 10 | 11 Ki Teẓe | 12 | 13 | 14 Va-Yishlaḥ |
| 4 | 4 | 6 | 5 | 7 | 7 | 9 Naso | 9 | 11 | 12 | 13 | 14 | 15 |
| 5 | 5 | 7 | 6 Terumah | 8 | 8 | 10 | 10 | 12 | 13 | 14 | 15 Va-Yera | 16 |
| 6 | 6 | 8 Bo | 7 | 9 | 9 | 11 | 11 | 13 Va-Etḥannan | 14 | 15 Sukkot | 16 | 17 |
| 7 | 7 | 9 | 8 | 10 | 10 Aḥarei Mot Kedoshim | 12 | 12 | 14 | 15 | 16 | 17 | 18 |
| 8 | 8 | 10 | 9 | 11 | 11 | 13 | 13 | 15 | 16 | 17 Ḥol ha-Mo'ed | 18 | 19 |
| 9 | 9 Va-Yiggash | 11 | 10 | 12 Ẓav Shabbat ha-Gadol | 12 | 14 | 14 Balak | 16 | 17 | 18 | 19 | 20 |
| 10 | 10 Fast | 12 | 11 Ta'anit Esther | 13 | 13 | 15 | 15 | 17 | 18 Ki Tavo | 19 | 20 | 21 Va-Yeshev |
| 11 | 11 | 13 | 12 | 14 | 14 | 16 Be-Ha'alotkha | 16 | 18 | 19 | 20 | 21 | 22 |
| 12 | 12 | 14 | 13 Teẓavveh Zakhor | 15 Pesaḥ | 15 | 17 | 17 Fast | 19 | 20 | 21 Hoshana Rabba | 22 Ḥayyei Sarah | 23 |
| 13 | 13 | 15 Be-Shallaḥ | 14 Purim | 16 Omer | 16 | 18 | 18 | 20 Ekev | 21 | 22 Shemini Aẓeret | 23 | 24 |
| 14 | 14 | 16 | 15 Shushan Purim | 17 Ḥol ha-Mo'ed | 17 Emor | 19 | 19 | 21 | 22 | 23 Simḥat Torah Ve-Ẓot Ha-Berakhah | 24 | 25 Ḥanukkah 1 |
| 15 | 15 | 17 | 16 | 18 | 18 Lag ba-Omer | 20 | 20 | 22 | 23 | 24 Bereshit | 25 | 26 2 |
| 16 | 16 Va-Yeḥi | 18 | 17 | 19 | 19 | 21 | 21 Pinḥas | 23 | 24 | 25 | 26 | 27 3 |
| 17 | 17 | 19 | 18 | 20 | 20 | 22 | 22 | 24 | 25 Niẓẓavim Va-Yelekh | 26 | 27 | 28 Mi-Keẓ 4 |
| 18 | 18 | 20 | 19 | 21 Pesaḥ | 21 | 23 Shelaḥ | 23 | 25 | 26 | 27 | 28 | 29 5 |
| 19 | 19 | 21 | 20 Ki Tissa Parah | 22 | 22 | 24 | 24 | 26 | 27 | 28 | 29 Toledot | 30 R. Ḥ. 6 |
| 20 | 20 | 22 Yitro | 21 | 23 | 23 | 25 | 25 | 27 Re'eh | 28 | 29 | 1 Kislev R. Ḥ. | 1 Tevet R. Ḥ. 7 |
| 21 | 21 | 23 | 22 | 24 | 24 Be-Har Be-Ḥukkotai | 26 | 26 | 28 | 29 | 30 R. Ḥ. | 2 | 2 8 |
| 22 | 22 | 24 | 23 | 25 | 25 | 27 | 27 | 29 | 1 Tishri Rosh Ha-Shanah | 1 Ḥeshvan R. Ḥ. No'aḥ | 3 | 3 |
| 23 | 23 Shemot | 25 | 24 | 26 Shemini | 26 | 28 | 28 Mattot Masei | 30 R. Ḥ. | 2 | 2 | 4 | 4 |
| 24 | 24 | 26 | 25 | 27 | 27 | 29 | 29 | 1 Elul R. Ḥ. | 3 Ha'azinu Shabbat Shuvah | 3 | 5 | 5 Va-Yiggash |
| 25 | 25 | 27 | 26 | 28 | 28 | 30 R. Ḥ. Koraḥ | 1 Av R. Ḥ. | 2 | 4 Fast | 4 | 6 | 6 |
| 26 | 26 | 28 | 27 Va-Yakhel Pekudei Ha-Ḥodesh | 29 | 29 | 1 Tammuz R. Ḥ. | 2 | 3 | 5 | 5 | 7 Va-Yeẓe | 7 |
| 27 | 27 | 29 Mishpatim Shekalim | 28 | 30 R. Ḥ. | 1 Sivan R. Ḥ. | 2 | 3 | 4 Shofetim | 6 | 6 | 8 | 8 |
| 28 | 28 | 30 R. Ḥ. | 29 | 1 Iyyar R. Ḥ. | 2 Be-Midbar | 3 | 4 | 5 | 7 | 7 | 9 | 9 |
| 29 | 29 | 1 Adar R. Ḥ. | 1 Nisan R. Ḥ. | 2 | 3 | 4 | 5 | 6 | 8 | 8 Lekh Lekha | 10 | 10 Fast |
| 30 | 1 Shevat R. Ḥ. Va-Era | | 2 | 3 Tazri'a Meẓora | 4 | 5 | 6 Devarim | 7 | 9 | 9 | 11 | 11 |
| 31 | 2 | | 3 | | 5 | | 7 | 8 | | 10 | | 12 Va-Yeḥi |

## 1961

**5721/22** — תשכ״א / תשכ״ב

| | January | February | March | April | May | June | July | August | September | October | November | December |
|---|---|---|---|---|---|---|---|---|---|---|---|---|
| 1 | 13 Tevet | 15 | 13 Ta'anit Esther | 15 Pesaḥ | 15 | 17 | 17 Balak | 19 | 20 | 21 Hoshana Rabba | 22 | 23 |
| 2 | 14 | 16 | 14 Purim | 16 Omer | 16 | 18 | 18 Fast | 20 | 21 Ki Tavo | 22 Shemini Aẓeret | 23 | 24 Va-Yeshev |
| 3 | 15 | 17 | 15 Shushan Purim | 17 | 17 | 19 Be-Ha'alotkha | 19 | 21 | 22 | 23 Simḥat Torah Ve-Zot Ha-Berakhah | 24 | 25 Ḥanukkah 1 |
| 4 | 16 | 18 Yitro | 16 Ki Tissa | 18 Ḥol ha-Mo'ed | 18 Lag ba-Omer | 20 | 20 | 22 | 23 | 24 | 25 Ḥayyei Sarah | 26 2 |
| 5 | 17 | 19 | 17 | 19 | 19 | 21 | 21 | 23 Ekev | 24 | 25 | 26 | 27 3 |
| 6 | 18 | 20 | 18 | 20 | 20 Emor | 22 | 22 | 24 | 25 | 26 | 27 | 28 4 |
| 7 | 19 Shemot | 21 | 19 | 21 Pesaḥ | 21 | 23 | 23 | 25 | 26 | 27 Bereshit | 28 | 29 5 |
| 8 | 20 | 22 | 20 | 22 | 22 | 24 | 24 Pinḥas | 26 | 27 | 28 | 29 | 1 Tevet R. H. 6 |
| 9 | 21 | 23 | 21 | 23 | 23 | 25 | 25 | 27 | 28 Niẓẓavim | 29 | 1 Kislev R. H. | 2 Mi-Keẓ 7 |
| 10 | 22 | 24 | 22 | 24 | 24 | 26 Shelaḥ | 26 | 28 | 29 | 30 R. H. | 2 | 3 8 |
| 11 | 23 | 25 Mishpatim Shekalim | 23 Va-Yakhel Pekudei Parah | 25 | 25 | 27 | 27 | 29 | 1 Tishri Rosh Ha-Shanah | 1 Ḥeshvan R. H. | 3 Toledot | 4 |
| 12 | 24 | 26 | 24 | 26 | 26 | 28 | 28 | 30 R. H. Re'eh | 2 | 2 | 4 | 5 |
| 13 | 25 | 27 | 25 | 27 | 27 Be-Har Be-Ḥukkotai | 29 | 29 | 1 Elul R. H. | 3 Fast | 3 | 5 | 6 |
| 14 | 26 Va-Era | 28 | 26 | 28 | 28 | 30 R. H. | 1 Av R. H. | 2 | 4 | 4 No'aḥ | 6 | 7 |
| 15 | 27 | 29 | 27 | 29 Shemini | 29 | 1 Tammuz R. H. | 2 Mattot Masei | 3 | 5 | 5 | 7 | 8 |
| 16 | 28 | 30 R. H. | 28 | 30 R. H. | 1 Sivan R. H. | 2 | 3 | 4 | 6 Va-Yelekh Shabbat Shuvah | 6 | 8 | 9 Va-Yiggash |
| 17 | 29 | 1 Adar R. H. | 29 | 1 Iyyar R. H. | 2 | 3 Koraḥ | 4 | 5 | 7 | 7 | 9 | 10 Fast |
| 18 | 1 Shevat R. H. | 2 Terumah | 1 Nisan Va-Yikra R. H. Ha-Ḥodesh | 2 | 3 | 4 | 5 | 6 | 8 | 8 | 10 Va-Yeẓe | 11 |
| 19 | 2 | 3 | 2 | 3 | 4 | 5 | 6 | 7 Shofetim | 9 | 9 | 11 | 12 |
| 20 | 3 | 4 | 3 | 4 Yom ha-Aẓma'ut | 5 Be-Midbar | 6 | 7 | 8 | 10 Yom Kippur | 10 | 12 | 13 |
| 21 | 4 Bo | 5 | 4 | 5 | 6 Shavuot | 7 | 8 | 9 | 11 | 11 Lekh Lekha | 13 | 14 |
| 22 | 5 | 6 | 5 | 6 Tazri'a Meẓora | 7 | 8 | 9 Devarim Tishah be-Av | 10 | 12 | 12 | 14 | 15 |
| 23 | 6 | 7 | 6 | 7 | 8 | 9 | 10 Fast | 11 | 13 Ha'azinu | 13 | 15 | 16 Va-Yeḥi |
| 24 | 7 | 8 | 7 | 8 | 9 | 10 Ḥukkat | 11 | 12 | 14 | 14 | 16 | 17 |
| 25 | 8 | 9 Teẓavveh Zakhor | 8 Ẓav Shabbat ha-Gadol | 9 | 10 | 11 | 12 | 13 | 15 Sukkot | 15 | 17 Va-Yishlaḥ | 18 |
| 26 | 9 | 10 | 9 | 10 | 11 | 12 | 13 | 14 Ki Teẓe | 16 | 16 | 18 | 19 |
| 27 | 10 | 11 | 10 | 11 | 12 Naso | 13 | 14 | 15 | 17 | 17 | 19 | 20 |
| 28 | 11 Be-Shallaḥ | 12 | 11 | 12 | 13 | 14 | 15 | 16 | 18 Ḥol ha-Mo'ed | 18 Va-Yera | 20 | 21 |
| 29 | 12 | | 12 | 13 Aḥarei Mot Kedoshim | 14 | 15 | 16 Va-Etḥannan | 17 | 19 | 19 | 21 | 22 |
| 30 | 13 | | 13 | 14 | 15 | 16 | 17 | 18 | 20 | 20 | 22 | 23 Shemot |
| 31 | 14 | | 14 | | 16 | | 18 | 19 | | 21 | | 24 |

## 1962

**5722/23** — תשכ״ב / תשכ״ג

| | January | February | March | April | May | June | July | August | September | October | November | December |
|---|---|---|---|---|---|---|---|---|---|---|---|---|
| 1 | 25 Tevet | 27 | 25 | 26 | 27 | 28 | 29 | 1 Av R. H. | 2 Shofetim | 3 Fast | 4 | 4 Toledot |
| 2 | 26 | 28 | 26 | 27 | 28 | 29 Be-Midbar | 30 R. H. | 2 | 3 | 4 | 5 | 5 |
| 3 | 27 | 29 Mishpatim | 27 Va-Yakhel Shekalim | 28 | 29 | 1 Sivan R. H. | 1 Tammuz R. H. | 3 | 4 | 5 | 6 No'aḥ | 6 |
| 4 | 28 | 30 R. H. | 28 | 29 | 30 R. H. | 2 | 2 | 4 Devarim | 5 | 6 | 7 | 7 |
| 5 | 29 | 1 Adar I R. H. | 29 | 1 Nisan R. H. | 1 Iyyar R. H. Kedoshim | 3 | 3 | 5 | 6 | 7 | 8 | 8 |
| 6 | 1 Shevat R. H. Va-Era | 2 | 30 R. H. | 2 | 2 | 4 | 4 | 6 | 7 | 8 Ha'azinu Shabbat Shuvah | 9 | 9 |
| 7 | 2 | 3 | 1 Adar II R. H. | 3 Tazri'a | 3 | 5 | 5 Koraḥ | 7 | 8 | 9 | 10 | 10 |
| 8 | 3 | 4 | 2 | 4 | 4 | 6 Shavuot | 6 | 8 | 9 Ki Teẓe | 10 Yom Kippur | 11 | 11 Va-Yeẓe |
| 9 | 4 | 5 | 3 | 5 | 5 Yom ha-Aẓma'ut | 7 | 7 | 9 Tishah be-Av | 10 | 11 | 12 | 12 |
| 10 | 5 | 6 Terumah | 4 Pekudei | 6 | 6 | 8 | 8 | 10 | 11 | 12 | 13 Lekh Lekha | 13 |
| 11 | 6 | 7 | 5 | 7 | 7 | 9 | 9 | 11 Va-Etḥannan | 12 | 13 | 14 | 14 |
| 12 | 7 | 8 | 6 | 8 | 8 Emor | 10 | 10 | 12 | 13 | 14 | 15 | 15 |
| 13 | 8 Bo | 9 | 7 | 9 | 9 | 11 | 11 | 13 | 14 | 15 Sukkot | 16 | 16 |
| 14 | 9 | 10 | 8 | 10 Meẓora Shabbat ha-Gadol | 10 | 12 | 12 Ḥukkat Balak | 14 | 15 | 16 | 17 | 17 |
| 15 | 10 | 11 | 9 | 11 | 11 | 13 | 13 | 15 | 16 Ki Tavo | 17 | 18 | 18 Va-Yishlaḥ |
| 16 | 11 | 12 | 10 | 12 | 12 | 14 Naso | 14 | 16 | 17 | 18 Ḥol ha-Mo'ed | 19 | 19 |
| 17 | 12 | 13 Teẓavveh | 11 Va-Yikra Zakhor | 13 | 13 | 15 | 15 | 17 | 18 | 19 | 20 Va-Yera | 20 |
| 18 | 13 | 14 | 12 | 14 | 14 | 16 | 16 | 18 Ekev | 19 | 20 | 21 | 21 |
| 19 | 14 | 15 | 13 Ta'anit Esther | 15 Pesaḥ | 15 Be-Har | 17 | 17 Fast | 19 | 20 | 21 Hoshana Rabba | 22 | 22 |
| 20 | 15 Be-Shallaḥ | 16 | 14 Purim | 16 Omer | 16 | 18 | 18 | 20 | 21 | 22 Shemini Aẓeret | 23 | 23 |
| 21 | 16 | 17 | 15 Shushan Purim | 17 | 17 | 19 | 19 Pinḥas | 21 | 22 | 23 Simḥat Torah Ve-Zot Ha-Berakhah | 24 | 24 |
| 22 | 17 | 18 | 16 | 18 Ḥol ha-Mo'ed | 18 Lag ba-Omer | 20 | 20 | 22 | 23 Niẓẓavim Va-Yelekh | 24 | 25 | 25 Va-Yeshev Ḥanukkah 1 |
| 23 | 18 | 19 | 17 | 19 | 19 | 21 Be-Ha'alotkha | 21 | 23 | 24 | 25 | 26 | 26 2 |
| 24 | 19 | 20 Ki Tissa | 18 Ẓav Parah | 20 | 20 | 22 | 22 | 24 | 25 | 26 | 27 Ḥayyei Sarah | 27 3 |
| 25 | 20 | 21 | 19 | 21 Pesaḥ | 21 | 23 | 23 | 25 Re'eh | 26 | 27 | 28 | 28 4 |
| 26 | 21 | 22 | 20 | 22 | 22 Be-Ḥukkotai | 24 | 24 | 26 | 27 | 28 | 29 | 29 5 |
| 27 | 22 Yitro | 23 | 21 | 23 | 23 | 25 | 25 | 27 | 28 | 29 Bereshit | 30 R. H. | 30 R. H. 6 |
| 28 | 23 | 24 | 22 | 24 Aḥarei Mot | 24 | 26 | 26 Mattot Masei | 28 | 29 | 30 R. H. | 1 Kislev R. H. | 1 Tevet R. H. 7 |
| 29 | 24 | | 23 | 25 | 25 | 27 | 27 | 29 | 1 Tishri Rosh Ha-Shanah | 1 Ḥeshvan R. H. | 2 | 2 Mi-Keẓ 8 |
| 30 | 25 | | 24 | 26 | 26 | 28 Shelaḥ | 28 | 30 R. H. | 2 | 2 | 3 | 3 |
| 31 | 26 | | 25 Shemini Ha-Ḥodesh | | 27 | | 29 | 1 Elul R. H. | | 3 | | 4 |

# 1963

5723/24 — תשכ״ג / תשכ״ד

| | January | February | March | April | May | June | July | August | September | October | November | December |
|---|---|---|---|---|---|---|---|---|---|---|---|---|
| 1 | 5 Tevet | 7 | 5 | 7 | 7 | 9 Naso | 9 | 11 | 12 | 13 | 14 | 15 |
| 2 | 6 | 8 Bo | 6 Terumah | 8 | 8 | 10 | 10 | 12 | 13 | 14 | 15 Va-Yera | 16 |
| 3 | 7 | 9 | 7 | 9 | 9 | 11 | 11 | 13 Va-Ethannan | 14 | 15 Sukkot | 16 | 17 |
| 4 | 8 | 10 | 8 | 10 | 10 Aḥarei Mot Kedoshim | 12 | 12 | 14 | 15 | 16 | 17 | 18 |
| 5 | 9 Va-Yiggash | 11 | 9 | 11 | 11 | 13 | 13 | 15 | 16 | 17 | 18 | 19 |
| 6 | 10 Fast | 12 | 10 | 12 Ẓav Shabbat ha-Gadol | 12 | 14 | 14 Balak | 16 | 17 | 18 Ḥol ha-Mo'ed | 19 | 20 |
| 7 | 11 | 13 | 11 Ta'anit Esther | 13 | 13 | 15 | 15 | 17 | 18 Ki Tavo | 19 | 20 | 21 Va-Yeshev |
| 8 | 12 | 14 | 12 | 14 | 14 | 16 Be-Ha'alotkha | 16 | 18 | 19 | 20 | 21 | 22 |
| 9 | 13 | 15 Be-Shallaḥ | 13 Teẓavveh Zakhor | 15 Pesaḥ | 15 | 17 | 17 Fast | 19 | 20 | 21 Ḥoshana Rabba | 22 Ḥayyei Sarah | 23 |
| 10 | 14 | 16 | 14 Purim | 16 Omer | 16 | 18 | 18 | 20 Ekev | 21 | 22 Shemini Aẓeret | 23 | 24 |
| 11 | 15 | 17 | 15 Shushan Purim | 17 | 17 Emor | 19 | 19 | 21 | 22 | 23 Simḥat Torah Ve-Zot Ha-Berakhah | 24 | 25 Ḥanukkah 1 |
| 12 | 16 Va-Yeḥi | 18 | 16 | 18 Ḥol ha-Mo'ed | 18 Lag ba-Omer | 20 | 20 | 22 | 23 | 24 Bereshit | 25 | 26 2 |
| 13 | 17 | 19 | 17 | 19 | 19 | 21 | 21 Pinḥas | 23 | 24 | 25 | 26 | 27 3 |
| 14 | 18 | 20 | 18 | 20 | 20 | 22 | 22 | 24 | 25 Niẓẓavim Va-Yelekh | 26 | 27 | 28 Mi-Keẓ 4 |
| 15 | 19 | 21 | 19 | 21 Pesaḥ | 21 | 23 Shelaḥ | 23 | 25 | 26 | 27 | 28 | 29 5 |
| 16 | 20 | 22 Yitro | 20 Ki Tissa Parah | 22 | 22 | 24 | 24 | 26 | 27 | 28 | 29 Toledot | 30 R. Ḥ. 6 |
| 17 | 21 | 23 | 21 | 23 | 23 | 25 | 25 | 27 Re'eh | 28 | 29 | 1 Kislev R. Ḥ. | 1 Tevet R. Ḥ. 7 |
| 18 | 22 | 24 | 22 | 24 | 24 Be-Har Be-Ḥukkotai | 26 | 26 | 28 | 29 | 30 R. Ḥ. | 2 | 2 8 |
| 19 | 23 Shemot | 25 | 23 | 25 | 25 | 27 | 27 | 29 | 1 Tishri Rosh Ha-Shanah | 1 Ḥeshvan R. Ḥ. No'aḥ | 3 | 3 |
| 20 | 24 | 26 | 24 | 26 Shemini | 26 | 28 | 28 Mattot Masei | 30 R. Ḥ. | 2 | 2 | 4 | 4 |
| 21 | 25 | 27 | 25 | 27 | 27 | 29 | 29 | 1 Elul R. Ḥ. | 3 Ha'azinu Shabbat Shuvah | 3 | 5 | 5 Va-Yiggash |
| 22 | 26 | 28 | 26 | 28 | 28 | 30 Koraḥ R. Ḥ. | 1 Av R. Ḥ. | 2 | 4 Fast | 4 | 6 | 6 |
| 23 | 27 | 29 Mishpatim Shekalim | 27 Va-Yakhel Pekudei Ha-Ḥodesh | 29 | 29 | 1 Tammuz R. Ḥ. | 2 | 3 | 5 | 5 | 7 Va-Yeẓe | 7 |
| 24 | 28 | 30 R. Ḥ. | 28 | 30 R. Ḥ. | 1 Sivan R. Ḥ. | 2 | 3 | 4 Shofetim | 6 | 6 | 8 | 8 |
| 25 | 29 | 1 Adar R. Ḥ. | 29 | 1 Iyyar R. Ḥ. | 2 Be-Midbar | 3 | 4 | 5 | 7 | 7 | 9 | 9 |
| 26 | 1 Shevat R. Ḥ. Va-Era | 2 | 1 Nisan R. Ḥ. | 2 | 3 | 4 | 5 | 6 | 8 | 8 Lekh Lekha | 10 | 10 Fast |
| 27 | 2 | 3 | 2 | 3 Tazri'a Meẓora | 4 | 5 | 6 Devarim | 7 | 9 | 9 | 11 | 11 |
| 28 | 3 | 4 | 3 | 4 | 5 | 6 | 7 | 8 | 10 Yom Kippur | 10 | 12 | 12 Va-Yeḥi |
| 29 | 4 | | 4 | 5 Yom ha-Aẓma'ut | 6 Shavuot | 7 Ḥukkat | 8 | 9 | 11 | 11 | 13 | 13 |
| 30 | 5 | | 5 Va-Yikra | 6 | 7 | 8 | 9 Tishah be-Av | 10 | 12 | 12 | 14 Va-Yishlaḥ | 14 |
| 31 | 6 | | 6 | | 8 | | 10 | 11 Ki Teẓe | | 13 | | 15 |

# 1964

5724/25 — תשכ״ד / תשכ״ה

| | January | February | March | April | May | June | July | August | September | October | November | December |
|---|---|---|---|---|---|---|---|---|---|---|---|---|
| 1 | 16 Tevet | 18 Yitro | 17 | 19 | 19 | 21 | 21 | 23 Ekev | 24 | 25 | 26 | 26 2 |
| 2 | 17 | 19 | 18 | 20 Ḥol ha-Mo'ed | 20 Emor | 22 | 22 | 24 | 25 | 26 | 27 | 27 3 |
| 3 | 18 | 20 | 19 | 21 Pesaḥ | 21 | 23 | 23 | 25 | 26 | 27 Bereshit | 28 | 28 4 |
| 4 | 19 Shemot | 21 | 20 | 22 | 22 | 24 | 24 Pinḥas | 26 | 27 | 28 | 29 | 29 5 |
| 5 | 20 | 22 | 21 | 23 | 23 | 25 | 25 | 27 | 28 Niẓẓavim | 29 | 30 R. Ḥ. | 30 R. Ḥ. Mi-Keẓ 6 |
| 6 | 21 | 23 | 22 | 24 | 24 | 26 Shelaḥ | 26 | 28 | 29 | 30 R. Ḥ. | 1 Kislev R. Ḥ. | 1 Tevet R. Ḥ. 7 |
| 7 | 22 | 24 | 23 Va-Yakhel Pekudei Parah | 25 | 25 | 27 | 27 | 29 | 1 Tishri Rosh Ha-Shanah | 1 Ḥeshvan R. Ḥ. | 2 Toledot | 2 8 |
| 8 | 23 | 25 Mishpatim Shekalim | 24 | 26 | 26 | 28 | 28 | 30 R. Ḥ. Re'eh | 2 | 2 | 3 | 3 |
| 9 | 24 | 26 | 25 | 27 | 27 Be-Har Be-Ḥukkotai | 29 | 29 | 1 Elul R. Ḥ. | 3 Fast | 3 | 4 | 4 |
| 10 | 25 | 27 | 26 | 28 | 28 | 30 R. Ḥ. | 1 Av R. Ḥ. | 2 | 4 | 4 No'aḥ | 5 | 5 |
| 11 | 26 Va-Era | 28 | 27 | 29 Shemini | 29 | 1 Tammuz R. Ḥ. | 2 Mattot Masei | 3 | 5 | 5 | 6 | 6 |
| 12 | 27 | 29 | 28 | 30 R. Ḥ. | 1 Sivan R. Ḥ. | 2 | 3 | 4 | 6 Va-Yelekh Shabbat Shuvah | 6 | 7 | 7 Va-Yiggash |
| 13 | 28 | 30 R. Ḥ. | 29 | 1 Iyyar R. Ḥ. | 2 | 3 Koraḥ | 4 | 5 | 7 | 7 | 8 | 8 |
| 14 | 29 | 1 Adar R. Ḥ. | 1 Nisan R. Ḥ. Va-Yikra Ha-Ḥodesh | 2 | 3 | 4 | 5 | 6 | 8 | 8 | 9 Va-Yeẓe | 9 |
| 15 | 1 Shevat R. Ḥ. | 2 Terumah | 2 | 3 | 4 | 5 | 6 | 7 Shofetim | 9 | 9 | 10 | 10 Fast |
| 16 | 2 | 3 | 3 | 4 Yom ha-Aẓma'ut | 5 Be-Midbar | 6 | 7 | 8 | 10 Yom Kippur | 10 | 11 | 11 |
| 17 | 3 | 4 | 4 | 5 | 6 Shavuot | 7 | 8 | 9 | 11 | 11 Lekh Lekha | 12 | 12 |
| 18 | 4 Bo | 5 | 5 | 6 Tazri'a Meẓora | 7 | 8 | 9 Devarim | 10 | 12 | 12 | 13 | 13 |
| 19 | 5 | 6 | 6 | 7 | 8 | 9 | 10 Tishah be-Av | 11 | 13 Ha'azinu | 13 | 14 | 14 Va-Yeḥi |
| 20 | 6 | 7 | 7 | 8 | 9 | 10 Ḥukkat | 11 | 12 | 14 | 14 | 15 | 15 |
| 21 | 7 | 8 | 8 Ẓav Shabbat ha-Gadol | 9 | 10 | 11 | 12 | 13 | 15 Sukkot | 15 | 16 Va-Yishlaḥ | 16 |
| 22 | 8 | 9 Teẓavveh Zakhor | 9 | 10 | 11 | 12 | 13 | 14 Ki Teẓe | 16 | 16 | 17 | 17 |
| 23 | 9 | 10 | 10 | 11 | 12 Naso | 13 | 14 | 15 | 17 | 17 | 18 | 18 |
| 24 | 10 | 11 | 11 | 12 | 13 | 14 | 15 | 16 | 18 Ḥol ha-Mo'ed | 18 Va-Yera | 19 | 19 |
| 25 | 11 Be-Shallaḥ | 12 | 12 | 13 Aḥarei Mot Kedoshim | 14 | 15 | 16 Va-Ethannan | 17 | 19 | 19 | 20 | 20 |
| 26 | 12 | 13 Ta'anit Esther | 13 | 14 | 15 | 16 | 17 | 18 | 20 | 20 | 21 | 21 Shemot |
| 27 | 13 | 14 Purim | 14 | 15 | 16 | 17 Balak | 18 | 19 | 21 Ḥoshana Rabba | 21 | 22 | 22 |
| 28 | 14 | 15 Shushan Purim | 15 Pesaḥ | 16 | 17 | 18 Fast | 19 | 20 | 22 Shemini Aẓeret | 22 | 23 Va-Yeshev | 23 |
| 29 | 15 | 16 Ki Tissa | 16 Omer | 17 | 18 | 19 | 20 | 21 Ki Tavo | 23 Simḥat Torah Ve-Zot Ha-Berakhah | 23 | 24 | 24 |
| 30 | 16 | | 17 Ḥol ha-Mo'ed | 18 Lag ba-Omer | 19 Be-Ha'alotkha | 20 | 21 | 22 | 24 | 24 | 25 Ḥanukkah 1 | 25 |
| 31 | 17 | | 18 | | 20 | | 22 | 23 | | 25 Ḥayyei Sarah | | 26 |

## 1965

**5725/26** תשכ״ה / תשכ״ו

| | January | February | March | April | May | June | July | August | September | October | November | December |
|---|---|---|---|---|---|---|---|---|---|---|---|---|
| 1 | 27 Tevet | 29 | 27 | 28 | **29** Aḥarei Mot | 1 Sivan R. Ḥ. | 1 Tammuz R. Ḥ. | 3 | 4 | 5 | 6 | 7 |
| 2 | **28** Va-Era | 30 R. Ḥ. | 28 | 29 | 30 R. Ḥ. | 2 | 2 | 4 | 5 | **6** Va-Yelekh Shabbat Shuvah | 7 | 8 |
| 3 | 29 | 1 Adar I R. Ḥ. | 29 | **1** Nisan Tazri'a R. Ḥ. Ha-Ḥodesh | 1 Iyyar R. Ḥ. | 3 | **3** Koraḥ | 5 | 6 | 7 | 8 | 9 |
| 4 | 1 Shevat R. Ḥ. | 2 | 30 R. Ḥ. | 2 | 2 | 4 | 4 | 6 | **7** Shofetim | 8 | 9 | **10** Va-Yeẓe |
| 5 | 2 | 3 | 1 Adar II R. Ḥ. | 3 | 3 | **5** Be-Midbar | 5 | 7 | 8 | 9 | 10 | 11 |
| 6 | 3 | **4** Terumah | **2** Pekudei | 4 | 4 Yom ha-Aẓma'ut | 6 Shavuot | 6 | 8 | 9 | 10 Yom Kippur | **11** Lekh Lekha | 12 |
| 7 | 4 | 5 | 3 | 5 | 5 | 7 | 7 | **9** Devarim Tishah be-Av | 10 | 11 | 12 | 13 |
| 8 | 5 | 6 | 4 | 6 | **6** Kedoshim | 8 | 8 | 10 Fast | 11 | 12 | 13 | 14 |
| 9 | **6** Bo | 7 | 5 | 7 | 7 | 9 | 9 | 11 | 12 | **13** Ha'azinu | 14 | 15 |
| 10 | 7 | 8 | 6 | **8** Meẓora Shabbat ha-Gadol | 8 | 10 | **10** Ḥukkat | 12 | 13 | 14 | 15 | 16 |
| 11 | 8 | 9 | 7 | 9 | 9 | 11 | 11 | 13 | **14** Ki Teẓe | 15 Sukkot | 16 | **17** Va-Yishlaḥ |
| 12 | 9 | 10 | 8 | 10 | 10 | **12** Naso | 12 | 14 | 15 | 16 | 17 | 18 |
| 13 | 10 | **11** Teẓavveh | **9** Va-Yikra Zakhor | 11 | 11 | 13 | 13 | 15 | 16 | 17 Ḥol ha-Mo'ed | **18** Va-Yera | 19 |
| 14 | 11 | 12 | 10 | 12 | 12 | 14 | 14 | **16** Va-Etḥannan | 17 | 18 | 19 | 20 |
| 15 | 12 | 13 | 11 | 13 | **13** Emor | 15 | 15 | 17 | 18 | 19 | 20 | 21 |
| 16 | **13** Be-Shallaḥ | 14 | 12 | 14 | 14 | 16 | 16 | 18 | 19 | **20** | 21 | 22 |
| 17 | 14 | 15 | 13 Ta'anit Esther | **15** Pesaḥ | 15 | 17 | **17** Balak | 19 | 20 | 21 Hoshana Rabba | 22 | 23 |
| 18 | 15 | 16 | 14 Purim | 16 Omer | 16 | 18 | 18 Fast | 20 | **21** Ki Tavo | 22 Shemini Aẓeret | 23 | **24** Va-Yeshev |
| 19 | 16 | 17 | 15 Shushan Purim | 17 Ḥol ha-Mo'ed | 17 | **19** Be-Ha'alotkha | 19 | 21 | 22 | 23 Simḥat Torah Ve-Ẓot Ha-Berakhah | 24 | 25 Ḥanukkah 1 |
| 20 | 17 | **18** Ki Tissa | **16** Ẓav | 18 | 18 Lag ba-Omer | 20 | 20 | 22 | 23 | 24 | **25** Ḥayyei Sarah | 26 2 |
| 21 | 18 | 19 | 17 | 19 | 19 | 21 | 21 | **23** Ekev | 24 | 25 | 26 | 27 3 |
| 22 | 19 | 20 | 18 | 20 | **20** Be-Har | 22 | 22 | 24 | 25 | 26 | 27 | 28 4 |
| 23 | **20** Yitro | 21 | 19 | 21 Pesaḥ | 21 | 23 | 23 | 25 | 26 | **27** Bereshit | 28 | 29 5 |
| 24 | 21 | 22 | 20 | **22** | 22 | 24 | **24** Pinḥas | 26 | 27 | 28 | 29 | 1 Tevet R. Ḥ. 6 |
| 25 | 22 | 23 | 21 | 23 | 23 | 25 | 25 | 27 | **28** Niẓẓavim | 29 | 1 Kislev R. Ḥ. | **2** Mi-Keẓ 7 |
| 26 | 23 | 24 | 22 | 24 | 24 | **26** Shelaḥ | 26 | 28 | 29 | 30 R. Ḥ. | 2 | 3 8 |
| 27 | 24 | **25** Va-Yakhel Shekalim | **23** Shemini Parah | 25 | 25 | 27 | 27 | 29 | 1 Tishri Rosh Ha-Shanah | 1 Ḥeshvan R. Ḥ. | **3** Toledot | 4 |
| 28 | 25 | 26 | 24 | 26 | 26 | 28 | 28 | **30** R. Ḥ. Re'eh | 2 | 2 | 4 | 5 |
| 29 | 26 | | 25 | 27 | **27** Be-Ḥukkotai | 29 | 29 | 1 Elul R. Ḥ. | 3 Fast | 3 | 5 | 6 |
| 30 | **27** Mishpatim | | 26 | 28 | 28 | 30 R. Ḥ. | 1 Av R. Ḥ. | 2 | 4 | **4** No'aḥ | 6 | 7 |
| 31 | 28 | | 27 | | 29 | | **2** Mattot Masei | 3 | | 5 | | 8 |

## 1966

**5726/27** תשכ״ו / תשכ״ז

| | January | February | March | April | May | June | July | August | September | October | November | December |
|---|---|---|---|---|---|---|---|---|---|---|---|---|
| 1 | **9** Va-Yiggash | 11 | 9 | 11 | 11 | 13 | 13 | 15 | 16 | **17** Ḥol ha-Mo'ed | 18 | 18 |
| 2 | 10 Fast | 12 | 10 | **12** Ẓav Shabbat ha-Gadol | 12 | 14 | **14** Balak | 16 | 17 | 18 | 19 | 19 |
| 3 | 11 | 13 | 11 Ta'anit Esther | 13 | 13 | 15 | 15 | 17 | **18** Ki Tavo | 19 | 20 | **20** Va-Yeshev |
| 4 | 12 | 14 | 12 | 14 | 14 | **16** Be-Ha'alotkha | 16 | 18 | 19 | 20 | 21 | 21 |
| 5 | 13 | **15** Be-Shallaḥ | **13** Teẓavveh Zakhor | 15 Pesaḥ | 15 | 17 | 17 | 19 | 20 | 21 Hoshana Rabba | **22** Ḥayyei Sarah | 22 |
| 6 | 14 | 16 | 14 Purim | 16 Omer | 16 | 18 | 18 | **20** Ekev | 21 | 22 Shemini Aẓeret | 23 | 23 |
| 7 | 15 | 17 | 15 Shushan Purim | 17 Ḥol ha-Mo'ed | **17** Emor | 19 | 19 | 21 | 22 | 23 Simḥat Torah Ve-Ẓot Ha-Berakhah | 24 | 24 |
| 8 | **16** Va-Yeḥi | 18 | 16 | 18 | 18 Lag ba-Omer | 20 | 20 | 22 | 23 | **24** Bereshit | 25 | 25 Ḥanukkah 1 |
| 9 | 17 | 19 | 17 | **19** | 19 | 21 | **21** Pinḥas | 23 | 24 | 25 | 26 | 26 2 |
| 10 | 18 | 20 | 18 | 20 | 20 | 22 | 22 | 24 | **25** Niẓẓavim Va-Yelekh | 26 | 27 | **27** Mi-Keẓ 3 |
| 11 | 19 | 21 | 19 | 21 Pesaḥ | 21 | **23** Shelaḥ | 23 | 25 | 26 | 27 | 28 | 28 4 |
| 12 | 20 | **22** Yitro | **20** Ki Tissa Parah | 22 | 22 | 24 | 24 | 26 | 27 | 28 | **29** Toledot | 29 5 |
| 13 | 21 | 23 | 21 | 23 | 23 | 25 | 25 | **27** Re'eh | 28 | 29 | 30 R. Ḥ. | 30 R. Ḥ. 6 |
| 14 | 22 | 24 | 22 | 24 | **24** Be-Har Be-Ḥukkotai | 26 | 26 | 28 | 29 | 30 R. Ḥ. | 1 Kislev R. Ḥ. | 1 Tevet R. Ḥ. 7 |
| 15 | **23** Shemot | 25 | 23 | 25 | 25 | 27 | 27 | 29 | 1 Tishri Rosh Ha-Shanah | **1** Ḥeshvan R. Ḥ. No'aḥ | 2 | 2 8 |
| 16 | 24 | 26 | 24 | **26** Shemini | 26 | 28 | **28** Mattot Masei | 30 R. Ḥ. | 2 | 2 | 3 | 3 |
| 17 | 25 | 27 | 25 | 27 | 27 | 29 | 29 | 1 Elul R. Ḥ. | **3** Ha'azinu Shabbat Shuvah | 3 | 4 | **4** Va-Yiggash |
| 18 | 26 | 28 | 26 | 28 | 28 | **30** R. Ḥ. Koraḥ | 1 Av R. Ḥ. | 2 | 4 Fast | 4 | 5 | 5 |
| 19 | 27 | **29** Mishpatim Shekalim | **27** Va-Yakhel Pekudei Ha-Ḥodesh | 29 | 29 | 1 Tammuz R. Ḥ. | 2 | 3 | 5 | 5 | **6** Va-Yeẓe | 6 |
| 20 | 28 | 30 R. Ḥ. | 28 | 30 R. Ḥ. | 1 Sivan R. Ḥ. | 2 | 3 | **4** Shofetim | 6 | 6 | 7 | 7 |
| 21 | 29 | 1 Adar R. Ḥ. | 29 | 1 Iyyar R. Ḥ. | **2** Be-Midbar | 3 | 4 | 5 | 7 | 7 | 8 | 8 |
| 22 | **1** Shevat R. Ḥ. Va-Era | 2 | 1 Nisan R. Ḥ. | 2 | 3 | 4 | 5 | 6 | 8 | **8** Lekh Lekha | 9 | 9 |
| 23 | 2 | 3 | 2 | **3** Tazri'a Meẓora | 4 | 5 | **6** Devarim | 7 | 9 | 9 | 10 | 10 Fast |
| 24 | 3 | 4 | 3 | 4 | 5 | 6 | 7 | 8 | 10 Yom Kippur | 10 | 11 | **11** Va-Yeḥi |
| 25 | 4 | 5 | 4 | 5 Yom ha-Aẓma'ut | 6 Shavuot | **7** Ḥukkat | 8 | 9 | 11 | 11 | 12 | 12 |
| 26 | 5 | **6** Terumah | **5** Va-Yikra | 6 | 7 | 8 | 9 Tishah be-Av | 10 | 12 | 12 | **13** Va-Yishlaḥ | 13 |
| 27 | 6 | 7 | 6 | 7 | 8 | 9 | 10 | **11** Ki Teẓe | 13 | 13 | 14 | 14 |
| 28 | 7 | 8 | 7 | 8 | **9** Naso | 10 | 11 | 12 | 14 | 14 | 15 | 15 |
| 29 | **8** Bo | | 8 | 9 | 10 | 11 | 12 | 13 | 15 Sukkot | **15** Va-Yera | 16 | 16 |
| 30 | 9 | | 9 | **10** Aḥarei Mot Kedoshim | 11 | 12 | **13** Va-Etḥannan | 14 | 16 | 16 | 17 | 17 |
| 31 | 10 | | 10 | | 12 | | 14 | 15 | | 17 | | **18** Shemot |

# 1967

**5727/28** — תשכ״ז / תשכ״ח

| | January | February | March | April | May | June | July | August | September | October | November | December |
|---|---|---|---|---|---|---|---|---|---|---|---|---|
| 1 | 19 Tevet | 21 | 19 | 20 Shemini Parah | 21 Pesah | 22 | 23 Korah | 24 | 26 | 26 | 28 | 28 |
| 2 | 20 | 22 | 20 | 21 | 22 | 23 | 24 | 25 | 27 Re'eh | 27 | 29 | 29 Toledot |
| 3 | 21 | 23 | 21 | 22 | 23 | 24 Be-Midbar | 25 | 26 | 28 | 28 | 30 R. H. | 1 Kislev R. H. |
| 4 | 22 | 24 Mishpatim | 22 Va-Yakhel | 23 | 24 | 25 | 26 | 27 | 29 | 29 | 1 Heshvan R. H. No'ah | 2 |
| 5 | 23 | 25 | 23 | 24 | 25 | 26 | 27 | 28 Masei | 30 R. H. | 1 Tishri Rosh Ha-Shanah | 2 | 3 |
| 6 | 24 | 26 | 24 | 25 | 26 Kedoshim | 27 | 28 | 29 | 1 Elul R. H. | 2 | 3 | 4 |
| 7 | 25 Va-Era | 27 | 25 | 26 | 27 | 28 | 29 | 1 Av R. H. | 2 | 3 Ha'azinu Shabbat Shuvah | 4 | 5 |
| 8 | 26 | 28 | 26 | 27 Tazri'a Ha-Hodesh | 28 | 29 | 30 R. H. Hukkat | 2 | 3 | 4 Fast | 5 | 6 |
| 9 | 27 | 29 | 27 | 28 | 29 | 1 Sivan R. H. | 1 Tammuz R. H. | 3 | 4 Shofetim | 5 | 6 | 7 Va-Yeze |
| 10 | 28 | 30 R. H. | 28 | 29 | 30 R. H. | 2 Naso | 2 | 4 | 5 | 6 | 7 | 8 |
| 11 | 29 | 1 Adar I R. H. Terumah | 29 Pekudei Shekalim | 1 Nisan R. H. | 1 Iyyar R. H. | 3 | 3 | 5 | 6 | 7 | 8 Lekh Lekha | 9 |
| 12 | 1 Shevat R. H. | 2 | 30 R. H. | 2 | 2 | 4 | 4 | 6 Devarim | 7 | 8 | 9 | 10 |
| 13 | 2 | 3 | 1 Adar II R. H. | 3 | 3 Emor | 5 | 5 | 7 | 8 | 9 | 10 | 11 |
| 14 | 3 Bo | 4 | 2 | 4 | 4 | 6 Shavuot | 6 | 8 | 9 | 10 Yom Kippur | 11 | 12 |
| 15 | 4 | 5 | 3 | 5 Mezora | 5 Yom ha-Azma'ut | 7 | 7 Balak | 9 Tishah be-Av | 10 | 11 | 12 | 13 |
| 16 | 5 | 6 | 4 | 6 | 6 | 8 | 8 | 10 | 11 Ki Teze | 12 | 13 | 14 Va-Yishlah |
| 17 | 6 | 7 | 5 | 7 | 7 | 9 Be-Ha'alotkha | 9 | 11 | 12 | 13 | 14 | 15 |
| 18 | 7 | 8 Tezavveh | 6 Va-Yikra | 8 | 8 | 10 | 10 | 12 | 13 | 14 | 15 Va-Yera | 16 |
| 19 | 8 | 9 | 7 | 9 | 9 | 11 | 11 | 13 Va-Ethannan | 14 | 15 Sukkot | 16 | 17 |
| 20 | 9 | 10 | 8 | 10 | 10 Be-Har | 12 | 12 | 14 | 15 | 16 | 17 | 18 |
| 21 | 10 Be-Shallah | 11 | 9 | 11 | 11 | 13 | 13 | 15 | 16 | 17 Hol ha-Mo'ed | 18 | 19 |
| 22 | 11 | 12 | 10 | 12 Aharei Mot Shabbat ha-Gadol | 12 | 14 | 14 Pinhas | 16 | 17 | 18 | 19 | 20 |
| 23 | 12 | 13 | 11 Ta'anit Esther | 13 | 13 | 15 | 15 | 17 | 18 Ki Tavo | 19 | 20 | 21 Va-Yeshev |
| 24 | 13 | 14 | 12 | 14 | 14 | 16 Shelah | 16 | 18 | 19 | 20 | 21 | 22 |
| 25 | 14 | 15 Ki Tissa | 13 Zav Zakhor | 15 Pesah | 15 | 17 | 17 Fast | 19 | 20 | 21 Hoshana Rabba | 22 Hayyei Sarah | 23 |
| 26 | 15 | 16 | 14 Purim | 16 Omer | 16 | 18 | 18 | 20 Ekev | 21 | 22 Shemini Azeret | 23 | 24 |
| 27 | 16 | 17 | 15 Shushan Purim | 17 Hol ha-Mo'ed | 17 Be-Hukkotai | 19 | 19 | 21 | 22 | 23 Simhat Torah Ve-Zot Ha-Berakhah | 24 | 25 Hanukkah 1 |
| 28 | 17 Yitro | 18 | 16 | 18 | 18 Lag ba-Omer | 20 | 20 | 22 | 23 | 24 Bereshit | 25 | 26 2 |
| 29 | 18 | | 17 | 19 | 19 | 21 | 21 Mattot | 23 | 24 | 25 | 26 | 27 3 |
| 30 | 19 | | 18 | 20 | 20 | 22 | 22 | 24 | 25 Nizzavim Va-Yelekh | 26 | 27 | 28 Mi-Kez 4 |
| 31 | 20 | | 19 | | 21 | | 23 | 25 | | 27 | | 29 5 |

# 1968

**5728/29** — תשכ״ח / תשכ״ט

| | January | February | March | April | May | June | July | August | September | October | November | December |
|---|---|---|---|---|---|---|---|---|---|---|---|---|
| 1 | 30 Kislev Hanukkah R. H. 6 | 2 | 1 Adar R. H. | 3 | 3 | 5 Be-Midbar | 5 | 7 | 8 | 9 | 10 | 10 |
| 2 | 1 Tevet R. H. 7 | 3 | 2 Terumah | 4 | 4 Yom ha-Azma'ut | 6 Shavuot | 6 | 8 | 9 | 10 Yom Kippur | 11 Lekh Lekha | 11 |
| 3 | 2 8 | 4 Bo | 3 | 5 | 5 | 7 | 7 | 9 Devarim Tishah be-Av | 10 | 11 | 12 | 12 |
| 4 | 3 | 5 | 4 | 6 | 6 Tazri'a Mezora | 8 | 8 | 10 Fast | 11 | 12 | 13 | 13 |
| 5 | 4 | 6 | 5 | 7 | 7 | 9 | 9 | 11 | 12 | 13 Ha'azinu | 14 | 14 |
| 6 | 5 Va-Yiggash | 7 | 6 | 8 Zav Shabbat ha-Gadol | 8 | 10 | 10 Hukkat | 12 | 13 | 14 | 15 | 15 |
| 7 | 6 | 8 | 7 | 9 | 9 | 11 | 11 | 13 | 14 Ki Teze | 15 Sukkot | 16 | 16 Va-Yishlah |
| 8 | 7 | 9 | 8 | 10 | 10 | 12 Naso | 12 | 14 | 15 | 16 | 17 | 17 |
| 9 | 8 | 10 | 9 Tezavveh Zakhor | 11 | 11 | 13 | 13 | 15 | 16 | 17 Hol ha-Mo'ed | 18 Va-Yera | 18 |
| 10 | 9 | 11 Be-Shallah | 10 | 12 | 12 | 14 | 14 | 16 Va-Ethannan | 17 | 18 | 19 | 19 |
| 11 | 10 Fast | 12 | 11 | 13 | 13 Aharei Mot Kedoshim | 15 | 15 | 17 | 18 | 19 | 20 | 20 |
| 12 | 11 | 13 | 12 | 14 | 14 | 16 | 16 | 18 | 19 | 20 | 21 | 21 |
| 13 | 12 Va-Yehi | 14 | 13 Ta'anit Esther | 15 Pesah | 15 | 17 | 17 Balak | 19 | 20 | 21 Hoshana Rabba | 22 | 22 |
| 14 | 13 | 15 | 14 Purim | 16 Omer | 16 | 18 | 18 Fast | 20 | 21 Ki Tavo | 22 Shemini Azeret | 23 | 23 Va-Yeshev |
| 15 | 14 | 16 | 15 Shushan Purim | 17 Hol ha-Mo'ed | 17 | 19 Be-Ha'alotkha | 19 | 21 | 22 | 23 Simhat Torah Ve-Zot Ha-Berakhah | 24 | 24 |
| 16 | 15 | 17 | 16 Ki Tissa | 18 | 18 Lag ba-Omer | 20 | 20 | 22 | 23 | 24 | 25 Hayyei Sarah | 25 Hanukkah 1 |
| 17 | 16 | 18 Yitro | 17 | 19 | 19 | 21 | 21 | 23 Ekev | 24 | 25 | 26 | 26 2 |
| 18 | 17 | 19 | 18 | 20 | 20 Emor | 22 | 22 | 24 | 25 | 26 | 27 | 27 3 |
| 19 | 18 | 20 | 19 | 21 Pesah | 21 | 23 | 23 | 25 | 26 | 27 Bereshit | 28 | 28 4 |
| 20 | 19 Shemot | 21 | 20 | 22 | 22 | 24 | 24 Pinhas | 26 | 27 | 28 | 29 | 29 5 |
| 21 | 20 | 22 | 21 | 23 | 23 | 25 | 25 | 27 | 28 Nizzavim | 29 | 30 R. H. | 30 R. H. Mi-Kez 6 |
| 22 | 21 | 23 | 22 | 24 | 24 | 26 Shelah | 26 | 28 | 29 | 30 R. H. | 1 Kislev R. H. | 1 Tevet R. H. 7 |
| 23 | 22 | 24 | 23 Va-Yakhel Pekudei Parah | 25 | 25 | 27 | 27 | 29 | 1 Tishri Rosh Ha-Shanah | 1 Heshvan R. H. | 2 Toledot | 2 8 |
| 24 | 23 | 25 Mishpatim Shekalim | 24 | 26 | 26 | 28 | 28 | 30 R. H. Re'eh | 2 | 2 | 3 | 3 |
| 25 | 24 | 26 | 25 | 27 | 27 Be-Har Be-Hukkotai | 29 | 29 | 1 Elul R. H. | 3 Fast | 3 | 4 | 4 |
| 26 | 25 | 27 | 26 | 28 | 28 | 30 R. H. | 1 Av R. H. | 2 | 4 | 4 No'ah | 5 | 5 |
| 27 | 26 Va-Era | 28 | 27 | 29 Shemini | 29 | 1 Tammuz R. H. | 2 Mattot Masei | 3 | 5 | 5 | 6 | 6 |
| 28 | 27 | 29 | 28 | 30 R. H. | 1 Sivan R. H. | 2 | 3 | 4 | 6 Va-Yelekh Shabbat Shuvah | 6 | 7 | 7 Va-Yiggash |
| 29 | 28 | 30 R. H. | 29 | 1 Iyyar R. H. | 2 | 3 Korah | 4 | 5 | 7 | 7 | 8 | 8 |
| 30 | 29 | | 1 Nisan R. H. Va-Yikra Ha-Hodesh | 2 | 3 | 4 | 5 | 6 | 8 | 8 | 9 Va-Yeze | 9 |
| 31 | 1 Shevat R. H. | | 2 | | 4 | | 6 | 7 Shofetim | | 9 | | 10 Fast |

# 1969

**5729/30** תשכ״ט / תש״ל

| | January | February | March | April | May | June | July | August | September | October | November | December |
|---|---|---|---|---|---|---|---|---|---|---|---|---|
| 1 | 11 Tevet | 13 Be-Shallaḥ | 11 Tezavveh Zakhor | 13 | 13 | 15 | 15 | 17 | 18 | 19 | 20 Va-Yera | 21 |
| 2 | 12 | 14 | 12 | 14 | 14 | 16 | 16 | 18 Ekev | 19 | 20 Hol ha-Mo'ed | 21 | 22 |
| 3 | 13 | 15 | 13 Ta'anit Esther | 15 Pesaḥ | 15 Emor | 17 | 17 Fast | 19 | 20 | 21 Hoshana Rabba | 22 | 23 |
| 4 | 14 Va-Yeḥi | 16 | 14 Purim | 16 Omer | 16 | 18 | 18 | 20 | 21 | 22 Shemini Aẓeret | 23 | 24 |
| 5 | 15 | 17 | 15 Shushan Purim | 17 Hol ha-Mo'ed | 17 | 19 | 19 Pinḥas | 21 | 22 | 23 Simḥat Torah Ve-Zot Ha-Berakhah | 24 | 25 Hanukkah 1 |
| 6 | 16 | 18 | 16 | 18 | 18 Lag ba-Omer | 20 | 20 | 22 | 23 Niẓẓavim Va-Yelekh | 24 | 25 | 26 Va-Yeshev 2 |
| 7 | 17 | 19 | 17 | 19 | 19 | 21 Be-Ha'alotkha | 21 | 23 | 24 | 25 | 26 | 27 3 |
| 8 | 18 | 20 Yitro | 18 Ki Tissa Parah | 20 | 20 | 22 | 22 | 24 | 25 | 26 | 27 Hayyei Sarah | 28 4 |
| 9 | 19 | 21 | 19 | 21 Pesaḥ | 21 | 23 | 23 | 25 Re'eh | 26 | 27 | 28 | 29 5 |
| 10 | 20 | 22 | 20 | 22 | 22 Be-Har Be-Ḥukkotai | 24 | 24 | 26 | 27 | 28 | 29 | 1 Tevet R.H. 6 |
| 11 | 21 Shemot | 23 | 21 | 23 | 23 | 25 | 25 | 27 | 28 | 29 Bereshit | 1 Kislev R.H. | 2 7 |
| 12 | 22 | 24 | 22 | 24 Shemini | 24 | 26 | 26 Mattot Masei | 28 | 29 | 30 R.H. | 2 | 3 8 |
| 13 | 23 | 25 | 23 | 25 | 25 | 27 | 27 | 29 | 1 Tishri Rosh Ha-Shanah | 1 Heshvan R.H. | 3 | 4 Mi-Keẓ |
| 14 | 24 | 26 | 24 | 26 | 26 | 28 Shelaḥ | 28 | 30 R.H. | 2 | 2 | 4 | 5 |
| 15 | 25 | 27 Mishpatim Shekalim | 25 Va-Yakhel Pekudei Ha-Hodesh | 27 | 27 | 29 | 29 | 1 Elul R.H. | 3 Fast | 3 | 5 Toledot | 6 |
| 16 | 26 | 28 | 26 | 28 | 28 | 30 R.H. | 1 Av R.H. | 2 Shofetim | 4 | 4 | 6 | 7 |
| 17 | 27 | 29 | 27 | 29 | 29 Be-Midbar | 1 Tammuz R.H. | 2 | 3 | 5 | 5 | 7 | 8 |
| 18 | 28 Va-Era | 30 R.H. | 28 | 30 R.H. | 1 Sivan R.H. | 2 | 3 | 4 | 6 | 6 No'aḥ | 8 | 9 |
| 19 | 29 | 1 Adar R.H. | 29 | 1 Iyyar R.H. Tazri'a Meẓora | 2 | 3 | 4 Devarim | 5 | 7 | 7 | 9 | 10 Fast |
| 20 | 1 Shevat R.H. | 2 | 1 Nisan R.H. | 2 | 3 | 4 | 5 | 6 | 8 Ha'azinu Shabbat Shuvah | 8 | 10 | 11 Va-Yiggash |
| 21 | 2 | 3 | 2 | 3 | 4 | 5 Koraḥ | 6 | 7 | 9 | 9 | 11 | 12 |
| 22 | 3 | 4 Terumah | 3 Va-Yikra | 4 | 5 | 6 | 7 | 8 | 10 Yom Kippur | 10 | 12 Va-Yeẓe | 13 |
| 23 | 4 | 5 | 4 | 5 Yom ha-Aẓma'ut | 6 Shavuot | 7 | 8 | 9 Ki Teẓe | 11 | 11 | 13 | 14 |
| 24 | 5 | 6 | 5 | 6 | 7 | 8 | 9 Tishah be-Av | 10 | 12 | 12 | 14 | 15 |
| 25 | 6 Bo | 7 | 6 | 7 | 8 | 9 | 10 | 11 | 13 | 13 Lekh Lekha | 15 | 16 |
| 26 | 7 | 8 | 7 | 8 Aharei Mot Kedoshim | 9 | 10 | 11 Va-Ethannan | 12 | 14 | 14 | 16 | 17 |
| 27 | 8 | 9 | 8 | 9 | 10 | 11 | 12 | 13 | 15 Sukkot | 15 | 17 | 18 Va-Yeḥi |
| 28 | 9 | 10 | 9 | 10 | 11 | 12 Ḥukkat Balak | 13 | 14 | 16 | 16 | 18 | 19 |
| 29 | 10 | | 10 Ẓav Shabbat ha-Gadol | 11 | 12 | 13 | 14 | 15 | 17 Hol ha-Mo'ed | 17 | 19 Va-Yishlaḥ | 20 |
| 30 | 11 | | 11 | 12 | 13 | 14 | 15 | 16 Ki Tavo | 18 | 18 | 20 | 21 |
| 31 | 12 | | 12 | | 14 Naso | | 16 | 17 | | 19 | | 22 |

# 1970

**5730/31** תש״ל / תשל״א

| | January | February | March | April | May | June | July | August | September | October | November | December |
|---|---|---|---|---|---|---|---|---|---|---|---|---|
| 1 | 23 Tevet | 25 | 23 | 24 | 25 | 26 | 27 | 28 Mattot Masei | 30 R.H. | 1 Tishri Rosh Ha-Shanah | 2 | 3 |
| 2 | 24 | 26 | 24 | 25 | 26 Aharei Mot | 27 | 28 | 29 | 1 Elul R.H. | 2 | 3 | 4 |
| 3 | 25 Shemot | 27 | 25 | 26 | 27 | 28 | 29 | 1 Av R.H. | 2 | 3 Ha'azinu Shabbat Shuvah | 4 | 5 |
| 4 | 26 | 28 | 26 | 27 Shemini Ha-Hodesh | 28 | 29 | 30 R.H. Koraḥ | 2 | 3 | 4 Fast | 5 | 6 |
| 5 | 27 | 29 | 27 | 28 | 29 | 1 Sivan R.H. | 1 Tammuz R.H. | 3 | 4 Shofetim | 5 | 6 | 7 Va-Yeẓe |
| 6 | 28 | 30 R.H. | 28 | 29 | 30 R.H. | 2 Be-Midbar | 2 | 4 | 5 | 6 | 7 | 8 |
| 7 | 29 | 1 Adar I R.H. Mishpatim | 29 Va-Yakhel Shekalim | 1 Nisan R.H. | 1 Iyyar R.H. | 3 | 3 | 5 | 6 | 7 | 8 Lekh Lekha | 9 |
| 8 | 1 Shevat R.H. | 2 | 30 R.H. | 2 | 2 | 4 | 4 | 6 Devarim | 7 | 8 | 9 | 10 |
| 9 | 2 | 3 | 1 Adar II R.H. | 3 | 3 Kedoshim | 5 | 5 | 7 | 8 | 9 | 10 | 11 |
| 10 | 3 Va-Era | 4 | 2 | 4 | 4 | 6 Shavuot | 6 | 8 | 9 | 10 Yom Kippur | 11 | 12 |
| 11 | 4 | 5 | 3 | 5 Tazri'a | 5 Yom ha-Aẓma'ut | 7 | 7 Ḥukkat | 9 Tishah be-Av | 10 | 11 | 12 | 13 |
| 12 | 5 | 6 | 4 | 6 | 6 | 8 | 8 | 10 | 11 Ki Teẓe | 12 | 13 | 14 Va-Yishlaḥ |
| 13 | 6 | 7 | 5 | 7 | 7 | 9 Naso | 9 | 11 | 12 | 13 | 14 | 15 |
| 14 | 7 | 8 Terumah | 6 Pekudei | 8 | 8 | 10 | 10 | 12 | 13 | 14 | 15 Va-Yera | 16 |
| 15 | 8 | 9 | 7 | 9 | 9 | 11 | 11 | 13 Va-Ethannan | 14 | 15 Sukkot | 16 | 17 |
| 16 | 9 | 10 | 8 | 10 | 10 Emor | 12 | 12 | 14 | 15 | 16 | 17 | 18 |
| 17 | 10 Bo | 11 | 9 | 11 | 11 | 13 | 13 | 15 | 16 | 17 Hol ha-Mo'ed | 18 | 19 |
| 18 | 11 | 12 | 10 | 12 Meẓora Shabbat ha-Gadol | 12 | 14 | 14 Balak | 16 | 17 | 18 | 19 | 20 |
| 19 | 12 | 13 | 11 Ta'anit Esther | 13 | 13 | 15 | 15 | 17 | 18 Ki Tavo | 19 | 20 | 21 Va-Yeshev |
| 20 | 13 | 14 | 12 | 14 | 14 | 16 Be-Ha'alotkha | 16 | 18 | 19 | 20 | 21 | 22 |
| 21 | 14 | 15 Tezavveh | 13 Va-Yikra Zakhor | 15 Pesaḥ | 15 | 17 | 17 Fast | 19 | 20 | 21 Hoshana Rabba | 22 Hayyei Sarah | 23 |
| 22 | 15 | 16 | 14 Purim | 16 Omer | 16 | 18 | 18 | 20 Ekev | 21 | 22 Shemini Aẓeret | 23 | 24 |
| 23 | 16 | 17 | 15 Shushan Purim | 17 | 17 Be-Har | 19 | 19 | 21 | 22 | 23 Simḥat Torah Ve-Zot Ha-Berakhah | 24 | 25 Hanukkah 1 |
| 24 | 17 Be-Shallaḥ | 18 | 16 | 18 | 18 Lag ba-Omer | 20 | 20 | 22 | 23 | 24 Bereshit | 25 | 26 2 |
| 25 | 18 | 19 | 17 | 19 Hol ha-Mo'ed | 19 | 21 | 21 Pinḥas | 23 | 24 | 25 | 26 | 27 3 |
| 26 | 19 | 20 | 18 | 20 | 20 | 22 | 22 | 24 | 25 Niẓẓavim Va-Yelekh | 26 | 27 | 28 Mi-Keẓ 4 |
| 27 | 20 | 21 | 19 | 21 Pesaḥ | 21 | 23 Shelaḥ | 23 | 25 | 26 | 27 | 28 | 29 5 |
| 28 | 21 | 22 Ki Tissa | 20 Ẓav Parah | 22 | 22 | 24 | 24 | 26 | 27 | 28 | 29 Toledot | 30 R.H. 6 |
| 29 | 22 | | 21 | 23 | 23 | 25 | 25 | 27 Re'eh | 28 | 29 | 1 Kislev R.H. | 1 Tevet R.H. 7 |
| 30 | 23 | | 22 | 24 | 24 Be-Ḥukkotai | 26 | 26 | 28 | 29 | 30 R.H. | 2 | 2 8 |
| 31 | 24 Yitro | | 23 | | 25 | | 27 | 29 | | 1 Heshvan R.H. No'aḥ | | 3 |

# 1971

**5731/32** תשל״א / תשל״ב

| | January | February | March | April | May | June | July | August | September | October | November | December |
|---|---|---|---|---|---|---|---|---|---|---|---|---|
| 1 | 4 Tevet | 6 | 4 | 6 | 6 *Tazri'a Mezora* | 8 | 8 | 10 Fast | 11 | 12 | 13 | 13 |
| 2 | 5 *Va-Yiggash* | 7 | 5 | 7 | 7 | 9 | 9 | 11 | 12 | 13 *Ha'azinu* | 14 | 14 |
| 3 | 6 | 8 | 6 | 8 *Zav* Shabbat ha-Gadol | 8 | 10 | 10 *Hukkat* | 12 | 13 | 14 | 15 | 15 |
| 4 | 7 | 9 | 7 | 9 | 9 | 11 | 11 | 13 | 14 *Ki Teze* | 15 Sukkot | 16 | 16 *Va-Yishlah* |
| 5 | 8 | 10 | 8 | 10 | 10 | 12 *Naso* | 12 | 14 | 15 | 16 | 17 | 17 |
| 6 | 9 | 11 *Be-Shallah* | 9 *Tezavveh* Zakhor | 11 | 11 | 13 | 13 | 15 | 16 | 17 Hol ha-Mo'ed | 18 *Va-Yera* | 18 |
| 7 | 10 Fast | 12 | 10 | 12 | 12 | 14 | 14 | 16 *Va-Ethannan* | 17 | 18 | 19 | 19 |
| 8 | 11 | 13 | 11 | 13 | 13 *Aharei Mot Kedoshim* | 15 | 15 | 17 | 18 | 19 | 20 | 20 |
| 9 | 12 *Va-Yehi* | 14 | 12 | 14 | 14 | 16 | 16 | 18 | 19 | 20 | 21 | 21 |
| 10 | 13 | 15 | 13 Ta'anit Esther | 15 Pesah | 15 | 17 | 17 *Balak* | 19 | 20 | 21 Hoshana Rabba | 22 | 22 |
| 11 | 14 | 16 | 14 Purim | 16 Omer | 16 | 18 | 18 Fast | 20 | 21 *Ki Tavo* | 22 Shemini Azeret | 23 | 23 *Va-Yeshev* |
| 12 | 15 | 17 | 15 Shushan Purim | 17 Hol ha-Mo'ed | 17 | 19 *Be-Ha'alotkha* | 19 | 21 | 22 | 23 Simhat Torah *Ve-Zot Ha-Berakhah* | 24 | 24 |
| 13 | 16 | 18 *Yitro* | 16 *Ki Tissa* | 18 | 18 Lag ba-Omer | 20 | 20 | 22 | 23 | 24 | 25 *Hayyei Sarah* | 25 Hanukkah 1 |
| 14 | 17 | 19 | 17 | 19 | 19 | 21 | 21 | 23 *Ekev* | 24 | 25 | 26 | 26 2 |
| 15 | 18 | 20 | 18 | 20 | 20 *Emor* | 22 | 22 | 24 | 25 | 26 | 27 | 27 3 |
| 16 | 19 *Shemot* | 21 | 19 | 21 Pesah | 21 | 23 | 23 | 25 | 26 | 27 *Bereshit* | 28 | 28 4 |
| 17 | 20 | 22 | 20 | 22 | 22 | 24 | 24 *Pinhas* | 26 | 27 | 28 | 29 | 29 5 |
| 18 | 21 | 23 | 21 | 23 | 23 | 25 | 25 | 27 | 28 *Nizzavim* | 29 | 30 R.H. | 30 R.H. *Mi-Kez* 6 |
| 19 | 22 | 24 | 22 | 24 | 24 | 26 *Shelah* | 26 | 28 | 29 | 30 R.H. | 1 Kislev R.H. | 1 Tevet R.H. 7 |
| 20 | 23 | 25 *Mishpatim* Shekalim | 23 *Va-Yakhel Pekudei* Parah | 25 | 25 | 27 | 27 | 29 | 1 Tishri Rosh Ha-Shanah | 1 Heshvan R.H. | 2 *Toledot* | 2 8 |
| 21 | 24 | 26 | 24 | 26 | 26 | 28 | 28 | 30 R.H. *Re'eh* | 2 | 2 | 3 | 3 |
| 22 | 25 | 27 | 25 | 27 | 27 *Be-Har Be-Hukkotai* | 29 | 29 | 1 Elul R.H. | 3 Fast | 3 | 4 | 4 |
| 23 | 26 *Va-Era* | 28 | 26 | 28 | 28 | 30 R.H. | 1 Av R.H. | 2 | 4 | 4 *No'ah* | 5 | 5 |
| 24 | 27 | 29 | 27 | 29 *Shemini* | 29 | 1 Tammuz R.H. | 2 *Mattot Masei* | 3 | 5 | 5 | 6 | 6 |
| 25 | 28 | 30 R.H. | 28 | 30 R.H. | 1 Sivan R.H. | 2 | 3 | 4 | 6 *Va-Yelekh* Shabbat Shuvah | 6 | 7 | 7 *Va-Yiggash* |
| 26 | 29 | 1 Adar R.H. | 29 | 1 Iyyar R.H. | 2 | 3 *Korah* | 4 | 5 | 7 | 7 | 8 | 8 |
| 27 | 1 Shevat R.H. | 2 *Terumah* | 1 Nisan *Va-Yikra* R.H. Ha-Hodesh | 2 | 3 | 4 | 5 | 6 | 8 | 8 | 9 *Va-Yeze* | 9 |
| 28 | 2 | 3 | 2 | 3 | 4 | 5 | 6 | 7 *Shofetim* | 9 | 9 | 10 | 10 Fast |
| 29 | 3 | | 3 | 4 Yom ha-Azma'ut | 5 *Be-Midbar* | 6 | 7 | 8 | 10 Yom Kippur | 10 | 11 | 11 |
| 30 | 4 *Bo* | | 4 | 5 | 6 Shavuot | 7 | 8 | 9 | 11 | 11 *Lekh Lekha* | 12 | 12 |
| 31 | 5 | | 5 | | 7 | | 9 *Devarim* Tishah be-Av | 10 | | 12 | | 13 |

# 1972

**5732/33** תשל״ב / תשל״ג

| | January | February | March | April | May | June | July | August | September | October | November | December |
|---|---|---|---|---|---|---|---|---|---|---|---|---|
| 1 | 14 Tevet *Va-Yehi* | 16 | 15 Shushan Purim | 17 Hol ha-Mo'ed | 17 | 19 | 19 *Pinhas* | 21 | 22 | 23 Simhat Torah *Ve-Zot Ha-Berakhah* | 24 | 25 Hanukkah 1 |
| 2 | 15 | 17 | 16 | 18 | 18 Lag ba-Omer | 20 | 20 | 22 | 23 *Nizzavim Va-Yelekh* | 24 | 25 | 26 *Va-Yeshev* 2 |
| 3 | 16 | 18 | 17 | 19 | 19 | 21 *Be-Ha'alotkha* | 21 | 23 | 24 | 25 | 26 | 27 3 |
| 4 | 17 | 19 | 18 *Ki Tissa* Parah | 20 | 20 | 22 | 22 | 24 | 25 | 26 | 27 *Hayyei Sarah* | 28 4 |
| 5 | 18 | 20 *Yitro* | 19 | 21 Pesah | 21 | 23 | 23 | 25 *Re'eh* | 26 | 27 | 28 | 29 5 |
| 6 | 19 | 21 | 20 | 22 | 22 *Be-Har Be-Hukkotai* | 24 | 24 | 26 | 27 | 28 | 29 | 1 Tevet R.H. 6 |
| 7 | 20 | 22 | 21 | 23 | 23 | 25 | 25 | 27 | 28 | 29 *Bereshit* | 1 Kislev R.H. | 2 7 |
| 8 | 21 *Shemot* | 23 | 22 | 24 *Shemini* | 24 | 26 | 26 *Mattot Masei* | 28 | 29 | 30 R.H. | 2 | 3 8 |
| 9 | 22 | 24 | 23 | 25 | 25 | 27 | 27 | 29 | 1 Tishri Rosh Ha-Shanah | 1 Heshvan R.H. | 3 | 4 *Mi-Kez* |
| 10 | 23 | 25 | 24 | 26 | 26 | 28 *Shelah* | 28 | 30 R.H. | 2 | 2 | 4 | 5 |
| 11 | 24 | 26 | *Va-Yakhel Pekudei* 25 Ha-Hodesh | 27 | 27 | 29 | 29 | 1 Elul R.H. | 3 Fast | 3 | 5 *Toledot* | 6 |
| 12 | 25 | 27 *Mishpatim* Shekalim | 26 | 28 | 28 | 30 R.H. | 1 Av R.H. | 2 *Shofetim* | 4 | 4 | 6 | 7 |
| 13 | 26 | 28 | 27 | 29 | 29 *Be-Midbar* | 1 Tammuz R.H. | 2 | 3 | 5 | 5 | 7 | 8 |
| 14 | 27 | 29 | 28 | 30 R.H. | 1 Sivan R.H. | 2 | 3 | 4 | 6 | 6 *No'ah* | 8 | 9 |
| 15 | 28 *Va-Era* | 30 R.H. | 29 | 1 R.H. Iyyar *Tazri'a Mezora* | 2 | 3 | 4 *Devarim* | 5 | 7 | 7 | 9 | 10 Fast |
| 16 | 29 | 1 Adar R.H. | 1 Nisan R.H. | 2 | 3 | 4 | 5 | 6 | 8 *Ha'azinu* Shabbat Shuvah | 8 | 10 | 11 *Va-Yiggash* |
| 17 | 1 Shevat R.H. | 2 | 2 | 3 | 4 | 5 *Korah* | 6 | 7 | 9 | 9 | 11 | 12 |
| 18 | 2 | 3 | 3 *Va-Yikra* | 4 | 5 | 6 | 7 | 8 | 10 Yom Kippur | 10 | 12 *Va-Yeze* | 13 |
| 19 | 3 | 4 *Terumah* | 4 | 5 Yom ha-Azma'ut | 6 Shavuot | 7 | 8 | 9 *Ki Teze* | 11 | 11 | 13 | 14 |
| 20 | 4 | 5 | 5 | 6 | 7 | 8 | 9 Tishah be-Av | 10 | 12 | 12 | 14 | 15 |
| 21 | 5 | 6 | 6 | 7 | 8 | 9 | 10 | 11 | 13 | 13 *Lekh Lekha* | 15 | 16 |
| 22 | 6 *Bo* | 7 | 7 | 8 *Aharei Mot Kedoshim* | 9 | 10 | 11 *Va-Ethannan* | 12 | 14 | 14 | 16 | 17 |
| 23 | 7 | 8 | 8 | 9 | 10 | 11 | 12 | 13 | 15 Sukkot | 15 | 17 | 18 *Va-Yehi* |
| 24 | 8 | 9 | 9 | 10 | 11 | 12 *Hukkat Balak* | 13 | 14 | 16 | 16 | 18 | 19 |
| 25 | 9 | 10 | 10 *Zav* Shabbat ha-Gadol | 11 | 12 | 13 | 14 | 15 | 17 Hol ha-Mo'ed | 17 | 19 *Va-Yishlah* | 20 |
| 26 | 10 | 11 *Tezavveh* Zakhor | 11 | 12 | 13 | 14 | 15 | 16 *Ki Tavo* | 18 | 18 | 20 | 21 |
| 27 | 11 | 12 | 12 | 13 | 14 *Naso* | 15 | 16 | 17 | 19 | 19 | 21 | 22 |
| 28 | 12 | 13 Ta'anit Esther | 13 | 14 | 15 | 16 | 17 | 18 | 20 | 20 *Va-Yera* | 22 | 23 |
| 29 | 13 *Be-Shallah* | 14 Purim | 14 | 15 *Emor* | 16 | 17 Fast | 18 *Ekev* | 19 | 21 Hoshana Rabba | 21 | 23 | 24 |
| 30 | 14 | | 15 Pesah | 16 | 17 | 18 | 19 | 20 | 22 Shemini Azeret | 22 | 24 | 25 *Shemot* |
| 31 | 15 | | 16 Omer | | 18 | | 20 | 21 | | 23 | | 26 |

# 1973

**5733/34** תשל״ג / תשל״ד

| | January | February | March | April | May | June | July | August | September | October | November | December |
|---|---|---|---|---|---|---|---|---|---|---|---|---|
| 1 | 27 **Tevet** | 29 | 27 | 28 | 29 | 1 **Sivan** R. H. | 1 **Tammuz** R. H. | 3 | **4** *Shofetim* | 5 | 6 | **6** *Va-Yeẓe* |
| 2 | 28 | 30 R. H. | 28 | 29 | 30 R. H. | **2** *Be-Midbar* | 2 | 4 | 5 | 6 | 7 | 7 |
| 3 | 29 | **1 Adar I** R. H. *Mishpatim* | **29** *Va-Yakhel* Shekalim | 1 **Nisan** R. H. | 1 **Iyyar** R. H. | 3 | 3 | 5 | 6 | 7 | **8** *Lekh Lekha* | 8 |
| 4 | 1 **Shevat** R. H. | 2 | 30 R. H. | 2 | 2 | 4 | 4 | **6** *Devarim* | 7 | 8 | 9 | 9 |
| 5 | 2 | 3 | 1 **Adar II** R. H. | 3 | **3** | 5 | 5 | 7 | 8 | 9 | 10 | 10 |
| 6 | **3** *Va-Era* | 4 | 2 | 4 | 4 | 6 Shavuot | 6 | 8 | 9 | **10** Yom Kippur | 11 | 11 |
| 7 | 4 | 5 | 3 | **5** *Tazri'a* | 5 Yom ha-Aẓma'ut | 7 | **7** *Ḥukkat* | 9 Tishah be-Av | 10 | 11 | 12 | 12 |
| 8 | 5 | 6 | 4 | 6 | 6 | 8 | 8 | 10 | **11** *Ki Teẓe* | 12 | 13 | **13** *Va-Yishlaḥ* |
| 9 | 6 | 7 | 5 | 7 | 7 | **9** *Naso* | 9 | 11 | 12 | 13 | 14 | 14 |
| 10 | 7 | **8** *Terumah* | **6** *Pekudei* | 8 | 8 | 10 | 10 | 12 | 13 | 14 | **15** *Va-Yera* | 15 |
| 11 | 8 | 9 | 7 | 9 | 9 | 11 | 11 | **13** *Va-Etḥannan* | 14 | 15 Sukkot | 16 | 16 |
| 12 | 9 | 10 | 8 | 10 | **10** *Emor* | 12 | 12 | 14 | 15 | 16 | 17 | 17 |
| 13 | **10** *Bo* | 11 | 9 | 11 | 11 | 13 | 13 | 15 | 16 | **17** Ḥol ha-Mo'ed | 18 | 18 |
| 14 | 11 | 12 | 10 | **12** *Meẓora* Shabbat ha-Gadol | 12 | 14 | **14** *Balak* | 16 | 17 | 18 | 19 | 19 |
| 15 | 12 | 13 | 11 Ta'anit Esther | 13 | 13 | 15 | 15 | 17 | **18** *Ki Tavo* | 19 | 20 | **20** *Va-Yeshev* |
| 16 | 13 | 14 | 12 | 14 | 14 | **16** *Be-Ha'alotkha* | 16 | 18 | 19 | 20 | 21 | 21 |
| 17 | 14 | **15** *Teẓavveh* | **13** *Va-Yikra* Zakhor | 15 Pesaḥ | 15 | 17 | 17 Fast | 19 | 20 | 21 Hoshana Rabba | **22** *Ḥayyei Sarah* | 22 |
| 18 | 15 | 16 | 14 Purim | 16 Omer | 16 | 18 | 18 | **20** *Ekev* | 21 | 22 Shemini Aẓeret | 23 | 23 |
| 19 | 16 | 17 | 15 Shushan Purim | 17 Ḥol ha-Mo'ed | **17** *Be-Har* | 19 | 19 | 21 | 22 | 23 Simḥat Torah *Ve-Zot Ha-Berakhah* | 24 | 24 |
| 20 | **17** *Be-Shallaḥ* | 18 | 16 | 18 | 18 Lag ba-Omer | 20 | 20 | 22 | 23 | **24** *Bereshit* | 25 | 25 Ḥanukkah 1 |
| 21 | 18 | 19 | 17 | **19** | 19 | 21 | **21** *Pinḥas* | 23 | 24 | 25 | 26 | 26 2 |
| 22 | 19 | 20 | 18 | 20 | 20 | 22 | 22 | 24 | **25** *Niẓẓavim Va-Yelekh* | 26 | 27 | **27** *Mi-Keẓ* 3 |
| 23 | 20 | 21 | 19 | 21 Pesaḥ | 21 | **23** *Shelah* | 23 | 25 | 26 | 27 | 28 | 28 4 |
| 24 | 21 | **22** *Ki Tissa* | **20** *Ẓav* Parah | 22 | 22 | 24 | 24 | 26 | 27 | 28 | **29** *Toledot* | 29 5 |
| 25 | 22 | 23 | 21 | 23 | 23 | 25 | 25 | **27** *Re'eh* | 28 | 29 | 30 R. H. | 30 R. H. 6 |
| 26 | 23 | 24 | 22 | 24 | **24** *Be-Ḥukkotai* | 26 | 26 | 28 | 29 | 30 R. H. | 1 **Kislev** R. H. | 1 **Tevet** R. H. 7 |
| 27 | **24** *Yitro* | 25 | 23 | 25 | 25 | 27 | 27 | 29 | 1 **Tishri** Rosh Ha-Shanah | **1 Ḥeshvan** R. H. *No'aḥ* | 2 | 2 8 |
| 28 | 25 | 26 | 24 | **26** *Aḥarei Mot* | 26 | 28 | **28** *Mattot Masei* | 30 R. H. | 2 | 2 | 3 | 3 |
| 29 | 26 | | 25 | 27 | 27 | 29 | 29 | 1 **Elul** R. H. | **3** *Ha'azinu* Shabbat Shuvah | 3 | 4 | **4** *Va-Yiggash* |
| 30 | 27 | | 26 | 28 | 28 | **30** R. H. *Koraḥ* | 1 **Av** R. H. | 2 | 4 Fast | 4 | 5 | 5 |
| 31 | 28 | | **27** *Shemini* Ha-Ḥodesh | | 29 | | 2 | 3 | | 5 | | 6 |

# 1974

**5734/35** תשל״ד / תשל״ה

| | January | February | March | April | May | June | July | August | September | October | November | December |
|---|---|---|---|---|---|---|---|---|---|---|---|---|
| 1 | 7 **Tevet** | 9 | 7 | 9 | 9 | **11** *Naso* | 11 | 13 | 14 | 15 Sukkot | 16 | 17 |
| 2 | 8 | **10** *Be-Shallaḥ* | **8** *Teẓavveh* Zakhor | 10 | 10 | 12 | 12 | 14 | 15 | 16 | **17** *Va-Yera* | 18 |
| 3 | 9 | 11 | 9 | 11 | 11 | 13 | 13 | **15** *Va-Etḥannan* | 16 | 17 Ḥol ha-Mo'ed | 18 | 19 |
| 4 | 10 Fast | 12 | 10 | 12 | **12** *Aḥarei Mot Kedoshim* | 14 | 14 | 16 | 17 | 18 | 19 | 20 |
| 5 | **11** *Va-Yeḥi* | 13 | 11 | 13 | 13 | 15 | 15 | 17 | 18 | **19** | 20 | 21 |
| 6 | 12 | 14 | 12 | **14** *Ẓav* Shabbat ha-Gadol | 14 | 16 | **16** *Balak* | 18 | 19 | 20 | 21 | 22 |
| 7 | 13 | 15 | 13 Ta'anit Esther | 15 Pesaḥ | 15 | 17 | 17 Fast | 19 | **20** *Ki Tavo* | 21 Hoshana Rabba | 22 | **23** *Va-Yeshev* |
| 8 | 14 | 16 | 14 Purim | 16 Omer | 16 | **18** *Be-Ha'alotkha* | 18 | 20 | 21 | 22 Shemini Aẓeret | 23 | 24 |
| 9 | 15 | **17** *Yitro* | **15** *Ki Tissa* Shushan Purim | 17 Ḥol ha-Mo'ed | 17 | 19 | 19 | 21 | 22 | 23 Simḥat Torah *Ve-Zot Ha-Berakhah* | **24** *Ḥayyei Sarah* | 25 Ḥanukkah 1 |
| 10 | 16 | 18 | 16 | 18 | 18 Lag ba-Omer | 20 | 20 | **22** *Ekev* | 23 | 24 | 25 | 26 2 |
| 11 | 17 | 19 | 17 | 19 | **19** *Emor* | 21 | 21 | 23 | 24 | 25 | 26 | 27 3 |
| 12 | **18** *Shemot* | 20 | 18 | 20 | 20 | 22 | 22 | 24 | 25 | **26** *Bereshit* | 27 | 28 4 |
| 13 | 19 | 21 | 19 | **21** Pesaḥ | 21 | 23 | **23** *Pinḥas* | 25 | 26 | 27 | 28 | 29 5 |
| 14 | 20 | 22 | 20 | 22 | 22 | 24 | 24 | 26 | **27** *Niẓẓavim* | 28 | 29 | **30** R. H. *Mi Keẓ* 6 |
| 15 | 21 | 23 | 21 | 23 | 23 | **25** *Shelaḥ* | 25 | 27 | 28 | 29 | 1 **Kislev** R. H. | 1 **Tevet** R. H. 7 |
| 16 | 22 | **24** *Mishpatim* | **22** *Va-Yakhel* Parah | 24 | 24 | 26 | 26 | 28 | 29 | 30 R. H. | **2** *Toledot* | 2 8 |
| 17 | 23 | 25 | 23 | 25 | 25 | 27 | 27 | **29** *Re'eh* | 1 **Tishri** Rosh Ha-Shanah | 1 **Ḥeshvan** R. H. | 3 | 3 |
| 18 | 24 | 26 | 24 | 26 | **26** *Be-Har Be-Ḥukkotai* | 28 | 28 | 30 R. H. | 2 | 2 | 4 | 4 |
| 19 | **25** *Va-Era* | 27 | 25 | 27 | 27 | 29 | 29 | 1 **Elul** R. H. | 3 Fast | **3** *No'aḥ* | 5 | 5 |
| 20 | 26 | 28 | 26 | **28** *Shemini* | 28 | 30 R. H. | **1** R. H. **Av** *Mattot Masei* | 2 | 4 | 4 | 6 | 6 |
| 21 | 27 | 29 | 27 | 29 | 29 | 1 **Tammuz** R. H. | 2 | 3 | **5** *Va-Yelekh* Shabbat Shuvah | 5 | 7 | **7** *Va-Yiggash* |
| 22 | 28 | 30 R. H. | 28 | 30 R. H. | 1 **Sivan** R. H. | **2** *Koraḥ* | 3 | 4 | 6 | 6 | 8 | 8 |
| 23 | 29 | **1 Adar** R. H. *Terumah* Shekalim | **29** *Pekudei* Ha-Ḥodesh | 1 **Iyyar** R. H. | 2 | 3 | 4 | 5 | 7 | 7 | **9** *Va-Yeẓe* | 9 |
| 24 | 1 **Shevat** R. H. | 2 | 1 **Nisan** R. H. | 2 | 3 | 4 | 5 | **6** *Shofetim* | 8 | 8 | 10 | 10 Fast |
| 25 | 2 | 3 | 2 | 3 Yom ha-Aẓma'ut | **4** *Be-Midbar* | 5 | 6 | 7 | 9 | 9 | 11 | 11 |
| 26 | **3** *Bo* | 4 | 3 | 4 | 5 | 6 | 7 | 8 | 10 Yom Kippur | **10** *Lekh Lekha* | 12 | 12 |
| 27 | 4 | 5 | 4 | **5** *Tazri'a Meẓora* | 6 Shavuot | 7 | **8** *Devarim* | 9 | 11 | 11 | 13 | 13 |
| 28 | 5 | 6 | 5 | 6 | 7 | 8 | 9 Tishah be-Av | 10 | **12** *Ha'azinu* | 12 | 14 | **14** *Va-Yeḥi* |
| 29 | 6 | | 6 | 7 | 8 | **9** *Ḥukkat* | 10 | 11 | 13 | 13 | 15 | 15 |
| 30 | 7 | | **7** *Va-Yikra* | 8 | 9 | 10 | 11 | 12 | 14 | 14 | **16** *Va-Yishlaḥ* | 16 |
| 31 | 8 | | 8 | | 10 | | 12 | **13** *Ki Teẓe* | | 15 | | 17 |

# 1975

**5735/36** תשל״ה / תשל״ו

| | January | February | March | April | May | June | July | August | September | October | November | December |
|---|---|---|---|---|---|---|---|---|---|---|---|---|
| 1 | 18 Tevet | 20 *Yitro* | 18 *Ki Tissa* Parah | 20 Hol ha-Mo'ed | 20 | 22 | 22 | 24 | 25 | 26 | 27 *Hayyei Sarah* | 27 3 |
| 2 | 19 | 21 | 19 | 21 Pesah | 21 | 23 | 23 | 25 *Re'eh* | 26 | 27 | 28 | 28 4 |
| 3 | 20 | 22 | 20 | 22 | 22 *Be-Har Be-Hukkotai* | 24 | 24 | 26 | 27 | 28 | 29 | 29 5 |
| 4 | 21 *Shemot* | 23 | 21 | 23 | 23 | 25 | 25 | 27 | 28 | 29 *Bereshit* | 30 R.H. | 30 R.H. 6 |
| 5 | 22 | 24 | 22 | 24 *Shemini* | 24 | 26 | 26 *Mattot Masei* | 28 | 29 | 30 R.H. | 1 Kislev R.H. | 1 Tevet R.H. 7 |
| 6 | 23 | 25 | 23 | 25 | 25 | 27 | 27 | 29 | 1 Tishri Rosh Ha-Shanah | 1 Heshvan R.H. | 2 | 2 *Mi-Kez* 8 |
| 7 | 24 | 26 | 24 | 26 | 26 | 28 *Shelah* | 28 | 30 R.H. | 2 | 2 | 3 | 3 |
| 8 | 25 | 27 *Mishpatim* Shekalim | 25 *Va-Yakhel Pekudei* Ha-Hodesh | 27 | 27 | 29 | 29 | 1 Elul R.H. | 3 Fast | 3 | 4 *Toledot* | 4 |
| 9 | 26 | 28 | 26 | 28 | 28 | 30 R.H. | 1 Av R.H. | 2 *Shofetim* | 4 | 4 | 5 | 5 |
| 10 | 27 | 29 | 27 | 29 | 29 *Be-Midbar* | 1 Tammuz R.H. | 2 | 3 | 5 | 5 | 6 | 6 |
| 11 | 28 *Va-Era* | 30 R.H. | 28 | 30 R.H. | 1 Sivan R.H. | 2 | 3 | 4 | 6 | 6 *No'ah* | 7 | 7 |
| 12 | 29 | 1 Adar R.H. | 29 | 1 Iyyar R.H. *Tazri'a Mezora* | 2 | 3 | 4 *Devarim* | 5 | 7 | 7 | 8 | 8 |
| 13 | 1 Shevat R.H. | 2 | 1 Nisan R.H. | 2 | 3 | 4 | 5 | 6 | 8 *Ha'azinu* Shabbat Shuvah | 8 | 9 | 9 *Va-Yiggash* |
| 14 | 2 | 3 | 2 | 3 | 4 | 5 *Korah* | 6 | 7 | 9 | 9 | 10 | 10 Fast |
| 15 | 3 | 4 *Terumah* | 3 *Va-Yikra* | 4 | 5 | 6 | 7 | 8 | 10 Yom Kippur | 10 | 11 *Va-Yeze* | 11 |
| 16 | 4 | 5 | 4 | 5 Yom ha-Azma'ut | 6 Shavuot | 7 | 8 | 9 *Ki Teze* | 11 | 11 | 12 | 12 |
| 17 | 5 | 6 | 5 | 6 | 7 | 8 | 9 Tishah be-Av | 10 | 12 | 12 | 13 | 13 |
| 18 | 6 *Bo* | 7 | 6 | 7 | 8 | 9 | 10 | 11 | 13 | 13 *Lekh Lekha* | 14 | 14 |
| 19 | 7 | 8 | 7 | 8 *Aharei Mot Kedoshim* | 9 | 10 | 11 *Va-Ethannan* | 12 | 14 | 14 | 15 | 15 |
| 20 | 8 | 9 | 8 | 9 | 10 | 11 | 12 | 13 | 15 Sukkot | 15 | 16 | 16 *Va-Yehi* |
| 21 | 9 | 10 | 9 | 10 | 11 | 12 *Hukkat Balak* | 13 | 14 | 16 | 16 | 17 | 17 |
| 22 | 10 | 11 *Tezavveh* Zakhor | 10 *Zav* Shabbat ha-Gadol | 11 | 12 | 13 | 14 | 15 | 17 Hol ha-Mo'ed | 17 | 18 *Va-Yishlah* | 18 |
| 23 | 11 | 12 | 11 | 12 | 13 | 14 | 15 | 16 *Ki Tavo* | 18 | 18 | 19 | 19 |
| 24 | 12 | 13 Ta'anit Esther | 12 | 13 | 14 *Naso* | 15 | 16 | 17 | 19 | 19 | 20 | 20 |
| 25 | 13 *Be-Shallah* | 14 Purim | 13 | 14 | 15 | 16 | 17 | 18 | 20 | 20 *Va-Yera* | 21 | 21 |
| 26 | 14 | 15 Shushan Purim | 14 | 15 *Emor* | 16 | 17 Fast | 18 *Ekev* | 19 | 21 Hoshana Rabba | 21 | 22 | 22 |
| 27 | 15 | 16 | 15 Pesah | 16 | 17 | 18 | 19 | 20 | 22 Shemini Azeret | 22 | 23 | 23 *Shemot* |
| 28 | 16 | 17 | 16 Omer | 17 | 18 | 19 *Pinhas* | 20 | 21 | 23 Simhat Torah *Ve-Zot Ha-Berakhah* | 23 | 24 | 24 |
| 29 | 17 | | 17 Hol ha-Mo'ed | 18 Lag ba-Omer | 19 | 20 | 21 | 22 | 24 | 24 | 25 *Va-Yeshev* Hanukkah 1 | 25 |
| 30 | 18 | | 18 | 19 | 20 | 21 | 22 | 23 *Nizzavim Va-Yelekh* | 25 | 25 | 26 2 | 26 |
| 31 | 19 | | 19 | | 21 *Be-Ha'alotkha* | | 23 | 24 | | 26 | | 27 |

# 1976

**5736/37** תשל״ו / תשל״ז

| | January | February | March | April | May | June | July | August | September | October | November | December |
|---|---|---|---|---|---|---|---|---|---|---|---|---|
| 1 | 28 Tevet | 30 R.H. | 29 | 1 Nisan R.H. | 1 Iyyar R.H. *Kedoshim* | 3 | 3 | 5 | 6 | 7 | 8 | 9 |
| 2 | 29 | 1 Adar I R.H. | 30 R.H. | 2 | 2 | 4 | 4 | 6 | 7 | 8 *Ha'azinu* Shabbat Shuvah | 9 | 10 |
| 3 | 1 Shevat R.H. *Va-Era* | 2 | 1 Adar II R.H. | 3 *Tazri'a* | 3 | 5 | 5 *Korah* | 7 | 8 | 9 | 10 | 11 |
| 4 | 2 | 3 | 2 | 4 | 4 | 6 Shavuot | 6 | 8 | 9 *Ki Teze* | 10 Yom Kippur | 11 | 12 *Va-Yeze* |
| 5 | 3 | 4 | 3 | 5 | 5 Yom ha-Azma'ut | 7 | 7 | 9 Tishah be-Av | 10 | 11 | 12 | 13 |
| 6 | 4 | 5 | 4 *Pekudei* | 6 | 6 | 8 | 8 | 10 | 11 | 12 | 13 *Lekh Lekha* | 14 |
| 7 | 5 | 6 *Terumah* | 5 | 7 | 7 | 9 | 9 | 11 *Va-Ethannan* | 12 | 13 | 14 | 15 |
| 8 | 6 | 7 | 6 | 8 | 8 *Emor* | 10 | 10 | 12 | 13 | 14 | 15 | 16 |
| 9 | 7 | 8 | 7 | 9 | 9 | 11 | 11 | 13 | 14 | 15 Sukkot | 16 | 17 |
| 10 | 8 *Bo* | 9 | 8 | 10 *Mezora* Shabbat ha-Gadol | 10 | 12 | 12 *Hukkat Balak* | 14 | 15 | 16 | 17 | 18 |
| 11 | 9 | 10 | 9 | 11 | 11 | 13 | 13 | 15 | 16 *Ki Tavo* | 17 Hol ha-Mo'ed | 18 | 19 *Va-Yishlah* |
| 12 | 10 | 11 | 10 | 12 | 12 | 14 *Naso* | 14 | 16 | 17 | 18 | 19 | 20 |
| 13 | 11 | 12 | 11 *Va-Yikra* Zakhor | 13 | 13 | 15 | 15 | 17 | 18 | 19 | 20 *Va-Yera* | 21 |
| 14 | 12 | 13 *Tezavveh* | 12 | 14 | 14 | 16 | 16 | 18 *Ekev* | 19 | 20 | 21 | 22 |
| 15 | 13 | 14 | 13 Ta'anit Esther | 15 Pesah | 15 *Be-Har* | 17 | 17 Fast | 19 | 20 | 21 Hoshana Rabba | 22 | 23 |
| 16 | 14 | 15 | 14 Purim | 16 Omer | 16 | 18 | 18 | 20 | 21 | 22 Shemini Azeret | 23 | 24 |
| 17 | 15 *Be-Shallah* | 16 | 15 Shushan Purim | 17 Hol ha-Mo'ed | 17 | 19 | 19 *Pinhas* | 21 | 22 | 23 Simhat Torah *Ve-Zot Ha-Berakhah* | 24 | 25 Hanukkah 1 |
| 18 | 16 | 17 | 16 | 18 | 18 Lag ba-Omer | 20 | 20 | 22 | 23 *Nizzavim Va-Yelekh* | 24 | 25 | 26 *Va-Yeshev* 2 |
| 19 | 17 | 18 | 17 | 19 | 19 | 21 *Be-Ha'alotkha* | 21 | 23 | 24 | 25 | 26 | 27 3 |
| 20 | 18 | 19 | 18 *Zav* Parah | 20 | 20 | 22 | 22 | 24 | 25 | 26 | 27 *Hayyei Sarah* | 28 4 |
| 21 | 19 | 20 *Ki Tissa* | 19 | 21 Pesah | 21 | 23 | 23 | 25 *Re'eh* | 26 | 27 | 28 | 29 5 |
| 22 | 20 | 21 | 20 | 22 | 22 *Be-Hukkotai* | 24 | 24 | 26 | 27 | 28 | 29 | 1 Tevet R.H. 6 |
| 23 | 21 | 22 | 21 | 23 | 23 | 25 | 25 | 27 | 28 | 29 *Bereshit* | 1 Kislev R.H. | 2 7 |
| 24 | 22 *Yitro* | 23 | 22 | 24 *Aharei Mot* | 24 | 26 | 26 *Mattot Masei* | 28 | 29 | 30 R.H. | 2 | 3 8 |
| 25 | 23 | 24 | 23 | 25 | 25 | 27 | 27 | 29 | 1 Tishri Rosh Ha-Shanah | 1 Heshvan R.H. | 3 | 4 *Mi-Kez* |
| 26 | 24 | 25 | 24 | 26 | 26 | 28 *Shelah* | 28 | 30 R.H. | 2 | 2 | 4 | 5 |
| 27 | 25 | 26 | 25 *Shemini* Ha-Hodesh | 27 | 27 | 29 | 29 | 1 Elul R.H. | 3 Fast | 3 | 5 *Toledot* | 6 |
| 28 | 26 | 27 *Va-Yakhel* Shekalim | 26 | 28 | 28 | 30 R.H. | 1 Av R.H. | 2 *Shofetim* | 4 | 4 | 6 | 7 |
| 29 | 27 | 28 | 27 | 29 | 29 *Be-Midbar* | 1 Tammuz R.H. | 2 | 3 | 5 | 5 | 7 | 8 |
| 30 | 28 | | 28 | 30 R.H. | 1 Sivan R.H. | 2 | 3 | 4 | 6 | 6 *No'ah* | 8 | 9 |
| 31 | 29 *Mishpatim* | | 29 | | 2 | | 4 *Devarim* | 5 | | 7 | | 10 Fast |

# 1977

**5737/38** תשל״ז / תשל״ח

| | January | February | March | April | May | June | July | August | September | October | November | December |
|---|---|---|---|---|---|---|---|---|---|---|---|---|
| 1 | **11** Tevet *Va-Yiggash* | 13 | 11 | 13 | 13 | 15 | 15 | 17 | 18 | **19** Hol | 20 | 21 |
| 2 | 12 | 14 | 12 | **14** *Zav* Shabbat ha-Gadol | 14 | 16 | **16** *Balak* | 18 | 19 | 20 ha-Mo'ed | 21 | 22 |
| 3 | 13 | 15 | 13 Ta'anit Esther | 15 Pesah | 15 | 17 | 17 Fast | 19 | **20** *Ki Tavo* | 21 Hoshana Rabba | 22 | **23** *Va-Yeshev* |
| 4 | 14 | 16 | 14 Purim | 16 Omer | 16 | **18** *Be-Ha'alotkha* | 18 | 20 | 21 | 22 Shemini Azeret | 23 | 24 |
| 5 | 15 | **17** *Be-Shallah* | **15** *Tezavveh* Shushan Purim | 17 | 17 | 19 | 19 | 21 | 22 | 23 Simhat Torah *Ve-Zot Ha-Berakhah* | **24** *Hayyei Sarah* | 25 Hanukkah 1 |
| 6 | 16 | 18 | 16 | 18 | 18 Lag ba-Omer | 20 | 20 | **22** *Ekev* | 23 | 24 | 25 | 26 2 |
| 7 | 17 | 19 | 17 | 19 Hol ha-Mo'ed | **19** *Emor* | 21 | 21 | 23 | 24 | 25 | 26 | 27 3 |
| 8 | **18** *Va-Yehi* | 20 | 18 | 20 | 20 | 22 | 22 | 24 | 25 | **26** *Bereshit* | 27 | 28 4 |
| 9 | 19 | 21 | 19 | **21** Pesah | 21 | 23 | **23** *Pinhas* | 25 | 26 | 27 | 28 | 29 5 |
| 10 | 20 | 22 | 20 | 22 | 22 | 24 | 24 | 26 | **27** *Nizzavim* | 28 | 29 | **30** R. H. *Mi-Kez* 6 |
| 11 | 21 | 23 | 21 | 23 | 23 | **25** *Shelah* | 25 | 27 | 28 | 29 | **1 Kislev** R. H. | **1 Tevet** R. H. 7 |
| 12 | 22 | **24** *Yitro* | **22** *Ki Tissa* Parah | 24 | 24 | 26 | 26 | 28 | 29 | 30 R. H. | **2** *Toledot* | 2 8 |
| 13 | 23 | 25 | 23 | 25 | 25 | 27 | 27 | **29** *Re'eh* | **1 Tishri** Rosh Ha-Shanah | 1 **Heshvan** R. H. | 3 | 3 |
| 14 | 24 | 26 | 24 | 26 | **26** *Be-Har Be-Hukkotai* | 28 | 28 | 30 R. H. | 2 | 2 | 4 | 4 |
| 15 | **25** *Shemot* | 27 | 25 | 27 | 27 | 29 | 29 | 1 **Elul** R. H. | 3 Fast | **3** *No'ah* | 5 | 5 |
| 16 | 26 | 28 | 26 | **28** *Shemini* | 28 | 30 R. H. | **1 Av** R. H. *Mattot Masei* | 2 | 4 | 4 | 6 | 6 |
| 17 | 27 | 29 | 27 | 29 | 29 | 1 **Tammuz** R. H. | 2 | 3 | **5** *Va-Yelekh* Shabbat Shuvah | 5 | 7 | **7** *Va-Yiggash* |
| 18 | 28 | 30 R. H. | 28 | 30 R. H. | 1 **Sivan** R. H. | **2** *Korah* | 3 | 4 | 6 | 6 | 8 | 8 |
| 19 | 29 | **1 Adar** R. H. *Mishpatim* Shekalim | **29** *Va-Yakhel Pekudei* Ha-Hodesh | 1 **Iyyar** R. H. | 2 | 3 | 4 | 5 | 7 | 7 | **9** *Va-Yeze* | 9 |
| 20 | 1 **Shevat** R. H. | 2 | 1 **Nisan** R. H. | 2 | 3 | 4 | 5 | **6** *Shofetim* | 8 | 8 | 10 | 10 Fast |
| 21 | 2 | 3 | 2 | 3 Yom ha-Azma'ut | **4** *Be-Midbar* | 5 | 6 | 7 | 9 | 9 | 11 | 11 |
| 22 | **3** *Va-Era* | 4 | 3 | 4 | 5 | 6 | 7 | 8 | 10 Yom Kippur | **10** *Lekh Lekha* | 12 | 12 |
| 23 | 4 | 5 | 4 | **5** *Tazri'a Mezora* | 6 Shavuot | 7 | **8** *Devarim* | 9 | 11 | 11 | 13 | 13 |
| 24 | 5 | 6 | 5 | 6 | 7 | 8 | 9 Tishah be-Av | 10 | **12** *Ha'azinu* | 12 | 14 | **14** *Va-Yehi* |
| 25 | 6 | 7 | 6 | 7 | 8 | **9** *Hukkat* | 10 | 11 | 13 | 13 | 15 | 15 |
| 26 | 7 | **8** Terumah Zakhor | **7** *Va-Yikra* | 8 | 9 | 10 | 11 | 12 | 14 | 14 | **16** *Va-Yishlah* | 16 |
| 27 | 8 | 9 | 8 | 9 | 10 | 11 | 12 | **13** *Ki Teze* | 15 Sukkot | 15 | 17 | 17 |
| 28 | 9 | 10 | 9 | 10 | **11** *Naso* | 12 | 13 | 14 | 16 | 16 | 18 | 18 |
| 29 | **10** *Bo* | | 10 | 11 | 12 | 13 | 14 | 15 | 17 Hol | **17** *Va-Yera* | 19 | 19 |
| 30 | 11 | | 11 | **12** *Aharei Mot Kedoshim* | 13 | 14 | **15** *Va-Ethannan* | 16 | 18 ha-Mo'ed | 18 | 20 | 20 |
| 31 | 12 | | 12 | | 14 | | 16 | 17 | | 19 | | **21** *Shemot* |

# 1978

**5738/39** תשל״ח / תשל״ט

| | January | February | March | April | May | June | July | August | September | October | November | December |
|---|---|---|---|---|---|---|---|---|---|---|---|---|
| 1 | 22 **Tevet** | 24 | 22 | **23** *Shemini* Parah | 24 | 25 | **26** *Shelah* | 27 | 29 | 29 | 1 R. H. **Heshvan** | 1 **Kislev** R. H. |
| 2 | 23 | 25 | 23 | 24 | 25 | 26 | 27 | 28 | **30** R. H. *Re'eh* | **1 Tishri** Rosh Ha-Shanah | 2 | **2** *Toledot* |
| 3 | 24 | 26 | 24 | 25 | 26 | **27** *Be-Hukkotai* | 28 | 29 | 1 **Elul** R. H. | 2 | 3 | 3 |
| 4 | 25 | **27** *Mishpatim* | **25** *Va-Yakhel* Shekalim | 26 | 27 | 28 | 29 | 1 **Av** R. H. | 2 | 3 Fast | **4** *No'ah* | 4 |
| 5 | 26 | 28 | 26 | 27 | 28 | 29 | 30 R. H. | **2** *Mattot Masei* | 3 | 4 | 5 | 5 |
| 6 | 27 | 29 | 27 | 28 | **29** *Aharei Mot* | 1 **Sivan** R. H. | 1 R. H. **Tammuz** | 3 | 4 | 5 | 6 | 6 |
| 7 | **28** *Va-Era* | 30 R. H. | 28 | 29 | 30 R. H. | 2 | 2 | 4 | 5 | **6** *Va-Yelekh* Shabbat Shuvah | 7 | 7 |
| 8 | 29 | 1 **Adar I** R. H. | 29 | **1** R. H. **Nisan** *Tazri'a* Ha-Hodesh | 1 **Iyyar** R. H. | 3 | **3** *Korah* | 5 | 6 | 7 | 8 | 8 |
| 9 | 1 **Shevat** R. H. | 2 | 30 R. H. | 2 | 2 | 4 | 4 | 6 | **7** *Shofetim* | 8 | 9 | **9** *Va-Yeze* |
| 10 | 2 | 3 | 1 **Adar II** R. H. | 3 | 3 | **5** *Be-Midbar* | 5 | 7 | 8 | 9 | 10 | 10 |
| 11 | 3 | **4** *Terumah* | **2** *Pekudei* | 4 | 4 Yom ha-Azma'ut | 6 Shavuot | 6 | 8 | 9 | 10 Yom Kippur | **11** *Lekh Lekha* | 11 |
| 12 | 4 | 5 | 3 | 5 | 5 | 7 | 7 | **9** *Devarim* Tishah be-Av | 10 | 11 | 12 | 12 |
| 13 | 5 | 6 | 4 | 6 | **6** *Kedoshim* | 8 | 8 | 10 Fast | 11 | 12 | 13 | 13 |
| 14 | **6** *Bo* | 7 | 5 | 7 | 7 | 9 | 9 | 11 | 12 | **13** *Ha'azinu* | 14 | 14 |
| 15 | 7 | 8 | 6 | **8** *Mezora* Shabbat ha-Gadol | 8 | 10 | **10** *Hukkat* | 12 | 13 | 14 | 15 | 15 |
| 16 | 8 | 9 | 7 | 9 | 9 | 11 | 11 | 13 | **14** *Ki Teze* | 15 Sukkot | 16 | **16** *Va-Yishlah* |
| 17 | 9 | 10 | 8 | 10 | 10 | **12** *Naso* | 12 | 14 | 15 | 16 | 17 | 17 |
| 18 | 10 | **11** *Tezavveh* | **9** *Va-Yikra* Zakhor | 11 | 11 | 13 | 13 | 15 | 16 | 17 Hol ha-Mo'ed | **18** *Va-Yera* | 18 |
| 19 | 11 | 12 | 10 | 12 | 12 | 14 | 14 | **16** *Va-Ethannan* | 17 | 18 | 19 | 19 |
| 20 | 12 | 13 | 11 | 13 | **13** *Emor* | 15 | 15 | 17 | 18 | 19 | 20 | 20 |
| 21 | **13** *Be-Shallah* | 14 | 12 | 14 | 14 | 16 | 16 | 18 | 19 | **20** | 21 | 21 |
| 22 | 14 | 15 | 13 Ta'anit Esther | **15** Pesah | 15 | 17 | **17** *Balak* | 19 | 20 | 21 Hoshana Rabba | 22 | 22 |
| 23 | 15 | 16 | 14 Purim | 16 Omer | 16 | 18 | 18 Fast | 20 | **21** *Ki Tavo* | 22 Shemini Azeret | 23 | **23** *Va-Yeshev* |
| 24 | 16 | 17 | 15 Shushan Purim | 17 | 17 | **19** *Be-Ha'alotkha* | 19 | 21 | 22 | 23 Simhat Torah *Ve-Zot Ha-Berakhah* | 24 | 24 |
| 25 | 17 | **18** *Ki Tissa* | **16** *Zav* | 18 Hol ha-Mo'ed | 18 Lag ba-Omer | 20 | 20 | 22 | 23 | 24 | **25** *Hayyei Sarah* | 25 Hanukkah 1 |
| 26 | 18 | 19 | 17 | 19 | 19 | 21 | 21 | **23** *Ekev* | 24 | 25 | 26 | 26 2 |
| 27 | 19 | 20 | 18 | 20 | **20** *Be-Har* | 22 | 22 | 24 | 25 | 26 | 27 | 27 3 |
| 28 | **20** *Yitro* | 21 | 19 | 21 Pesah | 21 | 23 | 23 | 25 | 26 | **27** *Bereshit* | 28 | 28 4 |
| 29 | 21 | | 20 | 22 | 22 | 24 | **24** *Pinhas* | 26 | 27 | 28 | 29 | 29 5 |
| 30 | 22 | | 21 | 23 | 23 | 25 | 25 | 27 | **28** *Nizzavim* | 29 | 30 R. H. | **30** R. H. *Mi-Kez* 6 |
| 31 | 23 | | 22 | | 24 | | 26 | 28 | | 30 R. H. | | 1 **Tevet** R. H. 7 |

# 1979

**5739/40** תשל״ט / תש״מ

| | January | February | March | April | May | June | July | August | September | October | November | December |
|---|---|---|---|---|---|---|---|---|---|---|---|---|
| 1 | 2 Tevet Ḥanukkah 8 | 4 | 2 | 4 | 4 | 6 Shavuot | 6 | 8 | 9 Ki Teẓe | 10 Yom Kippur | 11 | 11 Va-Yeẓe |
| 2 | 3 | 5 | 3 | 5 | 5 Yom ha-Aẓma'ut | 7 | 7 | 9 Tishah be-Av | 10 | 11 | 12 | 12 |
| 3 | 4 | 6 Bo | 4 Terumah | 6 | 6 | 8 | 8 | 10 | 11 | 12 | 13 Lekh Lekha | 13 |
| 4 | 5 | 7 | 5 | 7 | 7 | 9 | 9 | 11 Va-Ethannan | 12 | 13 | 14 | 14 |
| 5 | 6 | 8 | 6 | 8 | 8 Aḥarei Mot Kedoshim | 10 | 10 | 12 | 13 | 14 | 15 | 15 |
| 6 | 7 Va-Yiggash | 9 | 7 | 9 | 9 | 11 | 11 | 13 | 14 | 15 Sukkot | 16 | 16 |
| 7 | 8 | 10 | 8 | 10 Ẓav Shabbat ha-Gadol | 10 | 12 | 12 Ḥukkat Balak | 14 | 15 | 16 | 17 | 17 |
| 8 | 9 | 11 | 9 | 11 | 11 | 13 | 13 | 15 | 16 Ki Tavo | 17 Ḥol ha-Mo'ed | 18 | 18 Va-Yishlaḥ |
| 9 | 10 Fast | 12 | 10 | 12 | 12 | 14 Naso | 14 | 16 | 17 | 18 | 19 | 19 |
| 10 | 11 | 13 Be-Shallaḥ | 11 Teẓavveh Zakhor | 13 | 13 | 15 | 15 | 17 | 18 | 19 | 20 Va-Yera | 20 |
| 11 | 12 | 14 | 12 | 14 | 14 | 16 | 16 | 18 Ekev | 19 | 20 | 21 | 21 |
| 12 | 13 | 15 | 13 Ta'anit Esther | 15 Pesaḥ | 15 Emor | 17 | 17 Fast | 19 | 20 | 21 Hoshana Rabba | 22 | 22 |
| 13 | 14 Va-Yeḥi | 16 | 14 Purim | 16 Omer | 16 | 18 | 18 | 20 | 21 | 22 Shemini Aẓeret | 23 | 23 |
| 14 | 15 | 17 | 15 Shushan Purim | 17 Ḥol ha-Mo'ed | 17 | 19 | 19 Pinḥas | 21 | 22 | 23 Simḥat Torah Ve-Zot Ha-Berakhah | 24 | 24 |
| 15 | 16 | 18 | 16 | 18 | 18 Lag ba-Omer | 20 | 20 | 22 | 23 Niẓẓavim Va-Yelekh | 24 | 25 | 25 Va-Yeshev Ḥanukkah 1 |
| 16 | 17 | 19 | 17 | 19 | 19 | 21 Be-Ha'alotkha | 21 | 23 | 24 | 25 | 26 | 26 2 |
| 17 | 18 | 20 Yitro | 18 Ki Tissa Parah | 20 | 20 | 22 | 22 | 24 | 25 | 26 | 27 Ḥayyei Sarah | 27 3 |
| 18 | 19 | 21 | 19 | 21 Pesaḥ | 21 | 23 | 23 | 25 Re'eh | 26 | 27 | 28 | 28 4 |
| 19 | 20 | 22 | 20 | 22 | 22 Be-Har Be-Ḥukkotai | 24 | 24 | 26 | 27 | 28 | 29 | 29 5 |
| 20 | 21 Shemot | 23 | 21 | 23 | 23 | 25 | 25 | 27 | 28 | 29 Bereshit | 30 R. H. | 30 R. H. 6 |
| 21 | 22 | 24 | 22 | 24 Shemini | 24 | 26 | 26 Mattot Masei | 28 | 29 | 30 R. H. | 1 Kislev R. H. | 1 Tevet R. H. 7 |
| 22 | 23 | 25 | 23 | 25 | 25 | 27 | 27 | 29 | 1 Tishri Rosh Ha-Shanah | 1 Ḥeshvan R. H. | 2 | 2 Mi-Keẓ 8 |
| 23 | 24 | 26 | 24 | 26 | 26 | 28 Shelaḥ | 28 | 30 R. H. | 2 | 2 | 3 | 3 |
| 24 | 25 | 27 Mishpatim Shekalim | 25 Va-Yakhel Pekudei Ha-Ḥodesh | 27 | 27 | 29 | 29 | 1 Elul R. H. | 3 Fast | 3 | 4 Toledot | 4 |
| 25 | 26 | 28 | 26 | 28 | 28 | 30 R. H. | 1 Av R. H. | 2 Shofetim | 4 | 4 | 5 | 5 |
| 26 | 27 | 29 | 27 | 29 | 29 Be-Midbar | 1 Tammuz R. H. | 2 | 3 | 5 | 5 | 6 | 6 |
| 27 | 28 Va-Era | 30 R. H. | 28 | 30 R. H. | 1 Sivan R. H. | 2 | 3 | 4 | 6 | 6 No'aḥ | 7 | 7 |
| 28 | 29 | 1 Adar R. H. | 29 | 1 Iyyar R. H. Tazri'a Meẓora | 2 | 3 | 4 Devarim | 5 | 7 | 7 | 8 | 8 |
| 29 | 1 Shevat R. H. | | 1 Nisan R. H. | 2 | 3 | 4 | 5 | 6 | 8 Ha'azinu Shabbat Shuvah | 8 | 9 | 9 Va-Yiggash |
| 30 | 2 | | 2 | 3 | 4 | 5 Koraḥ | 6 | 7 | 9 | 9 | 10 | 10 Fast |
| 31 | 3 | | 3 Va-Yikra | | 5 | | 7 | 8 | | 10 | | 11 |

# 1980

**5740/41** תש״מ / תשמ״א

| | January | February | March | April | May | June | July | August | September | October | November | December |
|---|---|---|---|---|---|---|---|---|---|---|---|---|
| 1 | 12 Tevet | 14 | 13 Teẓavveh Zakhor | 15 Pesaḥ | 15 | 17 | 17 Fast | 19 | 20 | 21 Hoshana Rabba | 22 Ḥayyei Sarah | 23 |
| 2 | 13 | 15 Be-Shallaḥ | 14 Purim | 16 Omer | 16 | 18 | 18 | 20 Ekev | 21 | 22 Shemini Aẓeret | 23 | 24 |
| 3 | 14 | 16 | 15 Shushan Purim | 17 Ḥol ha-Mo'ed | 17 Emor | 19 | 19 | 21 | 22 | 23 Simḥat Torah Ve-Zot Ha-Berakhah | 24 | 25 Ḥanukkah 1 |
| 4 | 15 | 17 | 16 | 18 | 18 Lag ba-Omer | 20 | 20 | 22 | 23 | 24 Bereshit | 25 | 26 2 |
| 5 | 16 Va-Yeḥi | 18 | 17 | 19 | 19 | 21 | 21 Pinḥas | 23 | 24 | 25 | 26 | 27 3 |
| 6 | 17 | 19 | 18 | 20 | 20 | 22 | 22 | 24 | 25 Niẓẓavim Va-Yelekh | 26 | 27 | 28 Mi-Keẓ 4 |
| 7 | 18 | 20 | 19 | 21 Pesaḥ | 21 | 23 Shelaḥ | 23 | 25 | 26 | 27 | 28 | 29 5 |
| 8 | 19 | 21 | 20 Ki Tissa Parah | 22 | 22 | 24 | 24 | 26 | 27 | 28 | 29 Toledot | 1 Tevet R. H. 6 |
| 9 | 20 | 22 Yitro | 21 | 23 | 23 | 25 | 25 | 27 Re'eh | 28 | 29 | 1 Kislev R. H. | 2 7 |
| 10 | 21 | 23 | 22 | 24 | 24 Be-Har Be-Ḥukkotai | 26 | 26 | 28 | 29 | 30 R. H. | 2 | 3 8 |
| 11 | 22 | 24 | 23 | 25 | 25 | 27 | 27 | 29 | 1 Tishri Rosh Ha-Shanah | 1 Ḥeshvan R. H. No'aḥ | 3 | 4 |
| 12 | 23 Shemot | 25 | 24 | 26 Shemini | 26 | 28 | 28 Mattot Masei | 30 R. H. | 2 | 2 | 4 | 5 |
| 13 | 24 | 26 | 25 | 27 | 27 | 29 | 29 | 1 Elul R. H. | 3 Ha'azinu Shabbat Shuvah | 3 | 5 | 6 Va-Yiggash |
| 14 | 25 | 27 | 26 | 28 | 28 | 30 R. H. Koraḥ | 1 Av R. H. | 2 | 4 Fast | 4 | 6 | 7 |
| 15 | 26 | 28 | 27 Va-Yakhel Pekudei Ha-Ḥodesh | 29 | 29 | 1 Tammuz R. H. | 2 | 3 | 5 | 5 | 7 Va-Yeẓe | 8 |
| 16 | 27 | 29 Mishpatim Shekalim | 28 | 30 R. H. | 1 Sivan R. H. | 2 | 3 | 4 Shofetim | 6 | 6 | 8 | 9 |
| 17 | 28 | 30 R. H. | 29 | 1 Iyyar R. H. | 2 Be-Midbar | 3 | 4 | 5 | 7 | 7 | 9 | 10 Fast |
| 18 | 29 | 1 Adar R. H. | 1 Nisan R. H. | 2 | 3 | 4 | 5 | 6 | 8 | 8 Lekh Lekha | 10 | 11 |
| 19 | 1 Shevat R. H. Va-Era | 2 | 2 | 3 Tazri'a Meẓora | 4 | 5 | 6 Devarim | 7 | 9 | 9 | 11 | 12 |
| 20 | 2 | 3 | 3 | 4 | 5 | 6 | 7 | 8 | 10 Yom Kippur | 10 | 12 | 13 Va-Yeḥi |
| 21 | 3 | 4 | 4 | 5 Yom ha-Aẓma'ut | 6 Shavuot | 7 Ḥukkat | 8 | 9 | 11 | 11 | 13 | 14 |
| 22 | 4 | 5 | 5 Va-Yikra | 6 | 7 | 8 | 9 Tishah be-Av | 10 | 12 | 12 | 14 Va-Yishlaḥ | 15 |
| 23 | 5 | 6 Terumah | 6 | 7 | 8 | 9 | 10 | 11 Ki Teẓe | 13 | 13 | 15 | 16 |
| 24 | 6 | 7 | 7 | 8 | 9 Naso | 10 | 11 | 12 | 14 | 14 | 16 | 17 |
| 25 | 7 | 8 | 8 | 9 | 10 | 11 | 12 | 13 | 15 Sukkot | 15 Va-Yera | 17 | 18 |
| 26 | 8 Bo | 9 | 9 | 10 Aḥarei Mot Kedoshim | 11 | 12 | 13 Va-Ethannan | 14 | 16 | 16 | 18 | 19 |
| 27 | 9 | 10 | 10 | 11 | 12 | 13 | 14 | 15 | 17 Ḥol ha-Mo'ed | 17 | 19 | 20 Shemot |
| 28 | 10 | 11 Ta'anit Esther | 11 | 12 | 13 | 14 Balak | 15 | 16 | 18 | 18 | 20 | 21 |
| 29 | 11 | 12 | 12 Ẓav Shabbat ha-Gadol | 13 | 14 | 15 | 16 | 17 | 19 | 19 | 21 Va-Yeshev | 22 |
| 30 | 12 | | 13 | 14 | 15 | 16 | 17 | 18 Ki Tavo | 20 | 20 | 22 | 23 |
| 31 | 13 | | 14 | | 16 Be-Ha'alotkha | | 18 | 19 | | 21 | | 24 |

# 1981

**5741/42** תשמ״א / תשמ״ב

| | January | February | March | April | May | June | July | August | September | October | November | December |
|---|---|---|---|---|---|---|---|---|---|---|---|---|
| 1 | 25 Tevet | 27 | 25 | 26 | 27 | 28 | 29 | 1 Av R. H. *Masei* | 2 | 3 Fast | 4 | 5 |
| 2 | 26 | 28 | 26 | 27 | 28 *Kedoshim* | 29 | 30 R. H. | 2 | 3 | 4 | 5 | 6 |
| 3 | 27 *Va-Era* | 29 | 27 | 28 | 29 | 1 Sivan R. H. | 1 Tammuz R. H. | 3 | 4 | 5 *Va-Yelekh* Shabbat Shuvah | 6 | 7 |
| 4 | 28 | 30 R. H. | 28 | 29 *Tazri'a* Ha-Hodesh | 30 R. H. | 2 | 2 *Hukkat* | 4 | 5 | 6 | 7 | 8 |
| 5 | 29 | 1 Adar R. H. | 29 | 1 Nisan R. H. | 1 Iyyar R. H. | 3 | 3 | 5 | 6 *Shofetim* | 7 | 8 | 9 *Va-Yeze* |
| 6 | 1 Shevat R. H. | 2 | 30 R. H. | 2 | 2 | 4 *Naso* | 4 | 6 | 7 | 8 | 9 | 10 |
| 7 | 2 | 3 *Terumah* | 1 Adar II R. H. Shekalim *Pekudei* | 3 | 3 Yom ha-Azma'ut | 5 | 5 | 7 | 8 | 9 | 10 *Lekh Lekha* | 11 |
| 8 | 3 | 4 | 2 | 4 | 4 | 6 Shavuot | 6 | 8 *Devarim* | 9 | 10 Yom Kippur | 11 | 12 |
| 9 | 4 | 5 | 3 | 5 | 5 *Emor* | 7 | 7 | 9 Tishah be-Av | 10 | 11 | 12 | 13 |
| 10 | 5 *Bo* | 6 | 4 | 6 | 6 | 8 | 8 | 10 | 11 | 12 *Ha'azinu* | 13 | 14 |
| 11 | 6 | 7 | 5 | 7 *Mezora* | 7 | 9 | 9 *Balak* | 11 | 12 | 13 | 14 | 15 |
| 12 | 7 | 8 | 6 | 8 | 8 | 10 | 10 | 12 | 13 *Ki Teze* | 14 | 15 | 16 *Va-Yishlah* |
| 13 | 8 | 9 | 7 | 9 | 9 | 11 *Be-Ha'alotkha* | 11 | 13 | 14 | 15 Sukkot | 16 | 17 |
| 14 | 9 | 10 *Tezavveh* | 8 *Va-Yikra* Zakhor | 10 | 10 | 12 | 12 | 14 | 15 | 16 | 17 *Va-Yera* | 18 |
| 15 | 10 | 11 | 9 | 11 | 11 | 13 | 13 | 15 *Va-Ethannan* | 16 | 17 Hol ha-Mo'ed | 18 | 19 |
| 16 | 11 | 12 | 10 | 12 | 12 *Be-Har* | 14 | 14 | 16 | 17 | 18 | 19 | 20 |
| 17 | 12 *Be-Shallah* | 13 | 11 | 13 | 13 | 15 | 15 | 17 | 18 | 19 | 20 | 21 |
| 18 | 13 | 14 | 12 | 14 *Aharei Mot* Shabbat ha-Gadol | 14 | 16 | 16 *Pinhas* | 18 | 19 | 20 | 21 | 22 |
| 19 | 14 | 15 | 13 Ta'anit Esther | 15 Pesah | 15 | 17 | 17 Fast | 19 | 20 *Ki Tavo* | 21 Hoshana Rabba | 22 | 23 *Va-Yeshev* |
| 20 | 15 | 16 | 14 Purim | 16 Omer | 16 | 18 *Shelah* | 18 | 20 | 21 | 22 Shemini Azeret | 23 | 24 |
| 21 | 16 | 17 *Ki Tissa* | 15 *Zav* Shushan Purim | 17 Hol ha-Mo'ed | 17 | 19 | 19 | 21 | 22 | 23 Simhat Torah *Ve-Zot Ha-Berakhah* | 24 *Hayyei Sarah* | 25 Hanukkah 1 |
| 22 | 17 | 18 | 16 | 18 | 18 Lag ba-Omer | 20 | 20 | 22 *Ekev* | 23 | 24 | 25 | 26 2 |
| 23 | 18 | 19 | 17 | 19 | 19 *Be-Hukkotai* | 21 | 21 | 23 | 24 | 25 | 26 | 27 3 |
| 24 | 19 *Yitro* | 20 | 18 | 20 | 20 | 22 | 22 | 24 | 25 | 26 *Bereshit* | 27 | 28 4 |
| 25 | 20 | 21 | 19 | 21 Pesah | 21 | 23 | 23 *Mattot* | 25 | 26 | 27 | 28 | 29 5 |
| 26 | 21 | 22 | 20 | 22 | 22 | 24 | 24 | 26 | 27 *Nizzavim* | 28 | 29 | 30 R. H. *Mi-Kez* 6 |
| 27 | 22 | 23 | 21 | 23 | 23 | 25 *Korah* | 25 | 27 | 28 | 29 | 1 Kislev R. H. | 1 Tevet R. H. 7 |
| 28 | 23 | 24 *Va-Yakhel* | 22 *Shemini* Parah | 24 | 24 | 26 | 26 | 28 | 29 | 30 R. H. | 2 *Toledot* | 2 8 |
| 29 | 24 | | 23 | 25 | 25 | 27 | 27 | 29 *Re'eh* | 1 Tishri Rosh Ha-Shanah | 1 Heshvan R. H. | 3 | 3 |
| 30 | 25 | | 24 | 26 | 26 *Be-Midbar* | 28 | 28 | 30 R. H. | 2 | 2 | 4 | 4 |
| 31 | 26 *Mishpatim* | | 25 | | 27 | | 29 | 1 Elul R. H. | | 3 *No'ah* | | 5 |

# 1982

**5742/43** תשמ״ב / תשמ״ג

| | January | February | March | April | May | June | July | August | September | October | November | December |
|---|---|---|---|---|---|---|---|---|---|---|---|---|
| 1 | 6 Tevet | 8 | 6 | 8 | 8 *Aharei Mot Kedoshim* | 10 | 10 | 12 | 13 | 14 | 15 | 15 |
| 2 | 7 *Va-Yiggash* | 9 | 7 | 9 | 9 | 11 | 11 | 13 | 14 | 15 Sukkot | 16 | 16 |
| 3 | 8 | 10 | 8 | 10 *Zav* Shabbat ha-Gadol | 10 | 12 | 12 *Hukkat Balak* | 14 | 15 | 16 | 17 | 17 |
| 4 | 9 | 11 | 9 | 11 | 11 | 13 | 13 | 15 | 16 *Ki Tavo* | 17 Hol ha-Mo'ed | 18 | 18 *Va-Yishlah* |
| 5 | 10 Fast | 12 | 10 | 12 | 12 | 14 *Naso* | 14 | 16 | 17 | 18 | 19 | 19 |
| 6 | 11 | 13 *Be-Shallah* | 11 *Tezavveh* Zakhor | 13 | 13 | 15 | 15 | 17 | 18 | 19 | 20 *Va-Yera* | 20 |
| 7 | 12 | 14 | 12 | 14 | 14 | 16 | 16 | 18 *Ekev* | 19 | 20 | 21 | 21 |
| 8 | 13 | 15 | 13 Ta'anit Esther | 15 Pesah | 15 *Emor* | 17 | 17 Fast | 19 | 20 | 21 Hoshana Rabba | 22 | 22 |
| 9 | 14 *Va-Yehi* | 16 | 14 Purim | 16 Omer | 16 | 18 | 18 | 20 | 21 | 22 Shemini Azeret | 23 | 23 |
| 10 | 15 | 17 | 15 Shushan Purim | 17 Hol ha-Mo'ed | 17 | 19 | 19 *Pinhas* | 21 | 22 | 23 Simhat Torah *Ve-Zot Ha-Berakhah* | 24 | 24 |
| 11 | 16 | 18 | 16 | 18 | 18 Lag ba-Omer | 20 | 20 | 22 | 23 *Nizzavim Va-Yelekh* | 24 | 25 | 25 Hanukkah 1 *Va-Yeshev* |
| 12 | 17 | 19 | 17 | 19 | 19 | 21 *Be-Ha'alotkha* | 21 | 23 | 24 | 25 | 26 | 26 2 |
| 13 | 18 | 20 *Yitro* | 18 *Ki Tissa* Parah | 20 | 20 | 22 | 22 | 24 | 25 | 26 | 27 *Hayyei Sarah* | 27 3 |
| 14 | 19 | 21 | 19 | 21 Pesah | 21 | 23 | 23 | 25 *Re'eh* | 26 | 27 | 28 | 28 4 |
| 15 | 20 | 22 | 20 | 22 | 22 *Be-Har Be-Hukkotai* | 24 | 24 | 26 | 27 | 28 | 29 | 29 5 |
| 16 | 21 *Shemot* | 23 | 21 | 23 | 23 | 25 | 25 | 27 | 28 | 29 *Bereshit* | 30 R. H. | 30 R. H. 6 |
| 17 | 22 | 24 | 22 | 24 *Shemini* | 24 | 26 | 26 *Mattot Masei* | 28 | 29 | 30 R. H. | 1 Kislev R. H. | 1 Tevet R. H. 7 |
| 18 | 23 | 25 | 23 | 25 | 25 | 27 | 27 | 29 | 1 Tishri Rosh Ha-Shanah | 1 Heshvan R. H. | 2 | 2 *Mi-Kez* 8 |
| 19 | 24 | 26 | 24 | 26 | 26 | 28 *Shelah* | 28 | 30 R. H. | 2 | 2 | 3 | 3 |
| 20 | 25 | 27 *Mishpatim* Shekalim | 25 *Va-Yakhel Pekudei* Ha-Hodesh | 27 | 27 | 29 | 29 | 1 Elul R. H. | 3 Fast | 3 | 4 *Toledot* | 4 |
| 21 | 26 | 28 | 26 | 28 | 28 | 30 R. H. | 1 Av R. H. | 2 *Shofetim* | 4 | 4 | 5 | 5 |
| 22 | 27 | 29 | 27 | 29 | 29 *Be-Midbar* | 1 Tammuz R. H. | 2 | 3 | 5 | 5 | 6 | 6 |
| 23 | 28 *Va-Era* | 30 R. H. | 28 | 30 R. H. | 1 Sivan R. H. | 2 | 3 | 4 | 6 | 6 *No'ah* | 7 | 7 |
| 24 | 29 | 1 Adar R. H. | 29 | 1 Iyyar R. H. *Tazri'a Mezora* | 2 | 3 | 4 *Devarim* | 5 | 7 | 7 | 8 | 8 |
| 25 | 1 Shevat R. H. | 2 | 1 Nisan R. H. | 2 | 3 | 4 | 5 | 6 | 8 *Ha'azinu* Shabbat Shuvah | 8 | 9 | 9 *Va-Yiggash* |
| 26 | 2 | 3 | 2 | 3 | 4 | 5 *Korah* | 6 | 7 | 9 | 9 | 10 | 10 Fast |
| 27 | 3 | 4 *Terumah* | 3 *Va-Yikra* | 4 | 5 | 6 | 7 | 8 | 10 Yom Kippur | 10 | 11 *Va-Yeze* | 11 |
| 28 | 4 | 5 | 4 | 5 Yom ha-Azma'ut | 6 Shavuot | 7 | 8 | 9 *Ki Teze* | 11 | 11 | 12 | 12 |
| 29 | 5 | | 5 | 6 | 7 | 8 | 9 Tishah be-Av | 10 | 12 | 12 | 13 | 13 |
| 30 | 6 *Bo* | | 6 | 7 | 8 | 9 | 10 | 11 | 13 | 13 *Lekh Lekha* | 14 | 14 |
| 31 | 7 | | 7 | | 9 | | 11 *Va-Ethannan* | 12 | | 14 | | 15 |

# 1983

**5743/44** תשמ״ג / תשמ״ד

| | January | February | March | April | May | June | July | August | September | October | November | December |
|---|---|---|---|---|---|---|---|---|---|---|---|---|
| 1 | 16 **Tevet** *Va-Yeḥi* | 18 | 16 | 18 | 18 Lag ba-Omer | 20 | 20 | 22 | 23 | **24** *Bereshit* | 25 | 25 Ḥanukkah 1 |
| 2 | 17 | 19 | 17 | **19** Ḥol ha-Mo'ed | 19 | 21 | **21** *Pinḥas* | 23 | 24 | 25 | 26 | 26 2 |
| 3 | 18 | 20 | 18 | 20 | 20 | 22 | 22 | 24 | **25** *Niẓẓavim Va-Yelekh* | 26 | 27 | **27** *Mi-Keẓ* 3 |
| 4 | 19 | 21 | 19 | 21 Pesaḥ | 21 | **23** *Shelaḥ* | 23 | 25 | 26 | 27 | 28 | 28 4 |
| 5 | 20 | **22** *Yitro* | **20** *Ki Tissa* Parah | 22 | 22 | 24 | 24 | 26 | 27 | 28 | **29** *Toledot* | 29 5 |
| 6 | 21 | 23 | 21 | 23 | 23 | 25 | 25 | **27** *Re'eh* | 28 | 29 | 30 R. Ḥ. | 30 R. Ḥ. 6 |
| 7 | 22 | 24 | 22 | 24 | **24** *Be-Har Be-Ḥukkotai* | 26 | 26 | 28 | 29 | 30 R. Ḥ. | 1 **Kislev** R. Ḥ. | 1 **Tevet** R. Ḥ. 7 |
| 8 | **23** *Shemot* | 25 | 23 | 25 | 25 | 27 | 27 | 29 | 1 **Tishri** Rosh Ha-Shanah | 1 **Heshvan** R. Ḥ. *No'aḥ* | 2 | 2 8 |
| 9 | 24 | 26 | 24 | **26** *Shemini* | 26 | 28 | **28** *Mattot Masei* | 30 R. Ḥ. | 2 | 2 | 3 | 3 |
| 10 | 25 | 27 | 25 | 27 | 27 | 29 | 29 | 1 **Elul** R. Ḥ. | **3** *Ha'azinu* Shabbat Shuvah | 3 | 4 | **4** *Va-Yiggash* |
| 11 | 26 | 28 | 26 | 28 | 28 | **30** R. Ḥ. *Koraḥ* | 1 **Av** R. Ḥ. | 2 | 4 Fast | 4 | 5 | 5 |
| 12 | 27 | **29** *Mishpatim* Shekalim | **27** *Va-Yakhel Pekudei* Ha-Ḥodesh | 29 | 29 | 1 **Tammuz** R. Ḥ. | 2 | 3 | 5 | 5 | **6** *Va-Yeẓe* | 6 |
| 13 | 28 | 30 R. Ḥ. | 28 | 30 R. Ḥ. | 1 **Sivan** R. Ḥ. | 2 | 3 | **4** *Shofetim* | 6 | 6 | 7 | 7 |
| 14 | 29 | 1 **Adar** R. Ḥ. | 29 | 1 **Iyyar** R. Ḥ. | **2** *Be-Midbar* | 3 | 4 | 5 | 7 | 7 | 8 | 8 |
| 15 | 1 **Shevat** R. Ḥ. *Va-Era* | 2 | 1 **Nisan** R. Ḥ. | 2 | 3 | 4 | 5 | 6 | 8 | **8** *Lekh Lekha* | 9 | 9 |
| 16 | 2 | 3 | 2 | **3** *Tazri'a Meẓora* | 4 | 5 | **6** *Devarim* | 7 | 9 | 9 | 10 | 10 Fast |
| 17 | 3 | 4 | 3 | 4 | 5 | 6 | 7 | 8 | **10** Yom Kippur | 10 | 11 | **11** *Va-Yeḥi* |
| 18 | 4 | 5 | 4 | 5 Yom ha-Aẓma'ut | 6 Shavuot | **7** *Ḥukkat* | 8 | 9 | 11 | 11 | 12 | 12 |
| 19 | 5 | **6** *Terumah* | **5** *Va-Yikra* | 6 | 7 | 8 | 9 Tishah be-Av | 10 | 12 | 12 | **13** *Va-Yishlaḥ* | 13 |
| 20 | 6 | 7 | 6 | 7 | 8 | 9 | 10 | **11** *Ki Teẓe* | 13 | 13 | 14 | 14 |
| 21 | 7 | 8 | 7 | 8 | **9** *Naso* | 10 | 11 | 12 | 14 | 14 | 15 | 15 |
| 22 | **8** *Bo* | 9 | 8 | 9 | 10 | 11 | 12 | 13 | 15 Sukkot | **15** *Va-Yera* | 16 | 16 |
| 23 | 9 | 10 | 9 | **10** *Aḥarei Mot Kedoshim* | 11 | 12 | **13** *Va-Etḥannan* | 14 | 16 | 16 | 17 | 17 |
| 24 | 10 | 11 Ta'anit Esther | 10 | 11 | 12 | 13 | 14 | 15 | **17** | 17 | 18 | **18** *Shemot* |
| 25 | 11 | 12 | 11 | 12 | 13 | **14** *Balak* | 15 | 16 | 18 Ḥol ha-Mo'ed | 18 | 19 | 19 |
| 26 | 12 | **13** *Teẓavveh* Zakhor | **12** *Ẓav* Shabbat ha-Gadol | 13 | 14 | 15 | 16 | 17 | 19 | 19 | **20** *Va-Yeshev* | 20 |
| 27 | 13 | 14 Purim | 13 | 14 | 15 | 16 | 17 | **18** *Ki Tavo* | 20 | 20 | 21 | 21 |
| 28 | 14 | 15 Shushan Purim | 14 | 15 | **16** *Be-Ha'alotkha* | 17 Fast | 18 | 19 | 21 Hoshana Rabba | 21 | 22 | 22 |
| 29 | **15** *Be-Shallaḥ* | | 15 Pesaḥ | 16 | 17 | 18 | 19 | 20 | 22 Shemini Aẓeret | **22** *Ḥayyei Sarah* | 23 | 23 |
| 30 | 16 | | 16 Omer | **17** *Emor* | 18 | 19 | **20** *Ekev* | 21 | 23 Simḥat Torah *Ve-Zot Ha-Berakhah* | 23 | 24 | 24 |
| 31 | 17 | | 17 Ḥol ha-Mo'ed | | 19 | | 21 | 22 | | 24 | | **25** *Va-Era* |

# 1984

**5744/45** תשמ״ד / תשמ״ה

| | January | February | March | April | May | June | July | August | September | October | November | December |
|---|---|---|---|---|---|---|---|---|---|---|---|---|
| 1 | 26 **Tevet** | 28 | 27 | 28 | 29 | 1 **Sivan** R. Ḥ. | 1 **Tammuz** R. Ḥ. | 3 | **4** *Shofetim* | 5 | 6 | **7** *Va-Yeẓe* |
| 2 | 27 | 29 | 28 | 29 | 30 R. Ḥ. | **2** *Naso* | 2 | 4 | 5 | 6 | 7 | 8 |
| 3 | 28 | 30 R. Ḥ. | **29** *Pekudei* Shekalim | 1 **Nisan** R. Ḥ. | 1 **Iyyar** R. Ḥ. | 3 | 3 | 5 | 6 | 7 | **8** *Lekh Lekha* | 9 |
| 4 | 29 | 1 **Adar I** R. Ḥ. *Terumah* | 30 R. Ḥ. | 2 | 2 | 4 | 4 | **6** *Devarim* | 7 | 8 | 9 | 10 |
| 5 | 1 **Shevat** R. Ḥ. | 2 | 1 **Adar II** R. Ḥ. | 3 | **3** *Emor* | 5 | 5 | 7 | 8 | 9 | 10 | 11 |
| 6 | 2 | 3 | 2 | 4 | 4 | 6 Shavuot | 6 | 8 | 9 | **10** Yom Kippur | 11 | 12 |
| 7 | **3** *Bo* | 4 | 3 | **5** *Meẓora* | 5 Yom ha-Aẓma'ut | 7 | **7** *Balak* | 9 Tishah be-Av | 10 | 11 | 12 | 13 |
| 8 | 4 | 5 | 4 | 6 | 6 | 8 | 8 | 10 | **11** *Ki Teẓe* | 12 | 13 | **14** *Va-Yishlaḥ* |
| 9 | 5 | 6 | 5 | 7 | 7 | **9** *Be-Ha'alotkha* | 9 | 11 | 12 | 13 | 14 | 15 |
| 10 | 6 | 7 | **6** *Va-Yikra* | 8 | 8 | 10 | 10 | 12 | 13 | 14 | **15** *Va-Yera* | 16 |
| 11 | 7 | **8** *Teẓavveh* | 7 | 9 | 9 | 11 | 11 | **13** *Va-Etḥannan* | 14 | 15 Sukkot | 16 | 17 |
| 12 | 8 | 9 | 8 | 10 | **10** *Be-Har* | 12 | 12 | 14 | 15 | 16 | 17 | 18 |
| 13 | 9 | 10 | 9 | 11 | 11 | 13 | 13 | 15 | 16 | **17** | 18 | 19 |
| 14 | **10** *Be-Shallaḥ* | 11 | 10 | **12** *Aḥarei Mot* Shabbat ha-Gadol | 12 | 14 | **14** *Pinḥas* | 16 | 17 | 18 Ḥol ha-Mo'ed | 19 | 20 |
| 15 | 11 | 12 | 11 Ta'anit Esther | 13 | 13 | 15 | 15 | 17 | **18** *Ki Tavo* | 19 | 20 | **21** *Va-Yeshev* |
| 16 | 12 | 13 | 12 | 14 | 14 | **16** *Shelaḥ* | 16 | 18 | 19 | 20 | 21 | 22 |
| 17 | 13 | 14 | **13** *Ẓav* Zakhor | 15 Pesaḥ | 15 | 17 | 17 Fast | 19 | 20 | 21 Hoshana Rabba | **22** *Ḥayyei Sarah* | 23 |
| 18 | 14 | **15** *Ki Tissa* | 14 Purim | 16 Omer | 16 | 18 | 18 | **20** *Ekev* | 21 | 22 Shemini Aẓeret | 23 | 24 |
| 19 | 15 | 16 | 15 Shushan Purim | 17 | **17** *Be-Ḥukkotai* | 19 | 19 | 21 | 22 | 23 Simḥat Torah *Ve-Zot Ha-Berakhah* | 24 | 25 Ḥanukkah 1 |
| 20 | 16 | 17 | 16 | 18 Ḥol ha-Mo'ed | 18 Lag ba-Omer | 20 | 20 | 22 | 23 | **24** *Bereshit* | 25 | 26 2 |
| 21 | **17** *Yitro* | 18 | 17 | **19** | 19 | 21 | **21** *Mattot* | 23 | 24 | 25 | 26 | 27 3 |
| 22 | 18 | 19 | 18 | 20 | 20 | 22 | 22 | 24 | **25** *Niẓẓavim Va-Yelekh* | 26 | 27 | **28** *Mi-Keẓ* 4 |
| 23 | 19 | 20 | 19 | 21 Pesaḥ | 21 | **23** *Koraḥ* | 23 | 25 | 26 | 27 | 28 | 29 5 |
| 24 | 20 | 21 | **20** *Shemini* Parah | 22 | 22 | 24 | 24 | 26 | 27 | 28 | **29** *Toledot* | 30 R. Ḥ. 6 |
| 25 | 21 | **22** *Va-Yakhel* | 21 | 23 | 23 | 25 | 25 | **27** *Re'eh* | 28 | 29 | 1 **Kislev** R. Ḥ. | 1 **Tevet** R. Ḥ. 7 |
| 26 | 22 | 23 | 22 | 24 | **24** *Be-Midbar* | 26 | 26 | 28 | 29 | 30 R. Ḥ. | 2 | 2 8 |
| 27 | 23 | 24 | 23 | 25 | 25 | 27 | 27 | 29 | 1 **Tishri** Rosh Ha-Shanah | 1 **Heshvan** R. Ḥ. *No'aḥ* | 3 | 3 |
| 28 | **24** *Mishpatim* | 25 | 24 | **26** *Kedoshim* | 26 | 28 | **28** *Masei* | 30 R. Ḥ. | 2 | 2 | 4 | 4 |
| 29 | 25 | 26 | 25 | 27 | 27 | 29 | 29 | 1 **Elul** R. Ḥ. | **3** *Ha'azinu* Shabbat Shuvah | 3 | 5 | **5** *Va-Yiggash* |
| 30 | 26 | | 26 | 28 | 28 | **30** R. Ḥ. *Ḥukkat* | 1 **Av** R. Ḥ. | 2 | 4 Fast | 4 | 6 | 6 |
| 31 | 27 | | **27** *Tazri'a* Ha-Ḥodesh | | 29 | | 2 | 3 | | 5 | | 7 |

# 1985

**5745/46** תשמ״ה / תשמ״ו

| | January | February | March | April | May | June | July | August | September | October | November | December |
|---|---|---|---|---|---|---|---|---|---|---|---|---|
| 1 | 8 **Tevet** | 10 | 8 | 10 | 10 | **12** *Naso* | 12 | 14 | 15 | 16 | 17 | 18 |
| 2 | 9 | **11** *Be-Shallaḥ* | **9** *Teẓavveh* Zakhor | 11 | 11 | 13 | 13 | 15 | 16 | 17 | **18** *Va-Yera* | 19 |
| 3 | 10 Fast | 12 | 10 | 12 | 12 | 14 | 14 | **16** *Va-Etḥannan* | 17 | 18 Ḥol ha-Mo'ed | 19 | 20 |
| 4 | 11 | 13 | 11 | 13 | **13** *Aḥarei Mot Kedoshim* | 15 | 15 | 17 | 18 | 19 | 20 | 21 |
| 5 | **12** *Va-Yeḥi* | 14 | 12 | 14 | 14 | 16 | 16 | 18 | 19 | **20** | 21 | 22 |
| 6 | 13 | 15 | 13 Ta'anit Esther | **15** Pesaḥ | 15 | 17 | **17** *Balak* | 19 | 20 | 21 Hoshana Rabba | 22 | 23 |
| 7 | 14 | 16 | 14 Purim | 16 Omer | 16 | 18 | 18 Fast | 20 | **21** *Ki Tavo* | 22 Shemini Aẓeret | 23 | **24** *Va-Yeshev* |
| 8 | 15 | 17 | 15 Shushan Purim | 17 | 17 | **19** *Be-Ha'alotkha* | 19 | 21 | 22 | 23 Simḥat Torah *Ve-Zot Ha-Berakhah* | 24 | 25 Ḥanukkah 1 |
| 9 | 16 | **18** *Yitro* | **16** *Ki Tissa* | 18 Ḥol ha-Mo'ed | 18 Lag ba-Omer | 20 | 20 | 22 | 23 | 24 | **25** *Ḥayyei Sarah* | 26 2 |
| 10 | 17 | 19 | 17 | 19 | 19 | 21 | 21 | **23** *Ekev* | 24 | 25 | 26 | 27 3 |
| 11 | 18 | 20 | 18 | 20 | **20** *Emor* | 22 | 22 | 24 | 25 | 26 | 27 | 28 4 |
| 12 | **19** *Shemot* | 21 | 19 | 21 Pesaḥ | 21 | 23 | 23 | 25 | 26 | **27** *Bereshit* | 28 | 29 5 |
| 13 | 20 | 22 | 20 | **22** | 22 | 24 | **24** *Pinḥas* | 26 | 27 | 28 | 29 | 1 **Tevet** R. Ḥ. 6 |
| 14 | 21 | 23 | 21 | 23 | 23 | 25 | 25 | 27 | **28** *Niẓẓavim* | 29 | 1 **Kislev** R. Ḥ. | **2** *Mi Keẓ* 7 |
| 15 | 22 | 24 | 22 | 24 | 24 | **26** *Shelaḥ* | 26 | 28 | 29 | 30 R. Ḥ. | 2 | 3 8 |
| 16 | 23 | **25** *Mishpatim* Shekalim | *Va-Yakhel Pekudei* **23** Parah | 25 | 25 | 27 | 27 | 29 | 1 **Tishri** Rosh Ha-Shanah | 1 **Ḥeshvan** R. Ḥ. | **3** *Toledot* | 4 |
| 17 | 24 | 26 | 24 | 26 | 26 | 28 | 28 | **30** R. Ḥ. *Re'eh* | 2 | 2 | 4 | 5 |
| 18 | 25 | 27 | 25 | 27 | **27** *Be-Har Be-Ḥukkotai* | 29 | 29 | 1 **Elul** R. Ḥ. | 3 Fast | 3 | 5 | 6 |
| 19 | **26** *Va-Era* | 28 | 26 | 28 | 28 | 30 R. Ḥ. | 1 **Av** R. Ḥ. | 2 | 4 | **4** *No'aḥ* | 6 | 7 |
| 20 | 27 | 29 | 27 | **29** *Shemini* | 29 | 1 **Tammuz** R. Ḥ. | **2** *Mattot Masei* | 3 | 5 | 5 | 7 | 8 |
| 21 | 28 | 30 R. Ḥ. | 28 | 30 R. Ḥ. | 1 **Sivan** R. Ḥ. | 2 | 3 | 4 | **6** *Va-Yelekh* Shabbat Shuvah | 6 | 8 | **9** *Va-Yiggash* |
| 22 | 29 | 1 **Adar** R. Ḥ. | 29 | 1 **Iyyar** R. Ḥ. | 2 | **3** *Koraḥ* | 4 | 5 | 7 | 7 | 9 | 10 Fast |
| 23 | 1 **Shevat** R. Ḥ. | **2** *Terumah* | **1 Nisan** R. Ḥ. *Va-Yikra* Ha-Ḥodesh | 2 | 3 | 4 | 5 | 6 | 8 | 8 | **10** *Va-Yeẓe* | 11 |
| 24 | 2 | 3 | 2 | 3 | 4 | 5 | 6 | **7** *Shofetim* | 9 | 9 | 11 | 12 |
| 25 | 3 | 4 | 3 | 4 Yom ha-Aẓma'ut | **5** *Be-Midbar* | 6 | 7 | 8 | 10 Yom Kippur | 10 | 12 | 13 |
| 26 | **4** *Bo* | 5 | 4 | 5 | 6 Shavuot | 7 | 8 | 9 | 11 | **11** *Lekh Lekha* | 13 | 14 |
| 27 | 5 | 6 | 5 | **6** *Tazri'a Meẓora* | 7 | 8 | **9** *Devarim* Tishah be-Av | 10 | 12 | 12 | 14 | 15 |
| 28 | 6 | 7 | 6 | 7 | 8 | 9 | 10 Fast | 11 | **13** *Ha'azinu* | 13 | 15 | **16** *Va-Yeḥi* |
| 29 | 7 | | 7 | 8 | 9 | **10** *Ḥukkat* | 11 | 12 | 14 | 14 | 16 | 17 |
| 30 | 8 | | **8** *Ẓav* Shabbat ha-Gadol | 9 | 10 | 11 | 12 | 13 | 15 Sukkot | 15 | **17** *Va-Yishlaḥ* | 18 |
| 31 | 9 | | 9 | | 11 | | 13 | **14** *Ki Teẓe* | | 16 | | 19 |

# 1986

**5746/47** תשמ״ו / תשמ״ז

| | January | February | March | April | May | June | July | August | September | October | November | December |
|---|---|---|---|---|---|---|---|---|---|---|---|---|
| 1 | 20 **Tevet** | **22** *Yitro* | **20** *Ki Tissa* | 21 | 22 | 23 | 24 | 25 | 27 | 27 | **29** *Bereshit* | 29 |
| 2 | 21 | 23 | 21 | 22 | 23 | 24 | 25 | **26** *Mattot Masei* | 28 | 28 | 30 R. Ḥ. | 30 R. Ḥ. |
| 3 | 22 | 24 | 22 | 23 | **24** *Aḥarei Mot* | 25 | 26 | 27 | 29 | 29 | 1 **Ḥeshvan** R. Ḥ. | 1 **Kislev** R. Ḥ. |
| 4 | **23** *Shemot* | 25 | 23 | 24 | 25 | 26 | 27 | 28 | 30 R. Ḥ. | **1 Tishri** Rosh Ha-Shanah | 2 | 2 |
| 5 | 24 | 26 | 24 | **25** *Shemini* Ha-Ḥodesh | 26 | 27 | **28** *Shelaḥ* | 29 | 1 **Elul** R. Ḥ. | 2 | 3 | 3 |
| 6 | 25 | 27 | 25 | 26 | 27 | 28 | 29 | 1 **Av** R. Ḥ. | **2** *Shofetim* | 3 Fast | 4 | **4** *Toledot* |
| 7 | 26 | 28 | 26 | 27 | 28 | **29** *Be-Midbar* | 30 R. Ḥ. | 2 | 3 | 4 | 5 | 5 |
| 8 | 27 | **29** *Mishpatim* | **27** *Va-Yakhel* Shekalim | 28 | 29 | 1 **Sivan** R. Ḥ. | 1 **Tammuz** R. Ḥ. | 3 | 4 | 5 | **6** *No'aḥ* | 6 |
| 9 | 28 | 30 R. Ḥ. | 28 | 29 | 30 R. Ḥ. | 2 | 2 | **4** *Devarim* | 5 | 6 | 7 | 7 |
| 10 | 29 | 1 **Adar I** R. Ḥ. | 29 | 1 **Nisan** R. Ḥ. | **1 Iyyar** R. Ḥ. *Kedoshim* | 3 | 3 | 5 | 6 | 7 | 8 | 8 |
| 11 | **1 Shevat** R. Ḥ. *Va-Era* | 2 | 30 R. Ḥ. | 2 | 2 | 4 | 4 | 6 | 7 | **8** *Ha'azinu* Shabbat Shuvah | 9 | 9 |
| 12 | 2 | 3 | 1 **Adar II** R. Ḥ. | **3** *Tazri'a* | 3 | 5 | **5** *Koraḥ* | 7 | 8 | 9 | 10 | 10 |
| 13 | 3 | 4 | 2 | 4 | 4 | 6 Shavuot | 6 | 8 | **9** *Ki Teẓe* | 10 Yom Kippur | 11 | **11** *Va-Yeẓe* |
| 14 | 4 | 5 | 3 | 5 | 5 Yom ha-Aẓma'ut | **7** | 7 | 9 Tishah be-Av | 10 | 11 | 12 | 12 |
| 15 | 5 | **6** *Terumah* | **4** *Pekudei* | 6 | 6 | 8 | 8 | 10 | 11 | 12 | **13** *Lekh Lekha* | 13 |
| 16 | 6 | 7 | 5 | 7 | 7 | 9 | 9 | **11** *Va-Etḥannan* | 12 | 13 | 14 | 14 |
| 17 | 7 | 8 | 6 | 8 | **8** *Emor* | 10 | 10 | 12 | 13 | 14 | 15 | 15 |
| 18 | **8** *Bo* | 9 | 7 | 9 | 9 | 11 | 11 | 13 | 14 | **15** Sukkot | 16 | 16 |
| 19 | 9 | 10 | 8 | **10** *Meẓora* Shabbat ha-Gadol | 10 | 12 | **12** *Ḥukkat Balak* | 14 | 15 | 16 | 17 | 17 |
| 20 | 10 | 11 | 9 | 11 | 11 | 13 | 13 | 15 | **16** *Ki Tavo* | 17 | 18 | **18** *Va-Yishlaḥ* |
| 21 | 11 | 12 | 10 | 12 | 12 | **14** *Naso* | 14 | 16 | 17 | 18 Ḥol ha-Mo'ed | 19 | 19 |
| 22 | 12 | **13** *Teẓavveh* | **11** *Va-Yikra* Zakhor | 13 | 13 | 15 | 15 | 17 | 18 | 19 | **20** *Va-Yera* | 20 |
| 23 | 13 | 14 | 12 | 14 | 14 | 16 | 16 | **18** *Ekev* | 19 | 20 | 21 | 21 |
| 24 | 14 | 15 | 13 Ta'anit Esther | 15 Pesaḥ | **15** *Be-Har* | 17 | 17 Fast | 19 | 20 | 21 Hoshana Rabba | 22 | 22 |
| 25 | **15** *Be-Shallaḥ* | 16 | 14 Purim | 16 Omer | 16 | 18 | 18 | 20 | 21 | **22** Shemini Aẓeret | 23 | 23 |
| 26 | 16 | 17 | 15 Shushan Purim | **17** | 17 | 19 | **19** *Pinḥas* | 21 | 22 | 23 Simḥat Torah *Ve-Zot Ha-Berakhah* | 24 | 24 |
| 27 | 17 | 18 | 16 | 18 Ḥol ha-Mo'ed | 18 Lag ba-Omer | 20 | 20 | 22 | **23** *Niẓẓavim Va-Yelekh* | 24 | 25 | **25** *Va-Yeshev* Ḥanukkah 1 |
| 28 | 18 | 19 | 17 | 19 | 19 | **21** *Be-Ha'alotkha* | 21 | 23 | 24 | 25 | 26 | 26 2 |
| 29 | 19 | | **18** *Ẓav* Parah | 20 | 20 | 22 | 22 | 24 | 25 | 26 | **27** *Ḥayyei Sarah* | 27 3 |
| 30 | 20 | | 19 | 21 Pesaḥ | 21 | 23 | 23 | **25** *Re'eh* | 26 | 27 | 28 | 28 4 |
| 31 | 21 | | 20 | | **22** *Be-Ḥukkotai* | | 24 | 26 | | 28 | | 29 5 |

# 1987

**5747/48** תשמ״ז / תשמ״ח

| | January | February | March | April | May | June | July | August | September | October | November | December |
|---|---|---|---|---|---|---|---|---|---|---|---|---|
| 1 | 30 Kislev R. Ḥ. 6 Ḥanukkah | 2 | 30 R. Ḥ. | 2 | 2 | 4 | 4 | 6 Devarim | 7 | 8 | 9 | 10 |
| 2 | 1 Tevet R. Ḥ. 7 | 3 | 1 Adar R. Ḥ. | 3 | 3 Tazri'a Meẓora | 5 | 5 | 7 | 8 | 9 | 10 | 11 |
| 3 | 2 Mi-Keẓ 8 | 4 | 2 | 4 | 4 | 6 Shavuot | 6 | 8 | 9 | 10 Yom Kippur | 11 | 12 |
| 4 | 3 | 5 | 3 | 5 Va-Yikra | 5 Yom ha-Aẓma'ut | 7 | 7 Ḥukkat | 9 Tishah be-Av | 10 | 11 | 12 | 13 |
| 5 | 4 | 6 | 4 | 6 | 6 | 8 | 8 | 10 | 11 Ki Teẓe | 12 | 13 | 14 Va-Yishlaḥ |
| 6 | 5 | 7 | 5 | 7 | 7 | 9 Naso | 9 | 11 | 12 | 13 | 14 | 15 |
| 7 | 6 | 8 Bo | 6 Terumah | 8 | 8 | 10 | 10 | 12 | 13 | 14 | 15 Va-Yera | 16 |
| 8 | 7 | 9 | 7 | 9 | 9 | 11 | 11 | 13 Va-Ethannan | 14 | 15 Sukkot | 16 | 17 |
| 9 | 8 | 10 | 8 | 10 | 10 Aḥarei Mot Kedoshim | 12 | 12 | 14 | 15 | 16 | 17 | 18 |
| 10 | 9 Va-Yiggash | 11 | 9 | 11 | 11 | 13 | 13 | 15 | 16 | 17 | 18 | 19 |
| 11 | 10 Fast | 12 | 10 | 12 Ẓav Shabbat ha-Gadol | 12 | 14 | 14 Balak | 16 | 17 | 18 Ḥol ha-Mo'ed | 19 | 20 |
| 12 | 11 | 13 | 11 Ta'anit Esther | 13 | 13 | 15 | 15 | 17 | 18 Ki Tavo | 19 | 20 | 21 Va-Yeshev |
| 13 | 12 | 14 | 12 | 14 | 14 | 16 Be-Ha'alotkha | 16 | 18 | 19 | 20 | 21 | 22 |
| 14 | 13 | 15 Be-Shallaḥ | 13 Teẓavveh Zakhor | 15 Pesaḥ | 15 | 17 | 17 Fast | 19 | 20 | 21 Hoshana Rabba | 22 Ḥayyei Sarah | 23 |
| 15 | 14 | 16 | 14 Purim | 16 Omer | 16 | 18 | 18 | 20 Ekev | 21 | 22 Shemini Aẓeret | 23 | 24 |
| 16 | 15 | 17 | 15 Shushan Purim | 17 | 17 Emor | 19 | 19 | 21 | 22 | 23 Simḥat Torah Ve-Zot Ha-Berakhah | 24 | 25 Ḥanukkah 1 |
| 17 | 16 Va-Yeḥi | 18 | 16 | 18 Ḥol ha-Mo'ed | 18 Lag ba-Omer | 20 | 20 | 22 | 23 | 24 Bereshit | 25 | 26 2 |
| 18 | 17 | 19 | 17 | 19 | 19 | 21 | 21 Pinḥas | 23 | 24 | 25 | 26 | 27 3 |
| 19 | 18 | 20 | 18 | 20 | 20 | 22 | 22 | 24 | 25 Niẓẓavim Va-Yelekh | 26 | 27 | 28 Mi-Keẓ 4 |
| 20 | 19 | 21 | 19 | 21 Pesaḥ | 21 | 23 Shelaḥ | 23 | 25 | 26 | 27 | 28 | 29 5 |
| 21 | 20 | 22 Yitro | 20 Ki Tissa Parah | 22 | 22 | 24 | 24 | 26 | 27 | 28 | 29 Toledot | 30 R. Ḥ. 6 |
| 22 | 21 | 23 | 21 | 23 | 23 | 25 | 25 | 27 Re'eh | 28 | 29 | 1 Kislev R. Ḥ. | 1 Tevet R. Ḥ. 7 |
| 23 | 22 | 24 | 22 | 24 | 24 Be-Har Be-Ḥukkotai | 26 | 26 | 28 | 29 | 30 R. Ḥ. | 2 | 2 8 |
| 24 | 23 Shemot | 25 | 23 | 25 | 25 | 27 | 27 | 29 | 1 Tishri Rosh Ha-Shanah | 1 Ḥeshvan R. Ḥ. No'aḥ | 3 | 3 |
| 25 | 24 | 26 | 24 | 26 Shemini | 26 | 28 | 28 Mattot Masei | 30 R. Ḥ. | 2 | 2 | 4 | 4 |
| 26 | 25 | 27 | 25 | 27 | 27 | 29 | 29 | 1 Elul R. Ḥ. | 3 Ha'azinu Shabbat Shuvah | 3 | 5 | 5 Va-Yiggash |
| 27 | 26 | 28 | 26 | 28 | 28 | 30 R. Ḥ. Koraḥ | 1 Av R. Ḥ. | 2 | 4 Fast | 4 | 6 | 6 |
| 28 | 27 | 29 Mishpatim Shekalim | Va-Yakhel Pekudei 27 Ha-Ḥodesh | 29 | 29 | 1 Tammuz R. Ḥ. | 2 | 3 | 5 | 5 | 7 Va-Yeẓe | 7 |
| 29 | 28 | | 28 | 30 R. Ḥ. | 1 Sivan R. Ḥ. | 2 | 3 | 4 Shofetim | 6 | 6 | 8 | 8 |
| 30 | 29 | | 29 | 1 Iyyar R. Ḥ. | 2 Be-Midbar | 3 | 4 | 5 | 7 | 7 | 9 | 9 |
| 31 | 1 Shevat R. Ḥ. Va-Era | | 1 Nisan R. Ḥ. | | 3 | | 5 | 6 | | 8 Lekh Lekha | | 10 Fast |

# 1988

**5748/49** תשמ״ח / תשמ״ט

| | January | February | March | April | May | June | July | August | September | October | November | December |
|---|---|---|---|---|---|---|---|---|---|---|---|---|
| 1 | 11 Tevet | 13 | 12 | 14 | 14 | 16 | 16 | 18 | 19 | 20 Ḥol ha-Mo'ed | 21 | 22 |
| 2 | 12 Va-Yeḥi | 14 | 13 Ta'anit Esther | 15 Pesaḥ | 15 | 17 | 17 Balak | 19 | 20 | 21 Hoshana Rabba | 22 | 23 |
| 3 | 13 | 15 | 14 Purim | 16 Omer | 16 | 18 | 18 Fast | 20 | 21 Ki Tavo | 22 Shemini Aẓeret | 23 | 24 Va-Yeshev |
| 4 | 14 | 16 | 15 Shushan Purim | 17 | 17 | 19 Be-Ha'alotkha | 19 | 21 | 22 | 23 Simḥat Torah Ve-Zot Ha-Berakhah | 24 | 25 Ḥanukkah 1 |
| 5 | 15 | 17 | 16 Ki Tissa | 18 | 18 Lag ba-Omer | 20 | 20 | 22 | 23 | 24 | 25 Ḥayyei Sarah | 26 2 |
| 6 | 16 | 18 Yitro | 17 | 19 Ḥol ha-Mo'ed | 19 | 21 | 21 | 23 Ekev | 24 | 25 | 26 | 27 3 |
| 7 | 17 | 19 | 18 | 20 | 20 Emor | 22 | 22 | 24 | 25 | 26 | 27 | 28 4 |
| 8 | 18 | 20 | 19 | 21 Pesaḥ | 21 | 23 | 23 | 25 | 26 | 27 Bereshit | 28 | 29 5 |
| 9 | 19 Shemot | 21 | 20 | 22 | 22 | 24 | 24 Pinḥas | 26 | 27 | 28 | 29 | 1 Tevet R. Ḥ. 6 |
| 10 | 20 | 22 | 21 | 23 | 23 | 25 | 25 | 27 | 28 Niẓẓavim | 29 | 1 Kislev R. Ḥ. | 2 Mi-Keẓ 7 |
| 11 | 21 | 23 | 22 | 24 | 24 | 26 Shelaḥ | 26 | 28 | 29 | 30 R. Ḥ. | 2 | 3 8 |
| 12 | 22 | 24 | Va-Yakhel Pekudei 23 Parah | 25 | 25 | 27 | 27 | 29 | 1 Tishri Rosh Ha-Shanah | 1 Ḥeshvan R. Ḥ. | 3 Toledot | 4 |
| 13 | 23 | 25 Mishpatim Shekalim | 24 | 26 | 26 | 28 | 28 | 30 R. Ḥ. Re'eh | 2 | 2 | 4 | 5 |
| 14 | 24 | 26 | 25 | 27 | 27 Be-Har Be-Ḥukkotai | 29 | 29 | 1 Elul R. Ḥ. | 3 Fast | 3 | 5 | 6 |
| 15 | 25 | 27 | 26 | 28 | 28 | 30 R. Ḥ. | 1 Av R. Ḥ. | 2 | 4 | 4 No'aḥ | 6 | 7 |
| 16 | 26 Va-Era | 28 | 27 | 29 Shemini | 29 | 1 Tammuz R. Ḥ. | 2 Mattot Masei | 3 | 5 | 5 | 7 | 8 |
| 17 | 27 | 29 | 28 | 30 R. Ḥ. | 1 Sivan R. Ḥ. | 2 | 3 | 4 | 6 Va-Yelekh Shabbat Shuvah | 6 | 8 | 9 Va-Yiggash |
| 18 | 28 | 30 R. Ḥ. | 29 | 1 Iyyar R. Ḥ. | 2 | 3 Koraḥ | 4 | 5 | 7 | 7 | 9 | 10 Fast |
| 19 | 29 | 1 Adar R. Ḥ. | 1 Nisan Va-Yikra R. Ḥ. Ha-Ḥodesh | 2 | 3 | 4 | 5 | 6 | 8 | 8 | 10 Va-Yeẓe | 11 |
| 20 | 1 Shevat R. Ḥ. | 2 Terumah | 2 | 3 | 4 | 5 | 6 | 7 Shofetim | 9 | 9 | 11 | 12 |
| 21 | 2 | 3 | 3 | 4 Yom ha-Aẓma'ut | 5 Be-Midbar | 6 | 7 | 8 | 10 Yom Kippur | 10 | 12 | 13 |
| 22 | 3 | 4 | 4 | 5 | 6 Shavuot | 7 | 8 | 9 | 11 | 11 Lekh Lekha | 13 | 14 |
| 23 | 4 Bo | 5 | 5 | 6 Tazri'a Meẓora | 7 | 8 | 9 Tishah be-Av Devarim | 10 | 12 | 12 | 14 | 15 |
| 24 | 5 | 6 | 6 | 7 | 8 | 9 | 10 Fast | 11 | 13 Ha'azinu | 13 | 15 | 16 Va-Yeḥi |
| 25 | 6 | 7 | 7 | 8 | 9 | 10 Ḥukkat | 11 | 12 | 14 | 14 | 16 | 17 |
| 26 | 7 | 8 | 8 Ẓav Shabbat ha-Gadol | 9 | 10 | 11 | 12 | 13 | 15 Sukkot | 15 | 17 Va-Yishlaḥ | 18 |
| 27 | 8 | 9 Teẓavveh Zakhor | 9 | 10 | 11 | 12 | 13 | 14 Ki Teẓe | 16 | 16 | 18 | 19 |
| 28 | 9 | 10 | 10 | 11 | 12 Naso | 13 | 14 | 15 | 17 | 17 | 19 | 20 |
| 29 | 10 | 11 | 11 | 12 | 13 | 14 | 15 | 16 | 18 Ḥol ha-Mo'ed | 18 Va-Yera | 20 | 21 |
| 30 | 11 Be-Shallaḥ | | 12 | 13 Aḥarei Mot Kedoshim | 14 | 15 | 16 Va-Ethannan | 17 | 19 | 19 | 21 | 22 |
| 31 | 12 | | 13 | | 15 | | 17 | 18 | | 20 | | 23 Shemot |

## 1989

**5749/50** תשמ״ט / תש״נ

| | January | February | March | April | May | June | July | August | September | October | November | December |
|---|---|---|---|---|---|---|---|---|---|---|---|---|
| 1 | 24 Tevet | 26 | 24 | 25 Shemini Ha-Hodesh | 26 | 27 | 28 Shelah | 29 | 1 Elul R. H. | 2 Rosh Ha-Shanah | 3 | 3 |
| 2 | 25 | 27 | 25 | 26 | 27 | 28 | 29 | 1 Av R. H. | 2 Shofetim | 3 Fast | 4 | 4 Toledot |
| 3 | 26 | 28 | 26 | 27 | 28 | 29 Be-Midbar | 30 R. H. | 2 | 3 | 4 | 5 | 5 |
| 4 | 27 | 29 Mishpatim | 27 Va-Yakhel Shekalim | 28 | 29 | 1 Sivan R. H. | 1 Tammuz R. H. | 3 | 4 | 5 | 6 No'ah | 6 |
| 5 | 28 | 30 R. H. | 28 | 29 | 30 R. H. | 2 | 2 | 4 Devarim | 5 | 6 | 7 | 7 |
| 6 | 29 | 1 Adar I R. H. | 29 | 1 Nisan R. H. | 1 Iyyar R. H. Kedoshim | 3 | 3 | 5 | 6 | 7 | 8 | 8 |
| 7 | 1 Shevat R. H. Va-Era | 2 | 30 R. H. | 2 | 2 | 4 | 4 | 6 | 7 | 8 Ha'azinu Shabbat Shuvah | 9 | 9 |
| 8 | 2 | 3 | 1 Adar II R. H. | 3 Tazri'a | 3 | 5 | 5 Korah | 7 | 8 | 9 | 10 | 10 |
| 9 | 3 | 4 | 2 | 4 | 4 | 6 Shavuot | 6 | 8 | 9 Ki Teze | 10 Yom Kippur | 11 | 11 Va-Yeze |
| 10 | 4 | 5 | 3 | 5 | 5 Yom ha-Azma'ut | 7 | 7 | 9 Tishah be-Av | 10 | 11 | 12 | 12 |
| 11 | 5 | 6 Terumah | 4 Pekudei | 6 | 6 | 8 | 8 | 10 | 11 | 12 | 13 Lekh Lekha | 13 |
| 12 | 6 | 7 | 5 | 7 | 7 | 9 | 9 | 11 Va-Ethannan | 12 | 13 | 14 | 14 |
| 13 | 7 | 8 | 6 | 8 | 8 Emor | 10 | 10 | 12 | 13 | 14 | 15 | 15 |
| 14 | 8 Bo | 9 | 7 | 9 | 9 | 11 | 11 | 13 | 14 | 15 Sukkot | 16 | 16 |
| 15 | 9 | 10 | 8 | 10 Mezora Shabbat ha-Gadol | 10 | 12 | 12 Hukkat Balak | 14 | 15 | 16 | 17 | 17 |
| 16 | 10 | 11 | 9 | 11 | 11 | 13 | 13 | 15 | 16 Ki Tavo | 17 Hol ha-Mo'ed | 18 | 18 Va-Yishlah |
| 17 | 11 | 12 | 10 | 12 | 12 | 14 Naso | 14 | 16 | 17 | 18 | 19 | 19 |
| 18 | 12 | 13 Tezavveh | 11 Va-Yikra Zakhor | 13 | 13 | 15 | 15 | 17 | 18 | 19 | 20 Va-Yera | 20 |
| 19 | 13 | 14 | 12 | 14 | 14 | 16 | 16 | 18 Ekev | 19 | 20 | 21 | 21 |
| 20 | 14 | 15 | 13 Ta'anit Esther | 15 Pesah | 15 Be-Har | 17 | 17 Fast | 19 | 20 | 21 Hoshana Rabba | 22 | 22 |
| 21 | 15 Be-Shallah | 16 | 14 Purim | 16 Omer | 16 | 18 | 18 | 20 | 21 | 22 Shemini Azeret | 23 | 23 |
| 22 | 16 | 17 | 15 Shushan Purim | 17 Hol ha-Mo'ed | 17 | 19 | 19 Pinhas | 21 | 22 | 23 Simhat Torah Ve-Zot Ha-Berakhah | 24 | 24 |
| 23 | 17 | 18 | 16 | 18 | 18 Lag ba-Omer | 20 | 20 | 22 | 23 Nizzavim Va-Yelekh | 24 | 25 | 25 Hanukkah 1 Va-Yeshev |
| 24 | 18 | 19 | 17 | 19 | 19 | 21 Be-Ha'alotkha | 21 | 23 | 24 | 25 | 26 | 26 2 |
| 25 | 19 | 20 Ki Tissa | 18 Zav Parah | 20 | 20 | 22 | 22 | 24 | 25 | 26 | 27 Hayyei Sarah | 27 3 |
| 26 | 20 | 21 | 19 | 21 Pesah | 21 | 23 | 23 | 25 Re'eh | 26 | 27 | 28 | 28 4 |
| 27 | 21 | 22 | 20 | 22 | 22 Be-Hukkotai | 24 | 24 | 26 | 27 | 28 | 29 | 29 5 |
| 28 | 22 Yitro | 23 | 21 | 23 | 23 | 25 | 25 | 27 | 28 | 29 Bereshit | 30 R. H. | 30 R. H. 6 |
| 29 | 23 | | 22 | 24 Aharei Mot | 24 | 26 | 26 Mattot Masei | 28 | 29 | 30 R. H. | 1 Kislev R. H. | 1 Tevet R. H. 7 |
| 30 | 24 | | 23 | 25 | 25 | 27 | 27 | 29 | 1 Tishri Rosh Ha-Shanah | 1 Heshvan R. H. | 2 | 2 Mi-Kez 8 |
| 31 | 25 | | 24 | | 26 | | 28 | 30 R. H. | | 2 | | 3 |

## 1990

**5750/51** תש״נ / תשנ״א

| | January | February | March | April | May | June | July | August | September | October | November | December |
|---|---|---|---|---|---|---|---|---|---|---|---|---|
| 1 | 4 Tevet | 6 | 4 | 6 | 6 | 8 | 8 | 10 | 11 Ki Teze | 12 | 13 | 14 Va-Yishlah |
| 2 | 5 | 7 | 5 | 7 | 7 | 9 Naso | 9 | 11 | 12 | 13 | 14 | 15 |
| 3 | 6 | 8 Bo | 6 Terumah | 8 | 8 | 10 | 10 | 12 | 13 | 14 | 15 Va-Yera | 16 |
| 4 | 7 | 9 | 7 | 9 | 9 | 11 | 11 | 13 Va-Ethannan | 14 | 15 Sukkot | 16 | 17 |
| 5 | 8 | 10 | 8 | 10 | 10 Aharei Mot Kedoshim | 12 | 12 | 14 | 15 | 16 | 17 | 18 |
| 6 | 9 Va-Yiggash | 11 | 9 | 11 | 11 | 13 | 13 | 15 | 16 | 17 Hol ha-Mo'ed | 18 | 19 |
| 7 | 10 Fast | 12 | 10 | 12 Zav Shabbat ha-Gadol | 12 | 14 | 14 Balak | 16 | 17 | 18 | 19 | 20 |
| 8 | 11 | 13 | 11 Ta'anit Esther | 13 | 13 | 15 | 15 | 17 | 18 Ki Tavo | 19 | 20 | 21 Va-Yeshev |
| 9 | 12 | 14 | 12 | 14 | 14 | 16 Be-Ha'alotkha | 16 | 18 | 19 | 20 | 21 | 22 |
| 10 | 13 | 15 Be-Shallah | 13 Tezavveh Zakhor | 15 Pesah | 15 | 17 | 17 Fast | 19 | 20 | 21 Hoshana Rabba | 22 Hayyei Sarah | 23 |
| 11 | 14 | 16 | 14 Purim | 16 Omer | 16 | 18 | 18 | 20 Ekev | 21 | 22 Shemini Azeret | 23 | 24 |
| 12 | 15 | 17 | 15 Shushan Purim | 17 Hol ha-Mo'ed | 17 Emor | 19 | 19 | 21 | 22 | 23 Simhat Torah Ve-Zot Ha-Berakhah | 24 | 25 Hanukkah 1 |
| 13 | 16 Va-Yehi | 18 | 16 | 18 | 18 Lag ba-Omer | 20 | 20 | 22 | 23 | 24 Bereshit | 25 | 26 2 |
| 14 | 17 | 19 | 17 | 19 | 19 | 21 | 21 Pinhas | 23 | 24 | 25 | 26 | 27 3 |
| 15 | 18 | 20 | 18 | 20 | 20 | 22 | 22 | 24 | 25 Nizzavim Va-Yelekh | 26 | 27 | 28 Mi-Kez 4 |
| 16 | 19 | 21 | 19 | 21 Pesah | 21 | 23 Shelah | 23 | 25 | 26 | 27 | 28 | 29 5 |
| 17 | 20 | 22 Yitro | 20 Ki Tissa Parah | 22 | 22 | 24 | 24 | 26 | 27 | 28 | 29 Toledot | 30 R. H. 6 |
| 18 | 21 | 23 | 21 | 23 | 23 | 25 | 25 | 27 Re'eh | 28 | 29 | 1 Kislev R. H. | 1 Tevet R. H. 7 |
| 19 | 22 | 24 | 22 | 24 | 24 Be-Har Be-Hukkotai | 26 | 26 | 28 | 29 | 30 R. H. | 2 | 2 8 |
| 20 | 23 Shemot | 25 | 23 | 25 | 25 | 27 | 27 | 29 | 1 Tishri Rosh Ha-Shanah | 1 Heshvan R. H. No'ah | 3 | 3 |
| 21 | 24 | 26 | 24 | 26 Shemini | 26 | 28 | 28 Mattot Masei | 30 R. H. | 2 | 2 | 4 | 4 |
| 22 | 25 | 27 | 25 | 27 | 27 | 29 | 29 | 1 Elul R. H. | 3 Ha'azinu Shabbat Shuvah | 3 | 5 | 5 Va-Yiggash |
| 23 | 26 | 28 | 26 | 28 | 28 | 30 R. H. Korah | 1 Av R. H. | 2 | 4 Fast | 4 | 6 | 6 |
| 24 | 27 | 29 Mishpatim Shekalim | 27 Va-Yakhel Pekudei Ha-Hodesh | 29 | 29 | 1 Tammuz R. H. | 2 | 3 | 5 | 5 | 7 Va-Yeze | 7 |
| 25 | 28 | 30 R. H. | 28 | 30 R. H. | 1 Sivan R. H. | 2 | 3 | 4 Shofetim | 6 | 6 | 8 | 8 |
| 26 | 29 | 1 Adar R. H. | 29 | 1 Iyyar R. H. | 2 Be-Midbar | 3 | 4 | 5 | 7 | 7 | 9 | 9 |
| 27 | 1 Shevat R. H. Va-Era | 2 | 1 Nisan R. H. | 2 | 3 | 4 | 5 | 6 | 8 | 8 Lekh Lekha | 10 | 10 Fast |
| 28 | 2 | 3 | 2 | 3 Tazri'a Mezora | 4 | 5 | 6 Devarim | 7 | 9 | 9 | 11 | 11 |
| 29 | 3 | | 3 | 4 | 5 | 6 | 7 | 8 | 10 Yom Kippur | 10 | 12 | 12 Va-Yehi |
| 30 | 4 | | 4 | 5 Yom ha-Azma'ut | 6 Shavuot | 7 Hukkat | 8 | 9 | 11 | 11 | 13 | 13 |
| 31 | 5 | | 5 Va-Yikra | | 7 | | 9 Tishah be-Av | 10 | | 12 | | 14 |

## 1991

**5751/52** תשנ״א / תשנ״ב

| | January | February | March | April | May | June | July | August | September | October | November | December |
|---|---|---|---|---|---|---|---|---|---|---|---|---|
| 1 | 15 Tevet | 17 | 15 Shushan Purim | 17 | 17 | **19** *Be-Ha'alotkha* | 19 | 21 | 22 | 23 Simḥat Torah *Ve-Zot Ha-Berakhah* | 24 | 24 |
| 2 | 16 | **18** *Yitro* | **16** *Ki Tissa* | 18 Ḥol ha-Mo'ed | 18 Lag ba-Omer | 20 | 20 | 22 | 23 | 24 | **25** *Ḥayyei Sarah* | 25 Ḥanukkah 1 |
| 3 | 17 | 19 | 17 | 19 | 19 | 21 | 21 | **23** *Ekev* | 24 | 25 | 26 | 26 2 |
| 4 | 18 | 20 | 18 | 20 | **20** *Emor* | 22 | 22 | 24 | 25 | 26 | 27 | 27 3 |
| 5 | **19** *Shemot* | 21 | 19 | 21 Pesaḥ | 21 | 23 | 23 | 25 | 26 | **27** *Bereshit* | 28 | 28 4 |
| 6 | 20 | 22 | 20 | **22** | 22 | 24 | **24** *Pinḥas* | 26 | 27 | 28 | 29 | 29 5 |
| 7 | 21 | 23 | 21 | 23 | 23 | 25 | 25 | 27 | **28** *Niẓẓavim* | 29 | 30 R. Ḥ. | **30** R. Ḥ. *Mi-Keẓ* 6 |
| 8 | 22 | 24 | 22 | 24 | 24 | **26** *Shelaḥ* | 26 | 28 | 29 | 30 R. Ḥ. | 1 **Kislev** R. Ḥ. | 1 **Tevet** R. Ḥ. 7 |
| 9 | 23 | **25** *Mishpatim* Shekalim | *Va-Yakhel Pekudei* **23** Parah | 25 | 25 | 27 | 27 | 29 | 1 **Tishri** Rosh Ha-Shanah | 1 **Ḥeshvan** R. Ḥ. | **2** *Toledot* | 2 8 |
| 10 | 24 | 26 | 24 | 26 | 26 | 28 | 28 | **30** R. Ḥ. *Re'eh* | 2 | 2 | 3 | 3 |
| 11 | 25 | 27 | 25 | 27 | **27** *Be-Har Be-Ḥukkotai* | 29 | 29 | 1 **Elul** R. Ḥ. | 3 Fast | 3 | 4 | 4 |
| 12 | **26** *Va-Era* | 28 | 26 | 28 | 28 | 30 R. Ḥ. | 1 **Av** R. Ḥ. | 2 | 4 | **4** *No'aḥ* | 5 | 5 |
| 13 | 27 | 29 | 27 | **29** *Shemini* | 29 | 1 **Tammuz** R. Ḥ. | **2** *Mattot Masei* | 3 | 5 | 5 | 6 | 6 |
| 14 | 28 | 30 R. Ḥ. | 28 | 30 R. Ḥ. | 1 **Sivan** R. Ḥ. | 2 | 3 | 4 | **6** *Va-Yelekh* Shabbat Shuvah | 6 | 7 | **7** *Va-Yiggash* |
| 15 | 29 | 1 **Adar** R. Ḥ. | 29 | 1 **Iyyar** R. Ḥ. | 2 | **3** *Koraḥ* | 4 | 5 | 7 | 7 | 8 | 8 |
| 16 | 1 **Shevat** R. Ḥ. | **2** *Terumah* | **1** R. Ḥ. *Va-Yikra* **Nisan** Ha-Ḥodesh | 2 | 3 | 4 | 5 | 6 | 8 | 8 | **9** *Va-Yeẓe* | 9 |
| 17 | 2 | 3 | 2 | 3 | 4 | 5 | 6 | **7** *Shofetim* | 9 | 9 | 10 | 10 Fast |
| 18 | 3 | 4 | 3 | 4 Yom ha-Aẓma'ut | **5** *Be-Midbar* | 6 | 7 | 8 | 10 Yom Kippur | 10 | 11 | 11 |
| 19 | **4** *Bo* | 5 | 4 | 5 | 6 Shavuot | 7 | 8 | 9 | 11 | **11** *Lekh Lekha* | 12 | 12 |
| 20 | 5 | 6 | 5 | **6** *Tazri'a Meẓora* | 7 | 8 | **9** *Devarim* Tishah be-Av | 10 | 12 | 12 | 13 | 13 |
| 21 | 6 | 7 | 6 | 7 | 8 | 9 | 10 Fast | 11 | **13** *Ha'azinu* | 13 | 14 | **14** *Va-Yeḥi* |
| 22 | 7 | 8 | 7 | 8 | 9 | **10** *Ḥukkat* | 11 | 12 | 14 | 14 | 15 | 15 |
| 23 | 8 | **9** *Teẓavveh* Zakhor | **8** *Ẓav* Shabbat ha-Gadol | 9 | 10 | 11 | 12 | 13 | 15 Sukkot | 15 | **16** *Va-Yishlaḥ* | 16 |
| 24 | 9 | 10 | 9 | 10 | 11 | 12 | 13 | **14** *Ki Teẓe* | 16 | 16 | 17 | 17 |
| 25 | 10 | 11 | 10 | 11 | **12** *Naso* | 13 | 14 | 15 | 17 Ḥol ha-Mo'ed | 17 | 18 | 18 |
| 26 | **11** *Be-Shallaḥ* | 12 | 11 | 12 | 13 | 14 | 15 | 16 | 18 | **18** *Va-Yera* | 19 | 19 |
| 27 | 12 | 13 Ta'anit Esther | 12 | **13** *Aḥarei Mot Kedoshim* | 14 | 15 | **16** *Va-Etḥannan* | 17 | 19 | 19 | 20 | 20 |
| 28 | 13 | 14 Purim | 13 | 14 | 15 | 16 | 17 | 18 | **20** | 20 | 21 | **21** *Shemot* |
| 29 | 14 | | 14 | 15 | 16 | **17** *Balak* | 18 | 19 | 21 Hoshana Rabba | 21 | 22 | 22 |
| 30 | 15 | | **15** Pesaḥ | 16 | 17 | 18 Fast | 19 | 20 | 22 Shemini Aẓeret | 22 | **23** *Va-Yeshev* | 23 |
| 31 | 16 | | 16 Omer | | 18 | | 20 | **21** *Ki Tavo* | | 23 | | 24 |

## 1992

**5752/53** תשנ״ב / תשנ״ג

| | January | February | March | April | May | June | July | August | September | October | November | December |
|---|---|---|---|---|---|---|---|---|---|---|---|---|
| 1 | 25 **Tevet** | **27** *Mishpatim* | 26 | 27 | 28 | 29 | 30 R. Ḥ. | **2** *Mattot Masei* | 3 | 4 | 5 | 6 |
| 2 | 26 | 28 | 27 | 28 | **29** *Aḥarei Mot* | 1 **Sivan** R. Ḥ. | 1 **Tammuz** R. Ḥ. | 3 | 4 | 5 | 6 | 7 |
| 3 | 27 | 29 | 28 | 29 | 30 R. Ḥ. | 2 | 2 | 4 | 5 | **6** *Va-Yelekh* Shabbat Shuvah | 7 | 8 |
| 4 | **28** *Va-Era* | 30 R. Ḥ. | 29 | **1** **Nisan** *Tazri'a* R. Ḥ. Ha-Ḥodesh | 1 **Iyyar** R. Ḥ. | 3 | **3** *Koraḥ* | 5 | 6 | 7 | 8 | 9 |
| 5 | 29 | 1 **Adar I** R. Ḥ. | 30 R. Ḥ. | 2 | 2 | 4 | 4 | 6 | **7** *Shofetim* | 8 | 9 | **10** *Va-Yeẓe* |
| 6 | 1 **Shevat** R. Ḥ. | 2 | 1 **Adar II** R. Ḥ. | 3 | 3 | **5** *Be-Midbar* | 5 | 7 | 8 | 9 | 10 | 11 |
| 7 | 2 | 3 | **2** *Pekudei* | 4 | 4 Yom ha-Aẓma'ut | 6 Shavuot | 6 | 8 | 9 | 10 Yom Kippur | **11** *Lekh Lekha* | 12 |
| 8 | 3 | **4** *Terumah* | 3 | 5 | 5 | 7 | 7 | **9** *Devarim* Tishah be-Av | 10 | 11 | 12 | 13 |
| 9 | 4 | 5 | 4 | 6 | **6** *Kedoshim* | 8 | 8 | 10 Fast | 11 | 12 | 13 | 14 |
| 10 | 5 | 6 | 5 | 7 | 7 | 9 | 9 | 11 | 12 | **13** *Ha'azinu* | 14 | 15 |
| 11 | **6** *Bo* | 7 | 6 | **8** *Meẓora* Shabbat ha-Gadol | 8 | 10 | **10** *Ḥukkat* | 12 | 13 | 14 | 15 | 16 |
| 12 | 7 | 8 | 7 | 9 | 9 | 11 | 11 | 13 | **14** *Ki Teẓe* | 15 Sukkot | 16 | **17** *Va-Yishlaḥ* |
| 13 | 8 | 9 | 8 | 10 | 10 | **12** *Naso* | 12 | 14 | 15 | 16 | 17 | 18 |
| 14 | 9 | 10 | **9** *Va-Yikra* Zakhor | 11 | 11 | 13 | 13 | 15 | 16 | 17 Ḥol ha-Mo'ed | **18** *Va-Yera* | 19 |
| 15 | 10 | **11** *Teẓavveh* | 10 | 12 | 12 | 14 | 14 | **16** *Va-Etḥannan* | 17 | 18 | 19 | 20 |
| 16 | 11 | 12 | 11 | 13 | **13** *Emor* | 15 | 15 | 17 | 18 | 19 | 20 | 21 |
| 17 | 12 | 13 | 12 | 14 | 14 | 16 | 16 | 18 | 19 | **20** | 21 | 22 |
| 18 | **13** *Be-Shallaḥ* | 14 | 13 Ta'anit Esther | **15** Pesaḥ | 15 | 17 | **17** *Balak* | 19 | 20 | 21 Hoshana Rabba | 22 | 23 |
| 19 | 14 | 15 | 14 Purim | 16 Omer | 16 | 18 | 18 Fast | 20 | **21** *Ki Tavo* | 22 Shemini Aẓeret | 23 | **24** *Va-Yeshev* |
| 20 | 15 | 16 | 15 Shushan Purim | 17 Ḥol ha-Mo'ed | 17 | **19** *Be-Ha'alotkha* | 19 | 21 | 22 | 23 Simḥat Torah *Ve-Zot Ha-Berakhah* | 24 | 25 Ḥanukkah 1 |
| 21 | 16 | 17 | **16** *Ẓav* | 18 | 18 Lag ba-Omer | 20 | 20 | 22 | 23 | 24 | **25** *Ḥayyei Sarah* | 26 2 |
| 22 | 17 | **18** *Ki Tissa* | 17 | 19 | 19 | 21 | 21 | **23** *Ekev* | 24 | 25 | 26 | 27 3 |
| 23 | 18 | 19 | 18 | 20 | **20** *Be-Har* | 22 | 22 | 24 | 25 | 26 | 27 | 28 4 |
| 24 | 19 | 20 | 19 | 21 Pesaḥ | 21 | 23 | 23 | 25 | 26 | **27** *Bereshit* | 28 | 29 5 |
| 25 | **20** *Yitro* | 21 | 20 | **22** | 22 | 24 | **24** *Pinḥas* | 26 | 27 | 28 | 29 | 1 **Tevet** R. Ḥ. 6 |
| 26 | 21 | 22 | 21 | 23 | 23 | 25 | 25 | 27 | **28** *Niẓẓavim* | 29 | 1 **Kislev** R. Ḥ. | **2** *Mi-Keẓ* 7 |
| 27 | 22 | 23 | 22 | 24 | 24 | **26** *Shelaḥ* | 26 | 28 | 29 | 30 R. Ḥ. | 2 | 3 8 |
| 28 | 23 | 24 | **23** *Shemini* Parah | 25 | 25 | 27 | 27 | 29 | 1 **Tishri** Rosh Ha-Shanah | 1 **Ḥeshvan** R. Ḥ. | **3** *Toledot* | 4 |
| 29 | 24 | **25** *Va-Yakhel* Shekalim | 24 | 26 | 26 | 28 | 28 | **30** R. Ḥ. *Re'eh* | 2 | 2 | 4 | 5 |
| 30 | 25 | | 25 | 27 | **27** *Be-Ḥukkotai* | 29 | 29 | 1 **Elul** R. Ḥ. | 3 Fast | 3 | 5 | 6 |
| 31 | 26 | | 26 | | 28 | | 1 **Av** R. Ḥ. | 2 | | **4** *No'aḥ* | | 7 |

# 1993

**5753/54** תשנ״ג / תשנ״ד

| | January | February | March | April | May | June | July | August | September | October | November | December |
|---|---|---|---|---|---|---|---|---|---|---|---|---|
| 1 | 8 **Tevet** | 10 | 8 | 10 | **10** *Aharei Mot Kedoshim* | 12 | 12 | 14 | 15 | 16 | 17 | 17 |
| 2 | **9** *Va-Yiggash* | 11 | 9 | 11 | 11 | 13 | 13 | 15 | 16 | **17** | 18 | 18 |
| 3 | 10 Fast | 12 | 10 | **12** *Zav* Shabbat ha-Gadol | 12 | 14 | **14** *Balak* | 16 | 17 | 18 Hol ha-Mo'ed | 19 | 19 |
| 4 | 11 | 13 | 11 Ta'anit Esther | 13 | 13 | 15 | 15 | 17 | **18** *Ki Tavo* | 19 | 20 | **20** *Va-Yeshev* |
| 5 | 12 | 14 | 12 | 14 | 14 | **16** *Be-Ha'alotkha* | 16 | 18 | 19 | 20 | 21 | 21 |
| 6 | 13 | **15** *Be-Shallah* | **13** *Tezavveh* Zakhor | 15 Pesah | 15 | 17 | 17 Fast | 19 | 20 | 21 Hoshana Rabba | **22** *Hayyei Sarah* | 22 |
| 7 | 14 | 16 | 14 Purim | 16 Omer | 16 | 18 | 18 | **20** *Ekev* | 21 | 22 Shemini Azeret | 23 | 23 |
| 8 | 15 | 17 | 15 Shushan Purim | 17 | **17** *Emor* | 19 | 19 | 21 | 22 | 23 Simhat Torah *Ve-Zot Ha-Berakhah* | 24 | 24 |
| 9 | **16** *Va-Yehi* | 18 | 16 | 18 Hol ha-Mo'ed | 18 Lag ba-Omer | 20 | 20 | 22 | 23 | **24** *Bereshit* | 25 | 25 Hanukkah 1 |
| 10 | 17 | 19 | 17 | **19** | 19 | 21 | **21** *Pinhas* | 23 | 24 | 25 | 26 | 26 2 |
| 11 | 18 | 20 | 18 | 20 | 20 | 22 | 22 | 24 | **25** *Nizzavim Va-Yelekh* | 26 | 27 | **27** *Mi-Kez* 3 |
| 12 | 19 | 21 | 19 | 21 Pesah | 21 | **23** *Shelah* | 23 | 25 | 26 | 27 | 28 | 28 4 |
| 13 | 20 | **22** *Yitro* | **20** *Ki Tissa* Parah | 22 | 22 | 24 | 24 | 26 | 27 | 28 | **29** *Toledot* | 29 5 |
| 14 | 21 | 23 | 21 | 23 | 23 | 25 | 25 | **27** *Re'eh* | 28 | 29 | 30 R. H. | 30 R. H. 6 |
| 15 | 22 | 24 | 22 | 24 | **24** *Be-Har Be-Hukkotai* | 26 | 26 | 28 | 29 | 30 R. H. | 1 **Kislev** R. H. | 1 R. H. **Tevet** 7 |
| 16 | **23** *Shemot* | 25 | 23 | 25 | 25 | 27 | 27 | 29 | 1 **Tishri** Rosh Ha-Shanah | 1 R. H. **Heshvan** *No'ah* | 2 | 2 8 |
| 17 | 24 | 26 | 24 | **26** *Shemini* | 26 | 28 | **28** *Mattot Masei* | 30 R. H. | 2 | 2 | 3 | 3 |
| 18 | 25 | 27 | 25 | 27 | 27 | 29 | 29 | 1 **Elul** R. H. | **3** *Ha'azinu* Shabbat Shuvah | 3 | 4 | **4** *Va-Yiggash* |
| 19 | 26 | 28 | 26 | 28 | 28 | **30** R. H. *Korah* | 1 **Av** R. H. | 2 | 4 Fast | 4 | 5 | 5 |
| 20 | 27 | **29** *Mishpatim* Shekalim | **27** *Va-Yakhel Pekudei* Ha-Hodesh | 29 | 29 | 1 R. H. **Tammuz** | 2 | 3 | 5 | 5 | **6** *Va-Yeze* | 6 |
| 21 | 28 | 30 R. H. | 28 | 30 R. H. | 1 **Sivan** R. H. | 2 | 3 | **4** *Shofetim* | 6 | 6 | 7 | 7 |
| 22 | 29 | 1 **Adar** R. H. | 29 | 1 **Iyyar** R. H. | **2** *Be-Midbar* | 3 | 4 | 5 | 7 | 7 | 8 | 8 |
| 23 | 1 **Shevat** R. H. *Va-Era* | 2 | 1 **Nisan** R. H. | 2 | 3 | 4 | 5 | 6 | 8 | **8** *Lekh Lekha* | 9 | 9 |
| 24 | 2 | 3 | 2 | **3** *Tazri'a Mezora* | 4 | 5 | **6** *Devarim* | 7 | 9 | 9 | 10 | 10 Fast |
| 25 | 3 | 4 | 3 | 4 | 5 | 6 | 7 | 8 | **10** Yom Kippur | 10 | 11 | **11** *Va-Yehi* |
| 26 | 4 | 5 | 4 | 5 Yom ha-Azma'ut | 6 Shavuot | **7** *Hukkat* | 8 | 9 | 11 | 11 | 12 | 12 |
| 27 | 5 | **6** *Terumah* | **5** *Va-Yikra* | 6 | 7 | 8 | 9 Tishah be-Av | 10 | 12 | 12 | **13** *Va-Yishlah* | 13 |
| 28 | 6 | 7 | 6 | 7 | 8 | 9 | 10 | **11** *Ki Teze* | 13 | 13 | 14 | 14 |
| 29 | 7 | | 7 | 8 | **9** *Naso* | 10 | 11 | 12 | 14 | 14 | 15 | 15 |
| 30 | **8** *Bo* | | 8 | 9 | 10 | 11 | 12 | 13 | 15 Sukkot | **15** *Va-Yera* | 16 | 16 |
| 31 | 9 | | 9 | | 11 | | **13** *Va-Ethannan* | 14 | | 16 | | 17 |

# 1994

**5754/55** תשנ״ד / תשנ״ה

| | January | February | March | April | May | June | July | August | September | October | November | December |
|---|---|---|---|---|---|---|---|---|---|---|---|---|
| 1 | **18** **Tevet** *Shemot* | 20 | 18 | 20 Hol ha-Mo'ed | 20 | 22 | 22 | 24 | 25 | **26** *Bereshit* | 27 | 28 4 |
| 2 | 19 | 21 | 19 | **21** Pesah | 21 | 23 | **23** *Pinhas* | 25 | 26 | 27 | 28 | 29 5 |
| 3 | 20 | 22 | 20 | 22 | 22 | 24 | 24 | 26 | **27** *Nizzavim* | 28 | 29 | **30** R. H. *Mi-Kez* 6 |
| 4 | 21 | 23 | 21 | 23 | 23 | **25** *Shelah* | 25 | 27 | 28 | 29 | 1 **Kislev** R. H. | 1 **Tevet** R. H. 7 |
| 5 | 22 | **24** *Mishpatim* | **22** *Va-Yakhel* Parah | 24 | 24 | 26 | 26 | 28 | 29 | 30 R. H. | **2** *Toledot* | 2 8 |
| 6 | 23 | 25 | 23 | 25 | 25 | 27 | 27 | **29** *Re'eh* | 1 **Tishri** Rosh Ha-Shanah | 1 R. H. **Heshvan** | 3 | 3 |
| 7 | 24 | 26 | 24 | 26 | **26** *Be-Har Be-Hukkotai* | 28 | 28 | 30 R. H. | 2 | 2 | 4 | 4 |
| 8 | **25** *Va-Era* | 27 | 25 | 27 | 27 | 29 | 29 | 1 **Elul** R. H. | 3 Fast | **3** *No'ah* | 5 | 5 |
| 9 | 26 | 28 | 26 | **28** *Shemini* | 28 | 30 R. H. | **1** R. H. **Av** *Mattot Masei* | 2 | 4 | 4 | 6 | 6 |
| 10 | 27 | 29 | 27 | 29 | 29 | 1 R. H. **Tammuz** | 2 | 3 | **5** *Va-Yelekh* Shabbat Shuvah | 5 | 7 | **7** *Va-Yiggash* |
| 11 | 28 | 30 R. H. | 28 | 30 R. H. | 1 **Sivan** R. H. | **2** *Korah* | 3 | 4 | 6 | 6 | 8 | 8 |
| 12 | 29 | **1** R. H. **Adar** *Terumah* Shekalim | **29** *Pekudei* Ha-Hodesh | 1 **Iyyar** R. H. | 2 | 3 | 4 | 5 | 7 | 7 | **9** *Va-Yeze* | 9 |
| 13 | 1 **Shevat** R. H. | 2 | 1 **Nisan** R. H. | 2 | 3 | 4 | 5 | **6** *Shofetim* | 8 | 8 | 10 | 10 Fast |
| 14 | 2 | 3 | 2 | Yom ha-Azma'ut | **4** *Be-Midbar* | 5 | 6 | 7 | 9 | 9 | 11 | 11 |
| 15 | **3** *Bo* | 4 | 3 | 4 | 5 | 6 | 7 | 8 | 10 Yom Kippur | **10** *Lekh Lekha* | 12 | 12 |
| 16 | 4 | 5 | 4 | **5** *Tazri'a Mezora* | 6 Shavuot | 7 | **8** *Devarim* | 9 | 11 | 11 | 13 | 13 |
| 17 | 5 | 6 | 5 | 6 | 7 | 8 | 9 Tishah be-Av | 10 | **12** *Ha'azinu* | 12 | 14 | **14** *Va-Yehi* |
| 18 | 6 | 7 | 6 | 7 | 8 | **9** *Hukkat* | 10 | 11 | 13 | 13 | 15 | 15 |
| 19 | 7 | **8** *Tezavveh* Zakhor | **7** *Va-Yikra* | 8 | 9 | 10 | 11 | 12 | 14 | 14 | **16** *Va-Yishlah* | 16 |
| 20 | 8 | 9 | 8 | 9 | 10 | 11 | 12 | **13** *Ki-Teze* | 15 Sukkot | 15 | 17 | 17 |
| 21 | 9 | 10 | 9 | 10 | **11** *Naso* | 12 | 13 | 14 | 16 | 16 | 18 | 18 |
| 22 | **10** *Be-Shallah* | 11 | 10 | 11 | 12 | 13 | 14 | 15 | 17 | **17** *Va-Yera* | 19 | 19 |
| 23 | 11 | 12 | 11 | **12** *Aharei Mot Kedoshim* | 13 | 14 | **15** *Va-Ethannan* | 16 | 18 Hol ha-Moed | 18 | 20 | 20 |
| 24 | 12 | 13 Ta'anit Esther | 12 | 13 | 14 | 15 | 16 | 17 | **19** | 19 | 21 | **21** *Shemot* |
| 25 | 13 | 14 Purim | 13 | 14 | 15 | **16** *Balak* | 17 | 18 | 20 | 20 | 22 | 22 |
| 26 | 14 | **15** *Ki Tissa* Shushan Purim | **14** *Zav* Shabbat ha-Gadol | 15 | 16 | 17 Fast | 18 | 19 | 21 Hoshana Rabba | 21 | **23** *Va-Yeshev* | 23 |
| 27 | 15 | 16 | 15 Pesah | 16 | 17 | 18 | 19 | **20** *Ki-Tavo* | 22 Shemini Azeret | 22 | 24 | 24 |
| 28 | 16 | 17 | 16 Omer | 17 | **18** *Be-Ha'alotkha* | 19 | 20 | 21 | 23 Simhat Torah *Ve-Zot Ha-Berakhah* | 23 | 25 Hanukkah 1 | 25 |
| 29 | **17** *Yitro* | | 17 | 18 Lag ba-Omer | 19 | 20 | 21 | 22 | 24 | **24** *Hayyei Sarah* | 26 2 | 26 |
| 30 | 18 | | 18 Hol ha-Mo'ed | **19** *Emor* | 20 | 21 | **22** *Ekev* | 23 | 25 | 25 | 27 3 | 27 |
| 31 | 19 | | 19 | | 21 | | 23 | 24 | | 26 | | **28** *Va-Era* |

# 1995

**5755/56** תשנ״ה / תשנ״ו

| | January | February | March | April | May | June | July | August | September | October | November | December |
|---|---|---|---|---|---|---|---|---|---|---|---|---|
| 1 | 29 Tevet | 1 Adar I R. Ḥ. | 29 | 1 Nisan R. Ḥ. Tazri'a Ha-Ḥodesh | 1 Iyyar R. Ḥ. | 3 | 3 Koraḥ | 5 | 6 | 7 | 8 | 8 |
| 2 | 1 Shevat R. Ḥ. | 2 | 30 R. Ḥ. | 2 | 2 | 4 | 4 | 6 | 7 Shofetim | 8 | 9 | 9 Va-Yeẓe |
| 3 | 2 | 3 | 1 Adar II R. Ḥ. | 3 | 3 | 5 Be-Midbar | 5 | 7 | 8 | 9 | 10 | 10 |
| 4 | 3 | 4 Terumah | 2 Pekudei | 4 | 4 Yom ha-Aẓma'ut | 6 Shavuot | 6 | 8 | 9 | 10 Yom Kippur | 11 Lekh Lekha | 11 |
| 5 | 4 | 5 | 3 | 5 | 5 | 7 | 7 | 9 Devarim Tishah be-Av | 10 | 11 | 12 | 12 |
| 6 | 5 | 6 | 4 | 6 | 6 Kedoshim | 8 | 8 | 10 Fast | 11 | 12 | 13 | 13 |
| 7 | 6 Bo | 7 | 5 | 7 | 7 | 9 | 9 | 11 | 12 | 13 Ha'azinu | 14 | 14 |
| 8 | 7 | 8 | 6 | 8 Meẓora Shabbat ha-Gadol | 8 | 10 | 10 Ḥukkat | 12 | 13 | 14 | 15 | 15 |
| 9 | 8 | 9 | 7 | 9 | 9 | 11 | 11 | 13 | 14 Ki Teẓe | 15 Sukkot | 16 | 16 Va-Yishlaḥ |
| 10 | 9 | 10 | 8 | 10 | 10 | 12 Naso | 12 | 14 | 15 | 16 | 17 | 17 |
| 11 | 10 | 11 Teẓavveh | 9 Va-Yikra Zakhor | 11 | 11 | 13 | 13 | 15 | 16 | 17 | 18 Va-Yera | 18 |
| 12 | 11 | 12 | 10 | 12 | 12 | 14 | 14 | 16 Va-Etḥannan | 17 | 18 Ḥol ha-Mo'ed | 19 | 19 |
| 13 | 12 | 13 | 11 | 13 | 13 Emor | 15 | 15 | 17 | 18 | 19 | 20 | 20 |
| 14 | 13 Be-Shallaḥ | 14 | 12 | 14 | 14 | 16 | 16 | 18 | 19 | 20 | 21 | 21 |
| 15 | 14 | 15 | 13 Ta'anit Esther | 15 Pesaḥ | 15 | 17 | 17 Balak | 19 | 20 | 21 Hoshana Rabba | 22 | 22 |
| 16 | 15 | 16 | 14 Purim | 16 Omer | 16 | 18 | 18 Fast | 20 | 21 Ki Tavo | 22 Shemini Aẓeret | 23 | 23 Va-Yeshev |
| 17 | 16 | 17 | 15 Shushan Purim | 17 | 17 | 19 Be-Ha'alotkha | 19 | 21 | 22 | 23 Simḥat Torah Ve-Zot Ha-Berakhah | 24 | 24 |
| 18 | 17 | 18 Ki Tissa | 16 Ẓav | 18 Ḥol ha-Mo'ed | 18 Lag ba-Omer | 20 | 20 | 22 | 23 | 24 | 25 Ḥayyei Sarah | 25 Ḥanukkah 1 |
| 19 | 18 | 19 | 17 | 19 | 19 | 21 | 21 | 23 Ekev | 24 | 25 | 26 | 26 2 |
| 20 | 19 | 20 | 18 | 20 | 20 Be-Har | 22 | 22 | 24 | 25 | 26 | 27 | 27 3 |
| 21 | 20 Yitro | 21 | 19 | 21 Pesaḥ | 21 | 23 | 23 | 25 | 26 | 27 Bereshit | 28 | 28 4 |
| 22 | 21 | 22 | 20 | 22 | 22 | 24 | 24 Pinḥas | 26 | 27 | 28 | 29 | 29 5 |
| 23 | 22 | 23 | 21 | 23 | 23 | 25 | 25 | 27 | 28 Niẓẓavim | 29 | 30 R. Ḥ. | 30 R. Ḥ. Mi-Keẓ 6 |
| 24 | 23 | 24 | 22 | 24 | 24 | 26 Shelaḥ | 26 | 28 | 29 | 30 R. Ḥ. | 1 Kislev R. Ḥ. | 1 Tevet R. Ḥ. 7 |
| 25 | 24 | 25 Va-Yakhel Shekalim | 23 Shemini Parah | 25 | 25 | 27 | 27 | 29 | 1 Tishri Rosh Ha-Shanah | 1 Ḥeshvan R. Ḥ. | 2 Toledot | 2 8 |
| 26 | 25 | 26 | 24 | 26 | 26 | 28 | 28 | 30 R. Ḥ. Re'eh | 2 | 2 | 3 | 3 |
| 27 | 26 | 27 | 25 | 27 | 27 Be-Ḥukkotai | 29 | 29 | 1 Elul R. Ḥ. | 3 Fast | 3 | 4 | 4 |
| 28 | 27 Mishpatim | 28 | 26 | 28 | 28 | 30 R. Ḥ. | 1 Av R. Ḥ. | 2 | 4 | 4 No'aḥ | 5 | 5 |
| 29 | 28 | | 27 | 29 Aḥarei Mot | 29 | 1 Tammuz R. Ḥ. | 2 Mattot Masei | 3 | 5 | 5 | 6 | 6 |
| 30 | 29 | | 28 | 30 R. Ḥ. | 1 Sivan R. Ḥ. | 2 | 3 | 4 | 6 Va-Yelekh Shabbat Shuvah | 6 | 7 | 7 Va-Yiggash |
| 31 | 30 R. Ḥ. | | 29 | | 2 | | 4 | 5 | | 7 | | 8 |

# 1996

**5756/57** תשנ״ו / תשנ״ז

| | January | February | March | April | May | June | July | August | September | October | November | December |
|---|---|---|---|---|---|---|---|---|---|---|---|---|
| 1 | 9 Tevet | 11 | 10 | 12 | 12 | 14 Naso | 14 | 16 | 17 | 18 | 19 | 20 |
| 2 | 10 Fast | 12 | 11 Teẓavveh Zakhor | 13 | 13 | 15 | 15 | 17 | 18 | 19 Ḥol ha-Mo'ed | 20 Va-Yera | 21 |
| 3 | 11 | 13 Be-Shallaḥ | 12 | 14 | 14 | 16 | 16 | 18 Ekev | 19 | 20 | 21 | 22 |
| 4 | 12 | 14 | 13 Ta'anit Esther | 15 Pesaḥ | 15 Emor | 17 | 17 Fast | 19 | 20 | 21 Hoshana Rabba | 22 | 23 |
| 5 | 13 | 15 | 14 Purim | 16 Omer | 16 | 18 | 18 | 20 | 21 | 22 Shemini Aẓeret | 23 | 24 |
| 6 | 14 Va-Yeḥi | 16 | 15 Shushan Purim | 17 | 17 | 19 | 19 Pinḥas | 21 | 22 | 23 Simḥat Torah Ve-Zot Ha-Berakhah | 24 | 25 Ḥanukkah 1 |
| 7 | 15 | 17 | 16 | 18 Ḥol ha-Mo'ed | 18 Lag ba-Omer | 20 | 20 | 22 | 23 Niẓẓavim Va-Yelekh | 24 | 25 | 26 Va-Yeshev 2 |
| 8 | 16 | 18 | 17 | 19 | 19 | 21 Be-Ha'alotkha | 21 | 23 | 24 | 25 | 26 | 27 3 |
| 9 | 17 | 19 | 18 Ki Tissa Parah | 20 | 20 | 22 | 22 | 24 | 25 | 26 | 27 Ḥayyei Sarah | 28 4 |
| 10 | 18 | 20 Yitro | 19 | 21 Pesaḥ | 21 | 23 | 23 | 25 Re'eh | 26 | 27 | 28 | 29 5 |
| 11 | 19 | 21 | 20 | 22 | 22 Be-Har Be-Ḥukkotai | 24 | 24 | 26 | 27 | 28 | 29 | 1 Tevet R. Ḥ. 6 |
| 12 | 20 | 22 | 21 | 23 | 23 | 25 | 25 | 27 | 28 | 29 Bereshit | 1 Kislev R. Ḥ. | 2 7 |
| 13 | 21 Shemot | 23 | 22 | 24 Shemini | 24 | 26 | 26 Mattot Masei | 28 | 29 | 30 R. Ḥ. | 2 | 3 8 |
| 14 | 22 | 24 | 23 | 25 | 25 | 27 | 27 | 29 | 1 Tishri Rosh Ha-Shanah | 1 Ḥeshvan R. Ḥ. | 3 | 4 Mi-Keẓ |
| 15 | 23 | 25 | 24 | 26 | 26 | 28 Shelaḥ | 28 | 30 R. Ḥ. | 2 | 2 | 4 | 5 |
| 16 | 24 | 26 | 25 Va-Yakhel Pekudei Ha-Ḥodesh | 27 | 27 | 29 | 29 | 1 Elul R. Ḥ. | 3 Fast | 3 | 5 Toledot | 6 |
| 17 | 25 | 27 Mishpatim Shekalim | 26 | 28 | 28 | 30 R. Ḥ. | 1 Av R. Ḥ. | 2 Shofetim | 4 | 4 | 6 | 7 |
| 18 | 26 | 28 | 27 | 29 | 29 Be-Midbar | 1 Tammuz R. Ḥ. | 2 | 3 | 5 | 5 | 7 | 8 |
| 19 | 27 | 29 | 28 | 30 R. Ḥ. | 1 Sivan R. Ḥ. | 2 | 3 | 4 | 6 | 6 No'aḥ | 8 | 9 |
| 20 | 28 Va-Era | 30 R. Ḥ. | 29 | 1 Iyyar R. Ḥ. Tazri'a Meẓora | 2 | 3 | 4 Devarim | 5 | 7 | 7 | 9 | 10 Fast |
| 21 | 29 | 1 Adar R. Ḥ. | 1 Nisan R. Ḥ. | 2 | 3 | 4 | 5 | 6 | 8 Ha'azinu Shabbat Shuvah | 8 | 10 | 11 Va-Yiggash |
| 22 | 1 Shevat R. Ḥ. | 2 | 2 | 3 | 4 | 5 Koraḥ | 6 | 7 | 9 | 9 | 11 | 12 |
| 23 | 2 | 3 | 3 Va-Yikra | 4 | 5 | 6 | 7 | 8 | 10 Yom Kippur | 10 | 12 Va-Yeẓe | 13 |
| 24 | 3 | 4 Terumah | 4 | 5 Yom ha-Aẓma'ut | 6 Shavuot | 7 | 8 | 9 Ki Teẓe | 11 | 11 | 13 | 14 |
| 25 | 4 | 5 | 5 | 6 | 7 | 8 | 9 Tishah be-Av | 10 | 12 | 12 | 14 | 15 |
| 26 | 5 | 6 | 6 | 7 | 8 | 9 | 10 | 11 | 13 | 13 Lekh Lekha | 15 | 16 |
| 27 | 6 Bo | 7 | 7 | 8 Aḥarei Mot Kedoshim | 9 | 10 | 11 Va-Etḥannan | 12 | 14 | 14 | 16 | 17 |
| 28 | 7 | 8 | 8 | 9 | 10 | 11 | 12 | 13 | 15 Sukkot | 15 | 17 | 18 Va-Yeḥi |
| 29 | 8 | 9 | 9 | 10 | 11 | 12 Ḥukkat Balak | 13 | 14 | 16 | 16 | 18 | 19 |
| 30 | 9 | | 10 Ẓav Shabbat ha-Gadol | 11 | 12 | 13 | 14 | 15 | 17 Ḥol ha-Mo'ed | 17 | 19 Va-Yishlaḥ | 20 |
| 31 | 10 | | 11 | | 13 | | 15 | 16 Ki Tavo | | 18 | | 21 |

# 1997

**5757/58** תשנ״ז / תשנ״ח

| | January | February | March | April | May | June | July | August | September | October | November | December |
|---|---|---|---|---|---|---|---|---|---|---|---|---|
| 1 | 22 Tevet | 24 *Yitro* | 22 *Ki Tissa* | 23 | 24 | 25 | 26 | 27 | 29 | 29 | 1 R. H. Heshvan *No'ah* | 2 |
| 2 | 23 | 25 | 23 | 24 | 25 | 26 | 27 | 28 *Mattot Masei* | 30 R. H. | 1 Tishri Rosh Ha-Shanah | 2 | 3 |
| 3 | 24 | 26 | 24 | 25 | 26 *Aharei Mot* | 27 | 28 | 29 | 1 Elul R. H. | 2 | 3 | 4 |
| 4 | 25 *Shemot* | 27 | 25 | 26 | 27 | 28 | 29 | 1 Av R. H. | 2 | 3 *Ha'azinu* Shabbat Shuvah | 4 | 5 |
| 5 | 26 | 28 | 26 | 27 *Shemini* Ha-Hodesh | 28 | 29 | 30 R. H. *Korah* | 2 | 3 | 4 Fast | 5 | 6 |
| 6 | 27 | 29 | 27 | 28 | 29 | 1 Sivan R. H. | 1 R. H. Tammuz | 3 | 4 *Shofetim* | 5 | 6 | 7 *Va-Yeze* |
| 7 | 28 | 30 R. H. | 28 | 29 | 30 R. H. | 2 *Be-Midbar* | 2 | 4 | 5 | 6 | 7 | 8 |
| 8 | 29 | 1 Adar I R. H. *Mishpatim* | 29 *Va-Yakhel* Shekalim | 1 Nisan R. H. | 1 Iyyar R. H. | 3 | 3 | 5 | 6 | 7 | 8 *Lekh Lekha* | 9 |
| 9 | 1 R. H. Shevat | 2 | 30 R. H. | 2 | 2 | 4 | 4 | 6 *Devarim* | 7 | 8 | 9 | 10 |
| 10 | 2 | 3 | 1 Adar II R. H. | 3 | 3 *Kedoshim* | 5 | 5 | 7 | 8 | 9 | 10 | 11 |
| 11 | 3 *Va-Era* | 4 | 2 | 4 | 4 | 6 Shavuot | 6 | 8 | 9 | 10 Yom Kippur | 11 | 12 |
| 12 | 4 | 5 | 3 | 5 *Tazri'a* | 5 Yom ha-Azma'ut | 7 | 7 *Hukkat* | 9 Tishah be-Av | 10 | 11 | 12 | 13 |
| 13 | 5 | 6 | 4 | 6 | 6 | 8 | 8 | 10 | 11 *Ki Teze* | 12 | 13 | 14 *Va-Yishlah* |
| 14 | 6 | 7 | 5 | 7 | 7 | 9 *Naso* | 9 | 11 | 12 | 13 | 14 | 15 |
| 15 | 7 | 8 *Terumah* | 6 *Pekudei* | 8 | 8 | 10 | 10 | 12 | 13 | 14 | 15 *Va-Yera* | 16 |
| 16 | 8 | 9 | 7 | 9 | 9 | 11 | 11 | 13 *Va-Ethannan* | 14 | 15 Sukkot | 16 | 17 |
| 17 | 9 | 10 | 8 | 10 | 10 *Emor* | 12 | 12 | 14 | 15 | 16 | 17 | 18 |
| 18 | 10 *Bo* | 11 | 9 | 11 | 11 | 13 | 13 | 15 | 16 | 17 Hol ha-Mo'ed | 18 | 19 |
| 19 | 11 | 12 | 10 | 12 *Mezora* Shabbat ha-Gadol | 12 | 14 | 14 *Balak* | 16 | 17 | 18 | 19 | 20 |
| 20 | 12 | 13 | 11 Ta'anit Esther | 13 | 13 | 15 | 15 | 17 | 18 *Ki Tavo* | 19 | 20 | 21 *Va-Yeshev* |
| 21 | 13 | 14 | 12 | 14 | 14 | 16 *Be-Ha'alotkha* | 16 | 18 | 19 | 20 | 21 | 22 |
| 22 | 14 | 15 *Tezavveh* | 13 *Va-Yikra* Zakhor | 15 Pesah | 15 | 17 | 17 Fast | 19 | 20 | 21 Hoshana Rabba | 22 *Hayyei Sarah* | 23 |
| 23 | 15 | 16 | 14 Purim | 16 Omer | 16 | 18 | 18 | 20 *Ekev* | 21 | 22 Shemini Azeret | 23 | 24 |
| 24 | 16 | 17 | 15 Shushan Purim | 17 | 17 *Be-Har* | 19 | 19 | 21 | 22 | 23 Simhat Torah *Ve-Zot Ha-Berakhah* | 24 | 25 Hanukkah 1 |
| 25 | 17 *Be-Shallah* | 18 | 16 | 18 Hol ha-Mo'ed | 18 Lag ba-Omer | 20 | 20 | 22 | 23 | 24 *Bereshit* | 25 | 26 2 |
| 26 | 18 | 19 | 17 | 19 | 19 | 21 | 21 *Pinhas* | 23 | 24 | 25 | 26 | 27 3 |
| 27 | 19 | 20 | 18 | 20 | 20 | 22 | 22 | 24 | 25 *Nizzavim Va-Yelekh* | 26 | 27 | 28 *Mi-Kez* 4 |
| 28 | 20 | 21 | 19 | 21 Pesah | 21 | 23 *Shelah* | 23 | 25 | 26 | 27 | 28 | 29 5 |
| 29 | 21 | | 20 *Zav* Parah | 22 | 22 | 24 | 24 | 26 | 27 | 28 | 29 *Toledot* | 30 R. H. 6 |
| 30 | 22 | | 21 | 23 | 23 | 25 | 25 | 27 *Re'eh* | 28 | 29 | 1 Kislev R. H. | 1 Tevet R. H. 7 |
| 31 | 23 | | 22 | | 24 *Be-Hukkotai* | | 26 | 28 | | 30 R. H. | | 2 8 |

# 1998

**5758/59** תשנ״ח / תשנ״ט

| | January | February | March | April | May | June | July | August | September | October | November | December |
|---|---|---|---|---|---|---|---|---|---|---|---|---|
| 1 | 3 Tevet | 5 | 3 | 5 | 5 | 7 | 7 | 9 Tishah be-Av *Devarim* | 10 | 11 | 12 | 12 |
| 2 | 4 | 6 | 4 | 6 | 6 *Tazri'a Mezora* | 8 | 8 | 10 Fast | 11 | 12 | 13 | 13 |
| 3 | 5 *Va-Yiggash* | 7 | 5 | 7 | 7 | 9 | 9 | 11 | 12 | 13 *Ha'azinu* | 14 | 14 |
| 4 | 6 | 8 | 6 | 8 *Zav* Shabbat ha-Gadol | 8 | 10 | 10 *Hukkat* | 12 | 13 | 14 | 15 | 15 |
| 5 | 7 | 9 | 7 | 9 | 9 | 11 | 11 | 13 | 14 *Ki Teze* | 15 Sukkot | 16 | 16 *Va-Yishlah* |
| 6 | 8 | 10 | 8 | 10 | 10 | 12 *Naso* | 12 | 14 | 15 | 16 | 17 | 17 |
| 7 | 9 | 11 *Be-Shallah* | 9 *Tezavveh* Zakhor | 11 | 11 | 13 | 13 | 15 | 16 | 17 | 18 *Va-Yera* | 18 |
| 8 | 10 Fast | 12 | 10 | 12 | 12 | 14 | 14 | 16 *Va-Ethannan* | 17 | 18 Hol ha-Mo'ed | 19 | 19 |
| 9 | 11 | 13 | 11 | 13 | 13 *Aharei Mot Kedoshim* | 15 | 15 | 17 | 18 | 19 | 20 | 20 |
| 10 | 12 *Va-Yehi* | 14 | 12 | 14 | 14 | 16 | 16 | 18 | 19 | 20 | 21 | 21 |
| 11 | 13 | 15 | 13 Ta'anit Esther | 15 Pesah | 15 | 17 | 17 *Balak* | 19 | 20 | 21 Hoshana Rabba | 22 | 22 |
| 12 | 14 | 16 | 14 Purim | 16 Omer | 16 | 18 | 18 Fast | 20 | 21 *Ki Tavo* | 22 Shemini Azeret | 23 | 23 *Va-Yeshev* |
| 13 | 15 | 17 | 15 Shushan Purim | 17 | 17 | 19 *Be-Ha'alotkha* | 19 | 21 | 22 | 23 Simhat Torah *Ve-Zot Ha-Berakhah* | 24 | 24 |
| 14 | 16 | 18 *Yitro* | 16 *Ki Tissa* | 18 Hol ha-Mo'ed | 18 Lag ba-Omer | 20 | 20 | 22 | 23 | 24 | 25 *Hayyei Sarah* | 25 Hanukkah 1 |
| 15 | 17 | 19 | 17 | 19 | 19 | 21 | 21 | 23 *Ekev* | 24 | 25 | 26 | 26 2 |
| 16 | 18 | 20 | 18 | 20 | 20 *Emor* | 22 | 22 | 24 | 25 | 26 | 27 | 27 3 |
| 17 | 19 *Shemot* | 21 | 19 | 21 Pesah | 21 | 23 | 23 | 25 | 26 | 27 *Bereshit* | 28 | 28 4 |
| 18 | 20 | 22 | 20 | 22 | 22 | 24 | 24 *Pinhas* | 26 | 27 | 28 | 29 | 29 5 |
| 19 | 21 | 23 | 21 | 23 | 23 | 25 | 25 | 27 | 28 *Nizzavim* | 29 | 30 R. H. | 30 R. H. *Mi-Kez* 6 |
| 20 | 22 | 24 | 22 | 24 | 24 | 26 *Shelah* | 26 | 28 | 29 | 30 R. H. | 1 Kislev R. H. | 1 Tevet R. H. 7 |
| 21 | 23 | 25 *Mishpatim* Shekalim | 23 *Va-Yakhel Pekudei* Parah | 25 | 25 | 27 | 27 | 29 | 1 Tishri Rosh Ha-Shanah | 1 R. H. Heshvan | 2 *Toledot* | 2 8 |
| 22 | 24 | 26 | 24 | 26 | 26 | 28 | 28 | 30 R. H. *Re'eh* | 2 | 2 | 3 | 3 |
| 23 | 25 | 27 | 25 | 27 | 27 *Be-Har Be-Hukkotai* | 29 | 29 | 1 Elul R. H. | 3 Fast | 3 | 4 | 4 |
| 24 | 26 *Va-Era* | 28 | 26 | 28 | 28 | 30 R. H. | 1 Av R. H. | 2 | 4 | 4 *No'ah* | 5 | 5 |
| 25 | 27 | 29 | 27 | 29 *Shemini* | 29 | 1 R. H. Tammuz | 2 *Mattot Masei* | 3 | 5 | 5 | 6 | 6 |
| 26 | 28 | 30 R. H. | 28 | 30 R. H. | 1 Sivan R. H. | 2 | 3 | 4 | 6 *Va-Yelekh* Shabbat Shuvah | 6 | 7 | 7 *Va-Yiggash* |
| 27 | 29 | 1 Adar R. H. | 29 | 1 Iyyar R. H. | 2 | 3 *Korah* | 4 | 5 | 7 | 7 | 8 | 8 |
| 28 | 1 R. H. Shevat | 2 *Terumah* | 1 R. H. *Va-Yikra* Nisan Ha-Hodesh | 2 | 3 | 4 | 5 | 6 | 8 | 8 | 9 *Va-Yeze* | 9 |
| 29 | 2 | | 2 | 3 | 4 | 5 | 6 | 7 *Shofetim* | 9 | 9 | 10 | 10 Fast |
| 30 | 3 | | 3 | 4 Yom ha-Azma'ut | 5 *Be-Midbar* | 6 | 7 | 8 | 10 Yom Kippur | 10 | 11 | 11 |
| 31 | 4 *Bo* | | 4 | | 6 Shavuot | | 8 | 9 | | 11 *Lekh Lekha* | | 12 |

# 1999

**5759/60** תשנ״ט / תש״ס

| | January | February | March | April | May | June | July | August | September | October | November | December |
|---|---|---|---|---|---|---|---|---|---|---|---|---|
| 1 | 13 Tevet | 15 | 13 Ta'anit Esther | 15 Pesah | 15 Emor | 17 | 17 Fast | 19 | 20 | 21 Hoshana Rabba | 22 | 22 |
| 2 | 14 Va-Yeḥi | 16 | 14 Purim | 16 Omer | 16 | 18 | 18 | 20 | 21 | 22 Shemini Aẓeret | 23 | 23 |
| 3 | 15 | 17 | 15 Shushan Purim | 17 Ḥol ha-Mo'ed | 17 | 19 | 19 Pinḥas | 21 | 22 | 23 Simḥat Torah Ve-Zot Ha-Berakhah | 24 | 24 |
| 4 | 16 | 18 | 16 | 18 | 18 Lag ba-Omer | 20 | 20 | 22 | 23 Niẓẓavim Va-Yelekh | 24 | 25 | 25 Va-Yeshev Ḥanukkah 1 |
| 5 | 17 | 19 | 17 | 19 | 19 | 21 Be-Ha'alotkha | 21 | 23 | 24 | 25 | 26 | 26 2 |
| 6 | 18 | 20 Yitro | 18 Ki Tissa Parah | 20 | 20 | 22 | 22 | 24 | 25 | 26 | 27 Ḥayyei Sarah | 27 3 |
| 7 | 19 | 21 | 19 | 21 Pesah | 21 | 23 | 23 | 25 Re'eh | 26 | 27 | 28 | 28 4 |
| 8 | 20 | 22 | 20 | 22 | 22 Be-Har Be-Ḥukkotai | 24 | 24 | 26 | 27 | 28 | 29 | 29 5 |
| 9 | 21 Shemot | 23 | 21 | 23 | 23 | 25 | 25 | 27 | 28 | 29 Bereshit | 30 R. H. | 30 R. H. 6 |
| 10 | 22 | 24 | 22 | 24 Shemini | 24 | 26 | 26 Mattot Masei | 28 | 29 | 30 R. H. | 1 Kislev R. H. | 1 Tevet R. H. 7 |
| 11 | 23 | 25 | 23 | 25 | 25 | 27 | 27 | 29 | 1 Tishri Rosh Ha-Shanah | 1 Ḥeshvan R. H. | 2 | 2 Mi-Keẓ 8 |
| 12 | 24 | 26 | 24 | 26 | 26 | 28 Shelaḥ | 28 | 30 R. H. | 2 | 2 | 3 | 3 |
| 13 | 25 | 27 Mishpatim Shekalim | 25 Va-Yakhel Pekudei Ha-Ḥodesh | 27 | 27 | 29 | 29 | 1 Elul R. H. | 3 Fast | 3 | 4 Toledot | 4 |
| 14 | 26 | 28 | 26 | 28 | 28 | 30 R. H. | 1 Av R. H. | 2 Shofetim | 4 | 4 | 5 | 5 |
| 15 | 27 | 29 | 27 | 29 | 29 Be-Midbar | 1 Tammuz R. H. | 2 | 3 | 5 | 5 | 6 | 6 |
| 16 | 28 Va-Era | 30 R. H. | 28 | 30 R. H. | 1 Sivan R. H. | 2 | 3 | 4 | 6 | 6 No'aḥ | 7 | 7 |
| 17 | 29 | 1 Adar R. H. | 29 | 1 Iyyar R. H. Tazri'a Meẓora | 2 | 3 | 4 Devarim | 5 | 7 | 7 | 8 | 8 |
| 18 | 1 Shevat R. H. | 2 | 1 Nisan R. H. | 2 | 3 | 4 | 5 | 6 | 8 Ha'azinu Shabbat Shuvah | 8 | 9 | 9 Va-Yiggash |
| 19 | 2 | 3 | 2 | 3 | 4 | 5 Koraḥ | 6 | 7 | 9 | 9 | 10 | 10 Fast |
| 20 | 3 | 4 Terumah | 3 Va-Yikra | 4 | 5 | 6 | 7 | 8 | 10 Yom Kippur | 10 | 11 Va-Yeẓe | 11 |
| 21 | 4 | 5 | 4 | 5 Yom ha-Aẓma'ut | 6 Shavuot | 7 | 8 | 9 Ki Teẓe | 11 | 11 | 12 | 12 |
| 22 | 5 | 6 | 5 | 6 | 7 | 8 | 9 Tishah be-Av | 10 | 12 | 12 | 13 | 13 |
| 23 | 6 Bo | 7 | 6 | 7 | 8 | 9 | 10 | 11 | 13 | 13 Lekh Lekha | 14 | 14 |
| 24 | 7 | 8 | 7 | 8 Aḥarei Mot Kedoshim | 9 | 10 | 11 Va-Etḥannan | 12 | 14 | 14 | 15 | 15 |
| 25 | 8 | 9 | 8 | 9 | 10 | 11 | 12 | 13 | 15 Sukkot | 15 | 16 | 16 Va-Yeḥi |
| 26 | 9 | 10 | 9 | 10 | 11 | 12 Ḥukkat Balak | 13 | 14 | 16 | 16 | 17 | 17 |
| 27 | 10 | 11 Teẓavveh Zakhor | 10 Ẓav Shabbat ha-Gadol | 11 | 12 | 13 | 14 | 15 | 17 Ḥol ha-Mo'ed | 17 | 18 Va-Yishlaḥ | 18 |
| 28 | 11 | 12 | 11 | 12 | 13 | 14 | 15 | 16 Ki Tavo | 18 | 18 | 19 | 19 |
| 29 | 12 | | 12 | 13 | 14 Naso | 15 | 16 | 17 | 19 | 19 | 20 | 20 |
| 30 | 13 Be-Shallaḥ | | 13 | 14 | 15 | 16 | 17 | 18 | 20 | 20 Va-Yera | 21 | 21 |
| 31 | 14 | | 14 | | 16 | | 18 Ekev | 19 | | 21 | | 22 |

# 2000

**5760/61** תש״ס / תשס״א

| | January | February | March | April | May | June | July | August | September | October | November | December |
|---|---|---|---|---|---|---|---|---|---|---|---|---|
| 1 | 23 Tevet Shemot | 25 | 24 | 25 Shemini Ha-Ḥodesh | 26 | 27 | 28 Shelaḥ | 29 | 1 Elul R. H. | 2 Rosh Ha-Shanah | 3 | 4 |
| 2 | 24 | 26 | 25 | 26 | 27 | 28 | 29 | 1 Av R. H. | 2 Shofetim | 3 Fast | 4 | 5 Toledot |
| 3 | 25 | 27 | 26 | 27 | 28 | 29 Be-Midbar | 30 R. H. | 2 | 3 | 4 | 5 | 6 |
| 4 | 26 | 28 | 27 Va-Yakhel Shekalim | 28 | 29 | 1 Sivan R. H. | 1 Tammuz R. H. | 3 | 4 | 5 | 6 No'aḥ | 7 |
| 5 | 27 | 29 Mishpatim | 28 | 29 | 30 R. H. | 2 | 2 | 4 Devarim | 5 | 6 | 7 | 8 |
| 6 | 28 | 30 R. H. | 29 | 1 Nisan R. H. | 1 Iyyar R. H. Kedoshim | 3 | 3 | 5 | 6 | 7 | 8 | 9 |
| 7 | 29 | 1 Adar I R. H. | 30 R. H. | 2 | 2 | 4 | 4 | 6 | 7 | 8 Ha'azinu Shabbat Shuvah | 9 | 10 |
| 8 | 1 Shevat R. H. Va-Era | 2 | 1 Adar II R. H. | 3 Tazri'a | 3 | 5 | 5 Koraḥ | 7 | 8 | 9 | 10 | 11 |
| 9 | 2 | 3 | 2 | 4 | 4 | 6 Shavuot | 6 | 8 | 9 Ki Teẓe | 10 Yom Kippur | 11 | 12 Va-Yeẓe |
| 10 | 3 | 4 | 3 | 5 | 5 Yom ha-Aẓma'ut | 7 | 7 | 9 Tishah be-Av | 10 | 11 | 12 | 13 |
| 11 | 4 | 5 | 4 Pekudei | 6 | 6 | 8 | 8 | 10 | 11 | 12 | 13 Lekh Lekha | 14 |
| 12 | 5 | 6 Terumah | 5 | 7 | 7 | 9 | 9 | 11 Va-Etḥannan | 12 | 13 | 14 | 15 |
| 13 | 6 | 7 | 6 | 8 | 8 Emor | 10 | 10 | 12 | 13 | 14 | 15 | 16 |
| 14 | 7 | 8 | 7 | 9 | 9 | 11 | 11 | 13 | 14 | 15 Sukkot | 16 | 17 |
| 15 | 8 Bo | 9 | 8 | 10 Meẓora Shabbat ha-Gadol | 10 | 12 | 12 Ḥukkat Balak | 14 | 15 | 16 | 17 | 18 |
| 16 | 9 | 10 | 9 | 11 | 11 | 13 | 13 | 15 | 16 Ki Tavo | 17 Ḥol ha-Mo'ed | 18 | 19 Va-Yishlaḥ |
| 17 | 10 | 11 | 10 | 12 | 12 | 14 Naso | 14 | 16 | 17 | 18 | 19 | 20 |
| 18 | 11 | 12 | 11 Va-Yikra Zakhor | 13 | 13 | 15 | 15 | 17 | 18 | 19 | 20 Va-Yera | 21 |
| 19 | 12 | 13 Teẓavveh | 12 | 14 | 14 | 16 | 16 | 18 Ekev | 19 | 20 | 21 | 22 |
| 20 | 13 | 14 | 13 Ta'anit Esther | 15 Pesaḥ | 15 Be-Har | 17 | 17 Fast | 19 | 20 | 21 Hoshana Rabba | 22 | 23 |
| 21 | 14 | 15 | 14 Purim | 16 Omer | 16 | 18 | 18 | 20 | 21 | 22 Shemini Aẓeret | 23 | 24 |
| 22 | 15 Be-Shallaḥ | 16 | 15 Shushan Purim | 17 Ḥol ha-Mo'ed | 17 | 19 | 19 Pinḥas | 21 | 22 | 23 Simḥat Torah Ve-Zot Ha-Berakhah | 24 | 25 Ḥanukkah 1 |
| 23 | 16 | 17 | 16 | 18 | 18 Lag ba-Omer | 20 | 20 | 22 | 23 Niẓẓavim Va-Yelekh | 24 | 25 | 26 Va-Yeshev 2 |
| 24 | 17 | 18 | 17 | 19 | 19 | 21 Be-Ha'alotkha | 21 | 23 | 24 | 25 | 26 | 27 3 |
| 25 | 18 | 19 | 18 Ẓav Paraḥ | 20 | 20 | 22 | 22 | 24 | 25 | 26 | 27 Ḥayyei Sarah | 28 4 |
| 26 | 19 | 20 Ki Tissa | 19 | 21 Pesaḥ | 21 | 23 | 23 | 25 Re'eh | 26 | 27 | 28 | 29 5 |
| 27 | 20 | 21 | 20 | 22 | 22 Be-Ḥukkotai | 24 | 24 | 26 | 27 | 28 | 29 | 1 Tevet R. H. 6 |
| 28 | 21 | 22 | 21 | 23 | 23 | 25 | 25 | 27 | 28 | 29 Bereshit | 1 Kislev R. H. | 2 7 |
| 29 | 22 Yitro | 23 | 22 | 24 Aḥarei Mot | 24 | 26 | 26 Mattot Masei | 28 | 29 | 30 R. H. | 2 | 3 8 |
| 30 | 23 | | 23 | 25 | 25 | 27 | 27 | 29 | 1 Tishri Rosh Ha-Shanah | 1 Ḥeshvan R. H. | 3 | 4 Mi-Keẓ |
| 31 | 24 | | 24 | | 26 | | 28 | 30 R. H. | | 2 | | 5 |

# 2001

**5761/62** תשס"א / תשס"ב

| | January | February | March | April | May | June | July | August | September | October | November | December |
|---|---|---|---|---|---|---|---|---|---|---|---|---|
| 1 | 6 Tevet | 8 | 6 | 8 | 8 | 10 | 10 | 12 | **13** Ki Teẓe | 14 | 15 | **16** Va-Yishlaḥ |
| 2 | 7 | 9 | 7 | 9 | 9 | **11** Naso | 11 | 13 | 14 | 15 Sukkot | 16 | 17 |
| 3 | 8 | **10** Bo | **8** Terumah Zakhor | 10 | 10 | 12 | 12 | 14 | 15 | 16 | **17** Va-Yera | 18 |
| 4 | 9 | 11 | 9 | 11 | 11 | 13 | 13 | **15** Va-Etḥannan | 16 | 17 Ḥol ha-Mo'ed | 18 | 19 |
| 5 | 10 Fast | 12 | 10 | 12 | **12** Aḥarei Mot Kedoshim | 14 | 14 | 16 | 17 | 18 | 19 | 20 |
| 6 | **11** Va-Yiggash | 13 | 11 | 13 | 13 | 15 | 15 | 17 | 18 | **19** | 20 | 21 |
| 7 | 12 | 14 | 12 | **14** Ẓav Shabbat ha-Gadol | 14 | 16 | **16** Balak | 18 | 19 | 20 | 21 | 22 |
| 8 | 13 | 15 | 13 Ta'anit Esther | 15 Pesaḥ | 15 | 17 | 17 Fast | 19 | **20** Ki Tavo | 21 Hoshana Rabba | 22 | **23** Va-Yeshev |
| 9 | 14 | 16 | 14 Purim | 16 Omer | 16 | **18** Be-Ha'alotkha | 18 | 20 | 21 | 22 Shemini Aẓeret | 23 | 24 |
| 10 | 15 | **17** Be-Shallaḥ | **15** Teẓavveh Shushan Purim | 17 Ḥol ha-Mo'ed | 17 | 19 | 19 | 21 | 22 | 23 Simḥat Torah Ve-Zot Ha-Berakhah | **24** Ḥayyei Sarah | 25 1 |
| 11 | 16 | 18 | 16 | 18 | 18 Lag ba-Omer | 20 | 20 | **22** Ekev | 23 | 24 | 25 | 26 2 |
| 12 | 17 | 19 | 17 | 19 | **19** Emor | 21 | 21 | 23 | 24 | 25 | 26 | 27 3 |
| 13 | **18** Va-Yeḥi | 20 | 18 | 20 | 20 | 22 | 22 | 24 | 25 | **26** Bereshit | 27 | 28 4 |
| 14 | 19 | 21 | 19 | **21** Pesaḥ | 21 | 23 | **23** Pinḥas | 25 | 26 | 27 | 28 | 29 5 |
| 15 | 20 | 22 | 20 | 22 | 22 | 24 | 24 | 26 | **27** Niẓẓavim | 28 | 29 | **30** R. Ḥ. Mi-Keẓ 6 |
| 16 | 21 | 23 | 21 | 23 | 23 | **25** Shelaḥ | 25 | 27 | 28 | 29 | 1 Kislev R. Ḥ. | 1 Tevet R. Ḥ. 7 |
| 17 | 22 | **24** Yitro | **22** Ki Tissa Parah | 24 | 24 | 26 | 26 | 28 | 29 | 30 R. Ḥ. | **2** Toledot | 2 8 |
| 18 | 23 | 25 | 23 | 25 | 25 | 27 | 27 | **29** Re'eh | 1 Tishri Rosh Ha-Shanah | 1 Ḥeshvan R. Ḥ. | 3 | 3 |
| 19 | 24 | 26 | 24 | 26 | **26** Be-Har Be-Ḥukkotai | 28 | 28 | 30 R. Ḥ. | 2 | 2 | 4 | 4 |
| 20 | **25** Shemot | 27 | 25 | 27 | 27 | 29 | 29 | 1 Elul R. Ḥ. | 3 Fast | **3** No'aḥ | 5 | 5 |
| 21 | 26 | 28 | 26 | **28** Shemini | 28 | 30 R. Ḥ. | **1** Av R. Ḥ. Mattot Masei | 2 | 4 | 4 | 6 | 6 |
| 22 | 27 | 29 | 27 | 29 | 29 | 1 Tammuz R. Ḥ. | 2 | 3 | **5** Va-Yelekh Shabbat Shuvah | 5 | 7 | **7** Va-Yiggash |
| 23 | 28 | 30 R. Ḥ. | 28 | 30 R. Ḥ. | 1 Sivan R. Ḥ. | **2** Koraḥ | 3 | 4 | 6 | 6 | 8 | 8 |
| 24 | 29 | **1** Adar R. Ḥ. Mishpatim Shekalim | **29** Va-Yakhel Pekudei Ha-Ḥodesh | 1 Iyyar R. Ḥ. | 2 | 3 | 4 | 5 | 7 | 7 | **9** Va-Yeẓe | 9 |
| 25 | 1 Shevat R. Ḥ. | 2 | 1 Nisan R. Ḥ. | 2 | 3 | 4 | 5 | **6** Shofetim | 8 | 8 | 10 | 10 Fast |
| 26 | 2 | 3 | 2 | 3 Yom ha-Aẓma'ut | **4** Be-Midbar | 5 | 6 | 7 | 9 | 9 | 11 | 11 |
| 27 | **3** Va-Era | 4 | 3 | 4 | 5 | 6 | 7 | 8 | 10 Yom Kippur | **10** Lekh Lekha | 12 | 12 |
| 28 | 4 | 5 | 4 | **5** Tazri'a Meẓora | 6 Shavuot | 7 | **8** Devarim | 9 | 11 | 11 | 13 | 13 |
| 29 | 5 | | 5 | 6 | 7 | 8 | 9 Tishah be-Av | 10 | **12** Ha'azinu | 12 | 14 | **14** Va-Yeḥi |
| 30 | 6 | | 6 | 7 | 8 | **9** Ḥukkat | 10 | 11 | 13 | 13 | 15 | 15 |
| 31 | 7 | | **7** Va-Yikra | | 9 | | 11 | 12 | | 14 | | 16 |

# 2002

**5762/63** תשס"ב / תשס"ג

| | January | February | March | April | May | June | July | August | September | October | November | December |
|---|---|---|---|---|---|---|---|---|---|---|---|---|
| 1 | 17 Tevet | 19 | 17 | 19 Ḥol | 19 | **21** Be-Ha'alotkha | 21 | 23 | 24 | 25 | 26 | 26 2 |
| 2 | 18 | **20** Yitro | **18** Ki Tissa Parah | 20 ha-Mo'ed | 20 | 22 | 22 | 24 | 25 | 26 | **27** Ḥayyei Sarah | 27 3 |
| 3 | 19 | 21 | 19 | 21 Pesaḥ | 21 | 23 | 23 | **25** Re'eh | 26 | 27 | 28 | 28 4 |
| 4 | 20 | 22 | 20 | 22 | **22** Be-Har Be-Ḥukkotai | 24 | 24 | 26 | 27 | 28 | 29 | 29 5 |
| 5 | **21** Shemot | 23 | 21 | 23 | 23 | 25 | 25 | 27 | 28 | **29** Bereshit | 30 R. Ḥ. | 30 R. Ḥ. 6 |
| 6 | 22 | 24 | 22 | **24** Shemini | 24 | 26 | **26** Mattot Masei | 28 | 29 | 30 R. Ḥ. | 1 Kislev R. Ḥ. | 1 Tevet R. Ḥ. 7 |
| 7 | 23 | 25 | 23 | 25 | 25 | 27 | 27 | 29 | 1 Tishri Rosh Ha-Shanah | 1 Ḥeshvan R. Ḥ. | 2 | **2** Mi-Keẓ 8 |
| 8 | 24 | 26 | 24 | 26 | 26 | **28** Shelaḥ | 28 | 30 R. Ḥ. | 2 | 2 | 3 | 3 |
| 9 | 25 | **27** Mishpatim Shekalim | **25** Va-Yakhel Pekudei Ha-Ḥodesh | 27 | 27 | 29 | 29 | 1 Elul R. Ḥ. | 3 Fast | 3 | **4** Toledot | 4 |
| 10 | 26 | 28 | 26 | 28 | 28 | 30 R. Ḥ. | 1 Av R. Ḥ. | **2** Shofetim | 4 | 4 | 5 | 5 |
| 11 | 27 | 29 | 27 | 29 | **29** Be-Midbar | 1 Tammuz R. Ḥ. | 2 | 3 | 5 | 5 | 6 | 6 |
| 12 | **28** Va-Era | 30 R. Ḥ. | 28 | 30 R. Ḥ. | 1 Sivan R. Ḥ. | 2 | 3 | 4 | 6 | **6** No'aḥ | 7 | 7 |
| 13 | 29 | 1 Adar R. Ḥ. | 29 | **1** Iyyar R. Ḥ. Tazri'a Meẓora | 2 | 3 | **4** Devarim | 5 | 7 | 7 | 8 | 8 |
| 14 | 1 Shevat R. Ḥ. | 2 | 1 Nisan R. Ḥ. | 2 | 3 | 4 | 5 | 6 | **8** Ha'azinu Shabbat Shuvah | 8 | 9 | **9** Va-Yiggash |
| 15 | 2 | 3 | 2 | 3 | 4 | **5** Koraḥ | 6 | 7 | 9 | 9 | 10 | 10 Fast |
| 16 | 3 | **4** Terumah | **3** Va-Yikra | 4 | 5 | 6 | 7 | 8 | 10 Yom Kippur | 10 | **11** Va-Yeẓe | 11 |
| 17 | 4 | 5 | 4 | 5 Yom ha-Aẓma'ut | 6 Shavuot | 7 | 8 | **9** Ki Teẓe | 11 | 11 | 12 | 12 |
| 18 | 5 | 6 | 5 | 6 | **7** | 8 | 9 Tishah be-Av | 10 | 12 | 12 | 13 | 13 |
| 19 | **6** Bo | 7 | 6 | 7 | 8 | 9 | 10 | 11 | 13 | **13** Lekh Lekha | 14 | 14 |
| 20 | 7 | 8 | 7 | **8** Aḥarei Mot Kedoshim | 9 | 10 | **11** Va-Etḥannan | 12 | 14 | 14 | 15 | 15 |
| 21 | 8 | 9 | 8 | 9 | 10 | 11 | 12 | 13 | **15** Sukkot | 15 | 16 | **16** Va-Yeḥi |
| 22 | 9 | 10 | 9 | 10 | 11 | **12** Ḥukkat Balak | 13 | 14 | 16 | 16 | 17 | 17 |
| 23 | 10 | **11** Teẓavveh Zakhor | **10** Ẓav Shabbat ha-Gadol | 11 | 12 | 13 | 14 | 15 | 17 Ḥol ha-Mo'ed | 17 | **18** Va-Yishlaḥ | 18 |
| 24 | 11 | 12 | 11 | 12 | 13 | 14 | 15 | **16** Ki Tavo | 18 | 18 | 19 | 19 |
| 25 | 12 | 13 Ta'anit Esther | 12 | 13 | **14** Naso | 15 | 16 | 17 | 19 | 19 | 20 | 20 |
| 26 | **13** Be-Shallaḥ | 14 Purim | 13 | 14 | 15 | 16 | 17 | 18 | 20 | **20** Va-Yera | 21 | 21 |
| 27 | 14 | 15 Shushan Purim | 14 | **15** Emor | 16 | 17 Fast | **18** Ekev | 19 | 21 Hoshana Rabba | 21 | 22 | 22 |
| 28 | 15 | 16 | 15 Pesaḥ | 16 | 17 | 18 | 19 | 20 | **22** Shemini Aẓeret | 22 | 23 | **23** Shemot |
| 29 | 16 | | 16 Omer | 17 | 18 | **19** Pinḥas | 20 | 21 | 23 Simḥat Torah Ve-Zot Ha-Berakhah | 23 | 24 | 24 |
| 30 | 17 | | **17** Ḥol | 18 Lag ba-Omer | 19 | 20 | 21 | 22 | 24 | 24 | **25** Ḥanukkah Va-Yeshev 1 | 25 |
| 31 | 18 | | 18 ha-Mo'ed | | 20 | | 22 | **23** Niẓẓavim Va-Yelekh | | 25 | | 26 |

# 2003

**5763/64** תשס״ג / תשס״ד

| | January | February | March | April | May | June | July | August | September | October | November | December |
|---|---|---|---|---|---|---|---|---|---|---|---|---|
| 1 | 27 **Tevet** | **29** *Mishpatim* | **27** *Va-Yakhel* Shekalim | 28 | 29 | 1 **Sivan** R. H. | 1 **Tammuz** R. H. | 3 | 4 | 5 | **6** *No'aḥ* | 6 |
| 2 | 28 | 30 R. H. | 28 | 29 | 30 R. Ḥ. | 2 | 2 | **4** *Devarim* | 5 | 6 | 7 | 7 |
| 3 | 29 | 1 **Adar I** R. H. | 29 | 1 **Nisan** R. H. | 1 **Iyyar** R. H. *Kedoshim* | 3 | 3 | 5 | 6 | 7 | 8 | 8 |
| 4 | 1 **Shevat** R. H. *Va-Era* | 2 | 30 R. H. | 2 | 2 | 4 | 4 | 6 | 7 | **8** *Ha'azinu* Shabbat Shuvah | 9 | 9 |
| 5 | 2 | 3 | 1 **Adar II** R. H. | **3** *Tazri'a* | 3 | 5 | **5** *Koraḥ* | 7 | 8 | 9 | 10 | 10 |
| 6 | 3 | 4 | 2 | 4 | 4 | 6 Shavuot | 6 | 8 | **9** *Ki Teẓe* | 10 Yom Kippur | 11 | **11** *Va-Yeẓe* |
| 7 | 4 | 5 | 3 | 5 | 5 Yom ha-Aẓma'ut | **7** | 7 | 9 Tishah be-Av | 10 | 11 | 12 | 12 |
| 8 | 5 | **6** *Terumah* | **4** *Pekudei* | 6 | 6 | 8 | 8 | 10 | 11 | 12 | **13** *Lekh Lekha* | 13 |
| 9 | 6 | 7 | 5 | 7 | 7 | 9 | 9 | **11** *Va-Etḥannan* | 12 | 13 | 14 | 14 |
| 10 | 7 | 8 | 6 | 8 | **8** *Emor* | 10 | 10 | 12 | 13 | 14 | 15 | 15 |
| 11 | **8** *Bo* | 9 | 7 | 9 | 9 | 11 | 11 | 13 | 14 | **15** Sukkot | 16 | 16 |
| 12 | 9 | 10 | 8 | **10** *Meẓora* Shabbat ha-Gadol | 10 | 12 | **12** *Ḥukkat Balak* | 14 | 15 | 16 | 17 | 17 |
| 13 | 10 | 11 | 9 | 11 | 11 | 13 | 13 | 15 | **16** *Ki Tavo* | 17 | 18 | **18** *Va-Yishlaḥ* |
| 14 | 11 | 12 | 10 | 12 | 12 | **14** *Naso* | 14 | 16 | 17 | 18 Ḥol ha-Mo'ed | 19 | 19 |
| 15 | 12 | **13** *Teẓavveh* | **11** *Va-Yikra* Zakhor | 13 | 13 | 15 | 15 | 17 | 18 | 19 | **20** *Va-Yera* | 20 |
| 16 | 13 | 14 | 12 | 14 | 14 | 16 | 16 | **18** *Ekev* | 19 | 20 | 21 | 21 |
| 17 | 14 | 15 | 13 Ta'anit Esther | 15 Pesaḥ | **15** *Be-Har* | 17 | 17 Fast | 19 | 20 | 21 Hoshana Rabba | 22 | 22 |
| 18 | **15** *Be-Shallaḥ* | 16 | 14 Purim | 16 Omer | 16 | 18 | 18 | 20 | 21 | **22** Shemini Aẓeret | 23 | 23 |
| 19 | 16 | 17 | 15 Shushan Purim | **17** | 17 | 19 | **19** *Pinḥas* | 21 | 22 | 23 Simḥat Torah *Ve-Zot Ha-Berakhah* | 24 | 24 |
| 20 | 17 | 18 | 16 | 18 Ḥol ha-Mo'ed | 18 Lag ba-Omer | 20 | 20 | 22 | **23** *Niẓẓavim Va-Yelekh* | 24 | 25 | **25** Ḥanukkah *Va-Yeshev* 1 |
| 21 | 18 | 19 | 17 | 19 | 19 | **21** *Be-Ha'alotkha* | 21 | 23 | 24 | 25 | 26 | 26 2 |
| 22 | 19 | **20** *Ki Tissa* | **18** *Ẓav* Parah | 20 | 20 | 22 | 22 | 24 | 25 | 26 | **27** *Ḥayyei Sarah* | 27 3 |
| 23 | 20 | 21 | 19 | 21 Pesaḥ | 21 | 23 | 23 | **25** *Re'eh* | 26 | 27 | 28 | 28 4 |
| 24 | 21 | 22 | 20 | 22 | **22** *Be-Ḥukkotai* | 24 | 24 | 26 | 27 | 28 | 29 | 29 5 |
| 25 | **22** *Yitro* | 23 | 21 | 23 | 23 | 25 | 25 | 27 | 28 | **29** *Bereshit* | 30 R. H. | 30 R. H. 6 |
| 26 | 23 | 24 | 22 | **24** *Aḥarei Mot* | 24 | 26 | **26** *Mattot Masei* | 28 | 29 | 30 R. H. | 1 **Kislev** R. H. | 1 **Tevet** R. H. 7 |
| 27 | 24 | 25 | 23 | 25 | 25 | 27 | 27 | 29 | 1 **Tishri** Rosh Ha-Shanah | 1 **Ḥeshvan** R. H. | 2 | **2** *Mi-Keẓ* 8 |
| 28 | 25 | 26 | 24 | 26 | 26 | **28** *Shelaḥ* | 28 | 30 R. H. | 2 | 2 | 3 | 3 |
| 29 | 26 | | **25** *Shemini* Ha-Ḥodesh | 27 | 27 | 29 | 29 | 1 **Elul** R. H. | 3 Fast | 3 | **4** *Toledot* | 4 |
| 30 | 27 | | 26 | 28 | 28 | 30 R. H. | 1 **Av** R. H. | **2** *Shofetim* | 4 | 4 | 5 | 5 |
| 31 | 28 | | 27 | | **29** *Be-Midbar* | | 2 | 3 | | 5 | | 6 |

# 2004

**5764/65** תשס״ד / תשס״ה

| | January | February | March | April | May | June | July | August | September | October | November | December |
|---|---|---|---|---|---|---|---|---|---|---|---|---|
| 1 | 7 **Tevet** | 9 | 8 | 10 | **10** *Aḥarei Mot Kedoshim* | 12 | 12 | 14 | 15 | 16 | 17 | 18 |
| 2 | 8 | 10 | 9 | 11 | 11 | 13 | 13 | 15 | 16 | **17** | 18 | 19 |
| 3 | **9** *Va-Yiggash* | 11 | 10 | **12** *Ẓav* Shabbat ha-Gadol | 12 | 14 | **14** *Balak* | 16 | 17 | 18 Ḥol ha-Mo'ed | 19 | 20 |
| 4 | 10 Fast | 12 | 11 Ta'anit Esther | 13 | 13 | 15 | 15 | 17 | **18** *Ki Tavo* | 19 | 20 | **21** *Va-Yeshev* |
| 5 | 11 | 13 | 12 | 14 | 14 | **16** *Be-Ha'alotkha* | 16 | 18 | 19 | 20 | 21 | 22 |
| 6 | 12 | 14 | **13** *Teẓavveh* Zakhor | 15 Pesaḥ | 15 | 17 | 17 Fast | 19 | 20 | 21 Hoshana Rabba | **22** *Ḥayyei Sarah* | 23 |
| 7 | 13 | **15** *Be-Shallaḥ* | 14 Purim | 16 Omer | 16 | 18 | 18 | **20** *Ekev* | 21 | 22 Shemini Aẓeret | 23 | 24 |
| 8 | 14 | 16 | 15 Shushan Purim | 17 | **17** *Emor* | 19 | 19 | 21 | 22 | 23 Simḥat Torah *Ve-Zot Ha-Berakhah* | 24 | 25 Ḥanukkah 1 |
| 9 | 15 | 17 | 16 | 18 Ḥol ha-Mo'ed | 18 Lag ba-Omer | 20 | 20 | 22 | 23 | **24** *Bereshit* | 25 | 26 2 |
| 10 | **16** *Va-Yeḥi* | 18 | 17 | **19** | 19 | 21 | **21** *Pinḥas* | 23 | 24 | 25 | 26 | 27 3 |
| 11 | 17 | 19 | 18 | 20 | 20 | 22 | 22 | 24 | **25** *Niẓẓavim Va-Yelekh* | 26 | 27 | **28** *Mi-Keẓ* 4 |
| 12 | 18 | 20 | 19 | 21 Pesaḥ | 21 | **23** *Shelaḥ* | 23 | 25 | 26 | 27 | 28 | 29 5 |
| 13 | 19 | 21 | **20** *Ki Tissa* Parah | 22 | 22 | 24 | 24 | 26 | 27 | 28 | **29** *Toledot* | 1 **Tevet** R. H. 6 |
| 14 | 20 | **22** *Yitro* | 21 | 23 | 23 | 25 | 25 | **27** *Re'eh* | 28 | 29 | 1 **Kislev** R. H. | 2 7 |
| 15 | 21 | 23 | 22 | 24 | **24** *Be-Har Be-Ḥukkotai* | 26 | 26 | 28 | 29 | 30 R. H. | 2 | 3 8 |
| 16 | 22 | 24 | 23 | 25 | 25 | 27 | 27 | 29 | 1 **Tishri** Rosh Ha-Shanah | **1** **Ḥeshvan** R. H. *No'aḥ* | 3 | 4 |
| 17 | **23** *Shemot* | 25 | 24 | **26** *Shemini* | 26 | 28 | **28** *Mattot Masei* | 30 R. H. | 2 | 2 | 4 | 5 |
| 18 | 24 | 26 | 25 | 27 | 27 | 29 | 29 | 1 **Elul** R. H. | **3** *Ha'azinu* Shabbat Shuvah | 3 | 5 | **6** *Va-Yiggash* |
| 19 | 25 | 27 | 26 | 28 | 28 | **30** R. H. *Koraḥ* | 1 **Av** R. H. | 2 | 4 Fast | 4 | 6 | 7 |
| 20 | 26 | 28 | **27** *Va-Yakhel Pekudei* Ha-Ḥodesh | 29 | 29 | 1 **Tammuz** R. H. | 2 | 3 | 5 | 5 | **7** *Va-Yeẓe* | 8 |
| 21 | 27 | **29** *Mishpatim* Shekalim | 28 | 30 R. H. | 1 **Sivan** R. H. | 2 | 3 | **4** *Shofetim* | 6 | 6 | 8 | 9 |
| 22 | 28 | 30 R. H. | 29 | 1 **Iyyar** R. H. | **2** *Be-Midbar* | 3 | 4 | 5 | 7 | 7 | 9 | 10 Fast |
| 23 | 29 | 1 **Adar** R. H. | 1 **Nisan** R. H. | 2 | 3 | 4 | 5 | 6 | 8 | **8** *Lekh Lekha* | 10 | 11 |
| 24 | 1 **Shevat** R. H. *Va-Era* | 2 | 2 | **3** *Tazri'a Meẓora* | 4 | 5 | **6** *Devarim* | 7 | 9 | 9 | 11 | 12 |
| 25 | 2 | 3 | 3 | 4 | 5 | 6 | 7 | 8 | **10** Yom Kippur | 10 | 12 | **13** *Va-Yeḥi* |
| 26 | 3 | 4 | 4 | 5 Yom ha-Aẓma'ut | 6 Shavuot | **7** *Ḥukkat* | 8 | 9 | 11 | 11 | 13 | 14 |
| 27 | 4 | 5 | **5** *Va-Yikra* | 6 | 7 | 8 | 9 Tishah be-Av | 10 | 12 | 12 | **14** | 15 |
| 28 | 5 | **6** *Terumah* | 6 | 7 | 8 | 9 | 10 | **11** *Ki Teẓe* | 13 | 13 | 15 | 16 |
| 29 | 6 | 7 | 7 | 8 | **9** *Naso* | 10 | 11 | 12 | 14 | 14 | 16 | 17 |
| 30 | 7 | | 8 | 9 | 10 | 11 | 12 | 13 | 15 Sukkot | **15** *Va-Yera* | 17 | 18 |
| 31 | **8** *Bo* | | 9 | | 11 | | **13** *Va-Etḥannan* | 14 | | 16 | | 19 |

## 2005

**5765/66**　　　　　　　　　　　　　　　　　　　　　　　　　　　　　　　　　　　　　　　　　　　תשס״ה / תשס״ו

| | January | February | March | April | May | June | July | August | September | October | November | December |
|---|---|---|---|---|---|---|---|---|---|---|---|---|
| 1 | 20 Tevet Shemot | 22 | 20 | 21 | 22 | 23 | 24 | 25 | 27 | 27 Niẓẓavim | 29 | 29 |
| 2 | 21 | 23 | 21 | 22 Shemini Parah | 23 | 24 | 25 Korah | 26 | 28 | 28 | 30 R.H. | 1 Kislev R.H. |
| 3 | 22 | 24 | 22 | 23 | 24 | 25 | 26 | 27 | 29 Re'eh | 29 | 1 Heshvan R.H. | 2 Toledot |
| 4 | 23 | 25 | 23 | 24 | 25 | 26 Be-Midbar | 27 | 28 | 30 R.H. | 1 Tishri Rosh Ha-Shanah | 2 | 3 |
| 5 | 24 | 26 Mishpatim | 24 Va-Yakhel | 25 | 26 | 27 | 28 | 29 | 1 Elul R.H. | 2 | 3 No'ah | 4 |
| 6 | 25 | 27 | 25 | 26 | 27 | 28 | 29 | 1 Av R.H. Mas'ei | 2 | 3 Fast | 4 | 5 |
| 7 | 26 | 28 | 26 | 27 | 28 Kedoshim | 29 | 30 R.H. | 2 | 3 | 4 | 5 | 6 |
| 8 | 27 Va-Era | 29 | 27 | 28 | 29 | 1 Sivan R.H. | 1 Tammuz R.H. | 3 | 4 | 5 Va-Yelekh Shabbat Shuvah | 6 | 7 |
| 9 | 28 | 30 R.H. | 28 | 29 Tazri'a Ha-Hodesh | 30 R.H. | 2 | 2 Hukkat | 4 | 5 | 6 | 7 | 8 |
| 10 | 29 | 1 Adar I R.H. | 29 | 1 Nisan R.H. | 1 Iyyar R.H. | 3 | 3 | 5 | 6 Shofetim | 7 | 8 | 9 Va-Yeẓe |
| 11 | 1 Shevat R.H. | 2 | 30 R.H. | 2 | 2 | 4 | 4 | 6 | 7 | 8 | 9 | 10 |
| 12 | 2 | 3 Terumah | 1 R.H. Pekudei Adar II Shekalim | 3 | 3 Yom ha-Aẓma'ut | 5 | 5 | 7 | 8 | 9 | 10 Lekh Lekha | 11 |
| 13 | 3 | 4 | 2 | 4 | 4 | 6 Shavuot | 6 | 8 Devarim | 9 | 10 Yom Kippur | 11 | 12 |
| 14 | 4 | 5 | 3 | 5 | 5 Emor | 7 | 7 | 9 Tishah be-Av | 10 | 11 | 12 | 13 |
| 15 | 5 Bo | 6 | 4 | 6 | 6 | 8 | 8 | 10 | 11 | 12 Ha'azinu | 13 | 14 |
| 16 | 6 | 7 | 5 | 7 Meẓora | 7 | 9 | 9 Balak | 11 | 12 | 13 | 14 | 15 |
| 17 | 7 | 8 | 6 | 8 | 8 | 10 | 10 | 12 | 13 Ki Teẓe | 14 | 15 | 16 Va-Yishlah |
| 18 | 8 | 9 | 7 | 9 | 9 | 11 Be-Ha'alotkha | 11 | 13 | 14 | 15 Sukkot | 16 | 17 |
| 19 | 9 | 10 Tezavveh | 8 Va-Yikra Zakhor | 10 | 10 | 12 | 12 | 14 | 15 | 16 | 17 Va-Yera | 18 |
| 20 | 10 | 11 | 9 | 11 | 11 | 13 | 13 | 15 Va-Ethannan | 16 | 17 | 18 | 19 |
| 21 | 11 | 12 | 10 | 12 | 12 Be-Har | 14 | 14 | 16 | 17 | 18 Hol ha-Mo'ed | 19 | 20 |
| 22 | 12 Be-Shallaḥ | 13 | 11 | 13 | 13 | 15 | 15 | 17 | 18 | 19 | 20 | 21 |
| 23 | 13 | 14 | 12 | 14 Aharei-Mot Shabbat ha-Gadol | 14 | 16 | 16 Pinhas | 18 | 19 | 20 | 21 | 22 |
| 24 | 14 | 15 | 13 Ta'anit Esther | 15 Pesah | 15 | 17 | 17 Fast | 19 | 20 Ki Tavo | 21 Hoshana Rabba | 22 | 23 Va-Yeshev |
| 25 | 15 | 16 | 14 Purim | 16 Omer | 16 | 18 Shelaḥ | 18 | 20 | 21 | 22 Shemini Aẓeret | 23 | 24 |
| 26 | 16 | 17 Ki Tissa | 15 Shushan Purim | 17 Zav | 17 | 19 | 19 | 21 | 22 | 23 Simhat Torah Ve-Zot Ha-Berakhah | 24 Hayyei Sarah | 25 Hanukkah 1 |
| 27 | 17 | 18 | 16 | 18 Hol ha-Mo'ed | 18 Lag ba-Omer | 20 | 20 | 22 Ekev | 23 | 24 | 25 | 26 2 |
| 28 | 18 | 19 | 17 | 19 | 19 Be-Hukkotai | 21 | 21 | 23 | 24 | 25 | 26 | 27 3 |
| 29 | 19 Yitro | | 18 | 20 | 20 | 22 | 22 | 24 | 25 | 26 Bereshit | 27 | 28 4 |
| 30 | 20 | | 19 | 21 Pesah | 21 | 23 | 23 Mattot | 25 | 26 | 27 | 28 | 29 5 |
| 31 | 21 | | 20 | | 22 | | 24 | 26 | | 28 | | 30 R.H. Mi-Keẓ 6 |

## 2006

**5766/67**　　　　　　　　　　　　　　　　　　　　　　　　　　　　　　　　　　　　　　　　　　　תשס״ו / תשס״ז

| | January | February | March | April | May | June | July | August | September | October | November | December |
|---|---|---|---|---|---|---|---|---|---|---|---|---|
| 1 | 1 Tevet R.H. Hanukkah | 3 | 1 Adar R.H. | 3 Va-Yikra | 3 | 5 | 5 Korah | 7 | 8 | 9 | 10 | 10 |
| 2 | 2 8 | 4 | 2 | 4 | 4 | 6 Shavuot | 6 | 8 | 9 Ki Teẓe | 10 Yom Kippur | 11 | 11 Va-Yeẓe |
| 3 | 3 | 5 | 3 | 5 | 5 Yom ha-Aẓma'ut | 7 | 7 | 9 Tishah be-Av | 10 | 11 | 12 | 12 |
| 4 | 4 Bo | 6 | 4 Terumah | 6 | 6 | 8 | 8 | 10 | 11 | 12 | 13 Lekh Lekha | 13 |
| 5 | 5 | 7 | 5 | 7 | 7 | 9 | 9 | 11 Va-Ethannan | 12 | 13 | 14 | 14 |
| 6 | 6 | 8 | 6 | 8 | 8 Aharei Mot Kedoshim | 10 | 10 | 12 | 13 | 14 | 15 | 15 |
| 7 | 7 Va-Yiggash | 9 | 7 | 9 | 9 | 11 | 11 | 13 | 14 | 15 Sukkot | 16 | 16 |
| 8 | 8 | 10 | 8 | 10 Zav Shabbat ha-Gadol | 10 | 12 | 12 Hukkat Balak | 14 | 15 | 16 | 17 | 17 |
| 9 | 9 | 11 | 9 | 11 | 11 | 13 | 13 | 15 | 16 Ki Tavo | 17 | 18 | 18 Va-Yishlah |
| 10 | 10 Fast | 12 | 10 | 12 | 12 | 14 Naso | 14 | 16 | 17 | 18 Hol ha-Mo'ed | 19 | 19 |
| 11 | 11 | 13 Be-Shallah | 11 Tezavveh Zakhor | 13 | 13 | 15 | 15 | 17 | 18 | 19 | 20 Va-Yera | 20 |
| 12 | 12 | 14 | 12 | 14 | 14 | 16 | 16 | 18 Ekev | 19 | 20 | 21 | 21 |
| 13 | 13 | 15 | 13 Ta'anit Esther | 15 Pesah | 15 Emor | 17 | 17 Fast | 19 | 20 | 21 Hoshana Rabba | 22 | 22 |
| 14 | 14 Va-Yehi | 16 | 14 Purim | 16 Omer | 16 | 18 | 18 | 20 | 21 | 22 Shemini Aẓeret | 23 | 23 |
| 15 | 15 | 17 | 15 Shushan Purim | 17 Hol ha-Mo'ed | 17 | 19 | 19 Pinhas | 21 | 22 | 23 Simhat Torah Ve-Zot Ha-Berakhah | 24 | 24 |
| 16 | 16 | 18 | 16 | 18 | 18 Lag ba-Omer | 20 | 20 | 22 | 23 Niẓẓavim Va-Yelekh | 24 | 25 | 25 Hanukkah 1 Va-Yeshev |
| 17 | 17 | 19 | 17 | 19 | 19 | 21 Be-Ha'alotkha | 21 | 23 | 24 | 25 | 26 | 26 2 |
| 18 | 18 | 20 Yitro | 18 Ki Tissa Parah | 20 | 20 | 22 | 22 | 24 | 25 | 26 | 27 Hayyei Sarah | 27 3 |
| 19 | 19 | 21 | 19 | 21 Pesah | 21 | 23 | 23 | 25 Re'eh | 26 | 27 | 28 | 28 4 |
| 20 | 20 | 22 | 20 | 22 | 22 Be-Har Be-Hukkotai | 24 | 24 | 26 | 27 | 28 | 29 | 29 5 |
| 21 | 21 Shemot | 23 | 21 | 23 | 23 | 25 | 25 | 27 | 28 | 29 Bereshit | 30 R.H. | 30 R.H. 6 |
| 22 | 22 | 24 | 22 | 24 Shemini | 24 | 26 | 26 Mattot Mas'ei | 28 | 29 | 30 R.H. | 1 Kislev R.H. | 1 Tevet R.H. 7 |
| 23 | 23 | 25 | 23 | 25 | 25 | 27 | 27 | 29 | 1 Tishri Rosh Ha-Shanah | 1 Heshvan R.H. | 2 | 2 Mi-Keẓ 8 |
| 24 | 24 | 26 | 24 | 26 | 26 | 28 Shelaḥ | 28 | 30 R.H. | 2 | 2 | 3 | 3 |
| 25 | 25 | 27 Mishpatim Shekalim | Va-Yakhel Pekudei 25 Ha-Hodesh | 27 | 27 | 29 | 29 | 1 Elul R.H. | 3 Fast | 3 | 4 Toledot | 4 |
| 26 | 26 | 28 | 26 | 28 | 28 | 30 R.H. | 1 Av R.H. | 2 Shofetim | 4 | 4 | 5 | 5 |
| 27 | 27 | 29 | 27 | 29 | 29 Be-Midbar | 1 Tammuz R.H. | 2 | 3 | 5 | 5 | 6 | 6 |
| 28 | 28 Va-Era | 30 R.H. | 28 | 30 R.H. | 1 Sivan R.H. | 2 | 3 | 4 | 6 | 6 No'ah | 7 | 7 |
| 29 | 29 | | 29 | 1 R.H. Tazri'a Iyyar Meẓora | 2 | 3 | 4 Devarim | 5 | 7 | 7 | 8 | 8 |
| 30 | 1 Shevat R.H. | | 1 Nisan R.H. | 2 | 3 | 4 | 5 | 6 | 8 Ha'azinu Shabbat Shuvah | 8 | 9 | 9 Va-Yiggash |
| 31 | 2 | | 2 | | 4 | | 6 | 7 | | 9 | | 10 Fast |

# 2007

**5767/68** תשס״ז / תשס״ח

| | January | February | March | April | May | June | July | August | September | October | November | December |
|---|---|---|---|---|---|---|---|---|---|---|---|---|
| 1 | 11 Tevet | 13 | 11 Ta'anit Esther | 13 | 13 | 15 | 15 | 17 | 18 *Ki Tavo* | 19 Hol | 20 | 21 *Va-Yeshev* |
| 2 | 12 | 14 | 12 | 14 | 14 | 16 *Be-Ha'alotkha* | 16 | 18 | 19 | 20 ha-Mo'ed | 21 | 22 |
| 3 | 13 | 15 *Be-Shallah* | 13 *Tezavveh* Zakhor | 15 Pesah | 15 | 17 | 17 Fast | 19 | 20 | 21 Hoshana Rabba | 22 *Hayyei Sarah* | 23 |
| 4 | 14 | 16 | 14 Purim | 16 Omer | 16 | 18 | 18 | 20 *Ekev* | 21 | 22 Shemini Azeret | 23 | 24 |
| 5 | 15 | 17 | 15 Shushan Purim | 17 Hol ha-Mo'ed | 17 *Emor* | 19 | 19 | 21 | 22 | 23 Simhat Torah *Ve-Zot Ha-Berakhah* | 24 | 25 Hanukkah 1 |
| 6 | 16 *Va-Yehi* | 18 | 16 | 18 | 18 Lag ba-Omer | 20 | 20 | 22 | 23 | 24 *Bereshit* | 25 | 26 2 |
| 7 | 17 | 19 | 17 | 19 | 19 | 21 | 21 *Pinhas* | 23 | 24 | 25 | 26 | 27 3 |
| 8 | 18 | 20 | 18 | 20 | 20 | 22 | 22 | 24 | 25 *Nizzavim Va-Yelekh* | 26 | 27 | 28 *Mi-Kez* 4 |
| 9 | 19 | 21 | 19 | 21 Pesah | 21 | 23 *Shelah* | 23 | 25 | 26 | 27 | 28 | 29 5 |
| 10 | 20 | 22 *Yitro* | 20 *Ki Tissa* Parah | 22 | 22 | 24 | 24 | 26 | 27 | 28 | 29 *Toledot* | 1 Tevet R H 6 |
| 11 | 21 | 23 | 21 | 23 | 23 | 25 | 25 | 27 *Re'eh* | 28 | 29 | 1 Kislev R H | 2 7 |
| 12 | 22 | 24 | 22 | 24 | 24 *Be-Har Be-Hukkotai* | 26 | 26 | 28 | 29 | 30 R H | 2 | 3 8 |
| 13 | 23 *Shemot* | 25 | 23 | 25 | 25 | 27 | 27 | 29 | 1 Tishri Rosh Ha-Shanah | 1 R H Heshvan *No'ah* | 3 | 4 |
| 14 | 24 | 26 | 24 | 26 *Shemini* | 26 | 28 | 28 *Mattot Masei* | 30 R H | 2 | 2 | 4 | 5 |
| 15 | 25 | 27 | 25 | 27 | 27 | 29 | 29 | 1 Elul R H | 3 *Ha'azinu* Shabbat Shuvah | 3 | 5 | 6 *Va-Yiggash* |
| 16 | 26 | 28 | 26 | 28 | 28 | 30 R H *Korah* | 1 Av R H | 2 | 4 Fast | 4 | 6 | 7 |
| 17 | 27 | 29 *Mishpatim* Shekalim | 27 *Va-Yakhel Pekudei* Ha-Hodesh | 29 | 29 | 1 Tammuz R H | 2 | 3 | 5 | 5 | 7 *Va-Yeze* | 8 |
| 18 | 28 | 30 R H | 28 | 30 R H | 1 Sivan R H | 2 | 3 | 4 *Shofetim* | 6 | 6 | 8 | 9 |
| 19 | 29 | 1 Adar R H | 29 | 1 Iyyar R H | 2 *Be-Midbar* | 3 | 4 | 5 | 7 | 7 | 9 | 10 Fast |
| 20 | 1 R H Shevat *Va-Era* | 2 | 1 Nisan R H | 2 | 3 | 4 | 5 | 6 | 8 | 8 *Lekh Lekha* | 10 | 11 |
| 21 | 2 | 3 | 2 | 3 *Tazri'a Mezora* | 4 | 5 | 6 *Devarim* | 7 | 9 | 9 | 11 | 12 |
| 22 | 3 | 4 | 3 | 4 | 5 | 6 | 7 | 8 | 10 Yom Kippur | 10 | 12 | 13 *Va-Yehi* |
| 23 | 4 | 5 | 4 | 5 Yom ha-Azma'ut | 6 Shavuot | 7 *Hukkat* | 8 | 9 | 11 | 11 | 13 | 14 |
| 24 | 5 | 6 *Terumah* | 5 *Va-Yikra* | 6 | 7 | 8 | 9 Tishah be-Av | 10 | 12 | 12 | 14 *Va-Yishlah* | 15 |
| 25 | 6 | 7 | 6 | 7 | 8 | 9 | 10 | 11 *Ki Teze* | 13 | 13 | 15 | 16 |
| 26 | 7 | 8 | 7 | 8 | 9 *Naso* | 10 | 11 | 12 | 14 | 14 | 16 | 17 |
| 27 | 8 *Bo* | 9 | 8 | 9 | 10 | 11 | 12 | 13 | 15 Sukkot | 15 *Va-Yera* | 17 | 18 |
| 28 | 9 | 10 | 9 | 10 *Aharei Mot Kedoshim* | 11 | 12 | 13 *Va-Ethannan* | 14 | 16 | 16 | 18 | 19 |
| 29 | 10 | | 10 | 11 | 12 | 13 | 14 | 15 | 17 Hol | 17 | 19 | 20 *Shemot* |
| 30 | 11 | | 11 | 12 | 13 | 14 *Balak* | 15 | 16 | 18 ha-Mo'ed | 18 | 20 | 21 |
| 31 | 12 | | 12 *Zav* Shabbat ha-Gadol | | 14 | | 16 | 17 | | 19 | | 22 |

# 2008

**5768/69** תשס״ח / תשס״ט

| | January | February | March | April | May | June | July | August | September | October | November | December |
|---|---|---|---|---|---|---|---|---|---|---|---|---|
| 1 | 23 Tevet | 25 | 24 *Va-Yakhel* | 25 | 26 | 27 | 28 | 29 | 1 Elul R H | 2 Rosh Ha-Shanah | 3 *No'ah* | 4 |
| 2 | 24 | 26 *Mishpatim* | 25 | 26 | 27 | 28 | 29 | 1 R H Av *Masei* | 2 | 3 Fast | 4 | 5 |
| 3 | 25 | 27 | 26 | 27 | 28 *Kedoshim* | 29 | 30 R H | 2 | 3 | 4 | 5 | 6 |
| 4 | 26 | 28 | 27 | 28 | 29 | 1 Sivan R H | 1 Tammuz R H | 3 | 4 | 5 *Va-Yelekh* Shabbat Shuvah | 6 | 7 |
| 5 | 27 *Va-Era* | 29 | 28 | 29 *Tazri'a* Ha-Hodesh | 30 R H | 2 | 2 *Hukkat* | 4 | 5 | 6 | 7 | 8 |
| 6 | 28 | 30 R H | 29 | 1 Nisan R H | 1 Iyyar R H | 3 | 3 | 5 | 6 *Shofetim* | 7 | 8 | 9 *Va-Yeze* |
| 7 | 29 | 1 Adar I R H | 30 | 2 | 2 | 4 *Naso* | 4 | 6 | 7 | 8 | 9 | 10 |
| 8 | 1 Shevat R H | 2 | 1 R H Adar II *Pekudei* Shekalim | 3 | 3 Yom ha-Azma'ut | 5 | 5 | 7 | 8 | 9 | 10 *Lekh Lekha* | 11 |
| 9 | 2 | 3 *Terumah* | 2 | 4 | 4 | 6 Shavuot | 6 | 8 *Devarim* | 9 | 10 Yom Kippur | 11 | 12 |
| 10 | 3 | 4 | 3 | 5 | 5 *Emor* | 7 | 7 | 9 Tishah be-Av | 10 | 11 | 12 | 13 |
| 11 | 4 | 5 | 4 | 6 | 6 | 8 | 8 | 10 | 11 | 12 *Ha'azinu* | 13 | 14 |
| 12 | 5 *Bo* | 6 | 5 | 7 *Mezora* | 7 | 9 | 9 *Balak* | 11 | 12 | 13 | 14 | 15 |
| 13 | 6 | 7 | 6 | 8 | 8 | 10 | 10 | 12 | 13 *Ki Teze* | 14 | 15 | 16 *Va-Yishlah* |
| 14 | 7 | 8 | 7 | 9 | 9 | 11 *Be-Ha'alotkha* | 11 | 13 | 14 | 15 Sukkot | 16 | 17 |
| 15 | 8 | 9 | 8 *Va-Yikra* Zakhor | 10 | 10 | 12 | 12 | 14 | 15 | 16 | 17 *Va-Yera* | 18 |
| 16 | 9 | 10 *Tezavveh* | 9 | 11 | 11 | 13 | 13 | 15 *Va-Ethannan* | 16 | 17 Hol ha-Mo'ed | 18 | 19 |
| 17 | 10 | 11 | 10 | 12 | 12 *Be-Har* | 14 | 14 | 16 | 17 | 18 | 19 | 20 |
| 18 | 11 | 12 | 11 | 13 | 13 | 15 | 15 | 17 | 18 | 19 | 20 | 21 |
| 19 | 12 *Be-Shallah* | 13 | 12 | 14 *Aharei Mot* Shabbat ha-Gadol | 14 | 16 | 16 *Pinhas* | 18 | 19 | 20 | 21 | 22 |
| 20 | 13 | 14 | 13 Ta'anit Esther | 15 Pesah | 15 | 17 | 17 Fast | 19 | 20 *Ki Tavo* | 21 Hoshana Rabba | 22 | 23 *Va-Yeshev* |
| 21 | 14 | 15 | 14 Purim | 16 Omer | 16 | 18 *Shelah* | 18 | 20 | 21 | 22 Shemini Azeret | 23 | 24 |
| 22 | 15 | 16 | 15 *Zav* Shushan Purim | 17 Hol ha-Mo'ed | 17 | 19 | 19 | 21 | 22 | 23 Simhat Torah *Ve-Zot Ha-Berakhah* | 24 *Hayyei Sarah* | 25 Hanukkah 1 |
| 23 | 16 | 17 *Ki Tissa* | 16 | 18 | 18 Lag ba-Omer | 20 | 20 | 22 *Ekev* | 23 | 24 | 25 | 26 2 |
| 24 | 17 | 18 | 17 | 19 | 19 *Be-Hukkotai* | 21 | 21 | 23 | 24 | 25 | 26 | 27 3 |
| 25 | 18 | 19 | 18 | 20 | 20 | 22 | 22 | 24 | 25 | 26 *Bereshit* | 27 | 28 4 |
| 26 | 19 *Yitro* | 20 | 19 | 21 Pesah | 21 | 23 | 23 *Mattot* | 25 | 26 | 27 | 28 | 29 5 |
| 27 | 20 | 21 | 20 | 22 | 22 | 24 | 24 | 26 | 27 *Nizzavim* | 28 | 29 | 30 R H *Mi-Kez* 6 |
| 28 | 21 | 22 | 21 | 23 | 23 | 25 *Korah* | 25 | 27 | 28 | 29 | 1 Kislev R H | 1 Tevet R H 7 |
| 29 | 22 | 23 | 22 *Shemini* Parah | 24 | 24 | 26 | 26 | 28 | 29 | 30 R H | 2 *Toledot* | 2 8 |
| 30 | 23 | | 23 | 25 | 25 | 27 | 27 | 29 *Re'eh* | 1 Tishri Rosh Ha-Shanah | 1 Heshvan R H | 3 | 3 |
| 31 | 24 | | 24 | | 26 *Be-Midbar* | | 28 | 30 R H | | 2 | | 4 |

# 2009

**5769/70** תשס״ט / תש״ע

| | January | February | March | April | May | June | July | August | September | October | November | December |
|---|---|---|---|---|---|---|---|---|---|---|---|---|
| 1 | 5 Tevet | 7 | 5 | 7 | 7 | 9 | 9 | 11 Va-Ethannan | 12 | 13 | 14 | 14 |
| 2 | 6 | 8 | 6 | 8 | 8 Aharei Mot Kedoshim | 10 | 10 | 12 | 13 | 14 | 15 | 15 |
| 3 | 7 Va-Yiggash | 9 | 7 | 9 | 9 | 11 | 11 | 13 | 14 | 15 Sukkot | 16 | 16 |
| 4 | 8 | 10 | 8 | 10 Zav Shabbat ha-Gadol | 10 | 12 | 12 Hukkat Balak | 14 | 15 | 16 | 17 | 17 |
| 5 | 9 | 11 | 9 | 11 | 11 | 13 | 13 | 15 | 16 Ki Tavo | 17 Hol ha-Mo'ed | 18 | 18 Va-Yishlah |
| 6 | 10 Fast | 12 | 10 | 12 | 12 | 14 Naso | 14 | 16 | 17 | 18 | 19 | 19 |
| 7 | 11 | 13 Be-Shallah | 11 Tezavveh Zakhor | 13 | 13 | 15 | 15 | 17 | 18 | 19 | 20 Va-Yera | 20 |
| 8 | 12 | 14 | 12 | 14 | 14 | 16 | 16 | 18 Ekev | 19 | 20 | 21 | 21 |
| 9 | 13 | 15 | 13 Ta'anit Esther | 15 Pesah | 15 Emor | 17 | 17 Fast | 19 | 20 | 21 Hoshana Rabba | 22 | 22 |
| 10 | 14 Va-Yehi | 16 | 14 Purim | 16 Omer | 16 | 18 | 18 | 20 | 21 | 22 Shemini Azeret | 23 | 23 |
| 11 | 15 | 17 | 15 Shushan Purim | 17 Hol ha-Mo'ed | 17 | 19 | 19 Pinhas | 21 | 22 | 23 Simhat Torah Ve-Zot Ha-Berakhah | 24 | 24 |
| 12 | 16 | 18 | 16 | 18 | 18 Lag ba-Omer | 20 | 20 | 22 | 23 Nizzavim Va-Yelekh | 24 | 25 | 25 Hanukkah 1 Va-Yeshev |
| 13 | 17 | 19 | 17 | 19 | 19 | 21 Be-Ha'alotkha | 21 | 23 | 24 | 25 | 26 | 26 2 |
| 14 | 18 | 20 Yitro | 18 Ki Tissa Parah | 20 | 20 | 22 | 22 | 24 | 25 | 26 | 27 Hayyei Sarah | 27 3 |
| 15 | 19 | 21 | 19 | 21 Pesah | 21 | 23 | 23 | 25 Re'eh | 26 | 27 | 28 | 28 4 |
| 16 | 20 | 22 | 20 | 22 | 22 Be-Har Be-Hukkotai | 24 | 24 | 26 | 27 | 28 | 29 | 29 5 |
| 17 | 21 Shemot | 23 | 21 | 23 | 23 | 25 | 25 | 27 | 28 | 29 Bereshit | 30 R.H. | 30 R.H. 6 |
| 18 | 22 | 24 | 22 | 24 Shemini | 24 | 26 | 26 Mattot Masei | 28 | 29 | 30 R.H. | 1 Kislev R.H. | 1 Tevet R.H. 7 |
| 19 | 23 | 25 | 23 | 25 | 25 | 27 | 27 | 29 | 1 Tishri Rosh Ha-Shanah | 1 Heshvan R.H. | 2 | 2 Mi-Kez 8 |
| 20 | 24 | 26 | 24 | 26 | 26 | 28 Shelah | 28 | 30 R.H. | 2 | 2 | 3 | 3 |
| 21 | 25 | 27 Mishpatim Shekalim | 25 Va-Yakhel Pekudei Ha-Hodesh | 27 | 27 | 29 | 29 | 1 Elul R.H. | 3 Fast | 3 | 4 Toledot | 4 |
| 22 | 26 | 28 | 26 | 28 | 28 | 30 R.H. | 1 Av R.H. | 2 Shofetim | 4 | 4 | 5 | 5 |
| 23 | 27 | 29 | 27 | 29 | 29 Be-Midbar | 1 Tammuz R.H. | 2 | 3 | 5 | 5 | 6 | 6 |
| 24 | 28 Va-Era | 30 R.H. | 28 | 30 R.H. | 1 Sivan R.H. | 2 | 3 | 4 | 6 | 6 No'ah | 7 | 7 |
| 25 | 29 | 1 Adar R.H. | 29 | 1 R.H. Iyyar Tazri'a Mezora | 2 | 3 | 4 Devarim | 5 | 7 | 7 | 8 | 8 |
| 26 | 1 Shevat R.H. | 2 | 1 Nisan R.H. | 2 | 3 | 4 | 5 | 6 | 8 Ha'azinu Shabbat Shuvah | 8 | 9 | 9 Va-Yiggash |
| 27 | 2 | 3 | 2 | 3 | 4 | 5 Korah | 6 | 7 | 9 | 9 | 10 | 10 Fast |
| 28 | 3 | 4 Terumah | 3 Va-Yikra | 4 | 5 | 6 | 7 | 8 | 10 Yom Kippur | 10 | 11 Va-Yeze | 11 |
| 29 | 4 | | 4 | 5 Yom ha-Azma'ut | 6 Shavuot | 7 | 8 | 9 Ki Teze | 11 | 11 | 12 | 12 |
| 30 | 5 | | 5 | 6 | 7 | 8 | 9 Tishah be-Av | 10 | 12 | 12 | 13 | 13 |
| 31 | 6 Bo | | 6 | | 8 | | 10 | 11 | | 13 Lekh Lekha | | 14 |

# 2010

**5770/71** תש״ע / תשע״א

| | January | February | March | April | May | June | July | August | September | October | November | December |
|---|---|---|---|---|---|---|---|---|---|---|---|---|
| 1 | 15 Tevet | 17 | 15 Shushan Purim | 17 Hol ha-Mo'ed | 17 Emor | 19 | 19 | 21 | 22 | 23 Simhat Torah Ve-Zot Ha-Berakhah | 24 | 24 |
| 2 | 16 Va-Yehi | 18 | 16 | 18 | 18 Lag ba-Omer | 20 | 20 | 22 | 23 | 24 Bereshit | 25 | 25 Hanukkah 1 |
| 3 | 17 | 19 | 17 | 19 | 19 | 21 | 21 Pinhas | 23 | 24 | 25 | 26 | 26 2 |
| 4 | 18 | 20 | 18 | 20 | 20 | 22 | 22 | 24 | 25 Nizzavim Va-Yelekh | 26 | 27 | 27 Mi-Kez 3 |
| 5 | 19 | 21 | 19 | 21 Pesah | 21 | 23 Shelah | 23 | 25 | 26 | 27 | 28 | 28 4 |
| 6 | 20 | 22 Yitro | 20 Ki Tissa Parah | 22 | 22 | 24 | 24 | 26 | 27 | 28 | 29 Toledot | 29 5 |
| 7 | 21 | 23 | 21 | 23 | 23 | 25 | 25 | 27 Re'eh | 28 | 29 | 30 R.H. | 30 R.H. 6 |
| 8 | 22 | 24 | 22 | 24 | 24 Be-Har Be-Hukkotai | 26 | 26 | 28 | 29 | 30 R.H. | 1 Kislev R.H. | 1 Tevet R.H. 7 |
| 9 | 23 Shemot | 25 | 23 | 25 | 25 | 27 | 27 | 29 | 1 Tishri Rosh Ha-Shanah | 1 R.H. No'ah Heshvan | 2 | 2 8 |
| 10 | 24 | 26 | 24 | 26 Shemini | 26 | 28 | 28 Mattot Masei | 30 R.H. | 2 | 2 | 3 | 3 |
| 11 | 25 | 27 | 25 | 27 | 27 | 29 | 29 | 1 Elul R.H. | 3 Ha'azinu Shabbat Shuvah | 3 | 4 | 4 Va-Yiggash |
| 12 | 26 | 28 | 26 | 28 | 28 | 30 R.H. Korah | 1 Av R.H. | 2 | 4 Fast | 4 | 5 | 5 |
| 13 | 27 | 29 Mishpatim Shekalim | 27 Va-Yakhel Pekudei Ha-Hodesh | 29 | 29 | 1 Tammuz R.H. | 2 | 3 | 5 | 5 | 6 Va-Yeze | 6 |
| 14 | 28 | 30 R.H. | 28 | 30 R.H. | 1 Sivan R.H. | 2 | 3 | 4 Shofetim | 6 | 6 | 7 | 7 |
| 15 | 29 | 1 Adar R.H. | 29 | 1 Iyyar R.H. | 2 Be-Midbar | 3 | 4 | 5 | 7 | 7 | 8 | 8 |
| 16 | 1 R.H. Va-Era Shevat | 2 | 1 Nisan R.H. | 2 | 3 | 4 | 5 | 6 | 8 | 8 Lekh Lekha | 9 | 9 |
| 17 | 2 | 3 | 2 | 3 Tazri'a Mezora | 4 | 5 | 6 Devarim | 7 | 9 | 9 | 10 | 10 Fast |
| 18 | 3 | 4 | 3 | 4 | 5 | 6 | 7 | 8 | 10 Yom Kippur | 10 | 11 | 11 Va-Yehi |
| 19 | 4 | 5 | 4 | 5 Yom ha-Azma'ut | 6 Shavuot | 7 Hukkat | 8 | 9 | 11 | 11 | 12 | 12 |
| 20 | 5 | 6 Terumah | 5 Va-Yikra | 6 | 7 | 8 | 9 Tishah be-Av | 10 | 12 | 12 | 13 Va-Yishlah | 13 |
| 21 | 6 | 7 | 6 | 7 | 8 | 9 | 10 | 11 Ki Teze | 13 | 13 | 14 | 14 |
| 22 | 7 | 8 | 7 | 8 | 9 Naso | 10 | 11 | 12 | 14 | 14 | 15 | 15 |
| 23 | 8 Bo | 9 | 8 | 9 | 10 | 11 | 12 | 13 | 15 Sukkot | 15 Va-Yera | 16 | 16 |
| 24 | 9 | 10 | 9 | 10 Aharei Mot Kedoshim | 11 | 12 | 13 Va-Ethannan | 14 | 16 | 16 | 17 | 17 |
| 25 | 10 | 11 Ta'anit Esther | 10 | 11 | 12 | 13 | 14 | 15 | 17 Hol ha-Mo'ed | 17 | 18 | 18 Shemot |
| 26 | 11 | 12 | 11 | 12 | 13 | 14 Balak | 15 | 16 | 18 | 18 | 19 | 19 |
| 27 | 12 | 13 Tezavveh Zakhor | 12 Zav Shabbat ha-Gadol | 13 | 14 | 15 | 16 | 17 | 19 | 19 | 20 Va-Yeshev | 20 |
| 28 | 13 | 14 Purim | 13 | 14 | 15 | 16 | 17 | 18 Ki Tavo | 20 | 20 | 21 | 21 |
| 29 | 14 | | 14 | 15 | 16 Be-Ha'alotkha | 17 Fast | 18 | 19 | 21 Hoshana Rabba | 21 | 22 | 22 |
| 30 | 15 Be-Shallah | | 15 Pesah | 16 | 17 | 18 | 19 | 20 | 22 Shemini Azeret | 22 Hayyei Sarah | 23 | 23 |
| 31 | 16 | | 16 Omer | | 18 | | 20 Ekev | 21 | | 23 | | 24 |

## 2011

**5771/72** תשע״א / תשע״ב

| | January | February | March | April | May | June | July | August | September | October | November | December |
|---|---|---|---|---|---|---|---|---|---|---|---|---|
| 1 | 25 Tevet *Va-Era* | 27 | 25 | 26 | 27 | 28 | 29 | 1 Av R.H. | 2 | 3 *Ha'azinu* Shabbat Shuvah | 4 | 5 |
| 2 | 26 | 28 | 26 | 27 *Tazri'a* Ha-Ḥodesh | 28 | 29 | 30 R.H. *Ḥukkat* | 2 | 3 | 4 Fast | 5 | 6 |
| 3 | 27 | 29 | 27 | 28 | 29 | 1 Sivan R.H. | 1 Tammuz R.H. | 3 | 4 *Shofetim* | 5 | 6 | 7 *Va-Yeẓe* |
| 4 | 28 | 30 R.H. | 28 | 29 | 30 R.H. | 2 *Naso* | 2 | 4 | 5 | 6 | 7 | 8 |
| 5 | 29 | 1 Adar I R.H. *Terumah* | 29 *Pekudei* Shekalim | 1 Nisan R.H. | 1 Iyyar R.H. | 3 | 3 | 5 | 6 | 7 | 8 *Lekh Lekha* | 9 |
| 6 | 1 Shevat R.H. | 2 | 30 R.H. | 2 | 2 | 4 | 4 | 6 *Devarim* | 7 | 8 | 9 | 10 |
| 7 | 2 | 3 | 1 Adar II R.H. | 3 | 3 *Emor* | 5 | 5 | 7 | 8 | 9 | 10 | 11 |
| 8 | 3 *Bo* | 4 | 2 | 4 | 4 | 6 Shavuot | 6 | 8 | 9 | 10 Yom Kippur | 11 | 12 |
| 9 | 4 | 5 | 3 | 5 *Meẓora* | 5 Yom ha-Aẓma'ut | 7 | 7 *Balak* | 9 Tishah be-Av | 10 | 11 | 12 | 13 |
| 10 | 5 | 6 | 4 | 6 | 6 | 8 | 8 | 10 | 11 *Ki Teẓe* | 12 | 13 | 14 *Va-Yishlaḥ* |
| 11 | 6 | 7 | 5 | 7 | 7 | 9 *Be-Ha'alotkha* | 9 | 11 | 12 | 13 | 14 | 15 |
| 12 | 7 | 8 *Teẓavveh* | 6 *Va-Yikra* | 8 | 8 | 10 | 10 | 12 | 13 | 14 | 15 *Va-Yera* | 16 |
| 13 | 8 | 9 | 7 | 9 | 9 | 11 | 11 | 13 *Va-Ethannan* | 14 | 15 Sukkot | 16 | 17 |
| 14 | 9 | 10 | 8 | 10 | 10 *Be-Har* | 12 | 12 | 14 | 15 | 16 | 17 | 18 |
| 15 | 10 *Be-Shallaḥ* | 11 | 9 | 11 | 11 | 13 | 13 | 15 | 16 | 17 Ḥol ha-Mo'ed | 18 | 19 |
| 16 | 11 | 12 | 10 | 12 *Aharei Mot* Shabbat ha-Gadol | 12 | 14 | 14 *Pinḥas* | 16 | 17 | 18 | 19 | 20 |
| 17 | 12 | 13 | 11 Ta'anit Esther | 13 | 13 | 15 | 15 | 17 | 18 *Ki Tavo* | 19 | 20 | 21 *Va-Yeshev* |
| 18 | 13 | 14 | 12 | 14 | 14 | 16 *Shelaḥ* | 16 | 18 | 19 | 20 | 21 | 22 |
| 19 | 14 | 15 *Ki Tissa* | 13 *Ẓav* Zakhor | 15 Pesaḥ | 15 | 17 | 17 Fast | 19 | 20 | 21 Hoshana Rabba | 22 *Ḥayyei Sarah* | 23 |
| 20 | 15 | 16 | 14 Purim | 16 Omer | 16 | 18 | 18 | 20 *Ekev* | 21 | 22 Shemini Aẓeret | 23 | 24 |
| 21 | 16 | 17 | 15 Shushan Purim | 17 Ḥol ha-Mo'ed | 17 *Be-Ḥukkotai* | 19 | 19 | 21 | 22 | 23 Simḥat Torah *Ve-Zot Ha-Berakhah* | 24 | 25 Ḥanukkah 1 |
| 22 | 17 *Yitro* | 18 | 16 | 18 | 18 Lag ba-Omer | 20 | 20 | 22 | 23 | 24 *Bereshit* | 25 | 26 2 |
| 23 | 18 | 19 | 17 | 19 | 19 | 21 | 21 *Mattot* | 23 | 24 | 25 | 26 | 27 3 |
| 24 | 19 | 20 | 18 | 20 | 20 | 22 | 22 | 24 | 25 *Niẓẓavim Va-Yelekh* | 26 | 27 | 28 *Mi-Keẓ* 4 |
| 25 | 20 | 21 | 19 | 21 Pesaḥ | 21 | 23 *Koraḥ* | 23 | 25 | 26 | 27 | 28 | 29 5 |
| 26 | 21 | 22 *Va-Yakhel* | 20 *Shemini* Parah | 22 | 22 | 24 | 24 | 26 | 27 | 28 | 29 *Toledot* | 30 R.H. 6 |
| 27 | 22 | 23 | 21 | 23 | 23 | 25 | 25 | 27 *Re'eh* | 28 | 29 | 1 Kislev R.H. | 1 Tevet R.H. 7 |
| 28 | 23 | 24 | 22 | 24 | 24 *Be-Midbar* | 26 | 26 | 28 | 29 | 30 R.H. | 2 | 2 8 |
| 29 | 24 *Mishpatim* | | 23 | 25 | 25 | 27 | 27 | 29 | 1 Tishri Rosh Ha-Shanah | 1 Ḥeshvan R.H. *Noaḥ* | 3 | 3 |
| 30 | 25 | | 24 | 26 *Kedoshim* | 26 | 28 | 28 *Masei* | 30 R.H. | 2 | 2 | 4 | 4 |
| 31 | 26 | | 25 | | 27 | | 29 | 1 Elul R.H. | | 3 | | 5 *Va-Yiggash* |

## 2012

**5772/73** תשע״ב / תשע״ג

| | January | February | March | April | May | June | July | August | September | October | November | December |
|---|---|---|---|---|---|---|---|---|---|---|---|---|
| 1 | 6 Tevet | 8 | 7 | 9 | 9 | 11 | 11 | 13 | 14 *Ki Teẓe* | 15 Sukkot | 16 | 17 *Va-Yishlaḥ* |
| 2 | 7 | 9 | 8 | 10 | 10 | 12 *Naso* | 12 | 14 | 15 | 16 | 17 | 18 |
| 3 | 8 | 10 | 9 *Teẓavveh* Zakhor | 11 | 11 | 13 | 13 | 15 | 16 | 17 Ḥol ha-Mo'ed | 18 *Va-Yera* | 19 |
| 4 | 9 | 11 *Be-Shallaḥ* | 10 | 12 | 12 | 14 | 14 | 16 *Va-Ethannan* | 17 | 18 | 19 | 20 |
| 5 | 10 Fast | 12 | 11 | 13 | 13 *Aharei Mot Kedoshim* | 15 | 15 | 17 | 18 | 19 | 20 | 21 |
| 6 | 11 | 13 | 12 | 14 | 14 | 16 | 16 | 18 | 19 | 20 | 21 | 22 |
| 7 | 12 *Va-Yeḥi* | 14 | 13 Ta'anit Esther | 15 Pesaḥ | 15 | 17 | 17 *Balak* | 19 | 20 | 21 Hoshana Rabba | 22 | 23 |
| 8 | 13 | 15 | 14 Purim | 16 Omer | 16 | 18 | 18 Fast | 20 | 21 *Ki Tavo* | 22 Shemini Aẓeret | 23 | 24 *Va-Yeshev* |
| 9 | 14 | 16 | 15 Shushan Purim | 17 | 17 | 19 *Be-Ha'alotkha* | 19 | 21 | 22 | 23 Simḥat Torah *Ve-Zot Ha-Berakhah* | 24 | 25 Ḥanukkah 1 |
| 10 | 15 | 17 | 16 *Ki Tissa* | 18 Ḥol ha-Mo'ed | 18 Lag ba-Omer | 20 | 20 | 22 | 23 | 24 | 25 *Ḥayyei Sarah* | 26 2 |
| 11 | 16 | 18 *Yitro* | 17 | 19 | 19 | 21 | 21 | 23 *Ekev* | 24 | 25 | 26 | 27 3 |
| 12 | 17 | 19 | 18 | 20 | 20 *Emor* | 22 | 22 | 24 | 25 | 26 | 27 | 28 4 |
| 13 | 18 | 20 | 19 | 21 Pesaḥ | 21 | 23 | 23 | 25 | 26 | 27 *Bereshit* | 28 | 29 5 |
| 14 | 19 *Shemot* | 21 | 20 | 22 | 22 | 24 | 24 *Pinḥas* | 26 | 27 | 28 | 29 | 1 Tevet R.H. 6 |
| 15 | 20 | 22 | 21 | 23 | 23 | 25 | 25 | 27 | 28 *Niẓẓavim* | 29 | 1 Kislev R.H. | 2 *Mi-Keẓ* 7 |
| 16 | 21 | 23 | 22 | 24 | 24 | 26 *Shelaḥ* | 26 | 28 | 29 | 30 R.H. | 2 | 3 8 |
| 17 | 22 | 24 | 23 *Va-Yakhel Pekudei* Parah | 25 | 25 | 27 | 27 | 29 | 1 Tishri Rosh Ha-Shanah | 1 Ḥeshvan R.H. | 3 *Toledot* | 4 |
| 18 | 23 | 25 *Mishpatim* Shekalim | 24 | 26 | 26 | 28 | 28 | 30 R.H. *Re'eh* | 2 | 2 | 4 | 5 |
| 19 | 24 | 26 | 25 | 27 | 27 *Be-Har Be-Ḥukkotai* | 29 | 29 | 1 Elul R.H. | 3 Fast | 3 | 5 | 6 |
| 20 | 25 | 27 | 26 | 28 | 28 | 30 R.H. | 1 Av R.H. | 2 | 4 | 4 *Noaḥ* | 6 | 7 |
| 21 | 26 *Va-Era* | 28 | 27 | 29 *Shemini* | 29 | 1 Tammuz R.H. | 2 *Mattot Masei* | 3 | 5 | 5 | 7 | 8 |
| 22 | 27 | 29 | 28 | 30 R.H. | 1 Sivan R.H. | 2 | 3 | 4 | 6 *Va-Yelekh* Shabbat Shuvah | 6 | 8 | 9 *Va-Yiggash* |
| 23 | 28 | 30 R.H. | 29 | 1 Iyyar R.H. | 2 | 3 *Koraḥ* | 4 | 5 | 7 | 7 | 9 | 10 Fast |
| 24 | 29 | 1 Adar R.H. | 1 Nisan *Va-Yikra* R.H. Ha-Ḥodesh | 2 | 3 | 4 | 5 | 6 | 8 | 8 | 10 *Va-Yeẓe* | 11 |
| 25 | 1 Shevat R.H. | 2 *Terumah* | 2 | 3 | 4 | 5 | 6 | 7 *Shofetim* | 9 | 9 | 11 | 12 |
| 26 | 2 | 3 | 3 | 4 Yom ha-Aẓma'ut | 5 *Be-Midbar* | 6 | 7 | 8 | 10 Yom Kippur | 10 | 12 | 13 |
| 27 | 3 | 4 | 4 | 5 | 6 Shavuot | 7 | 8 | 9 | 11 | 11 *Lekh Lekha* | 13 | 14 |
| 28 | 4 *Bo* | 5 | 5 | 6 *Tazri'a Meẓora* | 7 | 8 | 9 *Devarim* Tishah be-Av | 10 | 12 | 12 | 14 | 15 |
| 29 | 5 | 6 | 6 | 7 | 8 | 9 | 10 Fast | 11 | 13 *Ha'azinu* | 13 | 15 | 16 *Va-Yeḥi* |
| 30 | 6 | | 7 | 8 | 9 | 10 *Ḥukkat* | 11 | 12 | 14 | 14 | 16 | 17 |
| 31 | 7 | | 8 *Ẓav* Shabbat ha-Gadol | | 10 | | 12 | 13 | | 15 | | 18 |

## 2013

**5773/74** תשע״ג / תשע״ד

| | January | February | March | April | May | June | July | August | September | October | November | December |
|---|---|---|---|---|---|---|---|---|---|---|---|---|
| 1 | 19 Tevet | 21 | 19 | 21 Pesah | 21 | 23 Shelah | 23 | 25 | 26 | 27 | 28 | 28 4 |
| 2 | 20 | 22 Yitro | 20 Ki Tissa Parah | 22 | 22 | 24 | 24 | 26 | 27 | 28 | 29 Toledot | 29 5 |
| 3 | 21 | 23 | 21 | 23 | 23 | 25 | 25 | 27 Re'eh | 28 | 29 | 30 R H | 30 R H 6 |
| 4 | 22 | 24 | 22 | 24 | 24 Be-Har Be-Hukkotai | 26 | 26 | 28 | 29 | 30 R H | 1 Kislev R H | 1 Tevet R H 7 |
| 5 | 23 Shemot | 25 | 23 | 25 | 25 | 27 | 27 | 29 | 1 Tishri Rosh Ha-Shanah | 1 Heshvan R H Noah | 2 | 2 8 |
| 6 | 24 | 26 | 24 | 26 Shemini | 26 | 28 | 28 Mattot Masei | 30 R H | 2 | 2 | 3 | 3 |
| 7 | 25 | 27 | 25 | 27 | 27 | 29 | 29 | 1 Elul R H | 3 Ha'azinu Shabbat Shuvah | 3 | 4 | 4 Va-Yiggash |
| 8 | 26 | 28 | 26 | 28 | 28 | 30 R H Korah | 1 Av R H | 2 | 4 Fast | 4 | 5 | 5 |
| 9 | 27 | 29 Mishpatim Shekalim | 27 Va-Yakhel Pekudei Ha-Hodesh | 29 | 29 | 1 Tammuz R H | 2 | 3 | 5 | 5 | 6 Va-Yeze | 6 |
| 10 | 28 | 30 R H | 28 | 30 R H | 1 Sivan R H | 2 | 3 | 4 Shofetim | 6 | 6 | 7 | 7 |
| 11 | 29 | 1 Adar R H | 29 | 1 Iyyar R H | 2 Be-Midbar | 3 | 4 | 5 | 7 | 7 | 8 | 8 |
| 12 | 1 Shevat R H Va-Era | 2 | 1 Nisan R H | 2 | 3 | 4 | 5 | 6 | 8 | 8 Lekh Lekha | 9 | 9 |
| 13 | 2 | 3 | 2 | 3 Tazri'a Mezora | 4 | 5 | 6 Devarim | 7 | 9 | 9 | 10 | 10 Fast |
| 14 | 3 | 4 | 3 | 4 | 5 | 6 | 7 | 8 | 10 Yom Kippur | 10 | 11 | 11 Va-Yehi |
| 15 | 4 | 5 | 4 | 5 Yom ha-Azma'ut | 6 Shavuot | 7 Hukkat | 8 | 9 | 11 | 11 | 12 | 12 |
| 16 | 5 | 6 Terumah | 5 Va-Yikra | 6 | 7 | 8 | 9 Tishah be-Av | 10 | 12 | 12 | 13 Va-Yishlah | 13 |
| 17 | 6 | 7 | 6 | 7 | 8 | 9 | 10 | 11 Ki Teze | 13 | 13 | 14 | 14 |
| 18 | 7 | 8 | 7 | 8 | 9 Naso | 10 | 11 | 12 | 14 | 14 | 15 | 15 |
| 19 | 8 Bo | 9 | 8 | 9 | 10 | 11 | 12 | 13 | 15 Sukkot | 15 Va-Yera | 16 | 16 |
| 20 | 9 | 10 | 9 | 10 Aharei Mot Kedoshim | 11 | 12 | 13 Va-Ethannan | 14 | 16 | 16 | 17 | 17 |
| 21 | 10 | 11 Ta'anit Esther | 10 | 11 | 12 | 13 | 14 | 15 | 17 Hol ha-Mo'ed | 17 | 18 | 18 Shemot |
| 22 | 11 | 12 | 11 | 12 | 13 | 14 Balak | 15 | 16 | 18 | 18 | 19 | 19 |
| 23 | 12 | 13 Tezavveh Zakhor | 12 Zav Shabbat ha-Gadol | 13 | 14 | 15 | 16 | 17 | 19 | 19 | 20 Va-Yeshev | 20 |
| 24 | 13 | 14 Purim | 13 | 14 | 15 | 16 | 17 | 18 Ki Tavo | 20 | 20 | 21 | 21 |
| 25 | 14 | 15 Shushan Purim | 14 | 15 | 16 Be-Ha'alotkha | 17 Fast | 18 | 19 | 21 Hoshana Rabba | 21 | 22 | 22 |
| 26 | 15 Be-Shallah | 16 | 15 Pesah | 16 | 17 | 18 | 19 | 20 | 22 Shemini Azeret | 22 Hayyei Sarah | 23 | 23 |
| 27 | 16 | 17 | 16 Omer | 17 Emor | 18 | 19 | 20 Ekev | 21 | 23 Simhat Torah Ve-Zot Ha-Berakhah | 23 | 24 | 24 |
| 28 | 17 | 18 | 17 Hol ha-Mo'ed | 18 Lag ba-Omer | 19 | 20 | 21 | 22 | 24 Bereshit | 24 | 25 Hanukkah 1 | 25 Va-Era |
| 29 | 18 | | 18 | 19 | 20 | 21 Pinhas | 22 | 23 | 25 | 25 | 26 2 | 26 |
| 30 | 19 | | 19 | 20 | 21 | 22 | 23 | 24 | 26 | 26 | 27 Mi-Kez 3 | 27 |
| 31 | 20 | | 20 | | 22 | | 24 | 25 Nizzavim Va-Yelekh | | 27 | | 28 |

## 2014

**5774/75** תשע״ד / תשע״ה

| | January | February | March | April | May | June | July | August | September | October | November | December |
|---|---|---|---|---|---|---|---|---|---|---|---|---|
| 1 | 29 Tevet | 1 R H Terumah Adar I | 29 Pekudei Shekalim | 1 Nisan R H | 1 Iyyar R H | 3 | 3 | 5 | 6 | 7 | 8 Lekh Lekha | 9 |
| 2 | 1 Shevat R H | 2 | 30 R H | 2 | 2 | 4 | 4 | 6 Devarim | 7 | 8 | 9 | 10 |
| 3 | 2 | 3 | 1 Adar II R H | 3 | 3 Emor | 5 | 5 | 7 | 8 | 9 | 10 | 11 |
| 4 | 3 Bo | 4 | 2 | 4 | 4 | 6 Shavuot | 6 | 8 | 9 | 10 Yom Kippur | 11 | 12 |
| 5 | 4 | 5 | 3 | 5 Mezora | 5 Yom ha-Azma'ut | 7 | 7 Balak | 9 Tishah be-Av | 10 | 11 | 12 | 13 |
| 6 | 5 | 6 | 4 | 6 | 6 | 8 | 8 | 10 | 11 Ki Teze | 12 | 13 | 14 Va-Yishlah |
| 7 | 6 | 7 | 5 | 7 | 7 | 9 Be-Ha'alotkha | 9 | 11 | 12 | 13 | 14 | 15 |
| 8 | 7 | 8 Tezavveh | 6 Va-Yikra | 8 | 8 | 10 | 10 | 12 | 13 | 14 | 15 Va-Yera | 16 |
| 9 | 8 | 9 | 7 | 9 | 9 | 11 | 11 | 13 Va-Ethannan | 14 | 15 Sukkot | 16 | 17 |
| 10 | 9 | 10 | 8 | 10 | 10 Be-Har | 12 | 12 | 14 | 15 | 16 | 17 | 18 |
| 11 | 10 Be-Shallah | 11 | 9 | 11 | 11 | 13 | 13 | 15 | 16 | 17 Hol ha-Mo'ed | 18 | 19 |
| 12 | 11 | 12 | 10 | 12 Aharei Mot Shabbat ha-Gadol | 12 | 14 | 14 Pinhas | 16 | 17 | 18 | 19 | 20 |
| 13 | 12 | 13 | 11 Ta'anit Esther | 13 | 13 | 15 | 15 | 17 | 18 Ki Tavo | 19 | 20 | 21 Va-Yeshev |
| 14 | 13 | 14 | 12 | 14 | 14 | 16 Shelah | 16 | 18 | 19 | 20 | 21 | 22 |
| 15 | 14 | 15 Ki Tissa | 13 Zav Zakhor | 15 Pesah | 15 | 17 | 17 Fast | 19 | 20 | 21 Hoshana Rabba | 22 Hayyei Sarah | 23 |
| 16 | 15 | 16 | 14 Purim | 16 Omer | 16 | 18 | 18 | 20 Ekev | 21 | 22 Shemini Azeret | 23 | 24 |
| 17 | 16 | 17 | 15 Shushan Purim | 17 Hol ha-Mo'ed | 17 Be-Hukkotai | 19 | 19 | 21 | 22 | 23 Simhat Torah Ve-Zot Ha-Berakhah | 24 | 25 Hanukkah 1 |
| 18 | 17 Yitro | 18 | 16 | 18 | 18 Lag ba-Omer | 20 | 20 | 22 | 23 | 24 Bereshit | 25 | 26 2 |
| 19 | 18 | 19 | 17 | 19 | 19 | 21 | 21 Mattot | 23 | 24 | 25 | 26 | 27 3 |
| 20 | 19 | 20 | 18 | 20 | 20 | 22 | 22 | 24 | 25 Nizzavim Va-Yelekh | 26 | 27 | 28 Mi-Kez 4 |
| 21 | 20 | 21 | 19 | 21 Pesah | 21 | 23 Korah | 23 | 25 | 26 | 27 | 28 | 29 5 |
| 22 | 21 | 22 Va-Yakhel | 20 Shemini Parah | 22 | 22 | 24 | 24 | 26 | 27 | 28 | 29 Toledot | 30 R H 6 |
| 23 | 22 | 23 | 21 | 23 | 23 | 25 | 25 | 27 Re'eh | 28 | 29 | 1 Kislev R H | 1 Tevet R H 7 |
| 24 | 23 | 24 | 22 | 24 | 24 Be-Midbar | 26 | 26 | 28 | 29 | 30 R H | 2 | 2 8 |
| 25 | 24 Mishpatim | 25 | 23 | 25 | 25 | 27 | 27 | 29 | 1 Tishri Rosh Ha-Shanah | 1 R H Noah Heshvan | 3 | 3 |
| 26 | 25 | 26 | 24 | 26 Kedoshim | 26 | 28 | 28 Masei | 30 R H | 2 | 2 | 4 | 4 |
| 27 | 26 | 27 | 25 | 27 | 27 | 29 | 29 | 1 Elul R H | 3 Ha'azinu Shabbat Shuvah | 3 | 5 | 5 Va-Yiggash |
| 28 | 27 | 28 | 26 | 28 | 28 | 30 R H Hukkat | 1 Av R H | 2 | 4 Fast | 4 | 6 | 6 |
| 29 | 28 | | 27 Tazri'a Ha-Hodesh | 29 | 29 | 1 Tammuz R H | 2 | 3 | 5 | 5 | 7 Va-Yeze | 7 |
| 30 | 29 | | 28 | 30 R H | 1 Sivan R H | 2 | 3 | 4 Shofetim | 6 | 6 | 8 | 8 |
| 31 | 30 R H | | 29 | | 2 Naso | | 4 | 5 | | 7 | | 9 |

## 2015

**5775/76** תשע"ה / תשע"ו

| | January | February | March | April | May | June | July | August | September | October | November | December |
|---|---|---|---|---|---|---|---|---|---|---|---|---|
| 1 | 10 **Tevet** Fast | 12 | 10 | 12 | 12 | 14 | 14 | **16** *Va-Ethannan* | 17 | 18 | 19 | 19 |
| 2 | 11 | 13 | 11 | 13 | **13** *Aharei Mot Kedoshim* | 15 | 15 | 17 | 18 | 19 Hol ha-Mo'ed | 20 | 20 |
| 3 | **12** *Va-Yehi* | 14 | 12 | 14 | 14 | 16 | 16 | 18 | 19 | **20** | 21 | 21 |
| 4 | 13 | 15 | 13 Ta'anit Esther | **15** Pesah | 15 | 17 | **17** *Balak* | 19 | 20 | 21 Hoshana Rabba | 22 | 22 |
| 5 | 14 | 16 | 14 Purim | 16 Omer | 16 | 18 | 18 Fast | 20 | **21** *Ki Tavo* | 22 Shemini Azeret | 23 | **23** *Va-Yeshev* |
| 6 | 15 | 17 | 15 Shushan Purim | 17 | 17 | **19** *Be-Ha'alotkha* | 19 | 21 | 22 | 23 Simhat Torah *Ve-Zot Ha-Berakhah* | 24 | 24 |
| 7 | 16 | **18** *Yitro* | **16** *Ki Tissa* | 18 Hol ha-Mo'ed | 18 Lag ba-Omer | 20 | 20 | 22 | 23 | 24 | **25** *Hayyei Sarah* | 25 Hanukkah 1 |
| 8 | 17 | 19 | 17 | 19 | 19 | 21 | 21 | **23** *Ekev* | 24 | 25 | 26 | 26 2 |
| 9 | 18 | 20 | 18 | 20 | **20** *Emor* | 22 | 22 | 24 | 25 | 26 | 27 | 27 3 |
| 10 | **19** *Shemot* | 21 | 19 | 21 Pesah | 21 | 23 | 23 | 25 | 26 | **27** *Bereshit* | 28 | 28 4 |
| 11 | 20 | 22 | 20 | **22** | 22 | 24 | **24** *Pinhas* | 26 | 27 | 28 | 29 | 29 5 |
| 12 | 21 | 23 | 21 | 23 | 23 | 25 | 25 | 27 | **28** *Nizzavim* | 29 | 30 R. H. | **30** R. H. *Mi-Kez* 6 |
| 13 | 22 | 24 | 22 | 24 | 24 | **26** *Shelah* | 26 | 28 | 29 | 30 R. H. | 1 **Kislev** R. H. | 1 **Tevet** R. H. 7 |
| 14 | 23 | **25** *Mishpatim* Shekalim | *Va-Yakhel Pekudei* **23** Parah | 25 | 25 | 27 | 27 | 29 | 1 **Tishri** Rosh Ha-Shanah | 1 **Heshvan** R. H. | **2** *Toledot* | 2 8 |
| 15 | 24 | 26 | 24 | 26 | 26 | 28 | 28 | **30** R. H. *Re'eh* | 2 | 2 | 3 | 3 |
| 16 | 25 | 27 | 25 | 27 | **27** *Be-Har Be-Hukkotai* | 29 | 29 | 1 **Elul** R. H. | 3 Fast | 3 | 4 | 4 |
| 17 | **26** *Va-Era* | 28 | 26 | 28 | 28 | 30 R. H. | 1 **Av** R. H. | 2 | 4 | **4** *No'ah* | 5 | 5 |
| 18 | 27 | 29 | 27 | **29** *Shemini* | 29 | 1 **Tammuz** R. H. | **2** *Mattot Masei* | 3 | 5 | 5 | 6 | 6 |
| 19 | 28 | 30 R. H. | 28 | 30 R. H. | 1 **Sivan** R. H. | 2 | 3 | 4 | **6** *Va-Yelekh* Shabbat Shuvah | 6 | 7 | **7** *Va-Yiggash* |
| 20 | 29 | 1 **Adar** R. H. | 29 | 1 **Iyyar** R. H. | 2 | **3** *Korah* | 4 | 5 | 7 | 7 | 8 | 8 |
| 21 | 1 **Shevat** R. H. | **2** *Terumah* | **1 Nisan** *Va-Yikra* R. H. Ha-Hodesh | 2 | 3 | 4 | 5 | 6 | 8 | 8 | **9** *Va-Yeze* | 9 |
| 22 | 2 | 3 | 2 | 3 | 4 | 5 | 6 | **7** *Shofetim* | 9 | 9 | 10 | 10 Fast |
| 23 | 3 | 4 | 3 | 4 Yom ha-Azma'ut | **5** *Be-Midbar* | 6 | 7 | 8 | 10 Yom Kippur | 10 | 11 | 11 |
| 24 | **4** *Bo* | 5 | 4 | 5 | 6 Shavuot | 7 | 8 | 9 | 11 | **11** *Lekh Lekha* | 12 | 12 |
| 25 | 5 | 6 | 5 | **6** *Tazri'a Mezora* | 7 | 8 | **9** *Devarim* Tishah be-Av | 10 | 12 | 12 | 13 | 13 |
| 26 | 6 | 7 | 6 | 7 | 8 | 9 | 10 Fast | 11 | **13** *Ha'azinu* | 13 | 14 | **14** *Va-Yehi* |
| 27 | 7 | 8 | 7 | 8 | 9 | **10** *Hukkat* | 11 | 12 | 14 | 14 | 15 | 15 |
| 28 | 8 | **9** *Tezavveh* Zakhor | **8** *Zav* Shabbat ha-Gadol | 9 | 10 | 11 | 12 | 13 | 15 Sukkot | 15 | **16** *Va-Yishlah* | 16 |
| 29 | 9 | | 9 | 10 | 11 | 12 | 13 | **14** *Ki Teze* | 16 | 16 | 17 | 17 |
| 30 | 10 | | 10 | 11 | **12** *Naso* | 13 | 14 | 15 | 17 Hol ha-Mo'ed | 17 | 18 | 18 |
| 31 | **11** *Be-Shallah* | | 11 | | 13 | | 15 | 16 | | **18** *Va-Yera* | | 19 |

## 2016

**5776/77** תשע"ו / תשע"ז

| | January | February | March | April | May | June | July | August | September | October | November | December |
|---|---|---|---|---|---|---|---|---|---|---|---|---|
| 1 | 20 **Tevet** | 22 | 21 | 22 | 23 | 24 | 25 | 26 | 28 | **28** *Nizzavim* | 30 R. H. | 1 **Kislev** R. H. |
| 2 | **21** *Shemot* | 23 | 22 | **23** *Shemini* Parah | 24 | 25 | **26** *Shelah* | 27 | 29 | 29 | 1 **Heshvan** R. H. | 2 |
| 3 | 22 | 24 | 23 | 24 | 25 | 26 | 27 | 28 | **30** R. H. *Re'eh* | 1 **Tishri** Rosh Ha-Shanah | 2 | **3** *Toledot* |
| 4 | 23 | 25 | 24 | 25 | 26 | **27** *Be-Hukkotai* | 28 | 29 | 1 **Elul** R. H. | 2 | 3 | 4 |
| 5 | 24 | 26 | **25** *Va-Yakhel* Shekalim | 26 | 27 | 28 | 29 | 1 **Av** R. H. | 2 | 3 Fast | **4** *No'ah* | 5 |
| 6 | 25 | **27** *Mishpatim* | 26 | 27 | 28 | 29 | 30 R. H. | **2** *Mattot Masei* | 3 | 4 | 5 | 6 |
| 7 | 26 | 28 | 27 | 28 | **29** *Aharei Mot* | 1 **Sivan** R. H. | 1 **Tammuz** R. H. | 3 | 4 | 5 | 6 | 7 |
| 8 | 27 | 29 | 28 | 29 | 30 R. H. | 2 | 2 | 4 | 5 | **6** *Va-Yelekh* Shabbat Shuvah | 7 | 8 |
| 9 | **28** *Va-Era* | 30 R. H. | 29 | **1 Nisan** *Tazri'a* R. H. Ha-Hodesh | 1 **Iyyar** R. H. | 3 | **3** *Korah* | 5 | 6 | 7 | 8 | 9 |
| 10 | 29 | 1 **Adar I** R. H. | 30 R. H. | 2 | 2 | 4 | 4 | 6 | **7** *Shofetim* | 8 | 9 | **10** *Va-Yeze* |
| 11 | 1 **Shevat** R. H. | 2 | 1 **Adar II** R. H. | 3 | 3 | **5** *Be-Midbar* | 5 | 7 | 8 | 9 | 10 | 11 |
| 12 | 2 | 3 | **2** *Pekudei* | 4 | 4 Yom ha-Azma'ut | 6 Shavuot | 6 | 8 | 9 | 10 Yom Kippur | **11** *Lekh Lekha* | 12 |
| 13 | 3 | **4** *Terumah* | 3 | 5 | 5 | 7 | 7 | **9** *Devarim* Tishah be-Av | 10 | 11 | 12 | 13 |
| 14 | 4 | 5 | 4 | 6 | **6** *Kedoshim* | 8 | 8 | 10 Fast | 11 | 12 | 13 | 14 |
| 15 | 5 | 6 | 5 | 7 | 7 | 9 | 9 | 11 | 12 | **13** *Ha'azinu* | 14 | 15 |
| 16 | **6** *Bo* | 7 | 6 | **8** *Mezora* Shabbat ha-Gadol | 8 | 10 | **10** *Hukkat* | 12 | 13 | 14 | 15 | 16 |
| 17 | 7 | 8 | 7 | 9 | 9 | 11 | 11 | 13 | **14** *Ki Teze* | 15 Sukkot | 16 | **17** *Va-Yishlah* |
| 18 | 8 | 9 | 8 | 10 | 10 | **12** *Naso* | 12 | 14 | 15 | 16 | 17 | 18 |
| 19 | 9 | 10 | **9** *Va-Yikra* Zakhor | 11 | 11 | 13 | 13 | 15 | 16 | 17 | **18** *Va-Yera* | 19 |
| 20 | 10 | **11** *Tezavveh* | 10 | 12 | 12 | 14 | 14 | **16** *Va-Ethannan* | 17 | 18 Hol ha-Mo'ed | 19 | 20 |
| 21 | 11 | 12 | 11 | 13 | **13** *Emor* | 15 | 15 | 17 | 18 | 19 | 20 | 21 |
| 22 | 12 | 13 | 12 | 14 | 14 | 16 | 16 | 18 | 19 | **20** | 21 | 22 |
| 23 | **13** *Be-Shallah* | 14 | 13 Ta'anit Esther | **15** Pesah | 15 | 17 | **17** *Balak* | 19 | 20 | 21 Hoshana Rabba | 22 | 23 |
| 24 | 14 | 15 | 14 Purim | 16 Omer | 16 | 18 | 18 Fast | 20 | **21** *Ki Tavo* | 22 Shemini Azeret | 23 | **24** *Va-Yeshev* |
| 25 | 15 | 16 | 15 Shushan Purim | 17 | 17 | **19** *Be-Ha'alotkha* | 19 | 21 | 22 | 23 Simhat Torah *Ve-Zot Ha-Berakhah* | 24 | 25 Hanukkah 1 |
| 26 | 16 | 17 | **16** *Zav* | 18 Hol ha-Mo'ed | 18 Lag ba-Omer | 20 | 20 | 22 | 23 | 24 | **25** *Hayyei Sarah* | 26 2 |
| 27 | 17 | **18** *Ki Tissa* | 17 | 19 | 19 | 21 | 21 | **23** *Ekev* | 24 | 25 | 26 | 27 3 |
| 28 | 18 | 19 | 18 | 20 | **20** *Be-Har* | 22 | 22 | 24 | 25 | 26 | 27 | 28 4 |
| 29 | 19 | 20 | 19 | 21 Pesah | 21 | 23 | 23 | 25 | 26 | **27** *Bereshit* | 28 | 29 5 |
| 30 | **20** *Yitro* | | 20 | **22** | 22 | 24 | **24** *Pinhas* | 26 | 27 | 28 | 29 | 1 **Tevet** R. H. 6 |
| 31 | 21 | | 21 | | 23 | | 25 | 27 | | 29 | | **2** *Mi-Kez* 7 |

## 2017

**5777/78** תשע״ז / תשע״ח

| | January | February | March | April | May | June | July | August | September | October | November | December |
|---|---|---|---|---|---|---|---|---|---|---|---|---|
| 1 | 3 Tevet Hanukkah 8 | 5 | 3 | 5 *Va-Yikra* | 5 Yom ha-Azma'ut | 7 | 7 *Hukkat* | 9 Tishah be-Av | 10 | 11 | 12 | 13 |
| 2 | 4 | 6 | 4 | 6 | 6 | 8 | 8 | 10 | **11** *Ki Teze* | 12 | 13 | **14** *Va-Yishlah* |
| 3 | 5 | 7 | 5 | 7 | 7 | **9** *Naso* | 9 | 11 | 12 | 13 | 14 | 15 |
| 4 | 6 | **8** *Bo* | **6** *Terumah* | 8 | 8 | 10 | 10 | 12 | 13 | 14 | **15** *Va-Yera* | 16 |
| 5 | 7 | 9 | 7 | 9 | 9 | 11 | 11 | **13** *Va-Ethannan* | 14 | 15 Sukkot | 16 | 17 |
| 6 | 8 | 10 | 8 | 10 | **10** *Aharei Mot Kedoshim* | 12 | 12 | 14 | 15 | 16 | 17 | 18 |
| 7 | **9** *Va-Yiggash* | 11 | 9 | 11 | 11 | 13 | 13 | 15 | 16 | **17** | 18 | 19 |
| 8 | 10 Fast | 12 | 10 | **12** *Zav* Shabbat ha-Gadol | 12 | 14 | **14** *Balak* | 16 | 17 | 18 Hol ha-Mo'ed | 19 | 20 |
| 9 | 11 | 13 | 11 Ta'anit Esther | 13 | 13 | 15 | 15 | 17 | **18** *Ki Tavo* | 19 | 20 | **21** *Va-Yeshev* |
| 10 | 12 | 14 | 12 | 14 | 14 | **16** *Be-Ha'alotkha* | 16 | 18 | 19 | 20 | 21 | 22 |
| 11 | 13 | **15** *Be-Shallah* | **13** *Tezavveh Zakhor* | 15 Pesah | 15 | 17 | 17 Fast | 19 | 20 | 21 Hoshana Rabba | **22** *Hayyei Sarah* | 23 |
| 12 | 14 | 16 | 14 Purim | 16 Omer | 16 | 18 | 18 | **20** *Ekev* | 21 | 22 Shemini Azeret | 23 | 24 |
| 13 | 15 | 17 | 15 Shushan Purim | 17 | **17** *Emor* | 19 | 19 | 21 | 22 | 23 Simhat Torah *Ve-Zot Ha-Berakhah* | 24 | 25 Hanukkah 1 |
| 14 | **16** *Va-Yehi* | 18 | 16 | 18 Hol ha-Mo'ed | 18 Lag ba-Omer | 20 | 20 | 22 | 23 | **24** *Bereshit* | 25 | 26 2 |
| 15 | 17 | 19 | 17 | **19** | 19 | 21 | **21** *Pinhas* | 23 | 24 | 25 | 26 | 27 3 |
| 16 | 18 | 20 | 18 | 20 | 20 | 22 | 22 | 24 | **25** *Nizzavim Va-Yelekh* | 26 | 27 | **28** *Mi-Kez* 4 |
| 17 | 19 | 21 | 19 | 21 Pesah | 21 | **23** *Shelah* | 23 | 25 | 26 | 27 | 28 | 29 5 |
| 18 | 20 | **22** *Yitro* | **20** *Ki Tissa Parah* | 22 | 22 | 24 | 24 | 26 | 27 | 28 | **29** *Toledot* | 30 R. H. 6 |
| 19 | 21 | 23 | 21 | 23 | 23 | 25 | 25 | **27** *Re'eh* | 28 | 29 | 1 Kislev R. H. | 1 Tevet R. H. 7 |
| 20 | 22 | 24 | 22 | 24 | **24** *Be-Har Be-Hukkotai* | 26 | 26 | 28 | 29 | 30 R. H. | 2 | 2 8 |
| 21 | **23** *Shemot* | 25 | 23 | 25 | 25 | 27 | 27 | 29 | 1 Tishri Rosh Ha-Shanah | **1** Heshvan R. H. *No'ah* | 3 | 3 |
| 22 | 24 | 26 | 24 | **26** *Shemini* | 26 | 28 | **28** *Mattot Masei* | 30 R. H. | 2 | 2 | 4 | 4 |
| 23 | 25 | 27 | 25 | 27 | 27 | 29 | 29 | 1 Elul R. H. | **3** *Ha'azinu* Shabbat Shuvah | 3 | 5 | **5** *Va-Yiggash* |
| 24 | 26 | 28 | 26 | 28 | 28 | **30** R. H. *Korah* | 1 Av R. H. | 2 | 4 Fast | 4 | 6 | 6 |
| 25 | 27 | **29** *Mishpatim Shekalim* | **27** *Va-Yakhel Pekudei* Ha-Hodesh | 29 | 29 | 1 Tammuz R. H. | 2 | 3 | 5 | 5 | **7** *Va-Yeze* | 7 |
| 26 | 28 | 30 R. H. | 28 | 30 R. H. | 1 Sivan R. H. | 2 | 3 | **4** *Shofetim* | 6 | 6 | 8 | 8 |
| 27 | 29 | 1 Adar R. H. | 29 | 1 Iyyar R. H. | **2** *Be-Midbar* | 3 | 4 | 5 | 7 | 7 | 9 | 9 |
| 28 | **1** Shevat R. H. *Va-Era* | 2 | 1 Nisan R. H. | 2 | 3 | 4 | 5 | 6 | 8 | **8** *Lekh Lekha* | 10 | 10 Fast |
| 29 | 2 | | 2 | **3** *Tazri'a Mezora* | 4 | 5 | **6** *Devarim* | 7 | 9 | 9 | 11 | 11 |
| 30 | 3 | | 3 | 4 | 5 | 6 | 7 | 8 | **10** Yom Kippur | 10 | 12 | **12** *Va-Yehi* |
| 31 | 4 | | 4 | | 6 Shavuot | | 8 | 9 | | 11 | | 13 |

## 2018

**5778/79** תשע״ח / תשע״ט

| | January | February | March | April | May | June | July | August | September | October | November | December |
|---|---|---|---|---|---|---|---|---|---|---|---|---|
| 1 | 14 Tevet | 16 | 14 Purim | 16 Omer | 16 | 18 | 18 Fast | 20 | **21** *Ki Tavo* | 22 Shemini Azeret | 23 | **23** *Va-Yeshev* |
| 2 | 15 | 17 | 15 Shushan Purim | 17 | 17 | **19** *Be-Ha'alotkha* | 19 | 21 | 22 | 23 Simhat Torah *Ve-Zot Ha-Berakhah* | 24 | 24 |
| 3 | 16 | **18** *Yitro* | **16** *Ki Tissa* | 18 Hol ha-Mo'ed | 18 Lag ba-Omer | 20 | 20 | 22 | 23 | 24 | **25** *Hayyei Sarah* | 25 Hanukkah 1 |
| 4 | 17 | 19 | 17 | 19 | 19 | 21 | 21 | **23** *Ekev* | 24 | 25 | 26 | 26 2 |
| 5 | 18 | 20 | 18 | 20 | **20** *Emor* | 22 | 22 | 24 | 25 | 26 | 27 | 27 3 |
| 6 | **19** *Shemot* | 21 | 19 | 21 Pesah | 21 | 23 | 23 | 25 | 26 | **27** *Bereshit* | 28 | 28 4 |
| 7 | 20 | 22 | 20 | **22** | 22 | 24 | **24** *Pinhas* | 26 | 27 | 28 | 29 | 29 5 |
| 8 | 21 | 23 | 21 | 23 | 23 | 25 | 25 | 27 | **28** *Nizzavim* | 29 | 30 R. H. | **30** R. H. *Mi-Kez* 6 |
| 9 | 22 | 24 | 22 | 24 | 24 | **26** *Shelah* | 26 | 28 | 29 | 30 R. H. | 1 Kislev R. H. | 1 Tevet R. H. 7 |
| 10 | 23 | **25** *Mishpatim Shekalim* | **23** *Va-Yakhel Pekudei* Parah | 25 | 25 | 27 | 27 | 29 | 1 Tishri Rosh Ha-Shanah | 1 Heshvan R. H. | **2** *Toledot* | 2 8 |
| 11 | 24 | 26 | 24 | 26 | 26 | 28 | 28 | **30** R. H. *Re'eh* | 2 | 2 | 3 | 3 |
| 12 | 25 | 27 | 25 | 27 | **27** *Be-Har Be-Hukkotai* | 29 | 29 | 1 Elul R. H. | 3 Fast | 3 | 4 | 4 |
| 13 | **26** *Va-Era* | 28 | 26 | 28 | 28 | 30 R. H. | 1 Av R. H. | 2 | 4 | **4** *No'ah* | 5 | 5 |
| 14 | 27 | 29 | 27 | **29** *Shemini* | 29 | 1 Tammuz R. H. | **2** *Mattot Masei* | 3 | 5 | 5 | 6 | 6 |
| 15 | 28 | 30 R. H. | 28 | 30 R. H. | 1 Sivan R. H. | 2 | 3 | 4 | **6** *Va-Yelekh* Shabbat Shuvah | 6 | 7 | **7** *Va-Yiggash* |
| 16 | 29 | 1 Adar R. H. | 29 | 1 Iyyar R. H. | 2 | **3** *Korah* | 4 | 5 | 7 | 7 | 8 | 8 |
| 17 | 1 Shevat R. H. | **2** *Terumah* | **1** Nisan *Va-Yikra* R. H. Ha-Hodesh | 2 | 3 | 4 | 5 | 6 | 8 | 8 | **9** *Va-Yeze* | 9 |
| 18 | 2 | 3 | 2 | 3 | 4 | 5 | 6 | **7** *Shofetim* | 9 | 9 | 10 | 10 Fast |
| 19 | 3 | 4 | 3 | 4 Yom ha-Azma'ut | **5** *Be-Midbar* | 6 | 7 | 8 | 10 Yom Kippur | 10 | 11 | 11 |
| 20 | **4** *Bo* | 5 | 4 | 5 | 6 Shavuot | 7 | 8 | 9 | 11 | **11** *Lekh Lekha* | 12 | 12 |
| 21 | 5 | 6 | 5 | **6** *Tazri'a Mezora* | 7 | 8 | **9** *Devarim* Tishah be-Av | 10 | 12 | 12 | 13 | 13 |
| 22 | 6 | 7 | 6 | 7 | 8 | 9 | 10 Fast | 11 | **13** *Ha'azinu* | 13 | 14 | **14** *Va-Yehi* |
| 23 | 7 | 8 | 7 | 8 | 9 | **10** *Hukkat* | 11 | 12 | 14 | 14 | 15 | 15 |
| 24 | 8 | **9** *Tezavveh Zakhor* | **8** *Zav* Shabbat ha-Gadol | 9 | 10 | 11 | 12 | 13 | 15 Sukkot | 15 | **16** *Va-Yishlah* | 16 |
| 25 | 9 | 10 | 9 | 10 | 11 | 12 | 13 | **14** *Ki Teze* | 16 | 16 | 17 | 17 |
| 26 | 10 | 11 | 10 | 11 | **12** *Naso* | 13 | 14 | 15 | 17 | 17 | 18 | 18 |
| 27 | **11** *Be-Shallah* | 12 | 11 | 12 | 13 | 14 | 15 | 16 | 18 Hol ha-Mo'ed | **18** *Va-Yera* | 19 | 19 |
| 28 | 12 | 13 Ta'anit Esther | 12 | **13** *Aharei Mot Kedoshim* | 14 | 15 | **16** *Va-Ethannan* | 17 | 19 | 19 | 20 | 20 |
| 29 | 13 | | 13 | 14 | 15 | 16 | 17 | 18 | **20** | 20 | 21 | **21** *Shemot* |
| 30 | 14 | | 14 | 15 | 16 | **17** *Balak* | 18 | 19 | 21 Hoshana Rabba | 21 | 22 | 22 |
| 31 | 15 | | **15** Pesah | | 17 | | 19 | 20 | | 22 | | 23 |

## 2019

**5779/80** תשע״ט / תש״פ

| | January | February | March | April | May | June | July | August | September | October | November | December |
|---|---|---|---|---|---|---|---|---|---|---|---|---|
| 1 | 24 **Tevet** | 26 | 24 | 25 | 26 | **27** *Be-Ḥukkotai* | 28 | 29 | 1 **Elul** R. Ḥ. | Rosh Ha-Shanah 2 | 3 | 3 |
| 2 | 25 | **27** *Mishpatim* | **25** *Va-Yakhel* Shekalim | 26 | 27 | 28 | 29 | 1 **Av** R. Ḥ. | 2 | 3 Fast | **4** *No'aḥ* | 4 |
| 3 | 26 | 28 | 26 | 27 | 28 | 29 | 30 R. Ḥ. | **2** *Mattot Masei* | 3 | 4 | 5 | 5 |
| 4 | 27 | 29 | 27 | 28 | **29** *Aḥarei Mot* | 1 **Sivan** R. Ḥ. | 1 **Tammuz** R. Ḥ. | 3 | 4 | 5 | 6 | 6 |
| 5 | **28** *Va-Era* | 30 R. Ḥ. | 28 | 29 | 30 R. Ḥ. | 2 | 2 | 4 | 5 | **6** *Va-Yelekh* Shabbat Shuvah | 7 | 7 |
| 6 | 29 | 1 **Adar I** R. Ḥ. | 29 | **1** **Nisan** *Tazri'a* R. Ḥ. Ha-Ḥodesh | 1 **Iyyar** R. Ḥ. | 3 | **3** *Koraḥ* | 5 | 6 | 7 | 8 | 8 |
| 7 | 1 **Shevat** R. Ḥ. | 2 | 30 R. Ḥ. | 2 | 2 | 4 | 4 | 6 | **7** *Shofetim* | 8 | 9 | **9** *Va-Yeẓe* |
| 8 | 2 | 3 | 1 **Adar II** R. Ḥ. | 3 | 3 | **5** *Be-Midbar* | 5 | 7 | 8 | 9 | 10 | 10 |
| 9 | 3 | **4** *Terumah* | **2** *Pekudei* | 4 | 4 Yom ha-Aẓma'ut | 6 Shavuot | 6 | 8 | 9 | 10 Yom Kippur | **11** *Lekh Lekha* | 11 |
| 10 | 4 | 5 | 3 | 5 | 5 | 7 | 7 | **9** *Devarim* Tishah be-Av | 10 | 11 | 12 | 12 |
| 11 | 5 | 6 | 4 | 6 | **6** *Kedoshim* | 8 | 8 | 10 Fast | 11 | 12 | 13 | 13 |
| 12 | **6** *Bo* | 7 | 5 | 7 | 7 | 9 | 9 | 11 | 12 | **13** *Ha'azinu* | 14 | 14 |
| 13 | 7 | 8 | 6 | **8** *Meẓora* Shabbat ha-Gadol | 8 | 10 | **10** *Ḥukkat* | 12 | 13 | 14 | 15 | 15 |
| 14 | 8 | 9 | 7 | 9 | 9 | 11 | 11 | 13 | **14** *Ki Teẓe* | 15 Sukkot | 16 | **16** *Va-Yishlaḥ* |
| 15 | 9 | 10 | 8 | 10 | 10 | **12** *Naso* | 12 | 14 | 15 | 16 | 17 | 17 |
| 16 | 10 | **11** *Teẓavveh* | **9** *Va-Yikra* Zakhor | 11 | 11 | 13 | 13 | 15 | 16 | 17 | **18** *Va-Yera* | 18 |
| 17 | 11 | 12 | 10 | 12 | 12 | 14 | 14 | **16** *Va-Etḥannan* | 17 | 18 | 19 | 19 |
| 18 | 12 | 13 | 11 | 13 | **13** *Emor* | 15 | 15 | 17 | 18 | 19 Ḥol ha-Mo'ed | 20 | 20 |
| 19 | **13** *Be-Shallaḥ* | 14 | 12 | 14 | 14 | 16 | 16 | 18 | 19 | **20** | 21 | 21 |
| 20 | 14 | 15 | 13 Ta'anit Esther | **15** Pesaḥ | 15 | 17 | **17** *Balak* | 19 | 20 | 21 Hoshana Rabba | 22 | 22 |
| 21 | 15 | 16 | 14 Purim | 16 Omer | 16 | 18 | 18 Fast | 20 | **21** *Ki Tavo* | 22 Shemini Aẓeret | 23 | **23** *Va-Yeshev* |
| 22 | 16 | 17 | 15 Shushan Purim | 17 | 17 | **19** *Be-Ha'alotkha* | 19 | 21 | 22 | 23 Simḥat Torah *Ve-Zot Ha-Berakhah* | 24 | 24 |
| 23 | 17 | **18** *Ki Tissa* | **16** *Ẓav* | 18 | 18 Lag ba-Omer | 20 | 20 | 22 | 23 | 24 | **25** *Ḥayyei Sarah* | 25 Ḥanukkah 1 |
| 24 | 18 | 19 | 17 | 19 Ḥol ha-Mo'ed | 19 | 21 | 21 | **23** *Ekev* | 24 | 25 | 26 | 26 2 |
| 25 | 19 | 20 | 18 | 20 | **20** *Be-Har* | 22 | 22 | 24 | 25 | 26 | 27 | 27 3 |
| 26 | **20** *Yitro* | 21 | 19 | 21 Pesaḥ | 21 | 23 | 23 | 25 | 26 | **27** *Bereshit* | 28 | 28 4 |
| 27 | 21 | 22 | 20 | **22** | 22 | 24 | **24** *Pinḥas* | 26 | 27 | 28 | 29 | 29 5 |
| 28 | 22 | 23 | 21 | 23 | 23 | 25 | 25 | 27 | **28** *Niẓẓavim* | 29 | 30 R. Ḥ. | **30** R. Ḥ. *Mi-Keẓ* 6 |
| 29 | 23 | | 22 | 24 | 24 | **26** *Shelaḥ* | 26 | 28 | 29 | 30 R. Ḥ. | 1 **Kislev** R. Ḥ. | 1 **Tevet** R. Ḥ. 7 |
| 30 | 24 | | **23** *Shemini* Parah | 25 | 25 | 27 | 27 | 29 | 1 **Tishri** Rosh Ha-Shanah | 1 **Ḥeshvan** R. Ḥ. | **2** *Toledot* | 2 8 |
| 31 | 25 | | 24 | | 26 | | 28 | **30** R. Ḥ. *Re'eh* | | 2 | | 3 |

## 2020

**5780/81** תש״פ / תשפ״א

| | January | February | March | April | May | June | July | August | September | October | November | December |
|---|---|---|---|---|---|---|---|---|---|---|---|---|
| 1 | 4 **Tevet** | **6** *Bo* | 5 | 7 | 7 | 9 | 9 | **11** *Va-Etḥannan* | 12 | 13 | 14 | 15 |
| 2 | 5 | 7 | 6 | 8 | **8** *Aḥarei Mot Kedoshim* | 10 | 10 | 12 | 13 | 14 | 15 | 16 |
| 3 | 6 | 8 | 7 | 9 | 9 | 11 | 11 | 13 | 14 | **15** Sukkot | 16 | 17 |
| 4 | **7** *Va-Yiggash* | 9 | 8 | **10** *Ẓav* Shabbat ha-Gadol | 10 | 12 | **12** *Ḥukkat Balak* | 14 | 15 | 16 | 17 | 18 |
| 5 | 8 | 10 | 9 | 11 | 11 | 13 | 13 | 15 | **16** *Ki Tavo* | 17 | 18 | **19** *Va-Yishlaḥ* |
| 6 | 9 | 11 | 10 | 12 | 12 | **14** *Naso* | 14 | 16 | 17 | 18 | 19 | 20 |
| 7 | 10 Fast | 12 | **11** *Teẓavveh* Zakhor | 13 | 13 | 15 | 15 | 17 | 18 | 19 Ḥol ha-Mo'ed | **20** *Va-Yera* | 21 |
| 8 | 11 | **13** *Be-Shallaḥ* | 12 | 14 | 14 | 16 | 16 | **18** *Ekev* | 19 | 20 | 21 | 22 |
| 9 | 12 | 14 | 13 Ta'anit Esther | 15 Pesaḥ | **15** *Emor* | 17 | 17 Fast | 19 | 20 | 21 Hoshana Rabba | 22 | 23 |
| 10 | 13 | 15 | 14 Purim | 16 Omer | 16 | 18 | 18 | 20 | 21 | **22** Shemini Aẓeret | 23 | 24 |
| 11 | **14** *Va-Yeḥi* | 16 | 15 Shushan Purim | **17** | 17 | 19 | **19** *Pinḥas* | 21 | 22 | 23 Simḥat Torah *Ve-Zot Ha-Berakhah* | 24 | 25 Ḥanukkah 1 |
| 12 | 15 | 17 | 16 | 18 | 18 Lag ba-Omer | 20 | 20 | 22 | **23** *Niẓẓavim Va-Yelekh* | 24 | 25 | **26** *Va-Yeshev* 2 |
| 13 | 16 | 18 | 17 | 19 Ḥol ha-Mo'ed | 19 | **21** *Be-Ha'alotkha* | 21 | 23 | 24 | 25 | 26 | 27 3 |
| 14 | 17 | 19 | **18** *Ki Tissa* Parah | 20 | 20 | 22 | 22 | 24 | 25 | 26 | **27** *Ḥayyei Sarah* | 28 4 |
| 15 | 18 | **20** *Yitro* | 19 | 21 Pesaḥ | 21 | 23 | 23 | **25** *Re'eh* | 26 | 27 | 28 | 29 5 |
| 16 | 19 | 21 | 20 | 22 | **22** *Be-Har Be-Ḥukkotai* | 24 | 24 | 26 | 27 | 28 | 29 | 1 **Tevet** R. Ḥ. 6 |
| 17 | 20 | 22 | 21 | 23 | 23 | 25 | 25 | 27 | 28 | **29** *Bereshit* | 1 **Kislev** R. Ḥ. | 2 7 |
| 18 | **21** *Shemot* | 23 | 22 | **24** *Shemini* | 24 | 26 | **26** *Mattot Masei* | 28 | 29 | 30 R. Ḥ. | 2 | 3 8 |
| 19 | 22 | 24 | 23 | 25 | 25 | 27 | 27 | 29 | **1** **Tishri** Rosh Ha-Shanah | 1 **Ḥeshvan** R. Ḥ. | 3 | **4** *Mi-Keẓ* |
| 20 | 23 | 25 | 24 | 26 | 26 | **28** *Shelaḥ* | 28 | 30 R. Ḥ. | 2 | 2 | 4 | 5 |
| 21 | 24 | 26 | **25** *Va-Yakhel Pekudei* Ha-Ḥodesh | 27 | 27 | 29 | 29 | 1 **Elul** R. Ḥ. | 3 Fast | 3 | **5** *Toledot* | 6 |
| 22 | 25 | **27** *Mishpatim* Shekalim | 26 | 28 | 28 | 30 R. Ḥ. | 1 **Av** R. Ḥ. | **2** *Shofetim* | 4 | 4 | 6 | 7 |
| 23 | 26 | 28 | 27 | 29 | **29** *Be-Midbar* | 1 **Tammuz** R. Ḥ. | 2 | 3 | 5 | 5 | 7 | 8 |
| 24 | 27 | 29 | 28 | 30 R. Ḥ. | 1 **Sivan** R. Ḥ. | 2 | 3 | 4 | 6 | **6** *No'aḥ* | 8 | 9 |
| 25 | **28** *Va-Era* | 30 R. Ḥ. | 29 | **1** R. Ḥ. **Iyyar** *Tazri'a Meẓora* | 2 | 3 | **4** *Devarim* | 5 | 7 | 7 | 9 | 10 Fast |
| 26 | 29 | 1 **Adar** R. Ḥ. | 1 **Nisan** R. Ḥ. | 2 | 3 | 4 | 5 | 6 | **8** *Ha'azinu* Shabbat Shuvah | 8 | 10 | **11** |
| 27 | 1 **Shevat** R. Ḥ. | 2 | 2 | 3 | 4 | **5** *Koraḥ* | 6 | 7 | 9 | 9 | 11 | 12 |
| 28 | 2 | 3 | **3** *Va-Yikra* | 4 | 5 | 6 | 7 | 8 | 10 Yom Kippur | 10 | **12** *Va-Yeẓe* | 13 |
| 29 | 3 | **4** *Terumah* | 4 | 5 Yom ha-Aẓma'ut | 6 Shavuot | 7 | 8 | **9** *Ki Teẓe* | 11 | 11 | 13 | 14 |
| 30 | 4 | | 5 | 6 | **7** | 8 | 9 Tishah be-Av | 10 | 12 | 12 | 14 | 15 |
| 31 | 5 | | 6 | | 8 | | 10 | 11 | | **13** *Lekh Lekha* | | 16 |

Based on *150 Year Calendar*, M. Greenfield, 1963.

EDITOR IN CHIEF:
**RABBI RAPHAEL POSNER**, D.H.L.

COORDINATOR:
**FERN SECKBACH**, B.A., M.A., C.Phil.

ADMINISTRATIVE MANAGER (Production Planning):
**RABBI HAYYIM SCHNEID**, B.A., M.Sc.

EDITORS:

**WENDY ELLIMAN**, B.A.
**MICHAEL FELDBERG**, B.A.
**DINA INGBER**, B.A., M.A.
**AARON LEWIN**, B.A., M.A.
**KATHY STANISLAWSKI**, B.A.
**HANNAH WEISS**, B.A., M.L.S.

ADMINISTRATIVE ASSISTANT:
**NECHAMA UNTERMAN**, B.A., M.A.

DESIGN AND ART DIRECTION:
**MURRAY BLOOM**, B.Sc., M.A., Prof. Dipl.

LAYOUT:
**OFRA LEVI**

GRAPHICS:
**ADRIENNE COHEN**, B.A., M.Sc.
**SHEMUEL KALDARON**

TYPING:
**ETHEL BASFORD**, Dipl. P.R.

PROOFREADING:
**ROSALYN SCHNEID**, B.A.

CONTRIBUTORS:

**RABBI DAVID BIN-NUN**
**ZIONA BIN-NUN**, B.A.
**RABBI ABRAHAM COHEN**, B.A., M.A.
**LEAH DARDICK**
**RUTH FEIGLIN**, B.A.
**RIVKA GORDON**
**RICHARD HAHN**
**HANAN LEMANN**, B.A.
**JUDITH LEHRFIELD**, B.A., A.A.S.

**JANET K. O'DEA**, B.A., B.H.L., M.A., Ph.D.
**DEBBIE PRAWER**
**HADASSAH RUDENSKY**, B.Ed.
**ARYEH RUBINSTEIN**, B.A., M.A., Ph.D.
**JUDY SIEGEL**, B.A., M.A.
**RABBI MOSHE TUTNAUER**, B.Sc., M.H.L.
**ROBERT A. VAUGHAN**, M.A.
**RABBI NAPHTALI WINTER**, B.A.
**PEARL YIZHAR**, B.A., M.A.

# ILLUSTRATION CREDITS

George Aarons, Gloucester, Massachusetts, 3:139.
Aberdeen University Library, 4:108.
R. Abramovitch (ed.), *The Vanished World,* New York, 1947, 1:17-2,3, 165-1; 2:84-3.
Affiliated Photo-Comay, 2:131-2.
AFLCIO, Washington, D.C., 2:176-2.
Agudath Israel of America, 5:183-2.
Photo V. Aharon, Jerusalem, 4:114-1.
Photo Leon Alaluf, Santiago, 2:15.
Fratelli Alinari, Florence, 1:96-1; 2:46, 56, 135-1, 172-2; 3:165, 185-3; 4:5, 131, 155-2; 5:81-1, 89.
Courtesy J. Altaras, Giessen, 6:111-2.
Altonaer Museum, Hamburg, 1:40; 5:92-2.
Ambrosian Library, Milan, 2:105; 5:167-3.
America Israel Cultural Foundation, 4:170-2.
American Jewish Archives, Cincinnati, Ohio, 1:156, 162; 5:98-2,3, 131-2; 6:67-1; 93-1.
American Jewish Congress, New York, 1:38-1.
American Jewish Historical Society, Waltham, Massachusetts, 5:3-1, 6-3, 142-1, 148-1.
American Joint Distribution Committee, 2:91-2.
Courtesy American Photo Offset Inc., New York, 3:9-2,3, 133-2; 5:43-1,2.
Photo Yiẓhak Amit, Kibbutz Ẓora, 2:120; 3:54, 175; 4:frontispiece.
Andover Newton Theological School, Harvard University, Cambridge, 4:121-1.
B.M. Ansbacher Collection, Jerusalem, 1:104-1, 166; 2:152; 3:7, 99, 118-1, 122-1; 4:184-2; 5:58-3, 68.
Archivo de Prensa, Buenos Aires; Photo S. Zimberoff, 1:71-1.
Photo by Arielli, Bat Yam, 3:142, 160-1,3.
Arizona Historical Foundation, 2:175-2.
Armenian Patriarchate, Jerusalem, 2:41; 6:35-1.
Thomas Arnold, *Painting in Islam,* New York, 4:164.
Ashmolean Museum, Oxford, 2:128; 6:96.
B. Aronson Collection, Amsterdam, 2:75.
Associated Press, Berlin, 1:162-2.
Associated Press, London, 1:88.
Australian Jewish Historical Society, Mitchell Library, Sydney, 1:89-1.
Avila Municipal Archives, Spain, 2:127.
O. Avissar (ed.), *Sefer Hebron,* Jerusalem, 1970, 1:94; 3:68-1.
Photo Fabian Bachrach, New York, 3:137-1.
Courtesy Baruch Bagg, Tel Aviv, 4:153-2.
Photo Oliver Baker, New York, 4:158.
Photo Stewart Bale, Liverpool, 4:63-2.
Courtesy *Ba-Maḥaneh,* Israel Ministry of Defense, Tel Aviv, 5:175-2, 177-1.
Photo Micha Bar-Am, Tel Aviv, 3:168-1.
Photo Nir Bareket, Jerusalem, 2:112-1.
Photo Emil Bauer, Bamberg, Germany, 1:57-3,4.
Bayerische Staatsgemaldesammlungen, Munich, 1:138.
Bayerische Landesamt für Denkmalpflege, Munich, 2:9-2.
Bayerische Staatsbibliothek, Munich, 5:178.
Beit Aaronsohn, Zikhron Ya'akov, 5:9-1.
Beit Loḥamei Ha-Getta'ot, Kibbutz Loḥamei Ha-Getta'ot, 4:63-1.
Belga, Brussels, 1:114-2.
Photo Benden, New York, 5:84-2.
Photo Ben Dov, Jerusalem, 4:16-2, 138-2; 5:106-3.
Courtesy E. Ben Eliahu, Kiryat Bialik, 2:26; 3:86-1,2.
Courtesy D. Benvenisti, Jerusalem, 2:183-2; 5:133-1.
Courtesy A.Z. Ben-Yishai, Tel Aviv, 3:36-1.
Photo Ben-Zvi, Rehovot, 4:13-2; 5:171-1; 6:88-1,2.
Photo Isaac Berez, New York, 5:5-2, 30-1.
Photo Ariel Berman, Haifa, 3:77-1.
Photo Alfred Bernheim, Jerusalem, 1:13-2; 2:102; 3:80-2; 4:111-1; 5:144-3.
Congregation Beth Emeth, Albany, N.Y., 1:74-3.
Beth Ya'akov Monthly, Jerusalem, 2:161-1.
Biblioteca Ambrosiana, Milan, 5:167-3.
Biblioteca Apostolica Vaticana, 1:27, 28-3, 37-2, 71-2; 2:112-2; 3:97-1, 183-1; 4:29-1; 5:153, 163-1.
Biblioteca Medicea Laurenziana, Florence, 5:83.
Bibliotheca Rosenthaliana, Amsterdam, 1:13-1.
Bibliotheek der Rijksuniversiteits, Leiden, 3:27-2.
Bibliotheque Municipale, Amiens, 2:101.
Bibliotheque Municipale, Lyons, 1:42.
Bibliotheque Municipale, Rheims, 2:89.
Bibliotheque Nationale, Paris, 2:frontispiece; 3:9-1; 5:85-1.
Bibliotheque Royale de Belgique, Brussels, 4:95-1.
Bodleian Library, Oxford, 1:76-1, 181-1; 3:32-1.
Boston Celtics, 1:89-2.
Photo Paul Brami, Tunis, 1:34-2.
Photo Werner Braun, Jerusalem, 1:107, 151, 177-1; 2:24-2, 106-1,3; 3:11-1, 58, 116-4, 117-4,126, 127-2, 144-1, 162-2, 167-2,4; 4:12-3, 24-2, 55-2, 98-1, 99-2, 106-1, 114-2, 128-2; 5:35-2, 93-2, 146-3, 177-2; 6:31-2, 101-1, 108.
The British Library Board, London, 1:29-2, 43-1, 68-3, 101-1, 118-1, 129, 144, 181-1; 2:28-1, 38-2, 136-1, 149-1; 3:8-1, 135-2, 183-2; 4:35-2, 40-2, 120-3, 145-1; 5:39-2, 135, 141-1, 182-2; 6:58.
The British Museum, London, 4:6; 5:151-1.
The Brooklyn Museum, Bequest of Miss Theodora Wilbour, 1:64-1.
Photo Jim Brown from *Black Star,* 4:17-1.
Photo H. Burger, Jerusalem, 4:106-2; 5:116-4.
Cambridge University Library, 2:180-1.
CJCongress, Montreal (Photo Mark Freedman),
Photo Eduardo Carreo, Oporto, 5:64-2.
Central Archives for the History of the Jewish People, Jerusalem, 1:17-1, 70-1 (Inv/1967), 110 (Inv/1628), 150 (Inv/1397); 2:4-1, 32, 102-3, 155-1 (Inv/2440(1)); 4:136-1, 174-2; 5:150-1,2; 6:75-3 (Inv/2440(1)).
Central Zionist Archives, Jerusalem, 1:24-1, 33-2,3, 61, 62-3, 72-1,2, 122-2, 125, 133-2, 167-1; 2:51-1, 76-2,3; 3:41-3, 50-1, 53-2, 56-1, 107-1, 107-3, 185; 4:15-1, 29-2, 45-3, 56, 138-1; 5:20-2, 32-2, 48, 99-4, 115-2, 143-1, 181-3; 6:20-4, 87-1,2, 115, 118, 120.
*Challenge,* the Lubavitch Foundation of Great Britain, London, 5:123.
Chester Beatty Library, Dublin, 3:180-2.
Christ Church Library, Oxford, 2:54; 4:18-1.
Photo Richard Cleave, Jerusalem, 1:77; 2:23, 166; 4:92-2, 179; 6:52-2,3.
Photo Yosaif Cohain, 2:150-2.
A. Cohen, *A People Apart,* New York, 1970, Photo Philip Garvin, 5:141-2.
Collections del Real Monasterio, Escorial, Spain, 3:177-2.
Committee to Save the Synagogue of Sardis, 5:139-3.
Columbia Pictures, New York, 4:15-3.
Columbia University, New York, 4:110-1; 6:86-2.
Photo Conti Press, Hamburg, 3:14-1.
Cooper Union Museum, New York, 3:133-1.
Corpus Inscriptionum Semiticarum, Paris, 1:64-2.
D. Corcas Collection, Jerusalem, 79-3
Culver Pictures Inc., 4:46-1.

"Dagon Collection," Archeological Museum of Grain Handling in Israel, Haifa, 2:139-1,3; 6:86-1.
S. Dagoni Collection, Haifa, 6:7-1,2,8-1,2,3.
Photo Frank J. Darmstaedter, New York, 1:184-2; 2:124-2, 130; 3:16-1; 5:25-2,3,124-1, 127-2.
Courtesy E. Dekel, Tel Aviv, 1:127; 3:79-1; 4-133-2.
Photo Dick de Maisico, New York, 5:4.
Deutsche Presse Agentur, Frankfort, 2:31; 4:74; 6:60-1.
Duke of Sutherland Collection, on loan to the National Gallery of Scotland, Edinburgh, 3:17.
Joseph Dunninger Collection, Cliffside Park, New Jersey, 3:72-1.
*Ecclesiastes, or the Preacher,* New York, 1965, 5:182-1.
Courtesy Z. Efron, Jerusalem, 1:116-1, 170; 5:19-1; 6:110-2.
Eglise Abbatiale de la Madeleine, Vezelay, 2:173.
J. Ehm, Prague, 4:81-2.
I. Einhorn Collection, Tel Aviv, 1:81; 2:6-2, 39-2, 116-1, 168-1; 4:80-2, 81-1; 5:130-1.
Photo David Eisenberg, Jerusalem, 2:177; 3:153-2, 6:34
Photo Y. Eisenstark, Jerusalem, 4:91-5.
Elia Photo Service, Jerusalem, 3:100-2.
E. E. Elias, Cochin, 2:26
Emergency Fund for Palestine, Tel Aviv, 3:107-2.
Photo-Emka Ltd., Jerusalem, 2:7; 3:148, 168-2; 4:59-1.
*Encyclopedia of the Jewish Diaspora,* Tel Aviv, 1956, 4:75-2.
*Epstein : An Autobiography,* London, 1955, 2:110-1-2.
Falasha Welfare Association, London, 2:114-2.
Federal Photos, Montreal, 5:30-3.
Formerly Feinberg Collection, Detroit, Michigan, 2:6-1; 6:48-2, 49-1.
Courtesy J. Feliks, Jerusalem, 1:52.
Courtesy Fogg Art Museum, Harvard University, Gift - Meta and Paul J. Sachs, Photo J.K. Ufford, 1:75-4.
Forbath Photo, Montreal, 4:150-2.
Courtesy J. Fraenkel, London, 2:85-2; 3:49-2; 5:63-1.
J. Fraenkel, *The Jewish Press of the World,* London, 1967, 5:77-3, 78-2.
H. Frankfort, *Stratified Cylinder Seals from the Diyala Region,* Chicago, 1955, 5:147-1.
Photo I. Freidin, Tel Aviv, 2:12-1; 3:1-2; 4:109-1, 122-2; 6:30.
D. Friedenberg Collection, New York, 2:121-2, 145-3; 5:26, 1,2.
Gabinetto Fotografico - Sopr. Gallerie, Florence, 2:70-1,2, 71.
*Gemeindeblatt der Juedischen Gemeinde zu Berlin,* Nov. 1928, 1:116-2.
Germanisches National Museum, Nuremberg, 1:155.
Courtesy Genazim, Tel Aviv, 5:92-1.
Ruth Gikow Collection, New York; Photo Geoffrey Clements, 4:185-1.
Saul Ginsberg Collection, Rivkind Archives, J.N.U.L., Jerusalem, 2:1.
Courtesy Giora Godik, Tel Aviv, 4:59-2.
Courtesy H. Gold, Tel Aviv, 4:168-2.
Photo Mike Goldberg, Neveh Ilan, 6:11-2.
The Golden Age of Second Avenue Co., New York, 6:39-1.
L.M. Goldman, *The History of the Jews of New Zealand,* Wellington, 1960, 6:76-1.
Ezra P. Gorodesky Collection, Jerusalem, 5:12-1,2,51-1; 6:67-2.
Courtesy Shmuel Gorr Photo Archives and Central Archives and Research Institute for the History of Gedolei Israel, Jerusalem, 3:2-1, 24-3, 25-2; 5:144-2.
S. Green, *The World of Musical Comedy,* New Jersey, 1968, 2:164; 4:37-1.
Photo F. Grubner, Jerusalem, 5:171-4.
Oscar Gruss Collection, New York, 1:184-2; 2:124-2, 130, 3:16-1; 5:25-2,3,127-2.
Ha'arez Museum, Tel Aviv, 2:22-2, 79; 3:13.
Hadassah Medical Organization, Jerusalem, 4:113-1; 5:6-4.
Haganah Historical Archives, Tel Aviv, 2:76-1, 176-1; 3:1-1, 5-2; 4:91-2,3; 5:35-1, 129-2.
Haifa Ethnological Museum and Folklore Archives, 1:44-2, 181-2.
I. Halperin (ed.), *Bet Israel be-Polin,* Jerusalem 1948-1954, 4:76-1.
Photo David Harris, Jerusalem, 1:30-1,2,3, 44-3, 47-2, 66-3, 81, 124, 169; 2:6-2, 9-1, 24-1, 39-2, 47, 116-1,2,3, 119-1, 168-1; 3:8-3, 18-1, 51-1, 52-2, 74, 145-2; 4:13-1, 33-1, 88 80-2, 81-1, 99-3, 4, 117, 137-2, 168-3 ; 5:20-1, 40-1,2, 41-2, 66-1, 69, 86-2, 118-1, 122-3, 130-1, 134-1, 146-1, 181-2; 6:9-4, 12-1, 21, 35-1, 35-2, 42, 47, 48-1, 84-2, 101-2.
Sigmund Harrison Collection, Villanova, Pennsylvania, 1:8-2, 28-2; 4:22-1, 144-1.
A.D. Hart, *The Jews in Canada,* Toronto, 1926, 1:104-2.
Hebrew Union College, Cincinnati, Ohio, 1:160-1,3; 3:46-1; 4:144-2; 5:42-1,2,140-3; 6:49-2.
Hebrew University, Jerusalem, Department of Archaeology, 3:44-2.
Hebrew University, Jerusalem, Institute of Contemporary Jewry, 5:77-1.
Hebrew University, Jerusalem, Public Relations Department, 2:172-1; 3:126-2, 150; 4:54-2; 6:17-1.
Hechal Shlomo, Sir Isaac and Lady Wolfson Museum, Jerusalem, 1:44-1 (Photo David Harris), 47-2, 66-3; 2:116-3, 119-1, 168-1; 3:18-1; 5:41-2, 66-1, 170-1, 181-2; 6:12-1.
R. Hecht Collection, Haifa, 5:146-1.
Photo Heliotipa Artistica Espanola, Madrid, 3:75.
*The Herald and Weekly Times,* Melbourne, 4:118, 147.
Hessischer Landes- und Hochschulbibliothek, Darmstadt, 3:8-1.
Photo Edgar Hirshbain, Jerusalem, 6:11-1.
Historisches Museum, Frankfurt am Main, 4:150-3.
B. Hoffmann (ed.), *Toyznt Yor Pinsk,* New York, 1941, 5:56-2.
Joseph B. Horwitz Judaica Collection, Cleveland, Ohio, 1:184-1; 5:74-1, 169-1; 6:84-1.
Photo Gadi Hoz, Toronto, 6:50-3.
Hungarian Academy of Sciences, Budapest, 2:59-2; 4:42; 6:8-4.
B. Hrushovski et al. (eds.), *A Shpigl Oyf a Shteyn,* Tel Aviv, 1964, 6:105-2.
A.L. Isaacs, *Jews of Majorca,* London, 1936, 4:86.
Israel Chess Federation, Tel Aviv, 2:11-2, 12-1.
Israel Department of Antiquities and Museums, Jerusalem, 1:9, 11-2, 23, 66-1, 67-5, 80-2, 132-2, 174, 177-2, 182-1; 2:49-2, 50-1, 139-2, 156-2 (courtesy Asher Ovadia), 160, 175-1; 3:32-3, 49-1, 130-2, 140-2, 141-1, 145-4, 147-2, 179-3; 4:35-2, 88-1, 115-2,3, 121-4; 5:13-1, 65-1,2,3; 6:32-3.
Israel Foreign Office, Jerusalem, 3:19-1, 163; 4:154-1; 5:60-2, 100-3, 157-2.
Israel Government Coins and Medals Corporation, 4:112-1,2.
Israel Government Press Office, Jerusalem, 1:11–1, 21–1, 34–1, 36–1, 63, 66–2,4, 68–2, 74–2, 78–1,2, 90, 105, 108–1, 111, 113, 122–1, 126, 129, 131–1,2, 154, 163–2, 171–2,172-2, 173, 175, 176; 2:24–3, 26–1, 30–1, 51–2, 55–2, 58, 66-1,2, 74, 84–1,2, 90, 93, 95, 98, 111–1, 122–1, 129–1,2,3, 140, 146, 150–1, 153, 174, 179; 3:3, 6–2, 11–3, 12, 20, 41-1,2, 44–1,3, 48–2, 51–2, 56–2, 59–1, 61–3, 71–1,2, 82, 83-1, 84–2,3,85–1, 102, 105–1,2, 106, 110–1, 111–1, 112–1,2, 115–1,3, 116–1, 118–1,3, 119–1, 120–2,3, 121–1, 122–1,2, 123, 124–1, 125–1,3,4, 141–1, 143–1, 145–1, 148–1,2, 151, 152–1,2,154, 157, 156–1, 157, 158–2,

161–2, 162–1,2, 167–7, 168–3, 169–2, 186–1,2; 4:14–2, 18–2, 19–2, 20–3, 28–2,3, 36–2,3 37–1, 46–3, 47, 58, 73–1, 76–2, 80–1, 87, 102–4, 107–1, 115–1, 116, 121–3, 122–1, 123–1,2, 128–2, 137–1, 160–1, 163–1, 167–2, 168–1, 172–1; 5:20–3,4, 39–1, 76–2, 93–1
104-4, 109-2, 111-1, 114-1,3, 129-1, 132-2, 134-2, 139-2, 146-4, 159, 161, 162-2,3, 168-1, 169-2, 172-2, 174-2, 175-1,3, 177-3, 181-4; 6: frontispiece, 3-1,2, 4-1,2,3,4,5, 12-2, 3, 31-1, 33, 37-2, 44-1, 46, 61, 71, 81-2, 92-2, 99, 100, 104-1, 107-1.
Israel Government Tourist Office, New York, 3:119-2, 4:23-3.
Israel Medical Association, Jerusalem, 2:20; 4:113-2; 6:78-1.
Israel Ministry of Religions, Jerusalem, 3:136-1; 4:4-2.
Israel Ministry of Tourism, Jerusalem, 1:15-1.
Israel Museum, Jerusalem, 1:8-1,3, 13-2, 18-1, 30-1,2,3, 37-1, 38-2, 66-3, 75-2; 2:9-1, 27-2, 40, 137-2; 3: frontispiece, 8-3, 52-2, 57, 74, 80-2; 4:13-1, 59-1, 70, 79-1, 99-3,4, 106-1, 117, 120-2, 126, 137-2, 142, 168-3; 5:20-1, 23-1, 52, 65-3, 69, 86-2, 107-2, 116-1, 118-1, 122-3, 141-3, 147-4; 6:9-4, 21, 35-2, 47, 48-1, 57, 101-2.
Israel Museum Department of Ethnography, Photo Collection, 2:63, 139-4; 4:152-2; 6:85-1.
Israel Museum Photo Archives, Jerusalem, 1:30, 133-1, 178-2; 4:151, 100-2, 101-1; 5:15-1, 162-1; 6:121.
Israel Press and Photo Agency, Tel Aviv, 3:167-3.
Israel State Archives, Jerusalem, 1:5-1, 68-1; 3:100-1, 178; 4:16-2, 78-2; 5:106-3, 137.
Italian Rite Synagogue, Jerusalem, 6:84-2.
Jabotinsky Institute, Tel Aviv, 3:92-2, 131, 132; 4:24-1, 65.
Photo Lotte Jacobi, Hillsboro, New York, 5:143-2.
Jerusalem Municipality Historical Archives, 2:30-3, 62; 4:27-2, 91-5, 138-2; 6:29.
Jewish Agency Photo Service, Jerusalem, 2:14-3, 65, 125-1; 3:30-2, 42, 50-3, 127-1, 158-1; 4:45-2, 82-2, 152-3; 5:91-1; 6:81-1, 82-1, 89.
*The Jewish Chronicle,* London, Photo David Kessler, 3:167-6; 6:94.
Jewish Colonization Association, London, 3:107-2.
Jewish Historical Society of England and the Librarian, University College, London, 1:3.
Jewish Immigrant Aid Services of Canada, 1:182-2.
Jewish Lads Brigade, Glasgow, Photo A.W. Middlemiss, Rothesay, 5:145.
Jewish Museum, Cape Town, 5:164-1,2.
Jewish Museum, London, 2:22-1; 4:130-1.
The Jewish Museum, New York, 3:16-2; 4: frontispiece, 122-1.
Jewish National Fund, Jerusalem, 1:98-1; 2:11-1, 14-2, 106-2, 129-4; 3:6-1, 19-2, 21-1, 22-2, 117-2, 118-2, 144-2, 145-3, 147-1, 153-1, 172-1,2; 4-20-1, 21-4, 25-1, 33-2, 36-1, 180-1; 5:71; 6:19-2, 52-1, 116.
Jewish National and University Library, Jerusalem, 1:7, 14, 24-2, 33-1, 36-2, 45, 48, 62-2, 86-2, 87-1, 115, 116-2, 136-2, 147, 150, 183; 2:4-2, 18-1,2, 39-1, 48, 83-1, 99, 103-1,2, 121-1, 122-2, 133-2, 151, 154, 157-1; 3:14-2, 23, 39-2, 76, 101, 181, 182-2; 4:1,7,50, 51-1, 53-1, 93, 95-2,3, 102-1, 103-1, 132, 166-1, 176-1, 177-1; 5:8-2, 17-1, 27-1,2, 46, 53, 67-1, 76-1, 77-2, 85-1,2,86-1, 88, 119, 138-1,2,3, 154,160, 163–2,165; 6:24,36, 43–1,2,3, 56–1,69, 75-2, 105-1, 114;
J.N.U.L. Photo Collection, Jerusalem, 2:42, 78-1; 4:25-2, 41, 97, 170-1; 6:2-2.
Jewish Publication Society, Philadelphia, 2:10.
Jewish Reconstructionist Foundation, New York, 4:12-2.
Jewish Theological Seminary of America, New York, 1:160-2; 2:167-1; 4:169-1; 5:18-1, 28, 70, 97-1.
Courtesy Jewish War Veterans of America, 4:54-1.
Johns Hopkins University, Maryland, 1:28-1.
Joint Distribution Committee, New York, 1:18-2; 4:114-3, 152-1.
Courtesy Y. Kahana, Ramat Gan, 5:133-2,3,
Y.D. Kamson Collection, Yad Vashem, Jerusalem, 4:61-1,2, 62-1,2, 77, 100-1; 6:32-2.
Keren Hayesod, United Jewish Appeal Photo Archives, Jerusalem, 1:60-1,2, 99, 100-2; 2-113, 117-1,2, 185; 3:4-2, 5-1, 50-2, 79-2, 80-1, 89, 94-2, 96, 103, 108, 110-2, 115-2, 149, 167-1, 168-4, 169-1, 170-1, 179-2; 4:19-1,3, 20-2, 21-2, 45-2, 91-4, 92-1, 181; 5:106-2, 114-2, 158-3, 172-1; 6:9-1, 82-3, 85-2.
Photo Keren-Or, Haifa, 1:181-2; 4:110-3.
Keystone Photo, Bar-David, Tel Aviv, 4:166-2.
Keystone Press Agency Ltd., New York, 4:3-2.
P.C. Kirchner, *Judisches Ceremoniel,* Nuremburg, 1734, 5:110.
Photo Kirschner, Newport, Rhode Island, 5:1.
Photo Kluger, Tel Aviv, 5:109-1, 120.
Photo R.M. Kneller, Jerusalem, 3:36-2; 4:120-2.
H. Kohl-C. Watzinger, *Antike Synagogen in Galilea,* Leipzig, 1916, 2:2.
L. Kolb (ed.), *The Woodcuts of Jakob Steinhardt,* San Francisco, 1959, 5:126-2.
Robert Körber, "Rassesieg in Wien," 1939, 3:66-2.
Photo D. Kroyanker, Jerusalem, 5:174-1.
E. Krausz, *Leeds Jewry,* Cambridge, 1964, 2:108-1.
Kupferstichkabinett der Oeffentlichen Kunstsammlung, Basel, 2:36-2.
Dr. Fredrick Lachman, New York, 3:137–1.
Harald Lamb, *Suleiman the Magnificent,* London, 1952, 2:14.
Landesbildstelle, Berlin, 2:69-2.
Photo P. Larsen, Jerusalem, 2:102-1; 3:15, 98; 4:8, 125, 185-2.
Leichter Collection, Jerusalem, 3:31.
Leo Baeck Institute, New York, 1:54; 5:49-3, 95-2.
Courtesy S. Levav, Jerusalem, 2:161-2.
Courtesy Harry Levine, Leominster, Mass., 5:7-1.
Jack Levine, New York, 4:185-1.
Library of the British and Foreign Aid Society, London, 2:29.
Library of the British & Foreign Bible Society, London, 4:157; 6:76-2.
Library of San Isodoro, Leon, Spain, 2:17-1; 3:141-2.
V.D. Lipman (ed.), *Three Centuries of Anglo-Jewish History,* Cambridge, c. 1961, 5:113-2.
London School of Economics, 4:39-1.
Los Angeles County Museum, History Division, 4:69.
The Louvre, Paris, 4:100-3; 6:59.
J.M. Lowy Collection, Montreal, 6:26.
Courtesy *Ma'ariv,* Tel Aviv, 2:155-2 (Kariel Gardosh); 6:22-2.
Photo Marcello Maggiori, Rome, 3:128-2.
March of Dimes, the National Foundation, 5:132-2.
Alexander Margulies Collection, London, 1:39.
Photo W. Margulies, London, 2:114-1.
Maritime Museum, Haifa, 4:94-1.
Marks and Spencer, London, 4:48-1.
Photo Ruben Maston, Tel Aviv, 1:106-2.
Photo G.E. Matson, Alhambra, California, 1:68-1; 3:124-2, 3; 4:91-1; 5:24, 31-1,2, 34-1, 134-3.
Mauritshuis, The Hague, 4:89-2.
Courtesy Mayor of New York City, 4:37-2.
T.J. Meek, *Excavations at Nuzi,* 3 (1935), 5:16.
A. Mendilow Collection, Jerusalem, 5:136-1.
The Metropolitan Museum of Art, New York, Gwynne M. Andrews Fund, 4:155-1.

The Metropolitan Museum of Art, New York, Rogers Fund, 1924, 6:32-1.
Charlotte Meyer Photo Studio, Haifa, 3:11-2.
Studio d'Art F. Meyer, Carpentras, France, 4:136-2.
Jakob Michael Collection of Jewish Music, J.N.U.L., Jerusalem, 3:29-1.
Photo R. Milon, Jerusalem, 2:137-2; 4:76-1, 126; 5:52, 157-2.
Photo R.J. Milch, New York, 2:44; 5:60-5.
Photo Mirlin-Yaron, Tel Aviv, 4:159.
Mishkan le Omanut, Ein Harod, 4:130-2,3; 5:33-2, 35-3, 87-2, 90-1, 122-2, 124-2, 127-1, 170-2; 6:9-3,5.
Mittelrheinisches Landesmuseum, Mainz, 4:12-1.
Mo-Bee Photo Service, Shawnee Mission, Kansas, 3:176-1.
P. Mocatta, *The Jews of Spain and Portugal and the Inquisition,* New York, 1928, 5:64-3.
Mosaiska Forsamlingen, Malmo, 5:146-2.
Photo Swapan Mukerji, Ace Studios Ltd., London, 4:67-1.
Photo Mula and Haramaty, Tel Aviv, 2:55-3.
Musee de Cluny, Paris, 4:1.
Musee de l'art juif, Paris, 5:121-1.
Museo Nacional de Arte Antigue, Lisbon, 4:60.
Museum of Modern Art, New York, 4:10.
The Museum of Modern Art, Stills Archives, New York, 6:9-2.
Museum of New Mexico, Santa Fe, New Mexico, 2:69-1.
National Air and Space Museum, Smithsonian Institution, Washington, D.C., 1:16-1,2.
National Gallery, London, 3:165; 5:100-1.
National Gallery of Art, Washington, D.C. (Widener Collection), 2:22-3.
National Gallery of Art, Washington, D.C. (Samuel Kress Collection), 4:141.
National Portrait Gallery, London, 5:179-2.
Itzhak Navon, 4:180-2.
New College, Oxford, 3:177-1.
From Roy Newquist, *Showcase,* New York, 1966, 2:57-2.
*New York News* Inc., 2:2-1,3.
New York Public Library, 2:50-2; 3:176-2; 5:95-1.
The New York Public Library, Jewish Division, Astor Lenox and Tilden Foundations, 6:106-1.
New York State Education Department, 1:22; 5:91-1.
Courtesy New York University, Photo W.R. Simmion, 2:168-2.
Photo Moshe Ninio, Jerusalem, 2:142-2; 5:36-2.
Courtesy Uriel Ofek, Herzliyah, 1:49-1; 3:37-1,2.
Photo Hanna Ophir-Rosenstein, Haifa, 2:139-3; 6:86-1.
Photo Joel Oront, Boston, 4:182-1.
ORT, Tel Aviv, 5:29-1,2,3.
Courtesy Moshe Oster, Tel Aviv, 5:62-1.
Photo Pach Bros., New York, 4:49-1.
Mrs. Y. Palombo, Har Zion, Jerusalem, 1:74-4.
Photo Palphot, Herzliyyah, 5:130-3.
Courtesy Mrs. A. Pann, Jerusalem, 1:75-1.
Photo J. Papp, Givatayim, 4:26-1.
A. Parrot, *Mission Archeologigue de Mari II,* Paris, 1959, 3:78-2.
A. Parrot, *Nineveh & Babylon,* London, 1961, 1:96-2.
B. Pasternak, *The Collected Prose Works,* London, 1945, 5:44-1.
Photo Harold P. Pearlman, New York, 5:183-1.
Personality Posters, United Kingdom, 4:161.
Pierpont Morgan Library, New York, 3:138.
*Pinkas Kletsk,* Tel Aviv, 1959, 3:21-2.
Photo H. Pinn, Tel Aviv, 3:85-2.
Pinakothek, Munich, 3:164-2.
Photo Paul Popper Ltd., London, 2:115.
Portuguese Jewish Community, Amsterdsm, 1:43-3; 5:64-1.
Photo David Posner, Jerusalem, 1:100-1, 108-2; 3:18-2,67; 4:68-2, 129-2, 173-1,2; 6:18.
Bernard Postal, J. Silver & R. Silver, *Encyclopaedia of Jews in Sports,* New York, 1965, 4:31-2; 6:5,6-1,2.
Prado Museum, Madrid, 1:5-2; 3:91; 4:57-2.
J. Prato, Jerusalem, 6:45-1.
Presse und Informationsamt der Bundesregierung, Bonn, 5:22.
Presses Universitaires de France, Paris, 2:88-1.
Photohouse Prior, Tel Aviv, 2:27-1.
Public Record Office, London, 4:140-1.
*Qadmoniot,* Vol. 1, Jerusalem, 1968, 4:172-2.
L.I. Rabinowitz Collection, Jerusalem, 1:128-2; 5:140-2; 6:113.
*Radom Memorial Book,* Jerusalem, 1961, 5:61-4.
Photo Zev Radovan, Jerusalem, 1:67–3; 2: 81–1, 3:44–2, 117-3, 147-3, 155, 161-1, 166-3, 167-5; 4:149-1, 70, 88-2; 5:65-3, 147-4.
Courtesy A. Rafaeli-Zenziper, Archive for Russian Zionism, Tel Aviv, 2:86-1, 92-1; 4:143-1.
Bernard Raskas Collection, St. Paul, Minnesota, 1:184-3.
Redwood Library and Athenaeum, Newport, R.I., 6:50-3.
Courtesy Louis Reens, New York, 6:17-2.
Photo A.B. Reportagebild, Stockholm, 1:20-2.
Reuters Ltd., 5:101-2.
Rhode Island Jewish Historical Society, 5:2; 6:64,66.
Rijksmuseum, Amsterdam, 5:112-3.
Rijksmuseum, The Hague, 6:3-3.
Courtesy L. Rochman, Jerusalem, 2:181; 6:106-2.
Franklin D. Roosevelt Library, Hyde Park, N.Y., 5:106-1.
Photo Teddy Rosentool, 2:139-1.
Cecil Roth Collection, 1:frontispiece, 32, 46, 59, 151, 172-1; 2:3-1, 5, 17-2, 36-1, 45-1,2, 78-3, 123, 126-1,2; 3:128-1, 152, 164-1; 4:40-1, 48-2, 66, 67-2, 75-1, 96-3, 120-1, 129-1, 148-1, 103-2; 5:13-2, 25-1, 54, 66-2, 116-2,3, 184-2; 6:38-1, 72.
Royal Library, Copenhagen, 1:85-1, 120-1; 2:180-2; 4:107-2; 5:166.
Alfred Rubens Collection, London, 2:162-3; 4:99-1; 5:26-4, 179-3; 6:38-2.
Photo David Rubinger, Jerusalem, 3:167-8; 6:74.
Helena Rubinstein Collection, 4:145-2.
Courtesy I. Russ, Givatayim, 5:61-5.
Photo Sadeh, Haifa, 4:94-1; 5:168-2.
G. Saige, *Les Juifs de Languedoc,* Paris, 1881, 5:147-2,3.
G. Salesky, *Famous Musicians of Jewish Origin,* New York, 1949, 2:29-2.
Sinai, St. Catherine's Monastery, 3:53-1; 5:78-3.
Sarajevo National Museum, 1:1, 2:80, 133-1.
S.D. Sassoon, *Massa Babel,* Jerusalem, 1955, 3:94-1,3.
Formerly Sassoon Collection, Letchworth, 4:38-1.
M. Schappes, *A Pictorial History of the Jews in America,* New York, 1965, 1:165-2; 2:13-1; 4:96-1; 6:62-2, 65-2, 78-2.
Photo C. Schieber, Netanya, 2:183-1; 4:84-2, 117; 5:103-1, 158-2; 6:1-1.
Photo Schleissner, Rehovot, 5:99-1.
Photo Emil Schlesinger, Manchester, 4:90-1.
A. Schoener (ed.), *Portal to America : The Lower East Side 1879-1925,* New York, 1967. Photo Lewis W. Hine, The Jewish Division, The N.Y. Public Library, Aston, Lenox and Tilden Foundation, 5:61.
T. Schrire, Cape Town, 4:78-1.
Schwadron Collection, J.N.U.L., Jerusalem, 1:167-2; 2:41-2, 85-1, 157-2; 3:4-1, 26, 28, 37-3, 43, 55-3, 77-2, 97-3, 182-1, 4:9, 11-1, 15-2, 27-3, 49-2, 87-1, 110-2, 119-2, 177-2; 5:5-1, 10-1, 18-2, 45-1, 99-3, 107-1, 118-2, 139-1, 179-1, 180-1; 6:54, 55-3, 80-2, 81-3, 122.

*Sefer Zikkaron li-Kehillat Lomza,* Tel Aviv, 1952, 6:102.
Seminario Vescovile, Vercelli, 3:135-1.
The Sentinel, Chicago, 13–1
Photo Maurice Seymour, New York, 6:56-2.
Sha'arei Zedek Hospital, Jerusalem, 4:16-1, 57-1.
From *The Alphabet of Creation,* illustrated by Ben Shahn, copyright 1954. Reprinted by permission of Pantheon Books, a division of Random House, Inc., 3:84-1.
Photo Joseph Shaw, London, 6:73.
The Shrine of the Book, Jerusalem, D. Samuel and Jeane H. Gottesman Center for Biblical Manuscripts, 1:67-1, 69, 124; 2:61; 3:59-2.
S. Siegmund Stahl Collection, New York, 5:124-1.
D. Silk, *Retrievements,* Jerusalem, 1969, 1:26-1.
Skirball Museum, H.U.C., Los Angeles, 5:55-2.
Society for Research on Jewish Com., Jerusalem, 1:56–1.
Photo S. Sonnenschein, Zurich, 4:140-2.
Soprintendenza alle Antichita di Roma, 4:121-2.
South African Library for Research Purposes, Cape Town, 6:51.
South African Press Services, Johannesburg, 5:186.
Courtesy L. Sowden, Jerusalem, 6:40-1.
Soziologische Texte, Neuwied, 5:180-2.
Staatliche Graphische Sammlung, Munich, 2:145-1.
Stadtliche Museen zu Berlin, 1:47-1.
Stadtsarchiv, Basel, 6:16-2.
Stadtsarchiv Landshut, 5:17-2.
Stadtarchive, Munich, 2:162-4; 4:165.
Stadlische Kulture Institute, Worms, 5:94.
Stadelschen Kunstinstitut, Frankfort, 5:100-2.
Stanford University, Stanford, California, 4:109-3.
C.H. Stark (ed.), *This is Gateshead,* Newcastle, 1967, 2:156-1.
State Jewish Museum, Prague, 1:75-5, 157; 5:67-2.
Courtesy State of Israel Bond Organization, 1:159; 2:97.
Stedelijk Museum, Amsterdam, 2:30-2, 59-1, 124-1, 131-1, 137-1; 5:55-1, 101-1.
B. Steibelman, Copenhagen, 3:68.
Strachan, *Early Bible Illustrations,* Cambridge University Press, 1957, 3:2-2.
Photo A. Strajmayster, Jerusalem, 1:49-2, 80-1; 3:125-1, 150; 4:139.
E.L. Sukenik, *The Ancient Synagogue of Beth Alpha,* Jerusalem, 1932, 1:25.
Photo Pat Sweeney, Dublin, 1:168.
N. Tamir, *Pinsk, II,* 1966, 5:60-3.
Tate Gallery, London, 1:140; 2:88-2; 3:174-2; 4:184-1.
Tel Aviv Museum, 4:71.
Tel Aviv University, the Institute of Archaeology, 1:66-5.
Temple Emanuel Museum, Montreal, 5:126-1.
Temple Emanu-el, Toronto, 1:74-1.
L. Trepp, *De Landesgemeinde der Juden in Oldenburg,* Oldenburg, 1965, 2:162-2.
The Harry S. Truman Research Center, Israel-Arab Documentation Unit, Hebrew University, Jerusalem, 1:62-1.
Union of American Hebrew Congregations, New York, 1:102; 3:69; 5:47-2, 98-1.
University Library, Bologna, 5:170-3.
University of the Witwatersrand, Johannesburg, 1:87-2.
U.P.I., N.Y., 4:133-1; 6:63.
U.S. Army Signal Corps, 3:65-2,4.
Victoria and Albert Museum, London, 2:78-2; 5:10-2.
Photo Roman Vishniak, N.Y., 2:43; 4:28–1, 72; 5:59–1,2, 60–4.
Wagner International Photos, New York, 5:144-1.
J. Wallersteiner Collection, Bene Berak, 1:76-2.
Courtesy Warsaw Ghetto Resistance Organization, New York, 5:6-2.
Photo Gabby Weill, Kiryat Ono, 4:23-1.
Wiesbaden Municipality, Photo J. Weber, 2:162-1.
Courtesy M. Weisgal, Rehovot, 6:55-2.
Photo K. Weiss, Jerusalem, 1:117; 2:55-1, 92-2; 3:156-2; 4:101–3, 167–1, 186; 5:32–1, 78–1, 141–4, 6:13, 76–3.
The White House, Washington, 5:9-2.
WIZO, Tel Aviv, 5:171-3.
Wuertembergishe Landesbibliothek, 3:137-2.
A. Ya'ari, *Hebrew Printers Marks,* Jerusalem, 1943, 4:89-1; 5:79-1,2,3, 80-1, 20.
Photo Yacoby, Jerusalem, 3:24-1.
Yad Vashem Archives, Jerusalem, 1:47-3, 57-2, 97-1, 98-2, 171-1; 2:14-1, 33-1,2, 85-3, 143, 165-1,2,3, 184, 186; 3:61-1, 65-1,3, 66-1,3; 4:30, 31-1, 32-1, 73-2, 79-2, 119-2, 182-3, 183-1; 5:14, 15-2, 37-2,3, 60-1,8, 99-2, 103-2, 104-1,2,3, 149-1; 6:75-1, 83, 93-2.
Yale University, New Haven, Conn., 1:53; 2:86-2,3, 87-1,2, 100; 3:78-1.
YIVO Institute of Jewish Studies, New York, 1:114-1; 2:45-1,2, 178; 3:25-1, 39-1; 4:135, 163-2; 5:58-4, 61-2,6, 157-1,2; 6:39-2, 40-2, 104-3.
*Yizkor Book of the Jewish Community of Ostrolenka,* 1963, 5:60-7.
Photo I. Zafrir, Tel Aviv, 4:71.
Zollkriminalinstitut, Cologne, 6:28.
Photo Aron Zuckerman, Jerusalem, 4:53-2.

# COVER CREDITS

Cover vol. 1: "Jewish Wedding" by Moritz Oppenheimer, 1861. Israel Museum, Jerusalem; photo David Harris, Jerusalem.

Cover vol. 2: Hannukah lamp. From the Collection of the Sir Isaac and Edith Wolfson Museum in Hechal Shlomo, Jerusalem; photo David Harris, Jerusalem.

Cover vol. 3: Call of Moses. London, British Museum, Add. ms. 27219, fol. 10v.

Cover vol. 4: Ketubbah Ancona, 1772. Hebrew University of Jerusalem; photo David Harris, Jerusalem.

Cover vol. 5: Medley of Passover items. From the collection of the Sir Isaac and Edith Wolfson Museum in Hechal Shlomo, Jerusalem; photo David Harris, Jerusalem.

Cover vol. 6: Great Synagogue in Florence. Photo Locci, Florence.

# COLOR CREDITS

Photo Murray Bloom, Jerusalem, 5: facing p. 154, plate 1.
Photo Werner Braun, Jerusalem, 2: facing p. 58, plates 2,4, facing p. 59, plate 2, facing p. 122, plate 2, facing p. 138; 3: facing p.10, plate 2, facing p. 27, plates 1,3; 5: facing p.42, plate 2, facing p.139, plates 1,2,3, facing p.155, plate 2.
The British Library, London, 1: facing p. 121, plate 2, p.136; 3: facing p.26; 4: facing p.106, plate 2, facing p. 107, plate 3; 5: facing p. 58.
Photo Hillel Burger, Jerusalem, 1: facing p. 73, plate 1.
Cambridge University Library, 4: facing p. 138.
Photo R. Cleave, Jerusalem, 3: facing p.106, plates 6,7.
I. Einhorn Collection, Tel Aviv, 3: facing p. 27, plate 2; 5: facing p.43, plate 1.
E. Erde Collection, Tel Aviv, 3: facing p.122, plate 2.
Photo A. Enis, Jerusalem, 3: facing p. 106, plates 2,3,5.
Photo Y. Feliks, Jerusalem, 3: facing p.106, plates 1, 4.
Shmuel Gorr Collection, Jerusalem, 6: facing p. 90, plate 2.
Oscar Gruss Collection, New York, 2: facing p.123, plate 2; 6: facing p. 27, plate 2.
Haifa Ethnological Museum, 2: facing p.74, plate 2.
Photo David Harris, Jerusalem, 1: facing p.88, plate 1, p.120, plate 3; 2: facing p.59, plate 1, facing p.74, plates 2,3, facing p.122, plate 3, facing p.139, plates 1,2,3,4; 3: facing p.27, plate 2, p.122, plates 1,2; 4: facing p.106, plate 1, facing p.107, plates 1,2, facing p.154, p.155, plate 2; 5: facing p.43, plate 1, facing p.59, plates 2, 3, facing p.139, plate 2, facing p.154, plate 3, facing p.155, plate 1.
Hebrew Union College, Cincinnati, 5: facing p.59, plate 1.
Israel Museum, Jerusalem, 1: facing p.73, plate 1, facing p.88, plates 1,2; 2: facing p.74, plate 3, facing p.122, plate 3, facing p.139, plates 2,3,4; 3: facing p.10, plate 1, facing p.122, plates 1,3, p.123, plate 1; 4: facing p.106, plate 1, facing p.107, plates 1,2, facing p.154; 5: facing p.42, plate 1, facing p.139, plate 2; 6: facing p.27, plate 1.
Israel Museum Photo Archives, Jerusalem, 1: facing p.72, plate 1; 4: facing p.139, plate 2.
Jewish Museum, London, 1: facing p.89, plate 3, facing p.121, plate 1; 6: facing p.42, facing p.90, plate 1, facing p.91, plate 1.
Jewish Museum, New York, 4: facing p.139, plate 1.
Jewish National Fund Photo Archives, Jerusalem, 3: facing p.10, plate 2.
Photo Peter Larsen, Jerusalem, 5: facing p.154, plate 2.
Library of the Hungarian Academy of Sciences, Budapest, 3: facing p.11; 4:facing p.91.
Photo Locci, Florence, 6: facing p.91, plate 2.
William Margulies Collection, London, 5: facing p.43, plate 2.
Mishkan Le-Omanut, Ein Harod, 1: facing p.73, plate 2, facing p.89, plate 2; 2: facing p.58, plate 1, facing p.74, plate 1; 6: facing p.26, plates 1, 2.
Musee de l'Art Juif, Paris, 5: facing p.138, plate 1.
National Library, Lisbon, 6: facing p.75.
National Museum, Sarajevo, 4: facing p.155, plate 1.
Photo Eric Politzer, New York, 4: facing p.139, plate 1.
Photo R. Posner, Jerusalem, 3: facing p.123, plate 3.
Rina Gallery (Bertha Urdang), Jerusalem, 3: facing p.123, plate 2.
Photo Hayyim Ron, Tel Aviv, 1: facing p.120, plate 1.
Cecil Roth Collection, 2: facing p.139, plate 1.
Photo David Rubinger, Jerusalem, 1: facing p.120, plate 2.
Formerly Sassoon Collection, Letchworth, 6: facing p.74.
Schocken Library, Jerusalem, 1: facing p.137.
Tel Aviv Museum, 2: facing p.59, plate 3.
Sir Isäac and Lady Wolfson Museum in Hechal Shlomo, Jerusalem, 4: facing p.155, plate 2; 5: facing p.59, plates 2,3, facing p.155, plate 1.
Worms Kulturinstute, 2: facing p.122, plate 1, facing p.123, plate 1.